ADOBE PHOTOSHOP

CREATIVE CLOUD

Elizabeth Eisner **REDING**

REVEALED

CENGAGE
Learning

Australia • Brazil • Mexico • Singapore • United Kingdom • United States

Adobe Photoshop Creative Cloud Revealed
Elizabeth Eisner Reding

Product Director: Kathleen McMahon

Senior Product Manager: Jim Gish

Content Developer: Megan Chrisman

Senior Marketing Manager: Eric La Scola

Senior Content Project Manager: Brooke Greenhouse

Developmental Editor: Karen Stevens

Technical Editor: Toni Toland

Managing Art Director: Jack Pendleton

Manufacturing Planner: Julio Esperas

IP Analyst: Sara Crane

Senior IP Project Manager: Kathy Kucharek

Production Service: Integra Software Services Pvt. Ltd

Text Designer: Liz Kingslein

Proofreader: Kim Kosmatka

Indexer: Alexandra Nickerson

Cover Image: Cengage Learning

© 2015, 2013, 2011 Cengage Learning

WCN: 01-100-101

For product information and technology assistance, contact us at **Cengage Learning Customer & Sales Support, 1-800-354-9706**

For permission to use material from this text or product, submit all requests online at **www.cengage.com/permissions.**

Further permissions questions can be emailed to **permissionrequest@cengage.com.**

Library of Congress Control Number: 2014944042

ISBN-13: 978-1-305-26053-5
ISBN-10: 1-305-26053-8

Cengage Learning
20 Channel Center Street
Boston, MA 02210
USA

Cengage Learning is a leading provider of customized learning solutions with office locations around the globe, including Singapore, the United Kingdom, Australia, Mexico, Brazil, and Japan. Locate your local office at **www.cengage.com/global**.

Cengage Learning products are represented in Canada by Nelson Education, Ltd.

To learn more about Cengage Learning Solutions, visit **www.cengage.com**.

Purchase any of our products at your local college store or at our preferred online store **www.cengagebrain.com**.

Printed in the United States of America

Print Number: 01   Print Year: 2014

Revealed Series Vision

The Revealed Series is your guide to today's hottest digital media applications. For years, the Revealed Series has kept pace with the dynamic demands of the digital media community, and continues to do so with the publication of 6 exciting titles covering the latest Adobe Creative Cloud products. Each comprehensive book teaches not only the technical skills required for success in today's competitive digital media market, but the design skills as well. From animation, to web design, to digital image-editing and interactive media skills, the Revealed Series has you covered.

We recognize the unique learning environment of the digital media classroom, and we deliver textbooks that include:

- Comprehensive step-by-step instructions
- In-depth explanations of the "Why" behind a skill
- Creative projects for additional practice
- Full-color visuals for a clear explanation of concepts
- Comprehensive online material offering additional instruction and skills practice

- **NEW** icons to highlight features that are new since the previous release of the software

With the Revealed Series, we've created books that speak directly to the digital media and design community—one of the most rapidly growing computer fields today.

—The Revealed Series

New to This Edition

The latest edition of Adobe Photoshop Creative Cloud includes many exciting new features, some of which are:

- Using Creative Cloud apps and services
- Isolation Mode Layer Filtering
- Smarter Smart Guides
- Font Search
- Focus Area Mask
- Linked Smart Objects
- 3D Imaging
- Min and Max Filters
- Blur Gallery
- Perspective Warp
- Multiple-Path Selection
- Rounded-Rectangle Properties panel
- Camera Raw Filter command
- Camera Shake Reduction

CourseMate

A CourseMate is available to accompany *Adobe Photoshop Creative Cloud Revealed*, which helps you make the grade!

This CourseMate includes:

- An interactive eBook, with highlighting, note-taking, read-aloud, and search capabilities
- Interactive learning tools including:
  - Chapter quizzes
  - Flash cards
  - Crossword puzzles
  - And more!

Go to login.cengagebrain.com to access these resources.

AUTHOR'S VISION

To the reader, a book magically appears on the shelf with each software revision, but to those of us "making it happen" it means not only working under ridiculous deadlines (which we're used to), but it also means working with slightly different teams with slightly different ways of doing things. Karen Stevens and I have worked together before on this project that has spanned more years than we care to admit. With this revision, we welcomed Megan Chrisman, Brooke Greenhouse, Gillian Daniels, and Toni Toland to the team. Thanks also to Jim Gish, Kathy Kucharek, Glenn Castle, and Meaghan Tomaso. Special thanks to John Freitas for tech editing the appendices at the last minute, Shanthi Guruswamy, and Ann Fisher, who oversees and compiles the Instructor Resources. Most of us have never met face-to-face, yet once again we managed to work together in a professional manner, while defying the time-space continuum with its many time zones, cultural holidays, and countless vacation plans.

I would also like to thank my husband, Michael, who is used to my disappearing acts when I'm facing deadlines, and to Bix and Jet, who know when it's time to take a break for food, water, and some good old-fashioned head-scratching.

—Elizabeth Eisner Reding

Introduction to Adobe Photoshop Creative Cloud

Welcome to *Adobe Photoshop Creative Cloud—Revealed.* This book offers creative projects, concise instructions, and coverage of basic to advanced Photoshop skills, helping you to create polished, professional-looking art work. Use this book both in the classroom and as your own reference guide. It also includes many of the new features of Adobe Photoshop Creative Cloud. This edition is written for the 2014 Photoshop CC release.

This text is organized into 18 chapters and two appendixes. In these chapters, you will learn many skills, including how to use the best tool for any particular task and how to navigate the Creative Cloud app, which, in this release, provides familiar functionality from one app to the next.

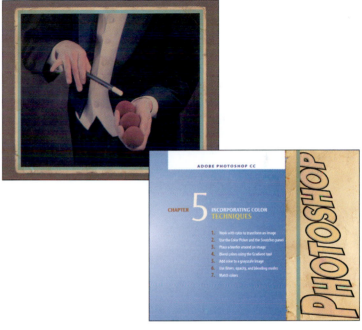

What You'll Do

A What You'll Do figure begins every lesson. This figure gives you an at-a-glance look at what you'll do in the chapter, either by showing you a file from the current project or a tool you'll be using.

Comprehensive Conceptual Lessons

Before jumping into instructions, in-depth conceptual information tells you "why" skills are applied. This book provides the "how" and "why" through the use of professional examples. Also included in the text are tips and sidebars to help you work more efficiently and creatively, or to teach you a bit about the history or design philosophy behind the skill you are using.

Step-by-Step Instructions

This book combines in-depth conceptual information with concise steps to help you learn Photoshop Creative Cloud. Each set of steps guides you through a lesson where you will create, modify, or enhance a Photoshop file. Step references to large colorful images and quick step summaries round out the lessons. The Data Files for the steps are provided on Cengage Brain.

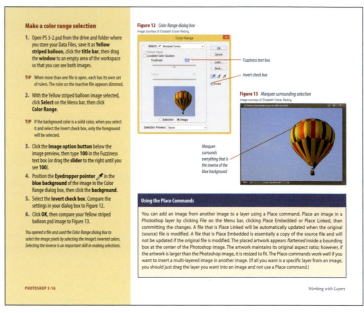

Make a color range selection

1. Open PS 3-2.psd from the drive and folder where you store your Data Files, save it as **Yellow striped balloon**, click the **title bar**, then drag the **window** to an empty area of the workspace so that you can see both images.

   TIP When more than one file is open, each has its own set of rulers. The ruler on the inactive file appears dimmed.

2. With the Yellow striped balloon image selected, click **Select** on the Menu bar, then click **Color Range**.

   TIP If the background color is a solid color, when you select it and select the Invert check box, only the foreground will be selected.

3. Click the **Image option button** below the image preview, then type **100** in the Fuzziness text box (or drag the **slider** to the right until you see **100**).

4. Position the **Eyedropper pointer** in the **blue background** of the image in the Color Range dialog box, then click the **background**.

5. Select the **Invert check box**. Compare the settings in your dialog box to Figure 12.

6. Click **OK**, then compare your Yellow striped balloon.psd image to Figure 13.

You opened a file and used the Color Range dialog box to select the image pixels by selecting the image's inverted colors. Selecting the inverse is an important skill in making selections.

Figure 12 *Color Range dialog box*
Image courtesy of Elizabeth Eisner Reding.

— Fuzziness text box
— Invert check box

Figure 13 *Marquee surrounding selection*
Image courtesy of Elizabeth Eisner Reding.

Marquee surrounds everything that is the inverse of the blue background

Using the Place Commands

You can add an image from another image to a layer using a Place command. Place an image in a Photoshop layer by clicking File on the Menu bar, clicking Place Embedded or Place Linked, then committing the changes. A file that is Place Linked will be automatically updated when the original (source) file is modified. A file that is Place Embedded is essentially a copy of the source file and will not be updated if the original file is modified. The placed artwork appears *flattened* inside a bounding box at the center of the Photoshop image. The artwork maintains its original aspect ratio; however, if the artwork is larger than the Photoshop image, it is resized to fit. The Place commands work well if you want to insert a multi-layered image in another image. (If all you want is a specific layer from an image, you should just drag the layer you want into an image and not use a Place command.)

Working with Layers

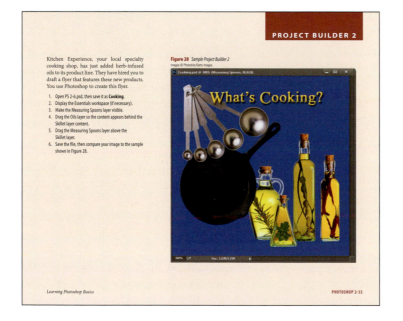

PROJECT BUILDER 2

Kitchen Experience, your local specialty cooking shop, has just added herb-infused oils to its product line. They have hired you to draft a flyer that features these new products. You use Photoshop to create this flyer.

1. Open PS 2-6.psd, then save it as **Cooking**.
2. Display the Essentials workspace (if necessary).
3. Make the Measuring Spoons layer visible.
4. Drag the Oils layer so the content appears behind the Skillet layer content.
5. Drag the Measuring Spoons layer above the Skillet layer.
6. Save the file, then compare your image to the sample shown in Figure 28.

Figure 28 *Sample Project Builder 2*
Images © Photodisc/Getty Images.

Learning Photoshop Basics

Projects

This book contains a variety of end-of-chapter materials for additional practice and reinforcement. The Power User Shortcuts table summarizes tasks covered in the chapter and offers the easiest way they can be completed. The Skills Review contains hands-on practice exercises that mirror the progressive nature of the lesson material. The chapter concludes with four projects: two Project Builders, one Design Project, and one Portfolio Project. The Project Builders and the Design Project require you to apply the skills you've learned in the chapter. The Portfolio Project encourages you to address and solve challenges based on the content explored in the chapter in order to create portfolio-quality work.

What Instructor Resources Are Available with this Book?

The Instructor Resources are Cengage's way of putting the resources and information needed to teach and learn effectively into your hands. All the resources are available for both Mac OS and Windows operating systems. These resources can be found online at: **http://login.cengage.com**. Once you login or create an account, search for the title under 'Add a product to your Instructor Resource Center' using the ISBN. Then select the instructor companion site resources and click 'Add Selected to Instructor Resource Center.'

Instructor's Manual

The Instructor's Manual includes chapter overviews and detailed lecture topics for each chapter, with teaching tips.

Sample Syllabus

The Sample Syllabus includes a suggested syllabus for any course that uses this book.

PowerPoint Presentations

Each chapter has a corresponding PowerPoint presentation that you can use in lectures, distribute to your students, or customize to suit your course.

Data Files for Students

To complete most of the chapters in this book, your students will need Data Files, which are available online. Instruct students to use the Data Files List at the end of this book. This list gives instructions on organizing files.

To access the Data Files for this book, take the following steps:

1. Open your browser and go to http://www.cengagebrain.com
2. Type the author, title, or ISBN of this book in the Search window. (The ISBN is listed on the back cover.)
3. Click the book title in the list of search results.
4. When the book's main page is displayed, click the Access Now button under Free Materials.
5. To download Data Files, select a chapter number and then click on the Data Files link on the left navigation bar to download the files.

Solutions to Exercises

Solution Files are Data Files completed with comprehensive sample answers. Use these files to evaluate your students' work. Or distribute them electronically so students can verify their work. Sample solutions to lessons and end-of-chapter material are provided, with the exception of some Portfolio Projects.

Test Bank and Test Engine

Cengage Learning Testing Powered by Cognero is a flexible, online system that allows you to:

- author, edit, and manage test bank content from multiple Cengage Learning solutions
- create multiple test versions in an instant
- deliver tests from your LMS, your classroom, or wherever you want

Start right away!

Cengage Learning Testing Powered by Cognero works on any operating system or browser.

- No special installs or downloads needed.
- Create tests from school, home, the coffee shop—anywhere with Internet access.

What Will You Find?

- Simplicity at every step. A desktop-inspired interface features drop-down menus and familiar, intuitive tools that take you through content creation and management with ease.
- Full-featured test generator. Create ideal assessments with your choice of 15 question types (including true/false, multiple choice, opinion scale/likert, and essay). Multi-language support, an equation editor, and unlimited metadata help ensure your tests are complete and compliant.
- Cross-compatible capability. Import and export content into other systems.

CONTENTS

CHAPTER 1: GETTING STARTED WITH ADOBE PHOTOSHOP CC

CHAPTER 2: LEARNING PHOTOSHOP BASICS

CHAPTER 3: WORKING WITH LAYERS

CHAPTER 4: MAKING SELECTIONS

CHAPTER 5: INCORPORATING COLOR TECHNIQUES

CHAPTER 6: PLACING TYPE IN AN IMAGE

CHAPTER 7: USING PAINTING TOOLS

CHAPTER 8: WORKING WITH SPECIAL LAYER FUNCTIONS

CHAPTER 9: CREATING SPECIAL EFFECTS WITH FILTERS

CHAPTER 10: ENHANCING SPECIFIC SELECTIONS

CHAPTER 11: ADJUSTING COLORS

CHAPTER 12: USING CLIPPING MASKS, PATHS, & SHAPES

CHAPTER 17: CREATING IMAGES FOR THE WEB

CHAPTER 18: WORKING WITH ANIMATION, VIDEO, & PHOTOGRAPHY

APPENDIX A: STORING AND EDITING IMAGES WITH THE ADOBE FAMILY OF REVEL APPS

APPENDIX B: PORTFOLIO PROJECTS AND EFFECTS

Intended Audience

This text is designed for the beginner or intermediate user who wants to learn how to use Photoshop CC. The book is designed to provide basic and in-depth material that not only educates, but also encourages you to explore the nuances of this exciting program. Features new to Photoshop and covered in this book are indicated by a New icon.

Approach

The text allows you to work at your own pace through step-by-step tutorials. A concept is presented and the process is explained, followed by the actual steps. To learn the most from the use of the text, you should adopt the following habits:

- Proceed slowly: Accuracy and comprehension are more important than speed.
- Understand what is happening with each step before you continue to the next step.
- After finishing a skill, ask yourself if you could do it on your own, without referring to the steps. If the answer is no, review the steps.

General

Throughout the initial chapters, students are given precise instructions regarding saving their work. Students should feel that they can save their work at any time, not just when instructed to do so.

Students are also given precise instructions regarding magnifying/reducing their work area. Once the student feels more comfortable, he/she should feel free to use the Zoom tool to make their work area more comfortable.

Icons, Buttons, and Pointers

Symbols for icons, buttons, and pointers are shown in the step each time they are used. Once an icon, button, or pointer has been used on a page, the symbol will be shown for subsequent uses on that page *without* showing its name.

Skills Reference

As a bonus, a Power User Shortcuts table is included at the end of the Photoshop chapters. This table contains the quickest method for completing tasks covered in the chapter. It is meant for the more experienced user, or for the user who wants to become more experienced. Tools are shown, not named. Brief directions are given, with no tool or command locations.

Fonts

The Data Files contain a variety of commonly used fonts, but there is no guarantee that these fonts will be available on your computer. In a few cases, fonts other than those common to a PC or a Macintosh are used. If any of the fonts in use is not available on your computer, you can make a substitution, realizing that the results may vary from those in the book.

Windows and Mac OS

Adobe Photoshop CC works virtually the same on Windows and Mac OS operating systems. In those cases where there is a significant difference, the abbreviations (Win) and (Mac) are used.

Preference Settings

The learning process will be much easier if you can see the file extensions for the files you will use in the lessons. To do this in Windows, open Windows Explorer, click Organize, Folder and Search Options, click the View tab, and then uncheck the Hide Extensions for Known File Types check box. To do this for a Mac, go to the Finder, click the Finder menu, and then click Preferences. Click the Advanced tab, and then select the Show all file extensions check box.

System Requirements

For a Windows operating system:

- Processor: Intel® Pentium® 4 processor or AMD Athlon® 64 processor (2 GHz or faster)
- Operating System: Microsoft® Windows 7 (with Service Pack 1), 8, or 8 .1
- Memory: 1 GB of RAM
- Storage space: 2.5 GB of available hard-disk space
- Monitor: 1024 × 768 resolution (1280 × 800 recommended)
- Video: 16-bit or higher OpenGL 2.0 video card; 512 MB RAM (1 GB recommended)
- Broadband Internet connection required for activation, Creative Cloud membership validation, and access to online services

For a Mac OS operating system:

- Processor: Multicore Intel® processor with 64-bit support
- Operating System: Mac OS X 10.7, v10.8, or v10.9
- Memory: 1 GB of RAM
- Storage space: 3.2 GB of available hard-disk space
- Monitor: 1024 × 768 or greater monitor resolution (1280 × 800 recommended)
- Video: 16-bit or greater OpenGL 2.0 video card; 512 MB of VRAM (1 GB recommended)
- Broadband Internet connection required for software activation, Creative Cloud membership validation, and access to online services

File Identification

Instead of printing a file, the owner of a Photoshop image can be identified by reading the File Info dialog box.

Use the following instructions to add your name to an image:

1. Click File on the Menu bar, then click File Info.
2. Click the Description, if necessary.
3. Click the Author text box.
4. Type your name, course number, or other identifying information.
5. Click OK.

There are no instructions with this text to use the File Info feature other than when it is introduced in Chapter 1. It is up to each user to use this feature so that his or her work can be identified.

Measurements

When measurements are shown, needed, or discussed, they are given in pixels. Use the following instructions to change the units of measurement to pixels:

1. Click Edit (Win) or Photoshop (Mac) on the Menu bar, point to Preferences, then click Units & Rulers.
2. Click the Rulers list arrow, then click pixels.
3. Click OK.

You can display rulers by clicking View on the Menu bar, and then clicking Rulers, or by pressing [Ctrl][R] (Win) or ⌘ [R] (Mac). A check mark to the left of the Rulers command indicates that the Rulers are displayed. You can hide visible rulers by clicking View on the Menu bar, then clicking Rulers, or by pressing [Ctrl] [R] (Win) or ⌘ [R] (Mac).

Menu Commands in Tables

In tables, menu commands are abbreviated using the following format:

Edit ➤ Preferences ➤ Units & Rulers

This command translates as follows: Click Edit on the Menu bar, point to Preferences, and then click Units & Rulers.

Grading Tips

Many students have web-ready accounts where they can post their completed assignments. The instructor can access the student accounts using a browser and view the images online. Using this method, it is not necessary for the student to include his/her name on a type layer, because all of their assignments are in an individual password-protected account.

Creating a Portfolio

One method for students to submit and keep a copy of all of their work is to create a portfolio of their projects that is linked to a simple web page that can be saved on a CD-ROM or a cloud-based drive. If it is necessary for students to print completed projects, work can be printed and mounted at a local copy shop; a student's name can be printed on the back of the image.

Data Files and Online Content

To complete most of the chapters in this book, your students will need Data Files, which are available online. Instruct students to use the Data Files List at the end of this book. This list gives instructions on organizing files.

To access the Data Files for this book, take the following steps:

1. Open your browser and go to http://www.cengagebrain.com
2. Type the author, title, or ISBN of this book in the Search window. (The ISBN is listed on the back cover.)
3. Click the book title in the list of search results.
4. When the book's main page is displayed, click the Access Now button under Free Materials.
5. To download Data Files, select a chapter number and then click on the Data Files link on the left navigation bar to download the files.

CHAPTER 1

GETTING STARTED WITH
ADOBE PHOTOSHOP CC

1. Start Adobe Photoshop CC 2014

2. Learn how to open and save an image

3. Examine the Photoshop window

4. Close a file and exit Photoshop

5. Learn about design principles and copyright rules

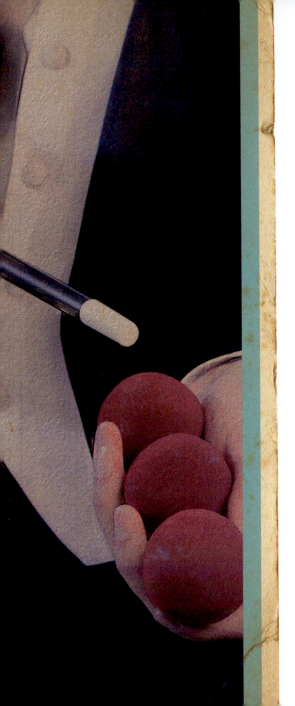

GETTING STARTED WITH
ADOBE PHOTOSHOP CC

Using Photoshop and the Creative Cloud

Adobe Photoshop CC is an image-editing program that lets you create and modify digital images. 'CC' stands for Creative Cloud, a complete design environment. Although Adobe makes Photoshop available as a stand-alone product, it is also available as part of the Creative Cloud subscription, whether your interests lie with print design, web design, or multimedia production.

QUICK TIP

The Creative Cloud offers many constantly evolving tools (such as Bridge, Dreamweaver, Illustrator, InDesign, and Photoshop) and services (such as Typekit and Kuler).

A **digital image** is a picture in electronic form, and may be referred to as a file, document, graphic, picture, or image. Using Photoshop, you can create original artwork, manipulate images, and retouch photographs. Popular with graphics professionals, Photoshop is practical for anyone who wants to enhance existing artwork or create new masterpieces. For example, you can repair and restore damaged areas within an image, combine images, and create graphics and special effects for the web.

Understanding Platform User Interfaces

Photoshop is available for both Windows and Mac OS platforms. Regardless of which platform you use, the features and commands are similar. Some Windows and Mac OS keyboard commands use different keys. For example, the [Ctrl] and [Alt] keys are used in Windows, and the [⌘] and [option] keys are used on Macintosh computers. There are also cosmetic differences between the Windows and Mac OS versions of Photoshop due to the user interface differences found in each platform.

Understanding Sources

Photoshop allows you to work with images from a variety of sources. You can create your own original artwork in Photoshop, use images downloaded from the web, or use images that have been scanned or created using a digital camera. Whether you create Photoshop images to print in high resolution or optimize them for multimedia presentations, web-based functions, or animation projects, Photoshop is a powerful tool for communicating your ideas visually.

QUICK TIP

This book examines features in the 2014 release of Photoshop CC.

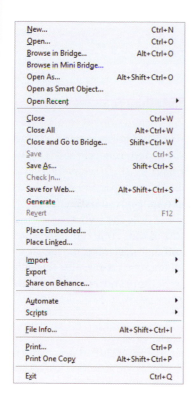

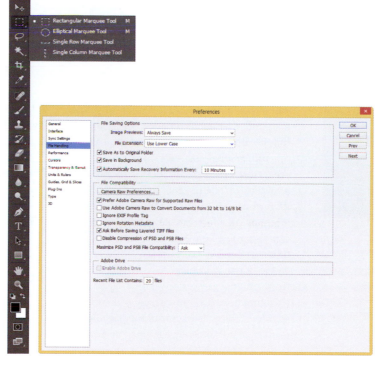

Options bar

Start Adobe
PHOTOSHOP CC 2014

What You'll Do

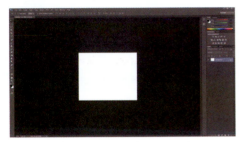

In this lesson, you'll start Photoshop for Windows or Mac OS, and then create a file.

Defining Image-Editing Software

Photoshop is an image-editing program. An **image-editing program** allows you to manipulate graphic images so that they can be posted on websites or reproduced by professional printers using full-color processes. Using panels, tools, menus, and a variety of techniques, you can modify a Photoshop image by rotating it, resizing it, changing its colors, or adding text. You can also use Photoshop to create and open different kinds of file formats, which enables you to create your own images, import them from a digital camera or scanner, or use files (in other formats) purchased from outside sources. Table 1 lists some of the graphics file formats that Photoshop can open and create.

Understanding Images

Every image is made up of very small squares, which are called **pixels**, and each pixel represents a color or shade. Pixels within an image can be added, deleted, or modified.

QUICK TIP

Photoshop files can become quite large. After a file is complete, you might want to **flatten** it, an irreversible process that combines all layers and reduces the file size.

Using Photoshop Features

Photoshop includes many tools that you can use to manipulate images and text. Within an image, you can add new items and modify existing elements, change colors, and draw shapes. For example, using the Lasso tool, you can outline a section of an image and drag the section onto another area of the image. You can also isolate a foreground or background image. You can extract all or part of a complex image from nearly any background and use it elsewhere.

QUICK TIP

You can create logos in Photoshop. A **logo** is a distinctive image that you can create by combining symbols, shapes, colors, and text. Logos give graphic identity to organizations such as corporations, universities, and retail stores.

You can also create and format text, called **type**, in Photoshop. You can apply a variety of special effects to type; for example, you can change the appearance of type and increase or decrease the distance between characters. You can also edit type after it has been created and formatted.

Adobe Dreamweaver CC, a web production app included in the Creative Cloud, allows you to optimize, preview, and animate images. Because Dreamweaver and Photoshop are both members of the Creative Cloud, you can jump seamlessly between the two apps.

Using these two apps, you can also quickly turn any graphics image into a gif animation.

Photoshop and Dreamweaver let you compress file size (while optimizing image quality) to ensure that your files download quickly from a web page. Using Photoshop optimization features, you can view multiple versions of an image and select the one that best suits your needs.

Starting Photoshop and Creating a File

The specific way you start Photoshop depends on whether you are using a Macintosh or Windows computer. When you start Photoshop in either platform, the computer displays a **splash screen**, which contains information about the software, and then the Photoshop window opens.

After you start Photoshop, you can create a file from scratch. You use the New dialog box to create a file. You can also use the New dialog box to set the size of the image you're about to create by typing dimensions in the Width and Height text boxes.

TABLE 1: SOME SUPPORTED GRAPHIC FILE FORMATS			
File format	**Filename extension**	**File format**	**Filename extension**
Bitmap	.bmp	PICT file	.pct, .pic, or .pict
Dicom	.dcm	Pixar	.pxr
Flash 3D	.fl3	Open EXR	.exr
Google Earth	.kmz	Radiance	.hdr, .rgbe, .xyze
Graphics Interchange Format	.gif	RAW	Varies
JPEG Picture Format	.jpg, .jpe, or .jpeg	Scitex CT	.sct
PC Paintbrush	.pcx	Tagged Image Format	.tif or .tiff
Photoshop	.psd	Targa	.tga or .vda
Photoshop EPS	.eps	Wavefront	.obj
Photoshop PDF	.pdf		

© 2013 Cengage Learning®

Start Photoshop (Windows 7, 8, or 8.1)

1. If using Windows 7, click the **Start button** 🅰 on the taskbar; if using Windows 8 or 8.1, click the **Windows logo button** 🔲 on the taskbar.

2. Type **ph**, click **Adobe Photoshop CC 2014** if necessary, as shown in Figure 1 using Windows 8.1, then click **Adobe Photoshop CC 2014**.

   If a 64-bit option is not available, click **Adobe Photoshop CC 2014**.

TIP In Windows 7, the text will be typed in the Search programs and files text box. The results of your search will display in the box above the Start button.

3. Click **File** on the Menu bar, then click **New** to open the New dialog box.

4. Double-click the **number in the Width text box**, type **500**, click the **Width list arrow**, then click **Pixels** if it is not already selected.

5. Double-click the **number in the Height text box**, type **400**, then specify a resolution of **72** pixels/inch if necessary.

6. Click **OK**.

TIP By default, the document window (the background of the active image) is dark gray. This color can be changed by right-clicking the background, then making a color selection.

7. Click the **menu arrow** ▶ on the status bar at the bottom of the image window, then click **Document Sizes** if it is not already selected.

You started Photoshop in Windows, then created a file with custom dimensions. Setting custom dimensions lets you specify the exact size of the image you are creating. You changed the display on the status bar to show the document size.

Figure 1 *Starting Photoshop CC (Windows)*

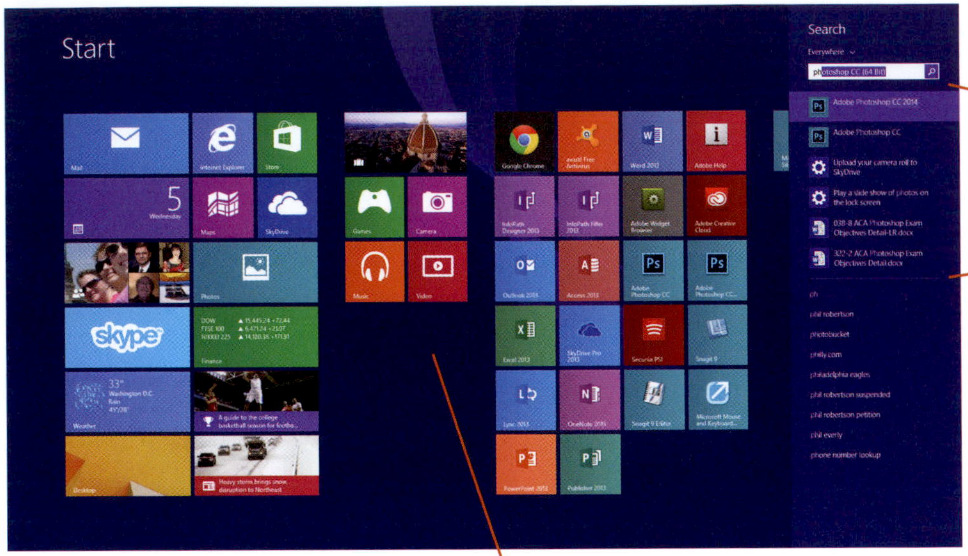

Your list may differ

Tiles on your screen will differ

Understanding Hardware Requirements (Windows)

Adobe Photoshop CC has the following minimum system requirements:

- Processor: Intel® Pentium® 4 processor or AMD Athlon® 64 processor (2 GHz or faster)
- Operating System: Microsoft® Windows 7 (with Service Pack 1), 8, or 8 .1
- Memory: 1 GB of RAM
- Storage space: 2.5 GB of available hard-disk space
- Monitor: 1024 x 768 resolution (1280 x 800 recommended)
- Video: 16-bit or higher OpenGL 2.0 video card; 512 MB RAM (1 GB recommended)
- Broadband Internet connection required for activation, Creative Cloud membership validation, and access to online services

Figure 2 *Starting Photoshop CC (Macintosh)*

Source: Apple Inc.

Understanding Hardware Requirements (Mac OS)

Adobe Photoshop CC has the following minimum system requirements:

- Processor: Multicore Intel® processor with 64-bit support
- Operating System: Mac OS X 10.7, v10.8, or v10.9
- Memory: 1 GB of RAM
- Storage space: 3.2 GB of available hard-disk space
- Monitor: 1024 x 768 or greater monitor resolution (1280 x 800 recommended)
- Video: 16-bit or greater OpenGL 2.0 video card; 512 MB of VRAM (1 GB recommended)
- Broadband Internet connection required for software activation, Creative Cloud membership validation, and access to online services

Start Photoshop (Mac OS)

1. Click the **Launchpad icon** in the Dock, then type **ph**. (The search field does not appear in Mac OS 10.7.) Compare your screen to Figure 2.

2. Click the **Adobe Photoshop CC 2014 program icon**.

3. Click **File** on the Menu bar, then click **New**.

4. Double-click the **number in the Width text box**, type **500**, click the **Width list arrow**, then click **Pixels**.

5. Double-click the **number in the Height text box**, type **400**, then verify a resolution of **72** pixels/inch.

6. Click **OK**.

TIP The gray document window background can be turned on by clicking Window on the Menu bar, then clicking Application Frame.

7. Click the **menu arrow** ▶ on the status bar at the bottom of the image window, then click **Document Sizes** if it is not already checked.

You started Photoshop for Mac OS, then created a file with custom dimensions. You verified that the document size is visible on the status bar.

Learn How to Open
AND SAVE AN IMAGE

What You'll Do

Source: Morguefile.

 In this lesson, you'll locate and open files using the File menu, Adobe Bridge, and Mini Bridge; flag and sort files; and then save a file with a new name.

Opening and Saving Files

Photoshop provides several options for opening and saving a file. Often, the project you're working on determines the techniques you use for opening and saving files. For example, you might want to preserve the original version of a file while you modify a copy. You can open a file, and then immediately save it with a different filename, as well as open and save files in many different file formats. When working with graphic images, you can open a Photoshop file that has been saved as a bitmap (.bmp) file, and then save it as a JPEG (.jpg) file to use on a web page.

Customizing How You Open Files

You can customize how you open your files by setting preferences. **Preferences** are options you can set that are based on your work habits. For example, you can use the Open Recent command on the File menu to instantly locate and open the files that you recently worked on, or you can allow others to preview your files as thumbnails. Figure 3 shows the Windows

Figure 3 *Preferences dialog box*

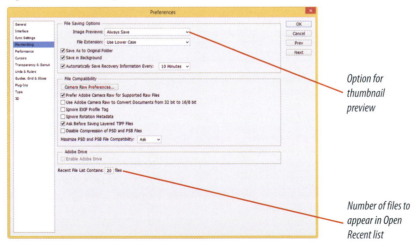

Option for thumbnail preview

Number of files to appear in Open Recent list

Getting Started with Adobe Photoshop CC

Preferences dialog box options for handling your files: the Mac dialog box differs slightly. Use the Preferences command on the Edit menu (Win) or the Photoshop menu (Mac) to open the Preferences dialog box.

Browsing Through Files

You can easily find the files you're looking for using Adobe Bridge, a separate download and stand-alone application that serves as the hub for Adobe Creative Cloud apps, or Adobe Mini Bridge, a less-powerful (and smaller) version of Bridge that opens within the Photoshop window. Mini Bridge provides less data than Bridge, but makes it easier to do simple tasks (like locating and opening files). Figure 4 shows the Magnifying Loupe tool in Adobe Bridge, the default when using the Filmstrip view. You can open Bridge or Mini Bridge using the File menu in Photoshop, but Bridge needs to be open in order to open Mini Bridge.

Figure 4 *Adobe Bridge window*
Source: Morguefile. Images © Photodisc/Getty Images. Image courtesy of Elizabeth Eisner Reding.

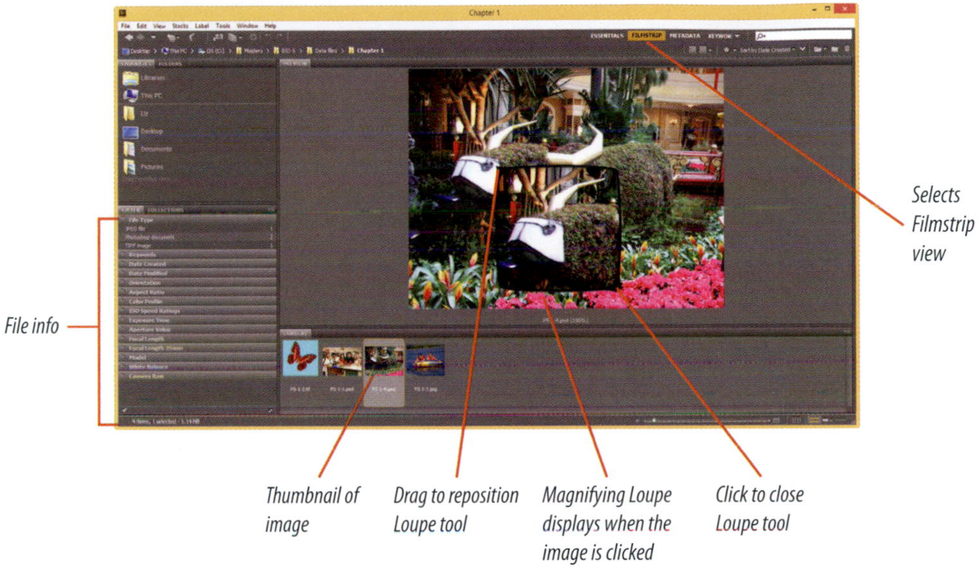

File info

Selects Filmstrip view

Thumbnail of image

Drag to reposition Loupe tool

Magnifying Loupe displays when the image is clicked

Click to close Loupe tool

Opening Scanned Images

You can open a scanned or uploaded image in Photoshop (which usually has a .jpg extension or another graphics file format) by clicking File on the Menu bar, and then clicking Open. All Formats is the default file type, so you should be able to see all available image files in the Open dialog box. (On the Mac, the term All Readable Documents is used instead of All Formats; Enable is used instead of File Type.) Locate the folder containing your scanned or digital camera images, click the file you want to open, and then click Open. A scanned or digital camera image contains all its imagery in a single layer. You can add layers to the image, but you can only save these new layers if you save the image as a Photoshop image (with the extension .psd).

When you open Bridge, a series of panels allows you to view the files on your hard drive as hierarchical files and folders. In addition to the Favorites and Folders panels in the upper-left pane of the Bridge window, there are other important areas. Directly beneath the Favorites and Folders panels is a grouping that includes the Filter panel, which allows you to review properties of images in the (center) Content panel. In the (default) Essentials view, the right column displays the Preview panel and the Metadata and Keywords panels, which store information about a selected file (such as keywords) that can then be used as search parameters. You can use the tree structure (visible when the Folders tab is active) to find the file you are seeking. When you locate a file, you can click its thumbnail to display a larger image in the Preview panel and to see information about its size, format, and creation and modification dates in the Metadata panel. You can open a file in Photoshop from Bridge by double-clicking its thumbnail. You can close Bridge by clicking File (Win) or Adobe Bridge CC (Mac) on the (Bridge) Menu bar, and then clicking Exit (Win) or Quit Adobe Bridge CC (Mac), or by clicking the window's Close button (Win).

QUICK TIP

You can select multiple non-contiguous images by pressing and holding [Ctrl] (Win) or ⌘ (Mac) each time you click an image. You can select contiguous images by clicking the first image, and then pressing and holding [Shift] and clicking the last image in the group.

QUICK TIP

You can reset the Adobe Bridge preferences to the factory default by holding [Ctrl][Alt] (Win) or ⌘ [option] (Mac) while clicking the Launch Bridge button.

Understanding the Power of Bridge

In addition to allowing you to see all your images, Bridge can be used to rate (assign importance), sort (organize by name, rating, and other criteria), and label your images. Figure 4, on the previous page, contains images shown in Filmstrip view. There are seven potential views in Bridge (Essentials, Filmstrip, Metadata, Keywords, Light Table, Folders, and Output) that are controlled by buttons to the left of the search text box. (The Adobe Output Module and Light Table may have to be installed separately.) To assist in organizing your images, you can assign a color label or rating to one or more images regardless of your current view. Any number of selected images can be assigned a label by clicking Label on the Menu bar, and then clicking one of the Rating or Label options.

QUICK TIP

You can use Bridge to view thumbnails of all files on your computer. You can open any file for software *installed* on your computer by double-clicking its thumbnail in Bridge.

Getting There with Mini Bridge

While not as powerful as Bridge, Mini Bridge can be used to easily filter, sort, locate, and open files from *within* Photoshop. Mini Bridge is opened in the Photoshop window once Bridge is running, by clicking the Browse in Mini Bridge command on the File menu. Mini Bridge can be resized to suit your needs, and closed and reopened whenever necessary. To navigate Mini Bridge, shown in Figure 5 after being undocked and resized, you can click the arrows within the Path bar to change the file source. Clicking each arrow in the Path bar reveals the file structure in your hard drive. When you locate a file you want to open in Photoshop, double-click its thumbnail image.

QUICK TIP

So when might you use Mini Bridge? Suppose you need a file but don't know where it is. Without closing or switching out of Photoshop, you can use Mini Bridge to locate the file, and then open it by double-clicking its thumbnail.

Using Save As Versus Save

Sometimes it's more efficient to create a new image by modifying an existing one, especially if it contains elements and special effects that you want to use again. The Save As command on the File menu (in Photoshop) creates a copy of the file, prompts you to give the duplicate file a new name, and then displays the new filename in the image's title bar. You use the Save As command to name an unnamed file or to save an existing file with a new name. For example, throughout this book, you will be instructed to open your Data Files and use the Save As command. Saving your Data Files with new names keeps the original files intact in case you have to start the lesson over again or you want to repeat an exercise. When you use the Save command, you save the changes you made to the open file.

QUICK TIP

You can also create a copy of the active file by clicking Image on the Menu bar, and then clicking Duplicate. Click OK to confirm the name of the duplicate file.

Getting Images into Photoshop

There are a zillion digital cameras available in the marketplace, and each brand is a little different, but you can still easily import your images into Bridge by connecting the camera to your computer using the camera's cable. Turn the camera on and once your computer recognizes the camera, open Adobe Bridge. Click File on the (Bridge) Menu bar, then click Get Photos from Camera. This opens the Adobe Bridge CC Photo Downloader. Select the correct camera device from the

Get Photos from list arrow and choose a location for the downloaded file, then click Get Media. Your images are probably in the JPEG or RAW format, and their clarity will be the result of the megapixel capacity of your camera and the resolution setting.

Figure 5 *Mini Bridge*
Source: Morguefile. Images © Photodisc/Getty Images. Image courtesy of Elizabeth Eisner Reding.

Path bar

Click to go to Bridge   Click to sort   Drag to enlarge/reduce thumbnail size   Drag to resize the Mini Bridge window

Resizing an Image

You may have created the perfect image, but the size may not be correct for your print format. Document size is a combination of the printed dimensions and pixel resolution. An image designed for a website, for example, might be too small for an image that will be printed in a newsletter. You can easily resize an image using the Image Size command on the Image menu. To use this feature, open the file you want to resize, click Image on the Menu bar, and then click Image Size. The Image Size dialog box, shown in Figure 6, opens. By changing the dimensions in the text boxes, you'll have your image resized in no time. Note the check mark next to Resample Image. With resampling checked, you can change the total number of pixels in the image and the print dimensions independently. With resampling off, you can change either the dimensions or the resolution; Photoshop will automatically adjust whichever value you ignore. The **canvas size**, which is the full editable area of an image, can be increased or decreased using the Canvas Size command on the Image menu. Decreasing an image's size crops the image whereas increasing the image's size adds to the background.

Figure 6 *Image Size dialog box*
Source: Morguefile.

Open a file using the Menu bar

1. Click **File** on the Menu bar, then click **Open**.

2. Click the **Look in list arrow** (Win) or the **Current file location list arrow** (Mac), then navigate to the drive and folder where you store your Data Files.

3. Click **PS 1-1.psd**, as shown in Figure 7, then click **Open**.

You used the Open command on the File menu to locate and open a file.

Open a file using the Folders panel in Adobe Bridge

1. Click **File** on the Menu bar, click **Browse in Bridge**, then click the **Folders panel tab** if the Folders panel is not active.

2. Navigate through the hierarchical tree to the drive and folder where you store your Chapter 1 Data Files, verify that Sort by Type and an up arrow (∧) display below the search box, then click **Essentials** on the workspace switcher if it is not already selected.

3. Click the **image of the butterfly**, then drag the **slider** (at the bottom of the Bridge window) a third of the way between the Smaller thumbnail size button 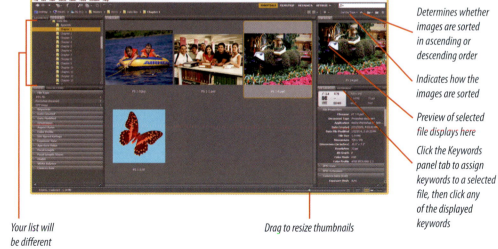 and the Larger thumbnail size button 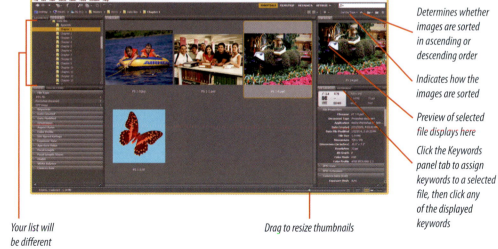, then click the image of the ox *once*. Compare your screen to Figure 8.

4. Double-click the **image of a butterfly** (PS 1-2.tif). Bridge is no longer visible.

5. Click the **Close button** in the butterfly image file tab in Photoshop.

You used the Folders panel in Adobe Bridge to locate and open a file. This feature makes it easy to find which file you want to use.

Figure 7 *Open dialog box for Windows and Macintosh*
Source: Morguefile. Images © Photodisc/Getty Images.

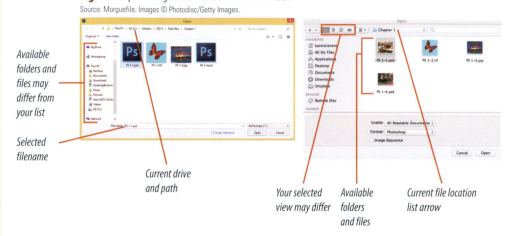

Available folders and files may differ from your list

Selected filename

Current drive and path

Your selected view may differ

Available folders and files

Current file location list arrow

Figure 8 *Adobe Bridge window*
Source: Morguefile. Images © Photodisc/Getty Images. Image courtesy of Elizabeth Eisner Reding.

Determines whether images are sorted in ascending or descending order

Indicates how the images are sorted

Preview of selected file displays here

Click the Keywords panel tab to assign keywords to a selected file, then click any of the displayed keywords

Your list will be different

Drag to resize thumbnails

Figure 9 *Adobe Mini Bridge window*

Source: Morguefile. Images © Photodisc/Getty Images. Image courtesy of Elizabeth Eisner Reding.

Timeline tab displays when Mini Bridge opens

Click to change the view options

Click to sort items

Move window by dragging this bar

Click to close Mini Bridge

Click to filter items

Resize window by dragging this (or any) corner

Path bar: yours will differ

Figure 10 *Save As dialog box*

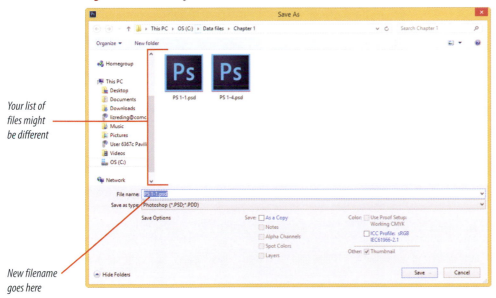

Your list of files might be different

New filename goes here

Open a file using Mini Bridge

1. Click **File** on the Menu bar, then click **Browse in Mini Bridge**.
2. Use the Path bar to locate the drive and folder where you store your Chapter 1 Data Files. See Figure 9.
3. Double-click the **image of a butterfly** (PS 1-2.tif).
4. Double-click the **Mini Bridge tab** to minimize the panel, then close PS 1-2.tif.

   By default, Mini Bridge is minimized at the bottom of the Photoshop workspace. Enlarge or minimize Mini Bridge by double-clicking its tab.

You opened Mini Bridge in Photoshop, navigated to where your Data Files are stored, opened a file, then minimized Mini Bridge.

Use the Save As command

1. Verify that the PS 1-1.psd window is active.
2. Click **File** on the Menu bar, click **Save As**, then compare your Save As dialog box to Figure 10.
3. If the drive containing your Data Files is not displayed, click the **Save in list arrow** (Win) or the **Current file location list arrow** (Mac), then navigate to the drive and folder where you store your Chapter 1 Data Files.
4. Select the current filename in the File name text box (Win) or Save As text box (Mac), type **Friends**, then click **Save**.

TIP Click OK to close the Maximize Compatibility dialog box if it appears now and in future lessons.

You used the Save As command on the File menu to save the file with a new name. This command lets you save a changed version of an image while keeping the original file intact.

Change from Tabbed to Floating Documents

1. Click **Window** on the Menu bar, point to **Arrange**, then click **2-up Horizontal**.

Each of the open files displays in a horizontal window.

N-up viewing allows you to edit one image while comparing it with another. You can drag layers from one image to another in N-up view. Use N-up viewing using the Arrange command on the Window menu, and then tiling either horizontally or vertically until the images are in the configuration that works best.

TIP You can display images in several arrangements which allows you to vary the grouping of open documents. To see these arrangements, click Window on the Menu bar, point to Arrange, then click any of the available menu choices.

TIP The options in the Arrange menu make a temporary change to the workspace that will be in effect for the current Photoshop session.

2. Click **Window** on the Menu bar, point to **Arrange**, then click **Float All in Windows**. Compare your Friends image to Figure 11.

TIP By default, each image is displayed in its own tab, but you can change this so each image floats in its own window.

You temporarily changed the arrangement of open documents from consolidated, or tabbed, to a 2-up Horizontal format, and then to the Float All in Windows format where each image displays in its own window.

Figure 11 *Friends image*
Source: Morguefile.

Duplicate file has new name

Ps Friends.psd @ 100% (RGB/8#)

100%   Doc: 550.8K/550.8K

Changing File Formats

In addition to using the Save As command to duplicate an existing file, the Save As command is a handy way of changing one format into another. For example, you can open an image you created using a digital camera, and then make modifications in the Photoshop format. To do this, open a JPEG file in Photoshop, click File on the Menu bar, and then click Save As. Name the file, click the Format list arrow, click Photoshop (*.psd, *.pdd) (Win) or Photoshop (Mac), and then click Save. You can also change formats using Bridge by selecting the file, clicking Tools on the Menu bar, pointing to Photoshop, and then clicking Image Processor. Section 3 of the Image Processor dialog box lets you determine the new file format.

Figure 12 *Images in Adobe Bridge*

Source: Morguefile. Images © Photodisc/Getty Images. Image courtesy of Elizabeth Eisner Reding.

Click to change sorting method

Rated and Approved file

Figure 13 *Sorted files*

Source: Morguefile. Images © Photodisc/Getty Images.

Click to change how items in the Content panel are sorted

Filter items by rating

Rate and filter with Bridge

1. Click **File** on the Menu bar, then click **Browse in Bridge** [Br] to make the program active.

2. Click the **Folders panel tab**, then click the drive and folder where you store your Chapter 1 Data Files on the File Hierarchy tree (if necessary).

3. Verify that file **PS 1-2.tif** (the butterfly image) is selected.

4. Press and hold [**Ctrl**] (Win) or [⌘] (Mac), click **PS 1-1.psd** (the image of the friends), then release [**Ctrl**] (Win) or [⌘] (Mac).

5. Click **Label** on the Bridge Menu bar, then click **Approved**.

6. Click **PS 1-1.psd**, click **Label** on the Bridge Menu bar, then click *******. See Figure 12.

7. Click the **Sort list arrow** on the Bridge Path bar, click **By Filename**, point to **Sort**, then verify that the **Ascending Order arrow** displays to the right of the sort list arrow. Compare your screen to Figure 13.

   The order of the files is changed.

TIP You can also change the order of files in the Content panel using the Sort command on the View menu. When you click the Sort by Filename list arrow, you'll see the same sorting options as on the View menu. Click the option you want and the files in the Content panel will be rearranged.

8. Click **View** on the Menu bar, point to **Sort**, then click **By Size**.

9. Click **File** (Win) or **Adobe Bridge CC** (Mac) on the (Bridge) Menu bar, then click **Exit** (Win) or **Quit Adobe Bridge CC** (Mac) to close Bridge.

You labeled and rated files using Bridge, sorted the files in a folder, then changed the sort order. When finished, you closed Bridge.

Examine
THE PHOTOSHOP WINDOW

What You'll Do

 In this lesson, you'll arrange documents and change the default display, select a tool on the Tools panel, use a shortcut key to cycle through the hidden tools, select and add a tool to the Tool Preset picker, use the Window menu to show and hide panels in the workspace, and create a customized workspace.

Learning About the Workspace

The Photoshop **workspace** is the area within the Photoshop program window that includes the entire window, from the command menus at the top of your screen to the status bar (Win) at the bottom. Desktop items may be visible between the menu commands and the document title bar (Mac). The (Windows) workspace is shown in Figure 14.

In Windows, the area containing the Photoshop commands is called the Menu bar. On the Mac, the main menus are at the top of the desktop, but not directly attached to the options bar. If the active image window is maximized, the filename of the open unnamed file is Untitled-1, because it has not been named. The Menu bar also contains the Close button and the Minimize/Maximize and Restore buttons (Win).

You can choose a menu command by clicking it or in Windows, by pressing [Alt], and then clicking the underlined letter in the menu name. Some commands display shortcut keys on the right side of the menu. Shortcut keys provide an alternative way to activate menu commands. Some commands might appear dimmed, which means they are not currently available. A right-pointing triangle after a command indicates additional choices.

DESIGN TIP

Overcoming Information Overload

One of the most common experiences shared by first-time Photoshop users is information overload. There are just too many panels and tools to look at! When you feel your brain overheating, take a moment and sit back. Remind yourself that the active image area is the central area where you can see a composite of your work. All the tools and panels are there to help you, not to add to the confusion. The tools and features in Photoshop CC are designed to be easier to find and use, making any given task faster to complete.

Finding Tools Everywhere

The **Tools panel** contains tools associated with frequently used Photoshop commands. The face of a tool contains a graphical representation (icon) of its function; for example, the Zoom tool shows a magnifying glass. The **zoom factor** (the amount of magnification applied to the image) is shown in the document title bar and allows you to better see the area you're working on. You can place the pointer over each tool to display a tool tip, which tells you the name or function of that tool. Some tools have additional hidden tools, indicated by a small gray triangle in the lower-right corner of the tool.

QUICK TIP

You can view the Tools panel in a 2-column format by clicking the expand arrow in its upper-left corner.

The **options bar**, located directly under the Menu bar, displays the current settings for the selected tool. For example, when you click the Type tool, the default font and font size appear on the options bar, which can be changed if desired. You can move the options bar anywhere in the workspace for easier access. The first button on the options bar is the Tool preset picker, which displays the active tool. You can click the list arrow on the Tool Preset picker to select another tool without having to use the Tools panel. Two vertical docks display to the right of the Document window, the panel icon dock and the expanded panel dock. Panels not displayed in a workspace can be collapsed and expanded from the icon dock, which also contains an area where you can assemble panels for quick access.

Panels are small windows used to access settings and modify images. By default, panels appear in stacked groups at the right side of the window. A collection of panels is called a **panel group**. A **dock** is a dark gray vertical bar that contains a collection of panels, panel groups or panel icons. The arrows in the dock are used to expand and collapse the panels. You can display a panel by simply clicking the panel tab, or making it the active panel by clicking its name in the Window menu, or by clicking its icon in the icon dock (if it's displayed). Panels can be separated and moved anywhere in the workspace by dragging their tabs to new locations. You can dock or undock a panel by dragging its tab in or out of a dock. As you move a panel within the dock, you'll see a blue highlighted drop zone. A **drop zone** is an area where you can move a panel. You can also change the order of tabs by dragging a tab to a new location within its panel. Each panel contains a menu that you can view by clicking the Panel options button in its upper-right corner.

QUICK TIP

You can reset panels to their default locations at any time by selecting Reset Essentials in the workspace switcher.

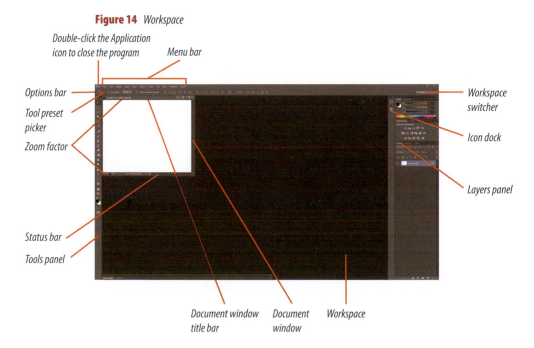

Figure 14 *Workspace*

Double-click the Application icon to close the program

Menu bar

Options bar

Tool preset picker

Zoom factor

Status bar

Tools panel

Workspace switcher

Icon dock

Layers panel

Document window title bar

Document window

Workspace

When images are displayed as tabbed documents, the **status bar** is located at the bottom of the program window (Win) or work area (Mac). When images are floating, the status bar is located at the bottom of each individual image. It displays information, such as the file size of the active window. You can display other information on the status bar by clicking the triangle to view a menu with more options.

Rulers can help you precisely measure and position an object in the workspace. The rulers do not appear the first time you use Photoshop, but you can display them by clicking Rulers on the View menu.

Using Tool Shortcut Keys

Each tool has a corresponding shortcut key. For example, the shortcut key for the Type tool is T. After you know a tool's shortcut key, you can select the tool on the Tools panel by pressing its shortcut key. To select and cycle through a tool's hidden tools, you press and hold [Shift], and then press the tool's shortcut key until the desired tool appears.

Customizing Your Environment

Photoshop makes it easy for you to position elements just where you want them. If you move elements around to make your environment more convenient, you can always return your workspace to its original appearance by resetting the default panel locations. Once you have your work area arranged the way you want it, you can create a customized workspace by clicking the workspace switcher on the Menu bar, and then clicking New Workspace. If you want to open a named workspace, click the workspace switcher, and then click the name of the workspace you want to use. Photoshop comes with many customized workspaces that are designed for specific tasks.

You can also change the color of your workspace by clicking Edit on the Menu bar, pointing to Preferences, then clicking Interface (Win) or by clicking Photoshop on the Menu bar, pointing to Preferences, then clicking Interface (Mac). Here you can choose one of four color themes. Color themes can be changed on a permanent or temporary basis. Using the Color list arrows in the Interface panel of the Preferences dialog box, you can permanently change the color theme using the four displayed themes, or any color you choose.

Figure 15 *Keyboard Shortcuts and Menus dialog box*

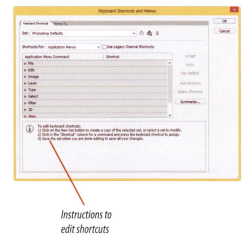

Instructions to edit shortcuts

Learning Shortcut Keys and Creating Customized Keyboard Shortcuts

Keyboard shortcuts can make your work with Photoshop faster and easier. As you become more familiar with Photoshop, you'll gradually pick up shortcuts for commands and tools you use most often, such as saving a file or the Move tool. You'll notice that as you learn to use shortcut keys, your speed while working with Photoshop will increase and you'll complete tasks with fewer mouse clicks. In fact, once you discover the power of keyboard shortcuts, you may never use menus again. You can find existing keyboard shortcuts by clicking Edit on the Menu bar, and then clicking Keyboard Shortcuts. The Keyboard Shortcuts and Menus dialog box, shown in Figure 15, allows you to add shortcuts or edit those that already exist. You can also display the list of shortcuts by exporting it to an HTML file, and then printing it or viewing it in a browser.

Figure 16 *Hidden tools*
Source: Morguefile.

Shortcut key

Select a tool

1. Click the **Lasso tool** on the Tools panel, press and hold the **mouse button** until a list of hidden tools appears, then release the **mouse button**. See Figure 16. Note the shortcut key, L, next to the tool name.

2. Click the **Polygonal Lasso tool** on the Tools panel.

3. Press and hold [**Shift**], press [**L**] three times to cycle through the Lasso tools, then release [**Shift**]. Did you notice how the options bar changes for each selected Lasso tool?

TIP You can return the tools to their default setting by clicking the Tool Preset picker list arrow on the options bar, clicking the More Options button, then clicking Reset All Tools.

You selected the Lasso tool on the Tools panel and used its shortcut key to cycle through the Lasso tools. Becoming familiar with shortcut keys can speed up your work and make you more efficient.

64-bit Version of Photoshop

You may have heard people talking about the 64-bit version of Photoshop. What does this mean? (Here's a good analogy: Imagine a bus that can hold 64 students versus one that can only hold 32 students. Because it has a larger capacity, the bus carrying 64 students will have to make fewer trips to pick up a greater number of students.) Prior to CS5, Photoshop was only available as a 32-bit application for both Windows and Mac. With CS6 and CC, Photoshop became a 64-bit application. This meant that the architecture of the program had been redesigned to accommodate huge files (those larger than 4 GB) and make better use of RAM. The net result is that the 64-bit version of Photoshop is faster and more efficient. Some features, however, still work only in 32-bit mode (until they're updated), whereas other features, such as video, are not supported on 32-bit mode. In Windows, you can launch either version from the Windows taskbar (or pin either or both versions to the taskbar). The Mac OS version of Photoshop is only available in 64-bit.

Select a tool from the Tool Preset picker

1. Click the **Tool Preset picker list arrow** ⬛▾ on the options bar.

2. Deselect the **Current Tool Only check box** if checked. See Figure 17.

   The name of a button is displayed in a tool tip, the descriptive text that appears when you point to the button. Your Tool Preset picker list will differ, and may contain no entries at all. This list can be customized by each user.

3. Double-click **Magnetic Lasso 24 pixels** in the list.

TIP Double-clicking a tool selects it and closes the Tool Preset picker list.

You selected the Magnetic Lasso tool using the Tool Preset picker. The Tool Preset picker makes it easy to access frequently used tools and their settings.

Figure 17 *Using the Tool Preset picker*

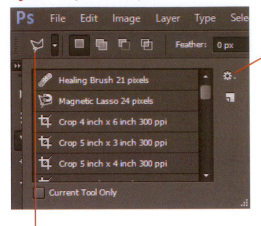

More Options button adds new tools and displays more options

Active tool displays in Tool Preset picker

Figure 18 *Full Screen Mode with Menu bar*
Source: Morguefile.

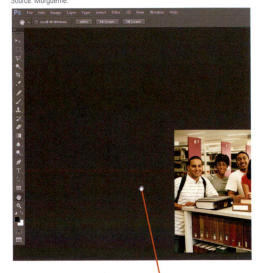

Use hand pointer to reposition image

Using the Full Screen Mode

By default, Photoshop displays images in consolidated tabs, although you can change this on a permanent or temporary basis. This means that each image is displayed within its own tab. There are also three modes for viewing the menus, panels, and tools: Standard Screen Mode, Full Screen Mode with Menu Bar, and Full Screen Mode. And why would you want to stray from the familiar Standard Screen Mode? Perhaps your image is so large that it's difficult to see it all in Standard Screen Mode, or perhaps you want a less cluttered screen. Maybe you just want to try something different. You can switch between modes by clicking View on the Menu bar, pointing to Screen Mode, then clicking one of the three modes. You can also change modes by pressing [Shift] F. When in Full Screen Mode with Menu bar, click the Hand tool (or press the keyboard shortcut H), and you can reposition the active image, as shown in Figure 18.

Getting Started with Adobe Photoshop CC

Figure 19 *Move tool added to Tool Preset picker*

Healing Brush 21 pixels

Move Tool 1

Magnetic Lasso 24 pixels

Crop 4 inch x 6 inch 300 ppi

Crop 5 inch x 3 inch 300 ppi

Current Tool Only

Click to display menu options

New tool added to panel

Selected check box displays only current tool

Setting Preferences

The Preferences dialog box contains several topics, each with its own settings: General; Interface; Sync Settings, File Handling; Performance; Cursors; Transparency & Gamut; Units & Rulers; Guides, Grid & Slices; Plug-Ins; Type; and 3D. To open the Preferences dialog box, click Edit (Win) or Photoshop (Mac) on the Menu bar, point to Preferences, and then click a topic that represents the settings you want to change. For example, if you move panels around the workspace or make other changes to them, those changes will be retained the next time you start the program. To reset panels to their default, click Interface on the Preferences menu, click the Restore Default Workspaces button, and then click OK.

Add a tool to the Tool Preset picker

1. Click the **Move tool** on the Tools panel.
2. Click the **Tool Preset picker list arrow** on the options bar.
3. Click the **More Options button** on the Tool Preset picker.
4. Click **New Tool Preset**, then click **OK** to accept the default name (Move Tool 1). Compare your list to Figure 19.

TIP You can display the currently selected tool alone by selecting the Current Tool Only check box.

You added the Move tool to the Tool Preset picker. Once you know how to add tools to the Tool Preset picker, you can quickly and easily customize your work environment.

Change the default display, theme color, and document display

1. Click **Edit** (Win) or **Photoshop** (Mac) on the Menu bar, point to **Preferences**, then click **Interface**.
2. Click the **far-right gray color box** (light gray).

   Did you notice that the workspace color changed?
3. Click the **far-left gray color box** (dark gray), click the **second from the right gray color box**, click the **second from the left gray color box**.

   The workspace theme display returns to the default.
4. Click the **Open Documents as Tabs check box** to deselect it, then click **OK**.

You examined each of the available color themes and changed the default display so that each time you open Photoshop, each image will display in its own window rather than in tabs.

Show and hide panels

1. If necessary, click the **Swatches tab** to make the Swatches panel active, as shown in Figure 20.
2. Click the **Collapse to Icons button** ▸▸ on the dock to collapse the panels.
3. Click the **Expand Panels button** ◂◂ on the dock to expand the panels.
4. Click **Window** on the Menu bar, then click **Swatches** to deselect it.

TIP You can hide all open panels by pressing [Shift] and [Tab] together, and then show them by pressing [Shift] and [Tab] again. To hide all open panels, the options bar, and the Tools panel, press [Tab], then show them by pressing [Tab] again. If you close a panel that is grouped with other panels, the other panels close as well.

5. Click **Window** on the Menu bar, then click **Swatches** to redisplay the Swatches panel.

You collapsed and expanded the panels, then used the Window menu to show and hide the Swatches panel. You might want to hide panels at times in order to enlarge your work area.

Figure 20 *Active Swatches panel*

Recently used color swatches (yours will differ)

Swatches tab is active

Figure 21 *Tool Preset picker More Options menu*

New Tool Preset...
Rename Tool Preset...
Delete Tool Preset
✔ Sort by Tool
✔ Show All Tool Presets
Show Current Tool Presets
Text Only
✔ Small List
Large List
Reset Tool
Reset All Tools
Preset Manager...
Reset Tool Presets...
Load Tool Presets...
Save Tool Presets...
Replace Tool Presets...
Airbrushes
Art History
Artists' Brushes
Brushes
Crop and Marquee
DP Presets
Dry Media
Pencil Brushes
Pencils Mixer Brush
Splatter Brush Tool Presets
Text

Modifying a Tool Preset

Once you've created tool presets, you'll probably want to know how they can be deleted and renamed. To delete any tool preset, select it on the Tool Preset picker panel. Click the More Options button on the Tool Preset picker panel to view the menu, shown in Figure 21, and then click Delete Tool Preset. To rename a tool preset, click the More Options button and then click Rename Tool Preset.

Figure 22 *New Workspace dialog box*

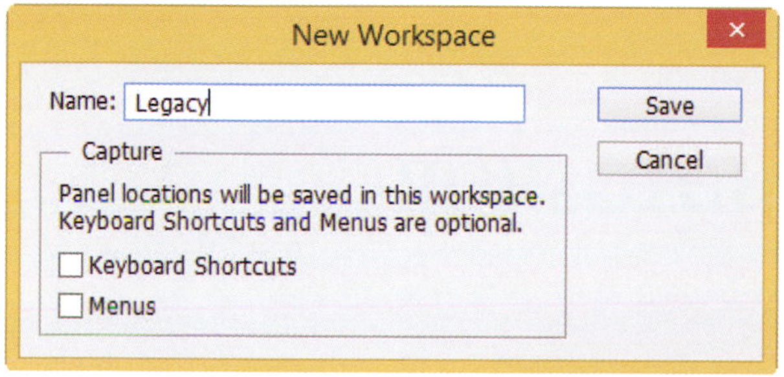

Figure 23 *Adobe Configurator 4*
Adobe Systems Incorporated.

Create a customized workspace

1. Click **Window** on the Menu bar, click **History**, then drag the newly displayed panel in the dark gray line *beneath* the Swatches panel. (*Hint*: When you drag one panel into another, you'll see a light blue line, indicating that the new panel will dock with the existing panels.)

2. Click **Window** on the Menu bar, point to **Workspace**, then click **New Workspace**.

3. Type **Legacy** in the Name text box, then verify that only Panel locations will be saved, as shown in Figure 22.

4. Click **Save**.

5. Click **Window** on the Menu bar, then point to **Workspace**.

   The name of the new workspace appears on the Workspace menu.

6. Click **Essentials (Default)**.

You created a customized workspace, then reset the panel locations to the default Essentials workspace. Customized workspaces provide you with a work area that is always tailored to your needs.

Creating Your Own Panels with Adobe Configurator

You've seen how you can customize your workspace by grouping panels, and then saving the settings for future use. Configurator 4, shown in Figure 23, lets you create a customized Photoshop workspace on steroids. Configurator is a downloadable app from Adobe that lets you create your own panels. Using drag-and-drop technology, you can pick and choose from the tools, commands, actions, widgets, and containers that are at your disposal in any session of Photoshop, and arrange them in any order you choose. And the great news is that you don't have to be a master programmer to do it! Once you've created a panel, you export it using a command on the File menu, then load the panel into Photoshop using the Extensions command on the Window menu. You can download Configurator from *labs.adobe .com/downloads/configurator.html.*

Close a File
AND EXIT PHOTOSHOP

What You'll Do

New...	Ctrl+N
Open...	Ctrl+O
Browse in Bridge...	Alt+Ctrl+O
Browse in Mini Bridge...	
Open As...	Alt+Shift+Ctrl+O
Open as Smart Object...	
Open Recent	▶
Close	Ctrl+W
Close All	Alt+Ctrl+W
Close and Go to Bridge...	Shift+Ctrl+W
Save	Ctrl+S
Save As...	Shift+Ctrl+S
Check In...	
Save for Web...	Alt+Shift+Ctrl+S
Generate	▶
Revert	F12
Place Embedded...	
Place Linked...	
Import	▶
Export	▶
Share on Behance...	
Automate	▶
Scripts	▶
File Info...	Alt+Shift+Ctrl+I
Print...	Ctrl+P
Print One Copy	Alt+Shift+Ctrl+P
Exit	Ctrl+Q

 In this lesson, you'll use the Close and Exit (Win) or Quit (Mac) commands to close a file and exit Photoshop.

Concluding Your Work Session

At the end of your work session, you might have opened several files; you now need to decide which ones you want to save.

QUICK TIP

If you share a computer with other people, it's a good idea to reset Photoshop's preferences back to their default settings. You can do so when you start Photoshop by clicking Window on the Menu bar, pointing to Workspace, and then clicking Essentials (Default).

Closing versus Exiting

When you are finished working on an image, you need to save and close it. You can close one file at a time, or close all open files at the same time by exiting the program. Closing a file leaves Photoshop open, which allows you to open or create another file. Exiting Photoshop closes the file, closes Photoshop, and returns you to the desktop, where you can choose to open another program or shut down the computer. Photoshop will prompt you to save any changes before it closes the files. If you do not modify a new or existing file, Photoshop will close it automatically when you exit.

QUICK TIP

To close all open files without exiting Photoshop, click File on the Menu bar, and then click Close All.

Maintaining Adobe Creative Cloud Tools and Services

When running Photoshop, you may see a small cloud icon (as part of the Creative Cloud installation, not Photoshop specifically) indicating that you have updates to installed Creative Cloud apps, an Update dialog box might appear, prompting you to search for updates or new information on the Adobe website. If you click Yes, Photoshop will automatically notify you that a download is available; however, you do not have to select it. You can also obtain information about Photoshop from the Adobe Photoshop website (www.adobe.com/products/photoshop.html), where you can link to downloads, tips, training, help, resources, and other support topics. The Creative Cloud desktop app in Windows will display the number of updates available. On the Mac, the number of updates will display next to the Creative Cloud icon at the top of the screen.

Figure 24 *Closing a file using the File menu*

New...	Ctrl+N
Open...	Ctrl+O
Browse in Bridge...	Alt+Ctrl+O
Browse in Mini Bridge...	
Open As...	Alt+Shift+Ctrl+O
Open as Smart Object...	
Open Recent	▶
Close	Ctrl+W
Close All	Alt+Ctrl+W
Close and Go to Bridge...	Shift+Ctrl+W
Save	Ctrl+S
Save As...	Shift+Ctrl+S
Check In...	
Save for Web...	Alt+Shift+Ctrl+S
Generate	▶
Revert	F12
Place Embedded...	
Place Linked...	
Import	▶
Export	▶
Share on Behance...	
Automate	▶
Scripts	▶
File Info...	Alt+Shift+Ctrl+I
Print...	Ctrl+P
Print One Copy	Alt+Shift+Ctrl+P
Exit	Ctrl+Q

Close command → Close

Exit command → Exit

Close a file and exit Photoshop

1. Click **File** on the Menu bar, then compare your menu to Figure 24.
2. Click **Close**.

TIP You can close an open file without closing Photoshop by clicking the Close button in the image window or tab. Photoshop will prompt you to save any unsaved changes before closing the file.

3. If asked to save your work, click **Yes** (Win) or **Save** (Mac).
4. Click **File** on the Menu bar, then click **Exit** (Win) or click **Photoshop** on the Menu bar, then click **Quit Photoshop** (Mac).
5. If asked to save your work (the untitled file), click **No** (Win) or **Don't Save** (Mac).

You closed the current file and exited the program by using the Close and Exit (Win) or Quit (Mac) commands.

DESIGNTIP

Using a Scanner and a Digital Camera

Scanners and digital cameras are two tools you can use to generate images in Photoshop. A digital camera captures images as digital files and stores them on some form of electronic medium, such as a SD/SDHC cards. After you upload the images from your camera to your computer, you can work with images in Photoshop. Digital cameras use **metering** which provides a way of compensating for a variety of lighting conditions. Examples of metering are spot metering, center-weighted average metering, average metering, partial metering, and multi-zone metering.

If you have a scanner, you can import print images, such as those taken from photographs, magazines, or line drawings, into Photoshop. Remember that images taken from magazines are owned by others and that you need permission to distribute them. There are many types of scanners, including flatbed, single-sheet feed, or handheld. Scanners are pretty commonplace, but *how* do they work? A flatbed scanner works by laying an image on a glass bed, and then a scanning array (which consists of a lamp, mirror, lens, and image sensor) moves back and forth to cover the whole surface. The image sensor may be a Charge-Coupled Device (CCD) in which a light beam is converted to an electrical signal, or a Compact Image Sensor (CIS), in which a single row of sensor elements are mounted very close to the document. Light from the lamp bounces off the original and is, with the CCD, reflected by the mirror into the lens, which focuses the image into the CCD. In the case of the CIS, the light and dark areas are picked up directly by the sensor. The CCD/CIS digitizes the results via an analog-to-digital converter, or ADC, and sends the resulting information to the scanner's own hardware, and then to the host computer.

Learn About Design Principles
AND COPYRIGHT RULES

What You'll Do

Image courtesy of Elizabeth Eisner Reding.

In this lesson, you'll learn about various design principles, the difference between designing for print media versus designing for the web, and copyright rules that define how images may be used.

Print Design Versus Web Design

Who's going to be viewing your images, and how? Will your image be printed in a lot of 5000, or will it be viewed on a monitor? Does it matter? When you think about it, the goals of print designers are quite different from those who design for the web. Table 2 illustrates some of the differences between these two art forms.

Composition 101

What makes one design merely okay and another terrific? While any such judgment is subjective, there are some rules governing image composition. It goes without saying that, as the artist, you have a message you're trying to deliver or something you're trying to say to the viewer. This is true whether the medium is oil painting, photography, or Photoshop imagery.

Elements under your control in your composition are tone, sharpness, scale, and arrangement. (You may see these items classified differently elsewhere, but they amount to the same concepts.)

- **Tone** is the brightness and contrast within an image. By using light and shadows you can shift the focus of the viewer's eye and control the mood.
- **Sharpness** is used to direct the viewer's eye to a specific area of an image.

TABLE 2: DIFFERENCES BETWEEN PRINT AND WEB DESIGN	
Print	**Web**
Mass-produced product that will all be identical and can be held in someone's hand.	Will be viewed on monitors of different size and resolution, with varying colors.
Designed for a limited size and area measured in inches.	Designed for a flexible web page measured in pixels.
You want to hold the reader's attention long to deliver the message: a *passive* experience.	You want the reader to stay as long as possible on your website and click links that delve deeper: an *active* experience.
Output is permanent and stable.	Output varies with user's hardware and software and content can evolve.

© 2013 Cengage Learning®

- **Scale** is the size relationship of objects to one another.
- **Arrangement** is how objects are positioned in space, relative to one another.

Are objects in your image contributing to clarity or clutter? Are similarly-sized objects confusing the viewer? Would blurring one area of an image change the viewer's focus?

These are tools you have to influence your artistic expression. Make sure the viewer understands what you want seen.

Arranging Elements

The appearance of elements in an image is important, but of equal importance is the way in which the elements are arranged. The components of any image should form a cohesive unit so that the reader is unaware of all the different parts, yet influenced by the way they work together to emphasize a message or reveal information. For example, if a large image is used, it should be easy for the reader to connect the image with any descriptive text. There should be an easily understood connection between the text and the artwork, and the reader should be able to seamlessly connect them.

QUICK TIP

Make peace with the fact that you cannot completely control how a web page will look on every conceivable device and browser.

In a newsletter, for example, it makes sense to organize text in a columnar fashion, but would you want snaking columns in a web page? Probably not. You wouldn't want to be scrolling up and down to read all the columnar text. At the very least, good web design has to consider the following items:

- layout, navigation, and flow
- interactivity as a design element
- imagery and text as content
- scrolling and linking

Overcoming the Fear of White Space

One design element that is often overlooked is white space. It's there on every page, and it doesn't seem to be doing much, does it? Take a look at a typical page in this book. Is every inch of space filled with either text or graphics? Of course not. If it were, the page would be impossible to read and would be horribly complex and ugly. The best example of the use of white space is the margins surrounding a page. This white space acts as a visual barrier—a resting place for the eyes. Without white space, the words on a page would crowd into each other, and the effect would be a cramped, cluttered, and hard-to-read page. Thoughtful use of white space makes it possible for you to guide the reader's eye from one location on the page to another. For many, one of the first design hurdles that must be overcome is the irresistible urge to put too much stuff on a page. When you are new to design, you may want to fill each page completely. Remember, less is more. Think of white space as a beautiful frame setting off an equally beautiful image.

Balancing Objects

The **optical center** of an image or a page occurs approximately three-eighths from the top of the page and is the point around which objects on the page are balanced. Once the optical center is located, objects can be positioned around it. A page can have a symmetrical or asymmetrical balance relative to an imaginary vertical line in the center of the page. In a **symmetrical balance**, objects are placed equally on either side of the vertical line. This type of layout tends toward a restful, formal design. In an **asymmetrical balance**, objects are placed unequally relative to the vertical line. Asymmetrical balance uses white space to balance the positioned objects, and is more dynamic and informal. A page with objects arranged asymmetrically tends to provide more visual interest because it is more surprising in appearance. See Figure 25 for an image having an obvious optical center.

Considering Ethical Implications

Because Photoshop makes it so easy for you to make so many dramatic changes to images, you should consider the ethical ramifications and implications of altering images. Is it proper or appropriate to alter an image just because you have the technical expertise to do so? Are there any legal responsibilities or liabilities involved in making these alterations? Because the general public is more aware about the topic of **intellectual property** (an image or idea that is owned and retained by legal control) with the increased availability of information and content, you should make sure you have the legal right to alter an image, especially if you plan on displaying or distributing the image to others. Know who retains the rights to an image, and if necessary, make sure you have written permission for its use, alteration, and/or distribution. Not taking these precautions could be costly.

Figure 25 *The optical center*
Image courtesy of Elizabeth Eisner Reding.

Getting Started with Adobe Photoshop CC

Understanding Copyright Terms

As you become more adept using Photoshop, you'll most likely obtain images from sources other than your own imagination and camera. It's of the utmost importance that you understand the legal and moral implications of using someone else's work. This means, among other things, that you have permission (verbal, or preferably, written) to use any part of the image, and that you understand terms such as copyright, fair use doctrine, intellectual property, and derivative works.

A **copyright** is protection extended to an author or creator of original work, which gives them the exclusive right to copy, distribute, and modify a thing, idea, or image. Copyright holders can give permission for others to copy, distribute, or modify their work. When something has been copyrighted, it is considered intellectual property. (The date of publication is the date the published work became generally available.) The length of time of a copyright is specific. In many cases, permission is *not* needed for education activities such as research and classroom use, but *is* required when you want to use someone else's property for profit.

Intellectual property includes ideas, inventions, or processes that derive from the work of the mind, and the corresponding body of laws, rights, and registrations relating to these properties. Intellectual property law grants certain exclusive rights to owners of intangible assets such as music, artistic works, discoveries, inventions, words, phrases, and designs. It includes the following protections: copyright, trademarks (a distinctive associated identifier), patents, design rights, and trade secrets.

Fair use doctrine allows a user to make a copy of all or part of a work, even if permission *has not* been granted, for purposes such as criticism, news reporting, research, teaching, or scholarship.

A **derivative work** is a new, original product that is based upon content from one or more previously existing works.

QUICK TIP

For copyright protection to extend to a derivative work, the derivative work must display a level of originality and new expression.

So, can you use a picture you saw on a website in a class project? **Yes**. Can you use that same picture in a project for a paying client? **No**.

Table 3 illustrates commonly used terms and an example of each.

TABLE 3: COMMONLY USED IMAGE-USE TERMS		
Term	**Definition**	**Example**
Copyright	Protection to an author of an original work, including the right to copy, distribute and adapt that work.	The author of a play (created after 1978) has copyright protection for his/her life + 70 years, after which the work passes into public domain. (The *public domain* indicates that ownership of the work is public and can be used freely by anyone.)
Intellectual property	Refers to both the products of the mind and the accompanying legal protection for these intangible assets.	Industrial icons such as the Nike swoosh, or the Lexus branding symbol.
Fair use doctrine	Conditions under which a work can be used *without* permission.	An image based on a well-known scene in the film The Godfather that appears in a newspaper article.
Derivative work	A new product created from an existing original product.	The Adobe Photoshop CC Revealed book, which is based on the pre-existing Adobe Photoshop CS6 Revealed book.

Licensing Your Work with Creative Commons

To many of us, the thought of dealing with lawyers or anything remotely legal makes us want to head for the hills. It is possible to license (and share) your work using licenses known as **Creative Commons licenses** without the use of lawyers or expensive fees. Creative Commons (*www.creativecommons.org*) is a nonprofit organization devoted to making it easier for people to share and build upon the works of others by offering free licenses and legal tools with which to mark creative work. Using a Creative Commons license allows you to keep your copyright, while allowing others to copy and distribute your work. You determine the conditions: you may insist that you be credited, you can decide if you will permit commercial use of your work or if your work can be modified. Figure 26 shows the Creative Commons licenses that can be applied to any work. The six licenses offered are then composed of combinations of license conditions, and consist of:

Attribution (*cc by*): The simplest of all Creative Commons licenses, in which any user (commercial or non-commercial) can distribute, modify, or enhance your work, provided you are credited.

Attribution Share Alike (*cc by-sa*): The same as Attribution, except that the new owner must create their license under the same terms you used.

Attribution No Derivatives (*cc by-nd*): Your work can be distributed by others, but not modified and in its entirety, with you being credited.

Attribution Non-Commercial (*cc by-nc*): Your work can be distributed, modified, or enhanced, with credit to you, for non-commercial purposes only. Derivative works do not have to be licensed.

Attribution Non-Commercial Share Alike (*cc by-nc-sa*): Your work can be distributed, modified, or enhanced, with credit to you, for non-commercial purposes only, but must be licensed under the identical terms. All derivative work must carry the same license, and be non-commercial.

Attribution Non-Commercial No Derivatives (*cc by-nc-nd*): This is the most restrictive license category. Redistribution is allowed as long as credit is given. The work cannot be modified or used commercially.

QUICK TIP

When determining project requirements, take into account the following criteria with respect to the audience: age, occupation, gender, education, geographic location, ethnicity, and computer literacy. Will the intended audience be able to read and comprehend the message?

Figure 26 *Creative Commons licenses conditions*
Creative Commons Attribution 4.0 International license.

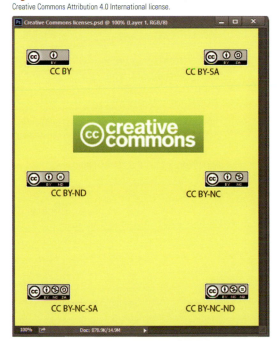

POWER USER SHORTCUTS			
To do this:	**Use this method:**	**To do this:**	**Use this method:**
Close a file	[Ctrl][W] (Win) ⌘ [W] (Mac)	Open Preferences dialog box	[Ctrl][K] (Win) ⌘ [K] (Mac)
Create a new file	[Ctrl][N] (Win) ⌘ [N] (Mac)	Reset preferences to default settings	[Shift][Alt][Ctrl] (Win) [shift][option] ⌘ (Mac)
Create a workspace	Window ➤ Workspace ➤ New Workspace or use the workspace switcher	Save a file	[Ctrl][S] (Win) ⌘ [S] (Mac)
Exit Photoshop	[Ctrl][Q] (Win) ⌘ [Q] (Mac)	Show hidden Lasso tools	[Shift] **L**
Lasso tool	⌀ or **L**	Show or hide all open panels	[Shift][Tab]
		Show or hide all open panels, the options bar, and the Tools panel	[Tab]
		Show or hide Swatches panel	Window ➤ Swatches
Open a file	[Ctrl][O] (Win) ⌘ [O] (Mac)	Use Save As	[Shift][Ctrl][S] (Win) ⌘ [shift] [S] (Mac)

Key: Menu items are indicated by ➤ between the menu name and its command. Blue bold letters are shortcuts for selecting tools on the Tools panel.

© 2013 Cengage Learning®

Start Adobe Photoshop CC 2014.

1. Start Photoshop.
2. Create a new image that is 500 x 600 pixels, accept the default resolution, then name and save it as **Review**.

Open and save an image.

1. Open PS 1-3.jpg from the drive and folder where you store your Data Files.
2. Save it as **Rafting**. (Use the default options when saving the file using a new name. If the JPEG Options dialog box opens, click OK.)

Examine the Photoshop window.

1. Locate the image title bar and the current zoom percentage, then change the color theme to Light Gray.
2. Locate the menu you use to open an image.
3. View the Tools panel, the options bar, and the panels that are showing.
4. Click the Move tool on the Tools panel, view the Move tool options on the options bar, then reset the Essentials workspace.
5. Create, save, and display a customized workspace (based on Essentials) called **History and Layers** that captures panel locations and displays the History panel above the Color panel.
6. Open Bridge, apply the To Do label to Friends.psd, close Bridge, then return the Photoshop color theme to the default (the second from the left color box).

Close a file and exit Photoshop.

1. Compare your screen to Figure 27, then close the Rafting file.
2. Close the Review file.
3. Exit (Win) or Quit (Mac) Photoshop.

Learn about design principles and copyright rules.

1. What elements of composition are under your control?
2. How can a page be balanced?
3. Name three differences between print and web design.
4. Under what conditions can an image *not* be used in a project?

Figure 27 *Completed Skills Review*
Source: Morguefile.

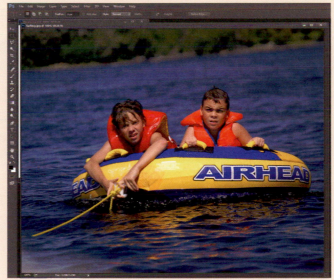

As a new Photoshop user, it's nice to know that there are so many tools to help you perform a task. Bridge and Mini Bridge seem to have many of the same features, yet Mini Bridge is available from within Photoshop and Bridge is a stand-alone program. You want to examine each of these tools to determine the best usage for each.

1. Open Photoshop, open Bridge, then open Mini Bridge.
2. Examine the folder containing the Data Files for this chapter and be prepared to discuss the differences between Bridge and Mini Bridge.
3. What are the sorting and printing limitations of Mini Bridge versus Bridge? Mini Bridge is shown in Figure 28.
4. Be prepared to discuss the best usages of Bridge and Mini Bridge.

Figure 28 *Sample Project Builder 1*

Source: Morguefile. Images © Photodisc/Getty Images. Image courtesy of Elizabeth Eisner Reding.

PROJECT BUILDER 2

At some point in your working with Photoshop, you'll probably have direct contact with one or more clients. Rather than take a sink-or-swim approach when this inevitable time comes, you decide to be proactive and use the web to research this process.

1. Open your favorite browser and search engine and find a website with relevant information about communicating with design clients.
2. Keep track of the most relevant website and make notes of key points on the information you've found. A client meeting is shown in Figure 29.
3. Be prepared to discuss how you'll effectively interact with your design clients when the time comes.

Figure 29 *Sample Project Builder 2*

Courtesy Parker Michael Knight.

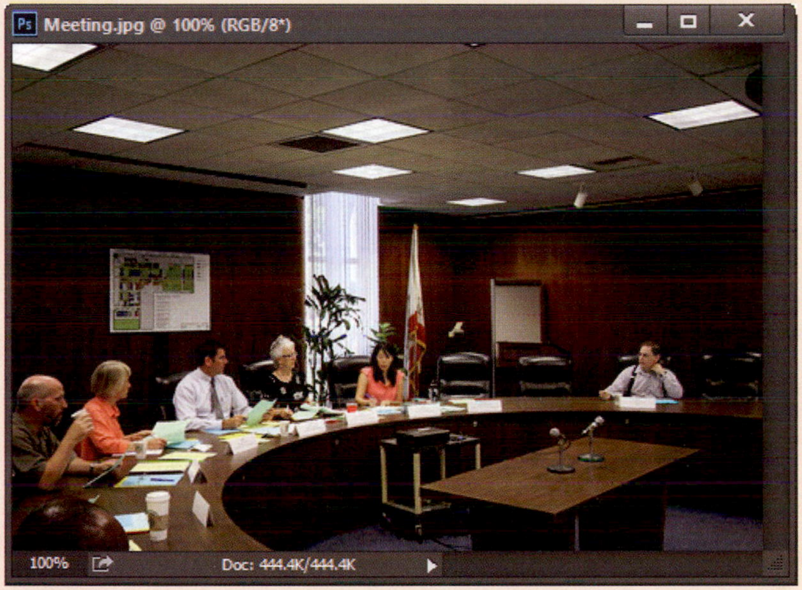

One of the best resources for learning about design principles is the web. You want to make sure you fully understand the differences between designing for print and designing for the web, so you decide to use the Internet to find out more.

1. Connect to the Internet, and use your browser to find at least two websites that have information about the differences between print and web design principles.
2. Find and download one image that serves as an example of good print design and one image of good web design. Save the images (in JPEG format) as Print design-1 and Web design-1. Figure 30 shows a sample print design.

Figure 30 *Sample Design Project*
Source: Morguefile.

Getting Started with Adobe Photoshop CC

You are preparing to work on a series of design projects to enhance your portfolio. You decide to see what information on digital imaging is available on the Adobe website. You also want to increase your familiarity with the Adobe website so that you can take advantage of product information and support, user tips and feedback, and become a more skilled Photoshop user. You'd also like to become more familiar with the concepts of intellectual property and copyright issues.

1. Connect to the Internet and go to the Adobe website at *www.adobe.com.*

2. Point to Products, then find the link for the Photoshop family, as shown in Figure 31. (Your screen may look different, as this page is updated often.)

3. Use the links on the web page to search for information about digital imaging options.

4. Print the relevant page(s).

5. Use your favorite browser and search engine to find several sites about intellectual property and copyright issues.

6. Print at least two of the sites you find the most interesting.

7. Evaluate the information in the documents, then compare any significant differences.

Figure 31 *Sample Portfolio Project*

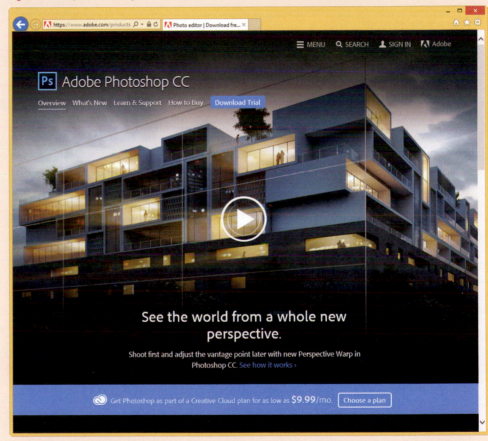

Getting Started with Adobe Photoshop CC

CHAPTER 2 LEARNING
PHOTOSHOP BASICS

1. Use organizational and management features
2. Use the Layers and History panels
3. Learn about Photoshop by using Help
4. View and print an image

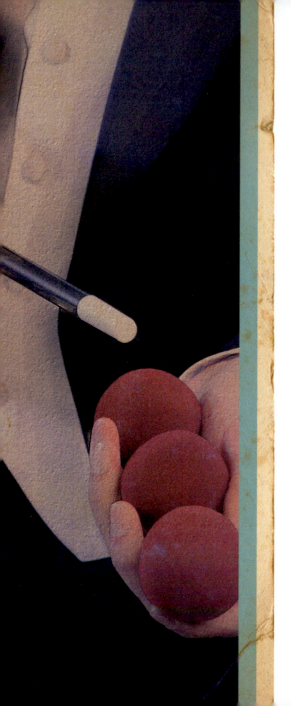

CHAPTER 2 LEARNING
PHOTOSHOP BASICS

Working Magic with Photoshop

Working with images in Photoshop is based on an understanding of layers. Every image opened in Photoshop is made up of one or more layers, and it is within these layers that you, as an artist, work your magic. The order of layers in an image, and the effects applied to them, can make one image very different from another.

Using Management Tools

Adobe Photoshop CC is an amazingly rich program that has a variety of tools that you can use to manage your digital images. Using services such as Acrobat.com, you'll be able to increase your productivity and work more efficiently individually and with coworkers.

Learning to Love Layers

Once you become more comfortable using Photoshop, you'll understand the importance of each of the panels. Some panels, such as the Layers panel, are vital to using Photoshop. Since layers are the key to creating and manipulating Photoshop images, the Layers panel is one that we depend on most, for it tells us at-a-glance the order and type of layers within an image. And if the Layers panel is the map of the Photoshop image, the History panel provides step-by-step instructions that let us know how we got to our destination.

Finding Help when You Need It

A complex program like Photoshop needs a robust Help system. You'll find that the Help system, which is accessed using your browser, doesn't disappoint.

Viewing and Printing

While not everyone prints each one of their images, nearly everyone needs to zoom in and out to get a better look at different areas. Using the Zoom tool, you can view the areas you need to focus on in as high or as low of a magnification as you want. If you do want to print out an image, Photoshop offers great tools to do so.

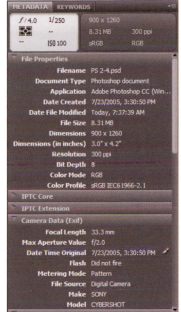

Source: Morguefile.

Use Organizational
AND MANAGEMENT FEATURES

What You'll Do

In this lesson, you'll learn about the Creative Cloud and Behance, and how to use Bridge, and Mini Bridge.

Learning About the Creative Cloud

Adobe Creative Cloud is a fee-based membership service that integrates Adobe Photoshop with apps in the Creative Cloud, as well as a variety of tools, Adobe Touch Apps, services, plus new features, products, and services as soon as they are released. Adobe Touch Apps are available for iOS and Android tablets and phones, and sync to your Creative Cloud desktop apps. With Adobe Creative Cloud, your files will be in sync regardless which device or desktop you're using. Also included is community training and support, and the opportunity to share your work and connect with peers. A Creative Cloud installation of Photoshop and Bridge, as well as some available apps is shown in Figure 1.

If you already have an Adobe ID, you can use this with Adobe Creative Cloud. Once a subscription is purchased, a redemption code is issued, which is required at installation. This code is what makes the connection between the Creative Cloud and the Photoshop program. 20 GB of cloud storage is provided with a free 30-day trial subscription, Single App, Upgrade, and Complete subscriptions.

QUICK TIP

As with any online service, the terms and instructions may change without notice.

Managing the Creative Cloud

Creative.adobe.com is a management feature of the Adobe Creative Cloud that can be used to organize your work whether you work in groups or by yourself. Adobe Creative Cloud is accessed using any browser. In addition to allowing you to share files with others in a virtual environment (also known as **cloud computing**), these services make it possible to take advantage of **file versioning**, which allows you to store multiple versions of your work. You can access creative.adobe.com using your favorite browser.

NEW If you access the Creative Cloud with multiple computers, you can duplicate settings in your personal workspace such as Preferences using the Sync feature. You can perform a sync by clicking Edit (Win) or Photoshop (Mac) on the menu bar, pointing to Sync Settings, then clicking either Upload Settings or Download Settings.

Files can be uploaded to the Creative Cloud web site (creative.adobe.com) by logging in with your Adobe ID, then dragging-and-dropping a file from your computer to the web page, or by clicking the File tab in the Creative Cloud window. Figure 2 shows sample files that have been uploaded to the Creative Cloud.

The Sync process also gives you access to the most up-to-date apps and services available and lets you sync files stored on the Creative Cloud.

Figure 1 *Sample of Creative Cloud apps*

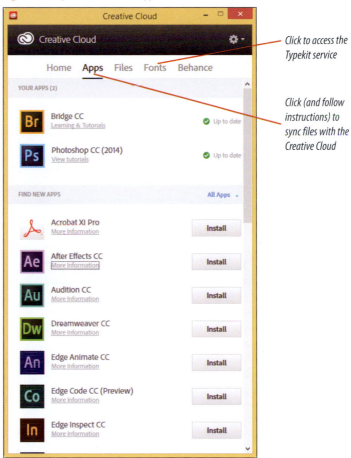

Click to access the Typekit service

Click (and follow instructions) to sync files with the Creative Cloud

Using Behance

Behance is a social network platform dedicated to the showcasing and promotion of creative work. This platform makes it possible to display your work, gaining you global reach. While using Behance gives you a wider audience, you can also view the work of others. When you join Behance (at www.behance.net) you can log in with your Adobe ID, as well as with Facebook and other social networks. During the initial process, you will be assigned a URL you can give to others to view your work.

Participation in Behance is free for creative professionals, and there are no restrictions on the number of projects you can create and post. Once your account is created, you can find people you know by syncing your Google or Facebook accounts.

Images on the Creative Cloud can be shared with Behance by opening the image in the Creative Cloud, clicking the Share icon (in the top-right corner to the right of the image title), then clicking Post Publicly. The image will be prepared for publishing, then you will be prompted to add a title, tags, comments, viewing and thumbnail cropping options.

Figure 2 *Creative Cloud Files*

Adobe Systems Incorporated. Images courtesy of Elizabeth Eisner Reding.

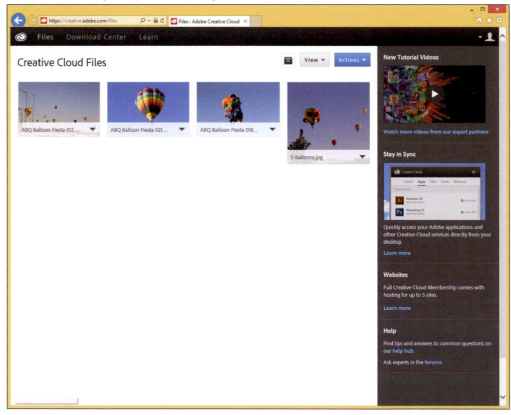

Using Adobe Exchange

Located in Photoshop in the Windows menu under the Extensions command, **Adobe Exchange** allows you to discover and install plug-ins, extensions, and other content for your Creative Cloud apps. This panel contains all sorts of free and paid content you can download.

NEW Adobe Typekit

If you're an Adobe Creative Cloud subscriber, you owe it to yourself to check out **Adobe Typekit** (located in the Fonts tab on the Creative Cloud desktop app). This service lets you select from a seemingly endless supply of really cool font families. Once downloaded, Typekit fonts can be used in any desktop applications.

When you choose fonts from the library and sync them with your desktop, the fonts will be available for use in other apps (even non-Adobe apps). Font families are organized in the Typekit website by classification, properties, or recommended usage. When you find a font family you want to use, click Use fonts, then click Sync selected fonts. Make sure you're logged into the Creative Cloud, the font sync setting is turned on in the Fonts tab in the Preferences section of the Creative Cloud desktop app and all your Typekit fonts will be ready for you. (You may have to reboot your computer for the fonts to appear in the Photoshop font list.) In Adobe apps, you'll notice a different Typekit icon next to the font name.

Figure 3 *Project Complexity triangle*
© 2013 Cengage Learning®

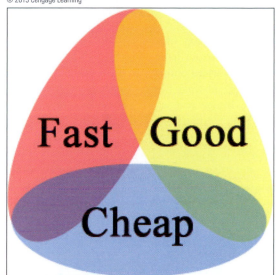

The Complexity of Projects

If you ask any client what they want in their project, they'll most likely say something to the effect that they want it now, they want it done well, and they want it to not cost a lot. These three variables (performance, time, and cost) that are shown in Figure 3 comprise the **project scope** and illustrate the complexity that exists in any project.

- If the project is a low price and completed quickly, will the quality be satisfactory?
- If the project is completed quickly and the quality is good, will the price be affordable?

Ask the client, and they'll say that they want all three elements. But is this a realistic expectation?

Reusing Housekeeping Tasks in Bridge and Mini Bridge

All those little housekeeping tasks you do, such as renaming files and copying files and folders from one location on your hard drive to another, can be easily carried out in Bridge and Mini Bridge. Once you select file thumbnails in Bridge or Mini Bridge, you can copy them to another location by dragging-and-dropping. Files can be renamed by clicking the filename until it is selected, typing the new name, and then pressing [Enter] (Win) or [return] (Mac).

Understanding Metadata

Metadata is descriptive standardized information about a file, and includes information such as the author's name, copyright, and keywords associated with it. In Bridge, you can also find information such as when the image was created, last modified, current size, resolution, bit depth, and color mode in the Metadata panel, shown in Figure 4. Metadata information is stored using the Extensible Metadata Platform (XMP) standard format, which was developed by Adobe and is commonly shared by their products. Sometimes metadata is stored separately in a **sidecar file**. This file can be applied to other files, making it possible to use metadata from one file as a template for another.

Assigning Keywords to an Image

The Keywords panel, as seen in Figure 5, is grouped with the Metadata panel and can be used to create your own system of identifying files based on their content.

Figure 4 *Metadata panel in Bridge*

Figure 5 *Keywords panel in Bridge*

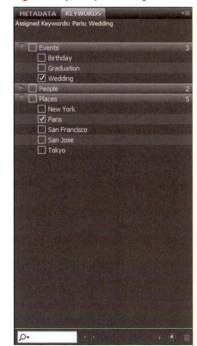

In conjunction with the options on the Filter panel (located beneath the Favorites and Folders panels on the left side of the screen in Bridge), keywords can be used to find images that meet specific criteria. Say, for example, that you have hundreds of images downloaded from your digital camera. Some could be assigned the keyword "New York," others "Paris," and still others "Rome." Viewing all images with the keyword "Rome" is as simple as making the folder containing all the images active, and then clicking the keyword Rome in the filter panel. Any file can be assigned multiple keywords, and those keywords can be renamed, deleted, or applied to other files.

Project Management Principles

Project management is the execution of a plan that brings a project to a successful completion. No longer is project management as simple as saying 'you do this' and 'I'll do that'. A good project manager has to wear many hats and needs to have a thorough understanding of many elements, including budgetary requirements, client needs, production limitations, availability of supplies (industrial and human resources), identification of deliverables (such as specifications, comps or sketches), and timeline management. Like an air traffic controller, a project manager must see what's in front, off to the side, and just around the bend.

Project management is not static: you don't get it all formulated and then just let it sit. Good project management requires periodic revisiting and revision. Without this periodic review, a project may suffer from **scope creep**, a condition to be avoided in which a project seems to have lost its way. Communication review methods vary, but can and should include periodic peer reviews and surveys, and are important feedback measurements. Scope creep can lead to budget overruns and failure to bring a product to market in a timely fashion. All too often, a project can become a victim of its own planning. Since a project plan is written down, many consider it to be 'written in stone'. In fact, a project has so many opportunities to fall off the track: project members become ill, weather becomes a limiting factor, suppliers fail to deliver when promised, or the plan may have been ill-conceived. See Table 1 for some commonly used project management terms.

TABLE 1: COMMONLY USED PROJECT MANAGEMENT TERMS		
Term	**Definition**	**Example**
Project scope	The goals and objectives of the project.	Creation of a website, including images.
Tasks	Specific goals that lead to the ultimate completion of the project.	Choose colors, collect photos, and create logo.
Due dates	When specific tasks must be completed in order to achieve the ultimate goal.	Secure image permissions before website goes live.
Resource allocation	How to best utilize resources, including budgetary constraints, human resources (including outsourcing), and supplies.	Ensure that image fees stay within budget and designer spends no more than 25% of her time.

© 2013 Cengage Learning®

Assigning a keyword

1. Launch **Bridge**.
2. Activate the **Folders tab**, if necessary, and locate the folder containing the Data Files for Chapter 2.
3. Select all the files in the folder and copy them to the folder for Solutions files for Chapter 2.

TIP It is *not necessary* to copy the files in order to complete the lesson. Copying the files just insures that the original data files are kept intact for future use.

4. Activate the **Chapter 2 folder** in the Solutions folder.
5. Click the **Sort by list arrow**, click **By Filename** if not already selected, then click the **Descending Order button** if the Ascending Order button is not already displayed.
6. Click the thumbnail in the Content panel for **PS 2-1.psd**, press and hold [**Shift**], click **PS 2-3.psd**, then release [**Shift**], as shown in Figure 6.
7. Click the **Keywords tab**, then click the **New Keyword button** in the Keywords panel.
8. Type **Sports** in the Keywords panel text box, press [**Enter**] (Win) or [**return**] (Mac), then click the **check box** to the left of Sports.

TIP You can apply keywords to individual images, but applying them to multiple images will speed up your workflow.

You created a new keyword that you applied to three images.

Figure 6 *Files selected in Bridge*
Source: Morguefile. Images © Photodisc/Getty Images.

Click to choose ascending or descending order

Click to choose the sort parameter

Keywords tab

Repurposing in Photoshop

Just because you create a new image in Photoshop, it doesn't mean you always start from scratch. You may use part of one image that already exists in another image, or you may drag an entire existing image into a new image. The idea of repurposing is not new, in fact, Photoshop encourages and promotes it. To this end, it provides you with many tools that make it easy to reuse skills and knowledge. Presets (established settings that perform specific tasks) are available in many Photoshop tools, such as brushes, actions, video styles, and custom shapes. Templates (predesigned files that have been developed by others and generally have a specific outcome, such as a label) are available from companies such as Avery, and can be downloaded from the web.

Figure 7 *Filtered files in Bridge*
Source: Morguefile.

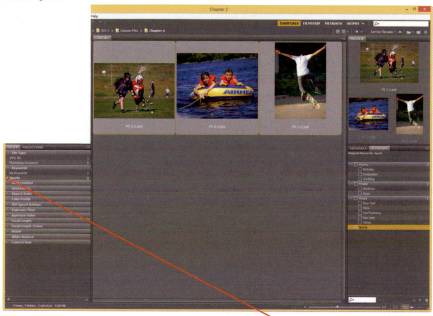

Check mark means
keyword filter is on

Filtering with Bridge

1. Click the **Keywords section** in the Filter panel, then click **Sports**.

   A check mark appears next to Sports in the Filter panel, as seen in Figure 7, and only the images with the keyword Sports are displayed.

2. Click **Sports** in the Keywords section in the Filter panel to restore all the images in the folder.

3. Close Bridge.

You used the Filter panel to see only those images that had a specific keyword applied, then you closed Bridge.

Basics of Project Management

The basics of project management include knowledge of the project scope, the tasks at hand, due dates for task completion, and effective resource allocation. And while all of this is extremely complicated, you must remember that most projects don't operate in a bubble: they are usually one of many projects competing for the same resources. In addition to competing with other projects, many tasks within a given project may be occurring simultaneously and repetitively. Not every project will have the same constraints. Some manufacturing projects, for example, may require more rigorous testing than others, and some projects may rely more heavily on outsourcing that others. Most projects will have deliverables, but the type and scope of those will vary.

Use the Layers
AND HISTORY PANELS

What You'll Do

 In this lesson, you'll hide and display a layer, move a layer on the Layers panel, and then undo the move by deleting the Layer Order state on the History panel.

You can think of layers in a Photoshop image as individual sheets of clear plastic that are in a stack. It's possible for your file to quickly accumulate dozens of layers. The **Layers panel** displays all the individual layers in an open file. You can use the Layers panel to create, copy, delete, display, hide, merge, lock, group, or reposition layers.

Learning About Layers

A **layer** is a section within an image that can be manipulated independently. Layers allow you to control individual elements within an image and create great dramatic effects and variations of the same image. Layers enable you to easily manipulate individual characteristics within an image. Each Photoshop file has at least one layer, and can contain many individual layers, or groups of layers.

QUICK TIP

In Photoshop, using and understanding layers is the key to success.

Understanding the Layers Panel

The order in which the layers appear on the Layers panel matches the order in which they appear in the image; the top layer in the Layers

panel is the top layer on the image. You can make a layer active by clicking its name on the Layers panel. When a layer is active, it is highlighted on the Layers panel, and the name of the layer appears in parentheses in the image title bar. Only one layer can be active at a time. Figure 8 shows an image with its Layers panel. Do you see that this image contains six layers? Each layer can be moved or modified individually on the panel to give a different effect to the overall image. If you look at the Layers panel, you'll see that the Finger Painting type layer is blue, indicating that it is currently active.

QUICK TIP

Get in the habit of shifting your eye from the image in the work area to the Layers panel. Knowing which layer is active will save you time and help you troubleshoot an image.

Filtering Layers

Layers can be filtered from within the Layers panel to build a short list of layers. This short list can be organized by Kind, Name, Effect, Mode, Attribute, Color, Smart Object, or Selected, and can be created by clicking the Filter list arrow on the Layers panel. You can also filter layers using any of the five preset filtering buttons. You can filter for layers containing images (pixel layers), adjustment layers, type layers, shape layers, and smart objects. (The different kinds of layers will be described in later chapters.)

Displaying and Hiding Layers

You can use the Layers panel to control which layers are visible in an image. You can show or hide a layer by clicking the Indicates layer visibility button next to the layer thumbnail. When a layer is hidden, you are not able to merge it with another, select it, or print it.

Using the History Panel

Photoshop records each task you complete in an image on the **History panel**. This record of events, called states, makes it easy to see what changes occurred and the tools or commands that you used to make the modifications. The History panel, shown in Figure 8, displays up to 20 states by default and automatically updates the list to display the most recently performed tasks. The list contains the name of the tool or command used to change the

Figure 8 *Layers and History panels*
Image courtesy of Elizabeth Eisner Reding.

image. You can delete a state on the History panel by selecting it and dragging it to the Delete current state button. Deleting a state is equivalent to using the Undo command. You can also use the History panel to create a new image from any state.

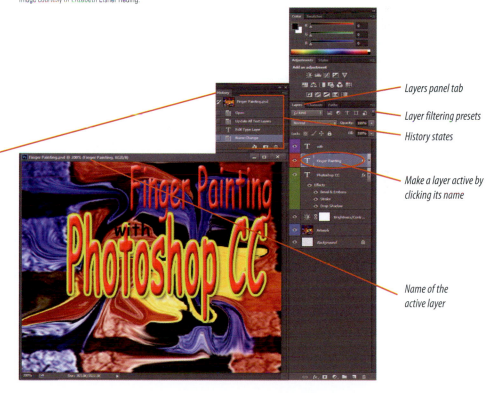

Layers panel tab

Layer filtering presets

History states

Make a layer active by clicking its name

Name of the active layer

History panel tab

Hide and display a layer

1. Open the file PS 2-4.psd, then rename it **Wedding Day.psd**.

2. Click the **Rings layer** on the Layers panel, then click the **Move tool** ▶⊕ if necessary.

   TIP Depending on the size of the window, you might only be able to see the initial characters of the layer name.

3. Verify that the **Show Transform Controls check box** on the options bar is not checked, then click the **Indicates layer visibility button** ▢ on the Rings layer to display the image, as shown in Figure 9.

   TIP By default, transparent areas of an image have a checkerboard display on the Layers panel.

4. Click the **Indicates layer visibility button** 👁 on the Rings layer to hide the layer.

You made the Rings layer active on the Layers panel, then clicked the Indicates layer visibility button to display and hide the layer. Hiding layers is an important skill that can be used to remove distracting elements. Once you've finished working on a specific layer, you can display the additional layers.

Figure 9 *Wedding Day*
Source: Morguefile.

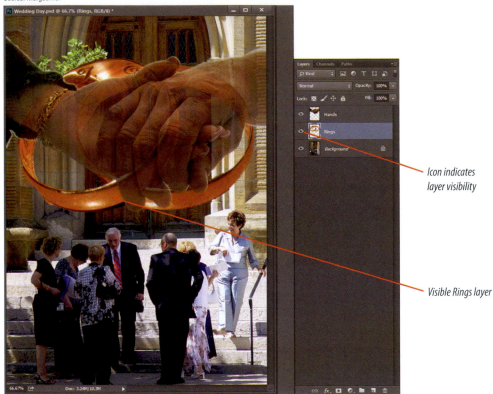

Icon indicates layer visibility

Visible Rings layer

DESIGN**TIP**

Visual Hierarchy

Projects that are visible in nature (such as a web page) should have a strong visual hierarchy. **Visual hierarchy** is the order in which the eye understands what it is seeing. For a web page, this would include fonts and font sizes, line spacing, indents, graphic images and their positioning. In graphic design, visual hierarchy is used to manipulate the reader's eye to see information in a particular location.

Figure 10 *Layer moved in Layers panel*

Figure 11 *Result of moved layer*
Source: Morguefile.

Result of moved layer

Figure 12 *Deleting a History state*

Selected state

Pointer when dragging a
history state to the trash

Move a layer on the Layers panel and delete a state on the History panel

1. Click the **Indicates layer visibility button** on the Rings layer on the Layers panel to display the layer.

2. Click on the Hands layer on the Layers panel to hide the layer.

3. Display the **Legacy workspace** you created in Chapter 1.

4. Click and drag the **Hands layer** on the Layers panel beneath the Rings layer, so your Layers panel looks like Figure 10.

   The hands are no longer visible as shown in Figure 11.

5. Click **Layer Order** on the History panel, then drag it to the **Delete current state button** on the History panel, as shown in Figure 12.

TIP Each time you close and reopen an image, the History panel is cleared.

   The original order of the layers in the Layers panel is restored.

6. Click **File** on the Menu bar, then click **Save**.

TIP An alternative to the deletion of history states is the Revert command. Located on the File menu, this command restores the image to its last saved state.

You moved the Hands layer beneath the Rings layer, then returned it to its original position by dragging the Layer Order state to the Delete current state button on the History panel. You can easily use the History panel to undo what you've done.

Learn About Photoshop
BY USING HELP

What You'll Do

In this lesson, you'll open Help, and then view and find information from the available topics and the Search feature.

Understanding the Power of Help

Photoshop features an extensive Help system that you can use to access definitions, explanations, and useful tips. Help information is displayed in a browser window, so you must have web browser software installed on your computer and an Internet connection to use Photoshop Help.

QUICKTIP

Since the Help contents displays in your browser, you already know how to print. Once the content is displayed, use the Print command on your browser to print the page(s) of interest.

Using Help Topics

The Home page of the Photoshop Help/Topics window, shown in Figure 13, displays detailed categories that you can use to retrieve information about Photoshop commands and features. The following topics are available:

- What's new
- Get started

- Workspace and workflow
- Image and color basics
- Layers
- Selecting
- Image adjustments
- Camera Raw
- Repair and restoration
- Reshaping and transforming
- Drawing and painting
- Text
- Video and animation
- Filters and effects
- Saving and exporting
- Printing
- Automation
- Web graphics
- 3D and technical imaging
- Color management
- System requirements

QUICKTIP

Due to the ever-changing nature of the Web, these categories can and will change.

When you click a link, Help takes you directly to the information you've selected. The Search feature is located in the left pane in the form of a text box. You can search the Photoshop Help System by typing your search terms in the text box, and then pressing [Enter] (Win) or [return] (Mac).

Figure 13 *Groups in Photoshop Online Help*

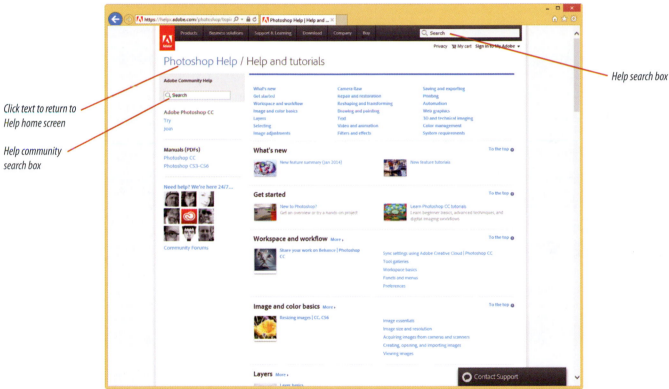

Find information in Adobe reference titles

1. Click **Help** on the Menu bar, then click **Photoshop Online Help**. If the Help Manager dialog box appears, click the red Close button to close this window (Mac).

   TIP You can also open the Help window by pressing [F1] (Win) or ⌘ [/] (Mac).

2. Click **Acquiring images from cameras and scanners** in the Image and color basics group. See Figure 14.

   TIP You can maximize the window if you want to take advantage of the full screen display.

   Bear in mind that Help is web-driven and, like any website, can change as updates are made and errors and inconsistencies are found.

3. Close the Photoshop Help window.

You used the Photoshop Online Help command on the Help menu to open the Help window and view a topic.

Figure 14 *A topic in the Image and color basics group*

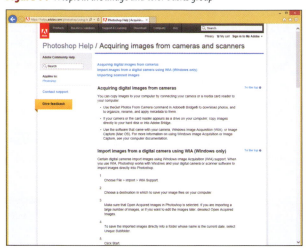

Understanding the Differences Between Monitor, Images, and Device Resolution

Image resolution is determined by the number of pixels per inch (ppi) that are printed on a page. Pixel dimensions (the number of pixels along the height and width of a bitmap image) determine the amount of detail in an image, while resolution controls the amount of space over which the pixels are printed. Think of the differences between the picture quality on a standard-definition 480i television versus a high-definition 1080i television. The high-definition image will be crisper and have more vibrant colors, whereas the standard-definition image may look weak and washed out. High resolution images show greater detail and more subtle color transitions than low resolution images. Lower resolution images can look grainy, like images in older newspapers.

Device resolution or printer resolution is measured by the ink dots per inch (dpi) produced by printers. You can set the resolution of your computer monitor to determine the detail with which images will be displayed. Each monitor should be calibrated to describe how the monitor reproduces colors. Monitor calibration is one of the first things you should do because it determines whether your colors are being accurately represented, which in turn determines how accurately your output will match your design intentions. **Screen frequency**, or *line screen*, is the number of printer dots or halftone cells per inch used to print grayscale images or color separations and is measured in lines per inch (lpi). Printer calibration ensures that what you see on your monitor is translated to paper.

Learning Photoshop Basics

Figure 15 *Photoshop Help Support Center*

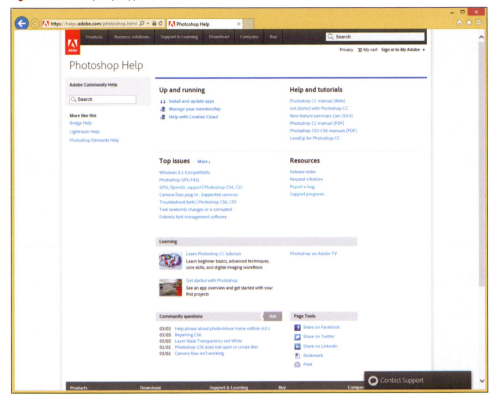

1. Click **Help** on the Menu bar, then click **Photoshop Support Center**.
2. Compare your Help window to Figure 15, then close the Photoshop Help window.

You accessed the Photoshop Help Support Center.

Using Help versus Support Center

So which helpful Help resource should you use? Use Help when you need instructions or basic how-to, or 'what is this' information. Use the Support Center if you want to see the latest issues and resource information on new and/or existing features.

The links listed in Figure 15 include top issues, such as operating system compatibility and troubleshooting, as well as installation and membership instructions. Also, look in this section for Release notes on new features.

Find information using Search

1. Open Photoshop Online Help, then click the **Search text box** in the browser window.

2. Type **rulers**, press [**Enter**] (Win) or [**return**] (Mac), then click the link for **Photoshop Help | Rulers**.

TIP You can search for multiple words by inserting a space.

3. Go to the top of the page, then compare your Help screen to Figure 16.

4. Close the Photoshop Help window.

You entered a search term, viewed search results, then closed the Help window.

Figure 16 *Result of a search in Help*

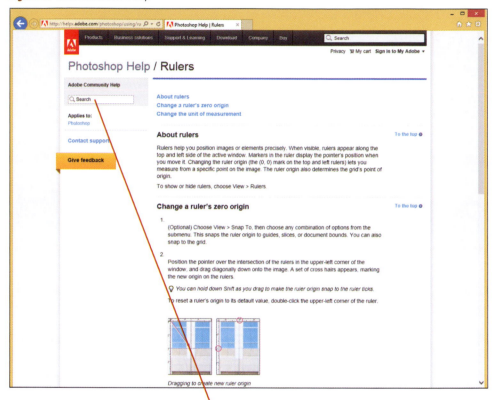

Search text box

Figure 17 *List of new features in Photoshop CC*

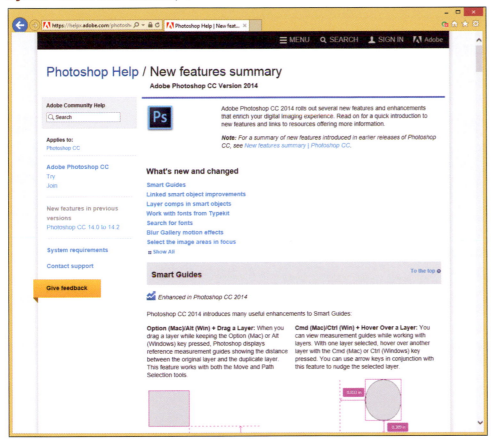

Learning what's new in Photoshop CC

TIP If you have some experience with a previous version of Photoshop or you just want to cut-to-the-chase and find out what's new in this version, you can find a list of new features in this version of Photoshop by clicking Help on the Menu bar, clicking Photoshop Online Help, and then clicking New feature summary in the What's new group. The list of new features, shown in Figure 17, contains a brief description of each feature and a link to more information.

View and PRINT AN IMAGE

What You'll Do

Source: Morguefile.

 In this lesson, you'll use the Zoom tool on the Tools panel to increase and decrease your views of the image. You'll also change the page orientation settings in the Print dialog box, and print the image.

Getting a Closer Look

When you edit an image in Photoshop, it is important that you have a good view of the area on which you want to focus. Photoshop has a variety of methods that allow you to enlarge or reduce your current view. You can use the Zoom tool by clicking the image to zoom in on (magnify the view) or zoom out of (reduce the view) areas of your image. Zooming in or out enlarges or reduces your *view*, not the actual image. The maximum zoom factor is 3200%. The current zoom percentage appears in the document's title bar, on the Navigator panel, and on the status bar. The View menu lets you zoom in and out, fit an image to the screen, change to 100% or 200% magnification, and see the print size.

When the Zoom tool is selected, the options bar provides additional choices for changing your view, as shown in Figure 18. For example, the Resize Windows To Fit check box automatically resizes the window whenever you magnify or reduce the view. You can also change the zoom percentage using the Navigator panel or the status bar by typing a new value in the Zoom text box, and then pressing [Enter] (Win) or [return] (Mac).

Viewing an Image in Multiple Views

You can use the New Window for *filename* command (accessed by pointing to Arrange on the Window menu) to open multiple

Figure 18 *Zoom tool options bar*

Selected check box resizes window

Displays image at 100% magnification

Fits the image on the screen

views of the same image. You can change the zoom percentage in each view so you can spotlight the areas you want to modify, and then modify the specific area of the image in each view. Because you are working on the same image in multiple views, not in multiple versions, Photoshop automatically applies the changes you make in one view to all views. Although you can close the views you no longer need at any time, Photoshop will not save any changes until you save the file.

Printing Your Image

In many cases, a professional print shop might be the best option for printing a Photoshop image to get the highest quality. Lacking a professional print shop, you can print a Photoshop image using a standard black-and-white or color printer from within Photoshop, or you can switch to Bridge and then choose to send output to a PDF or Web Gallery. The printed image will be a composite of all visible layers. The quality of your printer and paper will affect the appearance of your output. The Print dialog box displays options for printing, such as paper orientation. **Orientation** is the direction in which an image appears on the page. In **portrait orientation**, the image is printed with the shorter edges of the paper at the top and bottom. In **landscape orientation**, the image is printed with the longer edges of the paper at the top and bottom.

Use the Print command when you want to print multiple copies of an image. The Photoshop Print Settings dialog box allows you to handle color values using color management and printer profiles. Use the Print One Copy command to print a single copy without making dialog box selections.

Understanding Color Handling in Printing

The Photoshop Print Settings dialog box that opens when you click Print on the File menu lets you determine how colors are output. You can click the Color Management list arrow to choose whether Photoshop or the printing device should manage the colors. If you let Photoshop determine the colors, Photoshop performs any necessary conversions to color values appropriate for the selected printer. If you choose to let the printer determine the colors, the printer will convert document color values to the corresponding printer color values. In this scenario, Photoshop does not alter the color values.

Printed Images versus On-Screen Images

Why isn't what you see on your computer screen the same as your printer output? Well, these two items are different because video monitors and printers work very differently. The most obvious difference is that you can have a tiny monitor or an enormous monitor which can display an image in any zoom factor you choose while a printed image is limited to paper size. A printed image is measured in inches or centimeters, and its size is modified on paper by scaling. Also, an image size does not vary with its scanned resolution, and printed pixels are spaced using a specified scaled resolution (dpi). On paper, several printer ink dots are used to represent the color of one image pixel.

On a video monitor, the image size is measured on the screen in pixels, the image size is modified by resampling, and the size varies with the scanned resolution. Image pixels are located at each screen pixel location. On screen, one screen pixel location contains one image pixel, and can be of any RGB value.

Using the Photoshop File Info Dialog Box

You can use the File Info dialog box to identify a file, add a caption or other text, or add a copyright notice. The Description text box, shown in Figure 19, allows you to enter text that can be printed with the image. For example, to add information to an image, click File on the Menu bar, click File Info, and then click the Description text box. (You can move from field to field by pressing [Tab] or by clicking individual text boxes.) Type your name or other identifying information in the Description text box, or click stars to assign a rating. You can enter additional information in the other text boxes, and then save all the File Info data by clicking OK. To print data from the Description field of the File Info dialog box, click File on the Menu bar, and then click Print. Scroll down and click the right-pointing triangle to expand Printing Marks, and then select the Description check box. Additional printable options are listed.

To print the filename, select the Labels check box. You can also select check boxes that let you print crop marks and registration marks. If you choose, you can even add a background color or border to your image in the Functions category. After you select the items you want to print, click Print.

Figure 20 *Navigator panel*
Source: Morguefile.

Viewed area of image; also called the proxy view area

Figure 19 *File Info dialog box*

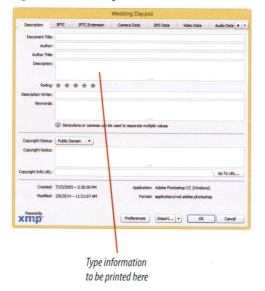

Type information to be printed here

Using the Navigator Panel

You can change the magnification factor of an image using the Navigator panel or the Zoom tool on the Tools panel. You can open the Navigator panel by clicking Window on the Menu bar, and then clicking Navigator. By double-clicking the Zoom text box on the Navigator panel, you can enter a new magnification factor, and then press [Enter] (Win) or [return] (Mac). The magnification factor—shown as a percentage—is displayed in the lower-left corner of the Navigator panel, as shown in Figure 20. The red border in the panel, called the proxy view area, defines the area of the image that is magnified. You can drag the proxy view area inside the Navigator panel to view other areas of the image at the current magnification factor.

Figure 21 *Reduced image*

Source: Morguefile.

Zoom percentage changed

Zoom tool on the Tools panel

Use the Zoom tool

1. Click the **Indicates layer visibility button** 👁 on the Layers panel for the Rings layer so the layer is no longer displayed.

2. Click the **Indicates layer visibility button** ⬛ on the Layers panel for the Hands layer so the layer is visible.

3. Click the **Zoom tool** 🔍 on the Tools panel.

TIP You can also change the magnification level by double-clicking the Zoom Level text box at the bottom-left corner of the image window and manually entering a zoom level.

4. Select the **Resize Windows To Fit check box** (if it is not already selected) on the options bar.

5. Position the **Zoom in pointer** ⊕ over the center of the image, then click the **image**.

TIP Position the pointer over the part of the image you want to keep in view.

6. Press [**Alt**] (Win) or [**option**] (Mac), then when the Zoom out pointer appears, click the **center of the image** twice with the **Zoom out pointer** ⊖.

7. Release [**Alt**] (Win) or [**option**] (Mac), then compare your image to Figure 21.

    The zoom factor for the image is 50%. Your zoom factor may differ.

You selected the Zoom tool on the Tools panel and used it to zoom in to and out of the image. The Zoom tool makes it possible to see the detail in specific areas of an image, or to see the whole image at once, depending on your needs.

Modify print settings

1. Click **File** on the Menu bar, then click **Print** to open the Print dialog box.

TIP If you have not selected a printer using the Print Center, a warning box might appear.

2. Click the **Print paper in landscape orientation button** ![icon].

3. Make sure that **1** appears in the Copies text box, compare your dialog box to Figure 22, click **Print**, then click **Print** after verifying that the correct printer is selected. (If you get a color-management dialog box, click OK.)

TIP You can use the handles surrounding the image preview in the Print dialog box to scale the print size.

4. Save your work.

You used the Print command on the File menu to open the Photoshop Print Settings dialog box, changed the page orientation, and then printed the image. Changing the page orientation can sometimes make an image fit better on a printed page.

Figure 22 *Print dialog box*
Source: Morguefile.

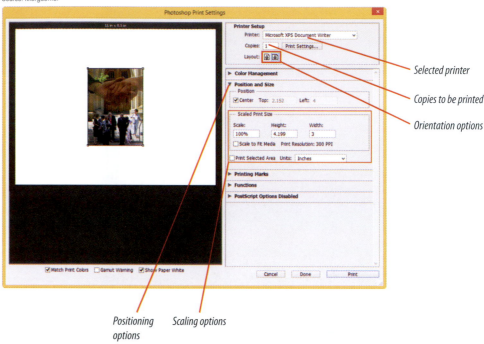

Selected printer

Copies to be printed

Orientation options

Positioning options

Scaling options

Previewing and Creating a Proof Setup

You can create and save a Proof Setup, which lets you preview your image to see how it will look when printed on a specific device. (How an image looks on specific hardware that has been calibrated and using a color management system is called a **soft proof**. The soft proof is an accurate representation of how an image will look when it has been printed.) This feature lets you see how colors can be interpreted by different devices. By using this feature, you can decrease the chance that the colors on the printed copy of the image will vary from what you viewed on your monitor. Create a custom proof by clicking View on the Menu bar, pointing to Proof Setup, and then clicking Custom. Specify the conditions in the Customize Proof Condition dialog box, and then click OK. Each proof setup has the .psf extension and can be loaded by clicking View on the Menu bar, pointing to Proof Setup, clicking Custom, and then clicking Load.

Figure 23 *PDF Output options in Bridge*

- Output workspace option
- PDF option
- Click to choose template layout
- Click to refresh preview screen
- Click to Save

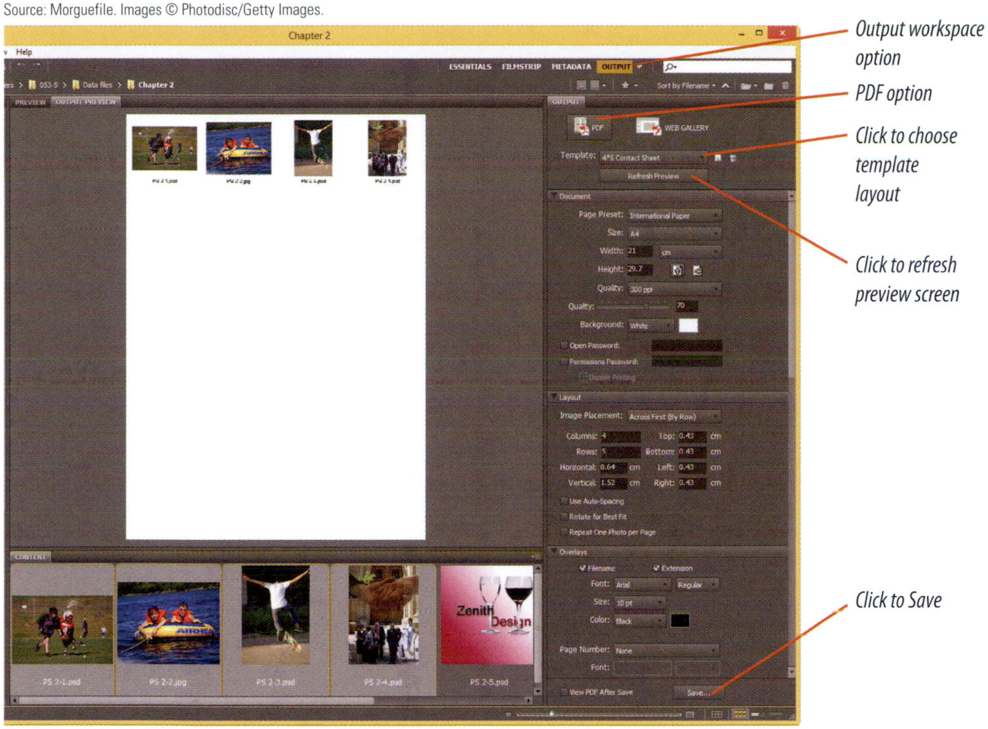

Create a PDF with Bridge

1. Open **Bridge**.

2. Click the **Folders tab** (if necessary), click **Chapter 2** in the location where your Data Files are stored in the Folders tab (if necessary), then verify that **Sort by Filename** is selected.

TIP Creating a PDF with Bridge requires the installation of the Adobe Output Module. If you don't see Output as a workspace option by clicking the workspace list arrow (to the left of the Bridge search text box), then the Output module has not been installed.

3. Click **Output** on the Bridge workspace switcher.

4. Click the **PDF button** in the Output tab.

5. Click **PS 2-1.psd**, hold [**Shift**], click **PS 2-4.psd** in the Content tab, then release [**Shift**].

6. Click the **Template list arrow** in the Output panel, click **4*5 Contact Sheet**, click **Refresh Preview**, then compare your screen to Figure 23. (The Generate PDF Contact Sheet dialog box will appear; the contact sheet will display in the Document window when processing is finished.)

You used Adobe Bridge to create a PDF, then selected specific images and an arrangement for the file.

DESIGN**TIP**

Installing the Adobe Output Module

When shipped, Bridge CC *might not* include the Adobe Output Module. This module allows you to create PDF presentation and web galleries. You can find this module by searching Bridge Help for Bridge CC Output. The resulting page will instruct you as to how to download and install the Adobe Output Module.

Save a PDF output file

1. Click **Save** (at the bottom of the Output panel), locate the folder where your Data Files are stored, type **your name Chapter 2 contact sheet** in the text box, then click **Save**.

2. Click **OK** to acknowledge that the contact sheet was successfully processed.

You generated a PDF that can be printed later using Adobe Acrobat, then saved and printed the PDF.

Figure 24 *Output panel in Bridge*
Source: Morguefile. Images © Photodisc/Getty Images.

Click to create output

Click to create PDF

Output preview

Selected thumbnails

Creating a PDF

Using Bridge you can create a PDF Presentation (a presentation in the PDF file format). Such a presentation can be viewed fullscreen on any computer monitor, or in Adobe Acrobat or Adobe Reader as a PDF file. You can create such a presentation by opening Bridge, locating and selecting images using the file hierarchy, and then clicking the Output button on the Bridge Menu bar. The Output panel, shown in Figure 24, opens and displays the images you have selected. You can add images by pressing [Ctrl] (Win) or ⌘ (Mac) while clicking additional images.

You can also create a PDF from a Photoshop file by clicking File on the menu bar, then clicking Print. Select Adobe PDF from the Print list arrow in the Printer Setup section of the Photoshop Print Settings dialog box, make any other necessary selections, then click Print. (These instructions are for Windows, Mac steps vary slightly.)

Figure 25 *Web Gallery options in Bridge*
Source: Morguefile.

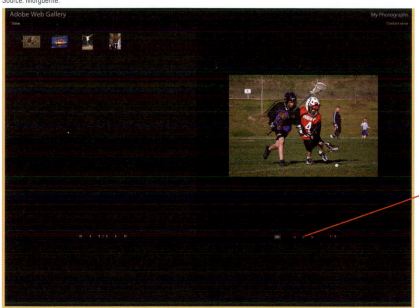

Click to view slideshow

Create a Web Gallery with Bridge

1. Verify that Bridge is open and that the images are still selected.

2. Click the **Web Gallery button** in the Output panel.

3. Click the **Preview in Browser button** in the Output Preview window, select a browser that will open the file if asked, click the **Play Slideshow button** in the browser window, then after reviewing the slideshow, click the **Pause Slideshow button**.

   Compare your screen to Figure 25.

4. Close the browser, return to Bridge, scroll down the Output panel to the Create Gallery section, click the **Save Location Browse button**, navigate to the location where your Data Files are stored if necessary, click **OK** (Win) or **Open** (Mac) in the Choose a Folder dialog box, then click **Save** at the bottom of the Output panel.

5. Click **OK** to close the Create Gallery dialog box.

6. Click **File** on the Bridge menu, then click **Exit** (Win) or click **Adobe Bridge CC** in Bridge, then click **Quit Adobe Bridge CC** (Mac).

You generated a Web Gallery using Adobe Bridge.

DESIGNTIP

Using Contrast to Add Emphasis

Contrast is an important design principle that uses opposing elements, such as colors or lines, to produce an intensified effect in an image, page, or publication. Just as you can use a font attribute to make some text stand out from the rest, you can use contrasting elements to make certain graphic objects stand out. You can create contrast in many ways: by changing the sizes of objects; by varying object weights, such as making a line surrounding an image heavier; by altering the position of an object, such as changing its location on the page or rotating it so that it is positioned on an angle; by drawing attention-getting shapes or a colorful box behind an object that makes it stand out (called a **matte**); or by adding carefully selected colors that emphasize an object.

POWER USER SHORTCUTS	
To do this:	**Use this method:**
Drag a layer	🖐
Hide a layer	👁
Open Help	[F1] (Win) ⌘ [/] (Mac)
Print File	File ➤ Print [Ctrl][P] (Win) ⌘ [P] (Mac)
Show a layer	▢
Show History panel	Window ➤ History 🔳
Zoom in	🔍 [Ctrl][+] (Win) ⌘ [+] (Mac)
Zoom out	[Alt] 🔍 (Win) [option] 🔍 (Mac) [Ctrl][-] (Win) ⌘ [−] (Mac)
Zoom tool	🔍 or **Z**

Key: Menu items are indicated by ➤ between the menu name and its command. Blue bold letters are shortcuts for selecting tools on the Tools panel.

Use organizational and management features.

1. Open Adobe Bridge.
2. Click the Folders tab, then locate the folder that contains your Data Files.
3. Close Adobe Bridge.

Use the Layers and History panels.

1. Open PS 2-5.psd from the drive and folder where you store your Data Files.
2. Save it as **Zenith Design Logo**.
3. Display the Legacy workspace.
4. Drag the Wine Glasses layer so it is above the Zenith layer, then use the History panel to undo the state.
5. Use the Indicates layer visibility button to hide the Wine Glasses layer.
6. Make the Wine Glasses layer visible again.
7. Hide the Zenith layer.
8. Show the Zenith layer.
9. Show the Tag Line layer.

Learn about Photoshop by using Help.

1. Open the Adobe Photoshop Online Help window.
2. Display information about Image size and resolution. (*Hint*: look in the Image and color basics group.).
3. Scroll down to information about file size.
4. Use your browser to print the information you find.
5. Close the Help window.

View and print an image.

1. Make sure that all the layers of the Zenith Design Logo are visible in the Layers panel.
2. Click the Zoom tool, then make sure the setting is selected to resize the window to fit.
3. Zoom in on the wine glasses twice.
4. Zoom out to the original perspective.
5. Print one copy of the image.
6. Save your work.
7. Compare your screen to Figure 26, then close the Zenith Design Logo file.

Figure 26 *Completed Skills Review*
Images © Photodisc/Getty Images.

As a new Photoshop user, you are comforted knowing that Photoshop's Help system provides definitions, explanations, procedures, and other helpful information. It also includes examples and demonstrations to show how Photoshop features work. You use the Help system to learn about moving document windows, switching workspaces, and the Tools panel.

1. Open the Photoshop Online Help window.
2. Click the Workspace basics link in the Workspace and workflow group.
3. Scroll down to the section on rearranging, docking, or floating document windows and read this information.
4. Scroll back to the top of the page, then click the Save and switch workspaces link.
5. Return to the Help home page, click Tool galleries in the Workspace and workflow group, compare your screen to the sample shown in Figure 27, then close the Help window.

Figure 27 *Sample Project Builder 1*

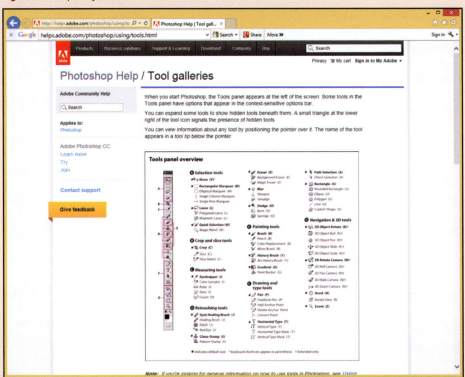

Kitchen Experience, your local specialty cooking shop, has just added herb-infused oils to its product line. They have hired you to draft a flyer that features these new products. You use Photoshop to create this flyer.

1. Open PS 2-6.psd, then save it as **Cooking**.
2. Display the Essentials workspace (if necessary).
3. Make the Measuring Spoons layer visible.
4. Drag the Oils layer so the content appears behind the Skillet layer content.
5. Drag the Measuring Spoons layer above the Skillet layer.
6. Save the file, then compare your image to the sample shown in Figure 28.

Figure 28 *Sample Project Builder 2*

Images © Photodisc/Getty Images.

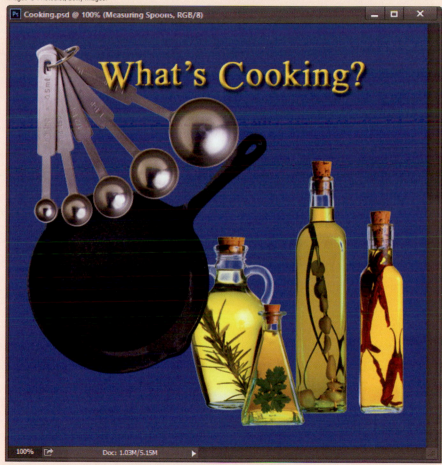

As an avid, albeit novice Photoshop user, you have grasped the importance of how layers affect your image. With a little practice, you can examine a single-layer image and guess which objects might display on their own layers. Now, you're ready to examine the images created by Photoshop experts and critique them on their use of layers.

1. Connect to the Internet, and use your browser and Behance, if possible, to find interesting artwork located on at least two websites.
2. Download a single-layer image (in its native format) from each website.
3. Start Photoshop, then open the downloaded images.
4. Save one image as **Critique-1** and the other as **Critique-2** in the Photoshop format (use the .psd extension).
5. Analyze each image for its potential use of layers.
6. Open the File Info dialog box for Critique-1.psd, then type in the Description section your speculation as to the number of layers there might be in the image, their possible order on the Layers panel, and how moving the layers would affect the image. Use the File Info dialog box to add a description for Critique-2.psd.
7. Close the dialog box.
8. Compare your image to the sample shown in Figure 29, then close the files.

Figure 29a *Sample Design Project*
Source: Morguefile.

Figure 29b *File Info dialog box for sample Design Project*

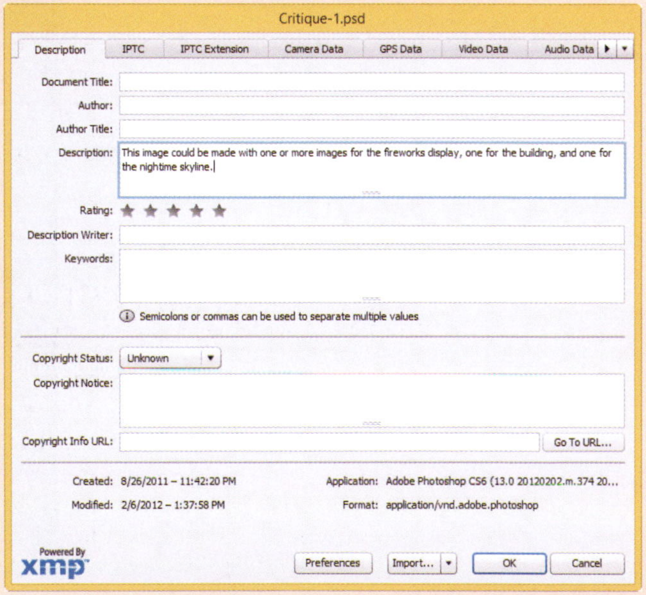

It seems that every major software manufacturer is including an element of 'cloud computing' in their latest version of their software. You've heard of it, but you're still not sure you fully understand it.

1. Connect to the Internet and use your favorite search engine to find information about cloud computing.
2. Using a sheet of paper or your favorite word processor, create a grid that contains the names of at least two or three major technology companies (such as Adobe, Microsoft, and Google) and find out about their forays into cloud computing. Figure 30 contains a sample document.
3. Print any relevant page(s).
4. Be prepared to discuss this topic and its relevance to your work in Photoshop.

Figure 30 *Sample Portfolio Project*

Cloud·Computing·Examples¶

¶

Manufacturer¤	Name¤	Specifications¤	¤
Adobe·Corporation¤	Adobe·Creative·Cloud¤	An·Adobe·Creative·Cloud·subscription·gives·you·immediate·access·to·the·latest·updates·and·features.·Creative·tools·for·photography,·video,·audio,·and·design·are·all·available.·Additional·services·exist·for·file·sharing,·collaboration,·and·publishing·apps·and·websites.·Individual·subscribers·get·20GB·of·storage;·team·subscribers·get·100GB.¤	¤
Apple·Corporation¤	iCloud¤	Allows·you·to·sync·your·apps,·music,·photos,·books,·mail,·and·documents·seamlessly·on·an·iPhone,·iPad,·iPod·Touch,·Mac,·or·PC.·Included·in·iCloud·is·Photos·Sharing,·iWork,·Keychain,·Mail,·Calendar,·and·Contacts,·Backup·and·Storage,·and·iCloud.com.·¤	¤
Google¤	Google·Drive¤	Google·Drive·is·a·place·where·you·can·safely·store·photos,·videos,·documents,·and·any·other·files·you·might·have·Users·get·15·GB.·Google·Drive·lets·you·edit·and·create·documents·and·spreadsheets·with·Docs·and·Sheets,·share·photos,·access·the·most·current·document·version·regardless·of·your·location,·and·make·files·available·for·offline·use.¤	¤
Microsoft·Corporation¤	OneDrive¤	OneDrive·is·free·online·storage·service·you·can·access·from·anywhere.·All·you·need·to·access·OneDrive·is·a·Microsoft·account,·such·as·Xbox,·Hotmail,·Skype,·or·Outlook.com.·¶ You·receive·7·GB·of·free·online·storage.·A·desktop·app·is·available·that·lets·you·sync·your·files·with·all·your·devices,·although·this·app·is·unnecessary·if·you're·running·Windows·8.1.·¤	¤

¶

CHAPTER 3

WORKING WITH LAYERS

1. Examine and convert layers

2. Add and delete layers

3. Add a selection from one image to another

4. Organize layers with layer groups and colors

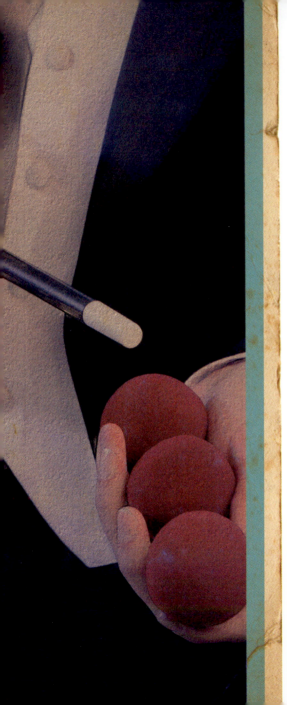

CHAPTER 3 WORKING WITH LAYERS

Layers Are Everything

You can use Photoshop to create sophisticated images in part because a Photoshop image can contain multiple layers. Each object created in Photoshop can exist on its own individual layer, making it easy to control the position and quality of each layer in the stack. Depending on your computer's resources, you can have a maximum of 8000 layers in each Photoshop image with each layer containing as much or as little detail as necessary.

Understanding the Importance of Layers

Layers make it possible to manipulate the tiniest detail within your image, which gives you tremendous flexibility when you make changes. By placing objects, effects, styles, and type on separate layers, you can modify them individually *without* affecting other layers. The advantage to using multiple layers is that you can isolate effects and images on one layer without affecting the others. The disadvantage of using multiple layers is that your file size might become very large.

However, once your image is finished, you can dramatically reduce its file size by combining all the layers into one using a process known as **flattening**.

QUICK TIP

The transparent areas in a layer do not increase file size.

Using Layers to Modify an Image

You can add, delete, and move layers in your image. You can also drag a portion of an image, called a **selection**, from one Photoshop image to another. When you do this, a new layer is automatically created. Copying layers from one image to another makes it easy to transfer a complicated effect, a simple image, or a piece of type. In addition to being able to hide and display each layer, you can also change its opacity. **Opacity** is the ability to see through a layer so that layers beneath it are visible. The more opacity a layer has, the less see-through (transparent) it is. You can continuously change the overall appearance of your image by changing the order of your layers, until you achieve just the look you want.

TOOLS YOU'LL USE

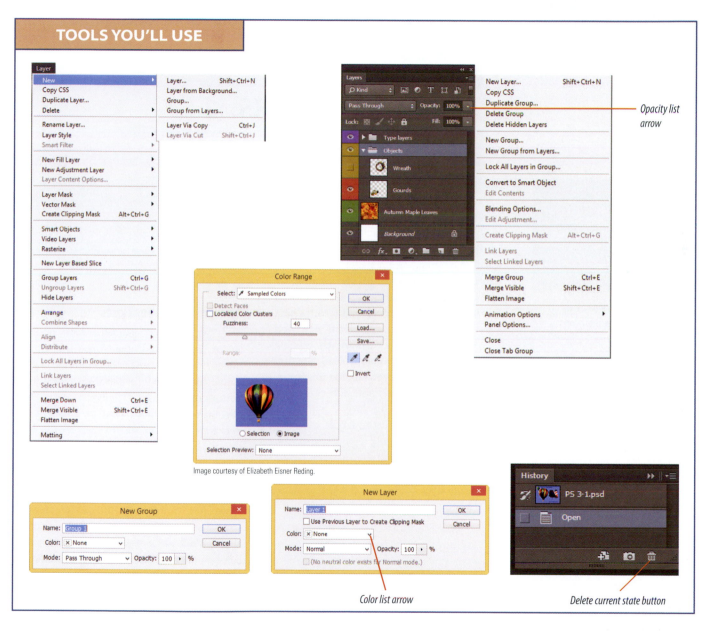

Image courtesy of Elizabeth Eisner Reding.

Opacity list arrow

Color list arrow

Delete current state button

Examine and
CONVERT LAYERS

What You'll Do

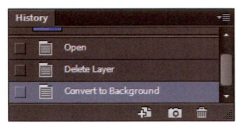

 In this lesson, you'll use the Layers panel to delete a Background layer and the Layer menu to create a Background layer from an image layer.

Learning About the Layers Panel

The Layers panel lists all the layers within a Photoshop file and makes it possible for you to manipulate one or more layers. By default, this panel is located in the lower-right corner of the screen, but it can be moved to a new location by dragging the panel's tab. In some cases, the entire name of the layer might not appear on the panel. If a layer name is too long, an ellipsis appears, indicating that part of the name is hidden from view. You can view a layer's entire name by holding the pointer over the name until the full name appears. The **layer thumbnail** appears to the left of the layer name and contains a miniature picture of the layer's content, as shown in Figure 1. To the left of the layer thumbnail, you can add color, which you can use to easily identify layers. The Layers panel also contains common buttons, such as the Delete layer button and the Create a new layer button.

Recognizing Layer Types

The Layers panel includes several types of layers: Background, type, adjustment, and image (non-type). The Background layer—whose name appears in italics—is always at the bottom of the stack. Type layers—layers that contain text—contain the type layer icon in the layer thumbnail, and image layers display a thumbnail of their contents. Adjustment layers, which affect the appearance of layers, have a variety of thumbnails depending on the kind of adjustment. Along with dragging selections from one Photoshop image to another, you can also drag objects created in other applications, such as Adobe Dreamweaver, Adobe InDesign, Adobe Illustrator, or Adobe Flash, onto a Photoshop image, which creates a layer containing the object you dragged from the other program window.

Organizing Layers

One of the benefits of using layers is that you can create different design effects by rearranging their order. Figure 2 contains the same layers as Figure 1, but they are arranged differently. Did you notice that the yellow-striped balloon is in front of both the black-striped balloon and the lighthouse balloon? This image was created by dragging the layer containing the yellow balloon (named Layer 2 on the Layers panel) above the Black striped balloon layer. When organizing layers, you may find it helpful to resize the Layers panel so you can see more layers within the image.

Figure 1 *Image with multiple layers*
Image courtesy of Elizabeth Eisner Reding.

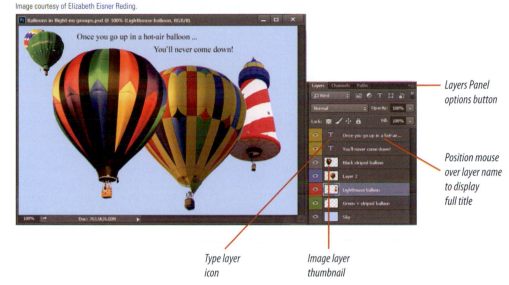

Layers Panel options button

Position mouse over layer name to display full title

Type layer icon

Image layer thumbnail

Figure 2 *Layers rearranged*
Image courtesy of Elizabeth Eisner Reding.

New layer order

Guideline

Overlapping balloons

Converting Layers

When you open an image created with a digital camera, you'll notice that the entire image appears in the Background layer. The Background layer of any image is the initial layer and is always located at the bottom of the stack. You cannot change its position in the stack, nor can you change its opacity or lighten or darken its colors. You can, however, convert a Background layer into an image layer (non-type layer), and you can convert an image layer into a Background layer. You might want to convert a Background layer into an image layer so that you can use the full range of editing tools on the layer content. You might want to convert an image layer into a Background layer after you have made all your changes and want it to be the bottom layer in the stack. Note that when you convert an image layer to a Background layer, you need to modify the image layer *before* converting it.

QUICK TIP

Before you can convert an image layer to a Background layer, you must first delete the existing Background layer. You delete a Background layer by selecting it on the Layers panel, and then dragging it to the Delete layer button on the Layers panel.

Figure 3 *Changing units of measurement*
Image courtesy of Elizabeth Eisner Reding.

Right-click (Win) or [control]-click (Mac) to display measurement choices

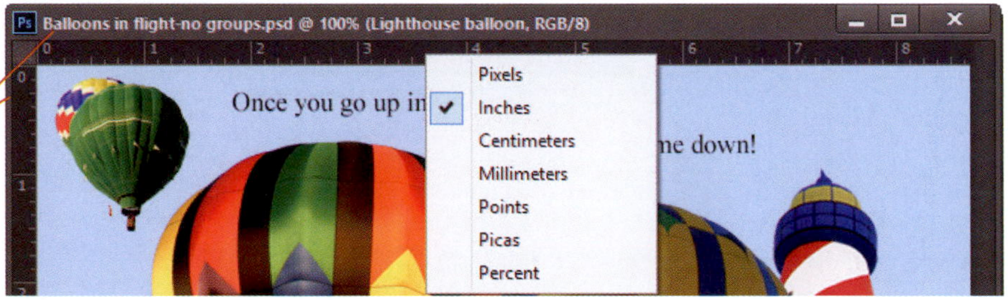

Using Rulers and Changing Units of Measurement

You can display horizontal and vertical rulers to help you better position elements. To display or hide rulers, click View on the Menu bar, and then click Rulers. (A check mark to the left of the Rulers command indicates that the rulers are displayed.)

In addition to displaying or hiding rulers, you can also choose from various units of measurement. Your choices include pixels, inches, centimeters, millimeters, points, picas, and percentages. Pixels, for example, display more tick marks and can make it easier to make tiny adjustments. You can change the units of measurement by clicking Edit [Win] or Photoshop [Mac] on the Menu bar, pointing to Preferences, and then clicking Units & Rulers. In the Preferences dialog box, click the Rulers list arrow, click the units you want to use, and then click OK. The easiest way to change units of measurement, however, is shown in Figure 3. Once the rulers are displayed, right-click (Win) or [control]-click (Mac) either the vertical or horizontal ruler, and then click the unit of measurement you want. When displayed, the Info panel shows the current X/Y coordinates of your pointer in your image, based on the units of measurement in use.

Pixel dimensions measure the number of pixels forming the width and height of an image, while *resolution* is the fineness of the detail in an image. The more pixels per inch, the greater the resolution.

Figure 4 *Warning box*

Figure 5 *Background layer deleted*

Background layer
no longer present

Figure 6 *New Background layer
added to Layers panel*

History state
indicating layer
conversion

New Background
layer

Convert an image layer into a Background layer

1. Open PS 3-1.psd from the drive and folder where you store your Data Files, then save it as **Up in the air**.

    TIP If you receive a warning box about maximum compatibility or a message stating that some of the text layers need to be updated before they can be used for vector-based output, click Update and/or click OK.

2. Click **View** on the Menu bar, click **Rulers** if your rulers are not visible, then make sure that the rulers are displayed in pixels.

    TIP If you are unsure which units of measurement are used, right-click (Win) or [control]-click (Mac) one of the rulers, then click Pixels if it is not already selected.

3. Click **Legacy** (created in a lesson in Chapter 1) in the workspace switcher on the options bar.

4. On the Layers panel, click the **Background layer**, then click the **Delete layer button** 🗑.

5. Click **Yes** in the dialog box, as shown in Figure 4, then compare your Layers panel to Figure 5.

6. Verify that the Sky layer in the Layers panel is active, click **Layer** on the Menu bar, point to **New**, then click **Background from Layer**.

    The Sky layer has been converted into the Background layer. Did you notice that in addition to the image layer being converted to the Background layer that a state now appears on the History panel that says Convert to Background? See Figure 6.

7. Save your work.

You displayed the rulers and switched to a previously created workspace, deleted the Background layer of an image, then converted an image layer into the Background layer. You can convert any layer into the Background layer, as long as you first delete the existing Background layer.

Add and Delete
LAYERS

What You'll Do

In this lesson, you'll create a new layer using the New command on the Layer menu, delete a layer, and create a new layer using buttons on the Layers panel.

Adding Layers to an Image

Because it's so important to make use of multiple layers, Photoshop makes it easy to add and delete layers. You can create layers in three ways:

- Use the New command on the Layer menu.
- Use the New Layer command on the Layers panel menu.
- Click the Create a new layer button on the Layers panel.

Objects on new layers have a default opacity setting of 100%, which means that objects on lower layers are not visible. Each layer has the Normal (default) blending mode

Merging Layers

You can combine multiple image layers into a single layer using the merging process. **Merging layers** is useful when you want to combine multiple layers in order to make specific edits permanent. (This merging process is different from flattening in that it's selective. Flattening merges *all* visible layers.) In order for layers to be merged, they must be visible. You can merge all visible layers within an image, or just the ones you select.

Type layers cannot be merged until they are **rasterized** (turned into a bitmapped image layer) or converted into uneditable text. To merge two layers, make sure that they are adjacent and that the Indicates layer visibility button is visible on each layer, and then click the layer in the higher position on the Layers panel. Click the Layers Panel options button, and then click Merge Down. The **active layer** (the layer that's currently selected) and the layer immediately beneath it will be combined into a single layer. To merge all visible layers, click the Layers Panel options button, and then click Merge Visible. Many layer commands that are available using the Layers Panel options button such as Merge Visible, are also available on the Layer menu.

applied to it. (A **blending mode** is a feature that affects a layer's underlying pixels, and is used to lighten or darken colors. Blending modes affect how pixels in two separate layers interact with each other.)

QUICK TIP

See Table 1 for tips on navigating the Layers panel.

Generating Assets from Layers

Imagine that you have an image with half a dozen or so layers. And these layers may have to be used elsewhere for a website, or for use by other departments. These other users are going to need these elements as gifs or jpgs, *not* Photoshop layers. Using **Adobe Generator**, you can have Photoshop create individual files (such as GIFs or JPGs) from the layers in an image. To do this, open the file for which you want the assets generated, click File on the Menu bar, point to Generate, then click Image Assets. (This option is a toggle switch so be sure to turn this off when you're finished.)

QUICK TIP

Adobe Generator is created to improve workflows, particularly for web designers, screen designers, and anyone who needs to extract image assets from a Photoshop image.

On each layer that you want to create as an asset, rename the layer with a sensible name, appended by the extension of the file format you want (.gif, .png, or .jpg). Photoshop generates the image assets in a subfolder (named *filename*-assets) in the same location as the source PSD file.

TABLE 1: SHORTCUTS FOR NAVIGATING THE LAYERS PANEL	
Use the combination:	**To navigate:**
[Alt] [[] (Win) or [option] [[] (Mac)	down the Layers panel
[Alt] [[] (Win) or [option] []] (Mac)	up the Layers panel
[Ctrl] [[] (Win) or ⌘ [[] (Mac)	to move a layer down one layer*
[Ctrl] []] (Win) or ⌘ []] (Mac)	to move a layer up one layer*
[Ctrl] [Shift] [[] (Win) or ⌘ [Shift] [[] (Mac)	to move a layer to the bottom of the stack*
[Ctrl] [Shift] []] (Win) or ⌘ [Shift] []] (Mac)	to move a layer to the top of the stack*

*Excluding the Background layer

© 2013 Cengage Learning®

Naming a Layer

Photoshop automatically assigns a sequential number to each new layer name, but you can rename a layer at any time. So, if you have four named layers and add a new layer, the default name of the new layer will be Layer 1. Although calling a layer "Layer 12" is fine, you might want to use a more descriptive name so it is easier to distinguish one layer from another. If you use the New command on the Layer menu, you can name the layer when you create it. You can rename a layer at any time by using either of these methods:

- Click Layer on the Menu bar, click Rename Layer, type the new name when the existing text is selected, and then press [Enter] (Win) or [return] (Mac).

- Double-click the name on the Layers panel, type the new name, and then press [Enter] (Win) or [return] (Mac).

QUICK TIP

Pressing [Alt] (Win) or [option] (Mac) while clicking the Create a new layer button on the Layers panel opens the New Layer dialog box.

Isolation Mode Layer Filtering

Suppose you are working with a complex image that has so many layers that you become distracted by them. Using this isolaton enhancement, you can filter layers in an image and focus more clearly on a specific subset of layers. You can selectively filter specific layers by clicking them (click the initial layer, then [Ctrl]-click (Win) or [command]-click (Mac) each additional layer, clicking Select on the Menu bar, then clicking Isolate Layers. Only the selected layers will be displayed in the Layers panel. To return the Layers Panel to normal, click Select on the Menu bar, then click Isolate Layers. Once the layers are selected, you can enter isolation mode by clicking the Layer Filtering list arrow in the Layers panel, then clicking Selected.

Deleting Layers from an Image

You might want to delete an unused or unnecessary layer. You can use multiple methods to delete a layer:

■ Click the name on the Layers panel, click the Layers Panel options button, and then click Delete Layer, as shown in Figure 7.
■ Click the name on the Layers panel, click the Delete layer button on the Layers panel, and then click Yes in the warning box.
■ Click the name on the Layers panel, press and hold [Alt] (Win) or [option] (Mac), and then click the Delete layer button on the Layers panel.

■ Drag the layer name on the Layers panel to the Delete layer button on the Layers panel.
■ Right-click a layer (Win) or [Ctrl]-click a layer (Mac), and then click Delete Layer.

You should be certain that you no longer need a layer before you delete it. If you delete a layer by accident, you can restore it during the current editing session by deleting the Delete Layer state on the History panel, or by clicking Edit on the Menu bar, then clicking Undo Delete Layer.

Figure 7 *Layers panel menu*

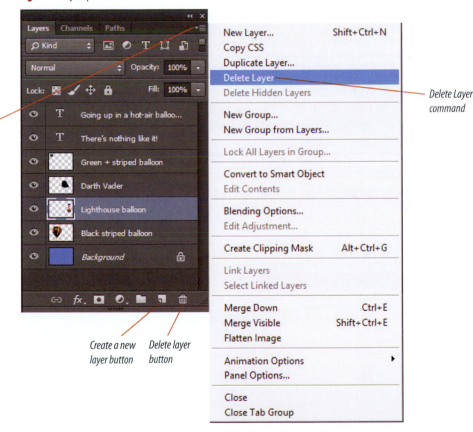

Layers Panel options button

Delete Layer command

Create a new layer button

Delete layer button

Modifying a workspace

1. Drag the History panel so it displays above the Layers panel.
2. Click **Window** on the Menu bar, point to **Workspace**, then click **New Workspace**.
3. Type **Legacy** in the Name text box, click **Save**, then click **Yes** in the New Workspace warning box.

You moved a panel in a saved workspace, then saved the change using the original name (making the change permanent).

Add a layer using the Layer menu

1. Click the **Lighthouse balloon layer** on the Layers panel.
2. Click **Layer** on the Menu bar, point to **New**, then click **Layer** to open the New Layer dialog box, as shown in Figure 8.

   A new layer will be added above the active layer.

TIP You can change the layer name in the New Layer dialog box before it appears on the Layers panel.

3. Click **OK**.

   The New Layer dialog box closes and the new layer, Layer 1, appears above the Lighthouse balloon layer on the Layers panel. The New Layer state is added to the History panel. See Figure 9.

You created a new layer above the Lighthouse balloon layer using the New command on the Layer menu. The layer does not yet contain any content.

Figure 8 *New Layer dialog box*

Figure 9 *New layer in Layers panel*

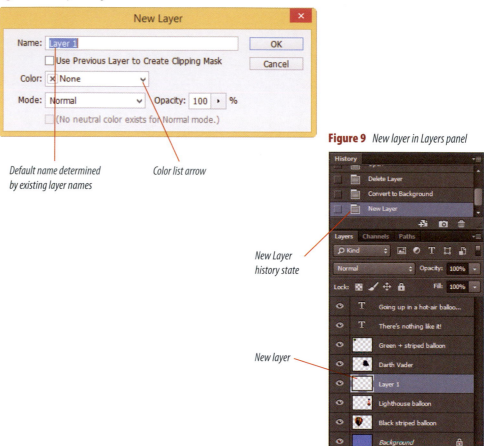

Default name determined by existing layer names

Color list arrow

New Layer history state

New layer

Inserting a Layer Beneath the Active Layer

When you add a layer to an image either by using the Layer menu or clicking the Create a new layer button on the Layers panel, the new layer is inserted above the active layer. But there might be times when you want to insert the new layer beneath, or in back of, the active layer. You can do so easily, by pressing [Ctrl] (Win) or ⌘ (Mac) while clicking the Create a new layer button on the Layers panel.

Figure 10 *New layer with default settings*

Default settings

Create a new layer button

Right-Clicking for Everyone (Mac)

Since some Mac mice only come with a single button, you may feel left out, unless you have a multitouch trackpad. Mac users can simulate the right-click menus by holding the [control] key while clicking. An alternative method is to use a 2-fingered click if you have a Mac multitouch trackpad. Once you've learned these simple tricks, you can right-click using the (Win) instructions in the steps. You can also assign the bottom-left corner of a Mac trackpad as a right-click zone. You can configure the trackpad using the Trackpad option in the System Preferences window. The Magic Mouse can be used with any Mac and can be customized to accommodate your own work style. Although it appears to have no buttons, its sleak surface can be programmed with multi-touch functionality, so it can single-click, right-click, multi-finger swipe, zoom, pan, or scroll and can be customized for right- and left-handed users.

Delete a layer

1. Position the **Layer selection pointer** over Layer 1 on the Layers panel.

2. Drag **Layer 1** to the **Delete layer button** on the Layers panel.

TIP You can also delete the layer by dragging the New Layer state on the History panel to the Delete current state button.

3. If the Delete the layer "Layer 1" dialog box opens, click the **Don't show again check box**, then click **Yes**.

TIP Many dialog boxes let you turn off this reminder feature by selecting the Don't show again check box. Selecting these check boxes can improve your efficiency.

You used the Delete layer button on the Layers panel to delete a layer.

Add a layer using the Layers panel

1. Click the **Lighthouse balloon layer** on the Layers panel, if it is not already selected.

2. Click the **Create a new layer button** on the Layers panel, then compare your Layers panel and History panel to Figure 10.

3. Save your work.

You used the Create a new layer button on the Layers panel to add a new layer.

Add a Selection
FROM ONE IMAGE TO ANOTHER

What You'll Do

Image courtesy of Elizabeth Eisner Reding.

 In this lesson, you'll use the Invert check box in the Color Range dialog box to make a selection, drag the selection to another image, and remove the fringe from a selection using the Defringe command.

Understanding Selections

Often the Photoshop file you want to create involves using an image or part of an image from another file. To use an image or part of an image, you must first select it. Photoshop refers to this as "making a selection." A selection is an area of an image surrounded by a **marquee**, a dashed line that encloses the area you want to edit or move to another image, as shown in Figure 11. You can drag a marquee around a selection using four marquee tools: Rectangular Marquee, Elliptical Marquee, Single Row Marquee, and Single Column Marquee. Table 2 displays the four marquee tools along with other selection tools. You can set options for each tool on the options bar when the tool you want to use is active.

Making and Moving a Selection

You can use a variety of methods and tools to make a selection, which can then be used as a specific part of a layer or as the entire layer. You use selections to isolate an area you want to alter. For example, you can use the Magnetic Lasso tool to select complex shapes by clicking the starting point, tracing an approximate outline, and then clicking the ending point. Later, you can use the Crop tool to trim areas from a selection. When you use the Move tool to drag a selection to the destination image, Photoshop places the selection in a new layer above the previously active layer.

Cropping an Image

You might find an image that you really like, except that it contains a particular portion that you don't need. You can exclude, or **crop**, certain parts of an image by using the Crop tool on the Tools panel. Cropping hides areas of an image from view *without* decreasing resolution quality. To crop an image, click the Crop tool on the Tools panel, drag the pointer around the area you *want to keep,* and then press [Enter] (Win) or [return] (Mac).

Understanding Color Range Command

In addition to using selection tools, Photoshop provides more methods for incorporating imagery from other files. You can use the Color Range command, located on the Select menu, to select a particular color contained in an existing image. Depending on the area you want, you can use the Color Range dialog box to extract a portion of an image.

For example, you can select the Invert check box, choose one color, and then Photoshop will select the portion of the image that is every color *except* the color you chose. After you select all the imagery you want from another image, you can drag it into your open file. Simply put, the Invert feature allows you to flip whatever you currently have selected to include whatever is not currently selected.

Defringing Layer Contents

Sometimes when you make a selection and move it into another image, the newly selected image contains unwanted pixels that give the appearance of a fringe, or halo. You can remove this effect using a Matting command called Defringe. This command is available by pointing to Matting on the Layer menu and allows you to replace fringe pixels with the colors of other nearby pixels. You can determine a width for replacement pixels between 1 and 200. It's magic!

Figure 11 *Marquee selections*
Image courtesy of Elizabeth Eisner Reding.

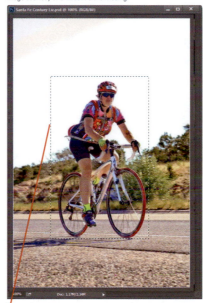
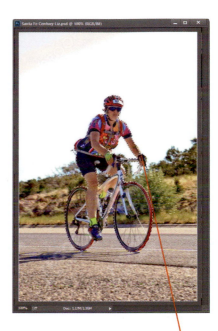

Area selected using the Rectangular Marquee tool

Specific element selected using the Magnetic Lasso tool

TABLE 2: SELECTION TOOLS			
Tool	**Tool name**	**Tool**	**Tool name**
	Rectangular Marquee tool		Quick Selection tool
	Elliptical Marquee tool		Lasso tool
	Single Row Marquee tool		Polygonal Lasso tool
	Single Column Marquee tool		Magnetic Lasso tool
	Crop tool		Slice tool
	Magic Wand tool		

© 2013 Cengage Learning®

Make a color range selection

1. Open PS 3-2.psd from the drive and folder where you store your Data Files, save it as **Yellow striped balloon**, click the **title bar**, then drag the **window** to an empty area of the workspace so that you can see both images.

   TIP When more than one file is open, each has its own set of rulers. The ruler on the inactive file appears dimmed.

2. With the Yellow striped balloon image selected, click **Select** on the Menu bar, then click **Color Range**.

   TIP If the background color is a solid color, when you select it and select the Invert check box, only the foreground will be selected.

3. Click the **Image option button** below the image preview, then type **100** in the Fuzziness text box (or drag the **slider** to the right until you see **100**).

4. Position the **Eyedropper pointer** 🖋 in the **blue background** of the image in the Color Range dialog box, then click the **background**.

5. Select the **Invert check box**. Compare the settings in your dialog box to Figure 12.

6. Click **OK**, then compare your Yellow striped balloon.psd image to Figure 13.

You opened a file and used the Color Range dialog box to select the image pixels by selecting the image's inverted colors. Selecting the inverse is an important skill in making selections.

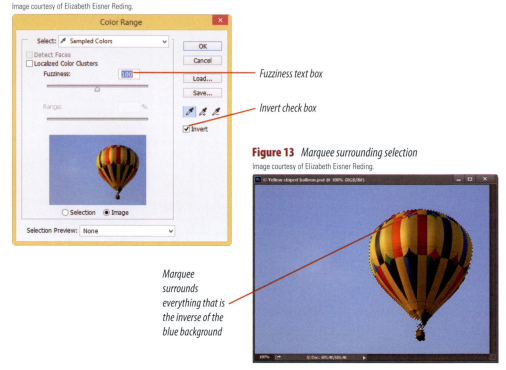

Figure 12 *Color Range dialog box*
Image courtesy of Elizabeth Eisner Reding.

Fuzziness text box

Invert check box

Figure 13 *Marquee surrounding selection*
Image courtesy of Elizabeth Eisner Reding.

Marquee surrounds everything that is the inverse of the blue background

Using the Place Commands

You can add an image from another image to a layer using a Place command. Place an image in a Photoshop layer by clicking File on the Menu bar, clicking Place Embedded or Place Linked, then committing the changes. A file that is Place Linked will be automatically updated when the original (source) file is modified. A file that is Place Embedded is essentially a copy of the source file and will not be updated if the original file is modified. The placed artwork appears *flattened* inside a bounding box at the center of the Photoshop image. The artwork maintains its original aspect ratio; however, if the artwork is larger than the Photoshop image, it is resized to fit. The Place commands work well if you want to insert a multi-layered image in another image. (If all you want is a specific layer from an image, you should just drag the layer you want into an image and not use a Place command.)

Working with Layers

Figure 14 *Yellow striped balloon image dragged to Up in the air image*
Image courtesy of Elizabeth Eisner Reding.

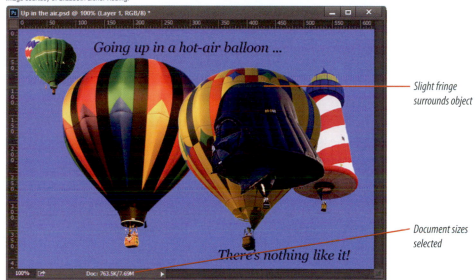

Slight fringe
surrounds object

Document sizes
selected

Figure 15 *New layer defringed*
Image courtesy of Elizabeth Eisner Reding.

Yellow striped
balloon in image

Yellow striped
balloon appears
on Layer 1

Move a selection to another image

1. Click the **Move tool** ▶⊹ on the Tools panel.
2. Position the **Move tool pointer** ▶⊠ anywhere over the selection in the Yellow striped balloon image.
3. Drag the **selection** to the Up in the air image, then release the mouse button.

   The Yellow striped balloon image moves to the Up in the air image appearing on Layer 1.
4. Use ▶⊹ to drag the yellow striped balloon to the approximate location shown in Figure 14.

   TIP When you drag an object, a box displays showing you how many horizontal and vertical pixels the object is moving.

5. Click the **menu arrow** ▶ in the document window status bar and verify that Document Sizes is selected.

You dragged a selection from one image to another. You verified that the document size is displayed in the window.

Defringe the selection

1. With Layer 1 selected, click **Layer** on the Menu bar, point to **Matting** then click **Defringe**.

   Defringing a selection gets rid of the halo effect that sometimes occurs when objects are dragged from one image to another.
2. Type **2** in the Width text box, then click **OK**.
3. Click the **Darth Vader layer** and defringe it using a width of **2**.
4. Save your work.
5. Close **Yellow striped ballon.psd**, then compare the Up in the air image to Figure 15.

You removed the fringe from a selection and a layer.

Organize Layers with
LAYER GROUPS AND COLORS

What You'll Do

Image courtesy of Elizabeth Eisner Reding.

 In this lesson, you'll use the Layers Panel options button to create, name, and color-code a layer group, and then add layers to it. You'll add finishing touches to the image, save it as a copy, and then flatten it.

Understanding Layer Groups

A **layer group** is a Photoshop feature that allows you to organize your layers on the Layers panel. A layer group contains individual layers, which are sometimes referred to as *nested layers*. For example, you can create a layer group that contains all the type layers in your image. To create a layer group, you click the Layers Panel options button, and then click New Group. As with layers, it is helpful to choose a descriptive name for a layer group.

> **QUICK TIP**
>
> You can press [Ctrl][G] (Win) or ⌘ [G] (Mac) to place the selected layer in a layer group.

Organizing Layers into Groups

After you create a layer group, you simply drag layers on the Layers panel directly on top of the layer group. You can remove layers from a layer group by dragging them out of the layer group to a new location on the Layers panel or by deleting them. Some changes made to a layer group, such as blending mode or opacity changes, affect every layer in the layer group. You can choose to expand or collapse layer groups, depending on the amount of information you need to see. Expanding a layer group shows all of the layers in the layer

Duplicating a Layer

When you add a new layer by clicking the Create a new layer button on the Layers panel, the new layer contains default settings. However, you might want to create a new layer that has the same settings as an existing layer. You can do so by duplicating an existing layer to create a copy of that layer and its settings. Duplicating a layer is also a good way to preserve your modifications, because you can modify the duplicate layer and not worry about losing your original work. To create a duplicate layer, select the layer you want to copy, click the Layers Panel options button, click Duplicate Layer, and then click OK. The new layer will appear above the original.

group, and collapsing a layer group hides all of the layers in a layer group. You can expand or collapse a layer group by clicking the triangle to the left of the layer group icon. Figure 16 shows one expanded layer group and one collapsed layer group.

Identifying a Layer with Color

If your image has relatively few layers, it's easy to locate the layers. However, if your image contains many layers, you might need some help in organizing them. You can organize layers by color-coding them, which makes it easy to find the layer or the group you want, regardless of its location on the Layers panel. For example, you can identify all type layers with red or color-code the layers associated with a particular portion of an image with blue. To color-code the Background layer, you must first convert it to a regular layer.

QUICK TIP

You can also color-code a layer group without losing the color-coding you applied to individual layers.

Flattening an Image

After you make all the necessary modifications to your image, you can greatly reduce the file size by flattening the image. Flattening merges all visible layers into a single Background layer and discards all hidden layers. Make sure that all layers that you want to display are visible before you flatten the image. Because flattening removes an image's individual layers, it's a good idea to make a copy of the original image *before* it is flattened. The status bar displays the file's current size and the size it will be when flattened.

Figure 16 *Layer groups*

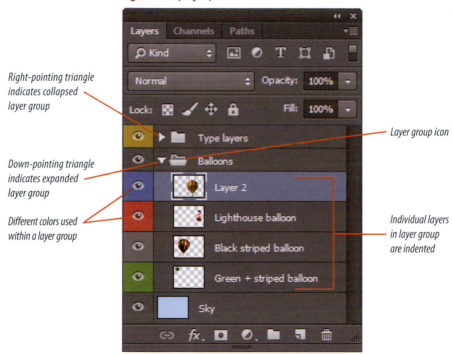

Right-pointing triangle indicates collapsed layer group

Down-pointing triangle indicates expanded layer group

Different colors used within a layer group

Layer group icon

Individual layers in layer group are indented

Understanding Layer Comps

The ability to create a **layer comp**, a variation on the arrangement and visibility of existing layers, is a powerful tool that can make your work more organized. You might, for example, want to create several variations of your single image that include different configurations of layers, and layer comps give you this ability. You open the Layer Comps panel by clicking Window on the Menu bar, and then clicking Layer Comps. Clicking the Create New Layer Comp button on the panel opens the New Layer Comp dialog box, shown in Figure 17, which allows you to name the layer comp and set parameters.

Using Layer Comps

Multiple layer comps, shown in Figure 18, make it easy to switch back and forth between variations on an image theme. The layer comp is an ideal tool for showing a client multiple layer arrangement options.

Figure 18 *Multiple layer comps in image*
Image courtesy of Elizabeth Eisner Reding.

Figure 17 *New Layer Comp dialog box*

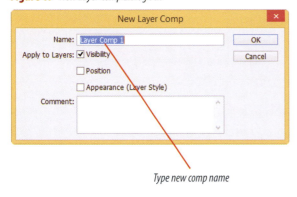

Type new comp name

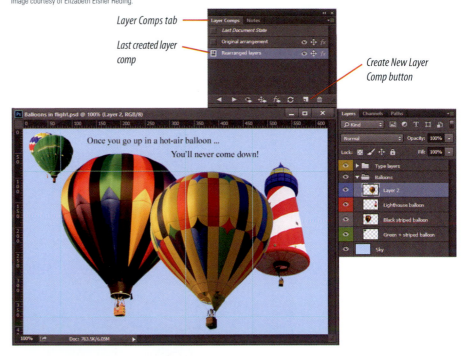

Layer Comps tab

Last created layer comp

Create New Layer Comp button

Figure 19 *New Group dialog box*

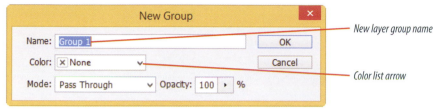

New layer group name

Color list arrow

Figure 20 *New layer group in Layers panel*

Down-pointing arrow indicates expanded layer group

New layer group

Figure 21 *Layers added to the All Type layer group*

Layers within group are indented

Layer group icon (folder)

Create a layer group

1. Click the **Green + striped balloon layer**, click the **Layers Panel options button** , then click **New Group**.

   The New Group dialog box opens, as shown in Figure 19.

   TIP Photoshop automatically places a new layer group above the active layer.

2. Type **All Type** in the Name text box.

3. Click the **Color list arrow**, click **Yellow**, then click **OK.**

   The New Group dialog box closes. Compare your Layers panel to Figure 20.

You used the Layers panel menu to create a layer group, then named and applied a color to it. This new group will contain all the type layers in the image.

Move layers to the layer group

1. Click the **Going up in a hot-air balloon** layer on the Layers panel, then drag it on to the **All Type layer group**.

2. Click the **There's nothing like it! layer**, drag it on to the **All Type layer group**, then compare your Layers panel to Figure 21.

   TIP If the There's nothing like it! layer is not below the Going up in a hot-air balloon layer, move the layers to match Figure 21.

3. Click the **triangle** to the left of the layer group icon (folder) to collapse the layer group.

You moved two layers into a layer group. Using layer groups is a great organizational tool, especially in complex images with many layers.

Rename a layer and adjust opacity

1. Double-click **Layer 1**, type **Yellow striped balloon**, then press [**Enter**] (Win) or [**return**] (Mac).

2. Double-click the **Opacity text box** on the Layers panel, type **85**, then press [**Enter**] (Win) or [**return**] (Mac).

3. Drag the **Yellow striped balloon layer** beneath the Lighthouse balloon layer, then compare your image to Figure 22.

4. Save your work.

You renamed the new layer, adjusted opacity, and rearranged layers.

Create layer comps

1. Click **Window** on the Menu bar, then click **Layer Comps**.

2. Click the **Create New Layer Comp button** on the Layer Comps panel.

3. Type **Green off/Yellow off** in the Name text box, as shown in Figure 23, then click **OK**.

4. Click the **Indicates layer visibility button** on the Green + striped balloon layer and the Yellow striped balloon layer.

5. Click the **Update Layer Comp button** on the Layer Comps panel. Compare your Layer Comps panel to Figure 24.

6. Save your work, then click the **Layer Comps Close button** on the icon dock to close the Layer Comps panel.

You created a Layer Comp in an existing image.

Figure 22 *Finished image*
Image courtesy of Elizabeth Eisner Reding.

Opacity text box

Renamed and moved layer

Overlapping balloon layers

Lower opacity allows pixels on lower layers to show through

Figure 23 *New Layer Comp dialog box*

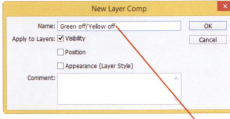

New Layer Comp name

Figure 24 *Layer Comps panel*

Active Layer Comp

Toggle Layer Comp Position

Apply Next Selected Layer Comp

Apply Previous Selected Layer Comp

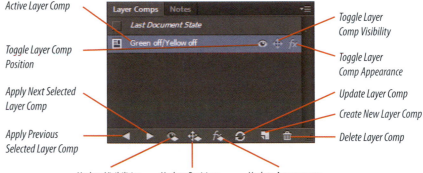

Toggle Layer Comp Visibility

Toggle Layer Comp Appearance

Update Layer Comp

Create New Layer Comp

Delete Layer Comp

Update Visibilities of Selected Layer Comps and Layers

Update Positions of Selected Layer Comps and Layers

Update Appearances of Selected Layer Comps and Layers

Figure 25 *Save As dialog box*

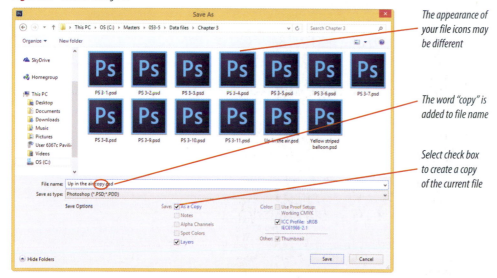

The appearance of your file icons may be different

The word "copy" is added to file name

Select check box to create a copy of the current file

Figure 26 *Flattened image layer*
Image courtesy of Elizabeth Eisner Reding.

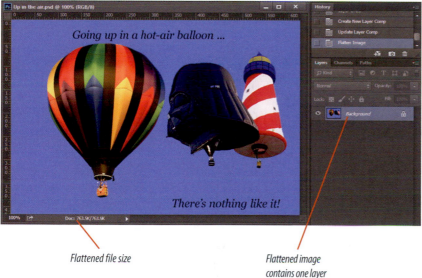

Flattened file size

Flattened image contains one layer

Flatten an image

1. Click **File** on the Menu bar, then click **Save As**.

2. Click the **As a Copy check box** to select it, then compare your dialog box to Figure 25.

   TIP If "copy" does not display in the File name text box, click this text box and type copy to add it to the name.

3. Click **Save**, then click **OK** to Maximize Compatibility, if necessary.

   Photoshop saves and closes a copy of the file containing all the layers and effects.

4. Click **Layer** on the Menu bar, then click **Flatten Image**.

5. Click **OK** in the warning box (to discard hidden layers), then save your work.

   Compare your Layers panel to Figure 26.

6. Click the **workspace switcher** on the options bar, then click **Essentials**.

7. Close all open images, then exit Photoshop.

You saved a copy of the file, then flattened the image. The image now has a single layer.

POWER USER SHORTCUTS	
To do this:	**Use this method:**
Adjust layer opacity	Click Opacity list arrow on Layers panel
	Drag Opacity slider
	Double-click Opacity text box, type a percentage
Add a layer to a group	Drag selected layer(s) to Group folder
Change measurements	Right-click ruler (Win)
	[Ctrl]-click ruler (Mac)
Color-code a layer	Right-click layer, click color
Create a layer comp	▣ on Layer Comps panel
Create a layer group	▾≡, New Group, or [Ctrl][G] (Win)
	⌘ [G] (Mac)
Delete a layer	🗑
Defringe a selection	Layer ➤ Matting ➤ Defringe
Flatten an image	Layer ➤ Flatten Image
Use the Move tool	▸⊕ or **V**
Make a new Background layer from existing layer	Layer ➤ New ➤ Background from Layer
Make a new layer	Layer ➤ New ➤ Layer
	or ▣
Rename a layer	Double-click layer name, type new name
Select color range	Select ➤ Color Range
Show/Hide Rulers	View ➤ Rulers
	[Ctrl][R] (Win)
	⌘ [R] (Mac)
Update a layer comp	🔄

Key: Menu items are indicated by ➤ *between the menu name and its command. Blue bold letters are shortcuts for selecting tools on the Tools panel.*

© 2013 Cengage Learning®

Examine and convert layers.

1. Start Photoshop.
2. Open PS 3-3.psd from the drive and folder where you store your Data Files, then save it as **Music Store**.
3. Make sure the rulers appear and that pixels are the unit of measurement.

TIP For now and future lessons, if you see a dialog box telling you that text layers might need to be updated, please update the layers.

4. Delete the Background layer.
5. Verify that the Rainbow blend layer is active, then convert the image layer to a Background layer.
6. Save your work.

Add and delete layers.

1. Make Layer 2 active.
2. Create a new layer above this layer using the Layer menu.
3. Accept the default name (Layer 5), and change the color of the layer to Red.
4. Delete (new) Layer 5.
5. Make Layer 2 active (if it is not already the active layer).
6. Save your work.

Add a selection from one image to another.

1. Open PS 3-4.psd.
2. Reposition this image of a horn by dragging the window to the right of the Music Store image.
3. Open the Color Range dialog box. (*Hint*: Use the Select menu.)
4. Verify that the Image option button is selected, the Invert check box is selected, and then set the Fuzziness to 0.
5. Sample the white background in the preview window in the dialog box, then click OK.
6. Use the Move tool to drag the selection into the Music Store image.
7. Position the selection so that the upper-left edge of the instrument matches the sample shown in Figure 27 on the next page.
8. Defringe the horn selection (in the Music Store image) using a 3 pixel width.
9. Close PS 3-4.psd.
10. Drag Layer 5 above the Notes layer.
11. Rename Layer 5 **Horn**.
12. Change the opacity for the Horn layer to 55%.
13. Drag the Horn layer so it is beneath Layer 2.
14. Hide Layer 1.
15. Hide the rulers.
16. Save your work.

Organize layers with layer groups and colors.

1. Create a Layer Group called **Type Layers** and assign the color Orange to the group.
2. Drag the following layers into the Type Layers folder: Allegro, Music Store, Layer 2.
3. Delete Layer 2, then collapse the Type Layers group.
4. Move the Notes layer beneath the Horn layer.
5. Create a layer comp called **Notes layer on**.
6. Update the layer comp.
7. Hide the Notes layer.
8. Create a new layer comp called **Notes layer off**, then update the layer comp.
9. Display the previous layer comp, save your work, then close the tab group. (*Hint*: Click the Layer Comps Panel options button, then click Close Tab Group.)
10. Save a copy of the Music Store file using the default naming scheme (add 'copy' to the end of the existing filename).
11. Flatten the original image. (*Hint*: Be sure to discard hidden layers.)
12. Save your work, then compare your image to Figure 27.

Figure 27 *Completed Skills Review*
Images © Photodisc/Getty Images.

A credit union is developing a hotline for members to use to help mitigate credit card fraud as soon as it occurs. They're going to distribute ten thousand refrigerator magnets over the next three weeks. As part of their effort to build community awareness of the project, they have sponsored a contest for the magnet design. You decide to enter the contest.

1. Open PS 3-5.psd, then save it as **Combat Fraud**. The PalatinoLinotype Roman font is used in this file. Please make a substitution if this font is not available on your computer.
2. Open PS 3-6.psd, use the Color Range dialog box or any selection tool on the Tools panel to select the cell phone image, then drag it to the Combat Fraud image.
3. Rename the newly created layer **Cell Phones**, then assign a color code to the layer on the Layers panel. Make sure the Cell Phones layer is beneath the type layers.
4. Convert the Background layer to an image layer, then rename it **Banner**.
5. Change the opacity of the Banner layer to any setting you like.
6. Defringe the Cell Phones layer using the pixel width of your choice.
7. Save your work, close PS 3-6.psd, then compare your image to the sample shown in Figure 28.

Figure 28 *Sample Project Builder 1*
Source: Morguefile.

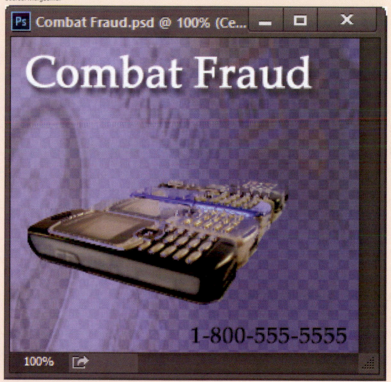

The local community can't get enough of the zoo's new giraffe exhibit, and they have hired you to create a promotional billboard commemorating this event. The Board of Directors wants the billboard to be humorous.

1. Open PS 3-7.psd, then save it as **Giraffe promotion**.
2. Open PS 3-8.psd, use the Color Range dialog box or any selection tool on the Tools panel to create a marquee around the giraffe, then drag the selection to the Giraffe promotion image.
3. Name the new layer **Giraffe**.
4. Change the opacity of the giraffe layer to 90% and defringe the layer containing the giraffe.
5. Reorder the layers so the Giraffe layer appears below the type layers.
6. Save your work, then compare your image to the sample shown in Figure 29.

Figure 29 *Sample Project Builder 2*
Images © Photodisc/Getty Images.

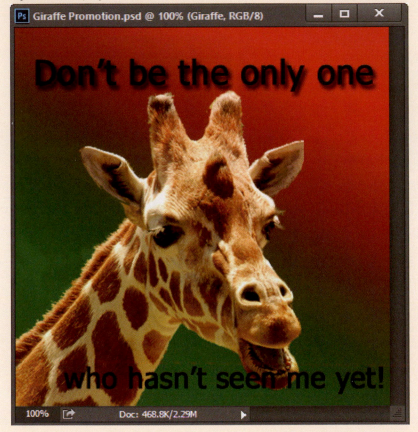

A friend of yours has designed a new heat-retaining coffee cup for take-out orders. She is going to present the prototype to a prospective vendor, but first needs to print a brochure. She's asked you to design an eye-catching cover.

1. Open PS 3-9.psd, then save it as **Coffee Cover**.
2. Open PS 3-10.psd, then drag the entire image to Coffee Cover.
3. Close PS 3-10.psd.
4. Rename Layer 1 with the name **Mocha**.
5. Delete the Background layer and convert the Mocha layer into a new Background layer.
6. Reposition the layer objects so they look like the sample. (*Hint*: You might have to reorganize the layers in the stack so all layers are visible. You can move type on a layer by selecting that layer, clicking the Move tool on the Tools panel, positioning the pointer over the type, then dragging until it is positioned where you want it.)
7. Create a layer group above Layer 2, name it **High Octane Text**, apply a color-code of your choice to the layer group, then drag the type layers to it. You can apply color-codes to any individual layers of your choosing.
8. Save your work, then compare your image to Figure 30.

Figure 30 *Sample Design Project*
Images © Photodisc/Getty Images.

Harvest Market, a line of natural food stores, and the trucking associations in your state have formed a coalition to deliver fresh fruit and vegetables to food banks and other food distribution programs. The truckers want to promote the project by displaying a sign on their trucks. Your task is to create a design that will become the Harvest Market logo. Keep in mind that the design will be seen from a distance.

1. Open PS 3-11.psd, then save it as **Harvest Market**.
2. Obtain at least two images of different-sized produce. You can obtain images by using what is available on your computer, scanning print media, or connecting to the Internet and downloading images.
3. Open one of the produce files, select it, then drag or copy it to the Harvest Market image. (*Hint*: Experiment with some of the other selection tools. Note that some tools require you to copy and paste the image after you select it.)
4. Repeat step 3, then close the two produce image files.
5. Set the opacity of the Market layer to 80%.
6. Arrange the layers so that smaller images appear on top of the larger ones. (You can move layers to any location in the image you choose.)
7. Create a layer group for the type layers, and apply a color-code to it.
8. You can delete any layers you feel do not add to the image. (In the sample image, the Veggies layer has been deleted.)
9. Save your work, then compare your image to Figure 31.
10. What are the advantages and disadvantages of using multiple images? How would you assess the ease and efficiency of the selection techniques you've learned?

Figure 31 *Sample Portfolio Project*

Source: Morguefile. Images © Photodisc/Getty Images.

CHAPTER **4** MAKING
SELECTIONS

1. Make a selection using shapes
2. Modify a marquee
3. Select using color and modify a selection
4. Add a vignette effect to a selection

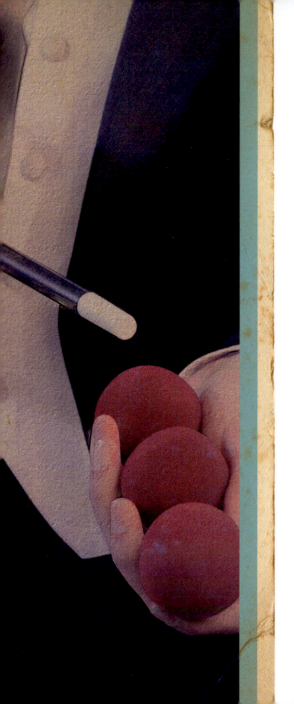

CHAPTER 4 MAKING
SELECTIONS

Combining Images

Most Photoshop images are created using a technique called **compositing**—combining images from different sources. These sources include other Photoshop images, royalty-free images, pictures taken with digital cameras, and scanned artwork. How you get those multiple images into your Photoshop images is an art unto itself. You can include additional images by using tools on the Tools panel and menu commands. And to work with all these images, you need to know how to select them—or how to select the parts you want to include.

Understanding Selection Tools

The two basic methods you can use to make selections are using a tool or using color. You can use three free-form tools to create your own unique selections, four fixed area tools to create circular or rectangular selections, and a wand tool to make selections using color. In addition, you can use menu commands to increase or decrease selections that you made

with these tools, or to make selections based on color.

Understanding Which Selection Tool to Use

With so many tools available, how do you know which one to use? After you become familiar with the different selection options, you'll learn how to look at images and evaluate selection opportunities. With experience, you'll learn how to identify edges that can be used to isolate imagery, and how to spot colors that can be used to isolate a specific object.

Combining Imagery

After you decide on an object that you want to place in a Photoshop image, you can add the object to another image by cutting, copying, and pasting or dragging and dropping objects using the selection tools, the Move tool, menu commands, or using the **Clipboard**, the temporary storage area provided by your operating system.

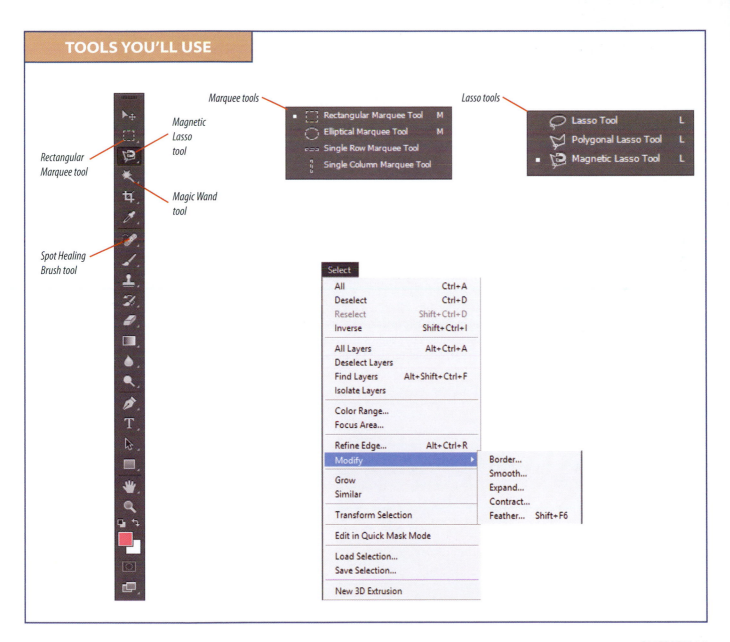

TOOLS YOU'LL USE

Marquee tools

Rectangular Marquee Tool   M
Elliptical Marquee Tool   M
Single Row Marquee Tool
Single Column Marquee Tool

Lasso tools

Lasso Tool   L
Polygonal Lasso Tool   L
Magnetic Lasso Tool   L

Magnetic Lasso tool

Rectangular Marquee tool

Magic Wand tool

Spot Healing Brush tool

Select

All	Ctrl+A
Deselect	Ctrl+D
Reselect	Shift+Ctrl+D
Inverse	Shift+Ctrl+I
All Layers	Alt+Ctrl+A
Deselect Layers	
Find Layers	Alt+Shift+Ctrl+F
Isolate Layers	
Color Range...	
Focus Area...	
Refine Edge...	Alt+Ctrl+R
Modify	▶
Grow	
Similar	
Transform Selection	
Edit in Quick Mask Mode	
Load Selection...	
Save Selection...	
New 3D Extrusion	

Border...
Smooth...
Expand...
Contract...
Feather...   Shift+F6

Make a Selection
USING SHAPES

What You'll Do

Source: Morguefile.

 In this lesson, you'll make selections using a marquee tool and a lasso tool, position a selection with the Move tool, deselect a selection, and drag a complex selection into another image.

Selecting by Shape

The Photoshop selection tools make it easy to select objects that are rectangular or elliptical in nature. However, it would be a boring world if every image we wanted fell into one of those categories, so fortunately they don't. While some objects are round or square, most are unusual in shape. Making selections can sometimes be a painstaking process because many objects don't have clearly defined edges. To select an object by shape, you need to click the appropriate tool on the Tools panel, and then drag the pointer around the object. The selected area is defined by a **marquee**, or series of dotted lines, as shown in Figure 1.

Creating a Selection

Drawing a rectangular marquee is easier than drawing an elliptical marquee, but with practice, you'll be able to create both types of marquees easily. Table 1 lists the tools you can use to make selections using shapes. Figure 2 shows a marquee surrounding an irregular shape.

Figure 1 *Elliptical Marquee tool used to create marquee*
Images © Photodisc/Getty Images.

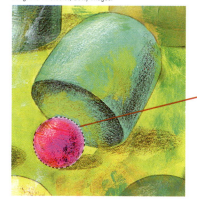

Elliptical Marquee surrounds object

Figure 2 *Marquee surrounding irregular shape*
Images © Photodisc/Getty Images.

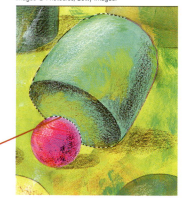

Marquee

Making Selections

Using Fastening Points

Each time you click one of the marquee tools, a fastening point is added to the image. A **fastening point** is an anchor within the marquee. When the marquee pointer reaches the initial fastening point (after making its way around the image), a very small circle appears on the pointer, indicating that you have reached the starting point. Clicking the pointer when this circle appears closes the marquee. Some fastening points, such as those in a circular marquee, are not visible, while others, such as those created by the Magnetic Lasso tools, are visible.

Selecting, Deselecting, and Reselecting

After a selection is made, you can move, copy, transform, or make adjustments to it. A selection stays selected until you unselect, or **deselect**, it. You can deselect a selection by clicking Select on the Menu bar, and then clicking Deselect. You can reselect a deselected object by clicking Select on the Menu bar, and then clicking Reselect.

TABLE 1: SELECTION TOOLS BY SHAPE		
Tool	**Button**	**Effect**
Rectangular Marquee tool		Creates a rectangular selection. Press [Shift] while dragging to create a square.
Elliptical Marquee tool		Creates an elliptical selection. Press [Shift] while dragging to create a circle.
Single Row Marquee tool		Creates a 1-pixel-wide row selection.
Single Column Marquee tool		Creates a 1-pixel-wide column selection.
Lasso tool		Creates a freehand selection.
Polygonal Lasso tool		Creates straight line selections. Press [Alt] (Win) or [option] (Mac) to create freehand segments.
Magnetic Lasso tool		Creates selections that snap to an edge of an object. Press [Alt] (Win) or [option] (Mac) to alternate between freehand and magnetic line segments.

© 2013 Cengage Learning®

Placing a Selection

You can place a selection in a Photoshop image in many ways. You can copy or cut a selection, and then paste it to a different location in the same image or to a different image. You can also use the Move tool to drag a selection to a new location. The Paste In Place command (found within the Paste Special option on the Edit menu) lets you paste Clipboard contents in the same relative location in the target document or layer as it occupied in the source document or layer.

Using Guides

Guides are non-printing horizontal and vertical lines that you can display on top of an image to help you position a selection.

You can create an unlimited number of horizontal and vertical guides. You create a guide by displaying the rulers, positioning the pointer on either ruler, and then clicking and dragging the guide into position. Figure 3 shows the creation of a horizontal guide in a file that already contains guides. You delete a guide by selecting the Move tool on the Tools panel, positioning the pointer over the guide, and then clicking and dragging it back to its ruler. If the Snap feature is enabled, as you drag an object toward a guide, the object will be pulled toward the guide. To turn on the Snap feature, click View on the Menu bar, and then click Snap. A check mark appears to the left of the command if the feature is enabled.

Figure 3 *Creating guides in image*
Image courtesy of Elizabeth Eisner Reding.

Dragging a guide to a new location

Taking Measurements

You can use any selection tool to select the object(s) you want measured. Measurements are recorded in the Measurement Log, which is grouped with the Mini Bridge and Timeline panels when it is opened. Sometimes you just need to know the dimensions of an object, such as the length, width, area, or density. Before you begin, you need to set the scale. This determines what unit of measurement will be used. You can do this by clicking the Measurement Log Panel options button, pointing to Set Measurement Scale, and then clicking Default or Custom. (The default scale uses pixel units.) Next, click Image on the Menu bar, point to Analysis, and then click Ruler Tool or Count Tool to select the measurement tool. If you select the Count Tool, the pointer will add a sequentially numbered object to the image so you can easily keep track of the count.

You can open the Measurement Log by clicking Window on the Menu bar, and then clicking Measurement Log. After you make a selection, click the Record Measurements button to record the measurement in a new row in the Measurement Log. Data in this log include label, date and time, document, source, scale, scale units, scale factor, count, length, and angle. Depending on what tool was used to define the area, measurements may also include area, perimeter, circularity, height, width, gray value (minimum), gray value (maximum), gray value (median), integrated density, and histogram. To measure a particular area, use a selection tool (including the Magic Wand or Quick Selection tool) to define an area. Click the Ruler tool, click a point on the selection area, then drag to another point on the selection area (which defines the area you want measured). Click the Record Measurements button on the Measurement Log panel and the measurement of the point-to-point area will display in the log. Repeat the process by clicking the next portion you want measured, then click Record Measurements. All your measurements will be recorded in the Measurement Log panel. You can skip the point-to-point measurement and simply collect data for a selection by clicking the Record Measurements button on the Measurement Log panel.

Figure 4 *Rectangular Marquee tool selection*

Source: Morguefile.

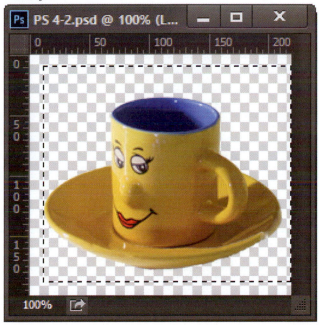

TABLE 2: WORKING WITH A SELECTION	
If you want to:	**Then do this:**
Move a selection (an image) using the mouse	Position ▶⊕ over the selection, then drag the marquee and its contents
Copy a selection to the Clipboard	Activate image containing the selection, click Edit ➢ Copy
Cut a selection to the Clipboard	Activate image containing the selection, click Edit ➢ Cut
Paste a selection from the Clipboard	Activate image where you want the selection, click Edit ➢ Paste
Delete a selection	Activate the image with the selection, then press [Delete] (Win) or [delete] (Mac)
Deselect a selection	Press [Ctrl][D] (Win) or ⌘ [D] (Mac)

© 2013 Cengage Learning®

Create a selection with the Rectangular Marquee tool

1. Start Photoshop, open PS 4-1.psd from the drive and folder where you store your Data Files, save it as **Kitchen Table**, click **OK** if the Maximize compatibility dialog box displays, then reset the **Essentials workspace**.

2. Open PS 4-2.psd, then display the rulers in pixels for this image if they do not already appear.

3. Click the **Rectangular Marquee tool** 🔲 on the Tools panel, then make sure the value in the Feather text box on the options bar is **0 px**.

   Feathering determines the amount of blur between the selection and the pixels surrounding it.

4. Drag the **Marquee pointer** ╬ to select the coffee cup from approximately **10 H/10 V** to **210 H/180 V**. See Figure 4.

   The first number in each coordinate refers to the horizontal ruler (H); the second number refers to the vertical ruler (V).

   TIP You can also use the X/Y coordinates displayed in the Info panel.

5. Click the **Move tool** ▶⊕ on the Tools panel, then drag the **coffee cup** to any location in the Kitchen Table image.

   The selection now appears in the Kitchen Table image on a new layer (Layer 1).

   TIP Table 2 describes methods you can use to work with selections in an image.

Using the Rectangular Marquee tool, you created a selection in an image, then you dragged that selection into another image. This left the original image intact, and created a copy of the selection in the destination image.

Position a selection with the Move tool

1. Verify that the **Move tool**  is active on the Tools panel, and display the rulers if they do not already appear.

2. If you do not see guides in the Kitchen Table image, click **View** on the Menu bar, point to **Show**, then click **Guides**.

   TIP You can use the Straighten Layer button on the Ruler options bar to straighten an image to any given angle. Select the Ruler tool on the Tools panel (which is grouped with the Eyedropper tool), click and drag the pointer from one area to another, release the mouse button, then click the Straighten Layer button on the options bar. The horizontal edge of the active layer will be made parallel with the drawn line.

3. Drag the **coffee cup** so that the lower-left corner snaps to the ruler guides at approximately **220 H/520 V**. Compare your image to Figure 5.

   Did you feel the snap to effect as you positioned the selection within the guides? This feature makes it easy to properly position objects within an image.

   TIP If you didn't feel the image snap to the guides, click View on the Menu bar, point to Snap To, then click Guides.

4. Rename Layer 1 **Coffee cup**.

You used the Move tool to reposition a selection in an existing image, then you renamed the layer.

Figure 5 *Rectangular selection in image*
Source: Morguefile.

Coffee cup snaps to guides

Using Smart Guides

Wouldn't it be great to be able to see a vertical or horizontal guide as you move an object? Using **Smart Guides**, you can do just that. Smart Guides are turned on/off by clicking View on the Menu bar, pointing to Show, and then clicking Smart Guides. (Smart Guides are turned on, by default.) When this feature is turned on, horizontal and vertical magenta guidelines appear automatically when you draw a shape or move an object. This feature allows you to align layer content as you move it. With the Smart Guides feature enabled, hold [Ctrl] (Win) or [command] (Mac) while dragging an object in the selected layer: as you drag, you'll see measurement guides displaying the dimensions of the active layer as well as the dimensions of nearby layers. As you move the object, the guides will also display spacing between other objects.

Figure 6 *Deselect command*
Source: Morguefile.

Shortcut can be
used instead of
clicking the menu

Deselect a selection

1. Click **Window** on the Menu bar, then
click **PS 4-2.psd**.

TIP If you can see the window of the image you want
anywhere on the screen, you can just click it to make
it active instead of using the Window menu.

2. Click **Select** on the Menu bar, then click
Deselect, as shown in Figure 6.

*You made another window active, then used the Deselect
command on the Select menu to deselect the object you
moved. When you deselect a selection, the marquee no longer
surrounds it.*

Figure 7 *Save Selection dialog box*

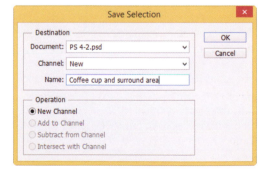

Saving and Loading a Selection

Any selection can be saved independently of the surrounding image, so that if you want to use it
again in the image, you can do so without having to retrace it using one of the marquee tools. Once
a selection is made, you can save it in the image by clicking Select on the Menu bar, and then clicking
Save Selection. The Save Selection dialog box opens, as shown in Figure 7; be sure to give the selection
a meaningful name. When you want to load a saved selection, click Select on the Menu bar, and then
click Load Selection. Click the Channel list arrow to display the Channel list, click the named selection,
and then click OK.

Create a selection with the Magnetic Lasso tool

1. Open PS 4-3.psd from the drive and folder where you store your Data Files.

2. Click the **Zoom tool** 🔍 on the Tools panel, then click the **tomato image** until the zoom factor is **200%**.

3. Click the **Magnetic Lasso tool** 🖈 on the Tools panel, then change the settings on the options bar so that they are the same as those shown in Figure 8. Table 3 describes Magnetic Lasso tool settings.

4. Click the **Magnetic Lasso tool pointer** 🖈 once anywhere on the edge of the tomato to create your first fastening point.

TIP If you click a spot that is not at the edge of the tomato, press [Esc] to undo the action, then start again.

5. Drag 🖈 slowly around the tomato (clicking at the top of each leaf may be helpful) until it is almost entirely selected, then click directly over the **initial fastening point**. See Figure 9.

TIP Zoom in or out of an image to see as much/little detail as you need.

Don't worry about all the nooks and crannies surrounding the leaves on the tomato; the Magnetic Lasso tool will select those automatically. You will see a small circle next to the pointer when it is directly over the initial fastening point, indicating that you are closing the selection. The individual segments turn into a marquee.

TIP If you feel that the Magnetic Lasso tool is missing some major details while you're tracing, you can insert additional fastening points by clicking the pointer while dragging. For example, click the mouse button at a location where you want to change the selection shape.

You created a selection with the Magnetic Lasso tool.

Figure 8 *Options for the Magnetic Lasso tool*

Figure 9 *Creating a selection with the Magnetic Lasso tool*
Source: Morguefile.

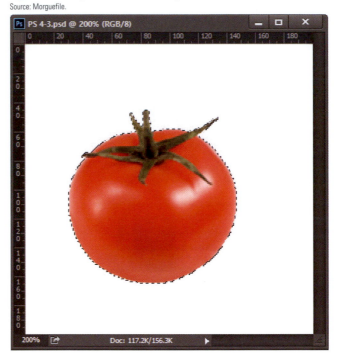

DESIGN**TIP**

Mastering the Art of Selections

You might feel that making selections is difficult when you first start. Making selections is a skill, and like most skills, it takes a lot of practice to become proficient. In addition to practice, make sure that you're comfortable in your work area, that your hands are steady, and that your mouse or other pointing device is working well. A non-optical mouse that is dirty will make selecting an onerous task, so make sure your mouse is well cared for and is functioning correctly.

Figure 10 *Selection dragged into image*
Source: Morguefile.

Defringing the layer reduces the amount of background that appears; your results will vary

Complex selection includes only object, no background

TABLE 3: MAGNETIC LASSO TOOL SETTINGS	
Setting	**Description**
Feather	The amount of blur between the selection and the surrounding pixels. This setting is measured in pixels and can be a value between 0 and 250.
Anti-alias	The smoothness of the selection, achieved by softening the color transition between edge and background pixels.
Width	The interior width, achieved by detecting an edge from the pointer. This setting is measured in pixels and can have a value from 1 to 40.
Contrast	The sensitivity of the tool. This setting can be a value between 1 percent and 100 percent; higher values detect high-contrast edges.
Frequency	The rate at which fastening points are applied. This setting can be a value between 0 and 100; higher values insert more fastening points.

© 2013 Cengage Learning®

Move a complex selection to an existing image

1. Click the **Move tool** on the Tools panel.

TIP You can also click the Tool Preset picker list arrow on the options bar, then double-click the Move tool.

2. Use the **Move tool pointer** to drag the tomato selection to the Kitchen Table image, then open the **Info panel** (using the Window command on the Menu bar).

   The selection appears on a new layer (Layer 1).

3. Drag the object so that the bottom of the tomato snaps to the guide at approximately **450 Y** and the left edge of the tomato snaps to the guide at **220 X** using the coordinates on the Info panel. (The coordinates in the Info panel track the location where you clicked to drag the object.)

4. Use the Layer menu to defringe the new Layer 1 at a width of **1** pixel.

5. Close the PS 4-3.psd image without saving your changes, then collapse the Info panel to the dock.

6. Rename the new layer **Tomato** in the Kitchen Table image, then reposition the Tomato layer so it is beneath the Coffee cup layer in the Layers panel.

7. Save your work, then compare your image to Figure 10.

8. Click **Window** on the Menu bar, then click **PS 4-2.psd**.

9. Close the PS 4-2.psd image without saving your changes.

You dragged a complex selection into an existing Photoshop image. You positioned the object using ruler guides and renamed and repositioned a layer. You also defringed a selection to eliminate its white border.

Modify
A MARQUEE

What You'll Do

Source: Morguefile.

In this lesson, you'll move and enlarge a marquee, drag a selection into a Photoshop image, and then position a selection.

Changing the Size of a Marquee

Not all objects are easy to select. Sometimes, when you make a selection, you might need to change the size or shape of the marquee.

The options bar contains selection buttons that help you add to and subtract from a marquee, or intersect with a selection. The marquee in Figure 11 was modified into the one shown in Figure 12 by clicking the Add to selection button. After the Add to selection button is active, you can draw an additional marquee, and it will be added to the current marquee.

One method you can use to increase the size of a marquee is the Grow command. After you make a selection, you can increase the marquee size by clicking Select on the Menu bar, and then clicking Grow. The Grow command selects pixels adjacent to the marquee that have colors similar to those specified by the Magic Wand tool. The Similar command, also located on the Select menu, selects both adjacent and non-adjacent pixels.

Modifying a Marquee

While a selection is active, you can modify the marquee by expanding or contracting it, smoothing out its edges, or enlarging it to add a border around the selection. These five commands, Expand, Contract, Smooth Feather, and Border, are located on the Modify command submenu, which is found on the Select menu. For example, you might want to enlarge your selection. Using the Expand command, you can increase the size of the selection, as shown in Figure 13.

> **QUICK TIP**
>
> While the Grow command selects adjacent pixels that have similar colors, the Expand command increases a selection by a specific number of pixels.

Moving a Marquee

After you create a marquee, you can move the marquee to another location in the same image or to another image entirely. You might want to move a marquee if you've drawn it in the wrong image or the wrong location. Sometimes it's easier to draw a marquee elsewhere on the page, and then move it to the desired location.

> **QUICK TIP**
>
> You can always hide and display layers as necessary to facilitate making a selection.

Making Selections

Using the Quick Selection Tool

The Quick Selection tool lets you paint-to-select an object from the interior using a resizeable brush. As you paint the object, the selection grows. Using the Auto-Enhance check box, rough edges and blockiness are automatically reduced to give you a perfect selection. As with other selection tools, the Quick Selection tool has options to add and subtract from your selection.

Figure 11 *New selection*
Image courtesy of Elizabeth Eisner Reding.

New selection button used to create a selection

Marquee surrounds rectangle

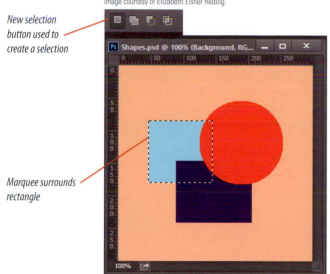

Figure 12 *Selection with additions*
Image courtesy of Elizabeth Eisner Reding.

Add to selection button adds new selection to the existing selection

Single marquee surrounds all shapes

Add to selection pointer

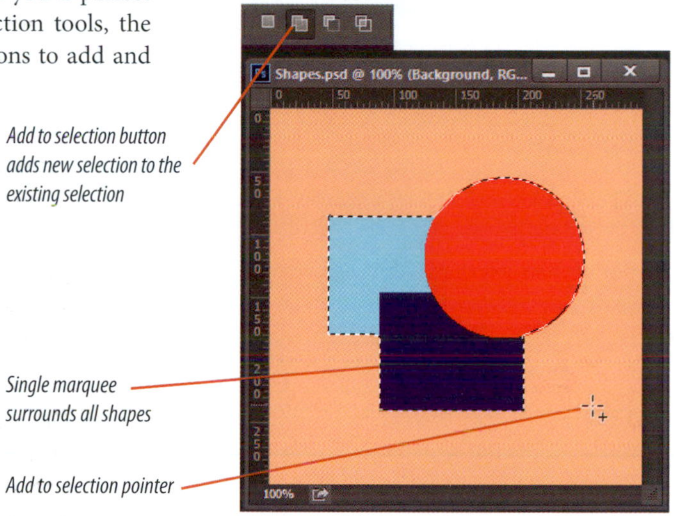

Figure 13 *Expanded selection*
Image courtesy of Elizabeth Eisner Reding.

Marquee expanded by 5 pixels

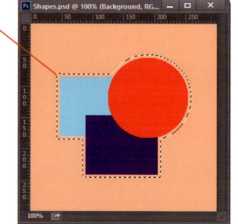

Adding To and Subtracting From a Selection

Of course knowing how to make a selection is important, but it's just as important to know how to make alterations in an existing selection. Sometimes it's almost impossible to create that perfect marquee on the first try. Perhaps your hand moved while you were tracing or you just got distracted. Using the Add to selection and Subtract from selection buttons (which appear with all selection tools), you can alter an existing marquee without having to start from scratch.

Move and enlarge a marquee

1. Open PS 4-4.psd from the drive and folder where you store your Data Files, then change the zoom factor to **200%**, enlarging the window as necessary.

2. Click the **Elliptical Marquee tool** on the Tools panel.

   TIP The Elliptical Marquee tool might be hidden under the Rectangular Marquee tool.

3. Click the **New selection button** on the options bar if it is not already active.

4. Drag the **Marquee pointer** to select the area from approximately **150 X/50 Y** to **400 X/250 Y**. Compare your image to Figure 14.

5. Position the **pointer** in the center of the selection, then drag the **Move pointer** so the marquee covers the casserole, at approximately **250 X/165 Y**, as shown in Figure 15.

   TIP You can also nudge a selection to move it by pressing the arrow keys. Each time you press an arrow key, the selection moves one pixel in the direction of the arrow.

6. Click **Select** on the Menu bar, then click **Similar**.

7. Click **Select** on the Menu bar, point to **Modify**, then click **Expand**.

8. Type **1** in the Expand Selection dialog box, click **OK**, then deselect the selection.

You created a marquee, then dragged the marquee to reposition it. You then enlarged a selection marquee by using the Similar and Expand commands then deselected the selection.

Figure 14 *Selection in image*
Source: Morguefile.

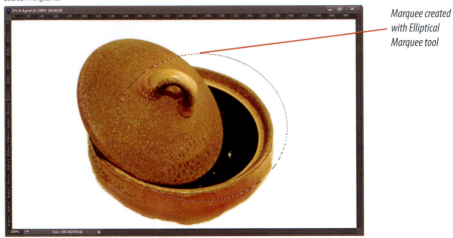

Marquee created with Elliptical Marquee tool

Figure 15 *Moved selection*
Source: Morguefile.

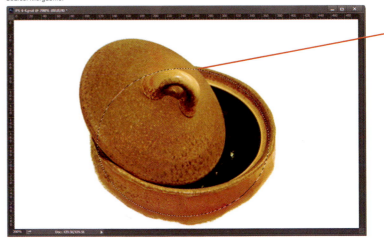

New marquee location

Figure 16 *Quick Selection tool settings*

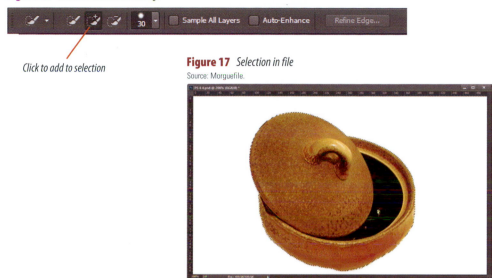

Click to add to selection

Figure 17 *Selection in file*
Source: Morguefile.

Figure 18 *Selection moved to the Kitchen Table image*
Source: Morguefile.

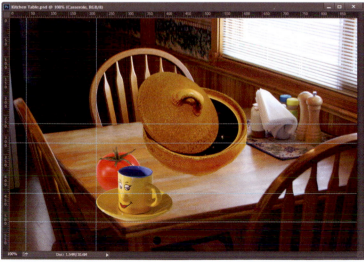

Use the Quick Selection tool

1. Click the **Quick Selection tool** on the Tools panel, then adjust your settings using Figure 16.

2. Verify that the Brush settings are 30 px diameter, 0% hardness, 1% spacing, 0° angle, 100% roundness, and Pen Pressure size.

TIP If you need to change the Brush settings, click the Brush picker list arrow on the options bar, then drag the sliders to the appropriate settings.

3. Position the pointer in the **center of the casserole**, then slowly drag the pointer to the outer edges until the object is selected. See Figure 17.

TIP Sometimes making a selection is easy, sometimes... not so much. Time and practice will hone your selection skills. It will get easier.

4. Change the zoom level to **100%**, then click the **Move tool** on the Tools panel.

5. Position the **Move pointer** over the selection, then drag the **casserole** to the Kitchen Table image.

6. Drag the **casserole** so that it is to the left of the napkins.

7. Defringe the casserole using a setting of **1** pixel.

8. Rename the new layer **Casserole**.

9. Save your work on the Kitchen Table image, then compare your work to Figure 18.

10. Make **PS 4-4.psd** active, then close PS 4-4.psd without saving your changes.

You selected an object using the Quick Selection tool, then you dragged the selection into an existing image.

Select Using Color and
MODIFY A SELECTION

What You'll Do

Source: Morguefile.

 In this lesson, you'll make selections using both the Color Range command and the Magic Wand tool. You'll also flip a selection, and then fix an image using the Healing Brush tool.

Selecting with Color

Selections based on color can be easy to make, especially when the background of an image is different from the image itself. High contrast between colors is an ideal condition for making selections based on color. You can make selections using color with the Color Range command on the Select menu, or you can use the Magic Wand tool on the Tools panel.

Using the Magic Wand Tool

When you select the Magic Wand tool, the following options are available on the options bar, as shown in Figure 19:

- The four selection buttons.
- Sample size, which defines the number of pixels sampled by the tool.

- The **Tolerance** setting, which allows you to specify how similar in color pixels must be in order to be selected. This setting has a value from 0 to 255; the lower the value, the closer in color the selected pixels will be.
- The Anti-alias check box softens the appearance of the edge of the selection.
- The Contiguous check box, which lets you select pixels that are next to one another.
- The Sample All Layers check box, which lets you select pixels from multiple layers at once.
- The Refine Edge button lets you easily improve the quality of the selection edges.

Figure 19 *Options for the Magic Wand tool*

Using the Color Range Command

You can use the Color Range command, located on the Select menu, to make the same selections as with the Magic Wand tool. When you use the Color Range command, the Color Range dialog box opens. This dialog box lets you use the pointer to identify which colors you want to use to make a selection. You can also select the Invert check box to *exclude* the chosen color from the selection. The **fuzziness** setting is similar to tolerance, in that the lower the value, the closer in color pixels must be to be selected.

QUICK TIP

Unlike the Magic Wand tool, the Color Range command does not give you the option of excluding contiguous pixels.

Transforming a Selection

After you place a selection in a Photoshop image, you can change its size and other qualities by clicking Edit on the Menu bar, pointing to Transform, and then clicking any of the commands on the submenu. After you select certain commands, small squares called **handles** surround the selection. To complete the command, you drag a handle until the image has the look you want, and then press [Enter] (Win) or [return] (Mac). You can also use the Transform submenu to flip a selection horizontally or vertically.

Understanding the Healing Brush Tool

If you place a selection then notice that the image has a few imperfections, you can fix the image. You can fix imperfections such as dirt, scratches, visible veins on skin, or wrinkles on a face using the Healing Brush tool on the Tools panel.

QUICK TIP

When correcting someone's portrait, make sure your subject looks the way he or she *thinks* they look. That's not always possible, but strive to get as close as you can to their ideal!

Using the Healing Brush Tool

This tool lets you sample an area, and then paint over the imperfections. What is the result? The less-than-desirable pixels seem to disappear into the surrounding image. In addition to matching the sampled pixels, the Healing Brush tool also matches the texture, lighting, and shading of the sample. This is why the painted pixels blend so effortlessly into the existing image. Corrections can be painted using broad strokes or using clicks of the mouse.

QUICK TIP

To take a sample, press and hold [Alt] (Win) or [option] (Mac) while dragging the pointer over the area you want to duplicate.

DESIGNTIP

Knowing Which Selection Tool to Use

The hardest part of making a selection might be determining which selection tool to use. How are you supposed to know if you should use a marquee tool or a lasso tool? The first question you need to ask yourself is, "What do I want to select?" Becoming proficient in making selections means that you need to assess the qualities of the object you want to select, and then decide which method to use. Ask yourself: Does the object have a definable shape? Does it have an identifiable edge? Are there common colors that can be used to create a selection?

Select using Color Range

1. Open PS 4-5.psd from the drive and folder where you store your Data Files.

2. Click **Select** on the Menu bar, then click **Color Range**.

3. Click the **Image option button** if it is not already selected.

4. Click the **Invert check box** to add a check mark if it does not already contain a check mark.

5. Verify that your settings match those shown in Figure 20, click anywhere in the white background area surrounding the sample image, then click **OK**.

   The Color Range dialog box closes and the teapot in the image is selected.

6. Click the **Move tool** ![move tool] on the Tools panel.

7. Drag the selection into Kitchen Table.psd, then position the selection as shown in Figure 21.

8. Rename the new layer **Teapot**.

9. Defringe the teapot using a setting of **2** pixels.

10. Activate **PS 4-5.psd**, then close this file without saving any changes.

You made a selection within an image using the Color Range command on the Select menu, and dragged the selection to an existing image.

Figure 20 *Completed Color Range dialog box*
Source: Morguefile.

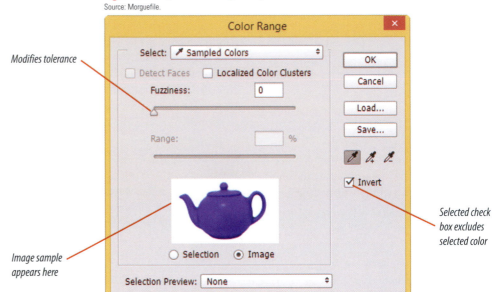

Modifies tolerance

Image sample appears here

Selected check box excludes selected color

Figure 21 *Selection in image*
Source: Morguefile.

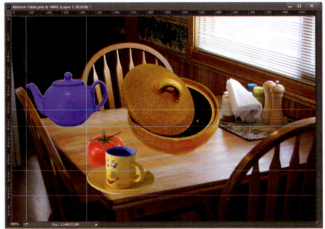

Figure 22 *Magic Wand tool settings*

Figure 23 *Selected area*

Source: Morguefile.

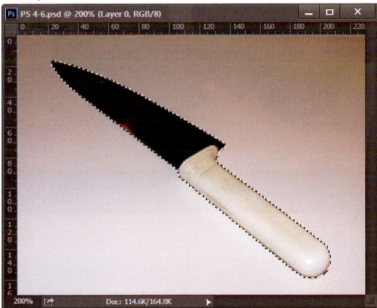

Select using the Magic Wand and the Quick Selection tools

1. Open PS 4-6.psd from the drive and folder where you store your Data Files, then change the zoom factor to **200%**.

2. Click the **Magic Wand tool** ![icon] on the Tools panel.

3. Change the settings on the options bar to match those shown in Figure 22.

4. Click anywhere in the **knife blade** of the image (such as **100 x/60 Y**).

5. Click the **Quick Selection tool** ![icon] on the Tools panel, click the **Add to selection button** ![icon], change the brush size to 20 (by clicking the Brush picker list arrow, dragging the Size slider to 20 px, then pressing **[Esc]**, then drag across the **knife handle**. Compare your selection to Figure 23.

   TIP If you get too many pixels in your selection, you can try using the Subtract from selection button on the options bar to modify your selection.

6. Click the **Move tool** ![icon] on the Tools panel, then drag the selection into Kitchen Table.psd.

You made a selection using the Magic Wand and Quick Selection tools, then dragged it into an existing image. The Magic Wand tool is just one more way you can make a selection. One advantage of using the Magic Wand tool (versus the Color Range tool) is the Contiguous check box, which lets you choose pixels that are next to one another. Combining tools is an effective way of making selections.

Flip a selection

1. Click **Edit** on the Menu bar, point to **Transform**, then click **Flip Vertical**.

2. Rename Layer 1 as **Knife**.

3. Defringe **Knife** using a **1** pixel setting.

4. Drag the **flipped selection** with the **Move tool pointer** ▶⊕ so it is positioned as shown in Figure 24.

5. Make **PS 4-6.psd** the active file, then close PS 4-6.psd without saving your changes.

6. Save your work.

You flipped and repositioned a selection. Sometimes it's helpful to flip an object to help direct the viewer's eye to a desired focal point.

Figure 24 *Flipped and positioned selection*
Source: Morguefile.

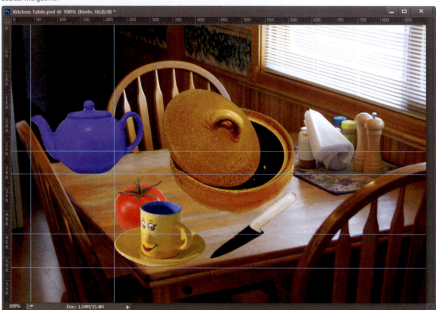

Getting Rid of Red Eye

When digital photos of your favorite people have that annoying red eye, what do you do? You use the Red Eye tool to eliminate this effect. To do this, select the Red Eye tool (which is grouped on the Tools panel with the Spot Healing Brush tool, the Healing Brush tool, and the Patch tool), and then either click a red area of an eye or draw a selection over a red eye. When you release the mouse button, the red eye effect is removed.

Figure 25 *Healing Brush tool options*

Figure 26 *Healed area*
Source: Morguefile.

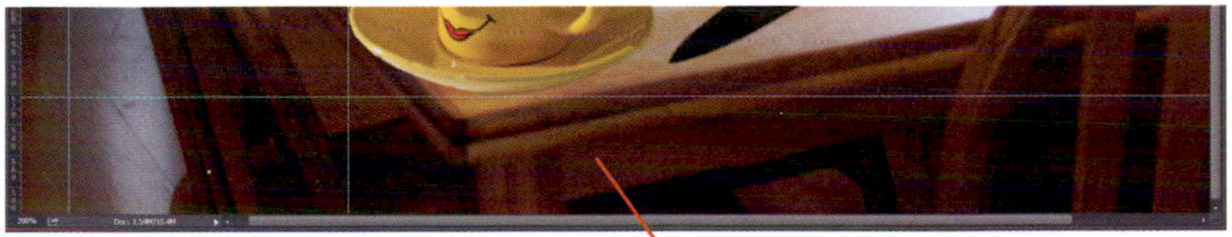

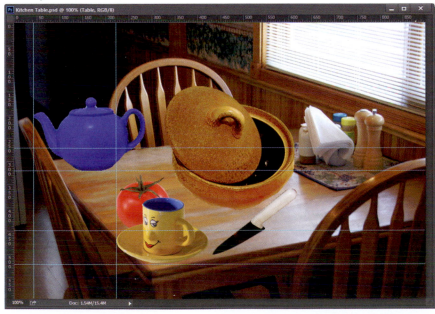

Stain removed from image

Figure 27 *Image after using the Healing brush*
Source: Morguefile.

Fix imperfections with the Healing Brush tool

1. Click the **Table layer** on the Layers panel, then zoom into the area below the coffee cup until the zoom factor is **200%** and you can see the black ink stain on the table.

2. Click the **Healing Brush tool** 🖌 on the Tools panel. Change the settings on the options bar to match those shown in Figure 25.

TIP If you need to change the Brush settings, click the Brush picker list arrow on the options bar, then drag the sliders so the settings are 25 px diameter, 100% hardness, 1% spacing, 0° angle, and 100% roundness.

3. Press and hold [**Alt**] (Win) or [**option**] (Mac), click the wood to the right of the stain, such as **410 X/565 Y**, then release [**Alt**] (Win) or [**option**] (Mac).

   You sampled an area of the table that is not stained so that you can use the Healing Brush tool to paint a damaged area with the sample.

4. Click the stain (at approximately **380 X/570 Y**).

   Notice that as you move the pointer over the stain, the sample shows you how the corrected area will look when healing is applied. Compare the repaired area to Figure 26.

5. Zoom out from the center of the image until the zoom factor is **100%**.

6. Save your work, then compare your image to Figure 27.

You used the Healing Brush tool to fix an imperfection in an image.

Add a Vignette Effect
TO A SELECTION

What You'll Do

Source: Morguefile.

In this lesson, you'll create a vignette effect, using a layer mask and feathering.

Understanding Vignettes

Traditionally, a **vignette** is a picture or portrait whose border fades into the surrounding color at its edges. You can use a vignette effect to give an image an old-world appearance. You can also use a vignette effect to tone down an overwhelming background. You can create a vignette effect in Photoshop by creating a mask with a blurred edge. A **mask** lets you protect or modify a particular area and is created using a marquee.

Creating a Vignette

A **vignette effect** uses feathering to fade a marquee shape. The feather setting blurs the area between the selection and the surrounding pixels, which creates a distinctive fade at the edge of the selection. You can create a vignette effect by using a marquee or lasso tool to create a marquee in an image layer. After the selection is created, you can modify the feather setting (a 10- or 20-pixel setting creates a nice fade) to increase the blur effect on the outside edge of the selection.

Getting that Healing Feeling

The Spot Healing Brush tool works in much the same way as the Healing Brush tool in that it removes blemishes and other imperfections. Unlike the Healing Brush tool, the Spot Healing Brush tool does not require you to take a sample. When using the Spot Healing Brush tool, you can choose from three option types:

- proximity match—which uses pixels around the edge of the selection as a patch.
- create texture—which uses all the pixels in the selection to create a texture that is used to fix the area.
- content-aware—which compares nearby image content to fill the selection while realistically maintaining key details such as shadows and edges.

You also have the option of sampling all the visible layers or only the active layer.

Figure 28 *Marquee in image*
Source: Morguefile.

Figure 29 *Layers panel*

Feathered mask creates vignette effect

Figure 30 *Vignette in image*
Source: Morguefile.

Vignette effect fades border and reveals background

Create a vignette

1. Verify that the **Table layer** is selected.
2. Click the **Rectangular Marquee tool** on the Tools panel.
3. Change the **Feather setting** on the options bar to **20px**.
4. Create a **selection** with the **Marquee pointer** from **50 X/50 Y** to **850 X/550 Y**, as shown in Figure 28.
5. Click **Layer** on the Menu bar, point to **Layer Mask**, then click **Reveal Selection**.

   The vignette effect is added to the layer and the mask blurs the selection and the background layer.

   Compare your Layers panel to Figure 29.
6. Click **View** on the Menu bar, then click **Rulers** to hide them.
7. Click **View** on the Menu bar, then click **Clear Guides**.
8. Save your work, then compare your image to Figure 30.
9. Close the Kitchen Table image, then exit Photoshop.

You created a vignette effect by adding a feathered layer mask. Once the image was finished, you hid the rulers and cleared the guides.

POWER USER SHORTCUTS			
To do this:	**Use this method:**	**To do this:**	**Use this method:**
Copy selection	Click Edit ➤ Copy or [Ctrl][C] (Win) or ⌘ [C] (Mac)	Move tool	⊹ or **V**
Create vignette effect	Marquee or Lasso tool, create selection, click Layer ➤ Layer Mask ➤ Reveal Selection	Paste selection	Edit ➤ Paste or [Ctrl][V] (Win) or ⌘ [V] (Mac)
Cut selection	Click Edit ➤ Cut or [Ctrl][X] (Win) or ⌘ [X] (Mac)	Polygonal Lasso tool	⟩ or [Shift] **L**
Deselect object	Select ➤ Deselect or [Ctrl][D] (Win) or ⌘ [D] (Mac)	Rectangular Marquee tool	⬚ or [Shift] **M**
Elliptical Marquee tool	⬯ or [Shift] **M**	Reselect a deselected object	Select ➤ Reselect or [Shift][Ctrl][D] (Win) or [Shift] ⌘ [D] (Mac)
Flip image	Edit ➤ Transform ➤ Flip Horizontal	Select all objects	Select ➤ All or [Ctrl][A] (Win) or ⌘ [A] (Mac)
Grow selection	Select ➤ Grow	Select using color range	Select ➤ Color Range, click sample area
Increase selection	Select ➤ Similar	Select using Magic Wand tool	⚡ or [Shift] **W**, then click image
Lasso tool	⟲ or [Shift] **L**	Select using Quick Selection tool	⟋ or [Shift] **W**, then drag pointer over image
Magnetic Lasso tool	⟨ or [Shift] **L**	Single Column Marquee tool	⫿
Move selection marquee	Position pointer in selection, drag ⬚ to new location	Single Row Marquee tool	▭

Key: *Menu items are indicated by* ➤ *between the menu name and its command. Blue bold letters are shortcuts for selecting tools on the Tools panel.*

Make a selection using shapes.

1. Open PS 4-7.psd from the drive and folder where you store your Data Files, update any text layers, then save it as **Lovely Felines**.
2. Select the Backdrop layer, then open PS 4-8.tif.
3. Display the rulers and any available guides in each image window if they are not displayed, and make sure that the Essentials workspace is selected.
4. Use the Rectangular Marquee tool to select the entire image in PS 4-8.tif. (*Hint*: Reset the Feather setting to 0 pixels, if necessary.)
5. Deselect the selection.
6. Use the Magnetic Lasso tool to create a selection surrounding only the block cat in the image. (*Hint*: You can use the Zoom tool to make the image larger.)
7. Drag the selection into the Powerful Felines image, positioning it so the right side of the cat is at 490 X, and the bottom of the right paw is at 450 Y.
8. Defringe the block cat, rename this new layer **Block cat**, then save your work.
9. Close PS 4-8.tif without saving any changes.

Modify a marquee.

1. Open PS 4-9.tif.
2. Use the Elliptical Marquee tool to create a marquee from 100 X/50 Y to 200 X/100 Y, using a setting of 0 in the Feather text box.
3. Use the Grow command on the Select menu.
4. Deselect the selection.
5. Use the Quick Selection tool to select the tabby cat.
6. Drag the selection into the Powerful Felines image, positioning it so the upper-left corner of the selection is near 0 X/0 Y.

7. Defringe the new layer using a width of 2 pixels.
8. Rename the layer **Tabby cat**, then save your work.
9. Close PS 4-9.tif without saving any changes.

Select using color and modify a selection.

1. Open PS 4-10.tif.
2. Use the Color Range dialog box to select only the kitten. (*Hint*: You can adjust any of the Color Range settings to get the best results.)
3. Drag the selection into the Powerful Felines image.
4. Flip the kitten image (in the Powerful Felines image) horizontally.

5. Position the kitten image so the bottom right snaps to the ruler guides at 230 X/450 y.
6. Defringe the kitten using a width of 3 pixels.
7. Rename the layer **Kitten**, then save your work.
8. Close PS 4-10.tif without saving any changes.

Add a vignette effect to a selection.

1. Use a 15-pixel feather setting and the Backdrop layer to create an elliptical selection surrounding the contents of the Powerful Felines image.
2. Add a layer mask that reveals the selection.
3. Hide the rulers and guides, then save your work.
4. Compare your image to Figure 31.

Figure 31 *Completed Skills Review project*
Images © Photodisc/Getty Images.

As a professional photographer, you often take photos of people for use in various publications. You recently took a photograph of a woman that will be used in a marketing brochure. The client is happy with the overall picture, but wants the facial lines smoothed out. You decide to use the Healing Brush tool to ensure that the client is happy with the final product.

1. Open PS 4-11.psd, then save it as **Portrait**.
2. Make a copy of the Background using the default name, or the name of your choice.
3. Use the Background copy layer and the Healing Brush tool to smooth the appearance of facial lines in this image. (*Hint*: You may have greater success if you use short strokes with the Healing Brush tool than if you paint long strokes.)
4. Create a vignette effect on the Background copy layer that reveals the selection using an elliptical marquee.
5. Reorder the layers (if necessary), so that the vignette effect is visible.
6. Save your work, then compare your image to the sample shown in Figure 32.

Figure 32 *Sample Project Builder 1*
Source: Morguefile.

The Clarksville Athletic Association, which sponsors the Clarksville Marathon, is holding a contest for artwork to announce the upcoming race. Submissions can be created on paper or computer-generated. You feel you have a good chance at winning this contest, using Photoshop as your tool.

1. Open PS 4-12.psd, then save it as **Marathon Contest**.
2. Locate at least two pieces of appropriate artwork—either on your hard disk, in a royalty-free collection, or from scanned images—that you can use in this file.
3. Use any appropriate methods to select imagery from the artwork.
4. After the selections have been made, copy each selection into Marathon Contest.
5. Arrange the images into a design that you think will be eye-catching and attractive.
6. Deselect the selections in the files you are no longer using, and close them without saving the changes.
7. Add a vignette effect to the Backdrop layer.
8. Display the type layers if they are hidden.
9. Defringe any layers, as necessary.
10. Save your work, then compare your screen to the sample shown in Figure 33.

Figure 33 *Sample Project Builder 2*

Images © Photodisc/Getty Images.

Making Selections

You are aware that there will be an opening in your firm's design department. Before you can be considered for the job, you need to increase your Photoshop compositing knowledge and experience. You have decided to teach yourself, using informational sources on the Internet and images that can be scanned or purchased.

1. Connect to the Internet and use your browser and favorite search engine to find information on image compositing. (Make a record of the site you found so you can use it for future reference, if necessary.)

2. Create a new Photoshop image, using the dimensions of your choice, then save it as **Sample Compositing**.

3. Locate at least two pieces of artwork—either on your hard disk, in a royalty-free collection, or from scanned images—that you can use. (The images can contain people, plants, animals, or inanimate objects.)

4. Select the images in the artwork, then copy each into the Sample Compositing image, using the method of your choice.

5. Rename each of the layers using meaningful names.

6. Apply a color-code to each new layer.

7. Arrange the images in a pleasing design. (*Hint*: Remember that you can flip any image, if necessary.)

8. Deselect the selections in the artwork, then close the files without saving the changes.

9. If desired, create a background layer for the image.

10. If necessary, add a vignette effect to a layer.

11. Defringe any images as you see necessary.

12. Save your work, then compare your screen to the sample shown in Figure 34.

Figure 34 *Sample Design Project*
Images © Photodisc/Getty Images.

At your design firm, a Fortune 500 client plans to start a 24-hour cable sports network called Total Sportz that will cover any nonprofessional sporting event. You have been asked to create some preliminary designs for the network using images from multiple sources.

1. Open PS 4-13.psd, then save it as **Total Sportz**.
2. Locate several pieces of sports-related artwork—either on your hard disk, in a royalty-free collection, or from scanned images. Remember that the images should not show professional sports figures, if possible.
3. Select imagery from the artwork and move it into the Total Sportz image.
4. Arrange the images in an interesting design. (*Hint*: Remember that you can flip any image, if necessary.)
5. Change each layer name to describe the sport in the layer image.
6. Deselect the selections in the files that you used, then close the files without saving the changes.
7. If you choose, you can add a vignette effect to a layer and/or adjust opacity.
8. Defringe any images (if necessary).
9. Save your work, then compare your image to the sample shown in Figure 35.

Figure 35 *Sample Portfolio Project*
Images © Photodisc/Getty Images.

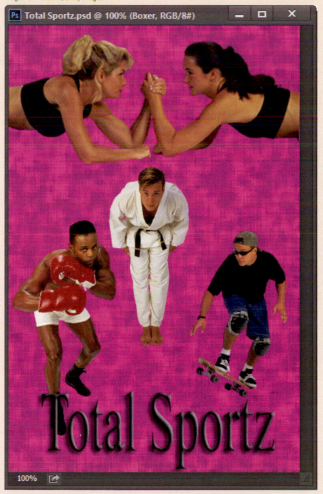

Making Selections

CHAPTER **5**

INCORPORATING COLOR
TECHNIQUES

1. Work with color to transform an image
2. Use the Color Picker and the Swatches panel
3. Place a border around an image
4. Blend colors using the Gradient tool
5. Add color to a grayscale image
6. Use filters, opacity, and blending modes
7. Match colors

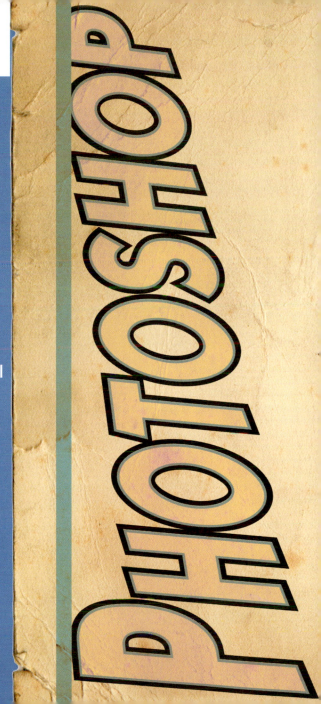

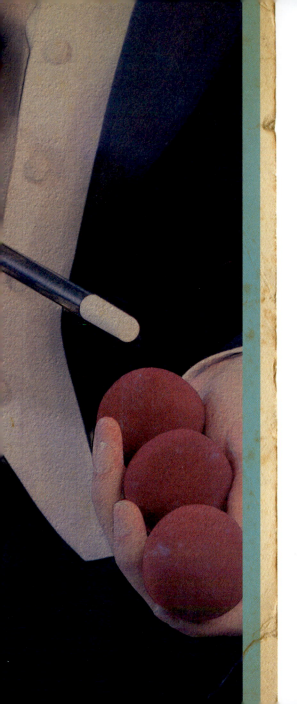

CHAPTER 5

INCORPORATING COLOR
TECHNIQUES

Using Color

Color can make or break an image. Sometimes colors can draw us into an image; other times they can repel us. We all know which colors we like, but when it comes to creating an image, it is helpful to have some knowledge of color theory and be familiar with color terminology.

Understanding how Photoshop measures, displays, and prints color can be valuable whether you create new images or modify existing images. Some colors you choose might be difficult for a professional printer to reproduce or might look muddy when printed. As you become more experienced using color, you will learn which colors reproduce well and which ones do not.

Understanding Color Modes and Color Models

Photoshop displays and prints images using specific color modes. A **color mode** is the amount of color data that can be stored in a given file format, based on an established model. A **color model** determines how pigments combine to produce resulting colors. This is the way your computer or printer associates a name or number with colors. Photoshop uses standard color models as the basis for its color modes. The *color mode* determines the number and range of colors displayed, as well as which color model will be used; the *color model* interprets the color mode information by a monitor and/or printer.

Displaying and Printing Images

An image displayed on your monitor, such as an icon on your desktop, is a **bitmap**, a geometric arrangement of different color dots on a rectangular grid. Each dot, called a **pixel**, represents a color or shade. Bitmapped images are *resolution-dependent* and can lose detail—often demonstrated by a jagged appearance—when highly magnified. When printed, images with high resolutions tend to show more detail and subtler color transitions than low-resolution images.

TOOLS YOU'LL USE

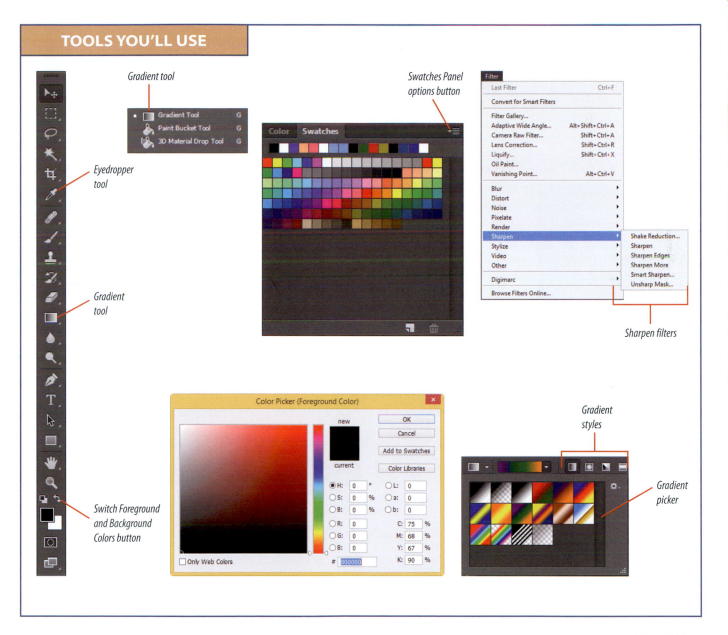

Gradient tool

	Gradient Tool	G
	Paint Bucket Tool	G
	3D Material Drop Tool	G

Eyedropper tool

Gradient tool

Switch Foreground and Background Colors button

Swatches Panel options button

Color   Swatches

Filter

Last Filter	Ctrl+F
Convert for Smart Filters	
Filter Gallery...	
Adaptive Wide Angle...	Alt+Shift+Ctrl+A
Camera Raw Filter...	Shift+Ctrl+A
Lens Correction...	Shift+Ctrl+R
Liquify...	Shift+Ctrl+X
Oil Paint...	
Vanishing Point...	Alt+Ctrl+V
Blur	▶
Distort	▶
Noise	▶
Pixelate	▶
Render	▶
Sharpen	▶
Stylize	▶
Video	▶
Other	▶
Digimarc	▶
Browse Filters Online...	

Shake Reduction...
Sharpen
Sharpen Edges
Sharpen More
Smart Sharpen...
Unsharp Mask...

Sharpen filters

Color Picker (Foreground Color)

new

current

OK
Cancel
Add to Swatches
Color Libraries

⦿ H:	0	°	◯ L:	0
◯ S:	0	%	◯ a:	0
◯ B:	0	%	◯ b:	0
◯ R:	0		C:	75	%
◯ G:	0		M:	68	%
◯ B:	0		Y:	67	%
			K:	90	%

☐ Only Web Colors   # 000000

Gradient styles

Gradient picker

Work with Color
TO TRANSFORM AN IMAGE

What You'll Do

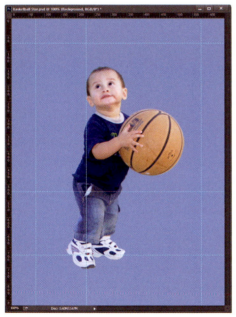

Source: Morguefile.

 In this lesson, you'll use the Color panel, the Paint Bucket tool, and the Eyedropper tool to change the background color of an image.

Learning About Color Models

Photoshop reproduces colors using models of color modes. The range of displayed colors, or **gamut**, for each model available in Photoshop is shown in Figure 1. The shape of each color gamut indicates the range of colors it can display. If a color is **out of gamut**, it is beyond the color space that your monitor can display or that your printer can print. You select the color mode from the Mode command on the Image menu. The available Photoshop color models include Lab Color, Indexed Color, RGB Color, CMYK Color, Bitmap, Duotone, Multichannel, and Grayscale. Photoshop uses color modes to determine how to display and print an image.

> **QUICK TIP**
>
> A color mode is used to determine which color model will be used to display and print an image.

> **DESIGN TIP**
>
> **Understanding the Psychology of Color**
>
> Have you ever wondered why some colors make you react a certain way? You might have noticed that some colors affect you differently than others. Color is such an important part of our lives, and in Photoshop, it's key. Specific colors are often used in print and web pages to evoke the following responses:
>
> - Blue tends to instill a feeling of safety and stability and is often used by financial services.
> - Certain shades of green can generate a soft, calming feeling, while others suggest youthfulness and growth.
> - Red commands attention and can be used as a call to action; it can also distract a reader's attention from other content.
> - White evokes the feeling of purity and innocence, looks cool and fresh, and is often used to suggest luxury.
> - Black conveys feelings of power and strength, but can also suggest darkness and negativity.

Lab Color Mode

The Lab color mode is based on the human perception of color. The numeric values describe all the colors a person with normal vision can see. The Lab color mode has one luminance (lightness) component and two chromatic components (from green to red, and from blue to yellow). Using the Lab color model has distinct advantages: you have the largest number of colors available to you and the greatest precision with which to create them. You can also create all the colors contained by other color models, which are limited in their respective color ranges. The Lab color model is device-independent—the colors will not vary, regardless of the hardware. Use this model when working with digital images so that you can independently edit the luminance and color values.

HSB Color Model

Based on the human perception of color, the HSB (Hue, Saturation, Brightness) model has three fundamental characteristics: hue, saturation, and brightness. The color reflected from or transmitted through an object is called **hue**. Expressed as a degree (between 0° and 360°), each hue is identified by a color name (such as red or green). **Saturation** (or *chroma*) is the strength or purity of the color, representing the amount of gray in proportion to hue. Saturation is measured as a percentage from 0% (gray) to 100% (fully saturated). **Brightness** is the measurement of relative lightness or darkness of a color and is measured as a percentage from 0% (black) to 100% (white). Although you can use the HSB model to define a color on the Color panel or in the Color Picker dialog box, Photoshop *does not* offer HSB mode as a choice for creating or editing images.

RGB Model

Each Photoshop color mode is based on established models used in color reproduction. Most colors in the visible spectrum can be represented by mixing various proportions and intensities of red, green, and blue (RGB) colored light known as the RGB color model. RGB images use three colors, or **channels**, to reproduce colors on screen. RGB colors are additive colors. **Additive colors** are used for lighting, video, and computer monitors; color is created by adding together red, green, and blue light. When red, green, and blue are combined at their highest value (255), the result is white; the absence of any color (when their values are zero) results in black. Photoshop assigns each component of the RGB mode an intensity value. Your colors can vary from monitor to monitor even if you are using the exact same RGB values on different computers.

Figure 1 *Photoshop color gamuts*

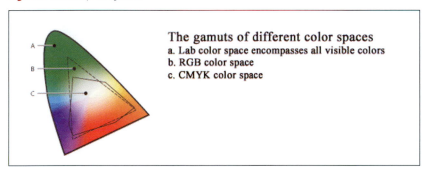

The gamuts of different color spaces
a. Lab color space encompasses all visible colors
b. RGB color space
c. CMYK color space

CMYK Model

The light-absorbing quality of ink printed on paper is the basis of the CMYK (Cyan, Magenta, Yellow, Black) mode. Unlike the **RGB mode**—in which components are combined to create new colors—the CMYK mode is based on colors being partially *absorbed* as the ink hits the paper and being partially *reflected* back to your eyes. CMYK colors are **subtractive colors**—the *absence* of cyan, magenta, yellow, and black creates white. Subtractive (CMYK) and additive (RGB) colors are complementary colors; a pair from one model creates a color in the other. When combined, cyan, magenta, and yellow absorb all color and produce black. The **CMYK mode**—in which the lightest colors are assigned the highest percentages of ink colors—is used in four-color process printing. Converting an RGB image into a CMYK image produces a **color separation** (the commercial printing process of separating colors for use with different inks). Note, however, that because your monitor uses RGB mode, you will not see the exact colors until you print the image, and even then the colors can vary depending on the printer and offset press.

Understanding the Bitmap and Grayscale Modes

In addition to the RGB and CMYK modes, Photoshop provides two specialized color modes: bitmap and grayscale. The **bitmap mode** uses black or white color values to represent image pixels, and is a good choice for images with subtle color gradations, such as photographs or painted images. The **grayscale mode** uses up to 256 shades of gray (in an 8-bit image), assigning a brightness value from 0 (black) to 255 (white) to each pixel. (The number of shades of gray in 16- and 32-bit images is much greater than 256.) The **Duotone mode** is used to create the following grayscale images: monotone, duotones (using two colors), tritones (using three colors), and quadtones (using four colors).

Changing Foreground and Background Colors

In Photoshop, the **foreground color** is black by default and is used to paint, fill, and apply a border to a selection. The **background color** is white by default and is used to make **gradient fills** (gradual blends of multiple colors) and to fill in areas of an image that have been erased. You can change foreground and background colors using the Color panel, the Swatches panel, the Color Picker, or the Eyedropper tool. One method of changing foreground and background colors is **sampling**, in which an existing color is used. You can restore the default colors by clicking the Default Foreground and Background Colors button on the Tools panel, shown in Figure 2. You can apply a color to the background of a layer using the Paint Bucket tool grouped with the Gradient tool. When you click an image with the Paint Bucket tool, the current foreground color on the Tools panel fills the active layer.

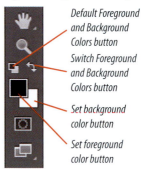

Figure 2 *Foreground and background color buttons*

Default Foreground and Background Colors button

Switch Foreground and Background Colors button

Set background color button

Set foreground color button

Figure 3 *Image with rulers displayed*
Source: Morguefile.

Figure 4 *Color Settings dialog box*

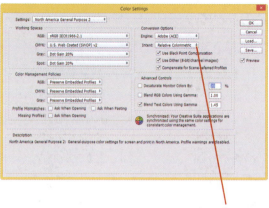

Intent list arrow

The use of a **rendering intent** determines how colors are converted by a color management system. A **color management system** is used to keep colors looking consistent as they move between devices. Colors are defined and interpreted using a **profile**. You can create a rendering intent by clicking Edit on the Menu bar, and then clicking Color Settings. Click the Intent list arrow in the Conversion Options area, shown in Figure 4, and then select one of the four rendering intent options. Since a gamut is the range of color that a color system can display or print, the rendering intent is constantly evaluating the color gamut and deciding whether or not the colors need adjusting. Although colors that fall inside the destination gamut are not changed, using a rendering intent allows colors that fall outside the destination gamut to be adjusted based on the intent you set.

Set the default foreground and background colors

1. Start Photoshop, open PS 5-1.psd from the drive and folder where you save your Data Files, then save it as **Basketball Star**.

TIP Whenever the Photoshop Format Options dialog box appears, click OK to maximize compatibility.

2. Click the **Default Foreground and Background Colors button** on the Tools panel, then reset the Essentials workspace.

TIP If you accidently click the Set foreground color button, the Color Picker (Foreground Color) dialog box opens.

3. Change the status bar so the document size displays, if it is not already displayed.

TIP Document sizes will not display in the status bar if the image window is too small. Drag the lower-right corner of the image window to expand the window and display the menu arrow and document sizes.

4. Display the rulers in pixels and show the guides if they are not already displayed, then compare your screen to Figure 3.

TIP You can right-click (Win) or [control]-click (Mac) one of the rulers to choose Pixels, Inches, Centimeters, Millimeters, Points, Picas, or Percent as a unit of measurement, instead of using the Rulers and Units Preferences dialog box.

You set the default foreground and background colors and displayed rulers in pixels.

Change the background color using the Color panel

1. Click the **Background layer** on the Layers panel.

2. Display the **Legacy workspace** (which was created in Chapter 1).

3. If necessary, display the **Color panel**.

4. Drag each **color slider** on the Color panel until you reach the values shown in Figure 5.

   The active color changes to the new color. Did you notice that this image is using the RGB mode?

   TIP You can also double-click each component's text box on the Color panel and type the color values.

5. Click the **Paint Bucket tool** 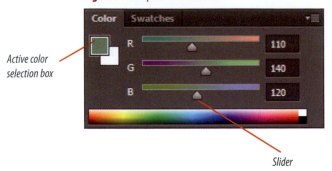 on the Tools panel.

   TIP If the Paint Bucket tool is not visible on the Tools panel, click the Gradient tool on the Tools panel, press and hold the mouse button until the list of hidden tools opens, then click the Paint Bucket tool.

6. Click the **image** with the **Paint Bucket pointer** .

7. Drag the **Paint Bucket state** on the History panel onto the Delete current state button .

   TIP You can also undo the last action by clicking Edit on the Menu bar, then clicking Undo Paint Bucket.

You set new values in the Color panel, used the Paint Bucket tool to change the background to that color, then undid the change. You can change colors on the Color panel by dragging the sliders or by typing values in the color text boxes.

Figure 5 *Color panel with new color*

Active color selection box

Slider

Figure 6 *Info panel*

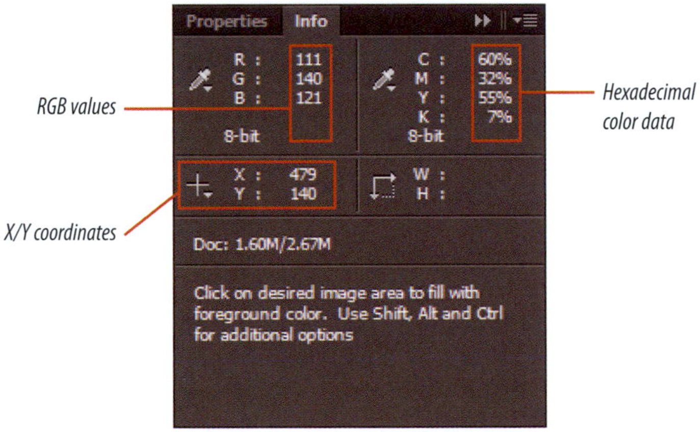

RGB values

Hexadecimal color data

X/Y coordinates

Using Ruler Coordinates

Photoshop rulers run along the top and left sides of the document window. Each point on an image has a horizontal and vertical location. These two numbers, called X and Y coordinates, appear on the Info panel (which is located with the Properties panel and can be opened with the Window menu) as shown in Figure 6. The X coordinate refers to the horizontal location, and the Y coordinate refers to the vertical location. You can use one or both sets of guides to identify coordinates of a location, such as a color you want to sample. If you have difficulty seeing the ruler markings, you can increase the size of the image; the greater the zoom factor, the more detailed the measurement hashes.

Figure 7 *New foreground color applied to Background layer*
Source: Morguefile.

New foreground color

Using Hexadecimal Values in the Info Panel

Colors can be expressed in a **hexadecimal value**, three pairs of letters or numbers that define the R, G, and B components of a color. The three pairs of letters/numbers are expressed in values from 00 (minimum luminance) to ff (maximum luminance). 000000 represents the value of black, ffffff is white, and ff0000 is red. To view hexadecimal values in the Info panel, click the Info Panel options button, and then click Panel Options. Click Web Color from either the First Color Readout or Second Color Readout Mode menu, and then click OK. This is just one more way you can precisely determine a specific color in an image.

Change the background color using the Eyedropper tool

1. Click the **Background layer** on the Layers panel, if it is not already selected.

2. Click the **Eyedropper tool** on the Tools panel.

3. Click the **light blue area on the boy's right shoe** in the image with the **Eyedropper pointer** .

    The Set foreground color button displays the light blue color that you clicked (or sampled).

    TIP Remember to zoom in or out of any image at any time during a lesson to improve your view.

4. Click the **Paint Bucket tool** on the Tools panel.

5. Click the **image**, then compare your screen to Figure 7.

    You might have noticed that in this instance, it doesn't matter where on the layer you click, as long as the correct layer is selected.

6. Save your work.

You used the Eyedropper tool to sample a color as the foreground color, then used the Paint Bucket tool to change the background color to the color you sampled. Using the Eyedropper tool is a convenient way of sampling a color in any Photoshop image.

Use the Color Picker
AND THE SWATCHES PANEL

What You'll Do

In this lesson, you'll use the Color Picker and the Swatches panel to select new colors, and then you'll add a new color to the background and to the Swatches panel. You'll also learn how to download and apply color themes from Kuler.

Making Selections from the Color Picker

Depending on the color model you are using, you can select colors using the **Color Picker**, a feature that lets you choose a color from a color spectrum or numerically define a custom color. You can change colors in the Color Picker dialog box by using the following methods:

- Drag the sliders along the vertical color bar.
- Click inside the vertical color bar.
- Click a color in the Color field.
- Enter a value in any of the text boxes.

Figure 8 shows a color in the Color Picker dialog box. A circular marker indicates the active color. The color slider displays the range of color levels available for the active color component. The adjustments you make by dragging or clicking a new color are reflected in the text boxes; when you choose a new color, the previous color appears below the new color in the preview area.

Using Kuler to Coordinate Colors

Kuler®, from Adobe, is a web application from which you can download pre-coordinated color themes or design your own. These collections can be saved and shared with others. Use Kuler as a fast, effective way of ensuring that your use of color is consistent and harmonious. If you decide to select an existing Kuler theme, you'll find that there are thousands from which to choose. Kuler themes can be seen by clicking the Window menu, pointing to Extensions, and then clicking Kuler, which opens a Kuler panel within Photoshop. You can also access Kuler through your browser at *kuler.adobe.com*, using the Kuler desktop (which requires the installation of Adobe AIR), or from Adobe Illustrator (CS4 or higher). When you pass the mouse over a theme in the Kuler website, icons appear over the current theme displaying options to get info, edit, copy link, download, and make a favorite. Click Info and the colors display at the top of the window. Click Edit to view the theme's color values. As a web-based app, the Kuler user interface and its available swatches change often. *Don't be alarmed* if your screens look different than those shown in this chapter.

Using the Swatches Panel

You can also change colors using the Swatches panel. The **Swatches panel** is a visual display of colors you can choose from, as shown in Figure 9. You can add your own colors to the panel by sampling a color from an image, and you can also delete colors. When you add a swatch to the Swatches panel, Photoshop assigns a default name that has a sequential number, or you can name the swatch whatever you like. Photoshop places new swatches in the first available space at the end of the panel. You can view swatch names by clicking the Swatches Panel options button, and then clicking Small List (or Large List).

QUICK TIP

You can reset the Swatches panel to its default settings by clicking the Swatches panel option button, then clicking Reset Swatches.

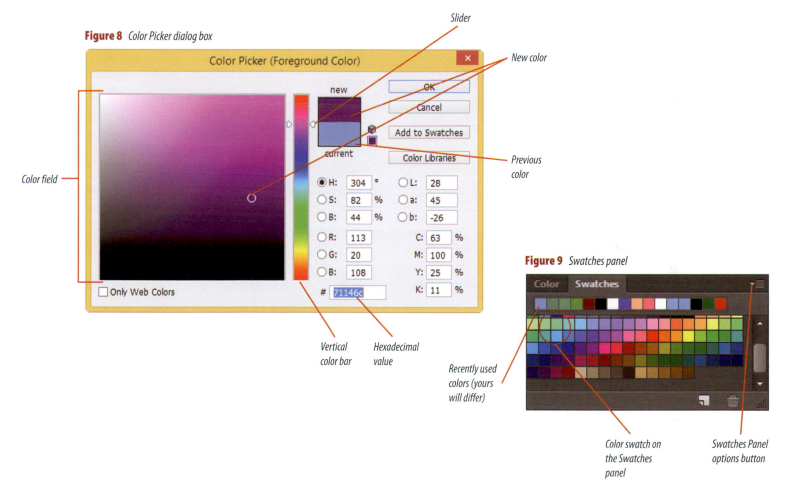

Figure 8 *Color Picker dialog box*

Slider

New color

Previous color

Color field

Figure 9 *Swatches panel*

Vertical color bar

Hexadecimal value

Recently used colors (yours will differ)

Color swatch on the Swatches panel

Swatches Panel options button

Select a color using the Color Picker dialog box

1. Click the **Set foreground color button** on the Tools panel, verify that the H: option button is selected in the Color Picker dialog box, then drag the slider in the Vertical color bar to the mid-point.

2. Click the **R: option button**.

3. Click the **bottom-right corner** of the Color field (purple), as shown in Figure 10.

TIP If the Warning: out-of-gamut for printing indicator appears next to the color, then this color is outside the printable range of colors.

4. Click **OK**.

You opened the Color Picker dialog box, selected a different color mode by clicking the R option button, and then selected a new color.

Select a color using the Swatches panel

1. Click the **Swatches panel option button**, click **Reset Swatches**, then click **OK** in the warning box.

2. Click the **third swatch from the right in the second row** (Pastel Red Orange), as shown in Figure 11 (the actual location of this color swatch may differ on your Swatches panel).

   Did you notice that the foreground color on the Tools panel changed to a pastel red orange?

3. Click the **Paint Bucket tool** on the Tools panel if necessary.

4. Click the **image** with the **Paint Bucket pointer**, then compare your screen to Figure 12.

You selected a color from the Swatches panel, and then used the Paint Bucket tool to change the background to that color.

Figure 10 *Color Picker dialog box*

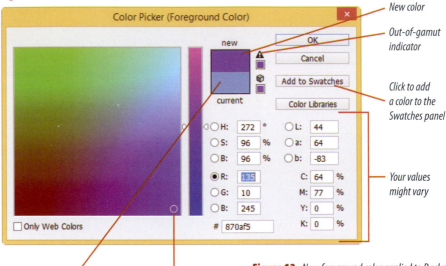

New color

Out-of-gamut indicator

Click to add a color to the Swatches panel

Your values might vary

Previous color

Click here for new color

Figure 11 *Swatches panel*

Your swatches on the last row might vary

Figure 12 *New foreground color applied to Background layer*
Source: Morguefile.

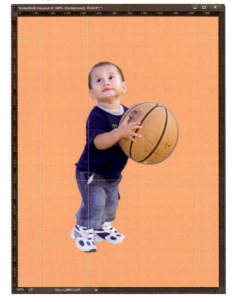

Figure 13 *Swatch added to Swatches panel*

New swatch appears
in last row

Maintaining Your Focus

Adobe Photoshop is probably unlike any other program you've used before. In other programs, there's a central area on the screen where you focus your attention. In Photoshop, there's the workspace containing your document, but you've probably already figured out that if you don't have the correct layer selected in the Layer's panel, things won't quite work out as you expected. In addition, you have to make sure you've got the right tool selected in the Tools panel. You also need to keep an eye on the History panel. As you work on your image, it might feel a lot like negotiating a grocery parking lot on the day before Thanksgiving. You've got to be looking in a lot of places at once.

Add a new color to the Swatches panel

1. Click the **Eyedropper tool** 🖊 on the Tools panel.
2. Click the **palm leaf** (on the boy's shirt) at coordinates **310 X/348 Y**.

TIP Use the Zoom tool whenever necessary to enlarge or decrease your workspace so you can better see what you're working on.

3. Scroll down the Swatches panel, then click the **empty area to the right of the last swatch** in the bottom row with the **Paint Bucket pointer** 🪣.
4. Type **Palm leaf** in the Name text box.
5. Click **OK** in the Color Swatch Name dialog box.

TIP To delete a color from the Swatches panel, press [Alt] (Win) or [option] (Mac), position the ✂ pointer over a swatch, then click the swatch.

6. Save your work, then compare the new swatch on your Swatches panel to Figure 13.

You used the Eyedropper tool to sample a color, added the color to the Swatches panel, and then gave it a descriptive name. Adding swatches to the Swatches panel makes it easy to reuse frequently used colors.

Use Kuler from a web browser

1. Open your favorite browser, type **kuler.adobe.com** in the URL text box, then press [**Enter**] (Win) or [**return**] (Mac).

   If you have an iPad, iPhone, or Android device, you can download and install a Kuler app by searching the App Store or Google Play (depending on your mobile device).

2. Click the **Sign In link**, type your **Adobe ID** and **password**, then Agree to the terms of the website if asked. (If you don't have an Adobe ID, click the Register link and follow the instructions.)

3. Click **Explore** on the Kuler menu bar, type **Johnny Cash Tribute** in the Search text box, press [**Enter**] (Win) or [**return**] (Mac). The swatches shown in Figure 14 will display, although your screen may contain other swatches.

4. Place your mouse over the swatch indicated in Figure 14 (top-right swatch), click the **Download button** , find the location where you save your Data Files in the Save As dialog box, then click **Save** (Win); on Mac OS, the downloaded file is automatically sent to the Downloads folder.

5. Click the **profile icon** in the upper-right of the screen, click the **Sign Out** button to sign out from Kuler, then activate Photoshop.

6. Click the **Swatches Panel options button** , then click **Load Swatches**.

7. Navigate to the location where you save your Data Files, (click the **Files of type button**, click **Swatch Exchange (*.ASE)** (Win)), click **Johnny Cash Tribute**, then click **Load** (Win) or **Open** (Mac).

You searched the Kuler website, downloaded a color theme, and then added it to your Photoshop Swatches panel.

Figure 14 *Themes in Kuler*

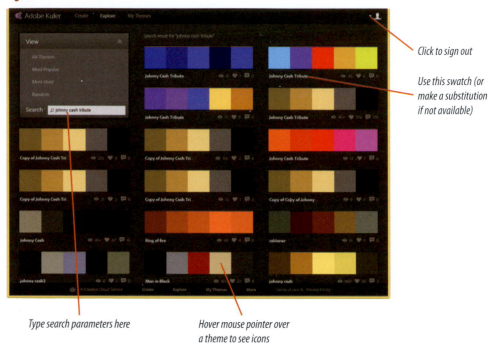

Click to sign out

Use this swatch (or make a substitution if not available)

Type search parameters here

Hover mouse pointer over a theme to see icons

Using the Kuler Mobile App

Using your iPhone, you can use the Kuler mobile app to copy colors you see when you're on the go. Imagine that you're out and about and you see a fabulous color that you'd really like to use in Photoshop. With the Kuler iPhone app and your phone's camera, you can capture the color and Kuler will not only save the color, but will also create a theme that includes complimentary colors. You can then save the theme on your phone for use in your Kuler account on your desktop. Once you've installed the Kuler mobile app and logged in, click the camera icon and point the camera at nearby images. The camera will pick up key colors within its view and create complimentary themes on-the-spot. You can then choose to see the hexadecimal values for those colors, name and save the theme (automatically added to your Kuler account), share the theme via Twitter or email, or delete the theme.

Figure 15 *Kuler panel*

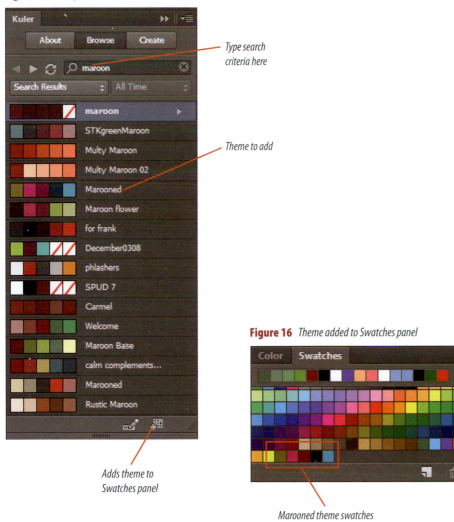

Type search criteria here

Theme to add

Adds theme to Swatches panel

Figure 16 *Theme added to Swatches panel*

Marooned theme swatches added to panel

Use Kuler from Photoshop

1. Click **Window** on the Menu bar, point to **Extensions**, then click **Kuler**.

2. Click the **Search text box**, type **maroon**, then press [**Enter**] (Win) or [**return**] (Mac). Compare your Kuler panel to Figure 15.

TIP Your Kuler panel may differ as themes change frequently.

3. Click the **Marooned theme** (or a similar theme if Marooned is not available), then click the **Add selected theme to swatches button** 🖳. Compare your Swatches panel to Figure 16.

4. Close the Kuler panel.

5. In the Swatches panel, click the **color box** for #F2CA80 (or the color of your choice if this color is not available) with the **Eyedropper pointer** 🖊.

TIP The locations of your color swatches may vary.

6. Verify that the Background layer is active, click the **Paint Bucket tool** 🪣 on the Tools panel, then click the **image**.

7. Save your work.

You opened Kuler in Photoshop, then added a color theme to the Swatches panel. You then applied a color downloaded from Kuler to the image.

Place a Border Around
AN IMAGE

What You'll Do

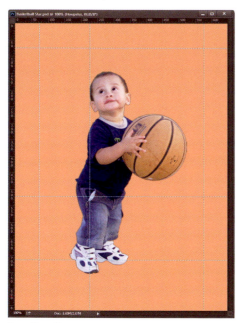

Source: Morguefile.

In this lesson, you'll add a border to an image.

Emphasizing an Image

You can emphasize an image by placing a border around its edges. This process is called **stroking the edges**. You add a border by selecting a layer or object, clicking Edit on the Menu bar, and then clicking Stroke. The default color of the border is the current foreground color on the Tools panel. You can change the width, color, location, and blending mode of a border using the Stroke dialog box. The location option buttons in the dialog box determine where the border will be placed. If you want to change the location of the stroke, you must first delete the previously applied stroke, or Photoshop will apply the new border over the existing one.

Locking Transparent Pixels

As you modify layers, you can lock some properties to protect their contents. The ability to lock—or protect—elements within a layer is controlled from within the Layers panel, as shown in Figure 17. It's a good idea to lock transparent pixels when you add borders so that stray marks will not be included in the stroke. You can lock the following layer properties:

- Transparency: Limits editing capabilities to areas in a layer that are opaque.
- Image: Makes it impossible to modify layer pixels using painting tools.
- Position: Prevents pixels within a layer from being moved.

Figure 17 *Layers panel locking options*

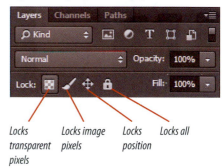

Locks transparent pixels

Locks image pixels

Locks position

Locks all

Figure 18 *Locking transparent pixels*

Locks transparent pixels button

Lock icon

Figure 19 *Stroke dialog box*

Your default stroke width might vary

Changes stroke color

Figure 20 *Border added to image*
Source: Morguefile.

Location options

Border

Create a border

1. Click the **Indicates layer visibility button** 👁 on the Background layer on the Layers panel to hide the layer.

   TIP You can click the Indicates layer visibility button to hide distracting layers.

2. Click the **Default Foreground and Background Colors button** ▣.

   The foreground color will become the default border color.

3. Click the **Hoopster layer** on the Layers panel.

4. Click the **Lock transparent pixels button** ▨ on the Layers panel. See Figure 18.

   The border will be applied only to the pixels on the edge of the boy and the ball.

5. Click **Edit** on the Menu bar, then click **Stroke** to open the Stroke dialog box. See Figure 19.

6. Verify that **1px** displays in the Width text box, click the **Outside option button**, then click **OK**.

   TIP Determining the correct border location can be confusing. The default stroke width is the setting last applied; you can apply a width from 1 to 150 pixels. Try different settings until you achieve the look you want.

7. Click the **Indicates layer visibility button** ▣ on the Background layer on the Layers panel.

8. Save your work, then compare your image to Figure 20.

You hid a layer, changed the foreground color to black, locked transparent pixels, then used the Stroke dialog box to apply a border to the image.

Blend Colors Using
THE GRADIENT TOOL

What You'll Do

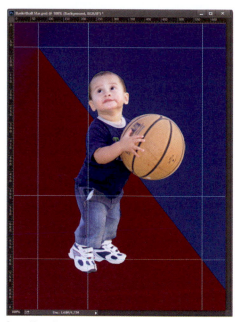

Source: Morguefile.

 In this lesson, you'll create a gradient fill from a sampled color and a swatch, and then apply it to the background.

Understanding Gradients

A **gradient fill**, or simply **gradient**, is a blend of colors used to fill a selection of a layer or an entire layer. A gradient's appearance is determined by its beginning and ending points, and its length, direction, and angle. Gradients allow you to create dramatic effects, using existing color combinations or your own colors. The Gradient picker, as shown in Figure 21, offers multicolor gradient fills and a few that use the current foreground or background colors on the Tools panel.

Using the Gradient Tool

You use the Gradient tool to create gradients in images. When you choose the Gradient tool, five gradient styles become available on the options bar. These styles—Linear, Radial,

Figure 21 *Gradient picker*

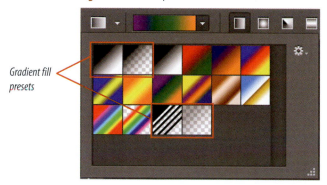

Gradient fill presets

Angle, Reflected, and Diamond—are shown in Figure 22. In each example, the gradient was drawn from 50 X/50 Y to 100 X/100 Y.

Customizing Gradients

Using the **gradient presets**—predesigned gradient fills that are displayed in the Gradient picker—is a great way to learn how to use gradients. But as you become more familiar with Photoshop, you might want to venture into the world of the unknown and create your own gradient designs. You can create your own designs by modifying an existing gradient using the Gradient Editor. You can open the Gradient Editor, shown in Figure 23, by clicking the selected gradient pattern that appears in the Gradient picker on the options bar. After it's open, you can use it to make the following modifications:

- Create a new gradient from an existing gradient.
- Modify an existing gradient.
- Add intermediate colors to a gradient.
- Create a blend between more than two colors.
- Adjust the opacity values.
- Determine the placement of the midpoint.

Figure 22 *Sample gradients*

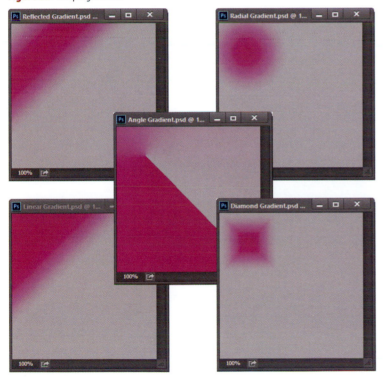

Figure 23 *Gradient Editor dialog box*

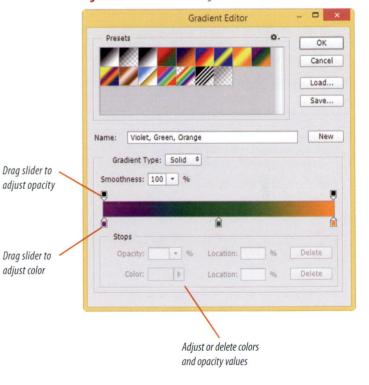

Drag slider to adjust opacity

Drag slider to adjust color

Adjust or delete colors and opacity values

Create a gradient from a sample color

1. Verify that the **Eyedropper tool** is selected.

2. Click the **blue shirt** in the image at coordinates **250 X/300 Y**.

   TIP To accurately select the coordinates, adjust the zoom factor as necessary.

3. Click the **Switch Foreground and Background Colors button** on the Tools panel.

4. Click the **Maroon swatch** (R=102 G=0 B=51) on the Swatches panel (or one of the new swatches you added) with the **Eyedropper pointer**.

5. Click the **Indicates layer visibility button** on the Hoopster layer to hide it, and make sure the Background layer is active, as shown in Figure 24.

6. Click the **Paint Bucket tool** on the Tools panel, then press and hold the mouse button until the panel of hidden tools opens.

7. Click the **Gradient tool** on the Tools panel, then click the **Angle Gradient button** on the options bar if it is not already selected.

8. Click the **Gradient picker list arrow** on the options bar, then double-click **Foreground to Background gradient fill** (first row, first column), as shown in Figure 25.

   TIP You can close the Gradient picker by pressing [Esc].

You sampled a color on the image to set the background color, changed the foreground color using an existing swatch, selected the Gradient tool, and then chose a gradient fill and style.

Figure 24 *Hoopster layer hidden*

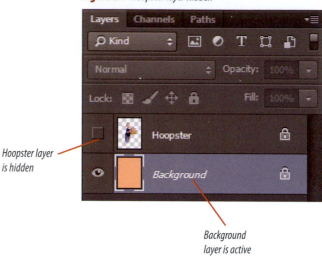

Hoopster layer is hidden

Background layer is active

Figure 25 *Gradient picker*

Gradient picker list arrow

Gradient styles

Foreground to Background

Gradient picker

Incorporating Color Techniques

Figure 26 *Gradient fill applied to Background layer*

Source: Morguefile.

Apply a gradient fill

1. Drag the **Gradient pointer** -‡- from **75 X/75 Y** to **575 X/710 Y** using the Info panel and the guides to help you create the gradient in the work area.

2. Click the **Indicates layer visibility button** ▢ on the Hoopster layer.

   The Hoopster layer appears against the new background, as shown in Figure 26.

3. Save your work.

TIP It is a good practice to save your work early and often in the creation process, especially before making significant changes or printing.

You applied the gradient fill to the background. You can create dramatic effects using the gradient fill in combination with foreground and background colors.

Add Color
TO A GRAYSCALE IMAGE

What You'll Do

Source: Morguefile.

In this lesson, you'll convert an image to grayscale, change the color mode, and then colorize a grayscale image using the Hue/Saturation dialog box.

Colorizing Options

Grayscale images can contain up to 256 shades of gray (at 8 bits per pixel), assigning a brightness value from 0 (black) to 255 (white) to each pixel. Since the earliest days of photography, people have been tinting grayscale images with color to create a certain mood or emphasize an image in a way that purely realistic colors could not. To capture this effect in Photoshop, you convert an image to the Grayscale mode, and then choose the color mode you want to work in before you continue. When you apply a color to a grayscale image, each pixel becomes a shade of that particular color instead of gray.

Converting Grayscale and Color Modes

When you convert a color image to grayscale, the data for light and dark values—called the **luminosity**—remain, while the color information is deleted. When you change from grayscale to a color mode, the foreground and background colors on the Tools panel change from black and white to the previously selected colors.

Tweaking Adjustments

Once you have made your color mode conversion to grayscale, you may want to make some adjustments. You can fine-tune

Converting a Color Image to Black and White

Using the Black & White command, you can easily convert a color image to black and white. This command lets you quickly make the color-to-black-and-white conversion while maintaining full control over how individual colors are converted. Tones can also be applied to the grayscale by applying color tones (the numeric values for each color). To use this feature, click Image on the Menu bar, point to Adjustments, and then click Black & White. The Black & White command can also be applied as an Adjustment layer.

the Brightness/Contrast, filters, and blending modes in a grayscale image.

Colorizing a Grayscale Image

In order for a grayscale image to be colorized, you must change the color mode to one that accommodates color. After you change the color mode and adjust settings in the Hue/Saturation dialog box, Photoshop determines the colorization range based on the hue of the currently selected foreground color. If you want a different colorization range, you need to change the foreground color.

Figure 27 *Gradient Map dialog box*

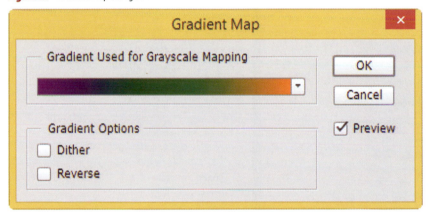

Applying a Gradient Effect

You can also use the Gradient Map to apply a colored gradient effect to a grayscale image. The Gradient Map uses gradient fills (the same ones displayed in the Gradient picker) to colorize the image, which can produce some stunning effects. You use the Gradient Map dialog box, shown in Figure 27, to apply a gradient effect to a grayscale image. You can access the Gradient Map dialog box using the Adjustments command on the Image menu.

Change the color mode

1. Open PS 5-2.psd from the drive and folder where you store your Data Files, then save it as **Basketball Star Colorized**.

2. Click **Image** on the Menu bar, point to **Mode**, then click **Grayscale**.

3. Click **Flatten** in the warning box, then click **Discard**.

   The color mode of the image is changed to grayscale, and the image is flattened so there is only a single layer. All the color information in the image has been discarded.

4. Click **Image** on the Menu bar, point to **Mode**, then click **RGB Color**.

   The color mode is changed back to RGB color, although there is still no color in the image. Compare your screen to Figure 28.

You converted the image to Grayscale, which discarded the existing color information. Then you changed the color mode to RGB color.

Figure 28 *Grayscale image converted to RGB mode*
Source: Morguefile.

Mode changed to RGB

Converting Color Images to Grayscale

Like everything else in Photoshop, there is more than one way of converting a color image into one that is black and white. Changing the color mode to grayscale is the quickest method. You can also make this conversion by converting to black and white or through desaturation by clicking Image on the Menu bar, pointing to Adjustments, and then clicking Black & White or Desaturate. Converting to Grayscale mode generally results in losing contrast, as does the desaturation method, while using the Black & White method retains the contrast of the original image.

Incorporating Color Techniques

Figure 29 *Hue/Saturation dialog box*

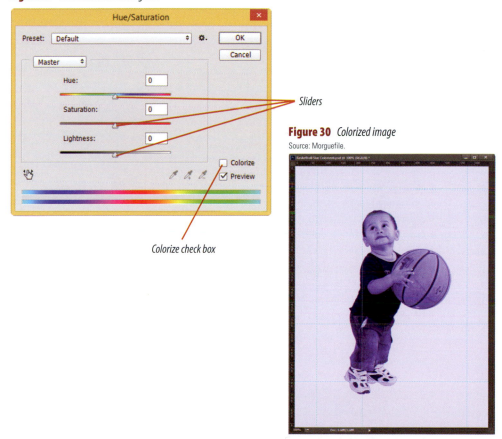

Sliders

Colorize check box

Figure 30 *Colorized image*
Source: Morguefile.

Colorize a grayscale image

1. Click **Image** on the Menu bar, point to **Adjustments**, then click **Hue/Saturation** to open the Hue/Saturation dialog box, as shown in Figure 29.

2. Click the **Colorize check box** in the Hue/Saturation dialog box to add a check mark.

3. Drag the **Hue slider** until the text box displays **240**.

TIP You can also type values in the text boxes in the Hue/Saturation dialog box. Negative numbers must be preceded by a minus sign or a hyphen. Positive numbers can be preceded by an optional plus sign (+).

4. Drag the **Saturation slider** until the text box displays **30**.

5. Drag the **Lightness slider** until the text box displays **-10**.

6. Click **OK**.

7. Compare your screen to Figure 30, then save your work.

You colorized a grayscale image by adjusting settings in the Hue/Saturation dialog box.

Understanding the Hue/Saturation Dialog Box

The Hue/Saturation dialog box is an important tool in the world of color enhancement. Useful for both color and grayscale images, the saturation slider can be used to boost a range of colors. By clicking the Master list arrow, you can isolate which colors (all, cyan, blue, magenta, red, yellow, or green) you want to modify. Using this tool requires patience and experimentation, but gives you great control over the colors in your image.

Use Filters, Opacity, AND BLENDING MODES

What You'll Do

Source: Morguefile.

In this lesson, you'll adjust the brightness and contrast in the Basketball Star Colorized image, apply a Sharpen filter, and adjust the opacity of the lines applied by the filter. You'll also adjust the color balance of the Basketball Star image.

Manipulating an Image

As you work in Photoshop, you might realize that some images have fundamental problems that need correcting, while others just need to be further enhanced. For example, you might need to adjust an image's contrast and sharpness, or you might want to colorize an otherwise dull image. You can use a variety of techniques to change the way an image looks. For example, you have learned how to use the Adjustments command on the Image menu to modify hue and saturation, but you can also use this command to adjust brightness and contrast, color balance, and a host of other visual effects.

Understanding Filters

Filters are Photoshop commands that can significantly alter an image's appearance. Experimenting with Photoshop's filters is a fun way to completely change the look of an image. For example, the Watercolor filter gives the illusion that your image was painted using traditional watercolors. Sharpen filters can appear to add definition to the entire image, or just the edges. Compare the

Fixing Blurry Scanned Images

An unfortunate result of scanning a picture is that the image can become blurry. You can fix this, however, using the Unsharp Mask filter. This filter both sharpens and smoothes the image by increasing the contrast along element edges. Here's how it works: the smoothing effect removes stray marks, and the sharpening effect emphasizes contrasting neighboring pixels. Most scanners come with their own Unsharp Masks built into the scanner driver, but using Photoshop, you have access to a more powerful version of this filter. You can use Photoshop's Unsharp Mask to control the sharpening process by adjusting key settings. In most cases, your scanner's Unsharp Mask might not give you this flexibility. Regardless of the technical aspects, the result is a sharper image. You can apply the Unsharp Mask by clicking Filter on the Menu bar, pointing to Sharpen, and then clicking Unsharp Mask.

Incorporating Color Techniques

different Sharpen filters applied in Figure 31. The **Sharpen More filter** increases the contrast of adjacent pixels and can focus a blurry image. Be careful not to overuse sharpening tools (or any filter), because you can create high-contrast lines or add graininess in color or brightness.

Choosing Blending Modes

A **blending mode** controls how pixels are made either darker or lighter based on colors on underlying layers. Photoshop provides a variety of commonly used blending modes, listed in Table 1, to combine the color of the pixels in the current layer with those in layer(s) beneath it. You can see a list of blending modes by clicking the Set the blending mode for the layer list arrow on the Layers panel, or by

clicking Blending Options, and then clicking the Blend Mode list arrow. You can also see a list of blending modes by clicking the Mode list arrow on the options bar when the Gradient tool is selected, or by clicking Layer on the Menu bar, pointing to Layer Style, and then clicking Blending Options.

Understanding Blending Mode Components

You should consider the following underlying colors when planning a blending mode: **base color**, which is the original color of the image; **blend color**, which is the color you apply with a paint or edit tool; and **resulting color**, which is the color that is created as a result of applying the blend color.

Softening Filter Effects

Opacity can soften the line that the filter creates, but it doesn't affect the opacity of the entire layer. After a filter has been applied, you can modify the opacity and apply a blending mode using the Layers panel or the Fade dialog box. You can open the Fade dialog box by clicking Edit on the Menu bar, and then clicking the Fade command.

Figure 31 *Sharpen filters*

Original image

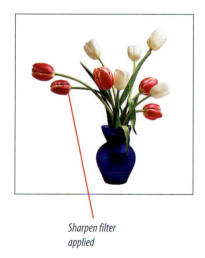

Sharpen filter applied

Sharpen More filter applied excessively

Images © Photodisc/Getty Images.

Balancing Colors

As you adjust settings, such as hue and saturation, you might create unwanted imbalances in your image. You can adjust colors to correct or improve an image's appearance. For example, you can decrease a color by increasing the amount of its opposite color. You open the Color Balance dialog box by clicking Image on the Menu bar, pointing to Adjustments, and then clicking Color Balance. This dialog box is used to balance the color in an image.

TABLE 1: BLENDING MODES	
Blending mode	**Description**
Dissolve mode	Dissolve mode creates a grainy, mottled appearance.
Multiply and Screen modes	Multiply mode creates semitransparent shadow effects. This mode assesses the information in each channel, and then multiplies the value of the base color by the blend color. The resulting color is always *darker* than the base color. The Screen mode multiplies the value of the inverse of the blend and base colors. After it is applied, the resulting color is always *lighter* than the base color.
Overlay mode	Dark and light values preserve the highlights and shadows of the base color while mixing the base color and blend color, dark base colors are multiplied (darkened), and light areas are screened (lightened).
Soft Light and Hard Light modes	Soft Light lightens a light base color and darkens a dark base color giving the effect of shining a diffuse spotlight on an image. The Hard Light blending mode creates the effect of a harsh spotlight, useful for adding highlights or shadows by providing a greater contrast between the base and blend colors.
Color Dodge and Color Burn modes	Color Dodge mode brightens the base color to reflect the blend color. The Color Burn mode darkens base color to reflect the blend color.
Darken and Lighten modes	Darken mode selects the base color or blend color based on whichever color is darker. The Lighten mode selects a new resulting color based on the lighter of the two colors.
Difference and Exclusion modes	The Difference mode subtracts the value of the blend color from the value of the base color, or vice versa, depending on which color has the greater brightness value. The Exclusion mode creates an effect similar to that of the Difference mode, but with less contrast between the blend and base colors.
Color and Luminosity modes	The Color mode creates a resulting color with the luminance of the base color and the hue and saturation of the blend color. The Luminosity mode creates a resulting color with the hue and saturation of the base color and the luminance of the blend color.
Hue and Saturation modes	The Hue mode creates a resulting color with the luminance and saturation of the base color and the hue of the blend color. The Saturation mode creates a resulting color with the luminance and hue of the base color and the saturation of the blend color.

Incorporating Color Techniques

Figure 32 *Brightness/Contrast dialog box*
Source: Morguefile.

Figure 33 *Shadow/Highlight dialog box*

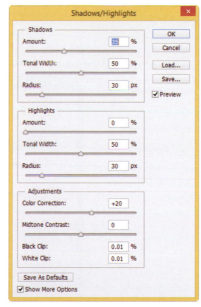

Adjust brightness and contrast

1. Click **Image** on the Menu bar, point to **Adjustments**, then click **Brightness/Contrast** to open the Brightness/Contrast dialog box.

2. Drag the **Brightness slider** until **15** appears in the Brightness text box.

3. Drag the **Contrast slider** until **30** appears in the Contrast text box. Compare your screen to Figure 32.

TIP Any dialog box containing a Preview check box can be toggled on and off to see the effects of your changes.

4. Click **OK**.

You adjusted settings in the Brightness/Contrast dialog box. The image now looks much brighter, with a higher degree of contrast, which obscures some of the finer detail in the image.

Correcting Shadows and Highlights

The ability to correct shadows and highlights will delight photographers everywhere. This image correction feature (opened by clicking Image on the Menu bar, pointing to Adjustments, and then clicking Shadows/Highlights) lets you modify overall lighting and make subtle adjustments. Figure 33 shows the Shadows/Highlights dialog box with the Show More Options check box selected. Check out this one-stop shopping for shadow and highlight adjustments!

Work with a filter, a blending mode, and an opacity setting

1. Click **Filter** on the Menu bar, point to **Sharpen**, then click **Sharpen More**.

   The border and other features of the image are intensified.

2. Click **Edit** on the Menu bar, then click **Fade Sharpen More** to open the Fade dialog box, as shown in Figure 34.

3. Drag the **Opacity slider** until **45** appears in the Opacity text box.

   The opacity setting softened the lines applied by the Sharpen More filter.

TIP You may have noticed the Fill list arrow (beneath the Opacity list arrow) on the Layers panel. The Fill list arrow lets you adjust the transparency of a layer (as does the Opacity setting) while ignoring any special effects (such as a drop shadow or stroke) you may have added.

4. Click the **Mode list arrow**, then click **Dissolve**.

   The Dissolve setting blends the surrounding pixels. Zoom in on the image if you need a closer look at the changes.

5. Click **OK**.

6. Save your work, then compare your image to Figure 35.

You applied the Sharpen More filter, then adjusted the opacity and changed the color mode in the Fade dialog box. The edge in the image looks crisper than before, with a greater level of detail.

Figure 34 *Fade dialog box*

Figure 35 *Image settings adjusted*
Source: Morguefile.

Incorporating Color Techniques

Figure 36 *Color Balance dialog box*

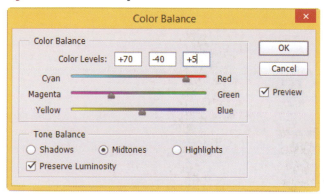

Figure 37 *Image with colors balanced*

Source: Morguefile.

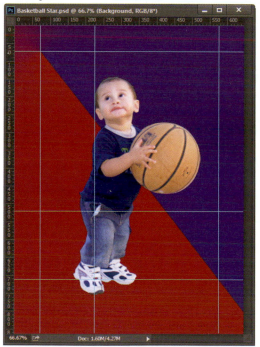

Adjust color balance

1. Switch to the **Basketball Star image**, with the Background layer active, then change the zoom factor to **66.7%**.

   The image you worked with earlier in this chapter becomes active.

2. Click **Image** on the Menu bar, point to **Adjustments**, then click **Color Balance**.

3. Drag the **Cyan-Red slider** until **+70** appears in the first text box.

4. Drag the **Magenta-Green slider** until **−40** appears in the middle text box.

5. Drag the **Yellow-Blue slider** until **+5** appears in the last text box, as shown in Figure 36.

   Subtle changes were made in the color balance in the image.

6. Click **OK**.

7. Save your work, then compare your image to Figure 37.

You balanced the colors in the Basketball Star image by adjusting settings in the Color Balance dialog box.

Match
COLORS

What You'll Do

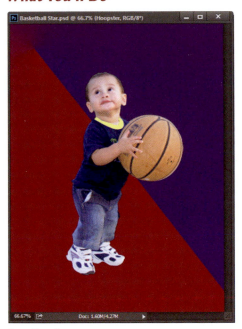

Source: Morguefile.

In this lesson, you'll make selections in source and target images, and then use the Match Color command to replace the target color.

Finding the Right Color

If it hasn't happened already, at some point you'll be working on an image and wish you could grab a color from another image to use in this one. Just as you can use the Eyedropper tool to sample any color in the current image for the foreground and background, you can sample a color from any other image to use in the current one. Perhaps the skin tones in one image look washed out; you can use the Match Color command to replace those tones with skin tone colors from another image. Or maybe the jacket color in one image would look better using a color in another image.

Using Selections to Match Colors

Remember that this is Photoshop, where everything is about layers and selections.

To replace a color in one image with one you've matched from another, you work with—you guessed it—layers and selections.

Suppose you've located the perfect color in another image. The image you are working with is the **target**, and the image that contains your perfect color is the **source**. By activating the layer on which the color lies in the source image, and making a selection around the color, you can have Photoshop match the color in the source and replace a color in the target. To accomplish this, you use the Match Color command, which is available by pointing to Adjustments on the Image menu.

Figure 38 *Selection in source image*

Images © Photodisc/Getty Images.

Selected area

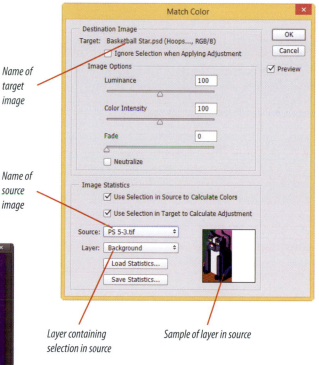

Figure 39 *Match Color dialog box*

Name of
target
image

Name of
source
image

Layer containing
selection in source

Sample of layer in source

Figure 40 *Image with matched color*

Source: Morguefile.

Modified
selection

Match a color

1. Click the **Hoopster layer** on the Layers panel, then zoom (once) into the boy's shirt collar.

2. Click **Select** on the Menu bar, then click **Load Selection**.

3. Click the **Channel list arrow**, click **collar**, then click **OK**.

4. Open PS 5-3.tif from the drive and folder where you store your Data Files, zoom into the image (if necessary), select the Magic Wand tool, change the tolerance to **4**, verify that the **Anti-alias** and **Contiguous check boxes** on the options bar are selected, then click the **yellow part of the cat's eye** (at **105 X/95 Y**) with the **Magic Wand pointer** ✳. Compare your selection to Figure 38.

5. Activate the **Basketball Star image**, click **Image** on the Menu bar, point to **Adjustments**, then click **Match Color**.

6. Click the **Source list arrow**, then click **PS 5-3.tif**. Compare your settings to Figure 39.

7. Click **OK**.

8. Deselect the selection, turn off the rulers and the guides, save your work, then compare your image to Figure 40.

9. Close all open images, display the **Essentials workspace**, then exit Photoshop.

You loaded a saved selection, then used the Match Color dialog box to replace a color in one image with a color from another image. The Match Color dialog box makes it easy to sample colors from other images, giving you even more options for incorporating color into an image.

POWER USER SHORTCUTS			
To do this:	**Use this method:**	**To do this:**	**Use this method:**
Apply a sharpen filter	Filter ➤ Sharpen	Hide or show rulers	[Ctrl][R] (Win) or ⌘ [R] (Mac)
Balance colors	Image ➤ Adjustments ➤ Color Balance	Hide or show the Color panel	[F6]
Change color mode	Image ➤ Mode	Lock transparent pixels check box on/off	[/]
Choose a background color from the Swatches panel	[Ctrl]Color swatch (Win) or ⌘ Color swatch (Mac)	Make Swatches panel active	Window ➤ Swatches
Delete a swatch from the Swatches panel	[Alt], click swatch with ✂ (Win) [option], click swatch with ✂ (Mac)	Paint Bucket tool	🪣 or **G**
Eyedropper tool	💉 or **I**	Return background and foreground colors to default	⬛ or **D**
Fill with background color	[Shift][Backspace] (Win) or ⌘ [delete] (Mac)	Show a layer	⬛
Fill with foreground color	[Alt][Backspace] (Win) or [option][delete] (Mac)	Show hidden Paint Bucket/Gradient tools	[Shift] **G**
Gradient tool	⬛ or **G**	Switch between open files	[Ctrl][Tab] (Win) or [control][tab] (Mac)
Guide pointer	⥮ or ⊣⊢	Switch foreground and background colors	↺ or **X**
Hide a layer	👁		

Key: Menu items are indicated by ➤ between the menu name and its command. Blue bold letters are shortcuts for selecting tools on the Tools panel.

© 2013 Cengage Learning®

Work with color to transform an image.

1. Start Photoshop.
2. Open PS 5-4.psd from the drive and folder where you store your Data Files, then save it as **Firetruck**.
3. Make sure the rulers display in pixels, and that the guides and the default foreground and background colors display.
4. Use the Eyedropper tool to sample the red color at 90 X/165 Y using the guides to help.
5. Use the Paint Bucket tool to apply the new foreground color to the Background layer.
6. Undo your last step using either the Edit menu or the History panel. (*Hint*: You can switch to another workspace that displays the necessary panels.)
7. Switch the foreground and background colors.
8. Save your work.

Use the Color Picker and the Swatches panel.

1. Use the Set foreground color button to open the Color Picker dialog box.
2. Click the R:, G:, and B: option buttons, one at a time. Note how the color panel changes.

3. With the B: option button selected, click the panel in the upper-left corner, then click OK.
4. Switch the foreground and background colors.
5. Add the foreground color (red) to the Swatches panel using a meaningful name of your choice.

Place a border around an image.

1. Make the Firetruck layer active.
2. Revert to the default foreground and background colors.
3. Create a border by applying a 2-pixel outside stroke to the firetruck.
4. Save your work.

Blend colors using the Gradient tool.

1. Change the foreground color to the fourth swatch from the left in the top row of the Swatches panel (RGB Cyan). (Your swatch location may vary.)
2. Switch foreground and background colors.
3. Use the new red swatch that you added previously as the foreground color.
4. Make the Background layer active, and verify that the blending mode is Normal.

5. Use the Gradient tool (Foreground to Background gradient fill) and the Radial Gradient style with its default settings, then using the guides to help, drag the pointer from 90 X/70 Y to 145 X/165 Y.
6. Save your work, and turn off the guides and rulers display.

Add color to a grayscale image.

1. Open PS 5–5.psd, then save it as **Firetruck Colorized**.
2. Change the color mode to RGB Color and flatten the image.
3. Open the Hue/Saturation dialog box, then select the Colorize check box.
4. Drag the sliders so the text boxes show the following values: 200, 56, and −30, then click OK.
5. Save your work.

SKILLS REVIEW
(CONTINUED)

Use filters, opacity, and blending modes.

1. Use the Sharpen filter to sharpen the image.
2. Open the Fade dialog box by using the Edit menu, change the opacity to 60%, change the mode to Overlay, then save your work.
3. Open the Color Balance dialog box.
4. Change the color level settings so the text boxes show the following values: +70, +25, and -15.
5. Turn off the guides and the rulers if necessary.
6. Save your work.

Match colors.

1. Open PS 5-6.tif, then use the Magic Wand tool to select the gray in the cat's left ear.
2. Using Firetruck.psd, select the lightest areas of the firetruck cab. (*Hint*: You can press [Shift] and click multiple areas using the Magic Wand tool.)
3. Use the Match Color dialog box to change the white in the Firetruck layer of the firetruck image to gray (in the cat's ear), then lock the Firetruck layer. Deselect the selection and compare your images to Figure 41. (The brightness of your colors may vary.)
4. Save your work.

Figure 41 *Completed Skills Review*

Image courtesy of Elizabeth Eisner Reding.

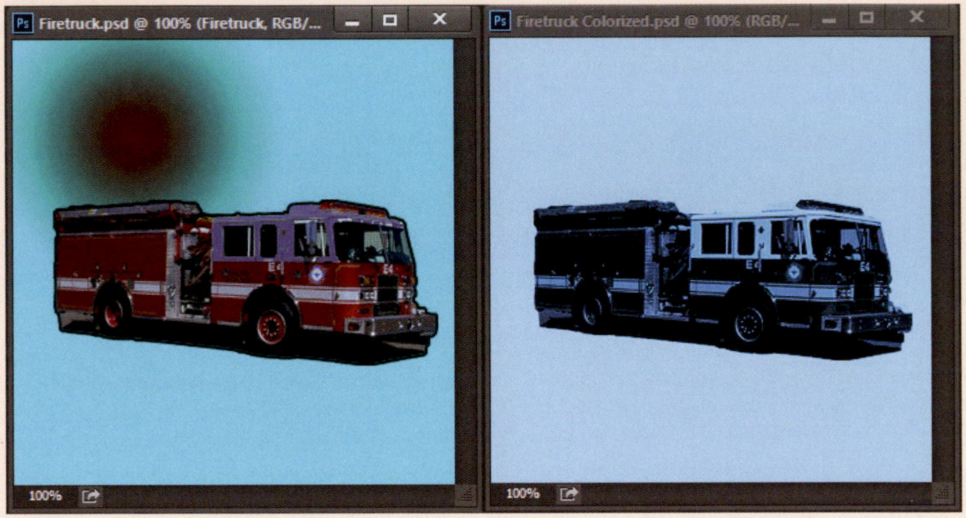

You are finally able to leave your current job and pursue your lifelong dream of opening a fix-it business. While you're waiting for business to increase, you start to work on a website design.

1. Open PS 5-7.psd, then save it as **Fix It!**.
2. Move the objects to any location to achieve a layout you think looks attractive and eye-catching.
3. Sample the blue pliers in the tool belt, then switch the foreground and background colors.
4. Sample another item in the image.
5. Use any Gradient tool to create an interesting effect on the Background layer.
6. Save the image, then compare your screen to the sample shown in Figure 42.

Figure 42 *Sample Project Builder 1*
Images © Photodisc/Getty Images.

You're working on the budget at the PB&J Preschool, when you notice a staff member struggling to redesign the school's website. Although the basic website is complete, it doesn't convey the high energy of the school. You offer to help, and soon find yourself in charge of creating an exciting background for the image.

1. Open PS 5-8.psd, then save it as **Preschool**.
2. Apply a foreground color of your choice to the Background layer.
3. Add a new layer above the Background layer, then select a background color and apply a gradient you have not used before to the layer. (*Hint*: Remember that you can immediately undo a gradient that you don't want.)
4. Add the foreground and background colors to the Swatches panel.
5. Apply a Sharpen filter to the Boy at blackboard layer and adjust the opacity of the filter.
6. Move any objects as you see fit.
7. Save your work.
8. Compare your screen to the sample shown in Figure 43.

Figure 43 *Sample Project Builder 2*
Images © Photodisc/Getty Images.

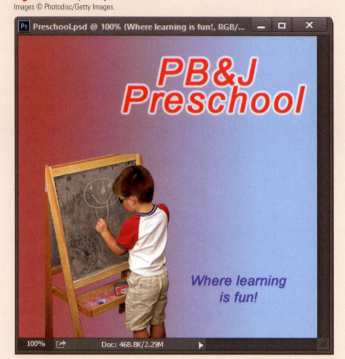

A local Top 40 morning radio show recently conducted a survey about chocolate, and discovered that only one in seven people knew about its health benefits. Now everyone is talking about chocolate. The station's web designer wants to incorporate chocolates into her fall campaign, and has asked you to create a design that will be featured on the radio station's website. You decide to highlight as many varieties as possible.

1. Open PS 5-9.psd, then save it as **Chocolate**.
2. If you choose, you can add any appropriate images that have been scanned or captured using a digital camera.
3. Activate the Background layer, then sample colors from the image for foreground and background colors. (*Hint*: Try to sample unusual colors, to widen your design horizons.)
4. Display the rulers, then move the existing guides to indicate the coordinates of the colors you sampled.
5. Add the sampled colors to the Swatches panel.
6. Create a gradient fill by using both the foreground and background colors and the gradient style of your choice.
7. Defringe the Chocolates layer, if necessary.
8. Hide the rulers and guides, save your work, then compare your image to the sample shown in Figure 44.

Figure 44 *Sample Design Project*
Source: Morguefile.

Incorporating Color Techniques

An educational toy and game store has hired you to create a design that will be used on the company's website to announce this year's Most Unusual Hobby contest. After reviewing the photos from last year's awards ceremony, you decide to build a design using the winner of the Handicrafts Award. You'll use your knowledge of Photoshop color modes to convert the color mode, adjust color in the image, and add a shaded background.

1. Open PS 5-10.psd, then save it as **Rubberband**.
2. Convert the image to Grayscale mode. (*Hint*: When Photoshop prompts you to flatten the layers, click Don't Flatten.)
3. Convert the image to RGB Color mode. (*Hint*: When Photoshop prompts you to flatten the layers, click Don't Flatten.)
4. Colorize the image and adjust the Hue, Saturation, and Lightness settings as desired.
5. Adjust Brightness/Contrast settings as desired.
6. Adjust Color Balance settings as desired.
7. Sample the image to create a new foreground color, then add a color of your choice as the background color.
8. Apply any Sharpen filter and adjust the opacity for that filter.
9. Add a reflected gradient to the Background layer that follows the path of one of the main bands on the ball.
10. Save your work, then compare your image to the sample shown in Figure 45.
11. Be prepared to discuss the color-correcting methods you used and why you chose them.

Figure 45 *Sample Portfolio Project*
Images © Photodisc/Getty Images.

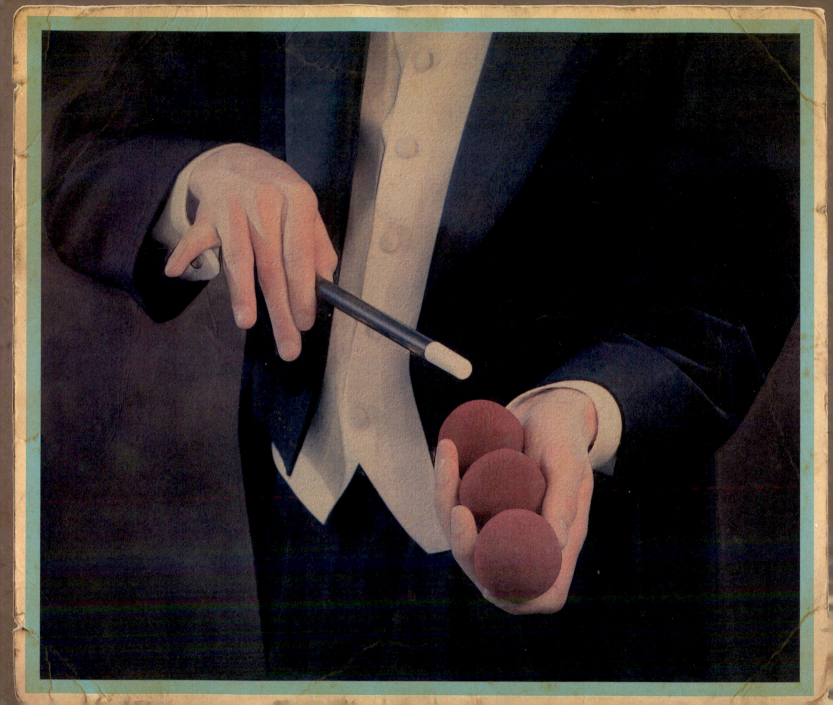

CHAPTER 6 **PLACING TYPE**
IN AN IMAGE

1. Learn about type and how it is created

2. Change spacing and adjust baseline shift

3. Use the Drop Shadow style

4. Apply anti-aliasing to type

5. Modify type with Bevel and Emboss and Extrude to 3D

6. Apply special effects to type using filters

7. Create text on a path

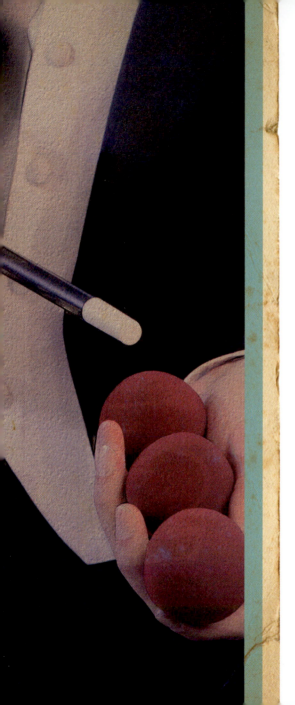

CHAPTER **6** **PLACING TYPE**
IN AN IMAGE

Learning About Type

Text plays an important design role when combined with images for posters, magazine and newspaper advertisements, and other graphics materials that are used to communicate detailed information. In Photoshop, text is referred to as **type**. You can use type to express the ideas conveyed in a file's imagery or to deliver an additional message. You can manipulate type in many ways to reflect or reinforce the meaning behind an image. As in other programs, type has its own unique characteristics in Photoshop. For example, you can change its appearance by using different fonts (also called **typefaces**) and colors.

Understanding the Purpose of Type

Type is typically used along with imagery to deliver a message quickly and with flare. Because type is used sparingly (often there's not a lot of room for it), its appearance is very important; color and imagery are frequently used to *complement* or *reinforce* the message within the text. Type should be limited, direct, and to the point. It should be large enough for easy reading, but should not overwhelm or distract from the central image. For example, a vibrant and daring advertisement should contain just enough type to interest the reader, without demanding too much reading.

Getting the Most Out of Type

Words can express an idea, but the appearance of the type is what drives the point home. After you decide on the content you want to use and create the type, you can experiment with its appearance by changing its **font** (a set of characters with a similar appearance, size, and color). You can also apply special effects that make it stand out or appear to pop off the page.

TOOLS YOU'LL USE

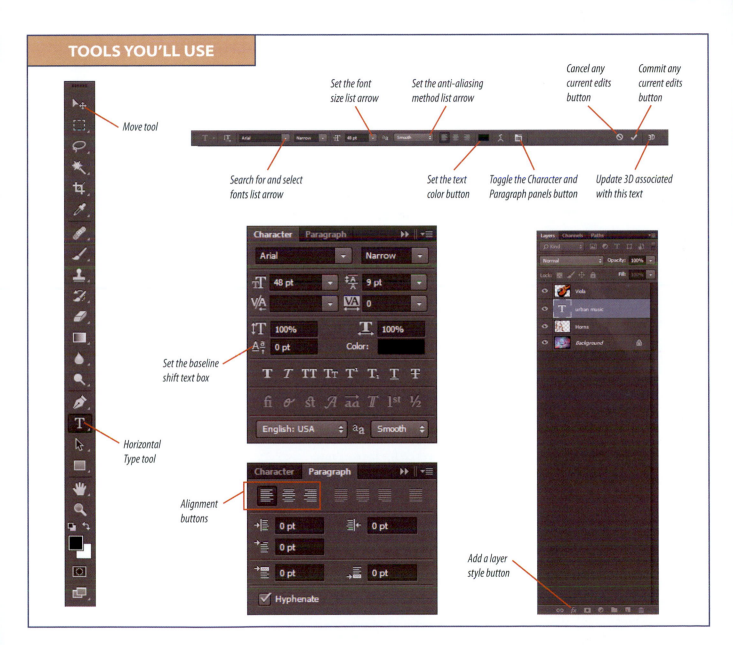

Move tool

Set the font size list arrow

Set the anti-aliasing method list arrow

Cancel any current edits button

Commit any current edits button

Search for and select fonts list arrow

Set the text color button

Toggle the Character and Paragraph panels button

Update 3D associated with this text

Set the baseline shift text box

Horizontal Type tool

Alignment buttons

Add a layer style button

Learn About Type and
HOW IT IS CREATED

What You'll Do

Source: Morguefile.

In this lesson, you'll create a type layer, and then change the font family, size, and color of the type.

Introducing Type Types

Outline type is mathematically defined, which means that it can be scaled to any size without losing its sharp, smooth edges. Some programs, such as Adobe Illustrator, create outline type, also known as **vector fonts**. **Bitmap type** is composed of pixels, and, like bitmap images, can develop jagged edges when enlarged. The type you create in Photoshop is initially outline type, but it is converted into bitmap type when you apply special filters. Using the type tools and the options bar, you can create horizontal or vertical type and modify font size and alignment. You use the Color Picker dialog box to change type color. Each time you create type in Photoshop, it is automatically placed on a new type layer on the Layers panel.

> **QUICK TIP**
>
> Keeping type on separate layers makes it much easier to modify and change its position within the image.

Getting to Know Font Families

Each **font family** represents a complete set of characters, letters, and symbols for a particular typeface. Font families are generally divided into three categories: serif, sans serif, and symbol. Characters in **serif fonts** have a tail, or stroke, at the ends of some characters. These tails make it easier for the eye to recognize words. For this reason, serif fonts are generally used in text passages as in the body text of this book. Emphasized text is a sans serif font. **Sans serif fonts** do not have tails and are commonly used in headlines. **Symbol fonts** are used to display unique characters (such as $, +, or ™). Table 1 lists some commonly used serif and sans serif fonts. After you select the Horizontal Type tool, you can change font families using the options bar.

> **QUICK TIP**
>
> The Verdana typeface was designed to be readable on a computer screen.

Measuring Type Size

The size of each character within a font is measured in **points**. **PostScript**, a programming language that optimizes printed text and graphics, was introduced by Adobe in 1984. In PostScript measurement, one inch is equivalent to 72 points or six picas. Therefore, one pica is equivalent to 12 points. In traditional character measurement, one inch is equivalent to 72.27 points. The default

Photoshop type size is 12 points. In Photoshop, you have the option of using PostScript or traditional character measurement.

Acquiring Fonts

Your computer has many fonts installed on it, but no matter how many fonts you have, you can probably use more. Fonts can be purchased from private companies, individual designers, computer stores, or catalog companies. Fonts are delivered on CD, DVD, or over the Internet from services such as Typekit (as part of your Creative Cloud subscription). Using your favorite search engine and the keywords "type foundry", you can locate websites where you can purchase or download fonts. Many websites offer specialty fonts, while others offer fonts free of charge or for a nominal fee. Figure 1 shows font samples in Photoshop (your list may differ). Notice that an icon may appear to the left of the font name: this indicates the origin or manufacturer of the font.

TABLE 1: COMMONLY USED SERIF AND SANS SERIF FONTS			
Serif fonts	**Sample**	**Sans serif fonts**	**Sample**
Lucida Handwriting	*Adobe Photoshop*	Arial	Adobe Photoshop
Rockwell	**Adobe Photoshop**	Bauhaus	Adobe Photoshop
Times New Roman	Adobe Photoshop	Century Gothic	Adobe Photoshop
Georgia	Adobe Photoshop	Verdana	Adobe Photoshop

© 2015 Cengage Learning®

Figure 1 *Fonts in Photoshop*

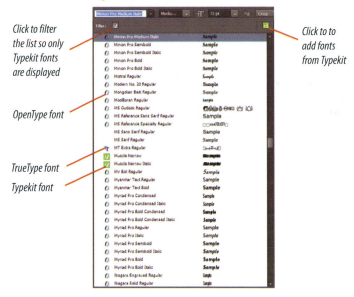

Click to filter the list so only Typekit fonts are displayed

Click to to add fonts from Typekit

OpenType font

TrueType font

Typekit font

Create and modify type

1. Start Photoshop, open PS 6-1.psd from the drive and folder where you store your Data Files, then save the file as **Urban Music**.

2. Display the document size in the status bar, guides, and rulers in pixels (if they are not already displayed), then change the workspace to **Typography**.

TIP You can quickly toggle the rulers on and off by pressing [Ctrl][R] (Win) or ⌘ [R] (Mac).

3. Click the **Default Foreground and Background Colors button** on the Tools panel.

4. Click the **Horizontal Type tool** T on the Tools panel.

5. Click the **Search for and select fonts list arrow** on the options bar, click **Arial Regular** (a sans serif font), click the **Set the font style list arrow**, then click **Italic**.

TIP If Arial is not available, make a reasonable substitution.

6. Click the **Set the font size list arrow** on the options bar, then click **48 pt**.

7. Click the **image** with the **Horizontal Type pointer** at approximately **430 X/510 Y**, then type **Live Music** as shown in Figure 2.

TIP It's okay if your text falls above or below the guide line.

You created a type layer by using the Horizontal Type tool on the Tools panel and modified the font family, font style, and font size.

Figure 2 *New type in image*
Source: Morguefile.

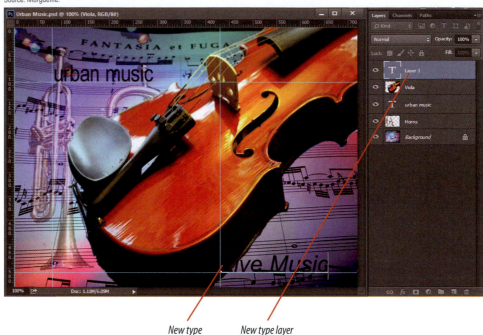

New type   New type layer

NEW Curing the Missing Font Blues

On occasion, you may see a dialog box telling you that the file you've opened in Photoshop contains fonts that are missing from your computer. Remember Typekit? That's the service available to Creative Cloud subscribers that contains hundreds of fonts. When you open an existing image, Photoshop automatically checks to see if any fonts within the document are available on your computer. If they are available, then everything is fine and the document opens. If they are not available, Photoshop checks Typekit to see if they (or a reasonable match) are available. If a match is found in Typekit, a dialog box will display asking if you want to replace the missing font with the Typekit font. And voilà! Your fonts are updated!

Figure 3 *Type with new color*

Source: Morguefile.

Type with
new color

Using the Swatches Panel to Change Type Color

You can also use the Swatches panel to change type color. Select the type, and then click a color on the Swatches panel. The new color that you click will appear in the Set foreground color button on the Tools panel and will be applied to type that is currently selected.

Change type color using an existing color in the image

1. Press [**Ctrl**][**A**] (Win) or ⌘ [**A**] (Mac) to select all the text.

2. Click the **Search for and select fonts list arrow** on the options bar, scroll down, then click **Times New Roman Regular**.

   TIP Click *in* the Set the font family text box and you can select a different font by typing the first few characters of the font name.

3. Click the **Set the font style list arrow**, then click **Bold Italic**.

4. Click the **Set the text color button** on the options bar.

   As you position the pointer over the image, the pointer automatically becomes an Eyedropper pointer.

5. Reposition the Color Picker (Text Color) dialog box if necessary, then click the **image** with the **Eyedropper pointer** anywhere in the orange area of the viola at approximately **250 X/250 Y**.

   The new color is now the active color in the Color Picker (Text Color) dialog box.

6. Click **OK** in the Color Picker (Text Color) dialog box.

7. Click the **Commit any current edits button** on the options bar.

   Click the Commit any current edits button to accept your changes and make them permanent.

8. Save your work, then compare your image to Figure 3.

You changed the font family, modified the color of the type by using an existing image color, and committed the current edits.

Change Spacing and ADJUST BASELINE SHIFT

What You'll Do

Source: Morguefile.

In this lesson, you'll adjust the spacing between characters, change the baseline of type, and then apply the same style to two different characters.

Adjusting Letter Spacing

Competition for readers on the visual landscape is fierce. To get and maintain an edge over other designers, Photoshop provides tools that let you make adjustments to your type, offering you the opportunity to make your type more distinctive. These adjustments might not be very dramatic, but they can influence readers in subtle ways. For example, type that is too small and difficult to read might make the reader impatient (at the very least), and he or she might not even look at the image (at the very worst). You can make finite adjustments, called **type spacing**, to the space between characters and between lines of type. Adjusting type spacing affects the ease with which words are read.

Understanding Character and Line Spacing

Fonts in desktop publishing and word-processing programs use proportional letter spacing, whereas typewriters use monotype spacing. In **monotype spacing**, each character occupies the same amount of space. This means that wide characters such as "o" and "w" take up the same real estate on the page as narrow ones such as "i" and "l". In **proportional spacing**, each character can take up a different amount of space, depending on its width. **Kerning** controls the amount of space between two characters and can affect several characters, a word, or an entire paragraph. **Tracking** inserts a *uniform* amount of space between selected characters. Figure 4 shows an example of type before and after it has been kerned. The second line of text takes up less room and has less space between its characters, making it easier to read. You can also change the amount of space, called **leading**, between lines of type, to add or decrease the distance between lines of text.

Using the Character Panel

The **Character panel**, shown in Figure 5, helps you manually or automatically control type properties such as kerning, tracking, and leading. You open the Character panel from the Type tool options bar, the icon dock, or from the Window menu on the Menu bar.

> **QUICK TIP**
>
> Click the Search for and select fonts list arrow on the options bar or Character panel to see previews of installed fonts.

Understanding Type Styles

You've probably noticed that within any publication you'll see certain formatting similarities occurring repeatedly. Since many people may be collaborating to make a publication possible, styles are often used to ensure consistency. A **style** is a collection of formatting attributes that can be saved and applied to specific characters or an entire paragraph. Perhaps a magazine has a five space indent at the start of each paragraph, or maybe sidebars that occur on certain pages have the same horizontal line spacing and justification. Photoshop allows you to define both character and paragraph styles that can be applied at any time. You can create and apply type styles by clicking Window on the Menu bar, then clicking either Character Styles or Paragraph Styles. Figure 6 shows the Paragraph Styles panel with two customized styles.

Creating a paragraph or character style is easy: for a paragraph, place your cursor anywhere within the paragraph containing the attributes you want and click the Create new paragraph style button at the bottom of the Paragraph Styles panel. The attributes in that paragraph will automatically be reflected in the Paragraph Style Options dialog box. For a character style, select type containing the attributes you want to preserve and reuse, then click the Create new character style button at the bottom of the Character Styles panel. This method is sometimes referred to as *style by example*. In the case of a new paragraph or character style, you are always free to define your attributes in the Paragraph Style Options dialog box or Character Style Options dialog box *without* first making a paragraph or character selection.

Adjusting the Baseline Shift

Type rests on an invisible line called a **baseline**. Using the Character panel, you can adjust the **baseline shift**, the vertical distance that type moves from its baseline. You can add interest to type by changing the baseline shift. Negative adjustments to the baseline move characters *below* the baseline, while positive adjustments move characters *above* the baseline.

QUICK TIP

Clicking the Set the text color button on either the options bar or the Character panel opens the Color Picker (Text Color) dialog box.

Figure 5 *Character panel*

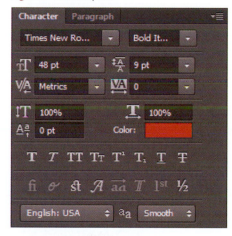

Figure 4 *Kerned characters*

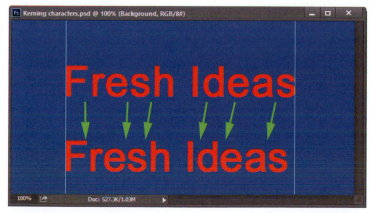

Figure 6 *Paragraph Styles panel*

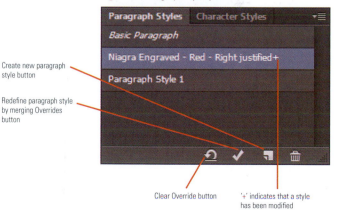

Create new paragraph style button

Redefine paragraph style by merging Overrides button

Clear Override button

'+' indicates that a style has been modified

Kern characters

1. Verify that the **Live Music type layer** is active and that the Horizontal Type tool is selected.

2. Click **between "L" and "i"** in the word "Live."

TIP Many of the changes you make throughout Photoshop will be subtle. Don't be disappointed when you only see slight change in your image. Those slight improvements add up, and you'll find that you might invest hours in individual details that no one notices. Taken together, these tweaks can take an image from blah to brilliant.

3. Click the **Set the kerning between two characters list arrow** on the Character panel, then click **–50**.

   The spacing between the two characters decreases.

TIP You can close the Character panel by clicking the Panel options button in the upper-right corner of its title bar, then clicking the Close command. You can also open and close the Character panel by clicking the Character icon on the dock if it's displayed, or by clicking the Character tab in the Character panel.

4. Click **between "M" and "u"** in the word "Music," as shown in Figure 7.

5. Click the **list arrow**, then click **–25**.

6. Click the **Commit any current edits button** on the options bar.

You modified the kerning between characters by using the Character panel.

Figure 7 *Kerned type*
Source: Morguefile.

Kerned type

Kerning adjustment

Correcting Spelling Errors

Are you concerned that your gorgeous image will be ruined by misspelled words? Photoshop understands your pain and has included a spelling checker to make sure you are never plagued by incorrect spellings. If you want, the spelling checker will check the type on the current layer, or on all the layers in the image. First, make sure the correct dictionary for your language is selected on the Character panel. English: USA is the default, but you can choose another language by clicking the Set the language on selected characters for hyphenation and spelling list arrow at the bottom of the panel. To check spelling, click Edit on the Menu bar, and then click Check Spelling. The spelling checker will automatically stop at each word not already appearing in the dictionary. One or more suggestions might be offered, which you can either accept or reject. (Note: The spelling checker does not correct for incorrect usage, such as their, there, and they're.)

Figure 8 *Character Style Options dialog box*

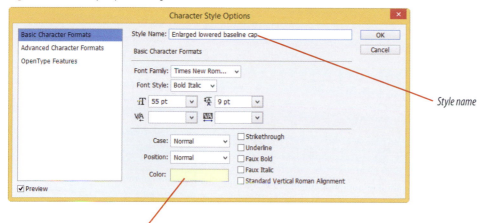

Style name

New font color

Figure 9 *Type with baseline shifted*
Source: Morguefile.

Lesson 2   Change Spacing and Adjust Baseline Shift

Shift the baseline

1. Use the **Horizontal Type pointer** to select the **"L"** in **"Live"**, then click the **Set the text color button** on the options bar.

2. Click **anywhere in the yellow area** in the center of the viola, such as **470 X/200**, then click **OK**.

3. Verify that the **"L"** in **"Live"** is selected, double-click **48** in the Set the font size text box on the Character panel, type **55**, double-click **0** in the Set the baseline shift text box on the Character panel, type **−5**, then click the **Commit any current edits button** on the options bar.

4. Select the **"L"** in **"Live"**, click the **Character Styles tab**, then click the **Create new Character Style button** on the Character Styles panel.

5. Double-click the name **Character Style 1** in the Character Styles panel, type **Enlarged lowered baseline cap** in the Style Name text box in the Character Style Options dialog box, as shown in Figure 8, then click **OK**.

TIP The application of a character style requires that you override the existing paragraph style by clicking the Clear Override button.

6. Select the **"M"** in **"Music"** with the **Horizontal Type pointer**, click **Enlarged lowered baseline cap** in the Character Styles panel, click **Clear Override** on the Character Styles panel, then click on the options bar. The "M" is *painted* with the same characteristics you created in the "L".

7. Save your work, compare your screen to Figure 9.

You changed the type color, adjusted the baseline of the first character in a word to make the first character stand out, created a character style, then applied the style to another character.

Use the
DROP SHADOW STYLE

What You'll Do

Source: Morguefile.

 In this lesson, you'll apply the drop shadow style to a type layer, and then modify drop shadow settings.

Adding Effects to Type

Layer styles (effects which can be applied to a type or image layer) can greatly enhance the appearance of type and improve its effectiveness. A type layer is indicated by the appearance of the T icon in the layer's thumbnail box on the Layers panel. When a layer style is applied to any layer, the Indicates layer effects icon (*fx*) appears in that layer when it is active. The Layers panel is a great source of information. You can see which effects have been applied to a layer by clicking the arrow to the right of the Indicates layer effects icon on the Layers panel whether the layer is active or inactive. Figure 10 shows a type layer that has a layer style applied to it. Layer styles are linked to the contents of a layer, which means that if a type layer is moved or modified, the layer's style will still be applied to the type.

Figure 10 *Effect applied to a type layer*

Layer styles applied

Indicates effect(s) applied in layer

Placing Type in an Image

Applying a Style

You can apply a style, such as a drop shadow, to the active layer, by clicking Layer on the Menu bar, pointing to Layer Style, and then clicking a style. The settings in the Layer Style dialog box are "sticky," meaning that they display the settings that you last used. An alternative method to using the Menu bar is to select the layer on the Layers panel that you want to apply the style to, click the Add a layer style button, and then click a style. Regardless of which method you use, the Layer Style dialog box opens. You use this dialog box to add all kinds of effects to type. Depending on which style you've chosen, the Layer Style dialog box displays options appropriate to that style.

QUICK TIP

You can apply styles to objects as well as to type.

Using the Drop Shadow

One method of placing emphasis on type is to add a drop shadow to it. A **drop shadow** creates an illusion that another colored layer of identical text is behind the selected type. The drop shadow default color is black, but it can be changed to another color using the Color Picker dialog box, or any of the other methods for changing color.

Controlling a Drop Shadow

You can control many aspects of a drop shadow's appearance, including its angle, its distance behind the type, the amount of blur it contains, and its opacity. The **angle** indicates the direction of the light source and determines where the shadow falls relative to the text, and the **distance** determines how far the shadow falls from the text. The **spread** determines the width of the shadow text, and the **size** determines the clarity of the shadow. Figure 11 shows samples of two different drop shadow effects. The first line of type uses the default background color (black), has an angle of 160 degrees, a distance of 10 pixels, a spread of 0%, and a size of five pixels. The second line of type uses a purple background color, has an angle of 120 degrees, a distance of 20 pixels, a spread of 10%, and a size of five pixels. As you modify the drop shadow, the preview window displays the changes.

Figure 11 *Sample drop shadows*

Add a drop shadow

1. Click the **layer thumbnail** on the urban music type layer.

2. Double-click **48** in the Set the font size text box in the Character panel, type **55**, then press [**Enter**] (Win) or [**return**] (Mac).

3. Click the **Add a layer style button** *fx*, on the Layers panel.

4. Click **Drop Shadow**.

5. Compare your Layer Style dialog box to Figure 12, and *do not close* the dialog box. (The settings are Blend Mode = Multiply, Opacity = 75, Angle = 30, Distance = 5, Spread = 0, Size = 5.)

   The default drop shadow settings are applied to the type. Table 2 describes the drop shadow settings.

TIP You can also open the Layer Style dialog box by double-clicking a layer on the Layers panel.

You created a drop shadow by using the Add a layer style button on the Layers panel and the Layer Style dialog box.

Figure 12 *Drop shadow settings*
Source: Morguefile.

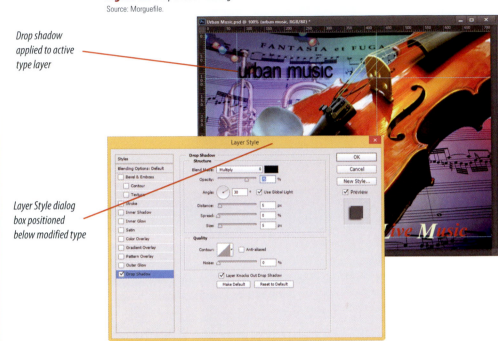

Drop shadow applied to active type layer

Layer Style dialog box positioned below modified type

TABLE 2: DROP SHADOW SETTINGS		
Setting	**Scale**	**Explanation**
Opacity	0–100%	Controls the opacity of the shadow. At 0%, the shadow is invisible.
Angle	0–360 degrees	At 0 degrees, the shadow appears on the baseline of the original text. At 90 degrees, the shadow appears directly below the original text.
Distance	0–30,000 pixels	A larger pixel size increases the distance from which the shadow text falls relative to the original text.
Spread	0–100%	A larger percentage increases the width of the shadow text.
Size	0–250 pixels	A larger pixel size increases the blur of the shadow text.

© 2015 Cengage Learning®

Placing Type in an Image

Figure 13 *Layer Style dialog box*

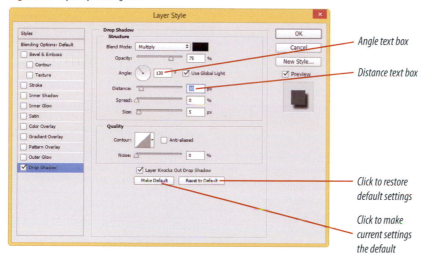

Angle text box

Distance text box

Click to restore default settings

Click to make current settings the default

Figure 14 *Drop shadow added to type layer*
Source: Morguefile.

Drop shadow appears behind text

Collapses effect(s) applied to layer

Modify drop shadow settings

1. Double-click the **number in the Angle text box**, then type **130**.

   Each style in the Layer Style dialog box shows different options in the center section. These options are displayed as you select each style from the Styles pane on the left.

TIP You can also set the angle by dragging the dial slider.

2. Double-click the **number in the Distance text box**, then type **10**. See Figure 13.

TIP You can create your own layer style in the Layer Style dialog box, by choosing your style options, clicking New Style, typing a new name or accepting the default, then clicking OK. Click Styles (at the top of the left pane), and the new style appears as a preset in the Styles list of the Layer Style dialog box. You can create a new style, rename, or delete a style from the list of presets by right-clicking the preset you want to change.

3. Click **OK**, then compare your screen to Figure 14.

4. Click the **Reveals layers effects in the panel arrow**, located to the right of the Indicates layer effects icon on the urban music layer, to collapse the list of layer styles.

5. Save your work.

You used the Layer Style dialog box to modify the settings for the drop shadow.

Apply Anti-Aliasing
TO TYPE

What You'll Do

Source: Morguefile.

 In this lesson, you'll view the effects of the anti-aliasing feature, and then use the History panel to return the type to its original state.

Eliminating the "Jaggies"

In the good old days of dot-matrix printers, jagged edges were obvious in many print ads. You can still see these jagged edges in designs produced on less sophisticated printers. To prevent the jagged edges (sometimes called "jaggies") that often accompany bitmap type, Photoshop offers an anti-aliasing feature. **Anti-aliasing** partially fills in pixel edges with additional colors, resulting in smooth-edge type and an increased number of colors in the image. Anti-aliasing is useful for improving the display of large type in print media; however, this can increase the file size.

Knowing When to Apply Anti-Aliasing

As a rule, type that has a point size greater than 12 should have some anti-aliasing method applied. Sometimes, smaller type sizes can become blurry or muddy when anti-aliasing is used. As part of the process, anti-aliasing adds intermediate colors to your image in an effort to reduce the jagged edges. As a designer, you need to weigh these three factors (type size, file size, and image quality) when determining if you should apply anti-aliasing.

DESIGN**TIP**

Using Type on the Web

While any typeface you use affects your reader, your choice of type has a larger impact on the web because it is more interactive than the print media. Since the goal of a website is to make your reader linger as long as possible, do you really want to offend or annoy that person with an ugly typeface? Of course not. So, you want to make sure that the typeface is not only appropriate, but can be seen as you intended.

In many cases, a typeface can only be seen on a web page if that font is installed on the reader's computer. Web-safe typefaces (which most computers can display with accuracy) are Times New Roman, Arial, Arial Black, or Helvetica (Mac), Lucida Console, Lucida Sans Unicode, Palatino Linotype, Book Antiqua, Verdana, and Comic Sans. There are other typefaces that can be downloaded from a variety of websites for free, such as Georgia and Trebuchet.

Understanding Anti-Aliasing

Anti-aliasing improves the display of type against the background. You can use five anti-aliasing methods: None, Sharp, Crisp, Strong, and Smooth. An example of each method is shown in Figure 15. The **None** setting applies no anti-aliasing, and can result in type that has jagged edges. The **Sharp** setting displays type with the best possible resolution. The **Crisp** setting gives type more definition and makes type appear sharper. The **Strong** setting makes type appear heavier, much like the bold attribute. The **Smooth** setting gives type more rounded edges.

Figure 15 *Anti-aliasing effects*

Anti-aliasing method: None

Anti-aliasing method: Sharp

Anti-aliasing method: Crisp

Anti-aliasing method: Strong

Anti-aliasing method: Smooth

Apply anti-aliasing

1. Double-click the **layer thumbnail** on the urban music layer to select the text, and verify that the Set the text color box displays yellow.
2. Click the **Set the anti-aliasing method list arrow** on the options bar.

TIP You've probably noticed that some items, such as the Set the anti-aliasing method list arrow, the Set the text color button, and the Set the font size list arrow are duplicated on the options bar and the Character panel. So which should you use? Whichever one you feel most comfortable using. These tasks are performed identically regardless of the feature's origin.

3. Click **Crisp**.
4. Click the **Commit any current edits button** on the options bar, then compare your work to Figure 16.

You applied the Crisp anti-aliasing setting to see how the setting affected the appearance of type.

Figure 16 *Effect of Crisp anti-aliasing*

Source: Morguefile.

Different Strokes for Different Folks

You're probably already aware that you can use multiple methods to achieve the same goals in Photoshop. For instance, if you want to see the Type options bar so you can edit a type layer, you can either double-click a type layer thumbnail or select the type layer and then click the Horizontal Type tool. The method you use determines what you'll see in the History panel.

Figure 17 *Deleting a state from the History panel*

Dragging state to Delete current state button

Undo anti-aliasing

1. Click **Legacy** in the workspace switcher.

   The History panel is now visible.

   TIP You can also display the History panel by clicking the History icon on the dock (if it's displayed). Once displayed, you can collapse the panel by clicking the Panel options button, then clicking Close.

2. Click the **Edit Type Layer state** listed at the bottom of the History panel, then drag it to the **Delete current state button**, as shown in Figure 17.

   Various methods of undoing actions are reviewed in Table 3.

   TIP Use the Undo command to undo the last edit, while using the Step Backward command lets you undo the last 20 edits you've done, one at a time. The Step Backward command is found on the Edit menu.

3. Return the workspace to the **Typography workspace**.

4. Save your work.

You changed the workspace to complete a specific task, deleted a state in the History panel to return the type to its original appearance, then changed the workspace again. The History panel offers an easy way of undoing previous steps.

TABLE 3: UNDOING ACTIONS		
Method	**Description**	**Shortcut**
Undo	Edit ➤ Undo	[Ctrl][Z] (Win) ⌘ [Z] (Mac)
Step Backward	Click Edit on the Menu bar, then click Step Backward	[Alt][Ctrl][Z] (Win) [option] ⌘ [Z] (Mac)
History panel	Drag state to the Delete current state button on the History panel, [Ctrl]-click or right-click state, then click [Delete], or click the Delete current state button on the History panel	[Alt] 🗑 (Win) [option] 🗑 (Mac)

© 2015 Cengage Learning®

Modify Type with Bevel and Emboss
AND EXTRUDE TO 3D

What You'll Do

Source: Morguefile.

 In this lesson, you'll apply the Bevel and Emboss style, modify the Bevel and Emboss settings, and then apply 3D Extrusion to a type layer.

Using the Bevel and Emboss Style

You use the Bevel and Emboss style to add combinations of shadows and highlights to a layer and make type appear to have dimension and shine. You can use the Layer menu or the Layers panel to apply the Bevel and Emboss style to the active layer. Like all Layer styles, the Bevel and Emboss style is linked to the type layer to which it is applied.

Understanding Bevel and Emboss Settings

You can use two categories of Bevel and Emboss settings: structure and shading. **Structure** determines the size and physical properties of the object, and **shading** determines the lighting effects. The shading used in the Bevel and Emboss style determines how and where light is projected on the type. You can control a variety of settings, including the angle, altitude, and gloss contour, to create a unique appearance. The **angle** setting indicates the direction of the light source and determines where the shadow falls relative to the text, and the **altitude** setting affects the amount of visible dimension. For example, an altitude of 0 degrees looks flat, while a setting of 90 degrees has a more three-dimensional appearance. The **gloss contour** setting determines the pattern with which light is reflected, and the **highlight mode** and **shadow mode** settings determine how pigments are combined. When the Use Global Light check box is selected, *all the type in the image* will be affected by your changes.

Filling Type with Imagery

You can use the imagery from a layer in one file as the fill pattern for another image's type layer. To create this effect, open a multilayer file that contains the imagery you want to use (the source), and then open the file that contains the type you want to fill (the target). In the source file, activate the layer containing the imagery you want to use, use the Select menu to select all, and then use the Edit menu to copy the selection. In the target file, press [Ctrl] (Win) or ⌘ (Mac) while clicking the layer thumbnail to which the imagery will be applied, click Edit on the Menu bar, point to Paste Special, and then click Paste Into. The imagery will appear within the type.

Learning About 3D Extrusion

3D Extrusion, formally called Repoussé (pronounced re-poo-say) is a tool for turning a 2-dimensional object (like type) into a 3-dimensional object. Extrusion tools allow you to rotate, roll, pan, slide, and scale an object, and this feature has a number of presets that help you learn its many uses. You can apply Extrusion to a type layer or image layer using the Type command on the Menu bar or the 3D panel or the 3D workspace. (Applying Extrusion to a type layer automatically rasterizes the type, a process that is covered in more detail later in this chapter.) With a existing type layer active and the 3D workspace open, click the 3D Extrusion option button (under Create New 3D Object) in the 3D panel, then click the Create button.

Each 3D extruded object displays on the image (sometimes on a grid or mesh), shown in Figure 18. A secondary window can be toggled, showing either the text in the document or by itself. Objects within the image are clickable, and when clicked, reveal **widgets** (tools that can be used to change the 3D object). Widgets exist for light, movement, and camera, to name a few. As you click on various elements within the image, take note that the Properties panel changes to reflect the active element.

Once you are finished adjusting the 3D settings, the image must be **rendered** for those settings to be applied to the image. The rendering process may take several minutes to complete: the amount of time remaining displays in the status bar at the bottom of the document window and a blue dotted line displays on the image indicating the rendering status.

QUICK TIP

Any formatting such as bold or italics, effects like a drop shadow or bevel, or warping can be applied to a 3D extrusion.

Elements with the image can be shown/hidden using the Show command on the View menu.

QUICK TIP

As you might imagine, 3D features are extremely memory- and hardware-intensive. 3D will not work if your computer does not have a GPU card, with a minimum of 512MB of Video RAM (VRAM). Please consult *www.adobe.com* for a list of supported video cards and requirements.

Figure 18 *3D Extrusion object*

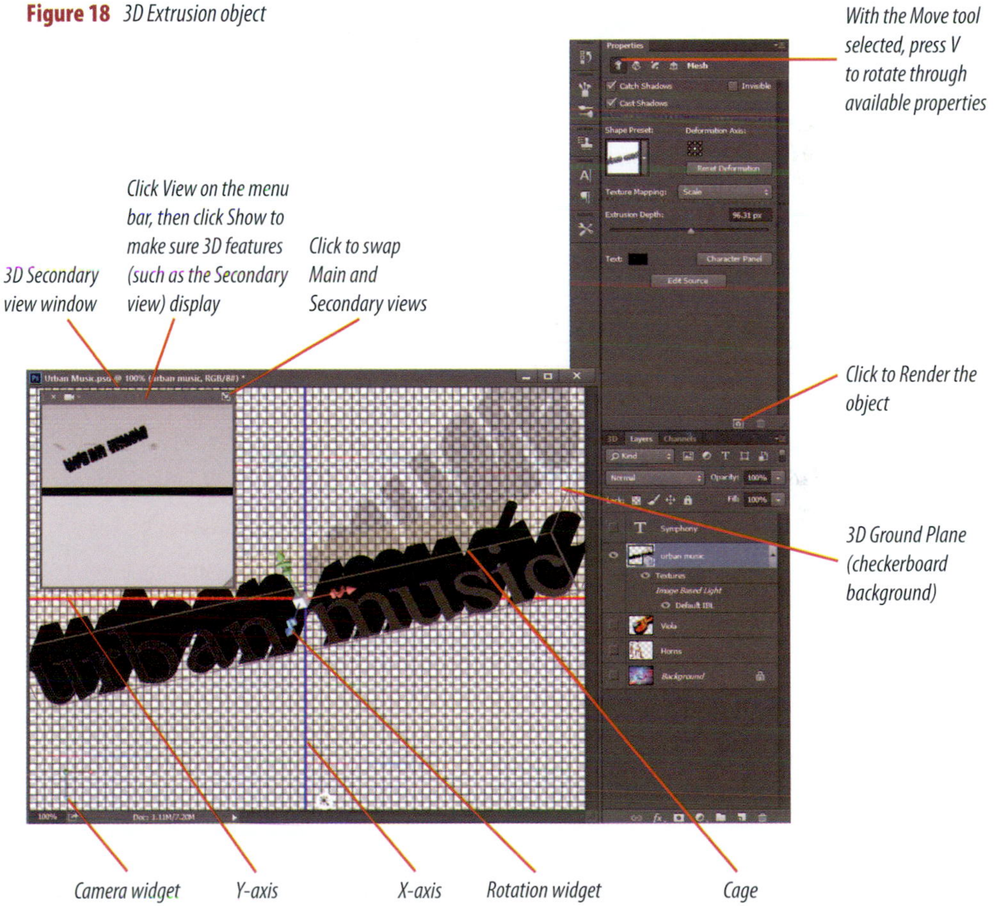

With the Move tool selected, press V to rotate through available properties
Click View on the menu bar, then click Show to make sure 3D features (such as the Secondary view) display
3D Secondary view window
Click to swap Main and Secondary views
Click to Render the object
3D Ground Plane (checkerboard background)
Camera widget
Y-axis
X-axis
Rotation widget
Cage

Add the Bevel and Emboss style with the Layer menu

1. Click the **Live Music layer** and verify that the Horizontal Type tool is active.

2. Click the **Set the text color button** ■ on the options bar, click the **pink area below the left horn** (at approximately **80 X/510 Y**), then click **OK**.

3. Click **Layer** on the Menu bar, point to **Layer Style**, click **Bevel & Emboss**.

4. Review the Layer Style dialog box shown in Figure 19, copying the settings shown to your dialog box, then move the Layer Style dialog box so that you can see the "Live Music" type, if necessary.

You applied the Bevel and Emboss style by using the Layer menu. This gave the text a three-dimensional look.

Figure 19 *Layer Style dialog box*

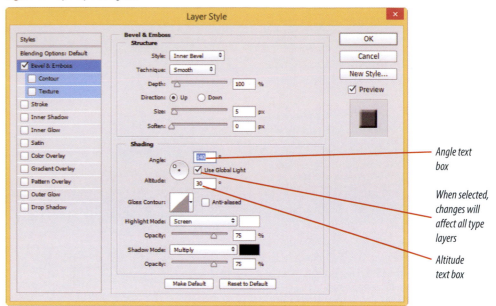

Angle text box

When selected, changes will affect all type layers

Altitude text box

Understanding GPU and OpenGL

Photoshop CC uses the GPU (graphics processing unit) rather than the main processor within your computer to speed screen redraw. (You can tell if your computer has OpenGL (Open Graphics Library) enabled by opening Preferences in Photoshop, clicking Performance, and then looking at the Graphics Processor Settings. If Use Graphics Processor is dimmed, your computer **does not** have OpenGL enabled or your graphics board may not be supported.) Once the GPU technology is detected, Photoshop automatically turns on the OpenGL technology which communicates with your display driver. OpenGL is necessary in Photoshop to operate many features, including 3D Extrusion, brush dynamic resize and hardness control, 3D overlays, 3D Acceleration, 3D Axis, Accelerated 3D Interaction via Direct to Screen, 3D Ground Plane, and 3D Selections via a Hi-light Overlay. In short, *no OpenGL means no 3D.*

Placing Type in an Image

Figure 20 *3D grid over type layer*
Source: Morguefile.

Figure 21 *3D Extrusion applied to type*
Source: Morguefile.

3D extrusion
applied to
layer

Thumbnail
indicates a
3D layer

Modify Bevel and Emboss settings and apply 3D Extrusion

1. Double-click the **number in the Angle text box**, then type **165**.

   You can use the Layer Style dialog box to change the structure of the bevel by adjusting style, technique, depth, direction, size, and soften settings.

2. Double-click the **Altitude text box**, then type **20**.

3. Click **OK**, then note the expanded Live Music layer in the Layers panel.

4. Click the **urban music layer** on the Layers panel.

   If you do not have OpenGL enabled on your computer, proceed to step 9.

5. Click **Type** on the Menu bar, click **Extrude to 3D**, click **Yes** to switch to the 3D workspace, drag the Secondary view out of the way if it obscures the type, then compare your screen to Figure 20.

6. If necessary, click the **Drag the 3D Object** ⊕ on the options bar, position the pointer ✛ **between the "n" and "m"**, then drag the type horizontally **to the right** until the "m" is at approximately **250X**.

7. Click the **Render button** 🖼 at the bottom of the Properties panel.

8. Click **View** on the Menu bar, point to **Show**, deselect any 3D options, then display the **Typography workspace**.

9. Save your work, turn off the ruler display, then compare your image to Figure 21.

You modified the default settings for the Bevel and Emboss style, then applied 3D Extrusion to a layer. Experimenting with different settings is crucial to achieve the effect you want.

Apply Special Effects to Type
USING FILTERS

What You'll Do

In this lesson, you'll rasterize a type layer, and then apply a filter to it to change its appearance.

Understanding Filters

Like an image layer, a type layer can have one or more filters applied to it to achieve special effects and make your text look unique, as shown in Figure 22. Some filters are available in the Filter Gallery while others have dialog boxes with preview windows that let you see the results of the particular filter before it is applied to the layer. Other filters must be applied to the layer before you can see the results. Before a filter can be applied to a type layer, the type layer must first be **rasterized**, or converted to an image layer. After it is rasterized, the type characters *can no longer be edited* because it is composed of pixels, just like artwork. When a type layer is rasterized, the T icon in the layer thumbnail becomes an image thumbnail while the Effects icons remain. Notice that none of the original type layers on the Layers panel in Figure 22 display the T icon in the layer thumbnail.

QUICK TIP

Because you cannot edit type after it has been rasterized, you should save your original type by making a copy of the layer *before* you rasterize it, and then hide it from view. This allows you to use the copy if you need to make changes to the type at a later time.

Producing Distortions

Distort filters let you create waves or curves in type. Some of the types of distortions you can produce include Pinch, Polar Coordinates, Ripple, Shear, Spherize, Twirl, Wave, and Zigzag. These effects are sometimes used as the basis of a corporate logo. The Twirl dialog box, shown in Figure 23, lets you determine the amount of twirl effect you want to apply. By dragging the Angle slider, you control how much twirl effect is added to a layer. Most filter dialog boxes have Zoom in and Zoom out buttons that make it easy to see the effects of the filter.

Using Relief

Many filters let you create the appearance of textures and **relief** (the height of ridges within an object). One of the Stylize filters, Wind, applies lines throughout the type, making it appear shredded. The Wind dialog box, shown in Figure 24, lets you determine the kind of wind and its direction.

Blurring Imagery

The Gaussian Blur filter, one of the Blur filter options, softens the appearance of type by blurring its edge pixels. You can control the amount of blur applied to the type by entering high or low values in the Gaussian Blur dialog box. The higher the blur value, the blurrier the effect.

QUICK TIP

Be careful: too much blur applied to type can make it unreadable.

Figure 22 *Sample filters applied to type*

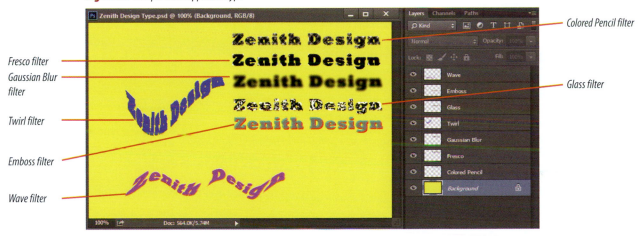

Colored Pencil filter

Fresco filter

Gaussian Blur filter

Twirl filter

Glass filter

Emboss filter

Wave filter

Figure 23 *Twirl dialog box*

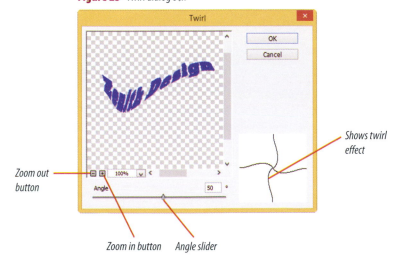

Shows twirl effect

Zoom out button

Zoom in button   Angle slider

Figure 24 *Wind dialog box*

Lesson 6   Apply Special Effects to Type Using Filters

Apply a filter to a type layer

1. Click the **Live Music** layer on the Layers panel.
2. Click **Filter** on the Menu bar, point to **Stylize**, then click **Diffuse**.
3. Click **OK** to rasterize the type and close the warning box shown in Figure 25.

   TIP You can also rasterize a type layer by clicking Layer on the Menu bar, pointing to Rasterize, then clicking Type.

   The Diffuse dialog box opens.

   You rasterized a type layer in preparation for applying a filter.

Figure 25 *Warning box*

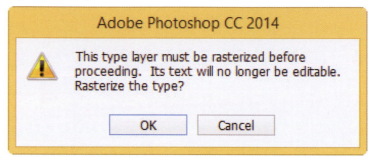

DESIGN**TIP**

Using Multiple Filters

Sometimes, adding one filter doesn't achieve the effect you had in mind. You can use multiple filters to create a unique effect. Before you try your hand at filters, though, it's a good idea to make a copy of the original layer. That way, if things don't turn out as you planned, you can always start over. You don't even have to write down which filters you used, because you can always look at the History panel to review which filters you applied.

Placing Type in an Image

Figure 26 *Type with Diffuse filter*
Source: Morguefile.

1. Drag in the preview window of the dialog box from the bottom to position the type so at least part of the type is visible.
2. Click the **Darken Only** and **Lighten Only option buttons**, notice the difference each makes, then click the **Normal option button**.
3. Click **OK**.
4. Save your work. Compare your modified type to Figure 26.

You modified the Diffuse filter settings to modify the appearance of the layer.

Creating a Neon Glow

Want to create a really cool effect that takes absolutely no time at all, and works on both type and objects? You can create a neon glow that appears to surround an object. You can apply the Neon Glow filter (one of the Artistic filters) to any flattened image. This effect works best by starting with any imagery—either type or objects—that has a solid color background. Flatten the image so there's only a Background layer. Click the Magic Wand tool on the Tools panel, and then click the solid color (in the background). Click Filter on the Menu bar, click Filter Gallery, click Artistic to expand the category, then click Neon Glow. Adjust the glow size, the glow brightness, and color, if you wish, and then click OK. (An example of this technique is used in the Design Project at the end of this chapter.)

Create Text
ON A PATH

What You'll Do

Source: Morguefile.

 In this lesson, you'll create a shape, and then add type to it.

Understanding Text on a Path

Although it is possible to create some cool type effects by adding layer styles such as bevel and emboss and drop shadow, you can also create some awesome warped text. Suppose you want type to conform to a shape, such as an oval, or a free-form outline you've drawn. No problem—just create the shape and add the text!

Creating Text on a Path

You start by creating a shape using one of the Photoshop shape tools on the Tools panel, setting the Pick tool mode to Path on the shape's options bar, and then adding type to that shape. Add type to a shape by clicking the Horizontal Type tool. When the pointer nears the path, you'll see that it changes to the Type on a Path pointer. Click the path when the Type on a Path pointer displays and begin typing. You can change fonts, font sizes, add styles, and any other interesting effects you've learned to apply with type. As you will see, the type is on a path!

> **QUICK TIP**
>
> Don't worry when you see the outline of the path on the screen. The path won't print, only the type will.

Warping Type

You can add dimension and style to your type by using the Warp Text feature. After you select the type layer you want to warp, click the Horizontal Type tool on the Tools panel. Click the Create warped text button on the options bar to open the Warp Text dialog box. If a warning box opens telling you that your request cannot be completed because the type layer uses a faux bold style, click the Character Panel options button, click Faux Bold to deselect it, and then click the Create warped text button again. You can click the Style list arrow to select from 15 available styles. After you select a style, you can modify its appearance by dragging the Bend, Horizontal Distortion, and Vertical Distortion sliders.

Figure 27 *Type on a path*

Source: Morguefile.

Path does not display
when image is printed

Create a path and add type

1. Turn on the ruler display, click the **Ellipse tool** on the Tools panel.

2. Click the **Pick tool mode list arrow** on the options bar, then click **Path**.

3. Drag the **Paths pointer** to create an elliptical path on the base of the viola from **150 X/350 Y** to **430 X/460 Y**.

4. Click the **Horizontal Type tool** on the Tools panel.

5. Change the font to **Times New Roman**, use the **Bold font style**, set the font size to **48,** then verify that the **Left align text button** is selected, and anti-aliasing is set to **Smooth**.

TIP You can change to any point size by typing the number in the Set the font size text box. You can also resize the circle by clicking Edit on the Menu bar, pointing to Transform Path, clicking Scale, then dragging the circle to make it larger.

6. Click the **Horizontal Type pointer** at approximately **200** on the ellipse.

7. Using the Color Picker, change the font color by sampling the blue at approximately **150 X/150 Y**, close the Color Picker, type **Symphony,** then commit any edits.

8. Drag the **Symphony layer** above the Viola layer, hide the rulers and guides, and return to the **Essentials workspace**. Compare your image to Figure 27.

9. Save your work, close the Urban Music.psd file, and exit Photoshop.

You created a path using a shape tool, then added type to it.

POWER USER SHORTCUTS

To do this:	Use this method:	To do this:	Use this method:
Apply anti-alias method	aa	Horizontal Type tool	T, or **T**
Apply Bevel and Emboss	fx, , Bevel & Emboss style	Kern characters	VA
Apply blur filter to type	Filter ➢ Blur ➢ Gaussian Blur	Move tool	or **V**
Apply Drop Shadow	fx, , Drop Shadow style	Save image changes	[Ctrl][S] (Win) or ⌘ [S] (Mac)
Cancel any current edits	⊘	See type effects (to collapse)	▾
Change font family	Myriad Pro	See type effects (to expand)	▴
Change font size	T	Select all text in layer	Double-click type layer icon
Change type color	▬	Shift baseline of type	Aa
Commit current edits	✓	Step Backward	[Alt][Ctrl][Z] (Win) or [option] ⌘ [Z] (Mac)
Cycle through 3D properties	Select Move tool, press V	Toggles Character and Paragraph panels from the options bar	▤
Display/hide rulers	[Ctrl][R] (Win) or ⌘ [R] (Mac)	Undo	[Ctll][Z] (Win) or ⌘ [Z] (Mac)
Erase a History state	Select state, drag to 🗑	Warp type	T

Key: Menu items are indicated by ➢ between the menu name and its command. Blue bold letters are shortcuts for selecting tools on the Tools panel.

Learn about type and how it is created.

1. Open PS 6-2.psd from the drive and folder where you store your Data Files, then save it as **ZD-Logo**.
2. Display the rulers with pixels, then change to the Typography workspace.
3. Use the Horizontal Type tool to create a type layer that starts at 45 X/95 Y.
4. Use a black 35 pt Lucida Sans Regular font or substitute another font.
5. Type **Zenith**, deselect the text, then reposition the type if necessary.
6. Use the Horizontal Type tool and a 16 pt type size to create a type layer at 70 X/180 Y, then type **Always the best**.
7. Save your work.

Change spacing and adjust baseline shift.

1. Use the Horizontal Type tool to create a new type layer at 210 X/95 Y.
2. Use a 35 pt Myriad Pro Regular font.
3. Type **Design**.
4. Select the Design type.
5. Change the type color to the color used in the lower-left of the background.
6. Change the type size of the D to 50 pt.
7. Adjust the baseline shift of the D to −5.
8. Select the Z, change the type size to 50 pt and the baseline shift to -5.
9. Save your work.

Use the Drop Shadow style.

1. Activate the Zenith type layer.
2. Apply the Drop Shadow style.

3. In the Layer Style dialog box, set the angle to 150°, then close the Layer Style dialog box.
4. Save your work.

Apply anti-aliasing to type.

1. Activate the Zenith type layer if necessary.
2. Change the Anti-Alias method to Smooth (if necessary).
3. Save your work.

Modify type with Bevel and Emboss and Extrude to 3D.

1. Activate the Design type layer.
2. Apply the Bevel and Emboss style.
3. In the Layer Style dialog box, set the style to Inner Bevel.
4. Set the angle to 150° and the altitude to 30°.
5. Close the Layer Style dialog box and apply the style.
6. Activate the Zenith type layer.
7. Apply the Bevel and Emboss style.
8. Set the style to Inner Bevel.
9. Verify that the angle is set to 150° and the altitude is set to 30°.

10. Close the Layer Style dialog box and apply the style.
11. Save your work.

Apply special effects to type using filters.

1. Apply a 1.0 pixel Gaussian Blur filter to the "Always the best" layer.
2. Save your work.

Create text on a path.

1. Use the Ellipse tool with Path selected to draw an ellipse from approximately 200 X/120 Y to 370 X/185 Y.
2. Click the path with the Horizontal Type tool at 250 X/120 Y.
3. Type **Since 1972** using the orange color in the lower-left triangle of the file, in a 16 pt Arial Regular font.
4. Change the anti-aliasing method to Crisp.
5. Change the opacity of the type (using the Opacity slider in the Layers panel) on the path to 45%.
6. Turn off the ruler display.
7. Save your work, then compare your image to Figure 28.

Figure 28 *Completed Skills Review*

A local flower shop, Nature's Beauty, asks you to design its color advertisement for website that features members of a group called *Florists United*. You have already started on the image, and need to add some type.

1. Open PS 6-3.psd, then save it as **Nature's Beauty Web Promo**.

2. Using the Horizontal Type tool, click at the top of the image, then type **Nature's Beauty** using a black 60 pt Times New Roman Regular font.

3. Create a catchy phrase of your choice, using a 24 pt Verdana Regular font.

4. Apply a drop shadow style to the name of the flower shop using the following settings: Multiply blend mode, 75% Opacity, 30° Angle, 5 pixel distance, 2% spread, and 5 pixel size.

5. Apply a Bevel and Emboss style to the catch phrase using the following settings: Emboss style, Chisel Soft technique, 100% depth, Up direction, 15 pixel size, 0 pixel soften, 30° angle, 25° altitude, and using global light.

6. If your computer has OpenGL enabled, add a 3D Extrusion effect to the Nature's Beauty type created in step 2.

7. Compare your image to the sample in Figure 29.

8. Save your work.

Figure 29 *Sample Project Builder 1*
Source: Morguefile.

You are a junior art director for an advertising agency. You have been working on a print ad that promotes milk and milk products. You have started the project, but still have a few details to finish up before it is complete.

1. Open PS 6-4.psd, then save it as **Milk Promotion**.
2. Create a shape using any shape tool, then use the shape as a text path and type a snappy phrase of your choosing on the shape.
3. Use a 24 pt Arial Regular font in the style and color of your choice for the catch phrase type layer. (If necessary, substitute another font.)
4. Create a Bevel and Emboss style on the type layer, setting the angle to 100° and the altitude to 30°.
5. Compare your image to the sample in Figure 30.
6. Save your work.

Figure 30 *Sample Project Builder 2*
Source: Morguefile.

You are a freelance designer. A local clothing store, Attitude, is expanding and has hired you to work on a print advertisement. You have already created the file, and inserted the necessary type layers. Before you proceed, you decide to explore the Internet to find information on using type to create an effective design.

1. Connect to the Internet and use your browser to find information about typography. (Make a record of the site you found so you can use it for future reference, if necessary.)

2. Find information about using type as an effective design element.

3. Open PS 6-5.psd, update the layers (if necessary), then save the file as **Attitude**.

4. Modify the existing type by changing fonts, font colors, and font sizes.

5. Edit the type, if necessary, to make it shorter and clearer.

6. Rearrange the position of the type to create an effective design.

7. Add a Bevel and Emboss style using your choice of settings, then compare your image to the sample in Figure 31.

8. Save your work.

Figure 31 *Sample Design Project*

© Photodisc/Getty Images.

Placing Type in an Image

You have been hired by your community to create an advertising campaign that promotes tourism on its website. Decide what aspect of the community you want to emphasize. Locate appropriate imagery (already existing on your hard drive, on the web, your own creation, or using a scanner), and then add type to create a meaningful Photoshop image.

1. Create an image with any dimensions you choose.
2. Save this file as **Community Promotion**.
3. Add at least two layers of type in the image, using multiple font sizes. (Use any fonts available on your computer. You can use multiple fonts if you want.)
4. Add a Bevel and Emboss style to at least one type layer and add a Drop Shadow style to at least one layer. (*Hint*: You can add both effects to the same layer.)
5. Position type layers to create an effective design.
6. Compare your image to the sample in Figure 32.
7. Save your work.

Figure 32 *Sample Portfolio Project*
Source: Morguefile.

CHAPTER 7 USING PAINTING TOOLS

1. Paint and patch an image
2. Create and modify a brush tip
3. Use the Smudge tool
4. Use a Brush library and an airbrush effect

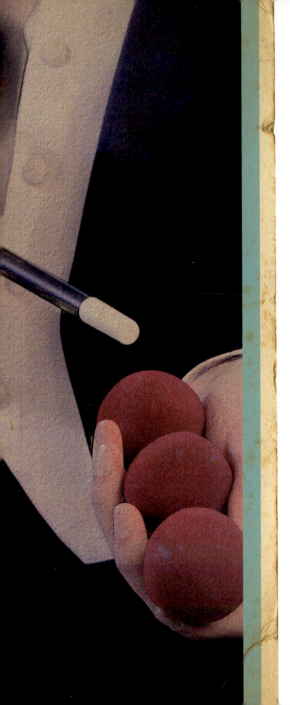

7

USING PAINTING
TOOLS

Painting Pixels

In addition to the color-enhancing techniques you've already learned, Photoshop has a variety of painting tools that allow you to modify colors. Unlike the tools an oil painter might use to *apply* pigment to a canvas, such as a brush or a palette knife, these virtual painting tools let you *change* existing colors and pixels.

Understanding Painting Tools

In most cases, you use a painting tool by selecting it, and then choosing a brush tip. Just like a real brush, the brush size and shape determines how colors are affected. You paint the image by applying the brush tip to an image, which is similar to the way pigment is applied to a real brush and then painted on a canvas. In Photoshop, the results of the painting process can be deeper, richer colors, bleached or blurred colors, or filter-like effects in specific areas. You can select the size and shape of a brush tip, and control the point at which the brush stroke fades.

Learning About Brush Libraries

Brushes that are used with painting tools are stored within a brush library. Each **brush library** contains a variety of brush tips that you can use, rename, delete, or customize. After you select a tool, you can select a brush tip from the default brush library, which is automatically available from the Brush Preset picker menu. Photoshop comes with the following additional brush libraries:

- Assorted Brushes
- Basic Brushes
- Calligraphic Brushes
- DP Brushes
- Drop Shadow Brushes
- Dry Media Brushes
- Faux Finish Brushes
- M Brushes
- Natural Brushes 2
- Natural Brushes
- Round Brushes with Size
- Special Effect Brushes
- Square Brushes
- Thick Heavy Brushes
- Wet Media Brushes

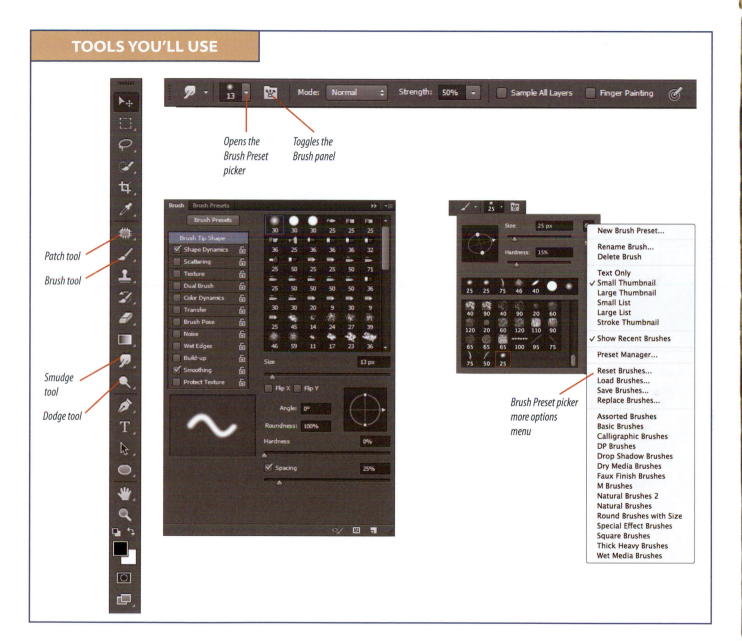

Opens the Brush Preset picker

Toggles the Brush panel

Patch tool

Brush tool

Smudge tool

Dodge tool

New Brush Preset...

Rename Brush...
Delete Brush

Text Only
✓ Small Thumbnail
Large Thumbnail
Small List
Large List
Stroke Thumbnail

✓ Show Recent Brushes

Preset Manager...

Reset Brushes...
Load Brushes...
Save Brushes...
Replace Brushes...

Brush Preset picker more options menu

Assorted Brushes
Basic Brushes
Calligraphic Brushes
DP Brushes
Drop Shadow Brushes
Dry Media Brushes
Faux Finish Brushes
M Brushes
Natural Brushes 2
Natural Brushes
Round Brushes with Size
Special Effect Brushes
Square Brushes
Thick Heavy Brushes
Wet Media Brushes

Paint and
PATCH AN IMAGE

What You'll Do

Source: Morguefile.

 In this lesson, you'll use the Sharpen tool to give pixels more definition, the Burn tool to darken specific areas, and then use fade settings to paint an area. You'll also use the Patch tool to hide unnecessary imagery.

Using Painting Tools

As you've probably realized, you can use many different methods to achieve similar effects in Photoshop. No one method is necessarily better than another. Like a mask that hides a specific area, Photoshop painting tools can be used to enhance specific areas of a layer. You can use the painting tools, shown in Table 1, to create some of the effects shown in Figure 1. Unlike a mask that is applied to a defined area within a layer, or a filter that is applied to an entire layer, the effects of painting tools are applied to whatever areas the pointer contacts. In some ways, Photoshop painting tools function very similarly to real painting brushes; in others, they go far beyond traditional tools to let you achieve some incredible effects.

Understanding Fade Options

When you dip a real brush in paint and then stroke the brush across canvas, the brush stroke begins to fade as more of the pigment is left on the canvas than on the brush. This effect can be duplicated in Photoshop using fade options. Fade options are brush settings that determine how and when colors fade toward the end of brush strokes. Fade option settings are measured in steps. A **step** is equivalent to one mark of the brush tip and can be any value from 1–9999. The larger the step value, the longer the fade. A factor that influences the shape of a brush stroke is jitter. **Jitter** is the randomness of dynamic elements such as size, angle, roundness, hue, saturation, brightness, opacity, and flow. You can set fade options for most of the painting tools using the Jitter control options on several of the Brush Tip Shape options within the Brush panel.

QUICK TIP

To picture a brush fade, imagine a skid mark left by a tire. The mark starts out strong and bold, and then fades out gradually or quickly, depending on conditions. This effect is analogous to a brush fade.

Learning About the Patch Tool

Photoshop offers many tools to work with damaged or unwanted imagery. One such tool is the Patch tool. Although this is not a painting tool, you might find as you work in Photoshop, you have to combine a variety of

Using Painting Tools

tool strategies to achieve the effect you want. The Patch tool is located on the Tools panel and is grouped with the Healing Brush tool, Content-Aware Move tool, Red Eye tool, and Spot Healing Brush tool. You can use the Patch tool to cover a selected area with pixels from another area or with a pattern. Both the Patch tool and the Healing Brush tool match the texture, lighting, and shading of the sampled pixels so your repaired area will look seamless. The Healing Brush tool, however, also matches the transparency of the pixels.

Using the Patch Tool

The Patch tool provides a quick and easy way to repair or remove an area within an image. You can use the Patch tool in the following ways:

■ Select the area you want to fix, click the Source option button on the options bar, and then drag the selection over the area you want to replicate.

■ Select the area you want replicated, click the Destination option button on the options bar, and then drag the selection over the area you want to fix.

QUICK TIP

There's not necessarily one "right tool" for any given job; there might be several methods of completing a task.

Figure 1 *Painting samples*

© Photodisc/Getty Images.

TABLE 1: PAINTING TOOLS		
Tool	**Button**	**Effect**
Blur tool		Decreases contrast between pixels, giving a soft, blurred look.
Sharpen tool		Increases contrast between pixels, giving a sharp, crisp look. (Grouped with the Blur tool.)
Smudge tool		Smears colors across an image as if you dragged your finger across wet ink. (Grouped with the Blur tool.)
Dodge tool		Lightens underlying pixels, giving a lighter, underexposed appearance.
Burn tool		Darkens underlying pixels, giving a richer, overexposed appearance. (Grouped with the Dodge tool.)
Sponge tool		Increases or decreases the purity of a color by saturating or desaturating the color. (Grouped with the Dodge tool.)

© 2015 Cengage Learning®

Use the Sharpen tool

1. Start Photoshop, open PS 7-1.psd from the drive and folder where you store your Data Files, then save it as **Painted Farm Scene**.

2. Display the rulers in pixels (if they are not already displayed), and make sure the document size displays in the status bar.

3. Use the workspace switcher to display the **Painting workspace**.

4. Click the **Sharpen tool** ▲ on the Tools panel.

TIP Look under the Blur tool or Smudge tool if the Sharpen tool is hidden.

5. Double-click the **Size text box** in the Brush Presets panel, type **30**, click the **sixth preset** (Hard Round Pressure Opacity) in the Brush Presets panel, then verify that 100% displays in the Strength text box on the options bar.

TIP You can also click the Brush Preset picker list arrow on the options bar to select brushes.

6. With the Scene layer active, drag the **Brush pointer** ⬭ from **35 X/345 Y** to **35 X/570 Y** to sharpen across the grassy area in the lower left of the image.

7. Press and hold [**Shift**], click the image in the lower-right corner at **860 X/570 Y**, then release [**Shift**].

TIP Instead of dragging to create a brush stroke from point to point, you can click a starting point, press and hold [Shift], click an ending point, then release [Shift] to create a perfectly straight brush stroke.

8. Press and hold [**Shift**], click the **image** in the middle right at **860 X/350 Y**, then release [**Shift**]. Compare your image to Figure 2.

You used the Sharpen tool to focus on the pixels around the perimeter of the grassy area in the lower part of the image. The affected pixels now appear sharper and crisper.

Figure 2 *Results of Sharpen tool*
Source: Morguefile.

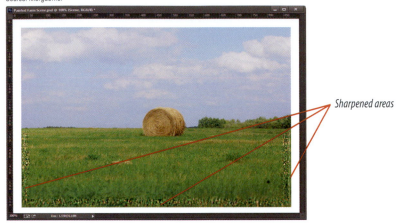

Sharpened areas

Figure 3 *Red eyes—before and after*
Source: Morguefile.

Red eyes

Getting Rid of Red-Eye

What do you do with that picture of your niece, who looks so cute except for that annoying red-eye? You use the Red Eye tool, that's what! The **red-eye effect** is the appearance of red eyes in photos due to the use of a flash. It is more evident in people, and animals, with light-colored eyes. Hidden in with the Patch tool and the Healing Brush tool, you can select the Red Eye tool and drag it over any red eye in an image and the eye will be magically corrected. If necessary, you can adjust the pupil size in the options bar. Figure 3 shows an image before (on the left) and after red-eye correction.

Figure 4 *Results of Burn tool*
Source: Morguefile.

Burned areas
(your results
may vary)

Painting with a Pattern and the Deco Pattern Feature

Suppose you have an area within an image that you want to replicate on a new or existing layer. You can paint an existing pattern using the desired area and the Pattern Stamp tool. To create this effect, select the Rectangular Marquee tool using a 0 pixel feather setting, and then drag the outline around an area in your image. With this area outlined, click Edit on the Menu bar, click Define Pattern, type a name in the Name text box, and then click OK. Deselect the marquee, click the Pattern Stamp tool on the Tools panel (hidden under the Clone Stamp tool), click the Pattern picker list arrow on the options bar, and then click the new pattern. Each time you click the pointer on a layer, the new pattern will be applied. You can delete a custom pattern by right-clicking the pattern swatch ([Ctrl]-click (Mac)) in the Pattern picker, and then clicking Delete Pattern.

You can create a wide variety of patterns using more than one input image patch. Now patterns can be offset, scaled, and rotated when filled using the Deco Pattern feature. To use the Deco Pattern feature, make a selection, click Edit on the Menu bar, then click Fill. Click Pattern from the Use list arrow, click the Scripted Patterns check box, click one of the choices from the Script list arrow, then click OK. After clicking OK, a dialog box specific to the selected pattern appears which contains options you can customize. Click OK, and the pattern is applied.

Burn an area

1. Click the **Burn tool** on the Tools panel.

   TIP Look under the Dodge tool or Sponge tool if the Burn tool is hidden.

2. Type **50** in the Size text box on the Brush Presets panel, click the **third preset** (Soft Round Pressure Size) on the Brush Presets panel, then set the Exposure on the options bar to **100%**.

   TIP You can change any brush tip size at any time. Press [ ]] to increase the brush tip or [[ ] to decrease the brush tip in increments of 10 (up to 100), increments of 25 (from 100 to 200), increments of 50 (from 200 to 300), and increments of 100 (above 300).

3. Drag the **Brush pointer** in the clouded area at approximately **50 X/150 Y** to **500 X/80 Y**.

   Did you notice that the area you painted became darker? It looks as though a storm may occur shortly.

4. Drag back and forth throughout the clouds in the upper-right area from **430 X/150 Y** to **860 X/150 Y**. Compare your image to Figure 4.

   TIP Use the Dodge tool to lighten image areas (its results are the opposite of the Burn tool and should be used sparingly, as it can easily degrade an image). Both the Dodge and Burn tools are best used on small, precise areas. To lighten larger areas, select the area you want to lighten, then make a Curves adjustment.

You used the Burn tool to intensify the pixels in the clouds of the image. This technique increases the darker tones, changing the mood of the image.

Set fade options

1. Click the **Eyedropper tool** on the Tools panel.

2. Use the **Eyedropper pointer** to click the dark green area of the image at **120 X/335 Y**, as shown in Figure 5.

3. Click the **Brush tool** on the Tools panel, then click the **Toggle the Brush panel button** on the options bar.

4. On the Brush panel, type **40** in the Size text box, then verify that Hardness is set to 100%.

5. Click the **sixth preset** (Hard Round Pressure Opacity) on the Brush Presets panel.

6. Click , click **Shape Dynamics** on the Brush panel, adjust your settings using Figure 6 as a guide, then click to close the Brush panel.

TIP When you open the Brush panel, Brush Tip Shape is selected and displays the option settings. Selecting an option's check box from the additional choices turns the option on, but doesn't display the settings. To adjust settings, you need to click the setting name (which displays its options).

Available fade options and their locations on the Brush panel are described in Table 2.

You modified the fade options using settings on the Brush panel.

Figure 5 *Location to sample*

Source: Morguefile.

Sampled pixel

Figure 6 *Brush panel*

Click to toggle the Brush Presets panel on/off

Indicates how many steps it takes for fade to occur

Figure 7 *Areas painted with fade*
Source: Morguefile.

Faded brush stroke

© 2015 Cengage Learning®

Paint an area

1. Press and hold [**Shift**], drag the **Brush pointer** [ ] from **40 X/50 Y** to **870 X/40 Y**, then release [**Shift**].

2. Use the **Brush pointer** [ ] to click the image at **40 X/70 Y**, press and hold [**Shift**], click the image at **40 X/575 Y**, then release [**Shift**], as shown in Figure 7.

You painted areas using the Brush tool.

TABLE 2: FADE OPTIONS		
Jitter option	**Brush Tip Shape option**	**Description**
Size Jitter	Shape Dynamics	Decreases the brush stroke size toward the end of the stroke. Available in the following tools: Brush 🖌 and Pencil ✏.
Opacity Jitter	Transfer	Decreases the brush stroke opacity toward the end of the stroke. Available in the following tools: Brush 🖌 and Pencil ✏.
Foreground/Background Jitter	Color Dynamics	Causes the foreground color to shift to the background color toward the end of the stroke. Available in the following tools: Brush 🖌 and Pencil ✏.

Create a patch for an area

1. Click the **Patch tool** 🔲 on the Tools panel.

TIP Look under the Healing Brush tool if the Patch tool is hidden.

2. Drag the **Patch tool pointer** ⬚ around the **outer edge of the hay bale,** being sure to complete the loop so you create the selection as shown in Figure 8.

TIP Make the selection area slightly larger than necessary to avoid awkward edges around the patched area.

3. Click the **Source button** on the options bar, if it is not already selected.

4. Position ⬚ within the left side of the selection, then drag to your left so that the left edge of the selection (the hay bale) is at approximately **250 X/335 Y**.

You used the Patch tool to define the source area for the patch, then dragged the selection within the image.

Figure 8 *Marquee surrounding source area*
Source: Morguefile.

Selection to be patched

Figure 9 *Results of Content-Aware Move tool*
Image courtesy of Elizabeth Eisner Reding

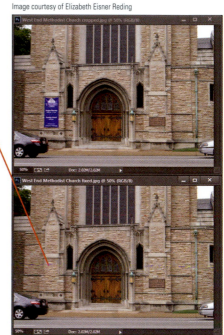

Repaired area

Using Content-Aware Fill and the Content-Aware Patch Tool to Replace Pixels

You can use the **Content-Aware fill** feature to easily fill an area, by allowing Photoshop to intelligently calculate the area in the selection. To use this feature, select an area in an image that you want to remove. (This area may contain content that you want to use elsewhere, like the hay bale in Figure 8.) Once you have the area selected, you can save it as a layer for later use, if you wish. With the selection intact, click Edit on the Menu bar, and then click Fill. When the Fill dialog box opens, make sure Content-Aware is selected from the Use list arrow, and then click OK and watch the magic happen!

The Content-Aware Patch mode in the Patch tool is an extension of the Content-Aware Fill feature where the user can use the fill process with the existing Patch tool. This new mode allows the user to use a rough guess that initializes the Fill feature and narrows the search region. Figure 9 shows an image before and after a banner was removed from the front of a historic church in Nashville, TN. Enhancements to this feature include option bar settings for Mode, Adaptation and Color Tolerance (to aid in color blending).

Figure 10 *Results of Patch tool*

Source: Morguefile.

The location of your tractor may vary

Complete patching an area

TIP As you drag a selection made with the Patch tool, look at the selection and you'll see what the pixels will be replaced with.

The selection is replaced with imagery from the destination that you defined with the selection. As you drag, you'll see the pixels that will be replacing the selection. When finished, the horizon should be aligned.

1. Click **Select** on the Menu bar, then click **Deselect**.

2. Activate and display the **Tractor** on the Layers panel.

You completed the patching process by deselecting the source area, then you activated and displayed a layer.

Adjust a patched area

1. Click the **Move tool** ▶⊕ on the Tools panel, then drag the tractor as needed until the engine area of the tractor covers any remnants of the hay bale. Compare your image to Figure 10.

   Selecting and patching are difficult skills to master. Your results might differ.

TIP You can undo steps using the History panel, then retry until you're satisfied with the results.

2. Click the **Scene layer** on the Layers panel.

3. Save your work.

You used the Move tool to properly position patched imagery.

Create and Modify
A BRUSH TIP

What You'll Do

Source: Morguefile.

 In this lesson, you'll create a brush tip and modify its settings, and then you'll use it to paint a border. This new brush tip will be wide and have a distinctive shape that adds an element of mystery to the image.

Understanding Brush Tips

You use brush tips to change the size and pattern of the brush used to apply color. Brushes are stored within libraries. In addition to the default brushes that are available from the Brush Preset picker list, you can also select a brush tip from one of the 15 brush libraries. You can access these additional libraries, shown in Figure 11, by clicking the Brush Preset picker list arrow on the options bar, and then clicking the More Options button or by clicking the panel options button on the Brush presets panel.

Learning About Brush Tip Modifications

You can adjust the many brush tip settings that help determine the shape of a brush. The number beneath the brush tip indicates the diameter, and the image of the tip changes as its values are modified. Figure 12 shows some of the types of modifications that you can make to a brush tip using the Brush panel. The shape of the brush tip pointer also reflects the shape of the brush tip. As you change the brush tip, its pointer also changes.

Figure 11 *Brush tip libraries*

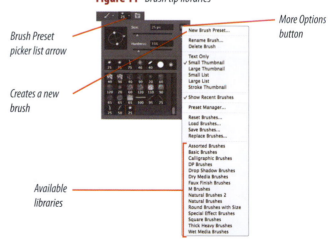

Brush Preset picker list arrow

Creates a new brush

More Options button

Available libraries

Using Painting Tools

Creating a Brush Tip

You can create your own brush tip by clicking the Brush Panel options button, and then clicking New Brush Preset to open the Brush Name dialog box, where you can enter a descriptive name in the Name text box. All the options on the Brush panel are available to you as you adjust the settings. As you select settings, a sample appears at the bottom of the panel. You can delete the current brush tip by clicking the Brush Preset picker list arrow, clicking the More Options button, and then clicking Delete Brush. Confirm the deletion by clicking OK in the warning dialog box. You can also right-click (Win) or [Ctrl]-click (Mac) a brush tip on the Brush Preset panel, and then click Delete Brush.

Figure 12 *Brush Presets in the Brush panel*

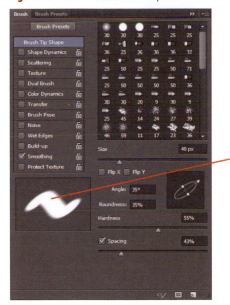

Sample brush tip

Figure 13 *Tinted image*
© Photodisc/Getty Images.

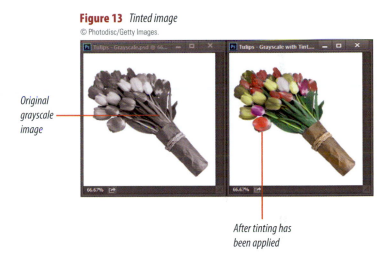

Original grayscale image

After tinting has been applied

Applying a Tint

You can use brush tips to apply a tint to a grayscale image. By changing the mode of a grayscale image to RGB color, you can use painting tools to tint an image. After you change the image mode, create a new layer using the Layer menu on the Menu bar or by clicking the Create a new layer button on the Layers panel while pressing [Alt] (Win) or [option] (Mac). Click the Mode list arrow in the New Layer dialog box, select a mode (such as Overlay), select colors from the Swatches panel, and then use the Brush tool to apply tints to the new layer. See Figure 13 for an example.

Create a brush tip

1. Click the **Brush tool** 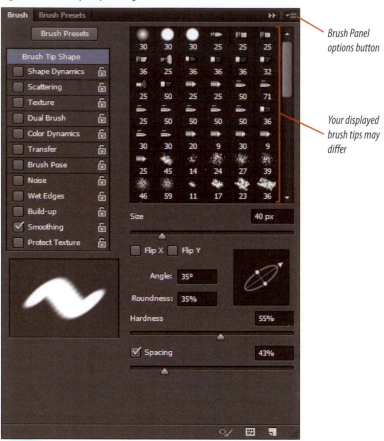 on the Tools panel, then click the **Toggle the Brush panel button** on the options bar to open the Brush panel.

2. Minimize or move the image window if it obscures your view of the Brush panel.

3. Click the **Brush Panel options button** on the Brush panel, then click **Clear Brush Controls**.

4. Click **Brush Tip Shape** on the Brush panel, then adjust your settings using Figure 14 as a guide.

5. Click again, then click **New Brush Preset**.

6. Type **Custom oval brush tip** to replace the current name, accept the selected check box, then click **OK**.

TIP A newly added brush tip generally is added in brush tip size order in the Brush Presets panel.

The new brush tip appears on the options bar or by opening the Brush Presets panel and scrolling to the bottom.

TIP If you have a pen tablet installed on your computer, you may periodically see a floating icon indicating that your tablet can be used to make entries.

You cleared the current brush settings, then created a brush tip using the Brush panel. You modified its settings to create a custom brush tip for painting a border.

Figure 14 *Brush Tip Shape settings*

Brush Panel options button

Your displayed brush tips may differ

Figure 15 *Painted image*

Source: Morguefile.

Effects of the custom brush tip

Customize Bristle Characteristics

You can customize the characteristics of bristle tips (using Brush Tip Shape options) by varying the shape, bristle density, length, thickness, and stiffness to create realistic, painterly brush strokes. To create even more realistic brush strokes, vary the Angle (which determines the brush tip angle) and Spacing (which controls the distance between the brush marks in a stroke), and then (if you have OpenGL enabled) use the Bristle Brush preview to display the sample brush tip. Bristle Tips are easily to identify in the Brush panel: their icons may be small, but they look like paint brushes rather than paint blots. The Bristle Brush preview is available for Bristle Tips. If your Cursor Preferences are set to Normal or Full Size Brush Tip, the Bristle Brush preview appears as an overlay on the active image with the shape and action acts as dictated by the brush dimensions. If you select a brush tip that has these modifications (indicated by a brush tip to the left of the brush sample in the Brush Presets panel, e.g. Round Point Stiff), you can see the preview.

Paint a border

1. With the new brush active, click the **Mode list arrow** on the options bar, then click **Multiply**.

   TIP The Multiply blend mode creates semitransparent shadow effects and multiplies the value of the base color by the blend color.

2. Double-click the **Opacity text box** on the options bar, then type **75**.

3. Click **Shape Dynamics** on the Brush panel.

4. In the Size Jitter section, click the **Control list arrow**, then click **Fade**.

5. Type **400** in the text box to the right of the Control list arrow, then press **[Enter]** (Win) or **[return]** (Mac).

6. Close the Brush panel, then make the Scene layer active if necessary.

7. Use the **Brush pointer** ⬭ to click the image near the upper-right corner at **850 X/50 Y**, press and hold **[Shift]**, click the image near the lower-right corner at **850 X/570 Y**, then release **[Shift]**.

8. Save your work, then compare your image to Figure 15.

Using the newly created brush tip, you painted an area of the image. You also made adjustments to the opacity and fade settings to make the brush stroke more dramatic.

Use the
SMUDGE TOOL

What You'll Do

Source: Morguefile.

 In this lesson, you'll smudge pixels to create a surreal effect in an image.

Blurring Colors

You can create the same finger-painted look in your Photoshop image that you did as a kid using paints in a pot. Using the Smudge tool, you can create the effect of dragging your finger through wet paint. Like the Brush tool, the Smudge tool has many brush tips that you can select from the Brush Presets panel, or you can create a brush tip of your own.

Smudging Options

Figure 16 shows an original image and three examples of Smudge tool effects. In each example, the same brush tip is used with different options on the options bar.

If you select the Smudge tool with the default settings, your smudge effect will be similar to the image shown in the upper-right corner of Figure 16.

Using Finger Painting

The image in the lower-right corner of Figure 16 shows the effect with the Finger Painting check box selected *prior* to the smudge stroke. The Finger Painting option uses the foreground color at the beginning of each stroke. Without the Finger Painting option, the color under the pointer is used at the beginning of each stroke. The image in the lower-left corner had the Finger Painting option off, but had the Sample All Layers check box selected. The Sample All Layers check box enables your smudge stroke to affect all the layers beneath the current layer.

Using Content-Aware Spot Healing

Get ready for some magic! You can use the Content-Aware Spot Healing Brush to fix all sorts of blemishes: from age-related stains to rips to eyeglass glare. This tool is grouped with the Healing Brush tool, the Patch tool, the Content-Aware Move tool, and the Red Eye tool. Open an image containing a blemish, click the Spot Healing Brush tool and click the Content-Aware option button, and then you can either paint or click to fix even the most stubborn problem areas. Figure 17 shows an old photograph before the Content-Aware Spot Healing tool was used, and after. Notice that the seam from a fold (on the left side of the photo, slightly lower than the girl's face) has miraculously vanished. Gone also are the yellow stains in the upper-left corner, and small white flecks throughout the image.

Figure 16 *Smudge samples*

© Photodisc/Getty Images.

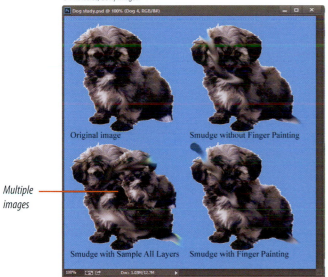

Multiple images

Figure 17 *Blemishes fixed with the Content-Aware Spot Healing Brush tool*

Image courtesy of Elizabeth Eisner Reding

Modify smudge settings

1. Click the **Smudge tool**  on the Tools panel.

TIP Look for the Smudge tool under the Sharpen tool.

2. Click the **Brush Preset picker list arrow** on the options bar, then click **46** (Spatter 46 pixels).

TIP This brush tip is located in the middle of the list.

3. Select the **Finger Painting check box** on the options bar if it is not already checked.

4. Make sure your settings match those shown in Figure 18.

You modified the existing smudge settings to prepare to smudge the image.

Figure 18 *Smudge tool options bar*

Figure 19 *Pen tablet*
Website © 2013–2014 Wacom.

Using a Graphics Tablet

If you really want to see Photoshop take off when you use brush tools, try using a graphics tablet. Although you can find a graphics tablet for as little as $50, this nifty high-end item might set you back several hundred dollars, but you'll love what you get in return.

Figure 19 shows a graphics tablet, with a cordless, battery-free pen. The benefits of using a graphics tablet include the following:

- Multiple levels of pressure sensitivity
- Use of pressure-sensitive tools already included in Photoshop
- Programmable menu buttons, touch strips, and a contoured grip pen
- The ability to move even faster than when you use shortcut keys

And as an added bonus, you'll probably experience fewer problems with repetitive stress injuries.

Figure 20 *Smudged area*

Source: Morguefile.

Unchanged
imagery

Figure 21a *Original image*

Source: Morguefile

Figure 21b *Painted image*

Source: Morguefile

Turning a Photo into a "Painting"

You can create a painting-like appearance using a photographic image and a few simple Photoshop brush tools. Take an image, like the one shown in Figure 21a, and make any necessary color adjustments. Define the entire image as a pattern by clicking Edit on the Menu bar, clicking Define Pattern, typing a name, and then clicking OK. Click the Create new fill or adjustment layer button on the Layers panel, and then click Solid Color. Choose white from the Color Picker, and then lower the opacity of the layer so you can see the image. Create another new layer, above the adjustment layer. Use the Pattern Stamp tool and set the Pattern picker (on the options bar) to the new pattern you created to paint over the existing image. You can also experiment with different blending modes and brushes. Figure 21b shows the same image after the painting treatment.

Smudge an image and correct a blemish

1. Verify that the **Scene layer** is active.
2. Drag the **Smudge tool pointer** 🐾 from **80 X/360 Y** to **350 X/550 Y**, zigzagging from left to right.

TIP Dragging the pointer up and down as you move from left to right creates an interesting smudge effect. The degree and effect of your smudging will vary.

An area on the current layer is smudged. Did you notice that the tractor layer is unchanged?

3. Click the **Spot Healing Brush tool** 🩹 on the Tools panel, then click the **Content-Aware button**.

TIP The Spot Healing Brush tool is grouped with the Patch tool.

4. Using a brush size of **25**, paint the dark green clump of grass at approximately **630 X/440 Y** to **720 X/440 Y**.
5. Save your work, then compare your image to Figure 20.

You used the Smudge tool to smear the pixels in the bottom third of the image. That area now has a dreamy quality. You also used the Content-Aware Spot Healing Brush tool to correct an area within the image.

Use a Brush Library and an
AIRBRUSH EFFECT

What You'll Do

Source: Morguefile

 In this lesson, you'll sample an area of the image, and then use brush tips from a library to create additional effects. You'll also use an airbrush effect to apply gradual tones.

Learning About the Airbrush Effect

You might have heard of professional photographers using an airbrush to minimize or eliminate flaws in faces or objects. In Photoshop, the effect simulates the photographer's technique by applying gradual tones to an image. Airbrushing creates a diffused effect on the edges of pixels. The airbrush effect button is located on the options bar. You can apply the airbrush effect with any brush tip size, using the Brush tool, Mixer Brush tool, History Brush tool, Dodge tool, Burn tool, and Sponge tool. The **flow** setting determines how much paint is sprayed (or the intensity of the effect of the tool you're using) while the mouse button is held.

> **QUICK TIP**
> When using the airbrush effect, you can accumulate intensity by holding the mouse button without dragging.

Using Brush Tip Libraries

Photoshop comes with 15 brush libraries that can replace or be appended to the current list of brushes. All the libraries are stored in a folder called Brushes. Each of the libraries, shown in Figure 22, is stored in its own file

(having the extension .abr). Libraries that are not included with Photoshop are loaded using the Load dialog box. When you use the Load Brushes command (found by clicking the Brush Presets Panel options button), the brush tips are added to the end of the brushes list. When you click the name of a brush tip library from the Brush Preset picker list, you are given the option of replacing the existing brush tips with the contents of the library, or appending the brush tips to the existing list.

Figure 22 *Available Brush sets*

Assorted Brushes
Basic Brushes
Calligraphic Brushes
DP Brushes
Drop Shadow Brushes
Dry Media Brushes
Faux Finish Brushes
M Brushes
Natural Brushes 2
Natural Brushes
Round Brushes with Size
Special Effect Brushes
Square Brushes
Thick Heavy Brushes
Wet Media Brushes

Managing the Preset Manager

The **Preset Manager** is a Photoshop feature that allows you to manage libraries of preset brushes, swatches, gradients, styles, patterns, contours, custom shapes, and tools. You can display the Preset Manager by clicking Edit on the Menu bar, pointing to Presets, and then clicking Preset Manager. Options for the Brushes type Preset Manager are shown in Figure 23. You can delete or rename individual elements for each type of library. Changes that you make in the Preset Manager dialog box are reflected on the corresponding panels.

Figure 23 *Preset Manager dialog box*

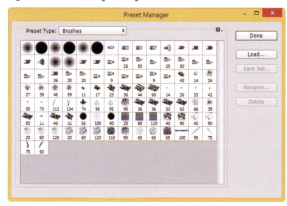

Figure 24 *Art History Brush tool options*

Click to control
opacity with
pressure

Restoring Pixel Data

You can use the History Brush tool to restore painted pixels. The History Brush tool makes a copy of previous pixel data, and then lets you paint with that data, making this tool another good source for undoing painting errors. The Art History Brush tool also lets you recreate imagery using pixel data, but with more stylized effects. This tool has many more options than the History Brush tool, including Style, Area, and Tolerance. Style controls the shape of the paint stroke. Area controls the area covered by the brush tip (a higher area value covers a larger area). Tolerance controls the region where the paint stroke is applied, based on color tolerance. A greater percentage value causes paint strokes to occur in areas that differ in color from the original tolerance. Some of the Art History Brush tool options are shown in Figure 24.

Load a brush library

1. Click the **Eyedropper tool**  on the Tools panel.

2. Use the **Eyedropper pointer** to click the **image** in the sky at approximately **700 X/100 Y**.

3. Click the **Brush tool** on the Tools panel.

4. Click the **Panel options button** on the Brush Presets panel, then click **Faux Finish Brushes**, as shown in Figure 25.

TIP This brush library is located in the Brushes folder. The Brushes folder is located in /Program Files/Adobe/ Adobe Photoshop CC (64 Bit)/Presets/Brushes (Win) and the Presets folder in the Adobe Photoshop CC folder in Applications (Mac).

5. Click **Append**.

6. Open the Brush panel, click **Brush Tip Shape**, scroll to the bottom of the list of brush tips, then click **75 (Veining Feather 1)** near the middle of the list.

The active brush tip is from the Faux Finish Brushes library.

You sampled a specific location in the image, then loaded the Faux Finish Brushes library. You selected a brush tip from this new library, which you will use to paint an area.

Figure 25 *List of brush libraries*

New Brush Preset...

Rename Brush...
Delete Brush

Text Only
Small Thumbnail
Large Thumbnail
Small List
Large List
✓ Stroke Thumbnail

✓ Show Recent Brushes

Preset Manager...

Reset Brushes...
Load Brushes...
Save Brushes...
Replace Brushes...

Assorted Brushes
Basic Brushes
Calligraphic Brushes
DP Brushes
Drop Shadow Brushes
Dry Media Brushes
Faux Finish Brushes
M Brushes
Natural Brushes 2
Natural Brushes
Round Brushes with Size
Special Effect Brushes
Square Brushes
Thick Heavy Brushes
Wet Media Brushes

Close
Close Tab Group

Added Benefits of Using a Graphics Tablet in Photoshop CC

If you are using a graphics tablet in Photoshop CC, you'll find that you have more options than ever for image fine-tuning. Using your graphics tablet in conjunction with Photoshop CC, you'll find that:

- A pressure-sensitive graphics tablet can be used to selectively apply adjustments to a layer mask using the presets in the Adjustments panel.
- By adjusting the intensity setting of your pen, you can use the Dodge, Burn, and Sponge tools with a higher degree of accuracy.
- You'll be able to get into hard-to-reach places by changing the Shape Dynamics setting to Pen Pressure.
- In OpenGL-enabled documents, you can use your pen in combination with the Rotate View tool (grouped with the Hand tool in the Tools panel or on the Menu bar) to spin your image canvas.
- You can easily pan your image using your pen.

Using Painting Tools

Figure 26 *Brush tool options*

Click to enable airbrush
capabilities

Figure 27 *Results of Airbrush option and style*
Source: Morguefile

Airbrushed effect;
your results may
differ

Creating Erodible Brush Tips

Erodible brush tips, which erode from thin to thick lines, like a crayon, let you draw lines with a tip that can be customized using the Brush panel. The Softness slider lets you adjust the erosion rate, and the Shape list arrow lets you set the shape of the brush. The Sharpen Tip button allows you to sharpen the brush point again.

Create an airbrush effect

1. Click **Enable airbrush-style build-up effects** on the options bar.

2. Change the settings on the options bar so they match those shown in Figure 26.

3. Drag the **Veining Feather Brush pointer** back and forth over the areas of the image containing the **sky** (from approximately **520 X/50 Y** to **750 X/80 Y**).

4. Hide the rulers.

5. Click the **Tractor layer** on the Layers panel.

6. Click the **Add a layer style button** *fx* on the Layers panel.

7. Click **Drop Shadow**, then click **OK** to accept the existing settings.

8. Save your work, return to the **Essentials workspace**, then compare your image to Figure 27.

9. Close the image and exit Photoshop.

You used an airbrush effect to paint the sky in the image. You applied the Drop Shadow style to a layer to add finishing touches.

POWER USER SHORTCUTS	
To do this:	**Use this method:**
Apply tint to grayscale image	Image ➤ Mode ➤ RGB Color, choose paint tool, apply color from Swatches panel
Blur an image	🔷
Burn an image	🔷 or [Shift] **O**
Create a brush tip	🔷 , 🔷 , click Panel options button, click New Brush Preset
Define a pattern	Edit ➤ Define Pattern, type name, click OK
Delete a brush tip	🔷 , in Brush Presets panel, click Delete Brush
Dodge an image	🔷 or [Shift] **O**
Load brush library	🔷 in Brush Presets panel, click library of your choice
Paint a straight line	Press and hold [Shift] while dragging pointer
Paint an image	🔷 or [Shift] **B**
Patch a selection	🔷 or [Shift] **J**
Restore default brushes	🔷 , click Reset Brushes in Brush Presets panel
Select Fade options	🔷 , click Shape Dynamics
Sharpen an image	🔷
Smudge an image	🔷

Key: Menu items are indicated by ➤ between the menu name and its command. Bold blue letters are shortcuts for selecting tools on the Tools panel.

Paint and patch an image.

1. Open PS 7-2.psd from the drive and folder where you store your Data Files, then save it as **The Maze**.
2. Display the rulers in pixels, display the Painting workspace, then reset the default brushes.
3. Select the Sharpen tool.
4. Select the Soft Round brush with a size of 27 pixels and a Strength of 100%.
5. Drag the pointer back and forth over the maze walls along the right edge of the image, as shown in Figure 28; start at 740 X/20 Y and finish at 840 X/540 Y.
6. Select the Burn tool.
7. Select the Hard Round brush tip with a size of 19 pixels and an Exposure of 100%.
8. Drag the pointer back and forth over the two dark red arrows.
9. Use the Eyedropper tool to sample the image at the ball's shadow (located at 50 X/100 Y) with the Eyedropper tool.
10. Select the Brush tool, then select the Soft Round brush tip with a size of 17 pixels.
11. Toggle the Brush panel if it is not already displayed, choose Shape Dynamics, set the Size Jitter Control to Fade, set the steps for size fade to 700 steps, then drag the pointer over the inside perimeter of the entire image. (You can perform this action several times.)
12. Select the Patch tool.
13. Select the far-left red arrow (located at 150 X/350 Y) by outlining it with the Patch tool.
14. Select the Destination option button.
15. Drag the selection up and to the right, to the cubicle located at approximately 500 X/140 Y.
16. Deselect the selection.
17. Save your work.

Create and modify a brush tip.

1. Change the existing settings (using the Brush Tip Shape area on the Brush panel) to the following: Size = 25 pixels, Angle = 15 degrees, Roundness = 80%, Hardness = 15%, Spacing = 65%. The opacity setting on the options bar should be 100%.
2. Create a brush called **25 Pixel Sample** using the Brush tool, Brush Presets panel, and Brush panel.
3. Use the new brush and the current foreground color to fill in the white space surrounding the perimeter of the image.
4. Save your work.

Use the Smudge tool.

1. Select the Smudge tool.
2. Select the Spatter 24 pixels brush tip.
3. Verify that the Finger Painting check box is selected.
4. Use the Normal mode and 70% strength settings.
5. Drag the pointer in a jagged line from the top left to the bottom right of the image.
6. Use the Spot Healing Brush tool with the Content-Aware setting on and your choice of brush size to clean the dirt in the area around 350 X/175 Y.
7. Save your work.

Use a library and an airbrush effect.

1. Use the Eyedropper tool to sample the aqua arrow in the lower-right corner of the image.
2. Select the Brush tool and enable the airbrush effect.
3. Replace the existing brushes with the Calligraphic Brushes library, but do not save the changes, if prompted.
4. Select brush tip 45 (Oval 45 px) towards the end of the list. Make a substitution if this brush tip is not available.
5. Drag the pointer over the aqua arrow.
6. Hide the rulers.
7. Create three type layers, using the text shown in Figure 28. The type layers were created using a black 35 pt Aparajita Regular font; use a different font if this one is not available on your computer. The first layer should read "Help Me," the second should read "Find," and the third should read "My Way Back." (*Hint*: You can create the vertical type effect shown using the Horizontal Type tool on the Tools panel, then using the Transform command on the Edit menu to rotate the type 90 degrees.)
8. Save your work.
9. Compare your image to Figure 28. The appearance of your image might differ.

Figure 28 *Completed Skills Review*
© Photodisc/Getty Images.

A national bank has hired you to create artwork for its new home loan division. The bank wants this artwork to be original; it will be used in print ads. They have instructed you to go wild, and make this ad look like a work of art. You have created a suitable image, but want to add some artistic touches.

1. Open PS 7-3.psd, then save it as **Bank Artwork**.
2. Use the Burn tool and any brush tip you think is appropriate to accentuate the money and the hand that is holding it.
3. Sample a dark brown area within the image (an area on the coat sleeve of the outstretched arm, located at 420 X/180 Y, was used in the sample).
4. Use a painting tool and brush tip of your choice (brush tip 27 is used in the sample) to paint areas within the suits. (*Hint:* In the sample, the suit lapels are painted.)
5. Create a brush tip using a size and shape of your choice, and give the brush tip a descriptive name.
6. Use any painting tool and any color to create a border that surrounds the image. Use the Fade options of your choice.
7. Use the Smudge tool and the settings of your choice to create an interesting effect in the image. (In the sample, the Smudge tool is used on the shaking hands.)
8. Use the Spot Healing Brush tool and the content-aware setting to rid the image of any blemishes.
9. Add a library of your choice, and apply an effect using the Burn tool and the airbrush effect. (The Drop Shadow Square 43 pixels brush from the Drop Shadow library is used in the sample on the hand holding the money.)
10. Make any color adjustments you want. (*Hint*: The Brightness was changed to −26, and the Contrast was changed to +15 in the sample.)
11. Add a type layer using the wording of your choice and any desired effects. (A 75 pt Perpetua Regular font is used on an elliptical path with the Bevel and Emboss effect applied in the sample. Substitute another font if this one is not available.)
12. Save your work, then compare your image to the sample in Figure 29.

Figure 29 *Sample Project Builder 1*
© Photodisc/Getty Images.

Using Painting Tools

The Robotics Department of a major chip manufacturer is conducting an art contest in the hopes of creating a new image for itself. The contest winner will be used in their upcoming advertising campaign, and they want the ad to be lighthearted and humorous. You have decided to enter the contest and have created a preliminary image. You still need to add the finishing touches.

1. Open PS 7-4.psd, then save it as **Robotics Contest Entry**.

2. Use the Sharpen tool to sharpen the pixels in an area of your choice.

3. Burn any area within the image, using any size brush tip.

4. Use any additional painting tools, libraries, and settings to enhance colors and imagery within the image.

5. Add descriptive type to the image, using the font and wording of your choice. (In the sample, a 36 pt Chaparral Pro Light Italic style font is used. A Bevel and Emboss effect was added to the type.)

6. Make any color adjustments you want. (In the sample, the Hue is modified to −15, the Saturation is modified to +34, and the Lightness is modified to −20.)

7. Save your work, then compare your image to the sample in Figure 30.

Figure 30 *Sample Project Builder 2*
© Photodisc/Getty Images.

You have been hired by a local art gallery, Expressions, to teach a course that describes how Photoshop can be used to create artwork. This gallery specializes in offbeat, avant-garde art and wants you to inspire the attendees to see the possibilities of this important software program. They hired you because you have a reputation for creating daring artwork. As you prepare your lecture, you decide to explore the Internet to see what information already exists.

1. Connect to the Internet and use your browser and favorite search engine to find information about digital artwork. (Record the URL of the site you found as reference.)
2. Identify and print a page containing an interesting piece of artwork that you feel could be created in Photoshop.
3. Using your word processor, create a document called **Art Course**. A sample document is shown in Figure 31. (Tip: You can capture your image, then paste it in your document by pressing [Print Scrn], then [Ctrl] [V] in your word processor (Win) or pressing ⌘ [C], then ⌘ [V] (Mac). You can also use Snipping Tool (Win) or Grab (Mac).)
4. In the document, analyze the image, pointing out which effects could be created in Photoshop, and which Photoshop tools and features you would use to achieve these effects.
5. Save your work.

Figure 31 *Sample Design Project*
Source: Morguefile.

|Art Course Discussion
Expressions Gallery

The image shown above is a great example of how the compositing technique can be used in Adobe Photoshop to create interesting effects. Various objects, can be added (and manipulated) to create this image.

Once the objects are positioned within the image, you can use various Photoshop painting tools to blend the different objects with one another so they appear to be a single, seamless image.

By hiding all the layers except the background, the Brush tool and the Airbrush option can be used to create the blended effect. (The images such as the building frame and flying bird have different opacities.)

Once the painting tools have been used, the layers can be displayed and rearranged to achieve the effect you want.

A local car dealer has hired you to create artwork that can be used in magazine ads. The dealership's only requirement is that an automobile be featured within the artwork. You can use any appropriate imagery (already existing on your hard drive, from the web, or your own creation, using a scanner or a digital camera), and then compile the artwork and use Photoshop's painting tools to create interesting effects. You should create a tag line for the image. You do not need to add a name for the dealership; it will be added at a later date.

1. Start Photoshop and create an image with any dimensions.
2. Save this file as **Dealership Ad**.
3. Make selections and create a composite image.
4. Use any painting tools and settings to create interesting effects.
5. Add at least one layer of type and an effect in the image. Use any fonts available on your computer. (The font shown in the sample is 136 pt Informal Roman Regular.)
6. Make color adjustments.
7. Save your work, then compare your image to the sample in Figure 32.

Figure 32 *Sample Portfolio Project*
© Photodisc/Getty Images.

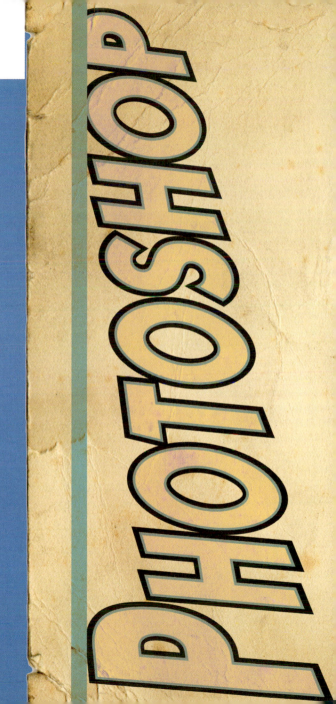

CHAPTER **8** **WORKING WITH SPECIAL**
LAYER FUNCTIONS

1. Use a layer mask with a selection
2. Work with multiple masked layers
3. Control pixels to blend colors
4. Eliminate a layer mask
5. Use an adjustment layer
6. Create a clipping mask

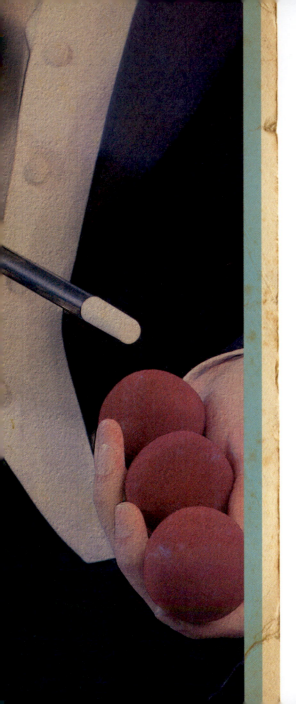

8 WORKING WITH SPECIAL LAYER FUNCTIONS

Designing with Layers

Photoshop is rich with tools and techniques for creating and enhancing images. After the imagery is in place, you can hide and modify objects to create special effects. When these special effects are used in conjunction with other relatively simple techniques, such as merging layers or duplicating layers, the results can be dramatic.

Making Non-Destructive Changes to a Layer

If you want to alter a layer, the easiest thing to do is to select the layer and then make the changes. But if you do that, the layer is changed forever, and once you save and exit Photoshop, there is *no* going back. Adjustment layers make it possible to alter a layer non-destructively, so you *can* go back and revise

(or reverse) your changes. There's no extra charge, so why not take advantage of this capability?

Modifying Specific Areas within a Layer

You can use special layer features to modify the entire image or a single layer of an image. For example, suppose that you have an image with objects in multiple layers. Perhaps you want to include certain elements from each layer, but you also want to hide some imagery in the finished image. You can *define* the precise area you want to manipulate in each layer, and then accurately adjust its appearance to exactly what you want, without permanently altering the original image. You can turn your changes on or off, align images, blend and adjust color, and combine elements to enhance your image.

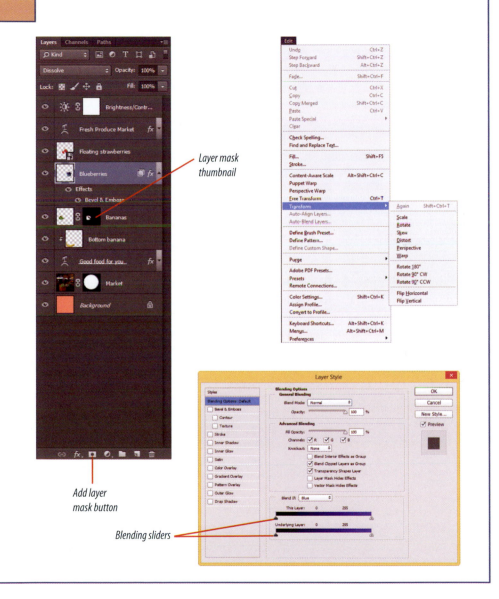

Layer mask
thumbnail

Add layer
mask button

Blending sliders

Use a Layer Mask
WITH A SELECTION

What You'll Do

Source: Morguefile.

 In this lesson, you'll use the Rectangular Marquee tool to make a selection and create a layer mask on the Soccer field layer and on the Opposition layer. You'll select the Brush tool and a brush tip, and then paint on the layer mask to hide pixels. The mask will be modified using the Refine Mask feature.

About Layer Masks

You can hide or reveal a selection within a layer by using a layer mask. A **layer mask** can cover an entire layer or specific areas within a layer. When a layer contains a mask, a layer mask thumbnail appears on the Layers panel between the layer thumbnail and the layer name. As you hide or reveal portions of a layer, the layer mask thumbnail mirrors the changes you make to the object. Some Photoshop features (such as filters or layer deletion) are permanent once you implement them. Masks, however, are extremely flexible—you can hide their effect when you view the image, or change them at will. Because you alter the mask and not the image, no actual pixels are harmed in the creation of your image. You can add an unlimited number of masks to an image, but only one mask to each layer. You can also continue to edit the layer without affecting the layer mask.

> **QUICK TIP**
>
> You can think of a mask as a type of temporary eraser. When you erase pixels from an image, they're gone. A mask can be used to cover pixels—either temporarily or permanently. You can also think of a mask as a cropping tool that offers flexible shapes.

Creating a Layer Mask

You can use any selection tool (such as the Rectangular Marquee tool) on the Tools panel to create the area you want to mask. You can apply a mask to the selection, or you can apply the mask to everything except the selection. You can also feather a selection (control the softness of its edges) by typing pixel values in the Feather text box on the options bar.

> **QUICK TIP**
>
> The term "mask" has its origin in printing. Traditionally, a mask was opaque material or tape used to block off an area of the artwork that you did not want to print.

Understanding Layers and Their Masks

The ability to repeatedly alter the appearance of an image without ever disturbing the actual pixels on the layer makes a layer mask a powerful editing tool. By default, Photoshop links the mask to the layer. This means that if you move the layer, the mask moves as well.

> **QUICK TIP**
>
> To move a layer mask from one layer to another, make sure that the layer mask that you want to move is active, and that the destination layer doesn't already have a layer mask. Drag the layer mask thumbnail from the layer containing the layer mask onto the layer where you want to move the mask.

Understanding the Link Icon

When you create a layer mask, the link icon automatically appears *between* the layer thumbnail and the layer mask thumbnail, indicating that the layer and the layer mask are linked together. To unlink the layer mask from its layer, click the link icon. The Unlink Mask state displays in the History panel. You can re-link a mask to its layer by clicking the space between the layer and mask thumbnails. The Link Mask state displays in the History panel.

Using the Properties Panel

Once you have created an area to be masked, you can create and refine the masked area using the Properties panel. This panel can be opened from the Window menu, and is grouped with the Info panel. It provides a central area where you can edit an existing mask. Using the Properties panel, you can adjust the mask density and feathering *non-destructively*. (Non-destructive changes are those that can be reversed even after the image has been closed.)

Painting a Layer Mask

After you add a layer mask to a layer, you can reshape the mask with the Brush tool and a specific brush size, or tip. Photoshop offers dozens of brush tips, so you can paint just the area you want. For example, you can create a smooth transition between the hidden and visible areas using a soft-edged brush.

Here are some important facts about painting a layer mask:

- When you paint the image with a black foreground, the size of the mask *increases*, and each brush stroke hides pixels on the image layer. *Paint with black to hide pixels.*
- When you paint an object using white as the foreground color, the size of the mask *decreases*, and each brush stroke restores pixels of the layer object. *Paint with white to reveal pixels.*

In Figure 1, the School Bus layer contains a layer mask. The area on the mask where the bus intersects with the camera has been painted in black so that the bus appears to be driving through the lens of the camera.

Figure 1 *Example of a layer mask*
© Photodisc/Getty Images.

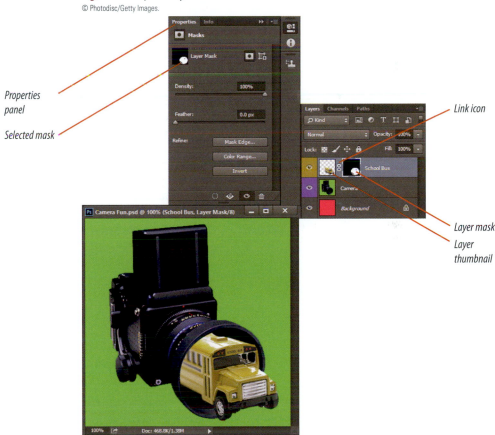

Properties panel

Selected mask

Link icon

Layer mask

Layer thumbnail

Create a layer mask using the Layer menu

1. Start Photoshop, open PS 8-1.psd from the drive and folder where you store your Data Files, then save it as **Soccer**.

TIP If you see a message stating that some text layers need to be updated before they can be used for vector-based output, click Update (Mac).

2. Click the **Default Foreground and Background Colors button** ▣ on the Tools panel.

3. Display the rulers in pixels, then display the **Photography workspace**.

4. Click the **Soccer field layer** to make it the active layer.

5. Click the **Rectangular Marquee tool** ⬚ on the Tools panel.

6. Change the Feather setting on the options bar to **10 px**.

7. Drag the **Marquee pointer** ╋ from **50 X/50 Y** to **1150 X/750 Y**, to create a marquee that includes the players, then compare your image to Figure 2.

8. Click **Layer** on the Menu bar, point to **Layer Mask**, then click **Reveal Selection**.

TIP You can deselect a marquee by clicking Select on the Menu bar, then clicking Deselect; by clicking another area of the image with the marquee tool that you are using; or by right-clicking the object, then clicking Deselect in the shortcut menu.

You used the Rectangular Marquee tool to create a selection, and created a layer mask on the Soccer field layer using the Layer Mask command on the Layer menu.

Figure 2 *Rectangular selection on the Soccer field layer*
Source: Morguefile.

Rectangular marquee selection

Layer Masks versus Vector Masks

A layer mask is resolution-dependent and edited with painting or selection tools, while a **vector mask** is resolution independent and is created with a pen or shape tool. Both masks are non-destructive and can be edited without any loss of original data. (A layer mask thumbnail displays a grayscale channel, while a vector mask thumbnail displays a path.) A vector mask creates a sharp-edged shape that is useful when you want to add a design element with a clean, well-defined edge. Multiple styles can be applied to a vector mask.

Figure 3 *Rectangular selection on the Opposition layer*
Source: Morguefile.

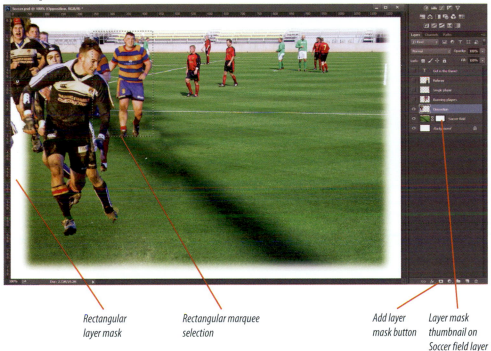

Rectangular
layer mask

Rectangular marquee
selection

Add layer
mask button

Layer mask
thumbnail on
Soccer field layer

Create a selection for a layer mask

1. Click the **Opposition layer** on the Layers panel, then make the layer visible.

2. Change the feather setting on the options bar to **0 px**, then drag the **Marquee pointer** ┼ from approximately **250 X/30 Y** to **435 X/360 Y** (to surround the two players wearing the striped jerseys), as shown in Figure 3.

You used the Rectangular Marquee tool to create a selection that will be used to create a mask.

Creating a Selection from a Quick Mask

Once you have created a selection, you can click the Edit in Quick Mask Mode button at the bottom of the Tools panel to create a mask that can be saved as a selection. When you click the Edit in Quick Mask Mode button, a red overlay displays. Use any painting tools to form a shape in and around the selection. When your mask is finished, click the Edit in Standard Mode button on the Tools panel, and the shape will be outlined by a marquee. You can then save the selection for future use, or use any other Photoshop tools and effects on it.

Create a layer mask using the Properties panel

1. Click **Window** on the Menu bar, then click **Properties**.

2. Click **Layer** on the Menu bar, point to **Layer Mask**, then click **Hide Selection**.

   The mask in the Opposition layer completely obscures the players wearing the striped jerseys, and partially obscures some of the opposition team. The layer mask thumbnail appears to the right of the layer thumbnail on the Layers panel and appears at the top of the Properties panel. Once the mask is created, the Properties panel options for masks are available.

   TIP You can also create a layer mask by clicking the Add layer mask button on the Layers panel. If you use this method, you can press and hold [Alt] (Win) or [option] (Mac) while clicking the Add layer mask button to add a mask that hides the selection, rather than reveals it.

3. Verify that the **layer mask thumbnail** on the Opposition layer is active, then compare your Layers and Properties panels to Figure 4.

   TIP You can tell whether the layer mask or the layer object is active by the outline surrounding the thumbnail and by its appearance in the Properties panel.

   You created a layer mask on the Opposition layer, then displayed the Properties panel.

Figure 4 *Layer mask icons on the Layers and Properties panels*

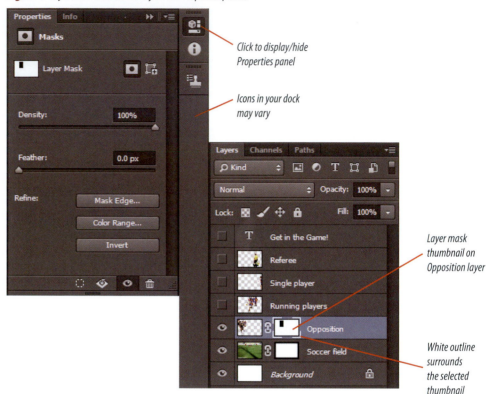

Click to display/hide Properties panel

Icons in your dock may vary

Layer mask thumbnail on Opposition layer

White outline surrounds the selected thumbnail

Figure 5 *Layer mask painted*
Source: Morguefile.

Painted area

Click to refine the
selected mask

Correcting and Updating a Mask

If you need to make a slight correction to a layer mask, you can just switch the foreground and background colors and paint over the mistake. The layer mask thumbnail on the Layers panel automatically updates itself to reflect changes you make to the mask.

Paint a layer mask

1. Zoom into the **opposition team** at approximately **250 X/150 Y** until the player is centered and the zoom factor is **200%**.

2. Click the **Brush tool** on the Tools panel.

3. Click the **Brush Preset picker list arrow** on the options bar, then select the **Hard Round brush tip** (second from the left although your brush tip position may vary), and choose a size of **10 pixels**.

4. Verify that the Mode on the options bar is **Normal** and the Opacity is **100%**.

   TIP Learning to paint a layer mask can be challenging. It's important to make sure the correct layer (and thumbnail) is active before you start painting to know whether you're adding to or subtracting from the mask, and to set your foreground and background colors correctly.

5. Verify that **White** is the foreground color and **Black** is the background color. (*Hint*: You may have to switch foreground and background colors.)

   TIP You can switch the foreground and background colors using the shortcut key X.

6. Drag the **Brush pointer** along the player in the foreground until he is completely visible. Compare your screen to Figure 5.

   As you painted, the shape of the mask thumbnail changed in both the Properties and Layers panels.

   TIP As you paint the layer mask to reveal the opposition player, you can zoom in and increase or decrease the brush size, if necessary. You can also reverse the foreground and background colors to make corrections to your painted mask.

You used the Zoom tool to keep a specific portion of the image in view as you increased the zoom percentage, selected a brush tip, and painted pixels on the layer mask to reveal a player.

Modify the layer mask with Refine Mask

1. Drag the **Brush pointer** 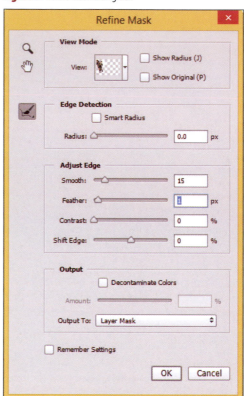 along the right edge of the player, until you reveal more of the player and the field in the Opposition layer.

TIP As you paint, a new History state is created each time you release the mouse button.

2. Click the **Mask Edge button** in the Properties panel.

   The Refine Mask dialog box opens with the On White option selected from the View list arrow. You can use the View list arrow options to see if you missed any areas that need to be painted away.

3. Change the Smooth setting to **15** and the Feather setting to **1 px**, as shown in Figure 6.

4. Click **OK** to close the Refine Mask dialog box, then use the brush pointer to paint away any omissions.

TIP The Horizontal and Vertical type mask tools can be used to create the effect of a picture coming through the outlines of text. When type has been created, the imagery behind the type will appear within the type.

You painted pixels to hide an unnecessary player, and used the Refine Mask dialog box to modify the mask.

Figure 6 *Refine Mask dialog box*

NEW Creating a Selection Using a Focus Area

Using the Focus Area feature, you can create a selection based on pixels that have the clearest focus. This feature works well on portraits, but also works well in images having high and low areas of pixel sharpness. On a given layer in a Photoshop image, click Select on the menu bar, then click Focus Area. Use the In-Focus Range slider (deselect the Auto checkbox) to change the range parameters, and the Brush tools to manually add or remove a selection. You can direct output to a selection, layer mask, new layer, new layer with layer mask, new document, or new document with layer mask. You can also open the Refine Edge dialog box from within the Focus Area dialog box.

Figure 7 *Modified layer mask*

Source: Morguefile.

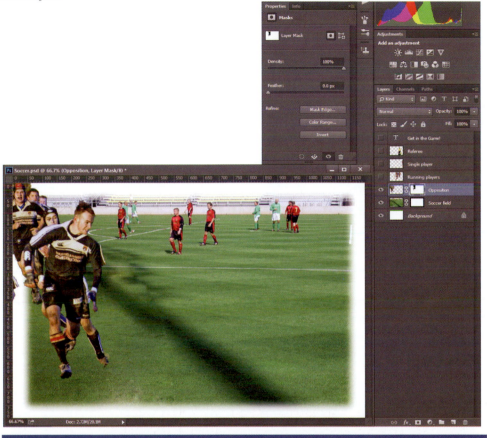

Selecting a Layer Mask versus the Layer Thumbnail

Modifying a layer mask can be tricky because you have to make sure that you've selected the layer mask and not the layer thumbnail. Even though the active thumbnail is surrounded by an outline, it can be difficult to see. To verify whether the layer mask or layer thumbnail is selected, click each one so you can see the difference, and then make sure the one you want is selected. You'll know if you've selected the wrong item as soon as you start painting!

Examine the refined mask

1. Zoom out until the zoom factor is **66.7%**.

2. Compare your screen to Figure 7, then close the Properties panel.

3. Save your work.

You reset the zoom percentage to 66.7% to examine the results of the modified mask.

Work with Multiple
MASKED LAYERS

What You'll Do

Source: Morguefile.

 In this lesson, you'll select two layers simultaneously, align the images on two layers, and then deselect the layers. You'll also scale the Referee and horizontally flip the Single player.

Selecting Multiple Layers

You can select more than one layer on the Layers panel to allow multiple layers to behave as one. Selecting multiple layers in Photoshop is analogous to grouping objects in other programs. You select multiple layers or layer sets by first clicking a layer on the Layers panel. To select contiguous layers (layers that are next to one another on the Layers panel), press and hold [Shift] while clicking additional layers on the Layers panel. To select non-contiguous layers, press and hold [Ctrl] (Win) or ⌘ (Mac) while clicking additional layers on the Layers panel. When selecting multiple layers make sure that you click the layer, *not the layer mask or thumbnail*. You can make multiple selections that include the active layer and any other layers on the Layers panel, even if they are in different layer sets. You can select entire layer sets along with a single layer or with other layer sets. Once you select multiple layers, you can link them so they will move together as a single layer.

> **QUICK TIP**
>
> When you move multiple selections of layers, the relocation of layers affects the objects' appearance in your image, as well as the layers' position on the Layers panel. This means that you can link two layers and then align them in your image. You can also select two non-contiguous layers and then move them simultaneously as a unit to the top of the Layers panel where they will become contiguous.

Working with Layers

After you select multiple layers, you can perform actions that affect the selection

---

Grouping Layers

You can quickly turn multiple selected layers into a group. Select as many layers as you'd like—even if they are not contiguous, click Layer on the Menu bar, and then click Group Layers. Each of the selected layers will be placed in a Group (sometimes called a **layer set**) on the Layers panel. You can ungroup the layers by selecting the group on the Layers panel, clicking Layer on the Menu bar, and then clicking Ungroup Layers.

Working with Special Layer Functions

such as moving their content as a single unit in your image. To deselect multiple layers, press [Ctrl] (Win) or ⌘ (Mac), click any selected layer on the Layers panel, and with the key pressed, click each layer you want to deselect. When you deselect each layer, each one returns to its independent state. You can also turn off a layer's display while it is part of a selection of layers by clicking the layer's Indicates layer visibility button.

Aligning Selected Layers

Suppose you have several type layers in your image and need to align them by their left edges. Rather than individually moving and aligning numerous layers, you can precisely position selected layers in your image. You can align the content in the image by first selecting layers on the Layers panel, and then choosing one of six subcommands from the Align command on the Layer menu. Photoshop aligns layers relative to each other or to a selection border. So, if you have four type layers and want to align them by their left edges, Photoshop will align them relative to the far-left pixels in those layers only, not to any other (nonselected) layers on the Layers panel or to other content in your image.

Distributing Selected Layers

To distribute (evenly space) the content on layers in your image, you must first select three or more layers, verify that their opacity settings are 50% or greater, and then select one of the six options from the Distribute command on the Layer menu. Photoshop spaces out the content in your image relative to pixels in the selected layers. For example, imagine an image that is 700 pixels wide and has four type layers that are 30 pixels wide each and span a range between 100 X and 400 Y. If you select the four type layers, click the Layer menu, point to Distribute, then click the Horizontal Centers command on the Distribute Layers menu, Photoshop will distribute them evenly, but only between 100 X and 400 Y. To distribute the type layers evenly across the width of your entire image, you must first move the left and right layers to the left and right edges of your image, respectively.

Transforming Objects

You can **transform** (change the shape, size, perspective, or rotation) of an object or objects on a layer, using one of 11 transform commands on the Edit menu. When you use some of the transform commands, eight selection handles surround the contents of the active layer. When you choose any transform command, a transform box appears around the object you are transforming. A **transform box** is a rectangle that surrounds an image and contains handles that can be used to change dimensions. You can pull the handles with the pointer to start transforming the object. After you transform an object, you can apply the changes by clicking the Commit transform (Enter) button on the options bar, or by pressing [Enter] (Win) or [return] (Mac). You can use transform commands individually or in a chain. After you choose your initial transform command, you can try out as many others as you like before you apply the changes by pressing [Enter] (Win) or [return] (Mac). If you attempt another command (something other than another transform command) before pressing [Enter] (Win) or [return] (Mac), a warning box will appear. Click Apply to accept the transformation you made to the layer.

Figure 8a *Original image*
Source: Morguefile.

Figure 8b *Image after using Content-Aware Scaling*
Source: Morguefile.

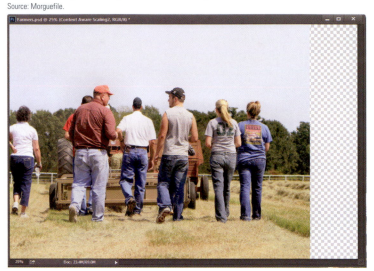

Using Content-Aware Scaling

If you appreciate Photoshop magic, you'll love this feature. Imagine that you have an image containing a group of people that you'd like to use, but there's too much space between the individual people, as in Figure 8a. You could use the transform box to change the dimensions of the box, and while that would change the amount of space the image takes up, it would incorrectly alter the amount of space between the people in the image. You could use various copy-and-paste techniques to physically move the people-pixels closer together, but you'd probably celebrate at least one birthday trying to complete this task, or you could use the Content-Aware Scale feature to resize the image without changing important content.

To use this feature, open an image and activate an image (non-Background) layer containing the content you want to change, or select the specific areas in the layer you want to scale. Click Edit on the Menu bar, and then click Content-Aware Scale. Handles surround the selection which you can drag to scale the pixels. As you drag the handles, you can see that the space between the individuals shrinks, while maintaining the correct scaling of the people, as shown in Figure 8b. Eventually, the image will experience some distortion using this feature, but not nearly what you'd experience if you used the Transform tools or if you resized the image by dragging the horizontal or vertical handles. Tools on the options bar let you control the amount of scaling so you can minimize distortion, and protect skin tones. The practical application of this feature will become obvious the first time you have imagery that doesn't quite fill the space you need. If you stretch it using the transform box, parts of it may look ridiculous. Use the Content-Aware Scaling feature, and it'll look just right!

Figure 9 *Running players layer selected with Opposition layer*

Layer selected with
Opposition layer

Select and align layers

1. Make the layer thumbnail of the **Opposition layer** on the Layers panel active, and verify that the **Running players** layer is visible.

2. Press and hold [**Ctrl**] (Win) or ⌘ (Mac), click the **Running players layer** on the Layers panel, then release [**Ctrl**] (Win) or ⌘ (Mac), and compare your Layers panel to Figure 9.

3. Click **Layer** on the Menu bar, point to **Align**, then click **Vertical Centers**.

   The centers of the Opposition and Running players layers are aligned with their vertical centers. Compare your image to Figure 10.

4. Click the **Opposition layer** on the Layers panel.

   The additional objects are no longer selected, yet all retain their new locations.

You selected two layers on the Layers panel, aligned the objects on those layers by their vertical centers using the Align Vertical Centers command on the Layer menu, then you deselected the layers.

Figure 10 *Aligned layers*
Source: Morguefile.

Center pixel of opposition
and running players
layers with their vertical
centers aligned

Transform a layer using Scale

1. Click the **Referee layer** on the Layers panel and make the layer visible.

2. Click **Edit** on the Menu bar, point to **Transform**, then click **Scale**.

3. Press and hold [**Shift**], position the **Scaling pointer** over the **upper-right sizing handle** using the ruler pixel measurements at approximately **1080 X/110 Y**, drag down and to the left to **1020 X/140 Y**, as shown in Figure 11, release [**Shift**], then release the **mouse button**.

TIP Holding [Shift] while transforming an image maintains the correct proportions so the image looks natural.

4. Click the **Commit transform (Enter) button** ✓ on the options bar.

   The image of the referee is reduced.

You resized the Referee layer using the Transform Scale command. This command makes it easy to resize an object.

Figure 11 *Referee layer scaled*
Source: Morguefile.

Smart Guides display dimensions as you resize an object (your coordinates may differ)

Drag handle to resize

Creating a Collage Effect

In the past, creating a collage meant physically cutting and pasting a variety of images onto a single object (such as an art board). With Photoshop, you can achieve this same result in a Photoshop image by assembling a variety of objects within a single file (and all without destroying existing images and getting paste all over yourself and everything around you). Images you acquire can be transformed into the dimensions you want, have effects applied, and positioned as you like to create just the right look. There are a variety of ways you can get objects from one image into another. You can drag a layer from one image into another, drag and drop a closed file into an open image, use the Paste in Place command to position a selection in the same relative position in the target document, use the Paste Into/Outside commands (Paste Special commands) to paste a selection into/outside another selection in an image.

Figure 12 *Single player layer transformed*
Source: Morguefile.

Single player layer flipped horizontally

Transform a layer using Flip Horizontal

1. Make the **Single player layer** visible and the active layer.

2. Click **Edit** on the Menu bar, point to **Transform**, then click **Flip Horizontal**.

   The single player now faces away from the referee instead of towards him.

3. Click the **Move tool** on the Tools panel, press and hold [**Shift**], move the **flipped player** to the left edge of the image as shown in Figure 12, then release [**Shift**].

4. Save your work.

You horizontally flipped the Single player layer using the Transform Flip Horizontal command, then moved the layer horizontally within the image. You can use this command to change the orientation of an object on a layer.

Scientific Applications of Photoshop Extended

Medical scans and scientific researchers often use the DICOM (Digital Imaging and Communications in Medicine) standard. These files generally contain multiple slices or frames which are read and converted to Photoshop layers, and can then be annotated or manipulated. In architecture and engineering applications, images can be overlaid, making complex analysis much easier, accurate, and effective.

Lesson 2   Work with Multiple Masked Layers

Control Pixels
TO BLEND COLORS

What You'll Do

Source: Morguefile.

  In this lesson, you'll apply styles to layers using the Layer Style dialog box. You'll also work with blending modes to blend pixels on various layers.

Blending Pixels

You can control the colors and form of your image by blending pixels on one layer with pixels on another layer. You can control *which* pixels from the active layer are blended with pixels from lower layers on the Layers panel. If you set the Blend If color to Red, then all pixels on the layer that are red will be blended based on your new settings. Blending options are found in the Layer Style dialog box and are available on the Layer menu. You can control *how* these pixels are blended by choosing a color as the Blend If color, and using the This Layer and Underlying Layer sliders. The

Blend If color determines the color range for the pixels you want to blend. You use the **This Layer** sliders to specify the range of pixels that will be blended on the active layer. You use the **Underlying Layer** sliders to specify the range of pixels that will be blended on all the lower—but still visible—layers. The color channels available depend on the color mode. For example, an RGB image will have Red, Green, and Blue color channels available.

> **QUICK TIP**
> Color channels contain information about the colors in an image.

Using Duplicate Layers

You can create interesting effects by duplicating layers. To duplicate a layer, first activate the layer you want to duplicate, click the Layers Panel options button, click Duplicate Layer, and then click OK. By default, the duplicate layer is given the same name as the active layer with "copy" attached to it. (You can also create a duplicate layer by dragging the layer to the Create a new layer button on the Layers panel.) You can modify the duplicate layer by applying effects or masks to it. In addition, you can alter an image's appearance by moving the original and duplicate layers to different positions on the Layers panel.

Using Color Sliders

When adjusting the This Layer and Underlying Layer sliders, the colors that are outside the pixel range you set with the color sliders will not be visible, and the boundary between the visible and invisible pixels will be sharp and hard. You can soften the boundary by adjusting the slider position and creating a gradual transition between the visible and invisible pixels. Normally, you determine the last visible color pixel by adjusting its slider position, just as you can set opacity by dragging a slider on the Layers panel. Photoshop also allows you to split the color slider in two. When you move the slider halves apart, you create a span of pixels for the visible boundary. Figure 13 shows two objects before they are blended and Figure 14 shows the two objects after they are blended. Do you see how the blended pixels conform to the shape of the underlying pixels?

Figure 13 *Pixels before they are blended*
© Photodisc/Getty Images.

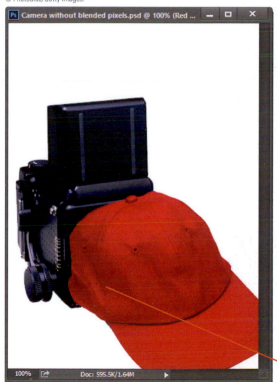

All red cap pixels are visible (unblended)

Figure 14 *Pixels after they are blended*
© Photodisc/Getty Images.

Red cap pixels blended using sliders in the Layer Style dialog box

Blend pixels with a color range

1. Double-click the **Single player thumbnail** on the Layers panel to open the Layer Style dialog box.

TIP Move the Layer Style dialog box if it obscures your view of the single player.

2. Click to highlight the **Blending Options: Default bar** at the top of the list if it is not already selected.

3. Select the **Drop Shadow check box**.

4. Click the **Blend If list arrow**, then click **Blue**.

5. Drag the left (black) **This Layer slider** to **18**, as shown in Figure 15.

TIP Slider position determines the bottom value of the pixels for the color channel you've selected.

6. Click **OK**, then view the fade-out effect on the Single player layer.

TIP If you want to really observe the fade-out effect, display the History panel, then delete the last state and redo steps 4 through 6.

You opened the Layer Style dialog box for the Single player layer, applied the Drop Shadow style, selected Blue as the Blend If color, then adjusted the This Layer slider to change the range of visible pixels. The result is that you blended pixels on the Single player layer so that blue pixels outside a specific range will not be visible.

Figure 15 *Layer Style dialog box*

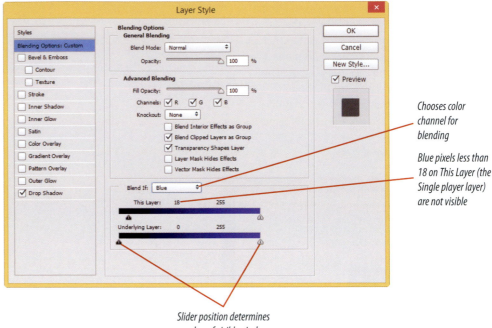

Chooses color channel for blending

Blue pixels less than 18 on This Layer (the Single player layer) are not visible

Slider position determines number of visible pixels

Figure 16 *Transition range for visible pixels*

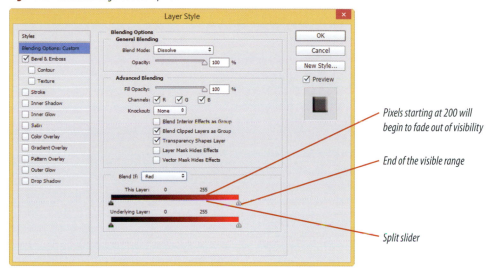

Pixels starting at 200 will begin to fade out of visibility

End of the visible range

Split slider

Figure 17 *Blended pixels*
Source: Morguefile.

Blended areas

Split sliders to select a color range

1. Double-click the **Running players thumbnail** on the Layers panel to open the Layer Style dialog box.

2. Click to highlight the **Blending Options: Default bar** at the top of the list if it is not already highlighted, then click the **Bevel & Emboss check box**.

3. Click the **Blend Mode list arrow**, then click **Dissolve**.

4. Click the **Blend If list arrow**, then click **Red**.

5. Press and hold [**Alt**] (Win) or [**option**] (Mac), click the right **This Layer slider**, drag the left half of the **Right slider** to **200**, then release [**Alt**] (Win) or [**option**] (Mac).

TIP Pressing [Alt] (Win) or [option] (Mac) splits the slider into two halves.

6. Compare your dialog box to Figure 16, then click **OK**.

7. Compare your image to Figure 17, then save your work.

You opened the Layer Style dialog box for the Running players layer, applied the Bevel and Emboss style to the layer and changed the blending mode to Dissolve, specifying the red pixels as the color to blend. To fine-tune the blend, you split the right This Layer slider and set a range of pixels that smoothed the transition between visible and invisible pixels.

Eliminate
A LAYER MASK

What You'll Do

Source: Morguefile.

 In this lesson, you'll use the Layer menu to temporarily disable a layer mask, and then discard a layer mask using the Layers panel.

Disposing of Layer Masks

As you have seen, layer masks enable you to radically change an image's appearance. However, you might not want to keep every layer mask you create, or you might want to turn the layer mask on or off, or you might want to apply the layer mask to the layer and move on to another activity. You can enable or disable the layer mask (turn it on or off), or remove it from the Layers panel by deleting it from the layer entirely or by permanently applying it to the layer.

QUICK **TIP**

You can select a layer mask by pressing [Ctrl][\] (Win) or [⌘][\] (Mac) .

Disabling a Layer Mask

Photoshop allows you to temporarily disable a layer mask from a layer to view the layer without the mask. When you disable a layer mask, Photoshop indicates that the layer mask is still in place, but not currently visible, by displaying a red X over the layer mask thumbnail in both the Layers and Properties panels, as shown in Figure 18. Temporarily disabling a layer mask has many advantages. For example, you can create duplicate layers and layer masks, apply different styles and effects to them, and then enable and disable (show and hide) layer masks individually until you decide which mask gives you the look you want.

QUICK **TIP**

The command available for a layer mask changes depending on whether the layer is visible or not. If the layer mask is enabled, the Layer Mask Disable command is active on the Layer menu. If the layer mask is disabled, the Layer Mask Enable command is active.

You can also right-click (or [ctrl]-click on the Mac) a layer mask to enable/disable it.

Removing Layer Masks

If you are certain that you don't want a layer mask, you can permanently remove it. Before you do so, Photoshop gives you two options:

- You can apply the mask to the layer so that it becomes a permanent part of the layer.
- You can discard the mask and its effect completely.

If you apply the mask, the layer will retain the *appearance* of the mask effect, but it will no longer contain the actual layer mask. If you discard the mask entirely, you delete the effects you created with the layer mask, and return the layer to its original state.

QUICK **TIP**

Each layer mask increases the file size, so it's a good idea to perform some routine maintenance as you finalize your image. Remove any unnecessary, unwanted layer masks, and then apply the layer masks you want to keep.

Figure 18 *Layer mask disabled*

Smart Object thumbnail

Red "X" indicates disabled layer mask

Enabled layer mask

Working with Smart Objects

Just as multiple layers can be selected, you can combine multiple objects into a **Smart Object**. This combination, which displays a visible indicator in the lower-right corner of the layer thumbnail, makes it possible to non-destructively scale, rotate, and warp layers without losing image quality. **Non-destructive editing** means you can always come back and either restore the pixels to their former state, or continue editing. Once the layers you want to combine are selected, you can create a Smart Object by clicking Layer on the Menu bar, pointing to Smart Objects, and then clicking Convert to Smart Object; or by clicking the Layers Panel options button, and then clicking Convert to Smart Object.

A Smart Object can be embedded or linked within an image. A **linked object** is a placeholder for the original object, while an **embedded object** is a copy of an object. When edited, changes in a *linked* Smart Object will be reflected elsewhere; changes in an *embedded* Smart Object will only display in the file where it is embedded.

You can place an embedded file within an image by clicking File on the Menu bar, pointing to Place Embedded, then locating and clicking the file. You can place a linked file by clicking File on the menu bar, pointing to Place Linked, then locating and clicking the file.

A linked Smart Object has an icon in the Layers panel that contains a link. Linked smart objects allows for shared source files across multiple Photoshop documents, which can be very useful for teams or when reusing assets. (Using Bridge, you can also place a linked file by dragging-and-dropping the file onto the image that will contain the linked image.)

Disable and enable a layer mask

1. Click the **Opposition layer** on the Layers panel.
2. Click **Layer** on the Menu bar, point to **Layer Mask**, then click **Disable**. See Figure 19.

   When you disable the mask, the formerly-hidden players are fully displayed.

   TIP You can also disable a layer mask by pressing [Shift] and clicking the layer mask thumbnail, then enable it by pressing [Shift] and clicking the layer mask thumbnail again.

3. Display the History panel.
4. Drag the **Disable Layer Mask history state** to the **Delete current state button** 🗑 on the History panel, then collapse the History panel to the dock.

   Deleting the Disable Layer Mask history state causes the remasking of the players.

You disabled the layer mask on the Opposition layer, using commands on the Layer menu, and then deleted the Disable Layer Mask history state using the History panel.

Figure 19 *Layer mask disabled*
Source: Morguefile.

Original view of players
without the layer mask

Disabled layer mask

Figure 20 *Warning box*

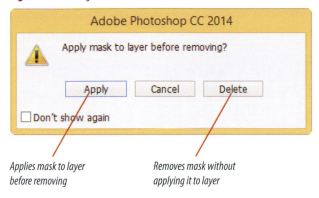

Applies mask to layer
before removing

Removes mask without
applying it to layer

Figure 21 *Soccer field layer with layer mask removed*
Source: Morguefile.

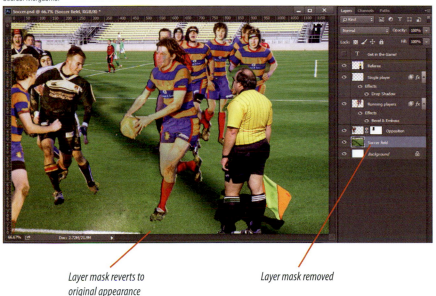

Layer mask reverts to
original appearance

Layer mask removed

Remove a layer mask

1. Click the **layer mask thumbnail** on the Soccer field layer on the Layers panel.
2. Click the **Delete layer button** 🗑 on the Layers panel, then compare your warning box to Figure 20.

TIP Before you remove a layer mask, verify that the layer mask, not just the layer, is active. Otherwise, if you use the Delete layer button on the Layers panel to remove the mask, you will delete the layer, not the layer mask.

3. Click **Delete** to remove the mask without first applying it to the Soccer field layer. Compare your screen to Figure 21.

TIP You can use the Delete Mask button in the Properties panel to delete the mask without seeing the warning box.

4. Click **Edit** on the Menu bar, then click **Undo Delete Layer Mask**.
5. Save your work.

You used the Delete layer button on the Layers panel to delete a layer mask, chose the Delete option in the warning box to remove the mask without applying it to the Soccer field layer, and then used the Edit menu to undo the action to restore the layer mask on the Soccer field layer.

Use an
ADJUSTMENT LAYER

What You'll Do

Source: Morguefile.

 In this lesson, you'll create an adjustment layer, choose Brightness/Contrast as the type of adjustment layer, adjust brightness and contrast settings for the layer, and then use the Layers panel to change the blending mode of the adjustment layer.

Understanding Adjustment Layers

An **adjustment layer** is a special layer that acts as a color filter for a single layer or for all the layers beneath it. Just as you can use a layer mask to edit the layer content without permanently deleting pixels on the image, you can create an adjustment layer to adjust color and tone. If you were to make changes directly on the original layer, the changes would be irreversible. (You could use the Undo feature or the History panel to undo your changes, but only in the current Photoshop session.) When you use an adjustment layer however, the color changes you make to the adjustment layer exist only in the adjustment layer.

Creating an Adjustment Layer

You can create an adjustment layer by selecting the layer you want to adjust, and then clicking the button for the preset in the Adjustments panel; by using the Layer menu to select the New Adjustment Layer command; or by clicking the Create new fill or adjustment layer button on the Layers panel. When you create an adjustment layer, it affects all the layers beneath it by default,

but you can change this setting so that it affects only the selected layer. When creating color adjustments, you must specify which layer you want to affect. In addition, color adjustment presets that can be made directly on a layer or by using an adjustment layer are described in Table 1. (Also included in Table 1 are the preset symbols used in the Adjustments panel.)

> **QUICK TIP**
>
> If you use the Create new fill or adjustment layer button on the Layers panel, you'll see three additional menu items: Solid Color, Gradient, and Pattern. You can use these commands to create fill layers, which fill a layer with a solid color.

Modifying an Adjustment Layer

When you double-click an adjustment layer thumbnail, its settings display in the Properties panel which can then be modified. Photoshop identifies the type of adjustment layer on the Layers panel by including the type of adjustment layer in the layer name.

> **QUICK TIP**
>
> An adjustment layer is created in the Adjustments panel, but modified in the Properties panel.

Working with Special Layer Functions

Adjusting Tone in an Image

Sometimes an image might have several problem areas that can be corrected with effective use of adjustments, either in the form of non-destructive Adjustment layers or by applying adjustments directly from the Image menu. Adjustments such as clarity (found in Camera Raw and similar to the contrast slider in Shadow/Highlight), temperature, exposure, levels, curves, shadow/highlight, dodge, and burn can be used on portions of any image to make effective changes that give your image that WOW factor.

TABLE 1: COLOR ADJUSTMENTS					
Symbol	Color adjustment	Description	Symbol	Color adjustment	Description
🔲	Black & White	Converts a color image to grayscale while controlling how individual colors are converted, and applies color tones such as a sepia effect.	📊	Levels	Sets highlights and shadows by setting the pixel distribution for individual color channels.
☀	Brightness/Contrast	Makes simple adjustments to a tonal range.		Match Color	Changes the color from one image or selection to another image or selection. (Available on the Image ➢ Adjustments menu.)
🔵	Channel Mixer	Modifies a color channel, using a mix of current color channels.	📷	Photo Filter	Similar to the practice of adding a color filter to a camera lens to adjust the color balance and color temperature.
⚖	Color Balance	Changes the overall mixture of color.	🔲	Posterize	Specifies the number of tonal levels for each channel.
▦	Color Lookup	Allows you to apply different *looks* to an image. These looks are derived using a look up table that maps colors in your image.		Replace Color	Replaces specific colors with new color values. (Available on the Image ➢ Adjustments menu.)
📈	Curves	Makes adjustments to an entire tonal range, using three variables: highlights, shadows, and midtones.	🔲	Selective Color	Increases or decreases the number of process colors in each of the additive and subtractive primary color components.
	Equalize	Redistributes brightness values of pixels so that they evenly represent the entire range of brightness levels. (Available on the Image ➢ Adjustments menu.)		Shadows/Highlights	Corrects images with silhouetted images due to strong backlighting, as well as brightening up areas of shadow in an otherwise well-lit image. (Available on the Image ➢ Adjustments menu.)
🔲	Exposure	Controls the tone.	🔲	Threshold	Converts images to high contrast, black-and-white images.
🔲	Gradient Map	Maps the equivalent grayscale range of an image to colors of a specific gradient fill.		Variations	Adjusts the color balance, contrast, and saturation of an image, and shows alternative thumbnails. (Available on the Image ➢ Adjustments menu.)
🔲	Hue/Saturation	Changes position on the color wheel (hue) or purity of a color (saturation).	🔽	Vibrance	Controls the color by adjusting color saturation.
🔲	Invert	Converts an image's brightness values to the inverse values on the 256-step color-values scale.			

Create and set an adjustment layer

1. Activate and display the **Get in the Game! type layer** on the Layers panel.

2. Click the **Brightness/Contrast button** ☼ in the Adjustments panel, which opens the Brightness/Contrast settings in the Properties panel. Compare your Properties panel to Figure 22.

TIP You can also create a new adjustment layer by clicking the Create new fill or adjustment layer button on the Layers panel, then selecting a color adjustment.

3. Type **−20** in the Brightness text box.

4. Type **35** in the Contrast text box, then collapse the Properties panel to the dock. Compare your Layers panel to Figure 23.

The new adjustment layer appears on the Layers panel above the Get in the Game! layer. The new layer is named Brightness/Contrast 1 because you chose Brightness/Contrast as the type of color adjustment.

You used the Adjustments and Properties panels to create a Brightness/Contrast adjustment layer, then adjusted the brightness and contrast settings.

Figure 22 *Adjustment settings in Properties panel*

This adjustment affects all layers below (click to clip to layer) button allows the adjustment layer to affect other layers

The Toggle layer visibility button or 'Peek back' button lets you display the previous document state

Figure 23 *Adjustment layer in Layers panel*

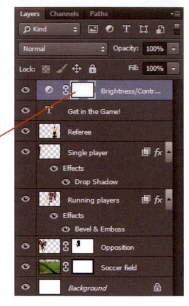

Brightness/Contrast adjustment layer thumbnail

Figure 24 *Adjustments panel*

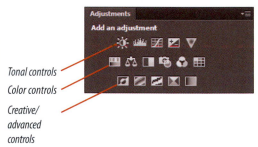

Tonal controls

Color controls

Creative/ advanced controls

Understanding Adjustment Panel Controls

The Adjustments panel, in Figure 24, allows you to apply 16 preset adjustment levels. Presets are available for selection by name, by clicking the Adjustments panel options button, then selecting the preset name. The top five presets (Brightness/Contrast, Levels, Curves, Exposure, and Vibrance) are tonal controls; the next six presets (Hue/Saturation, Color Balance, Black & White, Photo Filter, Channel Mixer, and Color Lookup) are color controls, and the remaining five presets are creative/advanced controls (Invert, Posterize, Threshold, Selective Color, and Gradient Map).

Working with Special Layer Functions

Figure 25 *Result of adjustment layer*

Source: Morguefile.

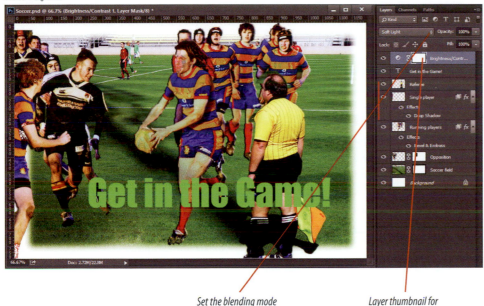

Set the blending mode
for the layer list arrow

Layer thumbnail for
adjustment layer

Applying an Adjustment Layer to a Single Layer

What if you've created an adjustment layer that affects all the layers beneath it, and then you decide you want it to only affect the previous layer? Do you have to delete this adjustment layer and start over? Certainly not. To toggle an adjustment layer between applying to all the layers beneath it and only the layer immediately beneath it, position the pointer between the adjustment layer and the layer beneath it. Press [Alt] (Win) and [option] (Mac), and then click between the two layers, or alternatively, select the adjustment layer, and then click the This adjustment affects all layers below (click to clip to layer) button on the Properties panel. When you see an Adjustment layer that is inset (not aligned with all the other layers), it applies only to the layer immediately beneath it. (A clipped adjustment layer also has a small downward-pointing arrow on the layer.)

Set the blending mode

1. Make sure that the **Brightness/Contrast 1 layer** is the active layer.

TIP If you choose, you can rename an adjustment layer by double-clicking its name on the Layers panel, typing the new name, then pressing [Enter] (Win) or [return] (Mac).

2. Click the **Set the blending mode for the layer list arrow** on the Layers panel, then click **Soft Light**.

TIP You can use as many adjustment layers as you want, but you must create them one at a time. At first glance, this might strike you as a disadvantage, but when you're working on an image, you'll find it to be very helpful. By adding one or more adjustment layers, you can experiment with a variety of colors and tones, then hide and show each one to determine the one that best suits your needs. Adjustment layers can also contain layer masks, which allow you to fine-tune your alterations by painting just the adjustment layer mask. When you are positive that the changes in your adjustment layers should be permanent, you can merge them with any visible layers in the image, including linked layers. You cannot, however, merge one adjustment layer with another adjustment layer. Merging layers reduces file size and ensures that your adjustments will be permanent.

3. Compare your image to Figure 25, then save your work.

You changed the blending mode for the adjustment layer to Soft Light using the Layers panel.

Create a
CLIPPING MASK

What You'll Do

Source: Morguefile.

 In this lesson, you'll create a clipping mask, adjust the opacity of the base layer, remove and restore the clipping mask, and then flatten the image.

Understanding Clipping Masks

A **clipping mask** (sometimes called a **clipping group**) is a group of two or more contiguous layers that are linked for the purpose of masking. Clipping masks are useful when you want one layer to act as the mask for other layers, or if you want an adjustment layer to affect only the layer directly beneath it. The bottom layer in a clipping mask is called the **base layer**, and it serves as the group's mask. For example, you can use a type layer as the base of a clipping mask so that a pattern appears through the text on the base layer, as shown in Figure 26. (On the left side of the figure is the imagery used as the pattern in the type.) The properties of the base layer determine the opacity and visible imagery of a clipping mask. You can, however, adjust the opacity of the individual layers in a clipping mask.

> **QUICK TIP**
>
> Not all clipping mask effects are so dramatic. You can use a clipping mask to add depth and texture to imagery.

Working with Special Layer Functions

Creating a Clipping Mask

To create a clipping mask, you need at least two layers: one to create the shape of the mask, and the other to supply the content for the mask. You can use a type or an image layer to create the clipping mask shape, and when the shape is the way you want it, you can position the pointer between the two layers, and then press [Alt] (Win) or [option] (Mac). The pointer changes to a white square with a black down-pointing arrow. Simply click the line between the layers to create the clipping mask. You can tell if a clipping mask exists by looking at the Layers panel. A clipping mask is indicated when one or more layers are indented and appear with a down arrow icon, and the base layer is underlined.

QUICK TIP

You can merge layers in a clipping mask with an adjustment layer, as long as the layers are visible.

Removing a Clipping Mask

When you create a clipping mask, the layers in the clipping mask are grouped together. To remove a clipping mask, press and hold [Alt] (Win) or [option] (Mac), position the clipping mask pointer over the line separating the grouped layers on the Layers panel, and then click. You can also select the mask layer, click Layer on the Menu bar, and then click Release Clipping Mask.

Figure 26 *Result of clipping group*
© Photodisc/Getty Images.

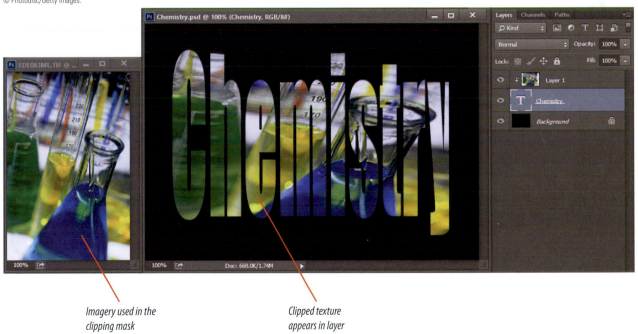

Imagery used in the clipping mask

Clipped texture appears in layer

Create a clipping mask

1. Click the **Get in the Game! layer** on the Layers panel to make it the active layer.

2. Drag the **active layer** below the **Soccer field** on the Layers panel.

3. Press and hold [**Alt**] (Win) or [**option**] (Mac), then point with the **Clipping mask pointer** ⌐ ☐ to the line between the Soccer field and the Get in the Game! layers. Compare your Layers panel to Figure 27.

4. Click the line between the two layers with the **Clipping mask pointer** ⌐ ☐, then release [**Alt**] (Win) or [**option**] (Mac).

   The Get in the Game! (base layer) is filled with the image from the Soccer field layer (member).

5. Verify that the clipping icon (a small downward-pointing arrow) appears in the Soccer field layer, then compare your Layers panel to Figure 28.

You created a clipping mask, using the Soccer field layer as the member and the Get in the Game! layer as the base, which makes the soccer field appear as the fill of the Get in the Game! layer.

Figure 27 *Creating a clipping group*

Clipping mask pointer

Figure 28 *Clipping group on Layers panel*

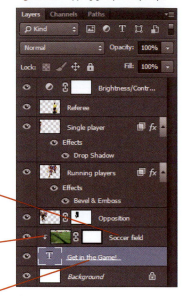

Clipping mask member; Soccer Field layer indented

Arrow indicates clipping group

Base layer name of clipping mask is underlined

Creating 3D Files in Photoshop

Photoshop CC allows you to open and work with three-dimensional files created in programs like Adobe Acrobat X, Autodesk products such as 3ds Max, Maya, and Alias, and Google Earth. Photoshop puts 3D models on a separate layer that you can move or scale, change the lighting, or change rendering modes. Although you must have a 3D authoring program to actually edit the three-dimensional model, you can add multiple 3D layers to an image, combine a 3D layer with a 2D layer, or convert a 3D layer into a 2D layer or Smart Object.

Textures within a 3D file appear as separate layers in Photoshop and can be edited using any painting or adjustment tools. With Photoshop CC you can paint directly on 3D models, and edit, enhance, and manipulate 3D images without using dialog boxes. In addition, 2D images can be wrapped around common 3D geometric shapes (such as cylinders and spheres) and gradient maps can be converted to 3D objects. 3D objects can be grouped within a scene using the 3D menu. These 3D layers can be shared using Sketchfab, a Web service used to publish and display interactive 3D models.

Working with Special Layer Functions

Figure 29 *Finished product*

Source: Morguefile.

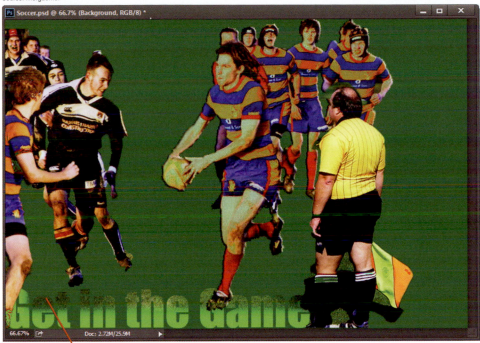

Get in the Game text filled
in with grass texture

Remove a clipping mask

1. Hide the rulers.
2. Click the **Soccer field layer** on the Layers panel, click **Layer** on the Menu bar, then click **Release Clipping Mask**.
3. Click **Edit** on the Menu bar, then click **Undo Release Clipping Mask**.
4. Click the **Get in the Game! layer** on the Layers panel, click the **Move tool** in the Tools panel, then reposition the type so it is in the lower-left corner of the image.
5. Make the **Background layer** active, then display the **Swatches panel**.
6. Click the **Dark Yellow Green color box** (in the sixth row, the sixth box from the left, although your location may vary), then collapse the Swatches panel to the dock.
7. Click the **Paint Bucket tool** on the Tools panel, then click the **image**.

   Compare your screen to Figure 29.
8. Save your work, then close the file and exit Photoshop.

You removed the clipping mask by using the Release Clipping Mask command on the Layer menu, then restored the clipping mask by using the Undo command on the Edit menu.

POWER USER SHORTCUTS			
To do this:	**Use this method:**	**To do this:**	**Use this method:**
Activate layer mask	Press and hold [Ctrl][\] (Win) or ⌘ [\] (Mac)	Disable layer mask	Layer ➢ Layer Mask ➢ Disable
Add an adjustment layer	[icon]	Flip layer content horizontally	Edit ➢ Transform ➢ Flip Horizontal
Align selected layers by vertical centers	Layer ➢ Align ➢ Vertical Centers	Previous or Next brush tip in Brush panel or Brush Presets panel	[,] or [.]
Blend pixels on a layer	Double-click a layer thumbnail, click Blend If list arrow, choose color, drag This Layer and Underlying Layer sliders	Remove a clipping mask	Select layer, then Layer ➢ Release Clipping Mask
Brush tool	[icon] or **B**	Remove a link	[icon]
Change brush tip	Select Brush tool, open Brush Preset picker, then select brush tip	Rotate a layer 90° to the left	Edit ➢ Transform ➢ Rotate 90° CCW
Create a clipping mask	Press and hold [Alt] (Win) or [option] (Mac), move the pointer to the line between two layers, then click	Scale a layer	Edit ➢ Transform ➢ Scale
Create a layer/vector mask	[icon]	Select first or last brush tip in Brushes panel	[Shift][,] or [Shift][.]
Create a layer mask that hides the selection	Press and hold [Alt] (Win) or [option] (Mac), click [icon]	Switch foreground and background colors	**X**
Create a layer mask that reveals the selection	Layer ➢ Layer Mask ➢ Reveal Selection	Use Content-Aware Scaling	Edit ➢ Content-Aware Scale
Delete layer	[icon]		

Key: Menu items are indicated by ➢ between the menu name and its command. Blue bold letters are shortcuts for selecting tools on the Tools panel.

Use a layer mask with a selection.

1. Start Photoshop, open PS 8-2.psd from the drive and folder where you store your Data Files, then save it as **Stripes**.
2. Make sure the rulers are displayed in pixels.
3. Change the zoom factor to 150% or 200%, to enlarge your view of the image.
4. Create a type layer title in black with the text **We must do lunch!** above the Zebra layer and add the drop shadow layer style (using default settings). (*Hint*: A 24 pt Segoe Print Regular font is shown in the sample. Use any other font on your computer if this font is not available.)
5. Make the Zebra layer active, then select the Elliptical Marquee tool.
6. Change the Feather setting on the options bar to 5 pixels.
7. Create a marquee selection from 35 X/35 Y to 235 X/360 Y (at the bottom of the image). (*Hint*: Feel free to add guides, if necessary.)
8. Use the Layers panel to add a layer mask.
9. Save your work.

Work with multiple masked layers.

1. Select the Brush tool, and reset the brushes.
2. Hide the type layer.
3. Change the existing brush tip to Soft Round with a size of 9 pixels.
4. Change the Painting mode to Normal, and the flow and opacity to 100% (if those are not the current settings).
5. Use the default foreground and background colors to paint the area from 20 X/70 Y to 65 X/290 Y.

(*Hint*: Make sure the layer mask thumbnail is selected and that white is the foreground color and black is the background color.)

6. Display the type layer.
7. Make the Fern layer active.
8. Unlink the Background layer from the Fern layer.
9. Rotate the fern so that its left edge barely touches the zebra's nose, then commit your edits.
10. Save your work.

Control pixels to blend colors.

1. Double-click the Fern layer thumbnail.
2. Using green as the Blend If color, drag the right This Layer slider to 200.
3. Split the right This Layer slider, drag the right half to 240, then click OK. (*Hint*: Press the [Alt] or [option] key to split the slider.)
4. Save your work.

Disable and enable a layer mask.

1. Click the layer mask thumbnail on the Zebra layer.
2. Use the Layer menu to disable the layer mask.
3. Use the Layer menu to enable the layer mask.
4. Save your work.

Use an adjustment layer.

1. Make the Fern layer active.
2. Using the Layer menu, create a Color Balance adjustment layer called Modifications.
3. Make sure Midtones is selected, drag the Cyan/Red, Magenta/Green, and Yellow/Blue sliders to +36, +12, and −19, respectively.
4. Create a Brightness/Contrast adjustment layer, above the Modifications layer.

---

5. Change the Brightness to −25 and the Contrast to +20.
6. Hide the Modifications layer.
7. Hide the Brightness/Contrast layer.
8. Display both adjustment layers.
9. Save your work.

Create a clipping mask.

1. Make the Background layer active.
2. Create a clipping mask (with the Background layer as the base layer) that includes the type layer. (*Hint*: Move the type layer to a new location, if necessary.)
3. Save your work, then compare your image to Figure 30.

Figure 30 *Completed Skills Review*
© Photodisc/Getty Images.

Your cousin has recently purchased a beauty shop and wants to increase the number of manicure customers. She's hired you to create an eye-catching image that can be used in print ads. You decided to take an ordinary image and use your knowledge of masks and adjustment layers to make the image look striking.

1. Open PS 8-3.psd, then save it as **Pro Nails**.
2. Duplicate the Polishes layer, then name the new layer **Red Polish**.
3. On the Red Polish layer, select the red nail polish bottle and cap, then delete everything else in the layer. (*Hint*: You can do this by deleting a selection.)
4. Hide the Red Polish layer, then make the Polishes layer active.
5. Create a layer mask that hides the red polish, then reveal the remaining items on the Polishes layer if necessary.
6. Use any tools at your disposal to fix (display areas you want visible; hide areas you want hidden) the area where the red polish (on the Polishes layer) has been masked.
7. Display the Red Polish layer.
8. Move the Red Polish layer below the Polishes layer on the Layers panel (if necessary).
9. Use the existing layer mask to hide the white polish (with the blue cap).
10. Position the red polish bottle so it appears where the white polish bottle was visible.
11. Use any tools necessary to fix areas you want to improve, such as the Blur tool to soften the edges of polish bottles.
12. Add an adjustment layer to the Red Polish layer that makes the polish color a darker red. (*Hint*: In the sample, a Hue/Saturation adjustment layer was used with the following settings: Hue: −16, Saturation: +42, and Lightness: −17.)
13. Add one or two brief type layers, and apply layer styles to at least one of them. (*Hint*: In the sample, the type used is a 36 pt Brush Script Std Regular and a 50 pt Cambria Math Regular font.)
14. Save your work, then compare your image to the sample in Figure 31.

Figure 31 *Sample Project Builder 1*
© Photodisc/Getty Images.

Working with Special Layer Functions

In exchange for free concert tickets, your hiking club has volunteered to promote keeping our environment clean. Before the concert, you have agreed to design a print poster to inspire concertgoers to throw trash in the trash barrels. You decide to create a Photoshop image that contains several unique illusions. Using any city or locale other than your own as a theme, you'll use your Photoshop skills to create and paint layer masks in an image that promotes your club and conveys a cleanup message.

1. Obtain the following images: a landscape, a sign, one large inanimate object, and two or more smaller objects that evoke a city or locale of your choice. You can use images that are available on your computer, scan print media, or use a digital camera. (*Hint*: Try to obtain images that fit your theme.)

2. Open the images you obtained, then create a new Photoshop image and save it as **Cleanup**.

3. Drag the landscape to the Cleanup image above the Background layer, then delete the Background layer.

4. Drag the large object image to the Cleanup image above the landscape layer.

5. Transform the large object as necessary to prepare it to be partially buried in the landscape. (*Hint*: The tower layer in the sample has been rotated and resized.)

6. Apply a layer mask to the large object, then paint the layer mask to reshape the mask and partially obscure the object.

7. Drag the sign image to the Cleanup image, then place it below the large object layer on the Layers panel.

8. Create a type layer for the sign layer with a message (humor optional), link the layers, then transform the layers as needed to fit in the image. (*Hint*: The sign layer and type layer in the sample have been skewed.)

9. Drag other images as desired to the Cleanup image, and add styles to them or transform them as necessary.

10. Create other type layers (humor optional) as desired, and apply a style to at least one layer. (*Hint*: The title layer in the sample has drop shadow and outer glow styles applied to it. An 18 pt Arial Regular font is used in the sign, and a 35 and 24 pt Arial Black Regular is used in the title.)

11. Add an adjustment layer to the landscape layer, and to any other layer that would benefit from it. (You can clip it to a layer if you choose.)

12. Save your work, then compare your image to the sample in Figure 32.

Figure 32 *Sample Project Builder 2*
© Photodisc/Getty Images.

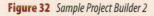

As the publishing director for a large accounting firm, you've been asked to design a banner for the new International Monetary Division website. They've asked that you include a flag, paper currency, and coinage of a country of your choice. You decide to use techniques to create an interesting collage of those three items.

1. Obtain several images of paper currency and coins, and a flag from a country (or countries) of your choice. You can use the images that are available on your computer, scan print media, or connect to the Internet and download images. (*Hint*: Try to obtain at least two denominations of both paper and coin.)

2. Create a new image in Photoshop and save it as **Currency**.

3. Open the paper money image files, then drag the paper money images to the currency image above the Background layer.

4. Transform the paper money layers as desired. (*Hint*: The paper money layers in the sample have been rotated and skewed.)

5. Add layer masks as desired.

6. Add an adjustment layer to the paper money layer, and apply at least one color adjustment. (*Hint*: The paper money layer in the sample have a Brightness/Contrast adjustment applied to them.)

7. Open the flag file, then drag the flag image to the Currency image, and position it to appear on top of the paper money layers, then resize it and adjust opacity, as necessary.

8. Apply a Curves adjustment layer to the flag.

9. Open the coin image files, drag the coin images to the Currency image, duplicate the coin layers as desired, position them above the flag layer, then apply at least one transformation and one layer style to them. (*Hint*: The coins in the sample have a Drop Shadow style and have been rotated.)

10. Blend the pixels for two of the coin layers.

11. Save your work, then compare your image to the sample in Figure 33.

Figure 33 *Sample Design Project*
© Photodisc/Getty Images.

Working with Special Layer Functions

Lost Horizons, a tragically hip coffeehouse, is hosting a regional multimedia Poetry Slam contest. You have teamed up with the Surreal Poetry Enclave, an eclectic poetry group. The contest consists of the poetry group reading poetry while you create a visual interpretation using two preselected images and as many elective images as you want. First, though, you must submit an entry design. Find a poem for inspiration, design the interpretation, obtain images, and write some creative copy (tag line or slogan) to be used in the design.

1. Obtain images for your interpretative design. The images you must include are a picture frame and a background image; the other pieces are up to you. You can use the images that are available on your computer, scan print media, or connect to the Internet and download images.

2. Create a new Photoshop image, then save it as **Poetry Poster**.

3. Open the background image file, drag the background image to the Poetry Poster image above the Background layer.

4. Open the picture frame image file, drag it to the Poetry Poster image above the Background layer, transform it as necessary, then apply styles to it if desired. (*Hint*: The frame in the sample has been skewed.)

5. Open the image files that will go in or on the picture frame, drag them to the Poetry Poster image, then transform them as necessary.

6. Arrange the image layers on the Layers panel in the configuration you want, and apply styles to them if you think they will enhance the image.

7. Apply a layer mask to two or more of the image layers.

8. Create a clipping mask using two or more of the image layers. (*Hint*: The clipping mask in the sample consists of the type layer as the base and the Books layer.)

9. Create type layers as desired and apply styles to them. (*Hint*: The type layer in the sample has Inner Glow and Outer Glow styles applied to it.)

10. Close the image files, save your work, then compare your image to the sample in Figure 34.

11. Be prepared to discuss the creative ways you can use clipping masks.

Figure 34 *Sample Portfolio Project*
Source: Morguefile.

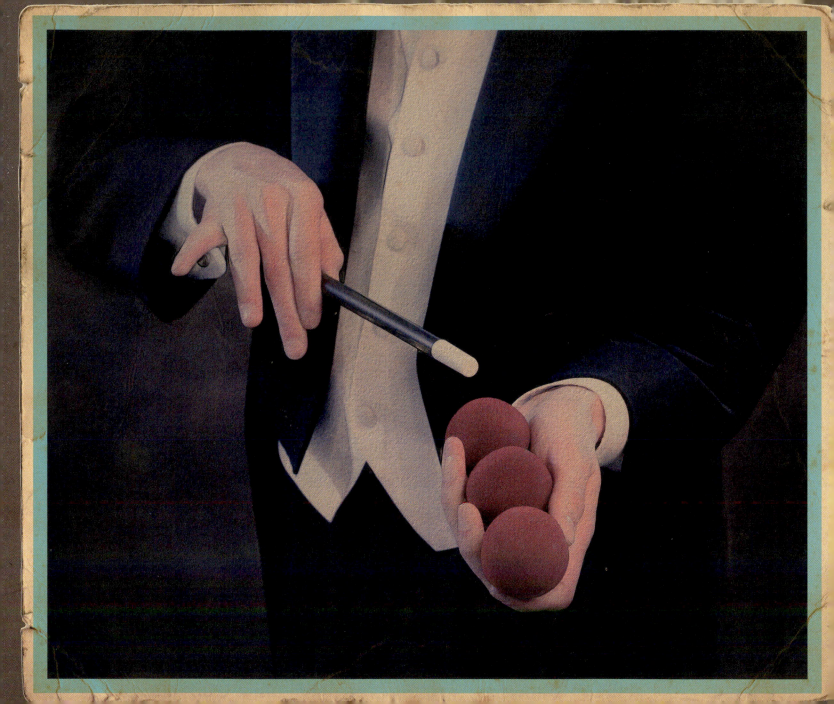

CHAPTER **9**

CREATING SPECIAL EFFECTS
WITH FILTERS

1. Learn about filters and how to apply them

2. Create an effect with an Artistic filter

3. Add unique effects with Stylize filters

4. Alter images with Distort and Noise filters

5. Alter lighting with a Render filter

6. Use Perspective Warp and Vanishing Point to add perspective

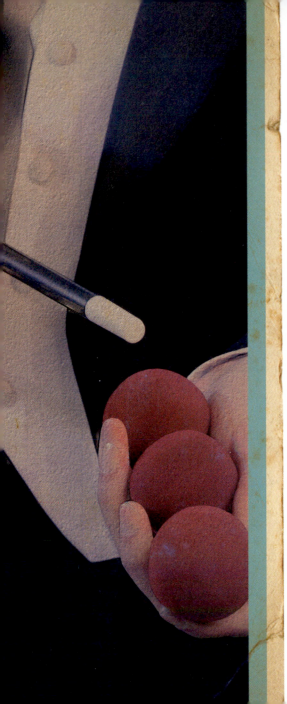

CHAPTER 9 CREATING SPECIAL EFFECTS
WITH FILTERS

Understanding Filters

You've already seen some of the filters that Photoshop offers. Filters modify the look of an image by altering pixels in a particular pattern or format, across a layer or a selection. This results in a unique, customized appearance. You use filters to apply special effects, such as realistic textures, distortions, changes in lighting, and blurring. Although you can use several types of filters and options, and can apply them to multiple layers in an image, the most important thing to remember when using filters is subtlety.

Applying Filters

You can apply filters to any layer (except the Background layer) using commands on the Filter menu. Most filters open in a dialog box where you can adjust filter settings and preview the effect before applying it. The preview window in the dialog box allows you to evaluate the precise effect of the filter on your selection. You can zoom in and out, and pan the image in the preview window to get a good look before making a final decision. Other filters—those whose menu command is not followed by an ellipsis (…)—apply their effects instantly as soon as you click the command.

QUICK **TIP**

Does your computer have enough RAM? You'll know for sure when you start using filters because they are very memory-intensive.

TOOLS YOU'LL USE

Blur filters

Filter	
Last Filter	Ctrl+F
Convert for Smart Filters	
Filter Gallery...	
Adaptive Wide Angle...	Alt+Shift+Ctrl+A
Camera Raw Filter...	Shift+Ctrl+A
Lens Correction...	Shift+Ctrl+R
Liquify...	Shift+Ctrl+X
Vanishing Point...	Alt+Ctrl+V
Blur	▶
Blur Gallery	▶
Distort	▶
Noise	▶
Pixelate	▶
Render	▶
Sharpen	▶
Stylize	▶
Video	▶
Other	▶
Digimarc	▶
Browse Filters Online...	

Average
Blur
Blur More
Box Blur...
Gaussian Blur...
Lens Blur...
Motion Blur...
Radial Blur...
Shape Blur...
Smart Blur...
Surface Blur...

Noise filters

Add Noise...
Despeckle
Dust & Scratches...
Median...
Reduce Noise...

Render filters

Clouds
Difference Clouds
Fibers...
Lens Flare...
Lighting Effects...

Diffuse...
Emboss...
Extrude...
Find Edges
Solarize
Tiles...
Trace Contour...
Wind...

Stylize filters

Learn About Filters and
HOW TO APPLY THEM

What You'll Do

Image courtesy of Elizabeth Eisner Reding

 In this lesson, you'll apply the Motion Blur filter to the Brown bar layer and convert the contents of a layer into a Smart Object.

Understanding the Filter Menu

The Filter menu sorts filters into categories and subcategories. Many filters are memory-intensive, so depending on the capabilities of your computer, you might need to wait several seconds while Photoshop applies the effect. Using filters might slow down your computer's performance and insufficient computer memory capacity may result in some filters being unavailable. Figure 1 shows samples of several filters and Table 1 (on page 9-6) describes the filter categories.

Learning About Filters

You can read about filters all day long, but until you apply one yourself, it's all academic. When you do, here are a few tips to keep in mind.

■ Distort filters can completely reshape an image; they are highly resource-demanding.
■ Photoshop applies a few of the Pixelate filters as soon as you click the command, without opening a dialog box.
■ Digimarc filters notify users that the image is copyright-protected.

Applying a Filter

You can apply a filter by clicking the Filter menu, pointing to the filter category, then clicking the filter name. When you click a filter name, the filter may be applied or a dialog box may open. If a dialog box opens, you can adjust setting properties. You can also apply one or more filters using the Filter Gallery. When you click a Filter menu name, the dialog box displays a sample of each filter in the category.

Using Smart Filters

Smart Objects, which are one or more objects on one or more layers that have been modified so that they can be scaled, rotated, or warped without losing image quality, can have filters applied to them. These filters are called **Smart Filters**. Smart Filters can be adjusted,

Figure 1 *Examples of filters*

Image courtesy of Elizabeth Eisner Reding

Destructive versus Nondestructive Editing

In the early days of Photoshop (the program celebrated its 20th anniversary in 2010), any editing change you made was *destructive*, in that it permanently altered the pixels in your image. There was no going back, except if you made duplicate layers of everything you ever did. *Nondestructive* editing, as the name implies, means that you can go back and edit what used to be a permanent change to pixels. An example of nondestructive editing is the application of adjustment layers versus applying an adjustment to a layer and hoping that you never have to remove or change it.

removed, or hidden, and are nondestructive. Any filter, with the exception of Extract, Liquify, Pattern Maker, and Vanishing Point, can be applied as a Smart Filter. You won't find the Smart Filter command on the Filter menu; simply apply a filter to a Smart

Object and it will be applied as a Smart Filter. Once the filter is applied, the Smart Filter appears in the Layers panel. Double-clicking the filter on the Layers panel opens the Filter Gallery, enabling you to modify or change the existing filter.

QUICK TIP

An active layer can become a Smart Object by clicking Filter on the menu bar, clicking Convert for Smart Filters, then clicking OK in the warning box, or by clicking Layer on the menu bar, pointing to Smart Objects, then clicking Convert to Smart Object.

Understanding the Filter Gallery

The **Filter Gallery** is a feature that lets you see the effects of each filter *before* its application. You can also use the Filter Gallery to apply filters (either individually, or in groups), rearrange filters, and change individual filter settings. The Filter Gallery is opened by clicking Filter on the Menu bar, and then clicking Filter Gallery. In Figure 2, the Patchwork filter (in the Texture category) is applied to the active layer, which has been enlarged for easier viewing in the preview window.

QUICKTIP

Not all filters in the Filter menu are available in the Filter Gallery.

Figure 2 *Filter Gallery dialog box*
Source: Morguefile.

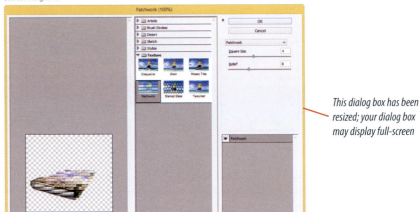

This dialog box has been resized; your dialog box may display full-screen

TABLE 1: FILTER CATEGORIES			
Category	**Use**	**Category**	**Use**
Artistic	Replicates traditional fine arts effects.	Sharpen	Refocuses blurry objects by increasing contrast in adjacent pixels.
Blur	Softens a selection or image; can use to retouch photographs.	Sketch	Applies a texture, or simulates a fine arts hard-drawn effect.
Brush Strokes	Mimics fine arts brushwork and ink effects.	Stylize	Produces a painted or impressionistic effect.
Distort	Reshapes an image.	Texture	Gives the appearance of depth or substance.
Noise	Gives an aged look; can use to retouch photographs.	Video	Restricts color use to those that are acceptable for television reproduction and smooths video images.
Pixelate	Adds small honeycomb shapes based on similar colors that sharply define a selection.	Other	Creates unique filters, modifies masks, and makes quick color adjustments.
Render	Creates three-dimensional shapes; simulates light reflections.	Digimarc	Embeds a digital watermark that stores copyright information.

© Cengage Learning®

Using the Blur Gallery to Soften an Image

The Blur Gallery is an intuitive, on-image, selective softening tool for generating shallow depth-of-field and tilt-shift effects and includes an Iris Blur that creates a post-camera vignette focus. The Blur Gallery consists of the Field Blur, Iris Blur, Tilt Shift, Path Blur, and Spin Blur filters all located within the Blur Gallery category in the Filter menu. The Spin Blur and Path Blur tools allow you to create a circular spin blur (a radial-style blur measured in degrees) and a camera motion blur. Regardless which Blur Gallery filter you choose, the Blur Tools and Blur Effects panels open displaying options for each of the filters. Each of the Blur Gallery filters has its own controls, and each has Bokeh Color controls. **Bokeh** (pronounced BOH-kay) is a Japanese term used to describe the qualities of an unfocused area within a photo.

Blur Gallery settings include:

- Adjust the Pin: move the Pin by clicking and dragging in the Center; delete the Pin by pressing the Delete key with the Pin selected; add a new Pin by clicking the image in a desired location.
- Adjust the Ellipse: adjust the size or rotation of the focus Ellipse by clicking and dragging the Ellipse handle; make the Ellipse more square by clicking and dragging the roundness knob.
- Adjust Focus: adjust the amount of focus using the Blur slider in the Blur Tools panel or click and drag the white ring next to the Focus Ring.
- Adjust the Feather Handles: move the feather edge by clicking and dragging a feather handle.
- In the Blur Effects panel, adjust the Light Bokeh Slider (used to enhance out-of-focus areas): use the Light Range controls to determine which Brightness values will be impacted by the Light Bokeh; swap the position of the dark and light sliders to get a different, less saturated effect.

Figure 3 *Current Layers panel*

Open a Blur filter

1. Start Photoshop, display the **Essentials workspace**, open PS 9-1.psd from the drive and folder where you store your Data Files, then save it as **Poolside**.

2. Click the **Default Foreground and Background Colors button** on the Tools panel to display the default settings.

TIP It's a good habit to check Photoshop settings and display the rulers before you begin your work if you'll need these features.

3. Click the **Indicates layer visibility button** on the plant LEFT layer on the Layers panel.

4. Click on the plant CENTER layer on the Layers panel.

5. Click on the plant RIGHT layer on the Layers panel.

6. Click the **Brown bar layer** on the Layers panel to make it active. Compare your Layers panel to Figure 3.

7. Zoom in until the zoom factor is **200%**.

8. Click **Filter** on the Menu bar, point to **Blur**, then click **Motion Blur**.

TIP The most recent filter applied to a layer appears at the top of the Filter menu.

You set default foreground and background colors, hid three layers, then opened the Motion Blur dialog box.

Apply a Blur filter

1. Position the **brown bar** in the preview window with the **Hand pointer** 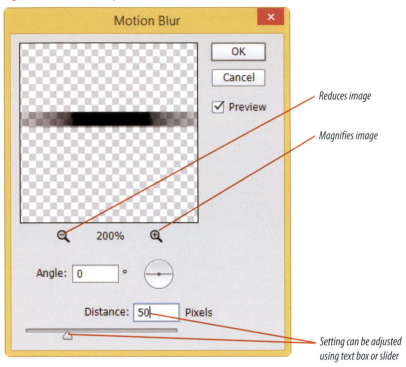, then reduce or enlarge the image using the buttons beneath the preview window so it displays in the center.

    The brown bar image is repositioned from the left area to the center of the preview window.

2. Verify that **0** is in the Angle text box.

3. Type **50** in the Distance text box, then compare your dialog box to Figure 4.

    TIP You can also adjust the settings in the Motion Blur dialog box by dragging the Angle wheel and/or the Distance slider.

4. Click **OK**.

    The Motion Blur filter is applied to the Brown bar layer.

    TIP You can use the Field blur filter when you need the most flexibility and control in blurring specific areas while maintaining clarity in other areas. The Tilt-Shift blur filter is used to control areas of blur by applying marking pins to blur all or part of a layer; the amount of blur can then be distorted or rotated.

    You repositioned the Brown bar layer in the preview window, then applied a Motion Blur filter to the layer.

Figure 4 *Motion Blur dialog box*

Reduces image

Magnifies image

Setting can be adjusted using text box or slider

Learning About Motion Filters

When you apply a Blur filter, keep in mind how you want your object to appear—perhaps to look as if it's moving or to create the illusion of depth. Blur filters smooth the transitions between different colors. The effect of the Blur More filter is four times stronger than the Blur filter. The Gaussian Blur filter produces more of a hazy effect. The direction of the blur is determined by the Angle setting—a straight horizontal path has an angle set to zero. The Motion Blur filter simulates taking a picture of an object in motion, and the Radial Blur filter simulates zooming or rotation. You can use the Smart Blur filter to set exactly how the filter will blur the image.

Creating Special Effects with Filters

Figure 5 *Motion Blur filter applied to layer*
Image courtesy of Elizabeth Eisner Reding

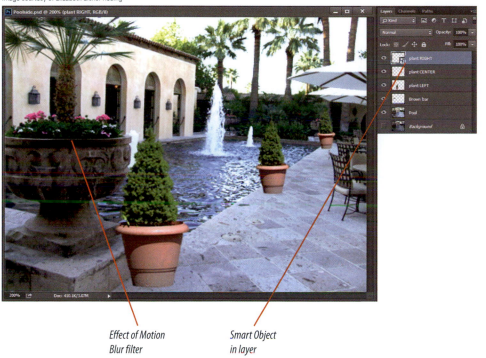

Effect of Motion
Blur filter

Smart Object
in layer

1. Click the **Indicates layer visibility button** ▢ on the plant RIGHT layer on the Layers panel.

2. Click ▢ on the plant CENTER layer on the Layers panel.

3. Click ▢ on the plant LEFT layer on the Layers panel.

TIP You can display/hide all layers *except* the one being clicked by pressing [Alt] 👁 /[Alt] ▢ (Win) or [option] 👁 /[option] ▢ (Mac).

4. Click the **plant RIGHT layer** on the Layers panel.

TIP Any layer can be turned into a Smart Object. Before you apply any filters to a layer, convert it to a Smart Object, which will give you full editing capabilities over your filter selections.

5. Click **Layer** on the Menu bar, point to **Smart Objects**, then click **Convert to Smart Object**.

6. Save your work, then compare your image and Layers panel to Figure 5.

You restored the visibility of three layers and converted one of the layers into a Smart Object. The ability to turn layers on and off while working on an image means you can reduce distracting elements and concentrate on specific objects.

Reducing Blur with the Smart Sharpen Filter

You can use the Smart Sharpen Filter to remove or reduce blurriness. This filter can be used to remove blur effects in images created by Gaussian Blur, Lens Blur, or Motion Blur filters. The Smart Sharpen Filter is available by clicking Filter on the Menu bar, pointing to Sharpen, and then clicking Smart Sharpen. Using the settings in the Smart Sharpen dialog box, you can change the amount as a percentage, adjust the radius in pixels, reduce noise, and choose the type of blur to be modified. You can also adjust shadow and highlight settings if desired.

Create an Effect with
AN ARTISTIC FILTER

What You'll Do

Image courtesy of Elizabeth Eisner Reding

 In this lesson, you'll apply the Poster Edges filter from the Artistic category to the plant RIGHT layer and then adjust the contrast and brightness of the layer.

Learning About Artistic Filters

You can dramatically alter an image by using Artistic filters. **Artistic filters** replicate traditional fine arts effects, are available from the Filter Gallery, and can be used for special effects in television commercials and other multimedia venues.

Taking Advantage of Smart Filters

Just as you can convert an object on a layer into a Smart Object to make your edits nondestructive, you can perform a similar operation to give the application of filters the same power. So, while you can apply a filter directly to a layer, you can just as easily apply a Smart Filter. If the active layer is not already a Smart Object, you can apply a Smart Filter on-the-fly using the Convert for Smart Filters command on the Filter menu. This command automatically converts your layer into a Smart Object.

> **QUICK TIP**
>
> A Smart Filter is nothing more than a filter that is applied to a Smart Object.

Using Artistic Filters

There are 15 Artistic filters. Figure 6 shows examples of some of the Artistic filters. The following list contains the names of each of the Artistic filters and their effects.

- Colored Pencil has a colored pencil effect and retains important edges.
- Cutout allows high-contrast images to appear in silhouette and has the effect of using several layers of colored paper.

> **Learning About Third-Party Plug-Ins**
>
> A **plug-in** is any external program that adds features and functionality to another program while working from within that program. Plug-ins enable you to obtain and work in additional file types and formats, add dazzling special effects, or take advantage of efficient shortcuts. You can purchase Photoshop plug-ins from third-party companies, or download them from freeware sites. To locate Photoshop plug-ins, you can use your favorite Internet search engine, or search for plug-ins on Adobe's website, *www.adobe.com*.

- Dry Brush simplifies an image by reducing its range of colors.
- Film Grain applies even color variations throughout an object.
- Fresco paints an image with short, rounded dabs of color.
- Neon Glow adds a glow effect to selected objects.
- Paint Daubs gives an image a painterly effect.
- Palette Knife reduces the level of detail in an image, revealing underlying texture.

- Plastic Wrap accentuates surface details and makes the contents of a layer appear to be covered in plastic.
- Poster Edges reduces the number of colors in an image and draws black lines on the edges of the image.
- Rough Pastels makes an image look as if it is stroked with colored pastel chalk on a textured background.
- Smudge Stick softens an image by smudging or smearing darker areas.
- Sponge creates highly textured areas, making an object look like it was painted with a sponge.

- Underpainting paints the image on a textured background.
- Watercolor simplifies the appearance of an object, making it look like it was painted with watercolors.

Adjusting Filter Effects

You can change the appearance of a filter by using any of the functions listed under the Adjustments command on the Image menu or the Adjustments panel. For example, you can modify the color balance or the brightness/contrast of a layer before or after you apply a filter to it.

Figure 6 *Examples of Artistic filters*

© Photodisc/Getty Images.

Apply a Smart Filter (Artistic filter) with the Filter Gallery

1. With the plant RIGHT layer active, click **Filter** on the Menu bar, click **Filter Gallery**, then move the image so that it is visible in the preview window.

   The Filter Gallery displays thumbnails of each filter as you expand each category, so you can see a quick overview of what effects are available.

   TIP The settings available for a filter in the Filter Gallery are the same as those in the individual dialog box that opens when you click the category name in the menu.

2. Click the **Zoom level list arrow** on the status bar of the Filter Gallery, then click **200%**.

   TIP You can zoom in and out of the Filter Gallery by pressing [Ctrl][+]/[Ctrl][−] (Win) or ⌘ [+]/⌘ [−] (Mac).

3. Click the **expand arrow** ▷ to the left of the Artistic folder, then click **Poster Edges**.

4. Type **10** in the Edge Thickness text box.

   The Edge Thickness determines the settings of the edges within the image.

5. Type **5** in the Edge Intensity text box.

   The Edge Intensity setting gives the edges more definition.

6. Type **3** in the Posterization text box, then compare your dialog box to Figure 7.

   The Posterization setting controls the number of unique colors the filter will reproduce in the image.

7. Click **OK**, then compare your image and Layers panel to Figure 8.

Using the Filter Gallery, you magnified the selected object, then applied the Poster Edges filter to the plant RIGHT layer. The far-right plant now looks less realistic than the other two potted plants, and shows poster effects.

Figure 7 *Poster Edges filter in Filter Gallery dialog box*

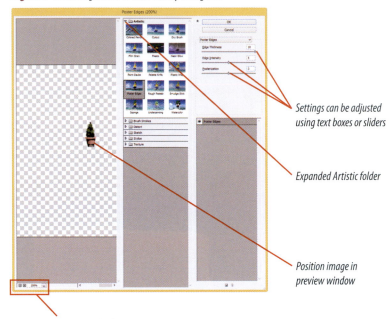

Settings can be adjusted using text boxes or sliders

Expanded Artistic folder

Position image in preview window

Click to change the zoom level in the preview window

Figure 8 *Poster Edges filter applied to layer*
Image courtesy of Elizabeth Eisner Reding

Indicates Smart Filter

Effect of Poster Edges filter

Figure 9 *Image adjusted*
Image courtesy of Elizabeth Eisner Reding

*Brightness and contrast
adjusted on image*

Adjust the filter effect and modify the Smart Filter

1. Click the **Brightness/Contrast button** ☼ on the Adjustments panel.

2. Type **30** in the Brightness text box.

3. Type **20** in the Contrast text box.

4. Double-click the **Filter Gallery effect** under the plant RIGHT layer on the Layers panel.

TIP To open the Filter Gallery and edit a Smart Filter, click (the words) Filter Gallery in the Layers panel.

5. Click **Smudge Stick** in the Artistic category, click **OK**, then collapse the Properties panel to the Dock.

6. Save your work, then compare your image to Figure 9.

You adjusted the brightness and contrast of the image and changed the existing filter type.

NEW   Using Filters to Refine Selection Masks

Hidden within the Other category of the Filters menu are the Minimum and Maximum filters. These two filters are typically used to refine selection masks. Selection masks can be refined with a bias towards either roundness or squareness using either decimals or whole numbers.

Add Unique Effects
WITH STYLIZE FILTERS

What You'll Do

Image courtesy of Elizabeth Eisner Reding

 In this lesson, you'll apply a solarize filter to a copy of the plant LEFT layer and a Wind filter to the Brown bar layer. You'll also apply the Poster Edges filter to two layers using the Filter Gallery.

Learning About Stylize Filters

Stylize filters produce a painted or impressionistic effect by displacing pixels and heightening the contrast within an image. Figure 10 shows several Stylize filters. Several commonly used Stylize filters and their effects are listed below:

- The Diffuse filter breaks up the image so that it looks less focused. The Darken Only option replaces light pixels with dark pixels, and the Lighten Only option replaces dark pixels with light pixels.
- The Extrude filter gives a 3D texture to a selection or layer.
- The Wind filter conveys directed motion.

- The Glowing Edges filter finds the edges of color and adds a neon-like glow to them.
- The Emboss filter makes a selection appear raised or stamped.

Applying a Filter to a Selection

Instead of applying a filter to an entire layer, you can specify a particular area of a layer to which you want to apply a filter. First, you define the area by using a selection tool, and then choose the desired filter, which will be applied to the selection by default. If you want to apply a filter to a layer that contains a mask, be sure to select the layer name, not the layer mask thumbnail.

Embedding a Watermark for Copyright

Before you can embed a watermark, you must first register with Digimarc Corporation. When Photoshop detects a watermark in an image, it displays the copyright image © in the image file's tab. To check if an image has a watermark, flatten the image if necessary, click Filter on the Menu bar, point to Digimarc, and then click Read Watermark.

Figure 10 *Examples of Stylize filters*

© Photodisc/Getty Images.

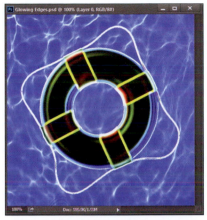

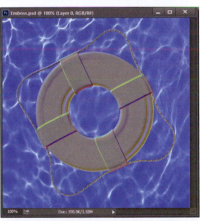

Browsing Filters Online

You might notice that at the bottom of the Filter menu is the option to Browse Filters Online. When you click this option, your browser will open and go to the Adobe Add-ons website which contains links for filter downloads, as well as plug-ins, extensions, and other content. You can also use your favorite browser to locate sites that offer Photoshop filters that are either available for free or for a small fee. (Some filters are available as plug-ins.)

Apply a Stylize filter

1. Click the **plant LEFT layer** on the Layers panel.

2. Drag the layer to the **Create a new layer button**  on the Layers panel. A new layer (called plant LEFT copy) displays above the plant LEFT layer in the Layers panel and is active.

3. Click the **Move tool** on the Tools panel, press and hold [**Shift**] while moving the new layer to the right of the existing plant LEFT, then release [**Shift**].

4. Click **Filter** on the Menu bar, point to **Stylize** as shown in Figure 11, then click **Solarize**.

TIP In addition to just looking interesting, the Solarize filter can be used to reduce shadows and make an image more equalized. In this effect, dark areas appear lighter and light areas appear darker.

5. Compare your image to Figure 12.

You copied the plant LEFT layer, moved the copy, then applied the Solarize filter to the copied layer.

Figure 11 *Stylize options on the Filter menu*

Figure 12 *Effect of Solarize filter*
Image courtesy of Elizabeth Eisner Reding

Pixels appear in a different color

Using Filters to Reduce File Size

If you apply a filter to a small area, you can view the effect while conserving your computer's resources. For example, you can test several filters on a small area, and then decide which one you want to apply to one or more layers. Alternatively, you can apply a filter to a large portion of a layer, such as applying a slight Motion Blur filter to a grassy background. Your viewers will not notice an appreciable difference when they look at the grass, but by applying the filter, you reduce the number of green colors Photoshop must save in the image, which reduces the size of the file.

Figure 13 *Elliptical Marquee selection*
Image courtesy of Elizabeth Eisner Reding

Marquee surrounds
the box

Figure 14 *Wind dialog box*
Image courtesy of Elizabeth Eisner Reding

Figure 15 *Effect of Wind filter*
Image courtesy of Elizabeth Eisner Reding

Wind filter applied
to copied layer

Apply a filter to a selection

1. Verify that the plant LEFT copy layer is active.

2. Click the **Rectangular Marquee tool** 🔲 on the Tools panel.

3. Change the Feather setting to **0 px** if it is not already set to 0.

4. Display the rulers, draw a **rectangle** around an area that includes the right side of the solarized plant (from approximately **260 X/140 Y** to **300 X/245 Y**) using the **Marquee pointer** ┼, as shown in Figure 13, then turn off the ruler display.

5. Click **Filter** on the Menu bar, point to **Stylize**, then click **Wind**.

6. Click the **Blast option button** in the Method section of the Wind dialog box.

7. Click the **From the Left option button** in the Direction section of the Wind dialog box if it is not already selected, then compare your dialog box to Figure 14.

8. Click **OK**.

9. Deselect the marquee, then compare your image to Figure 15.

You used the Rectangular Marquee tool to select a specific area on the plant LEFT copy layer, then applied the Wind filter to the selection.

Use the Filter Gallery to apply a previously used filter

1. Click the **plant CENTER layer** on the Layers panel.
2. Click **Filter** on the Menu bar, then click **Filter Gallery**. Compare your Filter Gallery to Figure 16.

TIP When the Filter Gallery opens, the filter that was last applied using the Filter Gallery is selected by default.

3. Click **OK**.

The filter last applied using the Filter Gallery is applied to the active layer.

You applied the Poster Edges filter to the plant CENTER layer using the Filter Gallery.

Figure 16 *Last filter applied on Filter Gallery*

Last applied filter

Figure 17 *Combining filters*

Multiple filters applied to image

Adds new filter layer

Using the Filter Gallery to Combine Effects

The Filter Gallery offers more than just another way of applying a single filter. Using this feature, you can apply multiple filters. And using the same principles as on the Layers panel, you can rearrange the filter layers and control their visibility. Figure 17 shows part of the Filter Gallery for an image to which four different filters have been applied, but only the effects of two are visible. Each time you apply, reorder, or turn off one of the filters, the preview image is updated, so you'll always know how your image is being modified.

Creating Special Effects with Filters

Figure 18 *Poster Edges filter applied to multiple layers*
Image courtesy of Elizabeth Eisner Reding

Poster Edges filter applied
to two layers

1. Click the **plant LEFT layer** on the Layers panel.
2. Click **Filter** on the Menu bar, then click the first instance of **Filter Gallery**.

   The plant LEFT and plant CENTER layers have the same filter applied.
3. Save your work, then compare your image to Figure 18.

You used the last filter applied on the Filter Gallery to apply the Poster Edges filter to the plant LEFT layer and the plant CENTER layer.

Getting Some Perspective with Vanishing Point

In the real world, perspective changes as you move towards and away from objects. If you use Photoshop to stretch the top of a skyscraper, to maintain proper perspective the modified shape should change so it appears to get taller and narrower. Using a grid, the Vanishing Point filter lets you do this by defining the area of any angle you want to modify so you can wrap objects around corners having multiple planes and into the distance while maintaining the correct perspective. The sky's the limit! The Vanishing Point feature is opened by clicking Filter on the Menu bar, and then clicking Vanishing Point.

Alter Images with Distort
AND NOISE FILTERS

What You'll Do

Image courtesy of Elizabeth Eisner Reding

 In this lesson, you'll apply the Ripple filter to the Pool layer and the Noise filter to the plant CENTER layer.

Understanding Distort and Noise Filters

Distort filters use the most memory, yet even a minimal setting can produce dramatic results. They can create a 3D effect or reshape an object. The Diffuse Glow filter mutes an image, similar to how classic film cinematographers layered cheesecloth or smeared Vaseline on the lens of a movie camera when filming leading ladies. Others, such as the Glass, Ocean Ripple, Ripple, and Wave filters make an object appear as if it is under or in water. The Twirl filter applies a circular effect to a layer. By adjusting the angle of the twirl, you can make images look as if they are moving or spinning. Figure 19 shows the diversity of the Distort filters.

Noise filters give an image an appearance of texture. You can apply them to an image layer or to the Background layer. If you want to apply a Noise filter to a type layer, you must rasterize the type layer to convert it to an image layer. You can apply effects to the rasterized type layer; however, you will no longer be able to edit the text.

Optimizing Memory in Photoshop

Many of the dynamic features in Photoshop are memory-intensive, particularly layer masks and filters. In addition to significantly increasing file size, they require a significant quantity of your computer memory to take effect. Part of the fun of working in Photoshop is experimenting with different styles and effects; however, doing so can quickly consume enough memory to diminish Photoshop's performance, or can cause you to not be able to work in other programs while Photoshop is running. You can offset some of the resource loss by freeing up memory as you work in Photoshop, and by adjusting settings in the Preferences dialog box.

Understanding Memory Usage

Every time you change your image, Photoshop stores the previous state in its buffer, which requires memory. You can control some of the memory that Photoshop uses by reducing the number of states available on the History panel. To change the number of states, point to Preferences on the Edit menu (Win) or

Photoshop menu (Mac), select Performance, and then enter a number in the History States text box. You can also liberate memory by clicking Edit on the Menu bar, pointing to Purge, and then clicking the option (Undo commands, History states, items on the Clipboard, or Video Cache) you want to purge. It's a good idea to use the Purge command after you've tried out several effects during a session, but be aware that you cannot undo the Purge command. For example, if you purge the History states, they will no longer appear on the History panel.

Controlling Memory Usage

Factors such as how much memory your computer has, the average size file you work with, and your need to multitask (have other programs open) can determine how Photoshop uses the memory currently allotted to it. To change your memory settings, click Edit (Win) or Photoshop (Mac) on the Menu bar, point to Preferences, and then click Performance. Make the desired change in the Let Photoshop Use text box in the Memory Usage section, and then click OK. You should carefully consider your program needs before changing the default settings. For additional tips on managing resources, visit Adobe's Photoshop Help website.

Figure 19 *Examples of Distort filters*
© Photodisc/Getty Images.

Apply a Ripple filter

1. Click the **Pool layer** on the Layers panel.

2. Hide the contents of the **plant LEFT copy layer**.

3. Display the rulers, then use the **Rectangular Marquee tool** ⬚ on the Tools panel to create a selection from approximately **210X/160Y** to **280X/185Y**.

TIP If you don't create a selection on the layer, the filter will be applied to the *entire* layer.

4. Click **Filter** on the Menu bar, point to **Distort**, then click **Ripple**.

5. Drag the **Amount slider** to **150%** (or type the value in the text box), as shown in Figure 20.

6. Click **OK**, turn off the ruler display, deselect the selection, then compare your image to Figure 21.

You applied a Ripple filter to a selection on the Pool layer.

Amount setting can be changed using text box or slider

Effect of Ripple filter

Correct Lens Distortion

Some distortions occur as a result of the camera lens. You can use the Lens Correction filter to counteract barrel (convex appearance), pincushion (concave appearance), and perspective distortions. You can also correct for chromatic aberrations and lens vignetting. These distortions can occur as a result of the focal length or f-stop in use. The Lens Correction filter can also be used to rotate an image or fix perspectives caused by camera tilt. Click Filter on the Menu bar, and then click Lens Correction.

Creating Special Effects with Filters

Figure 22 *Add Noise dialog box*
Image courtesy of Elizabeth Eisner Reding

Figure 23 *Add Noise filter applied to plant CENTER layer*
Image courtesy of Elizabeth Eisner Reding

*Effect of Add
Noise filter*

Figure 24 *Reduce Noise dialog box*
© Photodisc/Getty Images.

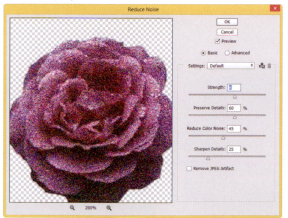

Apply a Noise filter

1. Click the **plant CENTER layer** on the Layers panel.

2. Click **Filter** on the Menu bar, point to **Noise**, then click **Add Noise**.

3. Center and/or enlarge the plant if necessary, drag the **Amount slider** to **20%** (or type the value in the text box), then compare your dialog box to Figure 22.

TIP The Uniform setting distributes color values using random numbers between 0 and a specified value, while the Gaussian setting distributes color values along a bell-shaped curve for a speckled effect.

4. Click **OK**.

    Flecks of noise are visible in the layer.

5. Save your work, then compare your image to Figure 23.

You applied a Noise filter to the active layer.

Adding or Reducing Noise

While some images look better when you've added some noise, others can benefit from a little noise reduction. Noise filters are a separate category found in the Filter menu and include the following commands: Add Noise, Despeckle, Dust & Scratches, Median, and Reduce Noise. You can quiet things down using the Reduce Noise dialog box shown in Figure 24. Here you can adjust the strength, details, and color noise, and can also sharpen the image. You can also use the Add Noise filter to remove **banding** (or **bands**) that may occur in an image during image conversion, resulting in tonal edges.

Alter Lighting with
A RENDER FILTER

What You'll Do

Image courtesy of Elizabeth Eisner Reding

 In this lesson, you'll add a lighting effect to the plant LEFT layer, add text, save a copy of the file, and then flatten the original image.

Understanding Lighting Effects

The Lighting Effects filter in the **Render** category of the Filter menu allows you to set an atmosphere or highlight elements in your image. (The Render category may not be functional on a Mac with insufficient memory.) You can select the style and type of light, adjust its properties, and texturize it. When the Render category is selected from the Filter menu, a lighting ellipse shows the light settings and allows you to position the light relative to your image. The ellipse displays *on the image* so that it looks like the light in the image is coming from a specific source. You can drag the handles on each circle, ellipse, or bar to change the direction and distance of the light sources. Figure 25 shows the Lighting Effects options bar using the Soft Spotlight style, as well as the darkened active layer and the lighting ellipse that is positioned over the image.

Adjusting Light by Setting the Style and Light Type

You can choose from over a dozen lighting presets, including spotlights, flood lights, and crossing. After you select a style, you choose the type of light—Spot, Point, or Infinite—and

Figure 25 *Lighting Effects options bar*
© Photodisc/Getty Images.

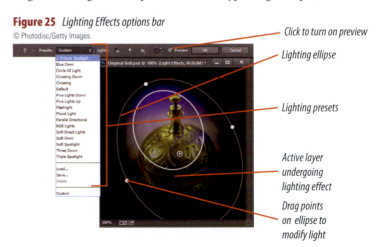

Click to turn on preview

Lighting ellipse

Lighting presets

Active layer undergoing lighting effect

Drag points on ellipse to modify light

set its intensity and focus. Directional lighting washes the surface with a constant light source, Omni casts light from the center, and Spotlight directs light outward from a single point. As shown in the Properties panel in Figure 26, you can adjust the brightness of the light by using the Intensity slider. You can drag the center circle (or one of its handles) on the image to adjust the size of the beam of light filling the ellipse. The light source begins where the radius touches the edge of the ellipse. The Color setting lets you modify the color of the light. You can also create custom lighting schemes and save them for use in other images. Custom lighting schemes will appear in the Presets list on the options bar.

Adjusting Surrounding Light Conditions

You can adjust the surrounding light conditions using the Exposure, Gloss, Metallic, or Ambience properties. The Exposure property lightens or darkens the ellipse (the area displaying the light source). The Gloss property controls the amount of surface reflection on the lighted surfaces. The Metallic property controls the parts of an image that reflect the light source color. The Ambience property controls the balance between the light source and the overall light in an image. The Color swatch changes the ambient light around the spotlight.

Adding Texture to Light

The Texture setting (located toward the bottom of the Properties panel) allows you to add 3D effects to the lighting filter. The Texture controls how light reflects off an image. If a color channel is selected, the colored parts of the channel will be raised; this lets you determine whether certain areas will appear to have the highest relief. To use this option, you select one of the three RGB color channels in the Texture list arrow on the Properties panel, and then drag the Height slider to the relief setting you want. Figure 27 shows a lighting effect texture with black colors highest.

> **QUICK TIP**
>
> QuickTips display at various points on the Lighting overlay: these hints let you know that *dragging* the points will affect the lighting.

Figure 26 *Properties panel showing Lighting Effects*

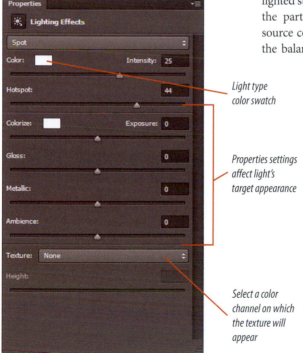

Light type color swatch

Properties settings affect light's target appearance

Select a color channel on which the texture will appear

Figure 27 *Texture added to lighting effect*
© Photodisc/Getty Images.

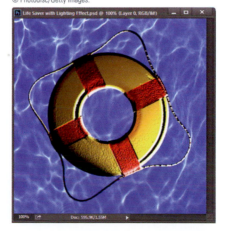

Select lighting settings

1. Click the **plant LEFT layer** on the Layers panel.

2. Click **Filter** on the Menu bar, point to **Render**, then click **Lighting Effects**.

3. Click the **Presets list arrow** on the options bar, then click **Flashlight**.

   A green circle displays over the image, indicating the selected style.

   TIP If the green circle doesn't display, click View on the menu bar, point to Show, then click All.

4. Click the **Light Type list arrow** on the Properties panel, then click **Infinite** if it is not already selected.

5. Verify that the **Preview check box** on the options bar is selected.

   The preview shows the settings for the Flashlight light source.

6. Click and hold the **center of the lighting overlay**, and drag towards the **third sconce** from the left in the image.

   As you drag the handle, the image automatically displays the change in the lighting direction and distance.

7. Use the following settings in the Properties panel: Lighting Effects=Infinite, Color Intensity=46, Exposure=0, Gloss=−100, Metallic=−100, Ambience=−23.

8. Compare your image to Figure 28.

You selected a lighting style and type, then changed the light source.

Figure 28 *Lighting overlay*
Image courtesy of Elizabeth Eisner Reding

Using Analysis and Measurement Tools

One of the commands on the Image menu is Analysis. This subgroup of commands allows you to set the measurement scale, set data points, or use the Ruler tool (which helps you position images or elements and calculates the distance between any two points) and may not be available on a computer with insufficient memory. The Count tool lets you manually count items. You can record measurements and place a scale marker at the top or bottom of the image. Recorded measurements are displayed in the Measurement Log panel (which appears grouped with the Mini Bridge and Timeline panels) and can be opened by clicking Window on the Menu bar, and then clicking Measurement Log.

Figure 29 *Lighting Effects filter applied to plant LEFT*
Image courtesy of Elizabeth Eisner Reding

Figure 30 *Type layer in flattened file*
Image courtesy of Elizabeth Eisner Reding

Apply a lighting effect

1. Click **OK** on the options bar.

   The light appears brightest to the left of the plant LEFT.

   TIP When there are multiple sources of light, you can delete a light source ellipse by dragging its center point off of the image.

2. Compare your image to Figure 29. Your results may vary, depending on your settings in the Lighting Effects dialog box.

You applied a lighting effect to the plant LEFT layer.

Apply finishing touches

1. Display the rulers, use a 30-point black Impact Regular font with a Crisp anti-aliasing setting to create a type layer at approximately **220 X/270 Y** that says **Meet us Poolside**, then hide the rulers. (*Hint:* Use a different size if your type looks different from Figure 30.)

2. Save a copy of this file using the default naming scheme, flatten the file discarding any hidden layers, then compare your image to Figure 30.

3. Save your work.

You added a type layer to the image, then saved a copy and flattened the file.

Use Perspective Warp and Vanishing
POINT TO ADD PERSPECTIVE

What You'll Do

Source: Morguefile.
Image Courtesy of Elizabeth Eisner Reding

 In this lesson, you'll use Perspective Warp and Vanishing Point to correct a perspective and apply a Photoshop image to the perspective created in another image.

NEW Adjusting with Perspective Warp

Sometimes an image that you know to be straight (such as a building) just doesn't appear that way. The **Perspective Warp** feature allows you to adjust the perspective, particularly in an image that has straight lines and flat surfaces. So a building that appears to be less than perpendicular to the street can be digitally corrected. The Perspective Warp command is located on the Edit menu and can be used in conjunction with the Vanishing Point feature.

Understanding Vanishing Point

Vanishing Point, which is found in the Filter menu, allows you to create planes which can visually adjust for perspective caused by width, height, and depth. With Vanishing Point, matching perspective is made easy. (Without this feature, you can fuss with Transform commands to try to create the illusion of perspective. You'll work very hard and may not be very happy with the results.) From within Vanishing Point, you can create an unlimited number of planes from which you can copy and clone objects around corners.

Creating Planes

You may find it helpful to use this feature on a newly created empty layer. That way, if you make a mistake, your original image will still be intact. Once you've opened Vanishing Point, you create an initial plane from which others can be drawn.

Each plane is surrounded by a light blue line, and while any image can have multiple planes, only one plane (and its related planes) can be active at a time in editing mode. The active plane is indicated by a grid. Figure 31 shows the Vanishing Point window, and an object containing two related drawn planes. As you draw each plane (using tools in the Vanishing Point window), the grid color lets you know if your perspective is realistic. A red box indicates that the drawn perspective is not possible. A yellow grid indicates that the perspective is unlikely; a blue grid means the perspective is correct.

Pasting One Image into Another

Using the Clipboard, you can copy an image that can then be pasted and manipulated in Vanishing Point. When imagery is initially pasted into Vanishing Point, it floats at the top until you pull it within the planes you have created. Figure 32 shows imagery that has been pulled onto the planes of a gift box.

Getting that Healing Feeling

Vanishing Point tools are located in the upper-left corner of the dialog box. You can use the Transform tool to flip images and the Stamp tool and Brush tool to paint over pixels.

QUICK TIP

You can use Vanishing Point and create a grid even if you don't have an image on which to create the grid. Simply create a new layer or open a new file, open Vanishing Point, create a grid, and then paste your graphic.

Figure 31 *Vanishing Point window*
Source: Morguefile.

Figure 32 *Image applied to multiple planes*
Source: Morguefile.

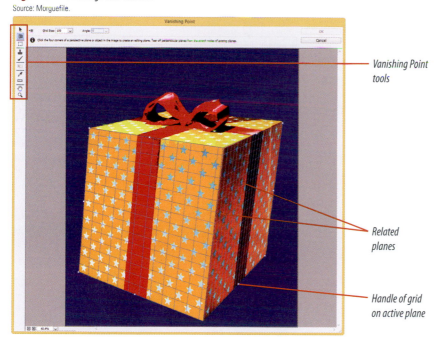

Vanishing Point tools

Related planes

Handle of grid on active plane

Using Perspective Warp

1. Open PS 9-2.psd from the drive and folder where you store your Data Files, then save it as **Poolside Grill-VP**.

2. Display the rulers, click **Edit** on the Menu bar, then click **Perspective Warp**. (You may see a visual tutorial on screen which you can close if you choose not to watch it.)

3. Click the **image** at **190 H/160 V**, then drag the **top-left** and **bottom-right corners** of the plane so they conform to the street-side of the building (approx. 190 H/620 V).

4. Click the **image** at **300 H/100 V** to display a new grid. (You may see a visual tutorial on screen, which you can close if you choose not to watch it.)

5. Adjust the top-right and bottom-right points of the new plane (which should automatically snap to the existing plane) so it conforms to the building, as shown in Figure 33.

6. Click **Warp** on the options bar, then drag the **top-left**, **top-center**, and **top-right points** until the building appears to be perpendicular to the street. Compare your image to Figure 34.

7. Click the **Commit Perspective Warp button** ✅ on the options bar, then save your work.

You used the Perspective Warp feature to make the building walls appear to be perpendicular to the street.

Figure 33 *Two planes in Perspective Warp*
Source: Morguefile.

Plane 1
Plane 2

Figure 34 *Straightened planes*
Source: Morguefile.

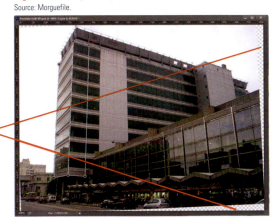

Lack of pixels due to distortion

Creating Special Effects with Filters

Figure 35 *Initial plane in Vanishing Point*
Source: Morguefile.

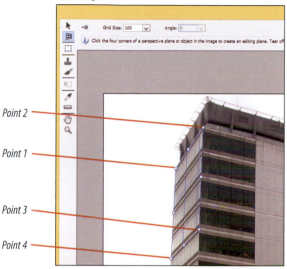

Point 2
Point 1
Point 3
Point 4

© 2015 Cengage Learning®

	TABLE 2: VANISHING POINT TOOLS	
Tool	**Name**	**Used to**
	Edit Plane tool	Selects, edits, moves, and resizes planes.
	Create Plane tool	Defines a plane, adjusts its size and shape, and tears off a new plane.
	Marquee tool	Makes square or rectangular selections, and moves and clones selections.
	Stamp tool	Paints with a sample of the image.
	Brush tool	Paints with a selected color in a plane.
	Transform tool	Scales, rotates, and moves a floating selection using handles.
	Eyedropper tool	Selects a color for painting when you click the preview image.
	Measure tool	Measures distances and angles of an item in a plane.
	Hand tool	Repositions the image in the preview window.
	Zoom tool	Magnifies/reduces the image in the preview window.

Prepare to use Vanishing Point

1. Display the flattened **Poolside** image.
2. Select the **entire flattened image**, copy the selection to the Clipboard, then minimize the image.
3. Create a new layer on the Poolside Grill-VP image.
4. Click **Filter** on the Menu bar, then click **Vanishing Point**.

   See Table 2 to learn about Vanishing Point tools.
5. If necessary, select the **Create Plane tool** .
6. Using Figure 35 as a guide, click **point 1** in the building, click **point 2**, click **point 3**, then click **point 4**.

You selected the contents of a flattened image, copied it to the Clipboard, opened Vanishing Point, then created an initial plane.

Create an additional plane

1. Click the **Create Plane tool** ⊞ .

2. Position the pointer over the right-center handle, then drag the **grid** along the long edge of the building, stopping at the extension towards the building's right edge.

3. With the **Edit Plane tool** ▶ selected, drag (Win) or ⌘-drag (Mac) the **right handles** so they cover the top four floors of the building, as shown in Figure 36.

You created an additional plane in Vanishing Point, then adjusted the points in the plane to include a specific area in an image.

Figure 36 *Grid covering four top floors of building*
Source: Morguefile.

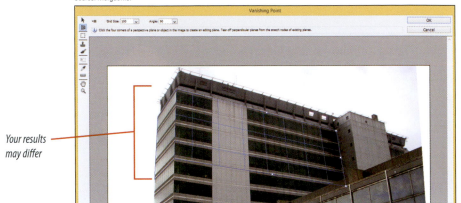

Your results
may differ

Creating Special Effects with Filters

Figure 37 *Pasted contents floating in Vanishing Point*

Source: Morguefile.
Image Courtesy of Elizabeth Eisner Reding

Pasted contents

Figure 38 *Repositioned Clipboard contents*

Source: Morguefile.
Image Courtesy of Elizabeth Eisner Reding

Paste image in Vanishing Point

1. Paste the copied image by pressing [**Ctrl**][**V**] (Win) or ⌘ [**V**] (Mac).

   The content of the Clipboard is copied into Vanishing Point, as shown in Figure 37.

2. Position the pointer ▶ over the pasted selection, then drag the **pointer** over the left side of the grid until you feel it pop into place.

3. Using the pointer ▶, drag the **image** up until the image fills the grid and the type displays. (*Hint*: If you need to reposition the pasted object, click it again with the pointer.)

4. Click **OK** to close Vanishing Point.

5. Click the **Crop tool** 🔲 on the Tools panel, drag the **top-, bottom-,** and **side-handles** to hide the missing side imagery, then click the **Commit current crop operation button** ✓ on the options bar.

6. Save your work, turn off the rulers, then compare your image to Figure 38. (Your zoom factor and results may differ.)

7. Close the file, then exit Photoshop.

You pasted the contents of the Clipboard into Vanishing Point, then adjusted the image within the grid.

Lesson 6   Use Perspective Warp and Vanishing Point to Add Perspective

POWER USER SHORTCUTS	
To do this:	**Use this method:**
Apply a filter	Filter ➤ Filter category ➤ Filter name
Apply last filter	[Ctrl][F] (Win) or ⌘ [F] (Mac)
Apply last filter, but set new options	[Ctrl][Alt][F] (Win) or ⌘ [option] [F] (Mac)
Ascend one layer at a time on the Layers panel	[Alt][]] (Win) or [option][]] (Mac)
Descend one layer at a time on the Layers panel	[Alt][[] (Win) or [option][[] (Mac)
Fades effect of previous filter	[Ctrl][Shift][F] (Win) or ⌘ [Shift][F] (Mac)
Open Filter Gallery	Filter ➤ Filter Gallery
Open Vanishing Point	Filter ➤ Vanishing Point
Zoom in/out of Filter Gallery	[Ctrl][+]/[Ctrl][−] (Win) or ⌘ [+]/⌘ [−] (Mac)

Key: Menu items are indicated by ➤ between the menu name and its command.

© 2015 Cengage Learning®

Learn about filters and how to apply them.

1. Start Photoshop, open PS 9-3.psd from the drive and folder where you store your Data Files, reset the Essentials workspace, then save it as **B&B Poster**.
2. Make the Dunes layer active.
3. Use the Elliptical Marquee tool to draw an ellipse around the bend in the driftwood limb.
4. Apply a Gaussian Blur filter (Blur category) with the following setting: Radius = 1.0 pixels. Remember to deselect the selection when you are finished.
5. Create four separate type layers with the text **Fish**, **Swim**, **Hike**, and **Relax**, and left align them vertically starting from below the bend in the tree limb down over the tree trunk on the left side of the image. (*Hint*: A 36 pt Pure Yellow Copperplate Gothic Bold Regular is used in the sample.)
6. Save your work.

Create an effect with an Artistic filter.

1. Make the B&B layer active, then convert the layer into a Smart Object.
2. Apply a Film Grain filter (Artistic category in Filter Gallery) with the following settings: Grain = 3, Highlight Area = 1, Intensity = 10.
3. Save your work.

Add unique effects with Stylize filters.

1. Make the Trout layer active.
2. Apply a Glowing Edges filter (Stylize category in Filter Gallery), with the following settings: Edge Width = 2, Edge Brightness = 2, Smoothness = 3.

3. Transform the Trout layer by resizing and rotating the trout so that it appears to be jumping, then drag it behind the Fish type layer.
4. Save your work.

Alter images with Distort and Noise filters.

1. Make the Swim type layer active.
2. Apply a Ripple filter (Distort category) with the following settings: Amount = 55%, Size = Medium. (*Hint*: Click OK to rasterize the layer.)
3. Make the Relax type layer active.
4. Recolor the type to the following settings: R = 227, G = 4, B = 178.
5. Apply an Add Noise filter (Noise category) with the following settings: Amount = 25%, Distribution = Uniform, Monochromatic = Selected.
6. Save your work.

Alter lighting with a Render filter.

1. Make the Dunes layer active.
2. Apply Lighting Effects (Render category) with the following settings: Preset = Crossing, Type = Spot.
3. Use the following Lighting Effects settings: Intensity = 28, Gloss = 0, Metallic = -100, Exposure = 0, Ambience = 11. (Your results may vary.)
4. Save your work as a copy using the default naming, flatten this file, then save your work.

Use Perspective Warp and Vanishing Point to add perspective.

1. Use the Image menu to change the image size to have a width of 3".

2. Select the contents of the flattened file, then copy it into the Clipboard.
3. Open PS 9-4.psd from the drive and folder where you store your Data Files, then save it as **Billboard**.
4. Create a new layer, then open Vanishing Point.
5. Create a realistic plane in the billboard, then paste the Clipboard contents into the image.
6. Center the B&B poster image in the sign, then return to Photoshop. (*Hint*: It's okay if Fish, Swim, Hike, Relax do not all display in the sign as the image and billboard have different dimensions.)
7. Save your work, close the flattened file without saving the changes, then compare your image to Figure 39. (Your results may vary.)

Figure 39 *Completed Skills Review*
Source: Morguefile.

Theatre in the Park, an outdoor production company, is adding Shakespeare's plays to their summer repertoire. The company has convinced several rollerbladers to wear sandwich boards promoting the event as they blade downtown during the noon hour. You've volunteered to design the print board for the Bard. You can use the title from any Shakespearian play in the sign.

1. Obtain the following images that reflect the production: a park, an image related to Shakespeare, and any other images that reflect a summer theater production. You can use the images that are available on your computer, scanned images, or images from a digital camera.
2. Create a new Photoshop image with the dimensions 630 × 450 pixels, then save it as **Play**.
3. Drag or copy the image of a park to the Play image above the Background layer, apply at least one filter to it, then rename the Background layer. (*Hint*: The Park layer in the sample has a Render category Lighting Effects filter applied to it.)
4. Drag the Shakespeare image to the Play image above the Park layer, and modify it as desired. (*Hint*: The face in the sample has an opacity setting of 64%, and has been rotated.)

5. Create a sign announcing the play, and apply at least one style and filter to it. (*Hint*: The sign in the sample was created using the Rectangle tool, and has the Drop Shadow, Satin, and Bevel and Emboss styles, and a Texture category Craquelure filter applied to it.)
6. Create type layers as desired, and apply at least one style or filter to them. (*Hint*: A 30 pt Trajan Pro 3 Regular font is used in the sample.)

7. Drag or copy the remaining images to the Play image, close the image files, then transform them or apply at least one style or filter to them.
8. Save your work, then compare your image to the sample in Figure 40.

Figure 40 *Sample Completed Project Builder 1*
© Photodisc/Getty Images.

Creating Special Effects with Filters

Local musical instrument shops in your town are producing a classic jazz and blues event. Last year, the poster displayed sponsor logos and never conveyed the feel of the genre. This year, they've decided not to include sponsor logos, and have asked you to design a print poster that focuses attention on the music itself. Use your Photoshop skills to express the feeling of the jazz and blues event.

1. Obtain images for the design, including at least one with one or more instruments that will dominate the image. You can use the images that are available on your computer, scanned images, or images from a digital camera.
2. Create a new Photoshop image of any dimension, then save it as **Jazz and Blues**.
3. Open the main instrument file, drag it to the Jazz and Blues image above the Background layer, then remove the Background layer.
4. Open the remaining image files, drag or copy them to the Jazz and Blues image, then close the image files.

5. Apply filters and styles and transform the other image layers as desired. (*Hint*: The Keyboard layer was converted into a Smart Object and has a Color Overlay layer applied to it.)
6. Create type layers as desired and apply filters or styles to them. (*Hint*: The event title type layer has a 43.83 pt

Times New Roman Bold font with the Drop Shadow, Inner Shadow, Bevel and Emboss, and Gradient Overlay styles applied to it. The text in the lower-left corner has a 12.83 pt Cambria Regular font.)
7. Save your work, then compare your image to the sample in Figure 41.

Figure 41 *Sample Completed Project Builder 2*
Source: Morguefile.

Destined Nations, a local travel agency, is looking to hire a freelance graphic artist to design their web marketing art. Rather than peruse portfolios, they are holding a contest to select a design. Each entrant is given the same image to modify as they see fit. As an incentive to get the very best entries, they're offering an all-expense paid week vacation to the winner. You really need a vacation, so you decide to enter the contest.

1. Obtain at least one image for the vacation destination design. You can use the images that are available on your computer, scanned images, or images from a digital camera.
2. Open PS 9-5.psd, then save it as **Shield.**
3. Verify that the Shield layer is active, open the Lighting Effects options bar, then choose a lighting style.
4. Continue working in the Lighting Effects options bar and Properties panel. Change the Light Color swatch to yellow. (*Hint:* To change color, click the color swatch.)
5. Place at least one other spotlight around the preview window using a different colored light. (*Hint:* To add a spotlight, click the Add new Spot Light button on the options bar.) Close the Lighting Effects options bar and view the image.
6. Apply a subtle texture to the Shield layer. (*Hint:* The Shield layer in the sample has the Smudge Stick Artistic filter applied to it.)
7. Delete the large center circle from the Shield layer. (*Hint:* To delete the circle quickly, select the Elliptical Marquee tool, draw a selection around the circle, then press [Delete], or you can apply a layer mask and paint the circle.)

8. Create a new layer at the bottom of the Layers panel, then fill it in black.
9. Create a new layer above the black layer and name it Blur.
10. Use a Lasso tool or any other selection tool to create a shape that fills the left side of the layer, then apply a fill color to the selection.
11. Apply at least one Blur filter to the Blur layer.
12. Transform the shield so that it has dimension, then move it to the left side of the window. (*Hint:* The Shield layer in the sample has been distorted.)

13. Add type layers as desired and apply styles or filters to them. (*Hint:* The Acapulco layer in the sample has a border applied by clicking the Rasterize, Type command on the Layer menu, then using the Stroke command on the Edit menu. The always great! layer in the sample is a 48 pt Verdana Italic.)
14. Open the image files, drag or copy them to the Shield image, close the image files, then apply filters or styles to them.
15. Save your work, then compare your image to the sample in Figure 42.

Figure 42 *Sample Design Project*
© Photodisc/Getty Images.

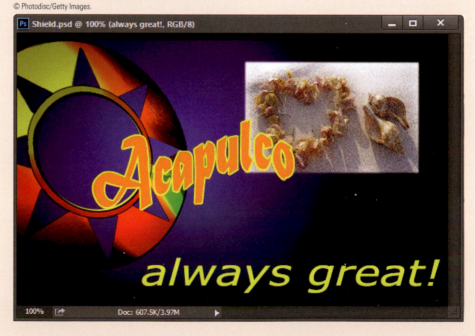

You have been asked to put together a presentation on traditional and modern dance styles from around the world. Choose a dance style and use your Photoshop skills to create artwork that will be used in print and on the web that conveys the feel of that style.

1. Obtain at least three images that reflect the style of dance you've chosen. You can use the images that are available on your computer, scanned images, images from a digital camera, or images downloaded from the Internet. Try to select images that you can transform and to which you can add styles and apply filters. Make sure that one image can be used as a background.

2. Create a new Photoshop image, then save it as **Dance**.

3. Drag or copy the background to the Dance image above the Background layer, then rename the Background layer and apply a fill color as desired.

4. Drag an image to the Dance image, transform it as desired, then apply a filter to it. (*Hint*: The Swan layer [dancer in lower-left corner] in the sample has an Artistic category Plastic Wrap filter applied to it.)

5. Drag or copy the remaining images, transform as needed, and apply at least one style or filter to them.

(*Hint*: The Large Ballerina layer has a layer mask applied to it, and the Shoes layer has a decreased opacity setting as well as the Distort category Diffuse Glow filter applied to it.)

6. Create type layers as desired, and apply at least one style or filter to them. (*Hint*: The Dancing type layer was created in a separate image using an image as a member of a clipping mask, then a variety of effects was applied to it. The keep dancing type layer in the sample uses a 20 pt Kalinga Regular font with Outer and Inner Glow layer styles applied.)

7. Be prepared to discuss the effects you generate when you add filters to styles and vice versa.

8. Save your work, then compare your image to the sample in Figure 43.

Figure 43 *Sample Portfolio Project*
Source: Morguefile.

CHAPTER 10

ENHANCING SPECIFIC
SELECTIONS

1. Create an alpha channel
2. Isolate an object
3. Erase areas in an image to enhance appearance
4. Use the Clone Stamp tool to make repairs
5. Use the Magic Wand tool to select objects
6. Learn how to create snapshots
7. Create multiple-image layouts

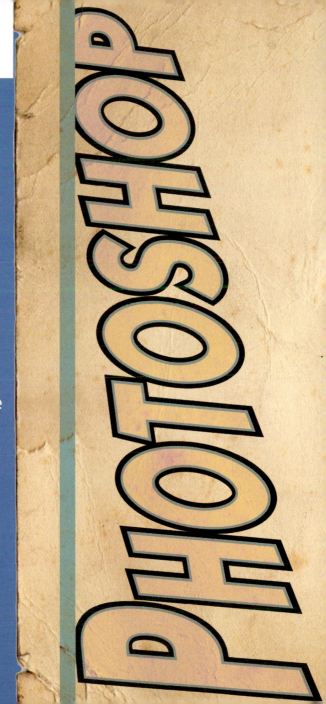

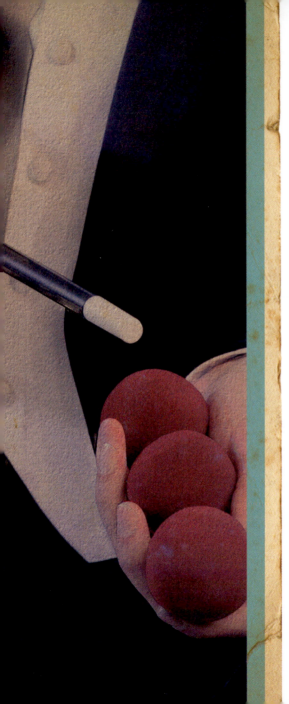

CHAPTER 10

ENHANCING SPECIFIC
SELECTIONS

Modifying Objects

As you have most likely figured out by now, a great part of the power of Photoshop resides in its ability to isolate graphics and text objects and make changes to them. This chapter focuses on several of the techniques used to separate graphic objects from an image and then make changes that enhance their appearance.

Using Channels

Nearly every image you open or create in Photoshop is separated into color channels. Photoshop uses **channels** to house the color information for each layer and layer mask in your image. The number of color information channels depends on the color mode of the image. You can also create specific channels for layer masks.

Fixing Imperfections

From time to time, you'll work with flawed images. Flawed images are not necessarily "bad," they just might contain imagery that does not fit your needs. Photoshop offers several ways to repair an image's imperfections. You can use the following methods—or combinations of these methods—to fix areas within an image that are less than ideal:

■ Isolate areas using the selection tools and the Refine Edge feature.
■ Erase areas using a variety of eraser tools.
■ Take a sample and then paint that sample over an area using the Clone Stamp tool.

Creating Snapshots

The Snapshot command lets you make a temporary copy of any state of an image. The snapshot is added to the top of the History panel and lets you work on a new version of the image. Snapshots are like the states found on the History panel but offer a few more advantages:

- You can name a snapshot to make it easy to identify and manage.
- You can compare changes to images easily. For example, you can take a snapshot before and after changing the color of a selection.
- You can recover your work easily. If your experimentation with an image doesn't satisfy your needs, you can select the snapshot to undo all the steps from the experiment.

Using Automation Features

After you complete an image that you want to share, you can create an image that contains various sizes of the same image, or several different images. Using a multiple-image layout, for example, makes it possible to print images in a variety of sizes and shapes on a single sheet. Another example is a contact sheet, a file that displays thumbnail views of a selection of images, so that you can easily catalog and preview them without opening each individual file.

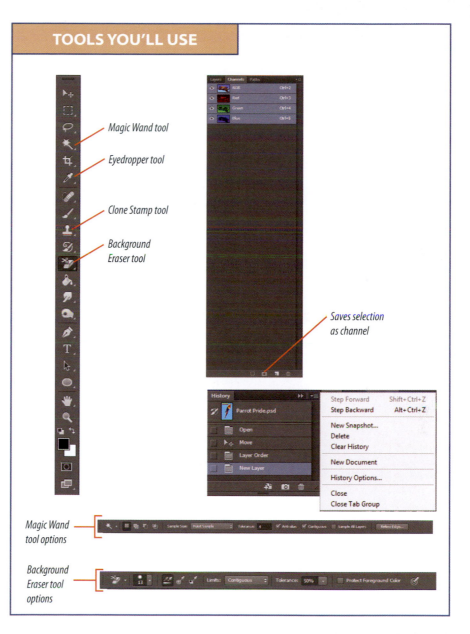

TOOLS YOU'LL USE

Magic Wand tool

Eyedropper tool

Clone Stamp tool

Background Eraser tool

Saves selection as channel

Magic Wand tool options

Background Eraser tool options

Create an
ALPHA CHANNEL

What You'll Do

Source: Morguefile.

In this lesson, you'll view the colors in the default color mode on the Channels panel. You'll also create a selection, save it as an alpha channel, and then change the color of the alpha channel.

Defining Channels

Photoshop uses channels to store color information about images. Channels, or **color channels**, are created at the same time the image is created, and the number of channels is determined by the image mode. For example, a CMYK image has at least four channels (one each for cyan, magenta, yellow, and black), whereas an RGB image has three channels (one each for red, green, and blue). Every Photoshop image has at least one channel, and can have a maximum of 24 color channels. The color channels contained in an image are known as **default channels**, which are created automatically by Photoshop.

You can add specific color information by adding an **alpha channel** or a **spot channel**. You use an alpha channel to create and store masks, which let you manipulate, isolate, and protect parts of an image. A spot channel contains information about special premixed inks used in CMYK color printing. The default number of channels is determined by the color mode you select in the New dialog box that opens when you

create a new file, as shown in Figure 1. You can add channels to images displayed in all color modes, except the bitmap modes.

Understanding Alpha Channels

You create alpha channels on the Channels panel. You can create an alpha channel that masks all or specific areas of a layer. For example, you can create a selection and then convert it into an alpha channel. Photoshop superimposes the color in an alpha channel onto the image; however, an alpha channel might appear in grayscale on the Channels panel thumbnail. You can use alpha channels to preserve a selection, to experiment with, to use later, to create special effects such as screens or shadows, or to save and reuse in other images. Photoshop supports the following formats for saving an alpha channel: PSD, PDF, PICT, TIFF, and Raw. If you use other formats, you might lose some channel information. You can copy the alpha channel to other images and instantly apply the same information. Alpha channels do not print—they will not be visible in print media.

Understanding the Channels Panel

The Channels panel lists all the default channels contained in a layer and manages all the image's channels. To access this panel, click the Channels tab next to the Layers tab, as shown in Figure 2. The top channel is a **composite channel**—a combination of all the other default channels. The additional default channels, based on the existing color mode, are shown below the composite channel, followed by spot color channels, and finally by the alpha channels.

Channels have many of the same properties as layers. You can hide channels in the same way as you hide layers, by clicking the Indicates channel visibility button to the left of the thumbnail on the Channels panel. Each channel has a thumbnail that mirrors the changes you make to the image's layers. You can also change the order of channels by dragging them up or down on the Channels panel.

The thumbnails on the Channels panel might appear in grayscale. To view the channels in their actual color, click Edit (Win) or Photoshop (Mac) on the Menu bar, point to Preferences, click Interface, select the Show Channels in Color check box, and then click OK. The default channels will appear in the color mode colors; the color assigned to an alpha channel will appear as the color selected in the Channel Options dialog box. You open the Channel Options dialog box by double-clicking the alpha channel on the Channels panel.

Figure 1 *New dialog box*

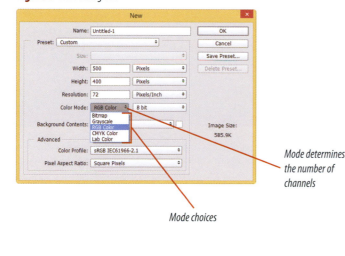

Mode determines the number of channels

Mode choices

Figure 2 *Channels on the Channels panel*
© Photodisc/Getty Images.

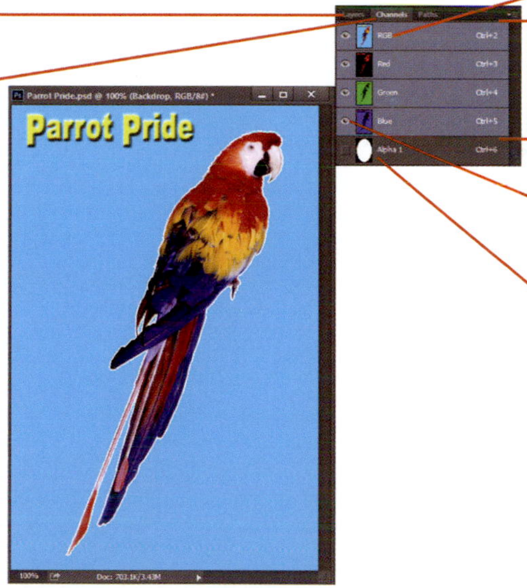

Layers tab

Channels tab

Composite channel

Default color mode channels

Indicates channel visibility button

Alpha channel, currently not visible

View the Channels panel

1. Start Photoshop, open PS 10-1.psd from the drive and folder where you store your Data Files, then save it as **Carnival ride**.

2. Click the **Default Foreground and Background Colors button**  on the Tools panel to display the default settings.

3. Verify that the **Essentials workspace** is selected and reset.

4. Display the rulers in pixels, verify that the zoom factor is **66.7%**, then display the guides if necessary.

5. Click **Edit** (Win) or **Photoshop** (Mac) on the Menu bar, point to **Preferences**, click **Interface**, click the **Show Channels in Color check box**, then click **OK** to close the Preferences dialog box.

6. Click the **Channels tab** next to the Layers tab on the Layers panel, then compare your Channels panel to Figure 3.

   The Channels panel is active and displays the four channels for RGB color mode: RGB (composite), Red, Green, and Blue.

You opened the Channels panel, and verified that colors are displayed in the default color channels. This allows you to see the actual colors contained in each channel when working with images.

Figure 3 *Channels panel*

Changes to the composite channel affect the entire layer

Displays the Channels panel

Changing Alpha Channel Colors

You can change the color that the alpha channel displays (to alter the appearance of the image) by picking a color in the Channel Options dialog box. To open the Channel Options dialog box, double-click the alpha channel (which appears at the bottom of the Channels panel once it is created), click the color box, select a color in the Color Picker (Channel Color) dialog box, and then click OK. Click an option button in the Channel Options dialog box to choose whether the color indicates masked areas, selected areas, or a spot color, and then click OK.

Figure 4 *Selection created*

Source: Morguefile.

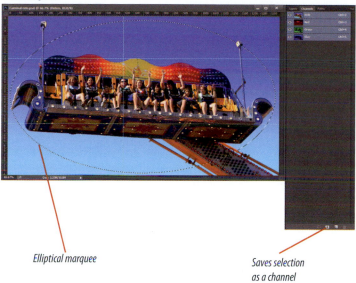

Elliptical marquee

*Saves selection
as a channel*

Figure 5 *Alpha channel created*

Source: Morguefile.

Alpha 1 channel

Create an alpha channel from a selection

1. Click the **Elliptical Marquee tool** on the Tools panel, then set the Feather setting on the options bar to **0 px** if it is not already set to 0.

2. Drag the **Marquee pointer** ─┼─ from approximately **10 X/10 Y** to **1380 X/800 Y**, then compare your image to Figure 4.

3. Click the **Save selection as channel button** on the Channels panel.

4. Double-click the **Alpha 1 thumbnail** on the Channels panel, then click the **color box** in the Channel Options dialog box.

5. Verify that the **R option button** is selected in the Color Picker (Channel Color) dialog box (R=255, G=0, B=0), then click **OK**.

6. Verify that the opacity setting is **50%** and that the **Masked Areas option button** is selected in the Channel Options dialog box, then click **OK**.

7. On the Channels panel, click the **RGB channel**, then click the **Indicates channel visibility button** for the Alpha 1 channel to view the alpha channel.

   The combination of the red alpha channel color overlaying blue produces the rose color at the edges of the figure.

8. Deselect the selection, then compare your image to Figure 5.

9. Save your work.

You used the Elliptical Marquee tool to create a selection, then saved the selection as an alpha channel. You also verified the alpha channel color and reviewed the results by displaying the alpha channel.

Isolate
AN OBJECT

What You'll Do

Source: Morguefile.

 In this lesson, you'll create a duplicate layer, and use tools to extract the star from the bottom of the chair so that you can adjust its color. You'll also adjust the color of the star by applying a Gradient Map to it.

Using Your Photoshop Knowledge

The goal in isolating an object is to use your knowledge of Photoshop tools to pick the best tool to select an object, and then place the selection on its own layer so you can perform any additional adjustments. Easier said than done.

Isolating Objects

You can use a variety of Photoshop tools to isolate a foreground object from its background. Using any of the tools at your disposal, you can define the object you want to extract, even if its edge is vaguely defined. When you extract an object from a layer,

Photoshop deletes the non-extracted portion of the image's background to underlying transparency. It's always a good idea to first copy the original layer and then extract an object from the duplicate layer. This preserves the original layer, which you can use as a reference, and helps you to avoid losing any of the original image information. After you extract an image, you can modify the extracted object layer as you wish.

QUICK TIP

To make sure you've correctly isolated content, add a layer filled with a contrasting color beneath the isolated content to highlight the selection. Once your selection is perfect, delete the color-filled layer.

Figure 6 *Settings in the Refine Edge dialog box*

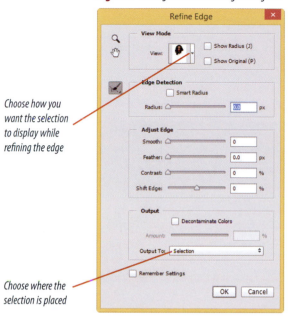

Choose how you
want the selection
to display while
refining the edge

Choose where the
selection is placed

Figure 7 *Results of refined edge*
Source: Morguefile.

Using the Refine Edge Option

The Refine Edge button is on the options bar of a variety of tools, including the Magic Wand tool. Once a selection is made, it lets you improve the quality of a selection's edges and allows you to view the selection against different backgrounds, making editing easier. It can also be used to find hard edges. (When a selection is made, Refine Edge is also available on the Select menu.) This feature would be great to use if you wanted to isolate a head of hair (the kind with stray strands through which you can see a background). Once you've made a selection, click the Refine Edge button on the options bar. Using the Refine Edge dialog box, you can make adjustments in the Edge Detection Radius (which determines the size of the region around the selection), Smooth (which reduces irregular areas), Feather (which creates a soft-edged transition), Contrast (which sharpens selection edges), and Shift Edge (which shrinks or enlarges the selection). See Figure 6.

The Refine Edge dialog box contains several View Modes. Each View Mode changes the way in which the selection is displayed, and you can make adjustments to your selection *while the dialog box is open*. You can use the On Layers mode (one of the View Mode options) to display the unmasked image data with the data of the revealed composite layers appearing below it. The Reveal Layer mode disables your layer mask so you can see the entire active layer; the only changes visible are color decontamination. **Color decontamination** is an Output option that allows you to remove color fringing around the edges of a masked image and is ideal for use in extracting a subject from its background. The Amount slider can be used to control the level of color replacement. Figure 7 shows the result of a selection made using the refine edge feature.

Isolate an object

1. Click the **Layers tab** on the Layers panel.

2. Click the **Riders layer** on the Layers panel, click the **Layers Panel options button** , then click **Duplicate Layer**.

3. Type **Center star** in the As text box, then click **OK** to close the Duplicate Layer dialog box.

   The new layer appears above the Riders layer on the Layers panel, and is now the active layer.

4. Click the **Channels tab**, click the **Indicates layer visibility button** for any channel that is not visible, then click the **Layers tab**.

5. Click the **Indicates layer visibility button** for the Riders layer, so the layer is not visible.

6. Click the **Zoom tool** on the Tools panel, then click the **center star** (under the riders) three times.

7. Click the **Magnetic Lasso tool** on the Tools panel.

8. Verify that the Feather setting is 0, drag the **pointer** around the inner edge of the center star, then compare your screen to Figure 8.

   The center star is selected.

You created and named a duplicate layer of the Riders layer, then used the Magnetic Lasso tool to outline the center star.

Figure 8 *Selection in image*
Source: Morguefile.

Selection

Figure 9 *Layer containing the extracted object*

Figure 10 *Sample gradients*

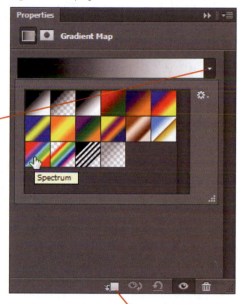

Gradient list arrow has the following ToolTip: Click to open the Gradient picker list arrow

Spectrum

This adjustment affects all layers below (click to clip layer)

Figure 11 *Extracted object with a Gradient Map applied*
Source: Morguefile.

Gradient Map adjustment on the extracted object

Exclude pixels

1. Zoom out until the zoom factor is **66.7%**.
2. Click **Select** on the Menu bar, then click **Inverse**.
3. Press [**Delete**], then deselect the selection. See Figure 9.

   The center star appears on the layer with a transparent background.

You inverted the pixel selection, then viewed the layer containing the extracted object.

Enhance an extracted object

1. Click the **Gradient Map button** on the Adjustments panel.
2. Click the **Gradient list arrow** in the Properties panel, click the **Spectrum gradient box**, as shown in Figure 10, then press [**Esc**] to close the gradient picker.
3. Click the **This adjustment affects all layers below (click to clip to layer) button** in the Properties panel, then collapse the Properties panel to the dock.
4. Click the **Indicates layer visibility button** on the Riders layer on the Layers panel.
5. Save your work, then compare your image to Figure 11.

You adjusted the color of the extracted center star by applying a Gradient Map to the layer, then viewed the color-adjusted image.

Erase Areas in an Image
TO ENHANCE APPEARANCE

What You'll Do

Source: Morguefile.

In this lesson, you'll use the Background Eraser tool to delete pixels on the Riders layer, and then equalize the brightness and contrast of the isolated object.

Learning How to Erase Areas

As you have learned, you can discard pixels by selecting and then inverting the selection. But there may be times when you want to simply erase an area *without* making a selection. Photoshop provides three eraser tools that can accommodate all your expunging needs. Figure 12 shows samples of the effects of each eraser tool. The specific use for each eraser tool is reflected in its options bar, as shown in Figure 13.

Understanding Eraser Tools

The **Eraser tool** has the opposite function of a brush. Instead of brushing *on* pixel color, you drag it *off*. When you erase a layer that has a layer beneath it, and the Lock transparent pixels button is inactive, you'll expose the color on the underlying layer when you erase. If there is no underlying layer, you'll expose transparency. If the Lock transparent pixels button *is* active, you'll expose the current background color on the Tools panel, regardless of the color of an underlying layer.

The **Magic Eraser tool** grabs similarly colored pixels based on the tool settings, and then exposes background color in the same way as the Eraser tool. However, instead of dragging the eraser, you click the areas you want to change. The Magic Eraser tool erases

---

Setting Options for Eraser Tools

Each eraser tool has its own options bar. You can select the mode (Brush, Pencil, or Block) for the Eraser tool, and the brush tip and size for both the Eraser tool and Background Eraser tool. Depending on the tool, you can also set the tolerance—how close a pixel color must be to another color to be erased with the tool. The lower the tolerance, the closer the color must be to the selection. You can also specify the opacity of the eraser strength. A 100% opacity erases pixels to complete transparency. To set options, click an eraser tool on the Tools panel, and then change the tolerance and opacity settings using the text boxes and list arrows on the options bar.

all pixels on the current layer that are close in color value to where you first click or just those pixels that are contiguous to that area.

The **Background Eraser tool** contains small crosshairs in the brush tip. When you click, the tool selects a color in the crosshairs, and then erases that particular color anywhere within the brush tip size. The Background Eraser tool exposes the color of the layer beneath it, or it exposes transparency if there is no layer beneath it. You can preserve objects in the foreground, while eliminating the background (it works best with a large brush tip size). The Background Eraser tool will sample the background colors of the current layer as you drag the tool in your image—you can watch the current background color change on the Tools panel.

Figure 12 *Examples of eraser tools*
© Photodisc/Getty Images.

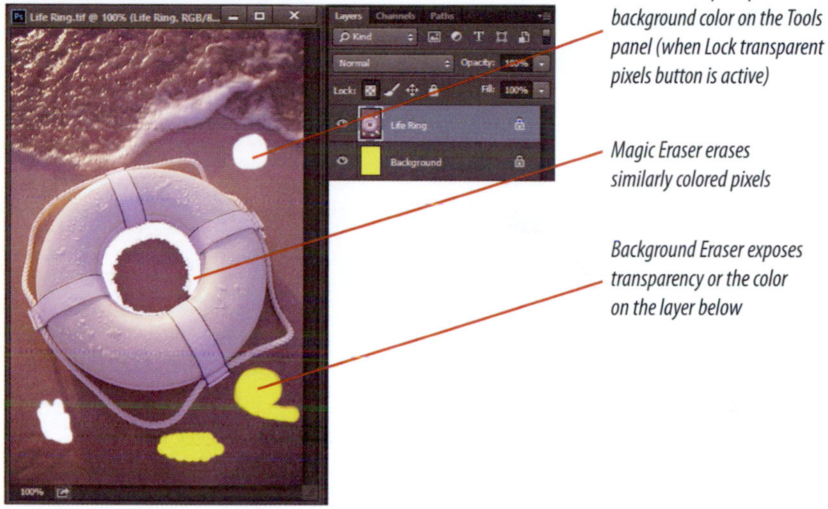

Eraser tools expose pixels of background color on the Tools panel (when Lock transparent pixels button is active)

Magic Eraser erases similarly colored pixels

Background Eraser exposes transparency or the color on the layer below

Figure 13 *Option bars for the eraser tools*

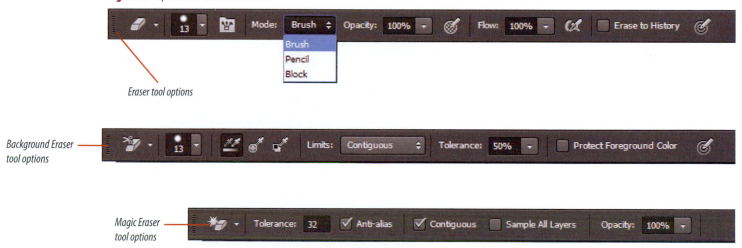

Eraser tool options

Background Eraser tool options

Magic Eraser tool options

Use the Background Eraser tool

1. Click the **Indicates layer visibility button** 👁 on the Center star layer to hide the layer.

2. Click the **Riders layer** to make it the active layer.

3. Zoom into the center star until the zoom factor is **300%**.

4. Click the **Background Eraser tool** 🖌 on the Tools panel.

TIP Look under the Eraser tool if the Background Eraser tool is hidden. To cycle through the eraser tools, press and hold [Shift], then press [E].

5. Click the **Brush Preset picker list arrow** on the options bar, set the Size to **5 px**, the Hardness to **100%**, and the Spacing to **15%** as shown in Figure 14.

6. Press [**Enter**] (Win) or [**return**] (Mac).

7. Keeping the crosshairs of the **Background Eraser pointer** ⊕ on the center star, drag the brush tip over the **center star** until it is completely erased, as shown in Figure 15.

TIP Try to use short strokes when erasing, rather than trying to erase in one pass. That way, if you make an erasure error (either under or over), you can display the History panel and undo any of your erasures.

You hid the Center star layer, zoomed in on the Riders layer, selected a brush tip for the Background Eraser tool, and erased the center star from the Riders layer.

Figure 14 *Brush Preset picker*

Figure 15 *Selection erased on layer*
Source: Morguefile.

Erased area exposes pixels on Layer 1

Figure 16 *Object adjusted in image*
Source: Morguefile.

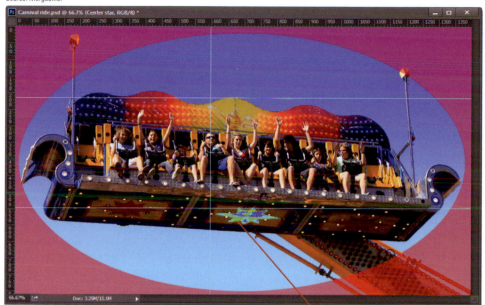

Equalize adjustment applied to Center star layer

Equalize brightness and contrast

1. Click the **Center star layer** on the Layers panel, then make the Center star layer visible.

2. Zoom out from the center star.

3. Click **Image** on the Menu bar, point to **Adjustments**, then click **Equalize**.

   The Equalize command evens out the brightness and contrast values in the center star, and changes its appearance.

4. Compare your image to Figure 16, then save your work.

You adjusted the color of the center star by equalizing the colors, then viewed the color-adjusted image.

Redistributing Brightness Values

The Equalize command changes the brightness values of an image's pixels so they more evenly display the entire range of brightness levels. This command can also be used when you want to balance color values in an image or selection to produce a lighter image. Photoshop changes the brightest and darkest values by remapping them so that the brightest values appear as white and the darkest values appear as black, and then it redistributes the intermediate pixel values evenly throughout the grayscale. You can use this command to "tone down" an image that is too bright. Conversely, you could use it on a dark image that you want to make lighter.

Use the Clone Stamp Tool
TO MAKE REPAIRS

What You'll Do

Source: Morguefile.

 In this lesson, you'll use the Clone Stamp tool to sample an undamaged portion of an image and use it to cover up a flaw on the image.

Touching Up a Damaged Area

Let's face it, many of the images you'll want to work with will have a visual flaw of some kind, such as a scratch, or a misplaced object spoiling what would otherwise be a great shot. While you cannot go back in time and move something out of the way, you can often use the Clone Stamp tool to remove an object or cover up a flaw.

Figure 17 *Clone Stamp tool in action*
© Photodisc/Getty Images.

Object to be deleted

Using the Clone Stamp Tool

The Clone Stamp tool can copy a sample (a pixel selection) in an image, and then paste it over what you want to cover up. The size of the sample taken with the Clone Stamp tool depends on the brush tip size you choose on the Brushes panel. Figure 17 shows the Clone Stamp tool in action. In addition to using the Clone Stamp tool to touch up images, you can use it to copy one image onto another. Using the Clone Stamp tool to copy an image differs from copying an image because you have extensive control over how much of the cloned area you expose and at what opacity.

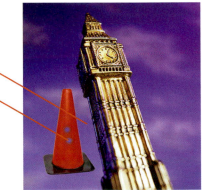

Sampled area

Sampled area applied twice to hide portions of the object

Figure 18 *Comparing images*

Source: Morguefile.

Perfecting Your Analytical Skills

An important step in making an adjustment to any image is to examine it critically and figure out what is wrong. An area that you select for fixing does not necessarily have to look bad or appear wrong. An image might be "wrong" because it simply does not convey the right meaning or mood. Compare the two images in Figure 18. They contain basically the same elements but express entirely different ideas. The figure on the left conveys a more positive image than the one on the right; clearly the grades are better for the student on the left, however, the positive feeling is also reflected in the lighter colored paper, which is in pristine condition. The elements that you choose for your content should depend on what you want to convey. For example, if you want to convey a positive mood, using the elements in the image on the right would be inappropriate for your image. Choosing the right content in the beginning can save you a lot of time in the end. It is much easier and quicker to reach your destination if you know where you are going before you begin.

Sample an area to clone

1. Click the **Riders layer** on the Layers panel.

2. Zoom into the far-right edge of the chair until the zoom factor is **300%** so you can clearly see the missing light.

3. Click the **Clone Stamp tool** ▣ on the Tools panel.

4. Click the **Brush Preset picker list arrow** on the options bar, select the **Hard Round brush tip** and set the Size to **15 px**, then press [**Esc**] to close the Brush Preset picker. (You may need to load the Round Brushes with Size brushes to see the Hard Round tip.)

5. Verify that the Opacity setting on the options bar is **100%**.

6. Position the **Brush pointer** ⊙ at approximately **1155 X/519 Y**, as shown in Figure 19.

7. Press [**Alt**] (Win) or [**option**] (Mac), click once, then release [**Alt**] (Win) or [**option**] (Mac).

   The sample is collected and is ready to be applied to the missing light.

You selected the Riders layer, set the zoom percentage, selected a brush tip for the Clone Stamp tool, and sampled a working light.

Figure 19 *Defining the area to be sampled*
Source: Morguefile.

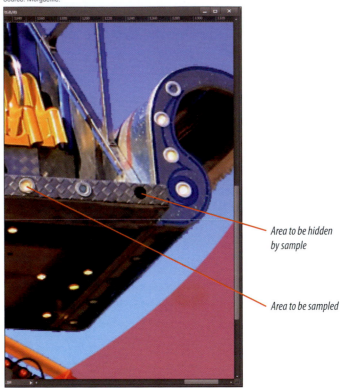

Area to be hidden by sample

Area to be sampled

Using the Clone Source Panel

You can open the Clone Source panel using the Window command on the Menu bar, the Toggle the Clone Source panel button on the options bar when the Clone Stamp tool is active, or by switching to the Motion workspace. Use the Clone Source panel to set up to five sample sources for use with the Clone Stamp tools or Healing Brush tools. The sample source can be displayed as an overlay of the brush pointer so you can more easily clone the source at a specific location. You can also rotate or scale the sample source at a specific size and orientation.

Figure 20 *Clone Stamp tool positioned over defect*
Source: Morguefile.

Clone Stamp tool
positioned over the
missing light

Figure 21 *Corrected image*
Source: Morguefile.

Missing light repaired

Use the Clone Stamp tool to fix an imperfection

1. Position the **Brush pointer** ⬜ *directly* over the missing light, as shown in Figure 20.
2. Click the **missing light**.

TIP Select a different brush size if your brush is too small or too large, then reapply the stamp.

3. Zoom out from the repaired light until the zoom factor is **66.7%**.
4. Compare your image to Figure 21, then save your work.

You fixed the damaged area of the chair by cloning the missing light.

Using Pressure-Sensitive Devices

For specialized painting that gives you maximum control when you create an image, you can purchase a pressure-sensitive stylus or graphics tablet. A pressure-sensitive device mimics the force you'd use with an actual brush; you paint lighter when you press softly and paint darker when you press harder. You can set the stylus or tablet pressure for the Magnetic Lasso, Pencil, Brush, Background Eraser, Color Replacement, Mixer Brush, Eraser, Spot Healing Brush, Healing Brush, Clone Stamp, Pattern Stamp, History Brush, Art History Brush, Blur, Sharpen, Smudge, Dodge, Burn, and Sponge tools. Also affected by pen pressure are the magnetic pen feature and the airbrush feature. To access the magnetic pen, select the Freeform Pen tool, and then click the Magnetic check box. To use the Airbrush feature, click the Brush, Mixer Brush, Clone Stamp, Pattern Stamp, History Brush, Eraser, Dodge, Burn, or Sponge tools, and then click the Enable airbrush-style build-up effects button on the options bar.

Use the Magic Wand Tool
TO SELECT OBJECTS

What You'll Do

Source: Morguefile.

 In this lesson, you'll open a new image, use the Magic Wand tool to select an object in the new image, and move the object to the Carnival ride image. You'll also readjust the Eyedropper tool sample size, reselect and move the object so you can compare the selection difference, and then delete the incomplete layer in the Carnival ride image.

Understanding the Magic Wand Tool

You can use the Magic Wand tool to select an object by selecting the color range of the object. The **Magic Wand tool** lets you choose pixels that are similar in color to the ones you first click in an image. You can control how the Magic Wand tool behaves by specifying tolerance settings and whether or not you want to select only contiguous pixels on the options bar. The Magic Wand tool options bar is shown in Figure 22.

Learning About Tolerance

The tolerance setting determines the range of colors you can select with the Magic Wand tool. For example, if you select a low tolerance and then click an image of the sky, you will only select a narrow range of blue pixels and probably not the entire sky. However, if you set a higher tolerance, you can expand the range of blue pixels selected by the Magic Wand tool. Each time you click the Magic Wand tool, you can choose from one of four buttons on the options bar to select a new area, add to the existing area (the effect is cumulative; the more you click, the more you add), subtract from the existing area, or intersect with the existing area.

> **QUICK TIP**
>
> You can also press and hold [Shift] and click to add pixels to your selection, or press and hold [Alt] (Win) or [option] (Mac), and then click to subtract pixels from your selection.

Figure 22 *Magic Wand tool options*

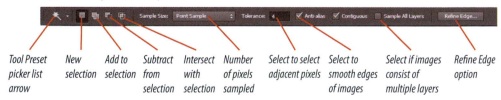

| Tool Preset picker list arrow | New selection | Add to selection | Subtract from selection | Intersect with selection | Number of pixels sampled | Select to select adjacent pixels | Select to smooth edges of images | Select if images consist of multiple layers | Refine Edge option |

Using the Eyedropper Tool and the Magic Wand Tool

The Contiguous and Tolerance settings are not the only determinants that establish the pixel area selected by the Magic Wand tool. The area that the Magic Wand tool selects also has an intrinsic relationship with the settings for the Eyedropper tool. The sample size, or number of pixels used by the Eyedropper tool to determine the color it picks up, affects the area selected by the Magic Wand tool. To understand this, you need to first examine the Eyedropper tool settings.

Understanding Sample Size

When the Eyedropper tool sample size is set to Point Sample, it picks up the one pixel where you click the image. When the sample size is set to 3 by 3 Average, the Eyedropper tool picks up the color values of the nine pixels that surround the pixel where you click the image and averages them. The sample area increases exponentially to 25 pixels for the 5 by 5 Average setting. The sample size of the Eyedropper tool influences the area selected by the Magic Wand tool. Figure 23 shows how different Eyedropper tool sample sizes change the Magic Wand tool selections, even when you sample an image at the same coordinates and use the same tolerance setting. As you become familiar with the Magic Wand tool, it's a good idea to verify or change the Eyedropper tool sample size as needed, in addition to changing the tolerance setting.

Figure 23a *Selection affected by Eyedropper tool sample size*

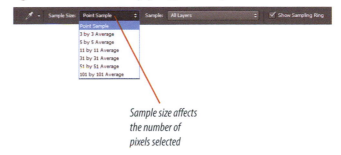

Sample size affects the number of pixels selected

Figure 23b *Point sample size*
© Photodisc/Getty Images.

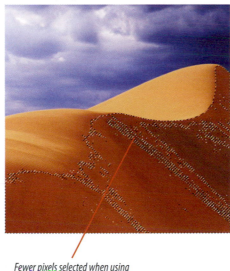

Fewer pixels selected when using Point Sample with Magic Wand

Figure 23c *101 by 101 Average sample size*
© Photodisc/Getty Images.

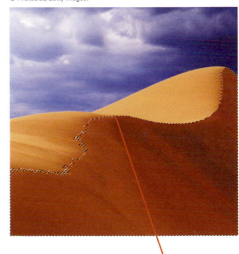

More pixels selected when using 101 by 101 Average sample with Magic Wand

Select an object using the Magic Wand tool

1. Verify that the **Riders layer** is the active layer.

2. Open PS 10-2.psd from the drive and folder where you store your Data Files, then save it as **Clown.psd**.

3. Change the zoom factor of the Carnival ride image to **50%**, drag the **Clown.psd window** to the right side of the workspace, and arrange your windows so that they look similar to those shown in Figure 24.

4. Click the **Eyedropper tool** on the Tools panel, then set the Sample Size to **101 by 101 Average** on the options bar.

5. Click the **Magic Wand tool** on the Tools panel.

6. Type **50** in the Tolerance text box on the options bar, then press [**Enter**] (Win) or [**return**] (Mac).

7. Select the **Contiguous check box** if it is not selected and verify that the New selection button is selected.

TIP If you use the Magic Wand tool when the Contiguous check box is selected, you'll select only the adjoining pixels that share the same color values.

8. In the Clown window, click the **clown face** at approximately **50 X/20 Y** to select the clown face, as shown in Figure 25.

9. Click the **Move tool** on the Tools panel.

10. Position the **Move pointer** over the **clown face**, drag the **selection** to the area above the center of the chair in the Carnival ride image, then compare your image to Figure 26.

You opened a new file, set the Eyedropper tool sample size to a different selection setting, used the Magic Wand tool to select the Clown image in the new file, then moved the selected image into the Carnival ride image.

Figure 24 *New image opened and positioned*
Source: Morguefile.

Figure 25 *Selection indicated by marquee*
Source: Morguefile.

Figure 26 *Selected object moved to current image*
Source: Morguefile.

Clown face

Enhancing Specific Selections

Figure 27 *Comparison of selections*
Source: Morguefile.

Selection made with 101 by 101 Average sample size captures more pixels

Selection made with 31 by 31 Average sample size captures fewer pixels

Figure 28 *Selection positioned in image*
Source: Morguefile.

Compare objects selected using different sample sizes

1. Activate **Clown.psd**.

2. Click **Select** on the Menu bar, then click **Deselect**.

3. Repeat Steps 4 through 10 on the previous page, but this time, set the sample size for the Eyedropper tool to **31 by 31 Average** in Step 4 and drag the **clown face** to the right of the existing face in Step 10.

4. Compare the two faces in the Carnival ride image, as shown in Figure 27.

TIP Your results may vary from the sample.

5. Delete **Layer 3** on the Layers panel.

6. Hide the rulers, zoom in to **66.7%**, compare your image to Figure 28, then save your work.

You changed the Eyedropper tool sample size to 31 by 31, reselected the clown face, moved it to the Carnival ride image for comparison, then deleted the new Clown image.

Learn How To
CREATE SNAPSHOTS

What You'll Do

Source: Morguefile.

 In this lesson, you'll edit an image, create a snapshot on the History panel, and then use the original snapshot to view the image as it existed prior to making changes.

Understanding Snapshots

As mentioned earlier in this chapter, it is a good work habit to make a copy of an original layer to help you avoid losing any of the original image information. Creating a snapshot is like creating that new copy. By default, the History panel records a maximum of 20 tasks, or states, that you perform. This setting can be changed to record a maximum of 1000 tasks by clicking Edit on the Menu bar (Win) or Photoshop on the Menu bar (Mac), pointing to Preferences, clicking Performance, clicking the History States list arrow, dragging the slider to a value, and then clicking OK. When the History panel reaches its limit, it starts deleting the oldest states to make room for new states. Rather than relying on the History panel, you can create a **snapshot** of your image, a temporary copy that contains the history states made to that point. It's a good idea to take a snapshot of your image before you begin an editing session and after you've made crucial changes because you can then use those snapshots to revert to or review your image from an earlier

stage of development. You can create multiple snapshots in an image, and you can switch between snapshots as necessary.

Creating a Snapshot

To create a snapshot, you can click the Create new snapshot button on the History panel, or click the History Panel options button and then click New Snapshot, as shown in Figure 29. Each new snapshot is numbered consecutively; snapshots appear in order at the top of the History panel. If you create a snapshot by clicking the New Snapshot command, you can name the snapshot in the Name text box in the New Snapshot dialog box. Otherwise, you can rename an existing snapshot in the same way that you rename a layer on the Layers panel: double-click the snapshot, and then edit the name once the existing name is highlighted. You can create a snapshot based on the entire image, merged layers, or just the current layer. A snapshot of the entire image (the Full Document option) includes all layers in the current image. A snapshot of merged layers combines all the layers in the current image on a single layer, and a snapshot of the current layer includes only the layer active at the time you took the snapshot. Figure 30 shows the New Snapshot dialog box.

Changing Snapshot Options

By default, Photoshop automatically creates a snapshot of an image when you open it. To change the default snapshot option, click the History Panel options button, click History Options, and then select one of the check boxes shown in Figure 31. You can open files faster by deselecting the Automatically Create First Snapshot check box.

Figure 29 *Snapshot commands on the History panel*

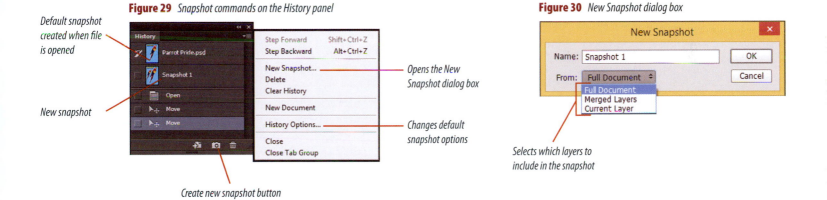

Default snapshot created when file is opened

New snapshot

Create new snapshot button

Opens the New Snapshot dialog box

Changes default snapshot options

Figure 30 *New Snapshot dialog box*

Selects which layers to include in the snapshot

Figure 31 *History Options dialog box*

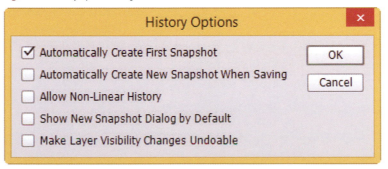

Create a snapshot

1. Deselect any selections in Clown.psd.
2. Click the **Invert button**  on the Adjustments panel.
3. Display the History panel, then compare your screen to Figure 32.
4. Click the **History Panel options button** , then click **New Snapshot**.
5. Type **After Invert** in the Name text box, as shown in Figure 33.
6. Click **OK**.

   The newly named snapshot appears on the History panel beneath the snapshot Photoshop created when you opened the image.

You deselected the selection in the Clown image, inverted the color in the image, then created and named a new snapshot.

Figure 32 *Inverted image*
Source: Morguefile.

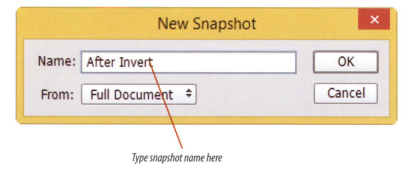

Figure 33 *New Snapshot dialog box*

Type snapshot name here

Enhancing Specific Selections

Figure 34 *Original snapshot view*

Source: Morguefile.

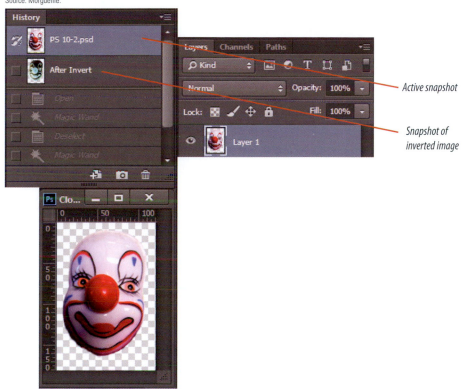

Active snapshot

Snapshot of inverted image

Use a snapshot

1. Scroll up the History panel if necessary, click the **PS 10-2.psd snapshot**, then compare your image to Figure 34.

   The image returns to its original color.

2. Click the **After Invert snapshot** on the History panel.

3. Collapse the History panel to the dock.

4. Close Clown.psd, saving any changes.

You used the snapshot to view the image as it was before you made changes.

Create Multiple-Image LAYOUTS

What You'll Do

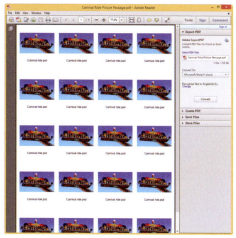

Source: Morguefile.

In this lesson, you'll create a multiple-image layout of the current image, and then create a folder containing a contact sheet of images.

Understanding Multiple-Image Layouts

With all the choices available for creating different variations of your images, you might get the idea that keeping track of all these choices is time-consuming or difficult. Not so; to facilitate the task, Adobe Bridge lets you generate multiple-image layouts. **Multiple-image layouts** are useful when you need to gather one or more Photoshop images in a variety of sizes for a variety of uses. For example, if you create an advertisement, you might want to have multiple image layouts for printing in different publications. Can you imagine what would be involved to create this type of arrangement of images manually? For each duplicate image, you'd have to create a layer, resize it, and then position it correctly on the page. A lot of work! You can generate a single layout that contains multiple images in a single file, as shown in Figure 35. The picture package option lets you choose from eight possible predesigned layouts of the same image, plus a custom layout, and then arranges them in a single printable image.

Creating a Web Gallery

You can display your image files on a website by creating a Web Gallery. A Web Gallery contains a thumbnail index page of all files you choose. To create a Web Gallery, open Bridge, click the Output tab in the Menu bar and the Web Gallery button in the Output panel. Click the Folders tab and the location of the files you want to include, and then click Refresh Preview in the Bridge Output panel to see the gallery display in Bridge, or click the Preview in Browser to see the images in your browser. [**Caution**: The Output panel in Adobe Bridge may require a separate download and installation.]

Assembling a Contact Sheet

Previewing and cataloging several related images could be a time-consuming and difficult chore, but Bridge makes it easy. It allows you to assemble a maximum of 30 thumbnail images in a specific folder, called a **contact sheet**, as shown in Figure 36. If the folder used to compile the contact sheet contains more than 30 files, Bridge automatically creates new sheets so that all the images appear.

Figure 35 *Sample picture package*

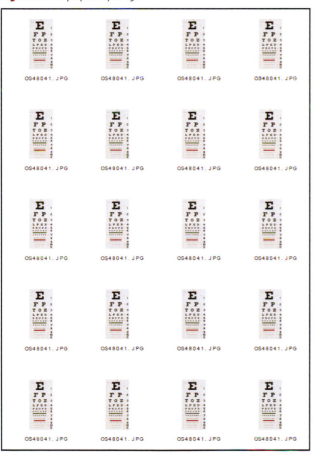

Figure 36 *Sample contact sheet*

Images of people © Photodisc/Getty Images.

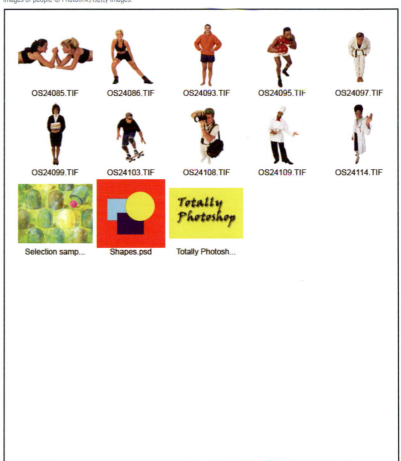

Create a multi-image layout

1. Click **File** on the Menu bar, then click **Browse in Bridge**.

2. Click the **Folders tab** if necessary.

3. Click the Folder where you store your Data Files, use the Content tab slider to locate the Carnival ride file, then click **Carnival ride.psd**.

4. Click **Output** at the top of the Bridge window if necessary, click the **PDF button** in the Output panel if necessary, then click the **Repeat One Photo per Page check box** in the Layout section and compare your settings to those shown in Figure 37, then click the **Refresh Preview** button.

TIP Creating a PDF with Bridge requires the installation of the Adobe Output Module.

5. Click the **View PDF After Save check box**, then click **Save**.

6. Save the multi-image layout as **Carnival Ride Picture Package** in the location where you store your Chapter 10 Data Files, then close the file and close Adobe Reader.

You opened Adobe Bridge to create a multi-image layout, selected a layout for a single-image picture package, then created and saved a layout using the Carnival ride image.

Figure 37 *Single-image settings in Adobe Bridge*
Source: Morguefile.

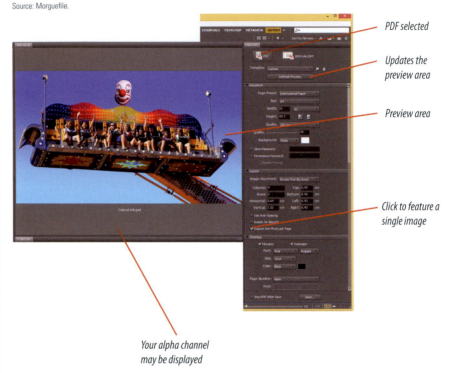

PDF selected

Updates the preview area

Preview area

Click to feature a single image

Your alpha channel may be displayed

Customizing a Layout

With so many layout options available, you might think it would be impossible to customize any further. Well, you'd be wrong. Using the Layout section of the Output panel, shown in Figure 38, you can change the number of columns and rows, the amount of space in the margins, and rotate the page for the best fit.

Figure 38 *Layout section of the Output panel*

Enhancing Specific Selections

Figure 39 *Contact Sheet settings*

© Photodisc/Getty Images. Source: Morguefile. Image courtesy of Elizabeth Eisner Reding

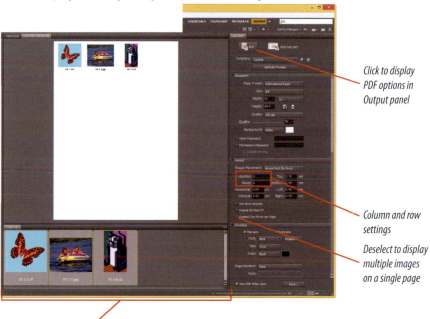

Click to display
PDF options in
Output panel

Column and row
settings

Deselect to display
multiple images
on a single page

Selected images in Content
panel: your images will differ

Create a contact sheet

1. Create a folder on your computer that contains copies of at least three Photoshop images you have created, then name the folder **Contact Sample**.

2. Click the **Folders tab** in Adobe Bridge, click the **Contact Sample folder**, then click the **PDF button** in the Output panel.

3. Select the files in the Contact Sample folder in the Content tab (use [Shift] to select multiple files), and use the settings in the Output panel shown in Figure 39, then click **Refresh Preview**.

   Bridge opens the files and places image thumbnails in a new file to which you can assign a meaningful name.

4. Click **Save** at the bottom of the Output panel, type the name **ContactSheet-001**, click **Save**, then close the file and exit Bridge, Photoshop, and Adobe Reader, if necessary.

You created a folder and placed images in it, then used Bridge to select files from which you created a contact sheet of the images.

POWER USER SHORTCUTS	
To do this:	**Use this method:**
Clone Stamp tool	🖋 or **S**
Create a snapshot	📷
Duplicate selection and move 1 pixel:	Press and hold [Ctrl][Alt] (Win) or ⌘ [option] (Mac), then press
Left	←
Right	→
Up	↑
Down	↓
Move selection 10 pixels:	Press and hold [Shift] (Win) or ⌘ [shift] (Mac), then press
Left	←
Right	→
Up	↑
Down	↓
Eraser tools	**E**
Magic Wand tool	✨ or **W**
Move selection 1 pixel:	▸⊹
Left	←
Right	→
Up	↑
Down	↓

Key: Menu items are indicated by ➢ between the menu name and its command. Blue bold letters are shortcuts for selecting tools on the Tools panel.

© Cengage Learning®

Create an alpha channel.

1. Open PS 10-3.psd from the drive and folder where you store your Data Files, then save it as **Tools**.
2. Make sure the rulers appear in pixels, zooming in and out of the image throughout this review as you see fit.
3. Display the Channels panel.
4. Select the Rectangular Marquee tool, then change the Feather to 25 on the options bar.
5. Create a selection from 70 X/50 Y to 400 X/270 Y, using the guides as a reference.
6. Save the selection as a channel, using the default name, on the Channels panel, then display the Alpha 1 channel.
7. Deselect the selection.
8. Open the Channel Options dialog box, select a blue color swatch of your choice, close the Color Picker (Channel Color) dialog box, enter 50% Opacity, then close the Channel Options dialog box.
9. Hide the Alpha 1 channel.
10. Save your work.

Isolate an object.

1. Display the Layers panel.
2. Duplicate the Tools layer, then name it **Red Tape**.
3. Use the Elliptical Marquee tool to surround the outer edge of the roll of red tape.
4. Select the inverse of the selection, then delete the selection.
5. Use the Elliptical Marquee tool to select the interior (hole) of the roll of red tape.
6. Delete the selection, then deselect the selection.
7. Save your work.

Erase areas in an image to enhance appearance.

1. Hide the Red Tape layer.
2. Make the Tools layer active.
3. Enlarge your view of the red tape.
4. Using the Background Eraser tool, erase the roll of red tape. (You can adjust the Tolerance setting to ensure a crisp deletion.)
5. Make the Red Tape layer active.
6. Adjust the Color Balance settings on the Red Tape layer to +75, −57, and −10, so that the adjustment affects only the Red Tape layer. (*Hint*: Click the Color Balance button on the Adjustments panel.)
7. Save your work.

Use the Clone Stamp tool to make repairs.

1. Make the Tools layer active.
2. Select the Clone Stamp tool on the Tools panel.
3. Use the Hard Round brush tip with a size of 5 pixels. (*Hint*: Use the Brush Preset picker.)
4. Sample the area at 325 X/50 Y by pressing [Alt] (Win) or [option] (Mac) and clicking over the wire cutters.
5. Click the red dot (at approximately 310 X/85 Y) to remove this imperfection.
6. Save your work.

Use the Magic Wand tool to select objects.

1. Open PS 10-4.psd, then save it as **Wrench**.
2. Select the Magic Wand tool, deselect the Contiguous check box if it is selected, then set the Tolerance to 0.
3. Click the wrench image anywhere on the white background.
4. Select the inverse of the selection.
5. Move the selection to the Tools image.
6. Move the top of the handle of the wrench to approximately 380 X/25 Y.
7. Deselect the selection, then close Wrench.psd.

Learn how to create snapshots.

1. Use the History Panel options button to create a new snapshot.
2. Name the snapshot **New**.
3. Save your work, zoom out to 100% magnification, hide the rulers and guides, then compare your image to Figure 40.

Create multiple-image layouts.

1. Use Bridge to create a 4 column, 3 row sheet containing the Tools image.
2. Select the Repeat One Photo per Page option.
3. Save the file as **Tools Picture Package** and close it.
4. Create a folder called **Contact Sample 2** with image files to use for a 3 column, 4 row contact sheet.
5. Save this file as **ContactSheet-002**, then close it.
6. Close Bridge.

Figure 40 *Completed Skills Review*
© Photodisc/Getty Images.

Science Discovery, a traveling educational show for children, is planning a piece on mathematics. For the first segment, the puppets will teach about different shapes, starting with spheres. You're going to design the spot graphic that will link users to the Science Discovery web page.

1. Obtain the following images for the graphic: a background that contains one or more round objects, at least two images that contain spheres whose content you can select, and any other images as desired. You'll use two of the sphere images for a clipping group.

2. Create a new Photoshop image, then save it as **Spheroid**.

3. Apply a color or style to the Background layer, or use any of the techniques you learned in this chapter to select and drag the image that will be the background of the Spheroid image, turn the Background layer into an image layer, then apply at least one style to it. (*Hint*: An Adjustment layer is applied to the grapes.)

4. Use any of the techniques you learned in this chapter to select and drag the image that will be the base of a clipping group to the Spheroid image above what was the Background layer, and modify it as desired. (*Hint*: The tennis ball in the sample is the base image and has been duplicated.)

5. Use any of the techniques you learned in this chapter to select and drag an image that will be the target of a clipping mask to the Spheroid image, and modify it as necessary. (*Hint*: The golf balls in the sample are the target image.)

6. Create a clipping mask using the two images, then modify the result as desired. (*Hint*: The tennis ball has been copied to another layer, which was adjusted to a lower opacity setting and moved above the clipping mask to create the illusion that the golf balls are inside it.)

7. Create type layers as desired, and apply at least one style or filter to at least one of the type layers.

8. Drag or copy any remaining images to the Spheroid image, transform them or apply at least one style or filter to them, then close the image files.

9. Save your work, then compare your image to the sample in Figure 41.

(*Hint*: The Oh, boy! type has a Vivid Light blending mode, and the Drop Shadow and Gradient Overlay styles applied to it.)

Figure 41 *Sample Project Builder 1*
© Photodisc/Getty Images.

Several resort hotels want to accommodate the unique vacation needs of their younger guests. They're going to give each child under 12 a bag of equipment, books, games, and other items that match their interests. Your job is to design the cover of the printed information booklet that will be included in the package.

1. Obtain images for the cover that are centered on a beach vacation theme. Include images whose content you can select or extract, and any other images as desired. You can use scanned images, images that are available on your computer, or you can connect to the Internet and download images. You'll need a background image and at least one layer to serve as the focal point.

2. Create a new Photoshop image, then save it as **Perfect Oasis**.

3. Apply a color or style to the Background layer, or use any of the techniques you learned in this chapter to select and drag the image that will be the background to the Perfect Oasis image, then convert the Background layer to an image layer.

4. Use any of the techniques you learned in this chapter to select and drag the image that will be the focal point of the Perfect Oasis image and add styles of your choice. (*Hint*: In the sample shown, the image of the boy and girl has a layer mask applied to it with Drop Shadow and Bevel and Emboss styles applied to it.)

5. Open the surrounding image files, then use any of the techniques you learned in this chapter to select and drag the images to the Perfect Oasis image.

6. Add layer masks, transform, or apply filters or styles to the images as desired. (*Hint*: In the sample, the image of the boy and girl has been enhanced and has a layer mask; the surf also has been enhanced.)

7. Create type layers as desired and apply filters or styles to at least one of them. (*Hint*: The is calling your name! type has Drop Shadow, Bevel and Emboss, and Gradient Overlay styles applied to it.)

8. Create a layer group called Title, add a color to the layer set, then add the type layers to it.

9. Save your work, close the image files, then compare your image to the sample in Figure 42.

Figure 42 *Sample Project Builder 2*
Source: Morguefile.

You're the senior graphics engineer at a 3D software simulation company and have just hired a few new graphic designers. Some of the work at your company involves reverse engineering, a process that your new artists will need to understand and capture visually. To better orient them to the practice, you've asked them to deconstruct a Photoshop image on the web, and then reinterpret the image using the techniques they identified. Before you assemble the staff, you want to walk through the process yourself.

1. Connect to the Internet to find digital artwork that contains images and type that appear to have styles or filters applied. (Make a record of the sites you find for future reference.)
2. Create a new Photoshop image and save it as **My Vision**.
3. Create a type layer named Techniques, then on the layer, type the skills and features that you believe were used to create the appearance of each letter and digital artwork and its background image. In addition to addressing the specifics for each letter, be sure to include the following general analyses:
   - Identify the light source for the image, and how light is handled for each letter and its background.
   - Discuss the relationship between the styles applied to the type and the styles or filters applied to the background image.
   - Evaluate any seemingly conflicting or unidentifiable techniques.
4. Complete your analyses and print the image.

5. Hide the Techniques layer, then obtain images to use for your own interpretation of the digital artwork. You can use scanned images or images that are available on your computer, or download images from the Internet.
6. Place the images in your image, create type layers for the letters, then apply the techniques you identified. Compare your image to the sample shown in Figure 43.

7. Create a snapshot, then update the Techniques layer as necessary, print the image so that the Techniques layer prints clearly, then compare your before and after analyses. (*Hint*: Hide distracting layers if necessary.)
8. Hide the Techniques layer, make the other layers active, then save your work.

Figure 43 *Sample Design Project*
© Photodisc/Getty Images.

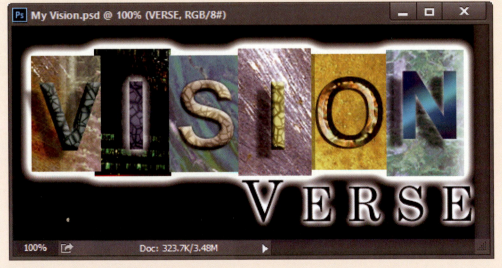

After years of lackluster advertising campaigns, you've decided to combine the talent of local photographers and your Photoshop skills to create new artwork for a local beach. You know that this is a grand public relations opportunity not to be missed. You decide to design a graphic that can be used in a print poster and a companion bumper sticker that highlights the beach. You can use any appropriate images of your choice in the design.

1. Obtain images for the poster and bumper sticker. Include those whose content you can select or extract, and any other images as desired. You can use scanned images, images that are available on your computer, or connect to the Internet and download images. You'll need a background image that might or might not include the animal, at least one small image (such as a snack, toy, or flower) to accompany the animal, and as many other images as desired.
2. Create a new Photoshop image and save it as **Beach Poster**.
3. Drag or copy the background to the Beach Poster image above the Background layer, then delete the Background layer, if necessary.
4. Select the animal in its image file, then copy the image to a new layer in the Beach Poster file. (*Hint*: The horses were selected using the Quick Selection tool.)
5. Duplicate the animal layer if desired, and apply filters or styles to it. (*Hint*: The horses were selected,

copied, then brightness and contrast settings were adjusted.)
6. Create type layers for the bumper sticker as desired, and apply at least one style or filter to them. (*Hint*: The background of the bumper sticker was created with the Rectangle tool and has Stroke and Drop Shadow effects applied to it, the heart was created with the Custom Shape tool, and the cut corners were created with the Eraser tool.)

7. Drag or copy the small image, transform it as needed, then apply at least one style or filter to it. (*Hint*: The type has been scaled, rotated, and background erased.)
8. Drag or copy other images as desired, then apply filters or styles to them.
9. Be prepared to discuss the effects you can generate when you select an image, copy it, and apply different opacity settings, filters, or styles to each copy.
10. Save your work, then compare your image to the sample in Figure 44.

Figure 44 *Sample Portfolio Project*
© Photodisc/Getty Images.

11

CHAPTER

ADJUSTING
COLORS

1. Correct and adjust color

2. Enhance colors by altering saturation

3. Modify color channels using levels

4. Create color samplers with the Info panel

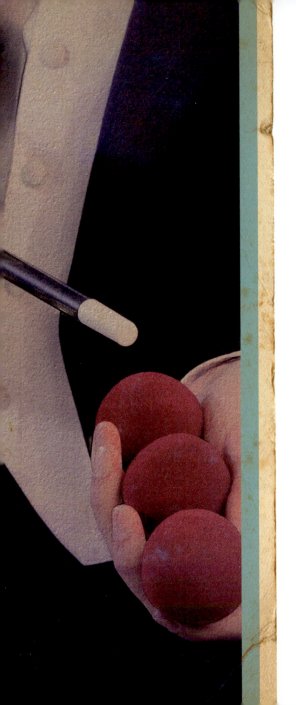

CHAPTER 11

ADJUSTING
COLORS

Enhancing Color

Photoshop places several color-enhancing tools at your disposal. By changing tonal values, these tools make it possible to change the mood or "personality" of a color. **Tonal values**, also called **color levels**, are the numeric values of an individual color and are crucial if you ever need to duplicate a color. For example, when you select a specific shade in a paint store that requires custom mixing, a recipe that contains the tonal values is used to create the color.

Using Tools to Adjust Colors

You can use color adjustment tools to make an image that is flat or dull appear to come to life. You can mute distracting colors to call attention to a central image. You can choose from several adjustment tools to achieve the same results, so the method you use depends on which one you *prefer*, not on which one is *better*.

Reproducing Colors

Accurate color reproduction is an important reason to learn about color measurement and modification. Because colors vary from monitor to monitor, and can be altered during the output process, knowing how to specify color levels will result in exactly how you want them to look. Professional printers know how to take your Photoshop settings and adapt them to get the colors that match your specifications. Color levels, depicted in a **histogram** (a graph that represents the frequency distribution—for example, the number of times a particular pixel color occurs), can be modified by making adjustments in the input and output levels. When working with color levels, moving the input sliders toward the center of the histogram increases the tonal range, resulting in increased contrast in the image. Moving the output sliders toward the center decreases the tonal range, resulting in decreased contrast.

QUICK **TIP**

You can make color adjustments directly on a layer, or by using an adjustment layer. Directly applying a color adjustment affects only the layer to which it is applied. Applying a color adjustment using an adjustment layer may or may not affect all visible layers beneath it.

TOOLS YOU'LL USE

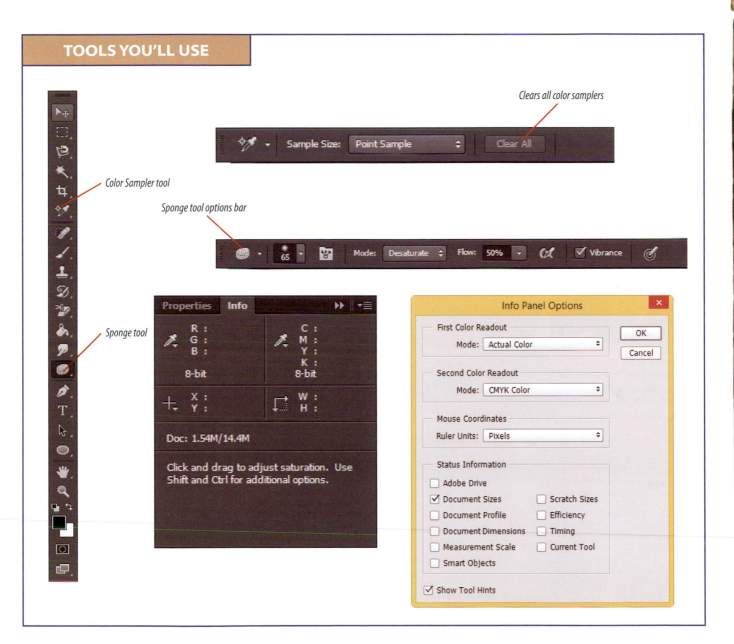

Clears all color samplers

Color Sampler tool

Sponge tool options bar

Sponge tool

Correct and ADJUST COLOR

What You'll Do

Source: Morguefile.

 In this lesson, you'll modify settings for color balance and curves to make dull colors look more vivid.

Making Color Corrections

Learning to recognize which colors need correction is one of the hardest skills to develop. Adjusting colors can be very difficult because, while there is a science to color correction, you must also consider the aesthetics of your image. Beauty is in the eye of the beholder, and you must choose how you want your work to look and feel. Add to this the problem of reconciling hardware differences, where *my* red may look very different from *your* red, and you can see how color management can become a can of worms. A **color management system** reconciles the differences between different devices.

> **QUICK TIP**
>
> Most color corrections can be made by clicking the appropriate button on the Adjustments panel, or by using a dialog box that is opened by clicking the Image menu on the Menu bar, pointing to Adjustments, and then clicking your desired adjustment.

Using a Color Management System

Photoshop has a way to deal with hardware discrepancies: the device profile. A **device profile** (also called an **ICC profile**) can be created for specific devices and embedded in an image, and is used to define how colors are interpreted by a specific device. The ICC specification was developed by the International Color Consortium, a group of software, camera, and printer vendors who came together to create a universal color management system. You can create a profile by clicking Edit on the Menu bar, and then clicking Color Settings. Use the list arrows in the Working Spaces section to specify the working color profile. An image's working space tells the color management system how RGB or CMYK values are interpreted. You don't have to use profiles, but you can assign a specific profile by selecting the ICC Profile check box (Win) or the Embed Color Profile check box (Mac) in the Save As dialog box. Doing so embeds the profile in the working space of an image.

Assigning an ICC profile is different from converting to an ICC profile. You should *assign* the color profile that looks the best on your calibrated monitor, and then *convert* to the profile you want if it is needed. During output preparation, you can select color management options in the Save Adobe PDF dialog box which you can access from the Save As dialog box by selecting the Photoshop PDF File type (Win) or Format (Mac), then clicking Save. The Save Adobe PDF dialog box allows you to fine-tune general options, as well as compression, output, and security.

Balancing Colors

You can balance colors by adding and subtracting tonal values from those already existing in a layer. You do this to correct oversaturated or undersaturated color and to remove color casts from an image. The Color Balance adjustment (by clicking Image on the Menu bar, pointing to Adjustments, then clicking Color Balance, or selecting the Color Balance button in the Adjustments panel and then making adjustments in the Properties panel) contains three sliders: one for Cyan-Red, one for Magenta-Green, and one for Yellow-Blue. You can adjust colors by dragging each of these sliders or by typing in values in the Color Levels text boxes. You can also use Color Balance to adjust the color balance of shadows or highlights by selecting Shadows or Highlights from the Tones list button.

Modifying Curves

Using the Curves adjustment shown in Figure 1, you can alter the output tonal value of any pixel input. Instead of just being able to make adjustments using three variables (highlights, shadows, and midtones), you can change as many as 16 points along the 0–255 scale in the Curves adjustment. The horizontal axis of the graph represents the original intensity values of the pixels (the Input levels), and the vertical axis represents the modified color values (the Output levels). The default curve appears as a diagonal line that shares the same input and output values. Each point on the line represents each pixel. You add curves to the line to adjust the tonal values.

Analyzing Colors

When you look at an image, ask yourself, "What's wrong with this picture?" Does the image need more blue than yellow? Preserve your work by creating an adjustment layer, and then try adjusting the color sliders, and see how the image changes. Then try modifying the curves. Much of the color correction process involves experimentation—with you, the artist, learning and applying the subtleties of shading and contrast.

Figure 1 *Curves Properties panel*

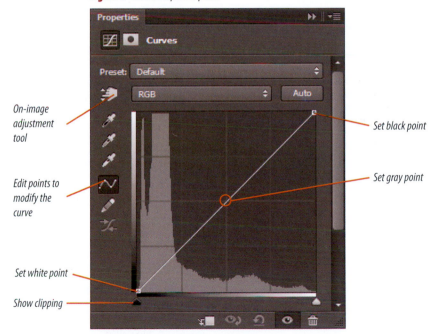

On-image adjustment tool

Edit points to modify the curve

Set white point

Show clipping

Set black point

Set gray point

Modify color balance settings

1. Start Photoshop, open PS 11-1.psd from the drive and folder where you store your Data Files, update any type layers if necessary, then save the file as **Valentine Candy**.

2. Click the **Default Foreground and Background Colors button** on the Tools panel, then change the zoom factor to **100%** if necessary.

3. Display the **Photography workspace**.

TIP Some panels such as Histogram have the option of displaying additional information. You can display this additional information by clicking the Panel options button in the panel of your choice, then clicking Expanded View. Use the display that best meets your needs.

4. Click the **Green heart layer** on the Layers panel.

5. Click the **Color Balance button** on the Adjustments panel, then click the **This adjustment affects all layers below (click to clip to layer) button** on the Properties panel.

6. Drag the **sliders** so that the Midtones settings in the Color Levels text boxes are **−40** for Cyan/Red, **+80** for Magenta/Green, and **−20** for Yellow/Blue, verify that the Preserve Luminosity check box is selected, then collapse the Properties panel to the dock.

TIP You can also use the [Tab] key to advance through the fields in this panel.

7. Compare your image to Figure 2.

You modified the color balance settings by creating an adjustment layer and using the sliders. As you drag the sliders, you can see changes in the image on the active layer.

Figure 2 *Color balanced layer*
Source: Morguefile.

Intensified green and yellow

Using the Auto Adjustments Commands

You can make color adjustments by clicking Image on the Menu bar and using one of the Auto Adjustments commands. You can use three Auto Adjustments commands (Auto Tone, Auto Contrast, and Auto Color) to make color adjustments automatically without any additional input. The Auto Tone command adjusts the intensity levels of shadows and highlights by identifying the lightest and darkest pixel in each color channel, and then redistributing the pixel's values across that range. You can use the Auto Contrast command to make simple adjustments to the contrast and mixture of colors in an RGB image; it works by analyzing the distribution of colors in the composite image, not in the individual color channels. The Auto Color command adjusts the contrast and color mixtures using the image itself to make the adjustment, resulting in neutralized midtones. You can use the Auto-Blend Layers command to combine multiple layers giving smooth transitions to your final image. You can use the Auto-Align Layers command to align multiple layers. (Both Auto-Blend Layers and Auto-Align Layers commands are found on the Edit menu.)

But beware: sometimes it's advantageous to use manual tonal adjustments. In the case where you're trying to create a special effect or fix a particularly damaged photograph, manual adjustments may give you an edge and enable you to create a special look.

Figure 3 *Curves graph in Properties panel*

Active channel

Active setting

Values for active settings

Click in the gray area, then the Curve values display while hovering over the graph

Figure 4 *Image with modified curves*

Source: Morguefile.

Modify curves

1. Click the **Green heart layer**, then click the **Curves button** on the Adjustments panel.

2. Click the **center of the graph** at the point on the line where the input and output values both equal **127**.

   TIP When you position the pointer over the Curves graph, input and output values display beneath the graph.

3. Drag the point down (or type the values) so that the input value equals **127** and the output value equals **99**.

   TIP This is not an exact science. Don't worry if you can't get the input and output values exactly as stated.

   Did you notice that the image's colors change as you drag the line? If you use the Curves dialog box, check the preview box to see the changes.

4. Click the **point where the curve intersects the right vertical gridline** (input value equals approximately **191**, and output value equals approximately **178**). (You may have to click in the gray area.)

   TIP The point that you click in the Curves graph is called the **active setting**.

5. Drag the **active setting** up as needed until the input and output values are both approximately **190**, as shown in Figure 3, and verify that the **This adjustment clips to the layer (click to affect all layers below) button** is selected.

   After you select the active setting, you can also change its location by changing the values in the Input and Output boxes.

6. Collapse the Properties panel to the dock.

7. Save your work, then compare your screen to Figure 4.

You modified curves settings by using Curves on the Adjustments panel.

Using the Color Settings Dialog Box

You can use the Color Settings dialog box to save common color management controls, such as working spaces, color management policies, conversion options, and advanced controls. You might want to create a custom color setting, for example, to match a specific proofing setup used by a commercial printer. To open the Color Settings dialog box, click Edit on the Menu bar, and then click Color Settings. In most cases, it's best to use preset color settings that have been tested by Adobe unless you are knowledgeable about color management. If you do make changes, you can save your new settings using the Color Settings dialog box.

Enhance Colors
BY ALTERING SATURATION

What You'll Do

Source: Morguefile.

 In this lesson, you'll modify the appearance of an image by altering color saturation.

Understanding Saturation

Saturation is the purity of a particular color. A higher saturation level indicates a color that is more intense. To understand saturation, imagine that you are trying to lighten a can of blue paint. For example, if you add some gray paint, you decrease the purity and the intensity of the original color—or desaturate it. Photoshop provides two methods of modifying color saturation: the Sponge tool and the Hue/Saturation adjustment.

QUICK TIP

Using the Sponge tool on an image is *destructive*; using the Hue/Saturation Adjustment layer is *non-destructive*.

Using the Sponge Tool

The Sponge tool is located on the Tools panel, and is used to increase or decrease the color saturation of a specific area within a layer. Settings for the Sponge tool are located on the options bar and include settings for the brush size, whether you want the sponge to saturate or desaturate, and how quickly you want the color to flow into or from the Sponge tool using the Airbrush feature.

QUICK TIP

You can reset the active tool to its default settings by clicking the tool on the options bar, clicking the More Options button, and then clicking Reset Tool.

Using the Hue/Saturation Adjustment

Hue is the amount of color that is reflected from or transmitted through an object. Hue is assigned a measurement (between 0 and 360 degrees) that is taken from a standard color wheel. In conversation, hue is the name of the color, such as red, blue, or gold and described in terms of its tints or shades, such as yellow-green or blue-green. Adjusting hue and saturation is similar to making modifications to color balance. You can make these adjustments by using the Hue, Saturation, and Lightness sliders, which are located in the Hue/Saturation dialog box or Hue/Saturation Properties panel. When modifying saturation levels using the Hue/Saturation setting, you have the option of adjusting the entire color range or preset color ranges. The available preset color ranges are shown in Figure 5. To choose any one of these color ranges, click the Master list button in the Hue/Saturation setting *before* modifying any of the sliders.

Using Saturation to Convert a Color Layer to Grayscale

Have you ever wondered how an image can contain both a color and a grayscale object, as shown in Figure 6? You can easily create this effect using the Hue/Saturation setting.

This image was created by selecting the layer containing the picnic table, clicking the Hue/Saturation button on the Adjustments panel, and then changing the Saturation setting to −100.

Figure 5 *Preset color ranges in the Hue/Saturation settings on the Properties panel*

Select colors to be changed

Figure 6 *Grayscale layer*
© Photodisc/Getty Images.

Saturate a color range

1. Click the **Yellow heart layer** on the Layers panel to make it active.

2. Click the **Hue/Saturation button**  on the Adjustments panel.

TIP When making color adjustments, you can use the preset buttons on the Properties panel, or select the desired adjustment from the Image menu.

3. Click the **Master list arrow** on the Properties panel, then click **Yellows**.

4. Click the **This adjustment affects all layers below (click to clip to layer) button** on the Properties panel.

5. Drag the **Saturation slider** to **+60**.

   The layer's yellow is intensified.

6. Collapse the Properties panel to the dock, then compare your image to Figure 7.

You used an adjustment layer to change the saturation of a preset color range. As you altered the saturation, the richness of the color became more defined.

Figure 7 *Modified yellow heart*
Source: Morguefile.

Saturated yellow

Getting More Color Data Using HDR Images

High Dynamic Range (HDR) images, which use 32 bits per channel, allow real-world levels of illumination to be represented. The level of detail afforded by using 32 bits per channel means that imagery is more realistic and better able to simulate light conditions and a wider range of color values. You can create an HDR image using multiple photographs, each captured at a different exposure. In Photoshop, you can create HDR images from multiple photographs by clicking File on the Menu bar, pointing to Automate, and then clicking Merge to HDR Pro command. You will also find this same command (Merge to HDR Pro) in Bridge by clicking Tools on the Menu bar, and then pointing to Photoshop. HDR Toning is also available in Photoshop by clicking Image on the Menu bar, pointing to Adjustments, and then clicking HDR Toning.

Figure 8 *Orange heart saturated with the Sponge tool*
Source: Morguefile.

Saturated orange area

Saturate using the Sponge tool

1. Click the **Orange heart layer** to make it active.
2. Click the **Sponge tool** on the Tools panel.

TIP The Sponge tool is grouped with the Dodge tool and the Burn tool on the Tools panel.

3. Click the **Brush Preset picker list arrow**, then select a **Hard Round brush tip** with a size of **13 px**.
4. Click the **Mode list arrow** on the options bar, click **Saturate**, then set the Flow to **100%**.
5. Click and drag the **Brush pointer** over the **orange heart** located in the upper-left area of the candy box.

   The orange color in the saturated area is brighter.
6. Save your work, then compare your screen to Figure 8.

You used the Sponge tool to saturate a specific area in an image. The Sponge tool lets you saturate spot areas.

Correcting Faulty Exposures

The Exposure adjustment feature allows you to correct for under- or over-exposure in images. By making adjustments to the black points (which can result in an image being too dark) or the white points (which can result in an image appearing too light), you can make corrections that will make an image's exposure settings just right. You can make exposure adjustments by clicking Image on the Menu bar, pointing to Adjustments, and then clicking Exposure, or by clicking the Exposure button on the Adjustments panel. The Sample in image to set black point eyedropper sets the Offset, the Sample in image to set white point eyedropper sets the Exposure, and the Sample in image to set gray point eyedropper makes the value you click middle gray.

Lesson 2 Enhance Colors by Altering Saturation

Modify Color Channels
USING LEVELS

What You'll Do

Source: Morguefile.

In this lesson, you'll use levels to make color adjustments.

Making Color and Tonal Adjustments

You can make color adjustments using the Levels button on the Adjustments panel or the Levels dialog box (which can be opened by clicking Image on the Menu bar, pointing to Adjustments, and then clicking Levels). This feature lets you make modifications across a tonal range, using the composite color channel or individual channels. The Levels setting takes the form of a histogram and displays light and dark color values on a linear scale. The plotted data indicates the total number of pixels for a given tonal value.

There is no "ideal" histogram shape. The image's character and tone determine the shape of the histogram. Some images will be lighter and their histogram will be bunched on the right; some will be darker and their histogram will be bunched on the left. When working with the Levels setting, three triangular sliders appear beneath the histogram representing shadows, midtones, and highlights. Three text boxes appear for input levels (one box each for the input shadows, midtones, and highlights). Two text boxes appear for output levels (one for output shadows and one for highlights).

Correcting Shadows and Highlights

You can modify the settings for shadows and highlights independently. By moving the output shadows slider to the right, you can decrease contrast and *lighten* the image on an individual layer. You can decrease contrast and *darken* an image by moving the output highlights slider to the left in the Levels setting.

Understanding the Histogram Panel

Using the Histogram panel, you can watch as you adjust color settings such as levels, curves, color balance, and hue/saturation. When the Histogram panel opens, you'll see the compact view: a single chart containing a composite channel for the image. You can view all the channels in color using the menu options on the options button on the panel. As you make color adjustments, the Histogram panel is updated.

Figure 9 *Levels dialog box and Histogram panel*

Shadows slider

Output shadows slider

Midtones slider

Highlights slider

Output highlights slider

Contains Histogram options

Shadow indicates original settings

Source list arrow

Each channel displayed in color

Figure 10 *Adjusted level of the Purple heart layer*
Source: Morguefile.

Modified purple heart

Lesson 3   Modify Color Channels Using Levels

Adjust color using the Levels setting

1. Click the **Purple heart layer** on the Layers panel to make it active.

2. Click the **Histogram Panel options button**, then click **Expanded View** if it is not already selected.

3. Click, then click **All Channels View**.

   TIP If you get an error message that there is not enough room to display the panel, close the other tab groups on the dock.

4. Click, verify that the **Show Statistics** and **Show Channels in Color commands** contain check marks, then click **RGB** in the Channels list arrow.

5. Click the **Source list arrow** on the Histogram panel, then click **Selected Layer**.

6. Click **Image** on the Menu bar, point to **Adjustments**, then click **Levels** to open the Levels dialog box. Type **40** in the Shadows text box, press [**Tab**], type **.90** in the Midtones text box, press [**Tab**], then type **200** in the Highlights text box. See Figure 9.

   TIP Making adjustments using the Image menu is destructive: the adjustment is made right on the layer and is irreversible. Making adjustments using the Adjustments panel is non-destructive and can be edited, eliminated, or flattened into a layer.

7. Click **OK**, reset the **Photography workspace**, then compare your work to Figure 10.

8. Save your work.

You modified levels for shadows, midtones, and highlights. You were also able to see how these changes were visible on the Histogram panel.

Create Color Samplers
WITH THE INFO PANEL

What You'll Do

Source: Morguefile.

 In this lesson, you'll take multiple color samples and use the Info panel to store color information.

Sampling Colors

In the past, you've used the Eyedropper pointer to take a sample of an existing color. By taking the sample, you were able to use the color as a background or a type color. This method is easy and quick, but it limited you to one color sample at a time. Photoshop has an additional feature, the **Color Sampler tool**, that makes it possible to sample—and store—up to four distinct colors.

> **QUICK TIP**
>
> The color samplers are saved with the image in which they are created.

Using Color Samplers

You can apply each of the four color samplers to an image or use the samplers to make color adjustments. Each time you click the Color Sampler tool, a color reading is taken and the number 1, 2, 3, or 4 appears on the image, depending on how many samples you have already taken. See Figure 11. A color sampler includes all visible layers and is dynamic. This means that if you hide a layer from which a sampler was taken, the next visible layer will contain a sampler that has

the same coordinates of the hidden layer, but the sampler will have the color reading of the visible layer.

Using the Info Panel

The Info panel is grouped with the Properties panel in the Photography workspace. The top-left quadrant displays actual color values for the current color mode. For example, if the

Figure 11 *Color samplers*
© Photodisc/Getty Images.

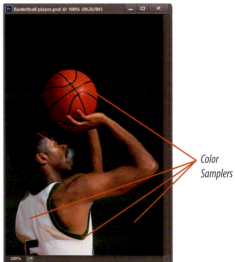

Color Samplers

current mode is RGB, and then RGB values are displayed. The Info panel also displays CMYK values, X and Y coordinates of the current pointer location, and the width and height of a selection (if applicable), as shown in Figure 12. When a color sampler is created, the Info panel expands to show the color measurement information from that sample. Figure 13 shows an Info panel containing four color samplers. After you have established your color samplers but no longer want them to be displayed, click the Info Panel options button, and then deselect Color Samplers. You can display hidden color samplers by clicking the Info Panel options button, and then clicking Color Samplers. Other options, such as which color modes, units of measure, and status details are displayed, can be controlled by clicking the Info Panel options button, and then clicking Panel Options.

Manipulating Color Samplers

Color samplers, like most Photoshop features, are designed to accommodate change. Each color sampler can be moved by dragging the sampler icon to a new location. After the sampler is moved to its new location, its color value information is updated on the Info panel. You can delete any of the samplers individually by selecting the Color Sampler tool, holding [Alt] (Win) or [option] (Mac),

and then clicking the sampler you want to delete. You can also delete all the samplers by clicking the Clear button on the options bar.

Figure 13 *Info panel with color samplers*

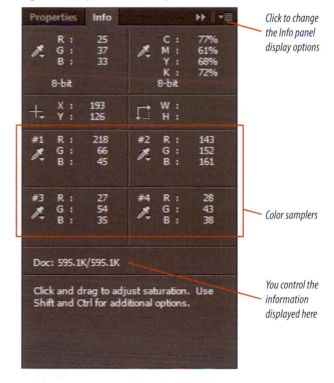

Click to change the Info panel display options

Color samplers

You control the information displayed here

Figure 12 *Information displayed in the Info panel*

Actual (RGB) color values

User-chosen (CMYK) color values

Pointer coordinates

Width and height of a selected area

Create color samplers and apply a filter

1. Display the rulers in pixels.

2. Expand the **Info panel** from the dock.

3. Click the **Color Sampler tool**  on the Tools panel, click the **Sample Size list arrow**, then click **Point Sample**, if necessary.

   TIP The Color Sampler tool is grouped with the Eyedropper tool, the 3D Material Eyedropper tool, the Ruler tool, the Note tool, and the Count tool on the Tools panel.

4. Using the **Color Sampler pointer** and Figure 14 as a guide, click the image in the four locations shown.

5. Click the **Info Panel options button**, then click **Color Samplers** to hide the color samplers.

6. Click, then click **Color Samplers** to display the color samplers.

7. Hide the rulers, then collapse the Info panel to the dock.

8. Make the **Pink heart layer** active.

9. Click **Filter** on the Menu bar, point to **Sharpen**, then click **Unsharp Mask**.

   You are now ready to put the finishing touches on your color-corrected image.

You sampled specific areas in the image, stored that color data on the Info panel, hid and revealed the color samplers, then opened the Unsharp Mask dialog box.

Figure 14 *Color samplers in image*
Source: Morguefile.

Sample 4 is the yellow heart

Sample 1 is the orange heart

Sample 3 is the purple heart

Sample 2 is the green heart

Creating a Spot Color Channel

Printing a Photoshop image can be a costly process, especially if a spot color is used. A **spot color** is one that can't easily be re-created by a printer, such as a specific color used in a client's logo. By creating a spot color channel, you can make it easier for your printer to create the ink for a difficult color, assure yourself of accurate color reproduction, and save yourself high printing costs. If you use this feature, you won't have to provide your printer with substitution colors; the spot color contains all of the necessary information. You can create a spot color channel by displaying the Channels panel, clicking the Channels Panel options button, and then clicking New Spot Channel. To create a meaningful name for the new spot channel, click the Color box, click the Color Libraries button in the Select spot color dialog box, click the Book list arrow located at the top of the Color Libraries dialog box, click a color-matching system, and then click a color from the list. You can also create a custom color by clicking the Picker button using the Select spot color dialog box. If you have created a color sampler, you can use this information to create the custom color for the spot color channel. Click OK to close the open dialog boxes, and then click OK to close the New Spot Channel dialog box.

Figure 15 *Unsharp Mask dialog box*
Source: Morguefile.

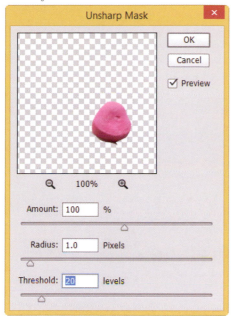

Figure 16 *Lighting Effects Properties panel*

Figure 17 *Lighting effect applied*
Source: Morguefile.

Color changed to match sample 3

Your lighting effect may look different

Lighting effect changes the appearance of the Box of candy layer

Unsharp Mask changes the appearance of the Pink heart layer

Apply a color sampler and add a lighting effect

1. Adjust your settings in the Unsharp Mask dialog box as necessary so they match those shown in Figure 15, then click **OK**.

TIP Drag the Pink heart into view if it does not appear in the Preview area.

These settings emphasize the edges and create the illusion of a sharper image.

2. Make the **Box of candy layer** active, click **Filter** on the Menu bar, point to **Render**, then click **Lighting Effects**.

3. In the Lighting Effects options bar select the **Soft Omni preset**, drag the **center of the light** over the green 'Yes Dear' heart, hover the mouse over the green circle, when it turns yellow, drag the **circle** towards the center of the light until a scale of approximately **300** displays and match the settings shown in the Properties panel in Figure 16, then click **OK** on the options bar.

4. Double-click the **Sweets for the Sweet layer thumbnail**, click the **Set the text color box** on the options bar, then expand the Info panel from the dock.

5. Type the **R, G, and B values from sample 1** on the Info panel in the R, G, and B text boxes in the Select text color dialog box, click **OK**, then click the **Commit any current edits button** ✓ on the options bar.

6. Save your work, hide the color samplers, collapse the Info panel to the dock, then compare your screen to Figure 17.

7. Close the Valentine Candy image, then exit Photoshop.

You applied Unsharp Mask settings to the Pink heart layer, then added the Lighting Effects filters to make the objects stand out more dramatically against the background. You also changed the type color using the values from a sampled color.

Lesson 4   Create Color Samplers with the Info Panel

POWER USER SHORTCUTS	
To do this:	**Use this method:**
Adjust color with thumbnails	Image ➤ Adjustments ➤ Variations (Win)
Adjust hue/saturation	on Adjustments panel
Balance colors	on Adjustments panel
Choose color range	Click Master list arrow in Hue/Saturation dialog box, click color range
Convert color layer to grayscale	or on Adjustments panel
Create color sampler	, click image using
Create spot color channel	Click Channels tab, , New Spot Channel
Delete color sampler	, [Alt] (Win) or [option] (Mac), click sampler using or click Clear on the Color Sampler tool options bar
Modify curves	on Adjustments panel
Modify levels	on Adjustments panel
Move color sampler	[Ctrl] (Win) or ⌘ (Mac), click sampler with
Open Histogram panel	Click Histogram tab
Open Info panel	Click Info tab, or [F8]
Saturate with Sponge tool	or **0**
Show/Hide color samplers	Click Info tab, , Color Samplers

Key: Menu items are indicated by ➤ between the menu name and its command. Blue bold letters are shortcuts for selecting tools on the Tools panel.

Correct and adjust color.

1. Start Photoshop.
2. Open PS 11-2.psd from the drive and folder where your Data Files are stored, then save it as **Big Bird**.
3. Make the Bird layer active (if it is not already active), then display the Photography workspace.
4. Display the Color Balance adjustment settings.
5. Change the Magenta-Green setting to +62, then collapse the Properties panel.
6. Display the Curves adjustment settings.
7. Click the point where the Input and Output both equal 64.
8. Drag the curve up so that the Output equals 128 while the Input remains at 64, then return to the adjustment list.
9. Save your work.

Enhance colors by altering saturation.

1. Display the Hue/Saturation settings using the Adjustments panel.
2. Edit the Master color range.
3. Change the Hue to −80 and the Saturation to −15, then collapse the Properties panel.
4. Use the Sponge tool to further saturate the purple in the bird's wings, feet, and beak.
5. Save your work.

Modify color channels using levels.

1. Display the Levels adjustment settings using the Adjustments panel.
2. Modify the Blue channel Input Levels to 95, 1.60, 185.
3. Modify the Red channel Input Levels to 0, 2, 200.
4. Collapse the Properties panel and save your work.

Create color samplers with the Info panel.

1. Click the Color Sampler tool.
2. Display the Info panel.
3. Create samplers for the following areas: the dark green tail feathers, the purple wing, the red head, and the maroon floor.

4. Compare your image to the sample shown in Figure 18. (Your colors may vary.)
5. Collapse the Info panel.
6. Save your work.

Figure 18 *Completed Skills Review*
© Photodisc/Getty Images.

Adjusting Colors

The Art Gallery has commissioned you to create a promotional (print) poster for an upcoming art show called Moods and Metaphors, which will be held during September of this year. The only guidance they have provided is that they want a piece that looks moody and evocative. You have already created a basic design, and you want to use color adjustments to heighten the mood.

1. Open PS 11-3.psd, then save it as **Gallery Poster**.
2. Make the Backdrop layer active.
3. Display the Curves settings and adjust your settings so they match those shown in Figure 19.
4. Display the Hue/Saturation settings and change the Saturation setting to +60.
5. Create two color samplers: one using the color of the man's tie, and the other using the yellow under the spotlight.
6. Create two type layers: one for the date and location of the art show and one for an expressive slogan that encourages people to come to the show, then position them appropriately in the image. Use either of the colors in the samplers for the font colors. For example, you can enter the color sampler RGB values in the Color Picker dialog box to create that color. (*Hint*: You can use any font and font size you want. The font used in the sample is Aparajita; the font size is 85 pt for the slogan layer and 36 pt for the Date and location layer.)
7. Hide the samplers.
8. Apply the following colors to the layer thumbnails: slogan = Red, Date and location = Green. (*Hint*: Make these modifications using the Layer Properties command.)
9. Apply any styles to the type you feel are appropriate. (*Hint*: The Bevel and Emboss style is applied to the slogan type layer in the sample. The Outer Glow and the Inner Glow styles are applied to the Date and location layer in the sample.)
10. Apply any lighting effect you feel adds to the theme of the show. (*Hint*: The Flood Light preset and Spot lighting effect are applied to the Backdrop layer in the sample.)
11. Save your work, then compare your image to the sample in Figure 20.

Figure 19 *Curves adjustment panel*

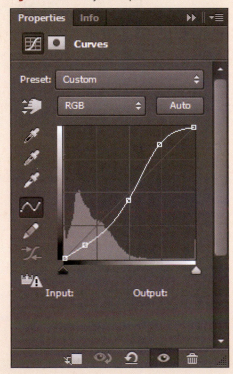

Figure 20 *Sample Project Builder 1*
© Photodisc/Getty Images.

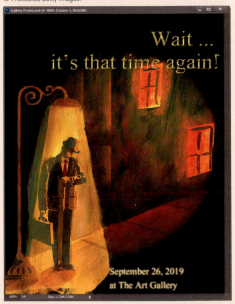

A new, unnamed e-commerce company has hired you to create an advertisement for their upcoming debut. While they are leaving the design to you, the only type they want in the imagery is "Explore your inner self." They want this print ad to be a teaser; more descriptive type will be added in the future. This is a cutting-edge company, and they want something really striking.

1. Open PS 11-4.psd, then save it as **Heads Up**.
2. Make the Backdrop layer active if it is not already active.
3. Use the Levels settings to modify the Input Levels of the RGB color settings. (*Hint*: The settings used in the sample are 82, 1.46, 200.)
4. Make the Head layer active.
5. Use the Hue/Saturation settings to modify the Head layer and all those beneath it. (*Hint*: The settings used in the sample are Hue = −39, Saturation = +25, Lightness = −5.)
6. Create a color sampler for the color of the neck, then hide the sampler.
7. Create a type layer for the image, then position it appropriately. (*Hint*: You can use any font, font size, and color you want. The font used in the sample is a blue italic Vivaldi; the font size is 100 pt.)

8. Apply the color Yellow to the type layer thumbnail.
9. Apply any styles to the type you feel are appropriate. (*Hint*: The Drop Shadow and Bevel and Emboss styles are applied to the type layer in the sample.)

10. Apply any filter you feel adds to the image. (*Hint*: The Lens Flare filter is applied to the Head layer in the sample.)
11. Save your work, then compare your image to the sample in Figure 21.

Figure 21 *Sample Project Builder 2*

© Photodisc/Getty Images.

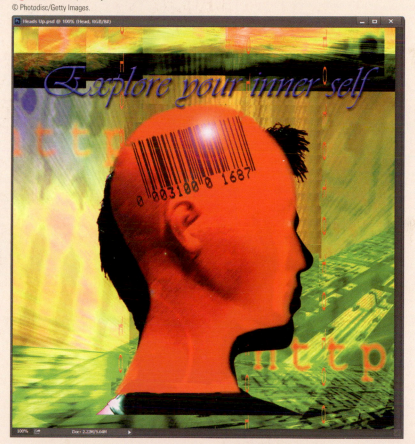

A friend of yours is a textile artist; she creates artwork that is turned into materials for clothing, curtains, and bedding. She has turned to you because of your Photoshop expertise and wants your advice on how she can jazz up her current project. You love the design, but think the colors need correction so they'll look more dynamic. Before you proceed, you decide to explore the Internet to find information on how Photoshop color correction techniques can be used to create an effective design.

1. Connect to the Internet, and use your browser to find information about adjusting colors in Photoshop. (Make a record of the site you found so you can use it for future reference.)
2. Read about color correction and take notes on any information that will help you incorporate new ideas into the image.
3. Open PS 11-5.psd, then save the file as **Puzzle Pieces**.
4. Use the skills you have learned to correct or adjust one or more of the colors in this image.
5. Create at least two color samplers from colors used in the image.
6. Apply any filter you feel enhances the image. (*Hint*: The Artistic Smudge Stick filter is applied to the Yellow Pieces layer in the sample. The Texture Craquelure filter is applied to the Blue Pieces layer.)
7. Save your work, then compare your image to the sample in Figure 22.

Figure 22 *Sample Design Project*
© Photodisc/Getty Images.

Each year, your company, Bullseye, has an art contest, and the winning entry is used as the cover of the Annual Report. Bullseye encourages employees to enter the contest. You decide to use your Photoshop skills to craft a winning entry. The Bullseye logo will be added once a winner of the contest has been selected.

1. Create an image with the dimensions 500 × 650 pixels.
2. Locate several pieces of artwork to use in the design. These can be located on your computer, from scanned images, or on the Internet. Remember that the images can show anything, but you want to demonstrate the flexibility of Photoshop and the range of your skills.
3. Save this file as **Annual Report Cover**.
4. Use any skills you have learned to correct or adjust the colors in this image.
5. Create a color sampler for at least two colors in the image, then hide the samplers.
6. Create one or two type layers for the name of the image (Bullseye Annual Report), then position the layer(s) appropriately in the image. Use your choice of font colors. (*Hint*: You can use any font and font size you want. The font used in the sample is Tempus Sans ITC; the font size is 110 pt in the title and 48 pt in the subtitle.)
7. Add any necessary effects to the type layer(s).
8. If necessary, apply any filters you feel add to the image.
9. If desired, apply sampled colors within the image.
10. Save the image, then compare your image to the sample in Figure 23.

Figure 23 *Sample Portfolio Project*
Source: Morguefile.

CHAPTER 12

USING CLIPPING MASKS, PATHS, & SHAPES

1. Use a clipping group as a mask
2. Use pen tools to create and modify a path
3. Work with shapes
4. Convert paths and selections

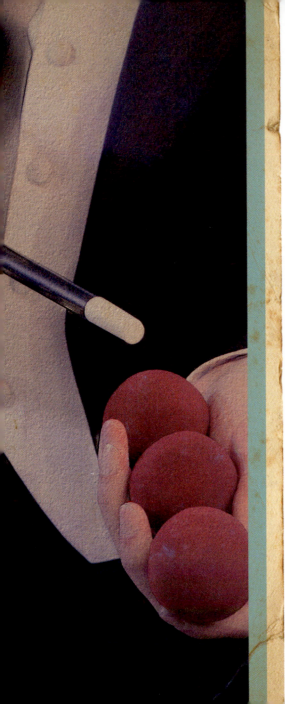

CHAPTER 12

USING CLIPPING MASKS, PATHS, & SHAPES

Working with Shapes

Photoshop provides several tools that help add stylistic elements, such as shapes, to your work. You can add either a shape or a rasterized shape to an image. A **shape** is simply a vector object that keeps its crisp appearance when it is resized, edited, moved, reshaped, or copied. A **rasterized shape** is converted into a bitmapped object that cannot be moved or copied without compromising quality; the advantage is that it can occupy a small file size, if compressed. The disadvantage is that a bitmapped object is resolution dependent. You can add either kind of shape as a predesigned shape, such as an ellipse, circle, or rectangle, or you can create a unique shape using a pen tool.

Defining Clipping Masks and Paths

A clipping mask (also called a clipping group) creates an effect in which the lower layer acts as a mask for all other layers in the group. You can use a path to turn an area defined within an object into an individual object—like an individual layer. A **path** is defined as one or more straight or curved line segments connected by **anchor points**, small squares similar to fastening points. Paths can be either

open or closed. An **open path**, such as a line, has two distinct **endpoints**, anchor points at each end of the open path. A **closed path**, such as a circle, is one continuous path without endpoints. A **path component** consists of one or more anchor points joined by line segments. You can use another type of path called a **clipping path**, to extract a Photoshop object from within a layer, place it in another app (such as Adobe InDesign or Adobe Illustrator), and retain its transparent background.

QUICK **TIP**

A shape and path are basically the same: the shape tools allow you to use a predefined path instead of having to create one by hand. A path has a hard edge and is vector-based.

Creating Paths

Using a path, you can manipulate images on a layer. Each path is stored on the **Paths panel**. You can create a path using the Pen tool or the Freeform Pen tool. Each **pen tool** lets you draw a path by placing anchor points along the edge of another image, or wherever you need them, to draw a specific shape. As you place anchor points, line segments automatically fall between them. The **Freeform Pen tool** acts just like a traditional pen or pencil. Just draw with it, and it automatically places *both* the anchor points and line segments wherever necessary to achieve the shape you want. With these tools, you can create freeform shapes or use existing edges within an image by tracing on top of it.

After you create a path, you can use the **Path Selection tool** to select the entire path, or the **Direct Selection tool** to select and manipulate individual anchor points and segments to reshape the path.

QUICK TIP

A path can be created from a selection.

Multiple paths can be saved using the Paths panel. When first created, a path is called a **work path**. The work path is temporary, but becomes a permanent part of your image when you save it or rename it. Paths, like layers, can be named, viewed, deleted, and duplicated.

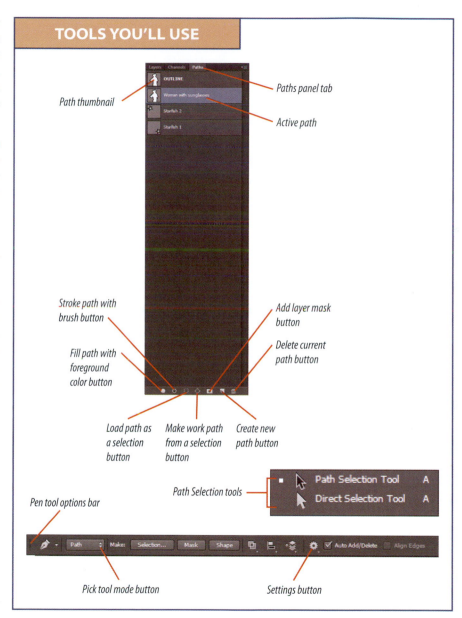

TOOLS YOU'LL USE

Path thumbnail

Paths panel tab

Active path

Stroke path with brush button

Add layer mask button

Fill path with foreground color button

Delete current path button

Load path as a selection button

Make work path from a selection button

Create new path button

Path Selection tools

Path Selection Tool   A
Direct Selection Tool   A

Pen tool options bar

Pick tool mode button

Settings button

Use a Clipping Group
AS A MASK

What You'll Do

 In this lesson, you'll rasterize a type layer, and then use a clipping group as a mask for imagery already in an image. You'll also use the Transform command to alter an object's appearance.

Understanding the Clipping Mask Effect

If you want to display type in one layer using an interesting image or pattern in another layer as the fill for the type, then look no further. You can create this effect using a clipping mask. With a clipping mask, you can isolate an area and make images outside the area transparent. This works very well with type, and can be used with a variety of images. Figure 1 shows an example of this effect in which type acts as a mask for imagery. In this effect, the (rasterized) type layer becomes the mask that reveals the layer containing the roses. The image of the roses is *masked* by the text. For this effect to work, the layer that is being masked (the imagery, in this case) must be positioned *above* the mask layer (in this case, the type layer) on the Layers panel.

QUICK **TIP**

Although this layer order may not seem logical to you, use the analogy of your face peering out from behind a Halloween mask. Your face is behind (above, in layer order) the mask.

Figure 1 *Sample clipping group effect*
© Photodisc/Getty Images.

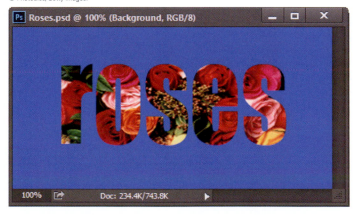

Rasterizing Text and Shape Layers

To use type or a shape in a clipping mask, the type or shape layer must first be rasterized, or changed from vector graphics into a normal object layer. Rasterizing changes the vector graphic into a bitmapped object, one that is made up of a fixed number of colored pixels. **Vector graphics** are made up of lines and curves defined by mathematical objects called vectors. The advantage to using vector graphics for shapes is that they can be resized and moved without losing image quality.

QUICK TIP

Bitmapped images contain a fixed number of pixels; as a consequence, they can appear jagged and lose detail when enlarged.

Using Transform Commands

Before you create a clipping mask, you might want to use one of the transform commands on the Edit menu to reshape layer contents so the shapes conform to the imagery that will be displayed. The transform commands are described in Table 1. Samples of the transform commands are shown in Figure 2. When a transform command is selected, a **bounding box** is displayed around the object. The bounding box contains handles that you can drag to modify the selection. A **reference point** is located in the center of the bounding box. This is the point around which the transform command takes place.

QUICK TIP

You can change the location of the reference point by dragging the point to a new location within the bounding box.

TABLE 1: TRANSFORM COMMANDS	
Command	**Use**
Scale	Changes the image size. Press [Shift] while dragging to scale proportionally. Press [Alt] (Win) or [option] (Mac) to scale from the reference point.
Rotate	Allows rotation of an image 360° around a reference point. Press [Shift] to rotate in increments of 15°.
Skew	Stretches an image horizontally or vertically, but cannot exceed the image boundary.
Distort	Stretches an image in all directions, and can exceed the image boundary.
Perspective	Changes opposite sides of an image equally, and can be used to make an oval appear circular, or change a rectangle into a trapezoid.
Warp	Changes the boundaries of an object using the Warp styles.
Rotate 180°	Rotates image 180° clockwise.
Rotate 90° CW	Rotates image 90° clockwise.
Rotate 90° CCW	Rotates image 90° counterclockwise.
Flip Horizontal	Produces a mirror image along the vertical axis.
Flip Vertical	Produces a mirror image along the horizontal axis.

© 2015 Cengage Learning®

Figure 2 *Sample transformations*
© Photodisc/Getty Images.

Transform a type layer for use in a clipping mask

1. Open PS 12-1.psd from the drive and folder where you store your Data Files, save the file as **Skatepark**, then reset the Essentials workspace.

   The intense type layer is active.

2. Click **Layer** on the Menu bar, point to **Rasterize**, then click **Type**.

   The intense layer is no longer a type layer, as shown in Figure 3.

3. Click **Edit** on the Menu bar, point to **Transform**, then click **Skew**.

4. Type **-15** in the Set horizontal skew text box on the options bar, as shown in Figure 4, so the type is slanted.

   TIP You can also drag the handles surrounding the object until the skew effect looks just right.

5. Click the **Commit transform (Enter) button** ✓ on the options bar, then compare your image to Figure 5.

You rasterized the existing type layer, then altered its shape using the Skew command by entering a new value in the Set horizontal skew text box on the options bar. This transformation slanted the image.

Figure 3 *Rasterized layer*

No longer a type layer

Figure 4 *Skew options bar*

Set horizontal skew text box

Figure 5 *Skewed layer*
Source: Morguefile.

Figure 6 *Preparing to create the clipping group*

Clipping mask pointer

Indent indicates inclusion in clipping mask

Figure 8 *Layers and History panels*

History state for clipping mask

Figure 7 *Effect of clipping mask*
Source: Morguefile.

Boards background visible through text

Create a clipping mask

1. Drag the **intense layer** beneath the Boards layer.

2. Click the **Indicates layer visibility button** 🔲 on the Boards layer on the Layers panel.

   The Boards layer will serve as the fill for the clipping mask.

   TIP It's a good idea to first position the layer that will act as a mask above the layer containing the pattern so that you can adjust the size and shape of the pattern. After the size and shape are the way you want them, reposition the mask layer beneath the pattern layer. (The size and shape have been positioned for you in this exercise.)

3. Display the **Legacy workspace** (created in Chapter 1).

4. Point to the **horizontal line** between the intense and Boards layers, press and hold [**Alt**] (Win) or [**option**] (Mac), then click using the **Clipping mask pointer** 🔲, as shown in Figure 6.

5. Release [**Alt**] (Win) or [**option**] (Mac).

   The clipping mask is created. The Boards image becomes visible through the text.

6. Save your work, compare your image to Figure 7 and the Layers and History panels to Figure 8.

   TIP There are two methods you can use to turn off the display of guides: you can hide them (using the Show command on the View menu) or clear them (using the Clear Guides command on the View menu). Hiding the guides means you can display them at a later date, while clearing them means they will no longer exist in your document. Unless you know that you'll never need the guides again, it's a good idea to hide them.

7. Display the **Essentials workspace**, then hide the guides display.

You created a clipping mask using the intense and Boards layers. This effect lets you use the imagery in one layer as the fill for an object in another layer.

Use Pen Tools to Create
AND MODIFY A PATH

What You'll Do

Source: Morguefile.

In this lesson, you'll create and name a path, expand the path to make sure it conforms to the skateboard, and then fill it with the foreground color.

Using Pen and Shape Tools

You have seen how you can use a clipping mask to create a mask effect. You can also create a path to serve as a mask by using any of the shape tools—the Pen tool, the Freeform Pen tool, or the Magnetic Pen tool. You can modify a path using any of the following Pen and Path Selection tools: the Add Anchor Point tool, Delete Anchor Point tool, Convert Point tool, Direct Selection tool, and the Path Selection tool. Table 2 describes some of these tools and their functions. When you select a pen tool, you can choose to create a shape layer or a path by choosing the appropriate option on the options bar.

> **QUICK TIP**
>
> Don't worry about creating a perfect path: you can perfect it later using the Pen tool as a direct selection tool.

Creating a Path

Unlike temporary selections, paths you create are saved with the image they were created in and stored on the Paths panel. Although you can't print paths unless they are filled or stroked, you can always display a path and make

TABLE 2: PEN TOOLS		
Tool	**Button**	**Use**
Pen tool		Creates curved or straight line segments, connected by anchor points.
Freeform Pen tool		Creates unique shapes by placing anchor points at each change of direction.
Magnetic option (Freeform Pen tool options bar)	Magnetic	Selecting the Magnetic check box on the options bar lets the Freeform Pen tool find an object's edge.
Add Anchor Point tool		Adds an anchor point to an existing path or shape.
Delete Anchor Point tool		Removes an anchor point from an existing path or shape.
Convert Point tool		Converts a smooth point to a corner point and a corner point to a smooth point.

© 2015 Cengage Learning®

modifications to it. You can create a path based on an existing object, or you can create your own shape with a pen tool. To create a closed path, you must position the pointer on top of the first anchor point. A small circle appears next to the pointer, indicating that the path will be closed when the pointer is clicked. Figure 9 shows an image of a young woman and the Paths panel containing four paths. The active path (Starfish 1) displays the starfish in the lower-right corner. Like the Layers panel, each path thumbnail displays a representation of its path. You can click a thumbnail on the Paths panel to see a specific path.

The way that you create a path depends on the tool you choose to work with. The Pen tool requires that you click using the pointer each time you want to add a smooth (curved) or corner anchor point, whereas the Freeform Pen tool only requires you to click once to begin creating the path, and places the anchor points for you as you drag the pointer.

Modifying a Path

After you establish a path, you can modify it and convert it into a selection. For example, you can add more curves to an existing path, widen it, or fill a path with the foreground color. Before you can modify an unselected path, you must select it with the Direct Selection tool. When

you do so, you can manipulate its individual anchor points without affecting the entire path. Moving an anchor point automatically forces the two line segments on either side of the anchor point to shrink or grow, depending on which direction you move the anchor point. You can also click individual line segments and move them to new locations. If you are working with a curved path, you can shorten or elongate the direction handles associated with each smooth point to adjust the amount of curve or length of the corresponding line segment.

Other methods for modifying a path include adding anchor points, deleting anchor points, and converting corner anchor points into

smooth anchor points, or vice versa. Adding anchor points splits an existing line segment into two, giving you more sides to your object. Deleting an anchor point does the reverse. Deleting anchor points is helpful when you have a bumpy path that is the result of too many anchors. Converting corner points into smooth points can give your drawing a softer appearance; converting smooth points into corner points can give your drawing a sharper appearance.

Figure 9 *Multiple paths in one image*
© Photodisc/Getty Images.

Current path

Current path thumbnail

Create a path

1. Click the **Indicates layer visibility button**  on the intense layer on the Layers panel so that it is no longer visible.

   Hiding layers can make it easier to work on a specific area of the image.

2. Click the **Skateboarder layer** on the Layers panel.

3. Click the **Freeform Pen tool** on the Tools panel.

4. Click the **Pick tool mode button** on the options bar and select **Path** if it is not already selected.

5. Click the **Settings options button** on the options bar, then adjust the settings so that your entire options bar matches Figure 10.

6. Use the **Magnetic Freeform Pen tool pointer** to trace the skateboard under the skater (excluding the three protruding wheels).

   TIP If you choose, you can zoom into the image to make it easier to trace the skateboard.

7. Click when you reach the **starting point** and the circle within a circle appears in the pointer.

   TIP If you enlarged the work area prior to creating the path, make sure you restore the zoom level.

8. Click the **Paths tab,** double-click the **Work Path layer** on the Paths panel, then type **Skateboard path** in the Name text box.

9. Click **OK**, then compare your path and Paths panel to Figure 11.

You created a path using the Magnetic Freeform Pen tool, then named the path in the Paths panel.

Figure 10 *Freeform Pen tool settings*

Pick tool mode button

Settings options button

Figure 11 *Path and Paths panel*
Source: Morguefile.

Path formed around board

New path name

Multiple-Path Selections

You can use the Path Selection or Direct Selection tool to drag more than one path, even if the paths are on different layers.

Using Clipping Masks, Paths, & Shapes

Figure 12 *Points added to path*
Source: Morguefile.

Area of adjusted path

Figure 13 *Fill Path dialog box*

Figure 14 *Modified path*
Source: Morguefile.

Path filled with color

Modify a path

1. Zoom into the skateboard so the zoom factor is **300%**, then click the **Add Anchor Point tool** on the Tools panel.

2. Click a **point near the curve at the left side of the skateboard**, then drag a **handle** so the curve conforms to the left side of the board using Figure 12 as a guide.

   As you drag the new anchor points, direction handles appear, indicating that you have added smooth points instead of corner points. You can drag any of these points so they conform to the shape you want for the path.

3. Repeat Step 2 until you are satisfied that you have corrected any irregularities in the path surrounding the skateboard.

4. Zoom out to the **100%** magnification, then click the **Eyedropper tool** on the Tools panel.

5. Click the **brown lace** on the skater's shoe to sample its color.

6. Verify that the Skateboard path is selected, click the **Paths Panel options button** on the Paths panel, click **Fill Path**, modify the settings in the Fill Path dialog box using Figure 13 as a guide, then click **OK**.

TIP The Skateboarder layer on the Layers panel must be selected or the Fill Path option on the Paths panel will not be available.

7. Deselect the path by clicking a blank area of the Paths panel.

8. Save your work, then compare your image to Figure 14.

You modified an existing path, then filled it with a color sampled from the image.

Work with
SHAPES

What You'll Do

Source: Morguefile.

 In this lesson, you'll create two shapes, and then modify and add a style to a shape layer.

Using Shape Tools

You might find that the imagery you are working with is not enough, and you need to create your own shapes. There are six shape tools on the Tools panel for creating shapes: the Rectangle tool, the Rounded Rectangle tool, the Ellipse tool, the Polygon tool, the Line tool, and the Custom Shape tool. A shape can occupy its own layer, called a **shape layer**. When you select a shape or pen tool, three buttons (Shape, Path, or Pixels) appear in the list box on the options bar to let you specify whether you want your shape to be on a new or existing shape layer (Shape), be a new work path (Path), or be rasterized and filled with a color (Pixels). Shapes and paths contain **vector data**, meaning that they will not lose their crisp appearance if resized or reshaped. You can create a rasterized shape using the Fill pixels button, which you can resize or reshape the using the Transform commands.

Creating Rasterized Shapes

You cannot create a rasterized shape on a vector-based layer, such as a type or shape layer. So, to create a rasterized shape, you must first select or create a non-vector-based layer, select the shape you desire, and then click the Fill pixels button on the options bar. You can change the blending mode to alter how the shape affects existing pixels in the image. You can change the opacity setting to make the shape more transparent or opaque. You can use the anti-aliasing option to blend the pixels on the shape's edge with the surrounding pixels. If you want to make changes to the content of a shape's blending mode, opacity, and anti-aliasing, you must make these changes *before* creating the rasterized shape; since the rasterization process converts the detail of the shape to an object layer. After you rasterize the shape, you can make changes to the blending mode and the opacity of the *layer* containing the shape.

Creating Shapes

A path and a shape are essentially the same, in that you edit them using the same tools. For example, you can modify a path and a shape using the Direct Selection tool. When selected, the anchor points are solid or hollow, and can then be moved to alter the appearance of the shape or path. When you click a shape or path with the Path Selection tool, the anchor points become solid. In this case, the entire path is selected, and the

Using Clipping Masks, Paths, & Shapes

individual components cannot be moved; the path or shape is moved as a single unit. A shape can be created on its own layer and can be filled with a color. Multiple shapes can also be added to a single layer, and you can specify how overlapping shapes interact. (Painting tools are used when individual pixels are edited, such as by changing a pixel's color on a rasterized shape.)

Embellishing Shapes

You can apply other features such as the Drop Shadow and the Bevel and Emboss style, or filters, to shapes. Figure 15 shows the Layers panel of an image containing two layer shapes. The top layer (Shape 2) has the Bevel and Emboss style applied to it.

Using the Puppet Warp Tool

You can use the **Puppet Warp tool** to add natural motion to rasterized images including still images, shapes, and rasterized text. The Puppet Warp tool is opened from an active bitmap layer or selection by clicking the Puppet Warp command on the Edit menu. A mesh overlays the layer's image; the density and expansion area can be increased or decreased using settings on the options bar. You can add pins to the mesh by clicking the pointer on any area of the mesh; you can delete

a push pin by holding [Alt] (Win) or [option] (Mac) over an existing pin and clicking when the pointer turns to scissors. The applied pins are used to create points on which the mesh can be dragged. When you move the pushpin pointer to an existing point, the pointer changes to a pushpin with the move symbol. At this time, you can click and drag the mesh to a new location. With as few as two points, you can easily pivot an image on a layer! You can also convert a layer to a SmartObject *before* using the Puppet Warp tool to take advantage of non-destructive editing. *Note*: When the Puppet Warp command is selected, the options bar for the currently selected tool is replaced with the Puppet Warp options bar shown in Figure 16.

Creating Custom Shapes

Although Photoshop comes with many interesting custom shapes, you still may not find the one you're looking for. If that's the case, consider creating your own using characters found within any symbol fonts installed on your computer, such as Wingdings or Webdings. First create a type layer using the symbol font of your choosing, and then click Type on the Menu bar, and click the Convert to Shape command. Use the Define Custom Shape command on the Edit menu to create your own custom shape. The Shape Name dialog box opens, allowing you to name and save the shape. Select the Custom Shape tool and then click the Custom Shape picker list arrow to see the shape you just created at the bottom of the panel.

Figure 15 *Shape layers on Layers panel*

Shape is displayed in thumbnail

Indicates that styles are applied

Figure 16 *Puppet Warp options bar*

Create a shape

1. Click the **Rectangle tool** ▭ on the Tools panel, then verify that **Shape** displays in the Pick tool mode list box on the options bar.
2. Make sure the Set shape stroke type button displays No Color, then display the rulers in pixels and display the guides.
3. Verify that the **Skateboarder layer** is active, click the **Set fill shape type option**, click **RGB Blue** (the 5th color box from the left in the 1st row), then click the **Set fill shape type option** to close the Swatches panel.
4. Drag the **Marquee pointer** ┼ from approx **245 X/105 Y** to **430 X/190 Y** using the guides, then close the Properties panel. Compare your Paths panel to Figure 17.
5. Compare your image to Figure 18.

   The shape is added to the image, and the Rectangle tool is still active.

You created a new shape layer using the Rectangle tool. The new shape was created on its own layer, and filled with a selected color.

Create a custom shape

1. Click the **Layers tab**, then verify that the **Rectangle 1 layer** is active and visible.
2. Click the **Custom Shape tool button** 🧩 on the Tools panel.
3. Click the **Custom Shape picker list arrow** Shape: ▼, then double-click **Checkmark**.
4. Drag the **Marquee pointer** ┼ from approximately **260 X/80 Y** to **280 X/120 Y**.
5. If necessary, drag the **Shape 2 layer** above the Shape 1 layer in the Layers panel, and click anywhere in the Layers panel to deselect the custom shape.

You created a custom shape using the Custom Shape picker, then moved the layer in the Layers panel for better visibility.

Figure 17 *Path created by shape*

Figure 18 *Shape in image*
Source: Morguefile.

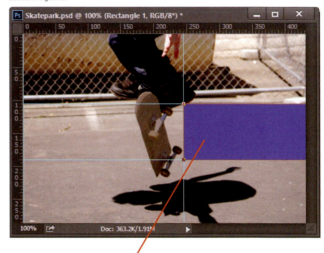

New shape

Export a Path into Another Program

As a designer, you might find yourself working with other programs, such as Adobe Illustrator or QuarkXPress. Many of the techniques you have learned, such as working with paths, can be used in all these programs. For example, you can create a path in Photoshop, and then export it to another program. Before you can export a path, it must be created and named. To export the path, click File on the Menu bar, point to Export, and then click Paths to Illustrator. The Paths list arrow in the Export Paths to File dialog box lets you determine which paths are exported. You can export all paths or one specific path. After you choose the path(s) that you want to export, choose a name and location for the path, and then click Save.

Figure 19 *Additional shape in image*
Source: Morguefile.

New shape

Figure 20 *Styles added to custom shape*
Source: Morguefile.

Custom shape with Bevel
and Emboss style

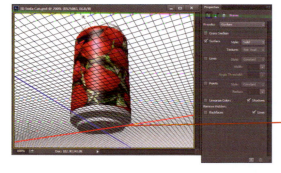

Figure 21 *Imagery applied to 3D shape*
© Photodisc/Getty Images.

Grid on which
object is rotated

Modify a custom shape

1. Select the **Shape 2 layer** in the Layers panel.
2. Click the **Set shape fill type button** on the options bar, click the **Pure Magenta Red** (first box on the right in the fifth row, but your location may vary) on the Swatches panel, then click the **Set shape fill type button** to close the swatch panel. Compare your image to Figure 19.
3. Verify that the **Shape 2 thumbnail** on the Layers panel is selected.
4. Click the **Add a layer style button** *fx.* on the Layers panel.
5. Click **Drop Shadow**, click **Bevel & Emboss**, then click **OK** to accept the current settings.
6. Save your work, turn off the guides and rulers, then compare your image to Figure 20.

You changed the color of a shape, then applied a style to the shape.

Creating Realistic 3D Shapes

Using the 3D workspace and your knowledge of shapes, you can create and rotate realistic 3D shapes that show naturalistic reflection using Photoshop CC. To do this, create an RGB file, and then fill the layer with any pattern. Make the layer containing the imagery active and visible, display the 3D workspace, click the Mesh from Preset option button on the 3D panel, then click one of the shapes listed, such as the Soda, then click the Create button. The image in the layer (the fill pattern) is wrapped around the 3D shape. Click the Move tool in the Tools panel, position the pointer over the shape, and then drag the shape to reposition it. Take note of the lifelike shadows and highlights as you reposition the shape. Using the 3D panel, you can treat the contents of a graphics file as a texture and wrap it around a shape, as shown in Figure 21. The original layer will automatically be converted into a Smart Object. (You may see a warning box if your video card does not meet the requirements necessary for 3D rendering. If you receive this message, you will still be able to complete the task, but your computer may run slower.) With Photoshop CC, 3D models can be printed on 3D printers. In preparation for printing, Photoshop automatically makes 3D models watertight and generates the necessary support structures. Once your 3D model is open, switch to the 3D Workspace, click 3D Print Utilities from the 3D menu, select options, then click the Print icon.

Convert Paths
AND SELECTIONS

What You'll Do

Source: Morguefile.

 In this lesson, you'll convert a selection into a path, and then apply a stroke to the path.

Converting a Selection into a Path

You can convert a selection into a path so that you can take advantage of clipping paths and other path features by using a button on the Paths panel. First, create your selection using any technique you prefer, such as the Magic Wand tool, lasso tools, or marquee tools. After the marquee surrounds the selection, then click the Make work path from selection button on the Paths panel, as shown in Figure 22.

Customizing Print Options

Because a monitor is an RGB device and a printer uses the CMYK model to print colors, even a well-calibrated monitor will never match the colors of your printer. Therefore, professional printers use standardized color systems such as Pantone or Toyo.

In the course of working with an image, you may need to print a hard copy. In order to get the output you want, you can set options in the Print dialog box. To open this dialog box, click File on the Menu bar, and then click Print. You can also print one copy of your document by clicking File on the menu bar, then clicking Print One Copy.

For additional printing options, click File on the Menu bar, click Print, and then expand the Printing Marks section (you may have to scroll to see the section). Here you can gain increased control over the way your image prints. For example, pages printed for commercial uses might often need to be trimmed after they are printed. The trim guidelines are called **crop marks**. These marks can be printed at the corners, center of each edge, or both. You can select the Corner Crop Marks check box and/or the Center Crop Marks check box to print these marks on your image.

Converting a Path into a Selection

You also can convert a path into a selection. You can do this by selecting a path on the Paths panel, and then clicking the Load path as a selection button on the Paths panel.

Figure 22 *Path created by selection*

Stroke path with brush   Load path as a selection   Make work path from selection

Choosing the Right Method

Are you totally confused about which method to use to make selections? You might have felt equally at sea after learning about all your paint tool choices. Well, as with painting, you need to experiment to find the method that works best for you. As you gain experience with Photoshop techniques, your comfort level—and personal confidence—will grow, and you'll learn which methods are *right for you*.

Figure 23 *Skewing a layer*
© Photodisc/Getty Images.

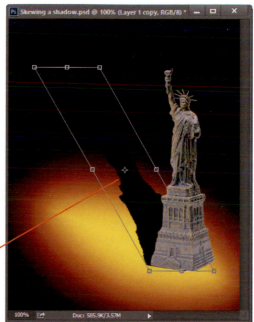

Black-filled layer being skewed

Using the Transform Command to Create a Shadow

You've already experienced using the Transform command to change the existing shape of an object or type. You can also use this command to simulate a shadow. To do so, you simply duplicate a layer containing the shape you want to have a shadow, and then fill the shape (that will become the shadow) with black using the Paint Bucket tool or the Fill command on the Edit menu. Make the black copy the active layer, and then use the Transform command to skew the object. Figure 23 shows an example of this technique.

Convert a selection into a path

1. Display the intense layer and the Boards layer.

2. Click the **intense layer** on the Layers panel, then change the zoom factor to **200%**.

3. Click the **Magic Wand tool** on the Tools panel, and verify that the Contiguous check box is *not* selected.

4. Click anywhere in the **blue color** behind the word intense.

5. Click **Select** on the Menu bar, then click **Inverse**. Compare your image to Figure 24.

6. Click the **Paths tab**.

7. Press and hold [**Alt**] (Win) or [**option**] (Mac), click the **Make work path from selection button** on the Paths panel, then release [**Alt**] (Win) or [**option**] (Mac).

TIP Pressing [Alt] (Win) or [option] (Mac) while clicking the Make work path from selection button causes the Make Work Path dialog box to open. You can use this to change the Tolerance setting. If you don't press and hold this key, the current tolerance setting is used.

8. Type **1.0** in the Tolerance text box, then click **OK**.

9. Double-click **Work Path** on the Paths panel.

10. Type **intense path** in the Name text box of the Save Path dialog box, then click **OK**. Compare your Paths panel to Figure 25.

You created a selection using the Magic Wand tool, then converted it into a path using the Make work path from selection button on the Paths panel.

Figure 24 *Selection in image*
Source: Morguefile.

Selected object

Figure 25 *Selection converted into path*

New path in thumbnail

Using Clipping Masks, Paths, & Shapes

Figure 26 *Stroke Path dialog box*

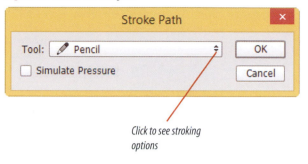

Click to see stroking options

Figure 27 *Layers panel*

Figure 28 *Completed image*

Source: Morguefile.

Stroke a path

1. Click the **Eyedropper tool** on the Tools panel.
2. Click the **RGB Yellow swatch** on the Swatches panel.
3. Activate the **Shape 2 layer** on the Layers panel, then create a new layer above it.
4. Click the **intense path** on the Paths panel, then click **Brush tool** on the Tools panel, and select the **Hard Round brush tip** with a size of **9 pixels** with 100% opacity (if necessary).

TIP You can select a path as a selection (rather than as a path) by holding [Ctrl] (Win) or [⌘] (Mac) while clicking the name of the path. When you do this, marching ants surround the path, which indicate that it's a selection.

5. Click the **intense path** if necessary, click the **Paths Panel options button** on the Paths panel, click **Stroke Path**, verify that the Pencil tool is selected as shown in Figure 26, click **OK**, then click the **Stroke path with brush button** on the Paths panel.
6. Click anywhere on the **Paths panel** to deselect the path.
7. Click the **Layers tab**, then compare your Layers panel to Figure 27.
8. Select the **Move tool** from the Tools panel, press [**Shift**], click the **intense layer** from the Layers panel, release [**Shift**], then press the [**right arrow key**] **seven times**.
9. Display the **Wheels layer** on the Layers panel, compare your image to Figure 28, then save your work.
10. Close the file and exit Photoshop.

You stroked a path, using a color from the Swatches panel and a command from the Paths Panel options button.

POWER USER SHORTCUTS

To do this:	Use this method:	To do this:	Use this method:
Add an anchor point		Distort a selection	Edit ➤ Transform ➤ Distort
Change perspective	Edit ➤ Transform ➤ Perspective	Distort with Puppet Warp	Edit ➤ Puppet Warp
Convert a selection into a path		Draw freeform shapes	or [Shift] **P**
Convert a point		Draw paths	or [Shift] **P**
Create a clipping mask	Press and hold [Alt] (Win) or [option] (Mac), position pointer between layers, then click using	Draw along the object's edge	, click the Magnetic check box
Create a custom shape	or [Shift] **U**	Export a path	File ➤ Export ➤ Paths to Illustrator
Create a line	or [Shift] **U**	Fill a shape with background color	[Ctrl][Shift][Backspace] (Win) or [shift] ⌘ [delete] (Mac)
Create a new work path		Flip a selection	Edit ➤ Transform ➤ Flip Horizontal or Flip Vertical
Create a polygon	or [Shift] **U**	Load path as a selection	
Create a rectangle	or [Shift] **U**	Repeat last transform command	Edit ➤ Transform ➤ Again or [Shift][Ctrl][T] (Win) or [shift] ⌘ [T] (Mac)
Create a rounded rectangle	or [Shift] **U**	Rotate a selection	Edit ➤ Transform ➤ Rotate
Create an ellipse	or [Shift] **U**	Scale a selection	Edit ➤ Transform ➤ Scale
Delete an anchor point		Skew a selection	Edit ➤ Transform ➤ Skew
Deselect a path	Click an empty space on Paths panel	Stroke a path with a brush	,

Key: Menu items are indicated by ➤ between the menu name and its command. Blue bold letters are shortcuts for selecting tools on the Tools panel.

Use a clipping group as a mask.

1. Open PS 12-2.psd from the drive and folder where you store your Data Files, then save it as **Numbers**.
2. Rasterize the Numbers type layer, then click the Move tool on the Tools panel.
3. Transform the rasterized type layer by distorting it, using Figure 29 as a guide. (*Hint:* Use the Perspective transform command.)
4. Drag the Numbers layer beneath the Symbols layer on the Layers panel.
5. Create a clipping mask with the Numbers and Symbols layers.
6. Apply the Bevel and Emboss style and a Drop Shadow (using the existing settings) to the Numbers layer.
7. Save your work.

Use pen tools to create and modify a path.

1. Make the Man layer active.
2. Click the Freeform Pen tool on the Tools panel.
3. Verify that Path is selected in the Pick tool mode list, and that the Magnetic check box is selected.
4. Open the Paths panel.
5. Trace the figure, *not the shadow*.
6. Change the name of the Work Path to **Figure path**.
7. Use the Eyedropper tool on the Tools panel to sample Dark Red using the Swatches panel.
8. Fill the path with the Foreground Color using 100% opacity.
9. Deselect the Figure path on the Paths panel.
10. Save your work.

Work with shapes.

1. Activate the Layers panel, then make the Megaphone layer active.
2. Use the Eyedropper tool to sample the RGB Red swatch on the Swatches panel.
3. Click the Custom Shape tool on the Tools panel.
4. Verify that Shape is selected in the Pick tool mode list on the options bar.
5. Open the Custom Shape picker on the options bar, then select the Scissors 2 custom shape.
6. Create the shape from 200 X/50 Y to 330 X/220 Y. (*Hint:* Use the guides to start the shape.)
7. Apply a Drop Shadow and Bevel and Emboss style (using the existing settings) to the Shape 1 layer.
8. Save your work.

Convert paths and selections.

1. Make the Megaphone layer active.
2. Hide the Backdrop, Numbers, and Shape 1 layers.

3. Use the Magnetic Lasso tool to select the megaphone. (*Hint:* Try using a 0-pixel Feather, a 5-pixel Width, and 10% Edge Contrast.)
4. Display the Paths panel, then make a path from the selection.
5. Change the name of the Work Path to **Megaphone path**.
6. Use the Eyedropper tool to sample the Pure Yellow Green swatch on the Swatches panel, then fill the megaphone path with this color.
7. Deselect the path, display the Layers panel, then show all layers.
8. Clear the guides, hide the rulers, then adjust the contrast of the Symbols layer to +42 directly on the layer.
9. Apply a Radial Blur filter, using the Spin method with Good quality and the Amount = 10, to the Backdrop layer.
10. Apply a 100% Spherize filter (Distort Filter) to the Backdrop layer.
11. Save your work, then compare your image to Figure 29.

Figure 29 *Completed Skills Review*
© Photodisc/Getty Images.

A cable manufacturer wants to improve its lackluster image—especially after a scandal that occurred earlier in the year. The company has hired you to create a dynamic image of one of its bestselling products, which they plan to use in an image advertising campaign. You have been provided with a picture of the product, and your job is to create a more exciting image suitable for print ads.

1. Open PS 12-3.psd, then save it as **Power Plug**.
2. Duplicate the Power Plug layer.
3. Add a type layer (using any font available on your computer) that says Power Plug. (In the sample, a 74 pt Cooper Std Regular font is used.)
4. Rasterize the type layer.
5. Transform the rasterized type layer, using a method of your choosing.
6. Apply any layer styles. (In the sample, a contoured Bevel and Emboss style, Drop Shadow, and Satin style are applied.)
7. Move the rasterized layer below the Power Plug copy layer, then create a clipping mask.
8. Adjust the Saturation of the Power Plug copy layer to +90.
9. Create an adjustment layer that changes the Yellow/Blue Color Balance of the Power Plug copy layer to +65.

10. Create an adjustment layer that changes the Color Balance of the (original) Power Plug layer so that the text is more visible. (In the sample, the color levels of the midtones are −80, +80, −80.)

11. Modify the Opacity of the Power Plug layer to 85%.
12. Save your work, then compare your image to the sample in Figure 30. Your results may vary.

Figure 30 *Sample Project Builder 1*
© Photodisc/Getty Images.

Using Clipping Masks, Paths, & Shapes

The National Initiative to Promote Reading has asked you to come up with a preliminary design for their upcoming season. They have provided you with an initial image you can use, as well as the promise of a fat paycheck if you can finish the project within the day. You can use any additional imagery to complete this task.

1. Open PS 12-4.psd, then save it as **Booklovers**.
2. Locate at least one piece of appropriate artwork— either on your computer, in a royalty-free collection, or from scanned images—that you can use in this image.
3. Use any appropriate methods to select imagery from the artwork.
4. After the selections have been made, copy them into Booklovers.
5. Transform any imagery.
6. Use your skills to create at least two paths in the image.
7. Add any special effects to a layer, such as a style or a vignette.
8. Add descriptive type to the image, using the font and wording of your choice. (In the sample, an 80 pt Onyx Regular font is used.)
9. Rasterize the type and create a mask.
10. Make any color adjustments or add filters as desired.
11. Save your work, then compare your image to the sample in Figure 31.

Figure 31 *Sample Project Builder 2*
© Photodisc/Getty Images.

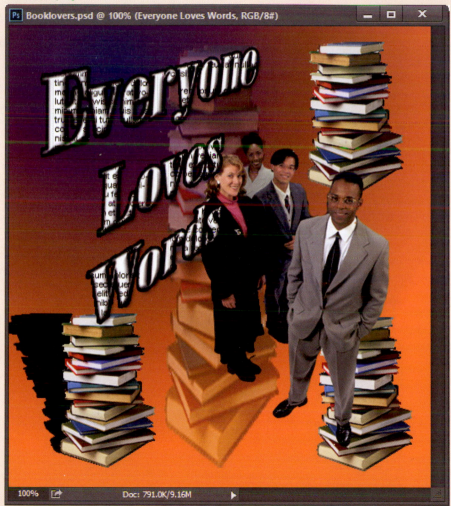

Booklovers.psd @ 100% (Everyone Loves Words, RGB/8#)

100%   Doc: 791.0K/9.16M

Using Clipping Masks, Paths, & Shapes

You can pick up some great design tips and tricks from the Internet. Because you are relatively new to using Photoshop shapes, you decide to see what information you can find about shapes on the web. Your goal is not only to increase your knowledge of shapes and paths, but to create attractive artwork.

1. Connect to the Internet and use your browser to find information about using paths and shapes in Photoshop. (Make a record of the sites you find so you can use it for future reference.)
2. Create a new Photoshop image, using the dimensions of your choice, then save it as **Shape Experimentation**.
3. Use paths and shapes to create an attractive image.
4. Create an attractive background, using any of your Photoshop skills.
5. Create at least two paths, using any shapes you want.
6. Add any special effects to the shapes.
7. If desired, make any color adjustments or add filters.
8. If you want, add a type layer, using any fonts available on your computer. (In the sample, the Adobe Caslon Pro Regular font of varying size is used.)
9. Save your work, then compare your image to the sample in Figure 32.

Figure 32 *Sample Design Project*

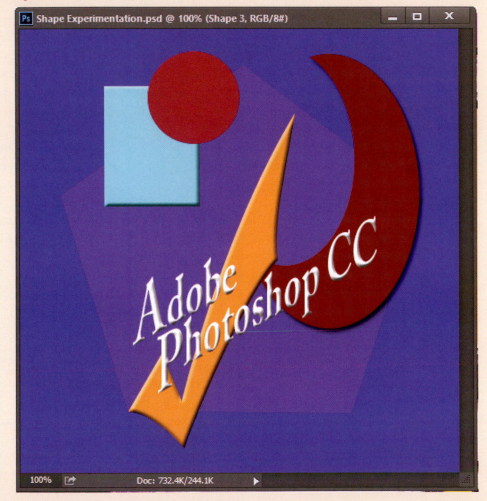

Using Clipping Masks, Paths, & Shapes

A Photoshop design contest, sponsored by a high-powered advertising agency, has you motivated. You have decided to submit the winning entry. Your entry must be completely original, and can use any imagery legally available to you.

1. Start Photoshop and create an image with any dimensions you want.
2. Save this file as **Contest Winner**.
3. Locate several pieces of artwork—either on your computer, in a royalty-free collection, or from scanned images. Although the images can show anything, remember that you want to show positive imagery so that the judges will select it.
4. Select imagery from the artwork and move it into Contest Winner.
5. Use your knowledge of shapes and paths to create interesting effects.
6. Add text to the image, and use any transform commands to enhance the text.
7. Add any filter effects if you decide they will make your image more dramatic. (In the sample, the Spatter filter was applied to the Computer layer.)
8. Make any color adjustments. (*Hint:* You can use Adjustment layers if you wish, but it is not necessary.)
9. Add type in any font available on your computer, then rasterize the type. (A 60 pt Britannic Bold font is shown in the sample. The following styles have been applied: Drop Shadow and Bevel and Emboss.)
10. Save your work, then compare your image to the sample in Figure 33.

Figure 33 *Sample Portfolio Project*
© Photodisc/Getty Images.

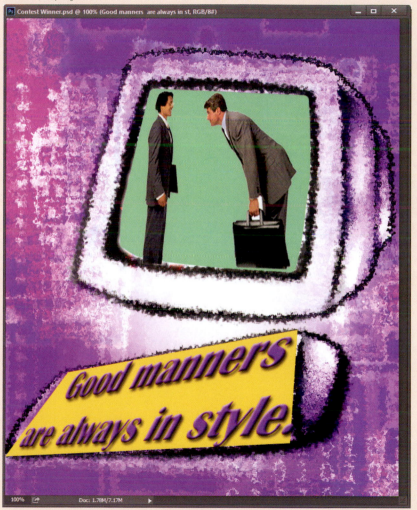

Using Clipping Masks, Paths, & Shapes

13

CHAPTER **TRANSFORMING**
TYPE

1. Modify type using a bounding box
2. Create warped type with a unique shape
3. Screen back type with imagery
4. Create a faded type effect

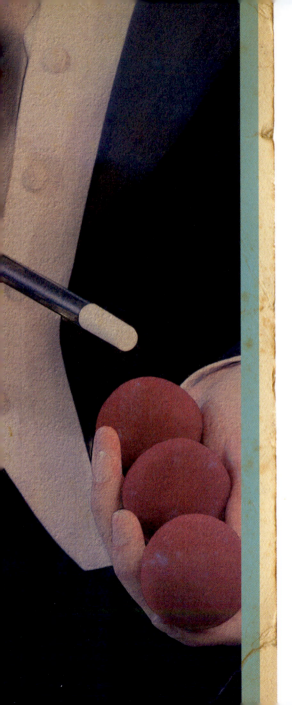

CHAPTER 13 TRANSFORMING TYPE

Working with Type

Type is usually not the primary focus of a Photoshop image, but it can be an important element when conveying a message. You have already learned how to create type and to embellish it using styles, such as the Drop Shadow and the Bevel and Emboss styles, and filters, such as the Twirl and Wind filters. You can further enhance type using techniques such as transforming or warping.

Transforming and Warping Type

When you want to modify text in an image, you can simply select the type layer, select the Horizontal Type tool, and then make changes using the options bar. You can also modify type by dragging the handles on the type's bounding box. A bounding box (or transform controls box) is a rectangle that surrounds type and contains handles that are used to change the dimensions.

Many of the Photoshop features that can be used to modify images can also be used to modify type layers. For example, type can be modified using all the transform commands on the Edit menu except Perspective and Distort. For more stylized type, you can use the Create warped text button to create exciting shapes by changing the dimensions. **Warping** makes it possible to distort type so that it conforms to a shape. Some of the distortions available through the warp feature are Arc, Arch, Bulge, Flag, Fish, and Twist. You *do not* have to rasterize type to use the warp text feature, so you can edit the type as necessary after you have warped it. (Likewise, you do not have to rasterize type in order to use the transform commands.)

QUICK TIP

If you want to use the Perspective or Distort commands, apply a filter to type, or create a clipping mask, you must first rasterize the type.

Using Type to Create Special Effects

In addition to adding styles to type, you can also create effects with your type and the imagery within your image. One popular effect is **fading type**, where the type appears to originate in darkness, and then gradually gets brighter, or vice versa. You can use the Gradient tool to fade type. The **screening back** effect displays imagery through the layer that contains type. One way to create the screened back effect is to convert a type layer into a shape layer, add a mask, and then adjust the levels of the shape layer. As with graphic objects, adding special effects to type changes the mood, style, and message of the content. You'll probably want to experiment with all your choices to strike just the right note for a particular project.

QUICK **TIP**

An **interruption** is a hesitation or omission in the text or design and can be used to guide a reader's eye to a specific area of an image or page.

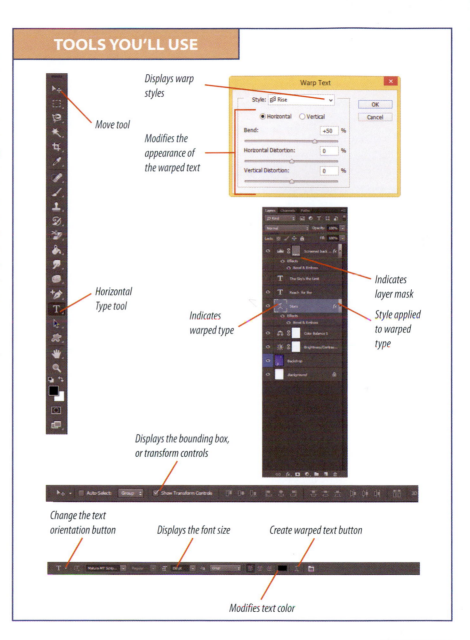

TOOLS YOU'LL USE

Displays warp styles

Move tool

Modifies the appearance of the warped text

Horizontal Type tool

Indicates layer mask

Indicates warped type

Style applied to warped type

Displays the bounding box, or transform controls

Change the text orientation button

Displays the font size

Create warped text button

Modifies text color

Modify Type Using
A BOUNDING BOX

What You'll Do

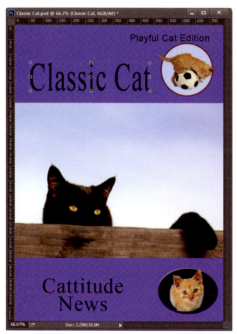

Source: Morguefile.

In this lesson, you'll change the dimensions of type using a bounding box.

Selecting the Bounding Box

A bounding box, such as the one shown in Figure 1, is a tool you can use to control the size and proportions of existing type. You can display the bounding box by clicking the Move tool on the Tools panel, and then selecting the Show Transform Controls check box on the options bar. After the transform controls (also known as the bounding box) feature is turned on, it will appear around type whenever a type layer is selected. Change the bounding box by positioning the pointer over a handle on the bounding box, as shown in Figure 2, and then dragging until you see the size you want. At the center of the bounding box (by default) is the **reference point**, the location from which distortions and transformations are measured.

> **QUICK TIP**
>
> You can resize the bounding box to visually change type size instead of specifying point sizes on the options bar. (Holding [Shift] while resizing the bounding box prevents distortion of the type.)

Figure 1 *Bounding box around type*
© Photodisc/Getty Images

Bounding box

Handle

Reference point

Figure 2 *Resizing the bounding box*
© Photodisc/Getty Images

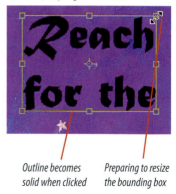

Outline becomes solid when clicked

Preparing to resize the bounding box

Changing the Bounding Box

When the bounding box around type is selected, the options bar displays additional tools for transforming type. Table 1 describes the bounding box options in detail. As you can see from the table, some of these tools are buttons and some are text boxes. You can change the size of the bounding box by placing the pointer over a handle. When you do this, the pointer changes to reflect the direction in which you can pull the box. When you resize a bounding box, the type within it reflows to conform to its new shape.

TABLE 1: TRANSFORM CONTROL TOOLS		
Tool	**Button**	**Use**
Reference point location button		The black dot determines the location of the reference point. Change the reference point by clicking any white dot on the button.
Set horizontal position of reference point text box	X: 0 px	Allows you to reassign the horizontal location of the reference point.
Use relative positioning for reference point button	△	Determines the point you want used as a reference.
Set vertical position of reference point text box	Y: 0 px	Allows you to reassign the vertical location of the reference point.
Set horizontal scale text box	W: 0%	Determines the percentage of left-to-right scaling.
Maintain aspect ratio button	⊖	Keeps the current proportions of the contents within the bounding box.
Set vertical scale text box	H: 0%	Determines the percentage of top-to-bottom scaling.
Rotate text box	△ 0.00 °	Determines the angle the bounding box will be rotated.
Set horizontal skew text box	H: 0.00 °	Determines the angle of horizontal distortion.
Set vertical skew text box	V: 0.00 °	Determines the angle of vertical distortion.
Switch between free transform and warp modes button		Toggles between manual entry of scaling and warp styles.
Interpolation list arrow	Interpolation: Bicubic ⬍	Calculates the values of pixels that are added or deleted during the transformation. Choose from Nearest Neighbor, Bilinear, Bicubic, Bicubic Smoother, Bicubic Sharper, Bicubic Automatic.
Cancel transform (Esc) button	⊘	Returns to the image without carrying out transformations.
Commit transform (Enter) button	✓	Returns to the image after carrying out transformations.

© 2013 Cengage Learning®

Display a bounding box

1. Open PS 13-1.psd from the drive and folder where you store your Data Files, update the text layers as needed, then save the file as **Classic Cat**.

2. Display the rulers in pixels and display the **Typography workspace**.

3. Make the **Classic Cat layer** active on the Layers panel.

4. Click the **Move tool** on the Tools panel.

5. Click the **Show Transform Controls check box** on the options bar. Compare your image to Figure 3.

   Transform control handles surround the bounding box. When you place the pointer on or near a handle, you can transform the shape of a bounding box. Table 2 describes the pointers you can use to transform a bounding box.

You displayed the bounding box of a text selection to make it easier to adjust the size and shape of the layer contents. Resizing a bounding box is the easiest way to change the appearance of an object or type layer.

Using Free Transform

Use the Free Transform command to apply any of the Transform commands (such as rotate, scale, skew, distort, and perspective) in one operation. You can use the Transform commands to:

- *scale proportionately* by pressing and holding [Shift] while dragging a corner,
- *rotate* in 15 degree increments by pressing and holding [Shift],
- *rotate numerically* by entering the number of degrees in the options bar,
- *distort freely* by pressing [Ctrl] (Win) or ⌘ (Mac) while dragging a handle,
- *distort* relative to the center of the bounding box by pressing [Alt] (Win) or [option] (Mac) while dragging a handle.

Figure 3 *Displayed bounding box*
Source: Morguefile.

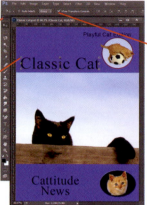

Move tool selected

Bounding box surrounds active type layer

Selected check box indicates that bounding box is displayed

TABLE 2: TRANSFORM POINTERS	
Pointer	**Use to**
↗	Resize bounding box; drag upper-right and lower-left handles.
↘	Resize bounding box; drag upper-left and lower-right handles.
↔	Resize bounding box; drag middle-left and middle-right handles.
↕	Resize bounding box; drag upper-center and lower-center handles.
↵	Rotate bounding box; appears below the lower-right handle.
↳	Rotate bounding box; appears below the lower-left handle.
↰	Rotate bounding box; appears above the upper-right handle.
↱	Rotate bounding box; appears above the upper-left handle.
↲	Rotate bounding box; appears to the left of the middle-left handle.
⌐	Rotate bounding box; appears below the lower-center handle.
⌐	Rotate bounding box; appears to the right of the middle-right handle.
⌐	Rotate bounding box; appears above the upper-middle handle.
▷	Skew content. Press and hold [Ctrl] (Win) or ⌘ (Mac) while dragging a handle.

© 2013 Cengage Learning®

Figure 4 *Modified bounding box*
Source: Morguefile.

Playful Cat Edition

Classic Cat

*Enlarged type and
bounding box*

Figure 5 *Bounding box before committing transformation*
Source: Morguefile.

*Bounding box (and text it contains)
has a narrower width*

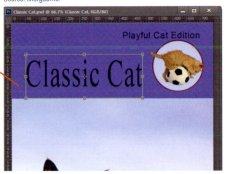

Playful Cat Edition

Classic Cat

Figure 6 *Transform settings*

*Current
reference
point*

*Set horizontal
position of
reference point*

*Set vertical
position of
reference point*

*Horizontal
scale set
to 90%*

*Cancel
transform
button*

*Commit
transform
button*

DESIGN**TIP**

Thinking Outside the (Bounding) Box

You're probably used to thinking in terms of font size: 10pt, 12pt, etc. Once you understand how to resize type using the bounding box, you'll realize that the rigid font size you apply is just a starting point. You really can have *any size* font you want!

Modify type using a bounding box

1. Drag the **top-center handle** ↕ with the Resizing pointer until you see that the Set vertical position of reference point text box (Y:) on the options bar displays approximately **194.00 px**. Compare your bounding box to Figure 4.

   TIP When you begin dragging the resizing handles, the option bar changes to display the bounding box transform tools. You can also type values in these text boxes.

2. Drag the **right-center handle** ←→ until the Set horizontal scale text box (W:) displays approximately **90.00%**.

3. Compare your bounding box to Figure 5 and your options bar to Figure 6. Your settings might differ.

   TIP You can use the Transform commands (Rotate, Scale, Skew, Distort, Perspective, and Warp) with any of the resizing pointers to distort a bounding box using an angle other than 90°.

4. Click the **Commit transform (Enter) button** ✓ on the options bar.

5. Save your work.

Using the bounding box, you modified the type by scaling disproportionately.

Create Warped Type
WITH A UNIQUE SHAPE

What You'll Do

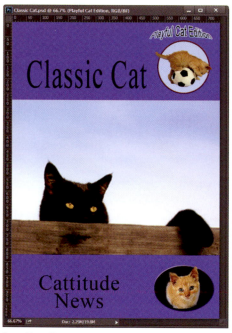

Source: Morguefile.

 In this lesson, you'll warp text, and then enhance the text with color and a layer style.

Warping Type

Have you ever wondered how designers create those ultra-cool wavy lines of text? They're probably using the Warp Text feature, which gives you unlimited freedom to create unique text shapes. You can distort a type layer beyond the limits of stretching a bounding box by using the Warp Text feature. You can choose from 15 warped text styles in the Warp Text dialog box. This dialog box can be opened by clicking a type tool on the

Tools panel, then clicking the Create warped text button on the options bar. Use the Style list arrow to access the styles as shown in Figure 7. You can warp type horizontally or vertically.

Figure 7 *Warp text styles*

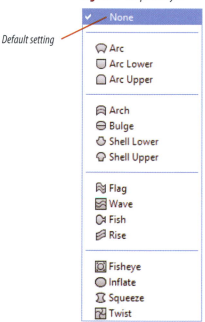

Default setting

Adding Panache to Warped Text

After you select a warp text style, you can further modify the type using the Bend, Horizontal Distortion, and Vertical Distortion sliders in the Warp Text dialog box. These settings and what they do are described in Table 3. A sample of warped text is shown in Figure 8. You adjust the warped style by using the sliders shown in Figure 9.

QUICK TIP

You cannot use the Distort and Perspective transform commands on non-rasterized type; however, you can achieve similar results by warping type.

Combining Your Skills

By this time, you've learned that many Photoshop features can be applied to more than one type of Photoshop object. The same is true for warped text. For example, after you warp text, you can apply a style to it, such as the Bevel and Emboss style, or a filter. You can also use the Stroke style to really make the text pop.

Figure 8 *Sample of warped type*
© Photodisc/Getty Images

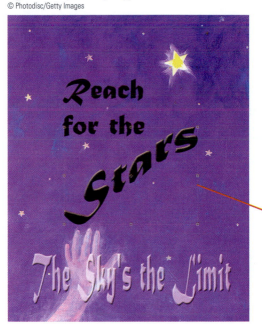

Bounding box surrounds warped type

Figure 9 *Warp Text dialog box*

Current style

Selects a new style

Options are displayed when style other than 'None' is selected

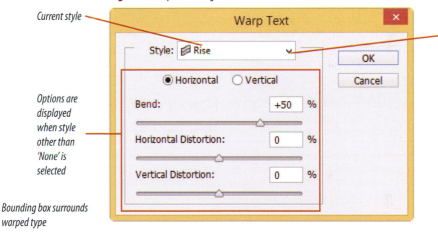

TABLE 3: WARPED TYPE SETTINGS	
Setting	**Use**
Horizontal	Determines the left-to-right direction of the warp style.
Vertical	Determines the top-to-bottom direction of the warp style.
Bend	Determines which side of the type will be affected.
Horizontal Distortion	Determines if the left or right side of the type will be warped, and applies perspective.
Vertical Distortion	Determines if the top or bottom of the type will be warped, and applies perspective.

© 2013 Cengage Learning®

Create warped text

1. Click the **Playful Cat Edition layer** on the Layers panel.

2. Zoom into the image until the magnification factor is **100%**.

3. Double-click the **Playful Cat Edition layer thumbnail** 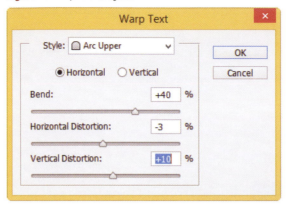 on the Layers panel.

4. Click the **Set the font size list arrow** on the options bar, then click **12 pt**.

5. Click the **Create warped text button** on the options bar.

6. Click the **Style list arrow** in the Warp Text dialog box, then click **Arc Upper**.

7. Verify that the **Horizontal option button** is selected.

8. Change the settings for the **Bend**, **Horizontal Distortion**, and **Vertical Distortion text boxes** so that they match those shown in Figure 10.

9. Click **OK** to close the Warp Text dialog box, commit any current edits, deselect any text, then compare your type to Figure 11.

10. Use the **Move tool** on the Tools panel to drag or nudge the type so it is centered over the logo of the playing kitten as shown in Figure 12.

TIP You can also use the (keyboard) arrow keys to nudge objects when the Move tool is active.

You transformed existing type into a unique shape using the Create warped text button. This feature lets you make type a much more dynamic element in your designs.

Figure 10 *Warp Text dialog box*

Figure 11 *Warped type*

Figure 12 *Moved type*

Source: Morguefile.

Selected warped type

Figure 13 *Sampled area*
Source: Morguefile.

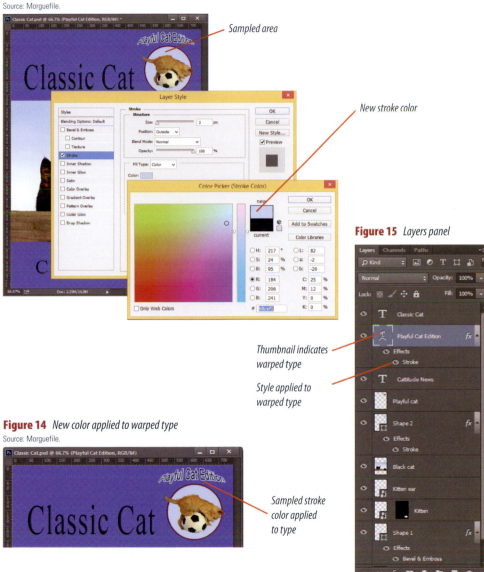

Sampled area

New stroke color

Figure 15 *Layers panel*

Thumbnail indicates warped type

Style applied to warped type

Figure 14 *New color applied to warped type*
Source: Morguefile.

Sampled stroke color applied to type

Enhance warped text with effects

1. Zoom out until the magnification level is at **66.7%**.

2. Click the **Add a layer style button** ƒx on the Layers panel, click **Stroke**, then move the Layer Style dialog box so the warped type is visible.

3. Click the **Set color of stroke box** in the Layer Style dialog box.

4. Verify that the **Only Web Colors check box** is *not* selected, then click the image anywhere on the light blue background (at approximately **650 X/90 Y**), as shown in Figure 13.

5. Click **OK** to close the Color Picker (Stroke Color) dialog box.

6. In the Layer Style dialog box, make sure the Size is set to **3 px** and the Position is set to **Outside**, click **OK**, then turn off the bounding box display if necessary.

TIP Creating fancy type is an important skill, but don't forget that type must be readable and shouldn't compete with (or distract from) its background.

7. Save your work, then compare your image to Figure 14 and the Layers panel to Figure 15.

You added a Stroke style to the warped text and changed the color of the stroke using a color already present in the image.

Screen Back Type
WITH IMAGERY

What You'll Do

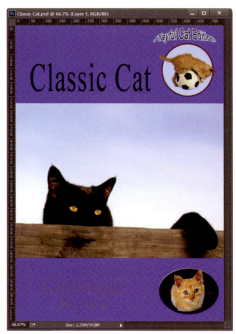

Source: Morguefile.

 In this lesson, you'll convert type to a shape layer using the Convert to Shape command, and then adjust the levels to create a screened back effect.

Screening Back Type

Using many of the techniques you already know, you can create the illusion that type appears to fade into the imagery below it. This is known as screening back or **screening** type. You can create a screened back effect in many ways. One method is to adjust the opacity of a type layer until you can see imagery behind it. Another method is to convert a type layer into a shape layer, which adds a **vector mask**, and then adjust the levels of the shape layer until you achieve the look you desire. A vector mask makes a shape's edges appear neat and defined on a layer. As part of this screening back process, the type assumes the shape of its mask. Figure 16 shows a sample of screened back type. Notice that the layer imagery beneath the type layer is visible.

Figure 16 *Screened back type*
© Photodisc/Getty Images

Image visible beneath screened back text

Screened back text

QUICK **TIP**

You can always adjust a layer's opacity so you can see more underlying imagery.

Creating the Screened Back Effect

Before converting a type layer, it's a good idea to duplicate the layer. That way, if you are not satisfied with the results, you can easily start from scratch with the original type layer. After the duplicate layer is created, you can convert it into a shape layer using the Layer menu. After the layer is converted, make sure the original layer is hidden. Using the Levels setting in the Properties panel, you can increase or decrease the midtones and shadows levels, as shown in Figure 17, to create different effects in the screened back type.

QUICK **TIP**

Whenever you select a shape layer, a path surrounds the shape.

Adding Finishing Touches

Adding effects to a layer can give your screened back type a more textured or three-dimensional look. For example, you can add the Bevel and Emboss style to a screened back shape layer, as shown in Figure 18. Here, the Bevel and Emboss style serves to accentuate the type. You can also add filter effects such as noise or lighting to make the text look more dramatic.

Figure 17 *Levels setting in Properties panel*

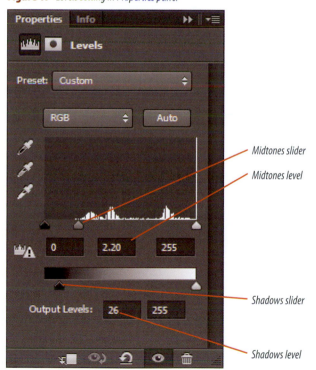

Midtones slider

Midtones level

Shadows slider

Shadows level

Figure 18 *Screened back type with Bevel and Emboss style*
© Photodisc/Getty Images

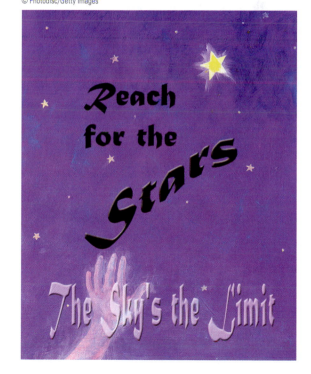

Convert a type layer to a shape layer

1. Click the **Cattitude News layer** on the Layers panel.

2. Click the **Layers Panel options button** ▤.

3. Click **Duplicate Layer**.

TIP When duplicating a layer, you have the option of keeping the duplicate in the current image, adding it to another image that is currently open, or placing it in a new image, by clicking the Document list arrow in the Duplicate Layer dialog box, then clicking another filename or New.

4. Type **Screened back type** in the As text box, then click **OK**.

5. Click the **Indicates layer visibility button** ◉ on the Cattitude News layer on the Layers panel, then compare your Layers panel to Figure 19.

6. Use the workspace switcher to display the **Legacy workspace** (created in Chapter 1).

7. Click **Type** on the Menu bar, then click **Convert to Shape**, as shown in Figure 20. (If working on a Mac, your menu may be slightly different.)

The type layer is converted to a shape layer. Figure 21 shows the Layers panel (with the converted type layer state and vector mask thumbnail) and the History panel (with the Convert to Shape state).

In preparation for screening back type, you created a duplicate layer, then hid the original from view. You then converted the duplicate layer into a shape layer.

Figure 19 *Duplicate layer*

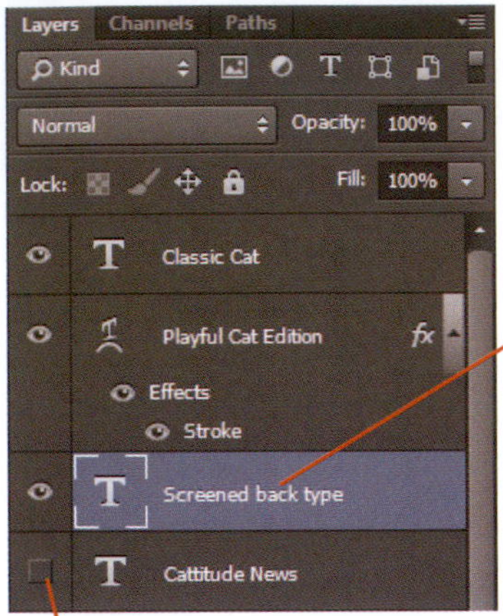

Renamed duplicate layer

Hidden layer

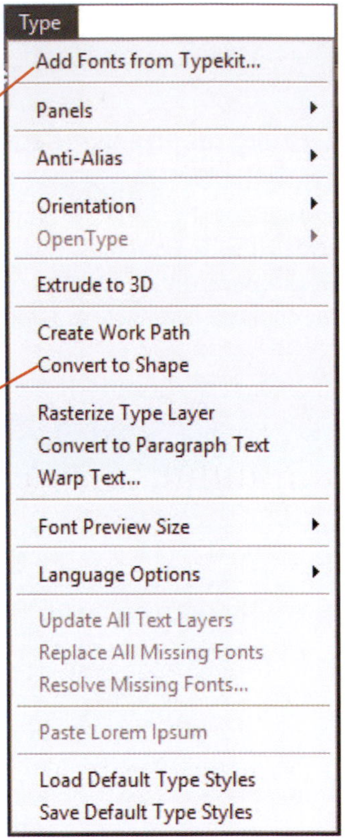

Figure 21 *History and Layers panels*

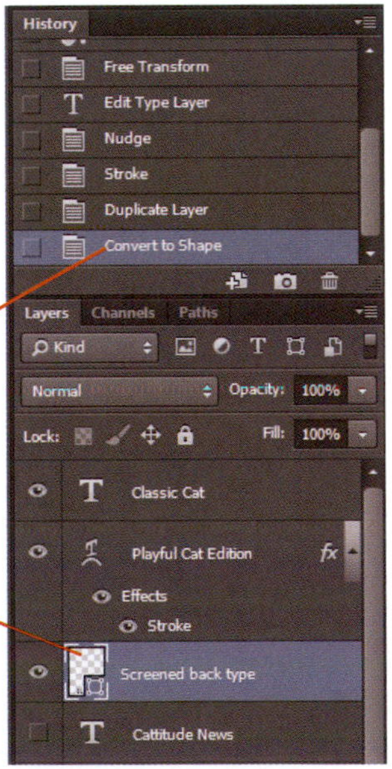

New History panel state shows conversion to Shape layer

Vector mask thumbnail

Figure 20 *Type menu*

Will not appear if Typekit is not installed

Converts a type layer to a shape layer

Figure 22 *Levels setting in Properties panel*

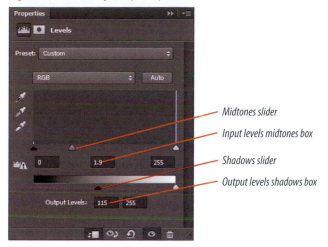

Midtones slider

Input levels midtones box

Shadows slider

Output levels shadows box

Figure 23 *Screened back type*
Source: Morguefile.

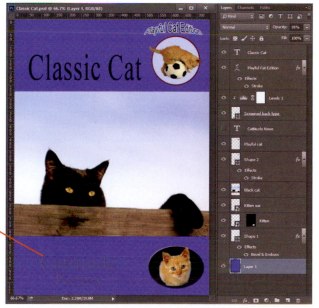

Screened back layer

Adjust layer content

1. Switch to the **Essentials workspace**, click the **Levels button** on the Adjustments panel, then click the **This adjustment affects all layers below (click to clip to layer) button** on the Properties panel.

2. Drag the **Input Levels midtones slider** to the left, until the middle Input Levels text box reads approximately **1.90**.

   The content of the layer now looks lighter.

3. Drag the **Output Levels shadows slider** to the right until the left Output Levels text box reads **115** as shown in Figure 22.

4. Collapse the Properties panel to the dock.

5. Click the **Screened back type layer** on the Layers panel, then adjust the opacity of the layer to **85%**.

   The content of the layer is now more transparent.

6. Click **Layer 1** on the Layers panel.

7. Save your work, then compare your image to Figure 23.

You modified the midtones and shadows levels on the shape layer to make the text more transparent. You adjusted the Output Levels shadows slider to make the pixels that make up the text appear lighter.

Create a
FADED TYPE EFFECT

What You'll Do

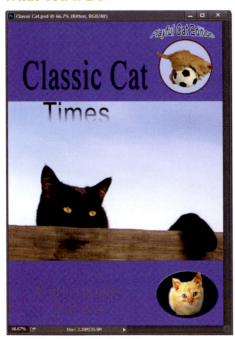

Source: Morguefile.

 In this lesson, you'll use the Gradient tool to make text appear faded in one area and brighter in another. You'll also apply a lighting filter.

Creating a Fade Effect

In addition to being able to change the font, size, color, and shape of your text, you might want to create the illusion that type is fading away in order to add an element of mystery to your masterpiece. You can create this effect using a type layer, a layer mask, and the Gradient tool. You can apply this effect to part of a type layer, if you want the text to look as if it's fading in or out, or to the entire layer.

QUICK **TIP**
Type does not have to be rasterized to create the fade effect.

Adding Styles to Type

You may have noticed the rather colorful Styles panel included in the Essentials workspace, although you can always open the Styles panel by clicking the Window menu on the Menu bar. You can apply these preset styles to any layer, much as you can use the Add a layer style button on the Layers panel.

Using the Gradient Tool

Before you can apply the fade effect, you need to create a layer mask for the type layer. You create the layer mask by clicking the Add layer mask button on the Layers panel. Then,

Creating Semitransparent Type

You can use blending options to create what appears to be semitransparent type. To do this, create a type layer and apply any layer styles you want. The Satin style, for example, can be used to darken the type, and the Pattern Overlay style can be used to create a patterned effect. In the Layer Style dialog box, drag the Set opacity of effect slider to the left and watch the preview until you get the amount of transparency you like. Any background images behind the type will be visible as the fill of the type.

you click the Gradient tool on the Tools panel. You can experiment with different types of gradient styles, but to create simple fading type, make sure Linear Gradient is selected on the options bar, click the Gradient picker list arrow, and then click the Black, White button on the Gradient picker.

Splitting Type

How easy is it to split type so that you get an effect similar to what's shown in Figure 24? The key to splitting type is rasterization. Once you've got a type layer in an image, rasterize it. Then, you can create a selection using your favorite tool (such as the Polygonal Lasso tool). Transform the selection using the Scale command on the Edit menu by manipulating any of the Transform Controls.

Figure 24 *Split type effect*

Figure 25 *White chrome type effect*

Creating White Chrome Type

By now, you've come to realize that not only can you create cool type by warping and fading it, you can also apply other techniques to create a variety of unique effects. For instance, you can give type the illusion of white chrome, and even add color to the chrome effect. To create this effect, start with black type in a large point size. Add a drop shadow, switch the foreground color to white, and then fill the type with the new foreground color by pressing [Alt][Backspace] (Win) or [option][delete] (Mac). Add an Inner Shadow style, and then the Satin style (with a low Distance setting). See the top of Figure 25. To add color to the effect (at the bottom of Figure 25), modify the Hue/Saturation setting and the Curves setting.

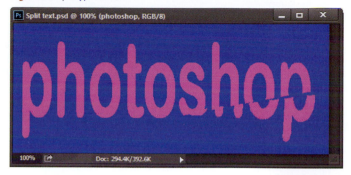

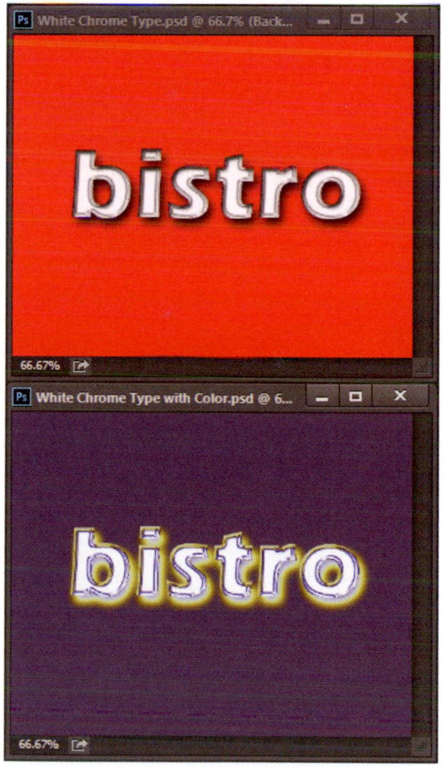

Create a fade effect

1. Click the **Black cat layer** on the Layers panel.

2. Click the **Horizontal Type tool**  on the Tools panel, click above the cat's right ear at approximately **120 X/350 Y**, set the font to **Arial Narrow Regular**, the font size to **48 pt**, the color to **Black**, the alignment to **Left align text**, then type **Times** as shown in Figure 26.

TIP Make similar font substitutions, if necessary.

3. Click the **Commit any current edits button** on the options bar.

4. Click the **Add layer mask button** on the Layers panel.

5. Click the **Gradient tool** on the Tools panel.

TIP The Gradient tool might be hidden under the Paint Bucket tool on the Tools panel.

6. Click the **Linear Gradient style button** on the options bar if not already selected.

7. Click the **Gradient picker list arrow** on the options bar.

8. Double-click the **Black, White style** (top row, third from left), then adjust the settings on your options bar to match Figure 27.

9. Verify that the **layer mask** on the Layers panel is selected, press and hold [**Shift**], drag the **Gradient pointer** -∔- from the bottom of the Times text to the top of the letter 'm' (to about 300 Y), then release [**Shift**]. Compare your text to Figure 28.

10. Save your work.

You added a layer mask and a gradient to create a faded type effect.

Figure 26 *New type in image*
Source: Morguefile.

New type layer

Figure 27 *Options for the Gradient tool*

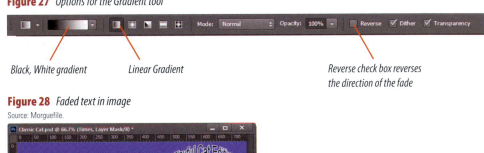

Black, White gradient   Linear Gradient   Reverse check box reverses the direction of the fade

Figure 28 *Faded text in image*
Source: Morguefile.

Bottom half of type is faded

Figure 29 *Styles panel*

Basic Drop Shadow style

Figure 30 *Lighting effect*
Source: Morguefile.

Apply a style to type

1. Click the **Classic Cat layer** on the Layers panel.
2. Click the **Styles tab**, click the **Basic Drop Shadow box** in the Styles panel, as shown in Figure 29.

You applied a preset style to type using the Styles panel.

Add a lighting effect

1. Click the **Kitten layer** on the Layers panel.

   Make sure the Smart Object thumbnail is selected, not the mask thumbnail.

   If working on a Mac with limited memory, proceed to step 4.
2. Click **Filter** on the Menu bar, point to **Render**, then click **Lighting Effects**.
3. Make sure that the **Default style** is selected on the options bar and **Point** is selected in the Properties panel, and that the light source is directly above the kitten's right ear (your left) in the black area, and has an Intensity of **50**, an Exposure of **20**, and an Ambiance of **−20**, then click **OK**.
4. Hide the rulers, save your work, then compare your image to Figure 30.
5. Close the image, then exit Photoshop.

You added a lighting filter to give the image a more polished appearance.

POWER USER SHORTCUTS	
To do this:	**Use this method:**
Adjust color levels	[icon] on Adjustments panel
Change warp type color	Double-click [icon], click [icon]
Commit a transformation	[icon], or press [Enter] (Win) or [return] (Mac)
Convert type to a shape	Type ➤ Convert to Shape
Create faded type	[icon], [icon], [icon], click Gradient picker list, then drag pointer over type
Create warped type	Double-click [icon], click [icon]
Display a bounding box	[icon] or **V**, click Show Transform Controls check box
Scale a bounding box	Press [Shift] while dragging handle, click [icon], or press [Enter] (Win) or [return] (Mac)
Screen back type	Duplicate layer, hide original layer, convert type to shape, then adjust Levels
Select Gradient tool	[icon] or [Shift] **G**
Skew a bounding box	Press [Ctrl] (Win) or [⌘] (Mac) while dragging handle, click [icon], or press [Enter] (Win) or [return] (Mac)
Stroke a type layer	[icon] *fx.*, Stroke, Set color of stroke button
Turn off bounding box display	[icon] or **V**, deselect Show Transform Controls check box

Key: Menu items are indicated by ➤ between the menu name and its command. Blue bold letters are shortcuts for selecting tools on the Tools panel.

Modify type using a bounding box.

1. Open PS 13-2.psd, update the text layers (if necessary), then save it as **Charge Card**.
2. Substitute a font available on your computer if necessary. (*Hint*: The font used in the sample is Courier New Regular.)
3. Display the rulers in pixels and make sure the guides are showing.
4. Select the Move tool and make sure that the Show Transform Controls check box is selected.
5. Make the Super Shopper layer active, drag the bounding box to the left so that the left edge of the S is just to the left of the guide at 135 X, then drag the top-middle handle of the bounding box to 290 Y.
6. Use the Transform command on the Edit menu to skew the text by dragging the upper-right handle of the bounding box to 500 X.
7. Commit the transformations, then save your work.

Create warped type with a unique shape.

1. Double-click the layer thumbnail on the Photoshop type layer on the Layers panel.
2. Change the font size to 72 pt, then commit the transformation.
3. Drag the type's bounding box to resize the type so that the bottom-left corner is at 135 X/150 Y. (*Hint*: This may take more than one step to complete.)
4. Open the Warp Text dialog box.
5. Change the Warp Text style to Arch.
6. Click the Horizontal option button (if it is not already selected).
7. Change the Bend setting to +52, the Horizontal Distortion setting to −20, and the Vertical Distortion setting to 0, then click OK.

8. Move the type so that the bottom-right corner of the bounding box is at 545 X/150 Y.
9. Change the type color using the Swatches panel (Dark Violet Magenta).
10. Apply the default Drop Shadow and Bevel and Emboss styles to the Photoshop type layer, then save your work.

Screen back type with imagery.

1. Make the CHARGE layer active.
2. Increase the font size to 80 pt.
3. Move the CHARGE layer so the bottom-left corner is at 90 X/275 Y.
4. Duplicate this layer, calling the new layer **Screened back type**.
5. Hide the CHARGE layer.
6. Convert the Screened back type layer to a shape layer.
7. Add a (clipped) Levels Adjustment layer that modifies the Midtones Input level to 0.45 and the Output levels shadow slider to 136.
8. Change the opacity of the Screened back type layer to 75%.

9. Make the Backdrop layer active, then use the Sponge tool to saturate the part of the image that is behind the text CHARGE.
10. Use any painting or erasure tools to make the hoop appear to be in front of the 't' in Photoshop.
11. Save your work.

Create a faded type effect.

1. Make the Super Shopper layer active, then add a mask to this layer.
2. Select the Gradient tool, set the opacity to 70%, select the Linear Gradient style, then select Black, White on the Gradient picker.
3. Drag a straight line the length of the text, starting at approximately 155 X/315 Y and ending at the right edge of the type.
4. Clear the guides, then hide the rulers.
5. Add the Add Noise filter with a 50% Uniform Distribution to the Background layer.
6. Save your work, then compare your image to Figure 31. (Your image may look slightly different.)

Figure 31 *Completed Skills Review*
© Photodisc/Getty Images

You have been asked to create cover art for a new pop-psychology book entitled *Battling Personalities: Outer Struggles*. The author has created some initial artwork that she wants on the cover. You can use any of your Photoshop skills to enhance this image, but you particularly want to transform the type to convey the mood and theme of the book.

1. Open PS 13-3.psd, then save it as **Battling Personalities**.
2. Create two type layers: **Battling Personalities** and **Outer Struggles**. (*Hint*: You can use any font available on your computer. In the sample, a 159.58 pt and 60 pt Trebuchet MS Regular font is shown.)
3. Position the type layers appropriately.
4. Make sure the Show Transform Controls check box is selected.
5. Warp the Battling Personalities type, using the Rise style and the settings of your choice in the Warp Text dialog box.
6. Use the bounding box to enlarge the warped text.
7. Duplicate the Outer Struggles type layer, choosing a suitable name for the duplicate layer.
8. Convert the copied layer to a shape, then change the levels using the settings of your choice. (In the sample, the Midtones input level is 2.26, and the Output shadows level is 20.)

9. Hide the original type layer.
10. Add a new type layer using the text and font of your choice in an appropriate location on the image.
11. Use the bounding box to scale the type layer to a smaller size.
12. Create a mask on this new layer.
13. Use the Gradient tool and the new type layer to create a fade effect.

14. Change any font colors, and add any enhancing effects to the type layers.
15. Add any filter effects or color adjustments that you determine are necessary to complete the image. (In the sample, the Brightness is adjusted to −15, the Contrast is adjusted to +15 using an Adjustment Layer, and the colors in the Fighting layer have been saturated.)
16. Save your work, then compare your image to the sample in Figure 32.

Figure 32 *Sample Project Builder 1*
© Photodisc/Getty Images

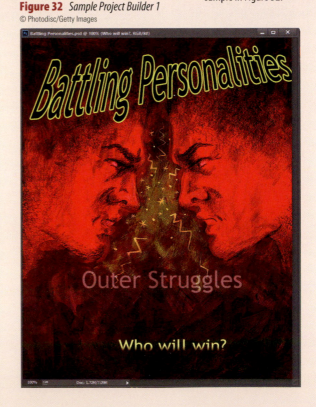

You work for Creativity, a graphic design firm that works almost exclusively with the high-tech business sector. As the newest member of the creative team, you have been assigned the design of the cover for the upcoming annual report. You have seen the annual reports for previous years, and they always feature dramatic, exciting designs. You have already started on the initial design, but need to complete the project.

1. Open PS 13-4.psd, then save it as **Creativity**.
2. Create a new layer containing just the dice. (*Hint*: You can duplicate the Backdrop layer, then use any of your Photoshop skills to isolate the dice in their own layer. Possible alternatives include creating a mask or erasing pixels.)
3. Create type layers for text appropriate for an annual report. (*Hint*: You can use any font available on your computer. In the sample, a Georgia Regular font is shown.)
4. Position the type layers appropriately.
5. Warp at least one of the type layers, using the style and settings of your choice. (*Hint*: In the sample, the Wave style [with both horizontal and vertical distortions] was used.)
6. Enlarge or skew at least one type layer.
7. Create a screened back effect using one of the type layers and the settings of your choice. (In the sample, the Midtones input level is 2.26, the Output shadows level is 20, and the opacity is 80%.)
8. Create a fade effect using one of the type layers.
9. Change any font colors, then add any enhancing effects to the type layers.

10. Add any filter effects or color adjustments (using the existing and newly created and modified layers) that you determine are necessary. In the sample, the Brightness is adjusted to +25, and the Contrast is adjusted to +10. The area underneath the dice in the Backdrop layer was saturated using the Sponge tool, and the default Lighting Effects filter was applied to the Backdrop layer. (The filter applied by your computer may vary.)
11. Save your work, then compare your image to the sample in Figure 33.

Figure 33 *Sample Project Builder 2*
© Photodisc/Getty Images

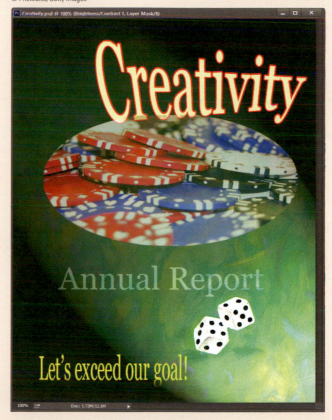

You have been asked to design a print advertisement for your favorite local television station that just won first place in a ratings race. Before you begin, you decide to see what information you can find about type enhancements on the Internet. You intend to use the information you find to improve your skills and create a dramatic image. Be prepared to discuss the design elements used in this project. (*Hint*: If you don't have a favorite television station, invent call letters that you can use in this exercise.)

1. Connect to the Internet and use your browser to find information about transforming type in Photoshop. (Make a record of the site you found so you can use it for future reference.)
2. Create a new Photoshop image, using the dimensions of your choice, then save it as **Television Station Ad**.
3. Create a type layer, using any color for the layer, any font available on your computer, and any text you want. (In the sample, an Onyx Regular font is used.)
4. Create a warped type effect, using any style and settings of your choice. (In the sample, the Flag style is used.)
5. Create an attractive background, using any of your Photoshop skills and any imagery available to you. You can use scanned or digital camera images, purchased imagery, or any images available on your computer.

6. Create any necessary additional type layers.
7. Resize any fonts, if necessary, using the bounding box.
8. Add any special effects to the type layers.
9. If necessary, make color adjustments or add filters.
10. Save your work, then compare your image to the sample in Figure 34.

Figure 34 *Sample Design Project*
© Photodisc/Getty Images

You are a member of a fan club devoted to your favorite musical group. The fan club is holding a contest to choose a cover design for the band's new CD. You decide to put your expert Photoshop skills to work on this print project. After the design is complete, take time to consider what you did, why you did it, and how your efforts contributed to the overall design of the image.

1. Create a Photoshop image using the dimensions of your choice, then save it as **CD Cover Artwork**.
2. Locate several pieces of artwork—either on your computer, in a royalty-free collection, or from scanned images. Although the images can show anything, you want to show positive imagery in keeping with the band's message.
3. Select imagery from the artwork and move it into CD Cover Artwork.
4. Create a warped type effect using any style and settings of your choice. (In the sample, the Viner Hand ITC font is used.)

5. Create any necessary additional type layers.
6. Resize any fonts, if necessary, using the bounding box.
7. Add any special effects to the type layers.
8. If necessary, make color adjustments or add filters.
9. Use at least one of the transformation skills you learned in this chapter to enhance the text.

10. Add any filter effects, if you decide they will make your image more dramatic. (In the sample, the Wind filter is applied to a layer.)
11. Make any color adjustments you feel would improve the look of the image.
12. Save your work, then compare your image to the sample in Figure 35.

Figure 35 *Sample Portfolio Project*
© Photodisc/Getty Images

CHAPTER 14 LIQUIFYING AN IMAGE

1. Use the Liquify tools to distort an image
2. Learn how to freeze and thaw areas
3. Use the mesh feature as you distort an image

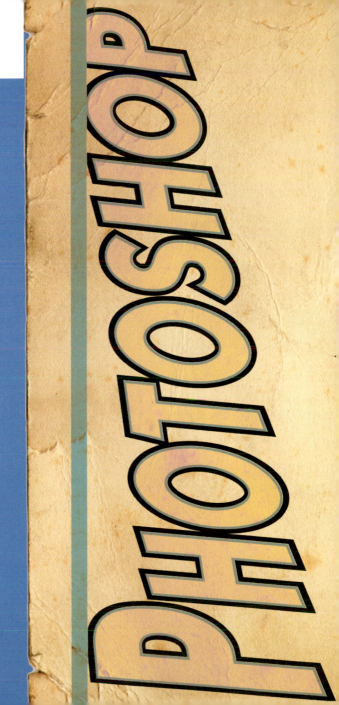

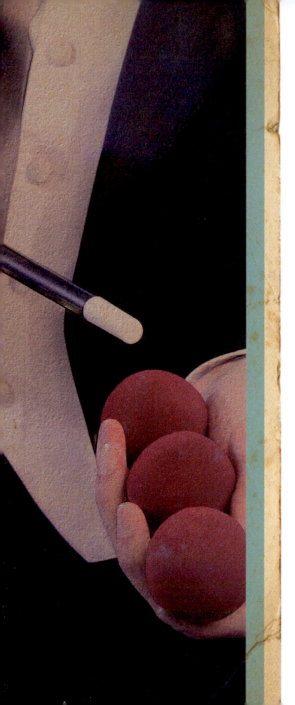

CHAPTER 14 LIQUIFYING AN IMAGE

Distorting Images

If you want to have some fun with an image, try your hand at the Liquify feature. Like the Smudge tool and the distort filters, you can use it to distort an image. But unlike those tools, the Liquify feature gives you much more control over the finished product. This feature contains eight distinct tools that you can use to create distortion effects.

Using the Liquify Feature

The Liquify feature lets you make an image look as if parts of it have melted. You can apply the seven Liquify distortions with a brush, and like other brush-based Photoshop tools, you can modify both the brush size and pressure to give you just the effect you want.

You can use the two non-distortion Liquify tools to freeze and thaw areas within the image. Freezing protects an area from editing and possible editing errors, whereas thawing a frozen area allows it to be edited. With these two tools, you can protect specific areas from Liquify distortions, and can determine with great accuracy which areas are affected.

Using Common Sense

Because the effects of the Liquify feature are so dramatic, you should take the proper precautions to preserve your original work. You can work on a copy of the original image, or create duplicate layers to ensure that you can always get back to your starting point.

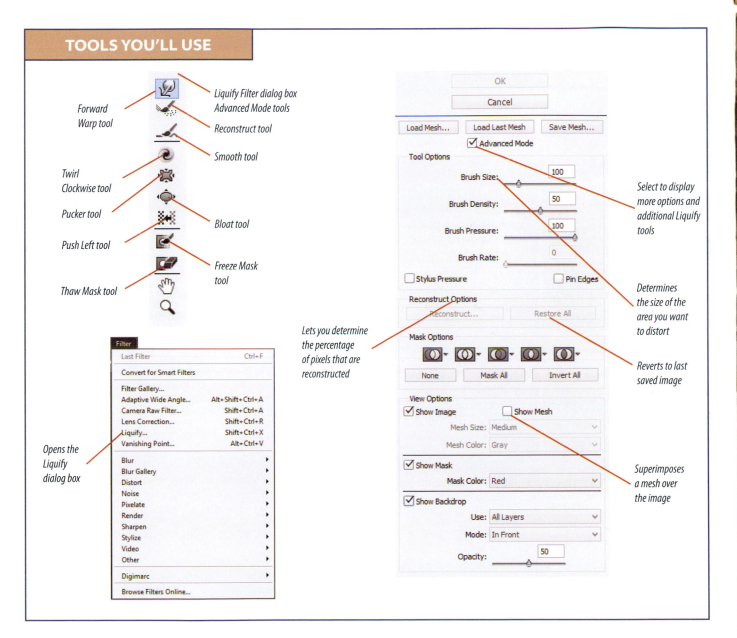

TOOLS YOU'LL USE

Forward Warp tool

Liquify Filter dialog box Advanced Mode tools

Reconstruct tool

Smooth tool

Twirl Clockwise tool

Pucker tool

Push Left tool

Bloat tool

Freeze Mask tool

Thaw Mask tool

OK

Cancel

Load Mesh...   Load Last Mesh   Save Mesh...

☑ Advanced Mode

Tool Options

Brush Size: 100

Brush Density: 50

Brush Pressure: 100

Brush Rate: 0

☐ Stylus Pressure   ☐ Pin Edges

Reconstruct Options

Reconstruct...   Restore All

Mask Options

None   Mask All   Invert All

View Options

☑ Show Image   ☐ Show Mesh

Mesh Size: Medium

Mesh Color: Gray

☑ Show Mask

Mask Color: Red

☑ Show Backdrop

Use: All Layers

Mode: In Front

Opacity: 50

Select to display more options and additional Liquify tools

Determines the size of the area you want to distort

Reverts to last saved image

Superimposes a mesh over the image

Lets you determine the percentage of pixels that are reconstructed

Opens the Liquify dialog box

Filter

Last Filter   Ctrl+F

Convert for Smart Filters

Filter Gallery...
Adaptive Wide Angle...   Alt+Shift+Ctrl+A
Camera Raw Filter...   Shift+Ctrl+A
Lens Correction...   Shift+Ctrl+R
Liquify...   Shift+Ctrl+X
Vanishing Point...   Alt+Ctrl+V

Blur   ▶
Blur Gallery   ▶
Distort   ▶
Noise   ▶
Pixelate   ▶
Render   ▶
Sharpen   ▶
Stylize   ▶
Video   ▶
Other   ▶

Digimarc   ▶

Browse Filters Online...

Use the Liquify Tools
TO DISTORT AN IMAGE

What You'll Do

Source: Morguefile.

 In this lesson, you'll use the Forward Warp tool in the Liquify dialog box to create distortions.

Using the Liquify Dialog Box

With the **Liquify feature**, you can apply distortions to any rasterized layer. When you use the Liquify command on the Filter menu, the contents of the active layer appear in a large preview window in the Liquify dialog box. The distortion tools—used to apply the Liquify effects—are displayed on the left side of the dialog box; the tool settings are displayed on the right side. Unlike other tools that you use in the image window, you can only access the Liquify tools from the Liquify dialog box. (The Liquify feature is similar to the Vanishing Point feature in this respect.) In this dialog box, you can create seven different types of distortions.

> **QUICK TIP**
>
> As you apply distortions, the effects are immediately visible in the preview window of the Liquify dialog box.

Exploring the Possibilities

Compare Figures 1 (the original image) and 2 (the distorted image). As you can see from the altered image, you can use this feature to make drastic changes in an image. The following Liquify tools were used for the distorted image:

- The Twirl Clockwise tool was used repeatedly on the top book.
- The Pucker tool was used on the corners of the third book. (The Pucker tool pulls the pixels toward the center of the brush tip.)
- The Bloat tool was used on the sixth and seventh book. (The Bloat tool pushes pixels away from the center of the brush tip, which can create a more subtle effect.)

> **QUICK TIP**
>
> The Liquify window is quite large. Feel free to resize it by dragging the sides or corners of the window.

Going Wild with Distortions

Of course, you can create strange, crazy distortions using the Liquify feature, and it is a lot of fun. As you can see from Figure 2, you can create some rather bizarre effects using these tools, but you can also use the distortion tools very conservatively to just correct a flaw or tweak an image.

Figure 1 *Undistorted image in Liquify dialog box*
© Photodisc/Getty Images

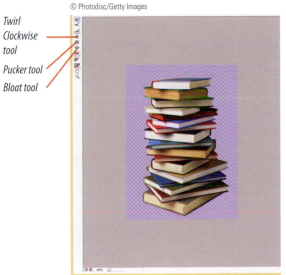

Twirl Clockwise tool

Pucker tool

Bloat tool

Figure 2 *Distortion samples*
© Photodisc/Getty Images

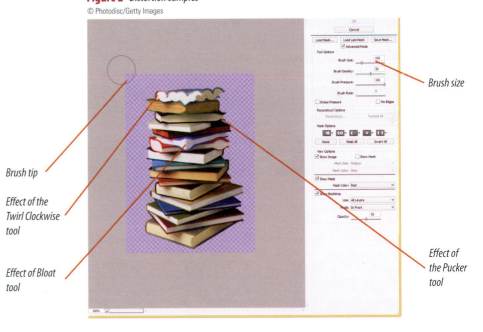

Brush size

Brush tip

Effect of the Twirl Clockwise tool

Effect of Bloat tool

Effect of the Pucker tool

Open the Liquify dialog box and modify the brush size

1. Open PS 14-1.psd from the drive and folder where you store your Data Files, then save the file as **Walk of Fame**.

2. Click **Filter** on the Menu bar, then click **Liquify**.

TIP After clicking Liquify, you may see a warning box about improving performance if your computer has insufficient graphics capabilities.

3. Click the **Zoom tool** 🔍 in the Liquify dialog box, then click the center of the image.

4. Select the Advanced Mode check box if necessary, then make sure the following check boxes are *not* selected: **Show Mesh**, **Show Mask**, and **Show Backdrop**.

5. Click the **Forward Warp tool** 🖉 in the Liquify dialog box.

   The Liquify tools are described in Table 1.

6. Double-click the **Brush Size text box**, type **35**, then press [**Enter**] (Win) or [**return**] (Mac).

TIP You can adjust the brush size by typing a value between 1 and 15,000 in the text box, pressing [[] to decrease by 10 or []] to increase by 10, or by dragging the slider to a new value.

7. Adjust your settings in the Liquify dialog box so that they match those shown in Figure 3.

TIP The Stylus Pressure check box will appear dimmed if you do not have a graphics tablet attached to your computer.

You opened the Liquify dialog box, then chose the Forward Warp tool and a brush size.

Figure 3 *Choosing a brush size*

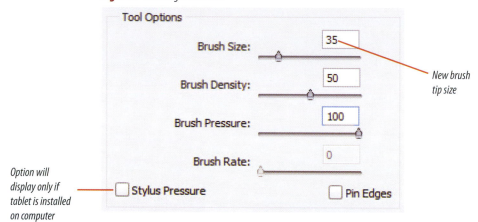

Option will display only if tablet is installed on computer

New brush tip size

TABLE 1: LIQUIFY TOOLS		
	Button	**Use**
Forward Warp tool	🖉	Pushes pixels forward during dragging.
Reconstruct tool		Unpaints recently distorted pixels completely or partially.
Smooth tool		Blurs unsightly artifacts.
Twirl Clockwise tool		Rotates pixels clockwise during dragging. (Hold [Alt] (Win) or [option] (Mac) to twirl counter-clockwise.)
Pucker tool		Moves pixels toward the center of the active brush tip.
Bloat tool		Moves pixels away from the center of the active brush tip.
Push Left tool		Moves pixels perpendicular to the brush stroke.
Freeze Mask tool		Protects an area from distortion.
Thaw Mask tool		Makes a frozen area available for distortions.

© 2015 Cengage Learning®

Liquifying an Image

Figure 4 *Positioned pointer*
Source: Morguefile.

Forward Warp tool
brush tip pointer

Figure 5 *Stretched bottle*
Source: Morguefile.

Stretched bottle
is distorted

Figure 6 *Effect of Forward Warp tool*
Source: Morguefile.

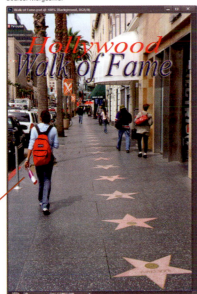

Your results will
be different

Use the Forward Warp tool

1. Position the **Forward Warp tool pointer** ○ over the pink area in the bottle, as shown in Figure 4.

   TIP Your results may vary slightly from those shown in the figures in this book.

2. Drag the **pink area in the bottle** down so it stretches the bottom of the bottle as shown in Figure 5.

   TIP You can return an image to its previous appearance by clicking the Restore All button in the Reconstruct Options section of the Liquify dialog box. The Reconstruct button undoes each action of the brush, much like the Undo command or History panel.

3. Click **OK** to close the Liquify dialog box.

4. Save your work, then compare your image to Figure 6.

You used the Forward Warp tool to distort the pixels of the bottle in an image. By dragging, you pushed the pixels downward giving the bottle a longer, distorted appearance.

Learn How to Freeze
AND THAW AREAS

What You'll Do

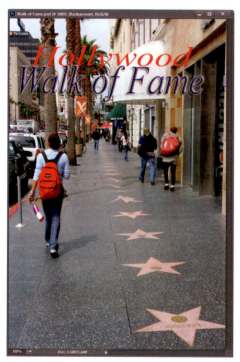

Source: Morguefile.

In this lesson, you'll freeze an area of an image, make distortions, and then thaw an area so that it can be edited.

Controlling Distortion Areas

Like storing food in the freezer to protect it from spoiling, you can **freeze** areas within an image so that the Liquify tools leave them unaffected. Using the Liquify dialog box, you can protect areas within an image, and then **thaw** them—or return them to a state that can be edited—and make necessary distortions. You control which areas are distorted by using the Freeze Mask and Thaw Mask tools in the Liquify dialog box.

Freezing Image Areas

You can selectively freeze areas by painting them with a pointer. The View Options section in the Liquify dialog box lets you display frozen areas in the preview window. By default, frozen areas are painted in red, but you can change this color to make it more visible. For example, Figure 7 shows an image that has not yet been distorted. If you froze areas of this image using the default red color, they would not be visible because of the colors in this image.

QUICK TIP

To isolate the exact areas you want to freeze, try painting a larger area, and then using the Thaw Mask tool to eliminate unwanted frozen areas.

Reconstructing Distortions

No matter how careful you are, you will most likely either create a distortion you don't like or need to do some sort of damage control. Unlike typical Photoshop states, individual distortions you make using the Liquify feature do not appear on the History panel, and therefore cannot be undone. You can, however, use the History panel to delete the effects of an entire **Liquify session**. When you delete a Liquify state from the History panel, your image is restored to its original condition. In order to correct or delete the effects of a liquify tool during a Liquify session, you need to use a reconstruction method. However, how distortions are reconstructed is determined by the mode used. If you want to reconstruct, you can do so by using the Reconstruct or Restore All buttons in the Liquify dialog box. Either choice affects the way pixels are reconstructed, relative to frozen areas in the image. This allows you to redo the changes in new and innovative ways.

QUICK TIP

You can use any combination of reconstruction tools and modes to get just the effect you want.

Liquifying an Image

Undergoing Reconstruction

Figure 8 shows a number of distortions that have been reconstructed using either the Reconstruct or Restore All buttons, as well as a frozen area painted in blue. Using the Reconstruct tool, the clockwise twirl on the chicken's beak was reconstructed by 20 percent. You can use several methods to reconstruct an image:

■ Click the Restore All button in the Liquify dialog box.

■ Click the Reconstruct button in the Liquify dialog box, then select a percentage that you want reverted.

■ Click the Reconstruct tool, drag the Revert Reconstruction slider to set the amount of reconstruction, and then drag the brush over distorted areas in the Liquify dialog box.

■ Click the Cancel button in the Liquify dialog box.

■ Make distortions in the Liquify dialog box, click OK, and then drag the Liquify state to the Delete current state button on the History panel.

Figure 7 *Original image*
© Photodisc/Getty Images

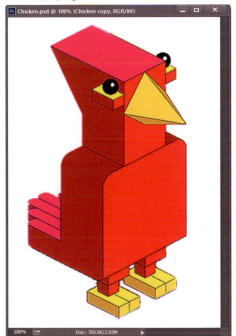

Figure 8 *Frozen areas and distortions in preview window*
© Photodisc/Getty Images

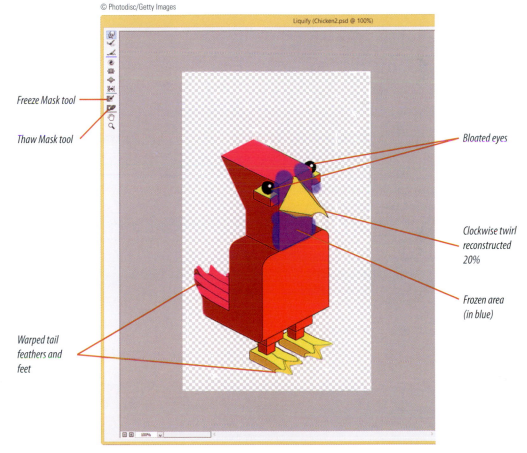

Freeze Mask tool

Thaw Mask tool

Bloated eyes

Clockwise twirl reconstructed 20%

Frozen area (in blue)

Warped tail feathers and feet

Freeze areas in an image

1. Click **Filter** on the Menu bar, then click (the second occurrence of) **Liquify**.

2. Use the **Zoom tool** 🔍 in the Liquify dialog box to magnify the **man with the striped shirt**.

TIP Use the Zoom tool in the Liquify dialog box as needed to increase the size of objects you're working on. Use the Hand tool to reposition objects for better visibility.

3. Click the **Freeze Mask tool** 🖌 in the Liquify dialog box.

TIP Toggle between the current tool and the Hand tool by holding the Spacebar. This works in the Liquify dialog box and throughout Photoshop!

4. Double-click the **Brush Size text box**, type **20**, then press [**Enter**] (Win) or [**return**] (Mac).

5. Click the **Show Mask check box**, click the **Mask Color list arrow**, then click **Red** if it is not already selected. Compare your Liquify dialog box settings to Figure 9 and make any necessary adjustments.

6. Drag the **Freeze mask pointer** ◯ around the perimeter of the **man in the striped shirt**, using Figure 10 as a guide. (Don't worry if your results differ.)

You modified Liquify settings, then froze an area within the image by using the Freeze Mask tool. Freezing the area protects it from any Liquify effects you apply going forward.

Figure 9 *Liquify settings*

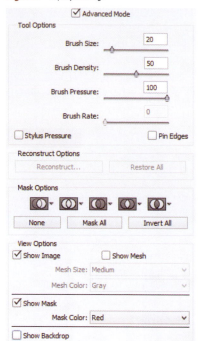

Figure 10 *Frozen area*
Source: Morguefile.

Red area is frozen

Liquifying an Image

Figure 11 *Distortions in image*
Source: Morguefile.

Shoulder bag
is distorted

Sixth star is reduced

Figure 12 *Distortions applied*
Source: Morguefile.

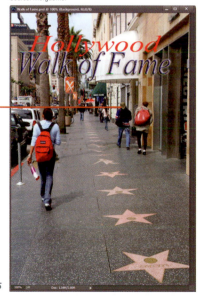

Distorted hat

Figure 13 *History panel*

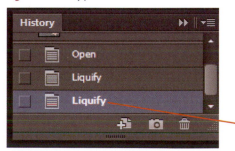

State indicates
most recent
distortions

Distort unprotected areas of an image

1. Click the **Pucker tool** in the Liquify dialog box.

2. Change the brush size to **100** if necessary.

3. Position the center of the **Pucker pointer** over the **sixth from the bottom star**, then press and hold the mouse button until the star is noticeably smaller.

4. Click the **Bloat tool** in the Liquify dialog box, center the **Bloat pointer** over the **red shoulder bag**, then press and hold the mouse button until the tip increases in size and fills the woman's back (on the left).

5. Click the **Thaw Mask tool** (in the Liquify dialog box) using the brush size of your choice, then paint the mask over the man's head to erase it.

6. Use the **Forward Warp tool** (in the Liquify dialog box) with a Brush Size of **25**, then drag the hat down to elongate it.

7. Compare your image to Figure 11.

8. Click the **None button** in the Mask Options section to remove the mask.

9. Click **OK**, then display the **History panel**.

   The distortions are applied to the image.

10. Save your work, compare your image to Figure 12 and the History panel to Figure 13.

After distorting three areas, you removed the frozen mask and reviewed the History panel.

Use the Mesh Feature
AS YOU DISTORT AN IMAGE

What You'll Do

Source: Morguefile.

In this lesson, you'll use the mesh feature to assist you when making distortions.

Using the Mesh Feature

The **mesh** is a series of horizontal and vertical gridlines superimposed on the preview window. You can easily see the effects of your distortions while working in an image by turning on the mesh. Although this feature is not necessary to create distortions, it can be helpful for seeing how much distortion you have added. The mesh can be controlled using the View Options section in the Liquify dialog box, shown in Figure 14. A magnified and distorted image with the large size (medium size is the default), yellow mesh displayed, is shown in Figure 15.

> **QUICK TIP**
>
> Distortions on the gridlines look similar to isobars on a thermal map or elevations on a topographic map.

Changing the Mesh Display

You can modify the appearance of the mesh so that it is displayed in another color or with larger or smaller gridlines. You may want to use large gridlines if your changes are so dramatic that the use of smaller gridlines would be distracting. You can use the gridlines to see where the distortions occur. If the mesh color

and the colors in the image are similar, you may want to change the mesh color so it will be easier to see the distortions. For example, a yellow mesh displayed on an image with a yellow background would be invisible. A blue mesh against a white background, as shown in Figure 16, is more noticeable.

Visualizing the Distortions

When the mesh feature is on and clearly visible, take a look at the gridlines as you make your distortions. Note where the gridlines have been adjusted and if symmetrical objects have equally symmetrical distortions. For example, distortions of a rectangular skyscraper can be controlled so that they are equivalent on all visible sides. If symmetry is what you want, the mesh feature gives you one method of checking your results.

Getting a Better View of Distortions

The active layer is always shown in the Liquify dialog box, but you might find it helpful to distort imagery with its companion layers visible. You can do this in two ways. One way is by selecting the Show Backdrop check box in the Liquify dialog box, and selecting which layer (or all layers) you want to be visible with

Liquifying an Image

the selected layer. You can then adjust the opacity of the backdrop layer(s) to make the layer(s) more visible. This technique distorts only the layer selected on the Layers panel. The other way is by merging visible layers: Click the highest layer on the Layers panel, click the Layers Panel options button, and then click Merge Visible. When you open the merged layers in the Liquify dialog box, all the imagery will be visible and can be altered by distortions. One way of ensuring that you can get back to your original layers—in case things don't turn out quite as you planned—is by making copies of the layers you want to combine before you merge the layers.

QUICK TIP

You can always turn off the mesh feature if it is distracting.

Figure 14 *Mesh display options*

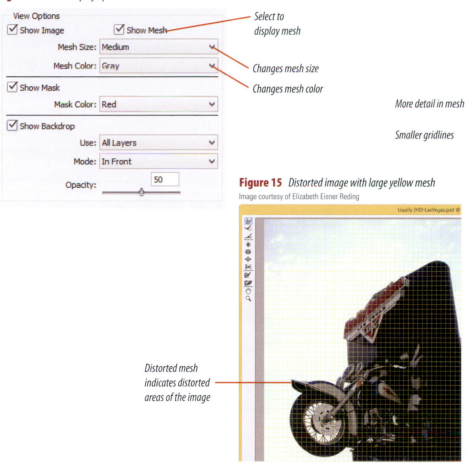

Select to display mesh

Changes mesh size

Changes mesh color

Distorted mesh indicates distorted areas of the image

Figure 16 *Distorted image with medium blue mesh*

Image courtesy of Elizabeth Eisner Reding

More detail in mesh

Smaller gridlines

Figure 15 *Distorted image with large yellow mesh*

Image courtesy of Elizabeth Eisner Reding

Turn on the mesh

1. Click **Filter** on the Menu bar, then click the second instance of **Liquify**.

2. Use the **Zoom tool** 🔍 in the Liquify dialog box to magnify the red backpack in the image.

3. Click the **Bloat tool** in the Liquify dialog box, then verify that the brush size is **100**.

4. Select the **Show Mesh check box**.

5. Click the **Mesh Color list arrow**, then click **Blue**. Verify that the **Mesh Size** is set to **Medium**.

6. Select the **Show Backdrop check box**. Compare your settings to Figure 17, then make any adjustments necessary so that your settings match those shown in the figure.

TIP   Turning on the backdrop allows you to see additional layers other than the layer being edited.

You turned on the mesh, changed the mesh color, then verified the setting of the mesh size.

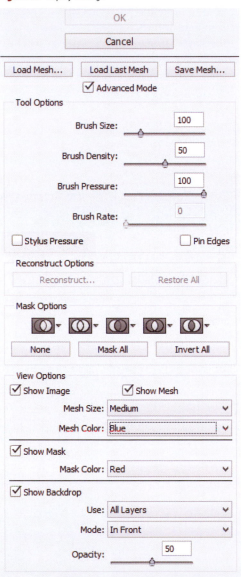

Figure 17   *Liquify settings*

Liquifying an Image

Figure 18 *Medium blue mesh over image*
Source: Morguefile.

Distorted mesh

Figure 19 *Distortions applied to image*
Source: Morguefile.

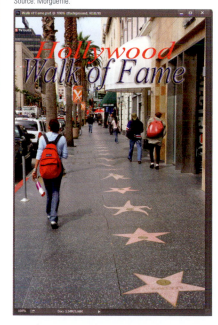

Distort an image with the mesh feature activated

1. Position the **Bloat pointer** ◯ over the middle of the **bottom of the red backpack**, press and hold the mouse button until you see the mesh being distorted, then release the mouse button.

2. Click the **Forward Warp tool** 〰 in the Liquify dialog box, then change the brush size to **25**.

3. Click the **Mesh Size list arrow**, then click **Small**.

    The gridlines appear smaller.

4. Drag the **Forward Warp pointer** ◯ in the points of the **third from the bottom star** using medium horizontal strokes so that it forms curved spikes, as shown in Figure 18.

5. Click the **Show Mesh check box** to turn off the mesh.

6. Click **OK**.

7. Save your work, then compare your image to Figure 19.

8. Close the image, then exit Photoshop.

You added new distortions to the image and changed the mesh size. After viewing the distortions with the smaller mesh, you turned off the mesh and viewed the image.

POWER USER SHORTCUTS

To do this:	Use this method:	To do this:	Use this method:
Bloat an area	Filter ➤ Liquify, 🔆 or **B**	Reconstruct pixels in an area	Filter ➤ Liquify, 🖌 or **R**
Blur unsightly artifacts	Filter ➤ Liquify, 🖌 or **E**	Return image to pre-Liquify state	Click Restore All in Liquify dialog box, click Cancel in Liquify dialog box, or drag state to 🗑 on the History panel
Change freeze color	Filter ➤ Liquify, click Show Mask check box, Mask Color list arrow	Shift pixels in an area	Filter ➤ Liquify, ▨◀ or **O**
Change mesh color	Filter ➤ Liquify, select Show Mesh check box, click the Mesh Color list arrow	Thaw frozen pixels	Filter ➤ Liquify, 🖌 or **D**
Change mesh size	Filter ➤ Liquify, select Show Mesh check box, click the Mesh Size list arrow	Turn mesh on/off	Filter ➤ Liquify, select Show Mesh check box
Change brush size	Filter ➤ Liquify, Brush Size text box, slider, or [[] or []]	Turn Backdrop on/off	Filter ➤ Liquify, select Show Backdrop check box
Freeze pixels	Filter ➤ Liquify, 🖌 or **F**	Twirl an area clockwise	Filter ➤ Liquify, 🌀 or **C**
Open Liquify dialog box	Filter ➤ Liquify or [Shift][Ctrl][X] (Win) or [shift] ⌘ [X] (Mac)	Warp an area	Filter ➤ Liquify, 🌀 or **W**
Pucker an area	Filter ➤ Liquify, ▨ or **S**		

Key: Menu items are indicated by ➤ between the menu name and its command. Blue bold letters are shortcuts for selecting tools in the dialog box.

© 2015 Cengage Learning®

Liquifying an Image

Use the Liquify tools to distort an image.

1. Open PS 14-2.psd, then save it as **Blurred Vision**.
2. Open the Liquify dialog box.
3. Select the Twirl Clockwise tool.
4. Change the Brush Size to 65.
5. Twirl the F in Line 2.
6. Twirl the P in Line 2. (*Hint*: The bloat effect appears as a gray overlay against the unbloated letters, almost like a preview of the Liquify effect.)
7. Close the Liquify dialog box, then save your work.

Learn how to freeze and thaw areas.

1. Open the Liquify dialog box.
2. Turn on the Show Mask feature, then change the Mask Color to Green.
3. Use the Freeze Mask tool to freeze the O in the middle of Line 3.
4. Select the Bloat tool.
5. Bloat both remaining letters in Line 3.
6. Use the Thaw Mask tool to thaw the frozen areas.
7. Click OK, then save your work.

Use the mesh feature as you distort an image.

1. Open the Liquify dialog box.
2. Turn on the Show Mesh feature.
3. Change the Mesh Color to Blue.
4. Change the Mesh Size to Large.
5. Select the Pucker tool, then change the Brush Size to 135.
6. Pucker the E on Line 1 and the numbers 3 and 7.
7. Use the Bloat tool and a 150 Brush Size to distort the green bar (between lines 6 and 7) and the red bar (between lines 8 and 9).
8. Distort the letter P in line 4 and the number 11 using the Bloat tool.
9. Close the Liquify dialog box, save your work, then compare your image to Figure 20.

Figure 20 *Completed Skills Review*
© Photodisc/Getty Images

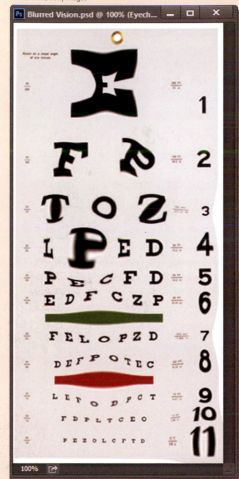

Your lifelong dream to open a restaurant is about to come true. In fact, even though you haven't found a location, you've already chosen a name: the Flying Star Cafe. Fortunately, you can use your Photoshop skills to save some money by designing your own promotional advertisements. You've created the initial background art, but need to complete the image.

1. Open PS 14-3.psd, then save it as **Flying Star**.
2. Activate the Flying Star layer, then open the Liquify dialog box.
3. Display the mesh in a size and color you think are appropriate.
4. Change the freeze mask color to Red (if necessary).
5. Use the brush size of your choice to freeze the face in the lower-left corner.
6. Use the Twirl Clockwise tool and a Brush Size of 60 to distort the bright shooting star.
7. Use the Bloat tool with a Brush Size of 250 to distort the shooting star.
8. Turn off the mesh, then click OK to close the Liquify dialog box.
9. Add a type layer that says **Flying Star Cafe**. (*Hint*: You can use any color and any font available on your computer. In the sample, a Poor Richard font is shown.)
10. Use the bounding box to change the size of the text.

11. Warp the type layer using the style and the settings of your choice. (*Hint*: Do not rasterize the type layer.)
12. Apply the type effects of your choice to the text.
13. Make any color adjustments you feel are necessary. (*Hint*: In the sample, the Levels were adjusted so that the input midtones are .69.)

14. Add any filter effects that you determine are necessary to enhance the image. (In the sample, the Lens Flare filter was set at 105mm Prime at 90% Brightness and positioned over the flying star.)
15. Save your work, then compare your image to the sample in Figure 21.

Figure 21 *Sample Project Builder 1*
© Photodisc/Getty Images

Liquifying an Image

Your friend is a film photographer and doesn't understand the power of Photoshop and digital photography. His birthday is coming soon, and you think it is a great opportunity to show him how useful Photoshop can be and to have a little fun with him. One of the things you like best about your friend is his great sense of humor. You decide to use the Liquify tools to distort a photo of him so it looks like a caricature.

1. Open PS 14-4.psd, then save it as **Photographer**.
2. Locate at least one piece of appropriate artwork— either a scanned image of a friend, an image on your computer, or an image from a royalty-free collection—that you can use in this file.
3. Use any appropriate methods to select imagery from the artwork.
4. After the selections have been made, copy each selection into Photographer.
5. Transform any imagery, if necessary.
6. Change the colors of the gradient fill in the Backdrop layer to suit the colors in your friend's image.
7. Open the Liquify dialog box.
8. Display any size mesh in any color you find helpful.
9. Change the freeze mask color to a color you find helpful.
10. Use the brush size of your choice to freeze an area within the image. (*Hint*: In the example, the face was protected while the hair was enlarged and brushed back.)

11. Use any distortion tool in any brush size of your choice to distort an area near the frozen area.
12. Thaw the frozen areas.
13. Use any additional distortion techniques to modify the image and distort the physical characteristics, as a caricaturist would do.
14. Turn off the mesh, then click OK to close the Liquify dialog box.
15. Add a type layer with a title for your friend. You can position it in any location you choose.
16. Save your work, then compare your image to the sample in Figure 22.

Figure 22 *Sample Project Builder 2*
© Photodisc/Getty Images. Source: Morguefile.

You really love the Photoshop Liquify feature and want to see other samples of how this tool can be used. You decide to look on the Internet, find a sample, and then cast a critical eye on the results.

1. Connect to the Internet and use your browser to find information about the Liquify feature in Photoshop. (Make a record of the site you found so you can use it for future reference.) You might find an image similar to a liquified image such as the sample shown in Figure 23.
2. Ask yourself the following questions about a specific image to which the Liquify feature has been applied.
   - Do you like this image? If so, why?
   - Does the distortion prevent you from determining what the image is?
   - In your opinion, does the distortion make the image more or less effective?
   - How was the distortion created?
   - After seeing this sample, what is your opinion as to the overall effectiveness of the Liquify feature? How can it best be used?
3. Be prepared to discuss your answers to these questions either in writing, in a group discussion, or in a presentation format.

Figure 23 *Sample Design Project*
Image courtesy of Elizabeth Eisner Reding

You have been asked to give a presentation to a group of students who are interested in taking computer design classes. The presentation should include general topics, such as layers, type, and making selections, and can also include more exotic features, such as Liquify. Make it clear that the Liquify feature can be used on people, objects, or abstract images. Create an image that you can use in your presentation.

1. Create a new Photoshop image with any dimensions.
2. Save the file as **Photoshop Presentation**.
3. Locate several pieces of artwork—either on your computer, in a royalty-free collection, or from scanned images. Remember that the images can show anything, but you want to demonstrate the flexibility of Photoshop and the range of your skills.
4. Select imagery from the artwork and move it into Photoshop Presentation.
5. Open the Liquify dialog box.
6. Display any size mesh in any color you find helpful.
7. Use the Freeze Mask tool and the brush size of your choice to isolate areas that you don't want to distort.
8. Use any distortion tool in any brush size of your choice to distort an area in the image.
9. Thaw the frozen areas.
10. Use any additional distortion techniques to modify the image.
11. Turn off the mesh, then click OK to close the Liquify dialog box.
12. Use any transformation skills to enhance the image.

13. Add any filter effects, if you decide they will make your image more dramatic. (In the sample, the Fresco filter was applied to the Abstract layer.)
14. Make any necessary color adjustments.
15. Add at least one type layer in any font available on your computer. (A Constantia Regular font is shown in the sample.)

16. Use your knowledge of special effects and the bounding box to enhance the type layer. (The following effects have been applied: Flag style warped text, Drop Shadow style, Bevel and Emboss style, and Stroke style.)
17. Save your work, then compare your image to the sample in Figure 24.

Figure 24 *Sample Portfolio Project*
© Photodisc/Getty Images

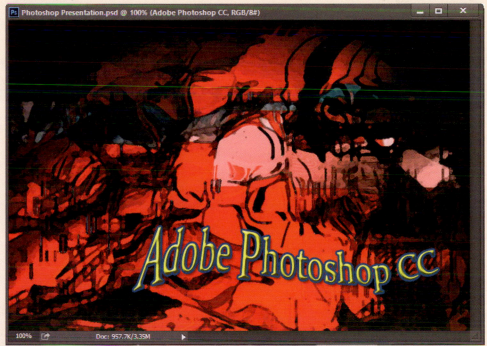

CHAPTER 15

PERFORMING
IMAGE SURGERY

1. Delete unnecessary imagery
2. Correct colors in an image
3. Tweak an image

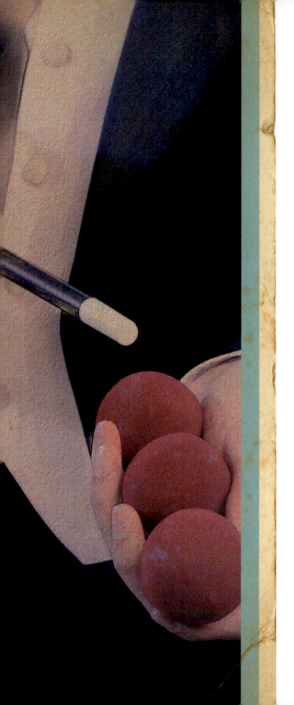

CHAPTER 15 PERFORMING IMAGE SURGERY

Understanding the Realities

By now you've realized that working with Photoshop is not always about creating cool effects and exciting images. Sometimes, your main task is problem solving. For example, you don't always have access to perfect images. If you did, you wouldn't need the arsenal of tools that Photoshop provides. Often, we find ourselves with images that need some "help." Perhaps the colors in an image are washed out, or maybe the image would be perfect except for one element that you don't want or need.

Assessing the Situation

In some situations, there may be many obvious ways to achieve the look you want in an image. A smart Photoshop user knows what tools are available, evaluates an image to see what is needed, and then decides which methods are best to fix the problem areas in the image.

Applying Knowledge and Making Decisions

People who can apply their Photoshop knowledge effectively are in demand in today's job market. The ability to assess which tools are needed in the first place is as much a part of Photoshop expertise as knowing how to use the tools. You can approach the same design problem in many ways; your job is to determine which approach to take in order to make an image look right. And it is up to you to determine what "right" is. By the time your image is finished, you may feel as if it has undergone major surgery.

QUICK TIP

Image surgery often goes unappreciated. You may spend a lot of time cleaning up edges and eliminating "dirt" and "smudges"—defects that often are noticeable in an image only when they've been neglected!

TOOLS YOU'LL USE

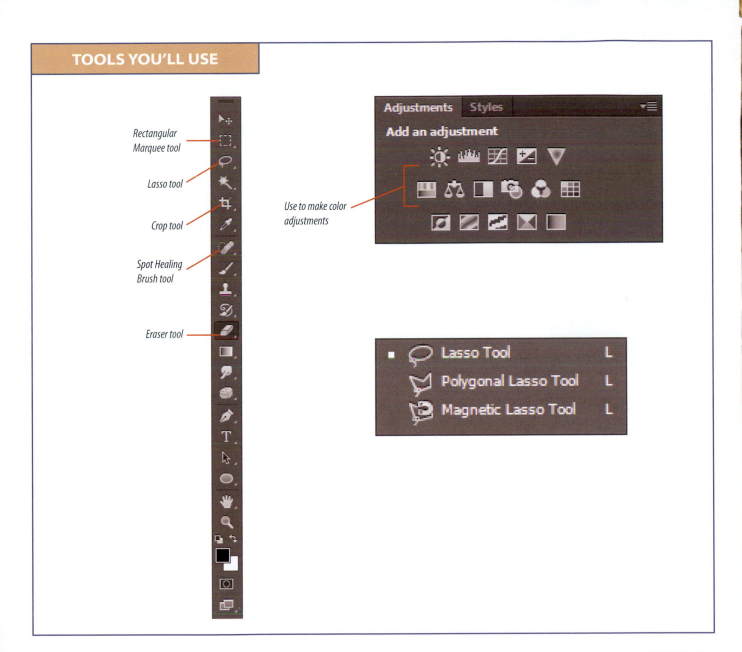

Rectangular Marquee tool

Lasso tool

Crop tool

Spot Healing Brush tool

Eraser tool

Adjustments   Styles

Add an adjustment

Use to make color adjustments

Lasso Tool   L

Polygonal Lasso Tool   L

Magnetic Lasso Tool   L

Delete
UNNECESSARY IMAGERY

What You'll Do

Source: Morguefile.

In this lesson, you'll use your skills and a variety of tools to conceal unwanted imagery. You'll also add a new layer from a selection.

Evaluating the Possibilities

Now that you have some experience creating and editing images, your assessment abilities have probably sharpened. You are more accustomed to deciding what imagery is useful for a particular project. You may also find that you've begun looking at images in terms of their potential usefulness for other projects. You might, for example, see a great element in one image and think, "That object has a crisp edge. I could isolate it using the Magnetic Lasso tool and use it for this other project."

QUICK TIP

Don't be surprised when a simple touch-up job that you thought would take a few minutes actually takes hours. Sometimes a seemingly simple effect is the one that requires the most work.

Performing Surgery

Removing unwanted imagery can be time-consuming and frustrating, but it can also be extremely gratifying (after you're finished). It's detailed, demanding, and sometimes complicated work. For example, Figures 1 and 2 show the same image *before* and *after* it underwent the following alterations:

- The .tif file was saved as a Photoshop .psd file.
- Selection tools were used to create separate layers for the background, the backdrop, and the candles.
- The candles layer was duplicated, as insurance—just in case it became necessary to start over. See the Layers panel in Figure 3.
- The backdrop color was changed from black to Dark Yellow Green.
- The candles on the left and right sides were eliminated using eraser tools.
- Extraneous "dirt" and "smudges" were eliminated using eraser tools.
- Contrast was added to the candles by using an adjustment layer.
- The Liquify feature was used to extend the individual flames and to smooth out the candleholder at the bottom of the image.
- The Noise filter was applied to the Backdrop layer, to give it more texture and dimension.

QUICK TIP

Developing critical thinking skills allows you to make decisions about images, such as discarding image information.

Understanding the Alternatives

Could these effects be achieved using other methods? Of course. For example, the bottom of the image was modified using the Forward Warp tool in the Liquify dialog box, but a similar effect could have been created using a painting tool such as the Smudge tool. The effect of the Noise filter could also have been created using the Grain filter. Using your Photoshop knowledge and skills, how many different ways can you think of to get the imagery from Figure 1 into what is shown in Figure 2? It's possible that you can create these effects in many ways. For example, you might want to use the Magnetic Lasso tool to select areas with clearly defined edges, and then zoom in and use the Eraser tool to clean up dirt and smudges. Or you just may decide to keep it simple and use the Rectangular Marquee tool to copy and paste pixels from one area to another.

Preparing for Surgery

Even if you think you've got it all figured out, sometimes your fixes do not go the way you planned. Doesn't it make sense to take the time to prepare for a worst-case scenario when using Photoshop? Of course. You can easily protect yourself against losing hours of work by building in some safety nets as you work. For example, you can duplicate your original image (or images) just in case things go awry. By creating a copy, you'll never have to complain that your original work was ruined. You can also save interim copies of your image at strategic stages of your work. Above all, make sure you plan your steps. To do this, perform a few trial runs on a practice image before starting on the *real* project. Until you get comfortable reading the states on the History panel, write down what steps you took and what settings you used. Careful planning will pay off.

Figure 1 *Original TIFF file*
© Photodisc/Getty Images

Figure 2 *Modified image*
© Photodisc/Getty Images

Flames extended using the Liquify feature's Warp tool

Noise filter added to new backdrop color to give texture

Eraser tool used to delete candles and eliminate smudges

Figure 3 *Layers panel of modified image*

Contrast applied using an Adjustment layer

Original Candles layer is hidden

Prepare the image for surgery

1. Open PS 15-1.jpg from the drive and folder where you store your Data Files.

2. Use the **Format list arrow** in the Save As dialog box to change the file from a JPEG to the **Photoshop (*.PSD, *.PDD)** (Win) or **Photoshop** (Mac) format, then save the file as **Street musicians.psd**.

3. Change the workspace to **Legacy** (created in Chapter 1).

4. Click **Layer** on the Menu bar, point to **New**, then click **Layer From Background**.

5. Type **Duo** in the Name text box.

6. Click the **Color list arrow** in the New Layer dialog box, click **Yellow**, then click **OK**.

7. Drag the **Duo layer** on the Layers panel to the **Create a new layer button** ⬚.

   A copy of the Duo layer (named Duo copy) is created. Compare your image and History and Layers panels to Figure 4.

8. Click the **Duo layer** on the Layers panel.

9. Click the **Indicates layer visibility button** 👁 on the **Duo copy layer** to hide the layer.

   Table 1 reviews some of the many possible selection methods you can use to remove unwanted imagery.

You saved a .JPEG in the Photoshop PSD format, converted a Background layer into an image layer, made a copy of the image layer, then hid the copy from view.

Figure 4 *Duplicated layer*
Source: Morguefile.

New file format

Copied layer

TABLE 1: IMAGE REMOVAL METHODS		
Tool	**Name**	**Method**
	Magnetic Lasso tool	Trace an object along its edge, then click Edit ➤ Clear.
	Magic Wand tool	Select by color, then click Edit ➤ Clear.
	Clone Stamp tool	Press and hold [Alt] (Win) or [option] (Mac), click sample area, release [Alt] (Win) or [option] (Mac), then click areas you want to remove.
	Rectangular Marquee tool	Select area, select Move tool, press and hold [Alt] (Win) or [option] (Mac), drag a copy of the selection to new location. (Without [Alt], the actual pixels in the selection are moved.)
	Elliptical Marquee tool	Select area, select Move tool, press and hold [Alt] (Win) or [option] (Mac), drag a copy of the selection to new location. (Without [Alt], the actual pixels in the selection are moved.)
	Eraser tool	Drag over pixels to be removed.
	Patch tool	Select source/destination, then drag to destination/source.
	Spot Healing Brush tool	Select brush size and type, select Content-Aware option, then click or paint over area.

Figure 5 *Selection in image*

Source: Morguefile.

Sample area

Figure 6 *Cleared selection*

Source: Morguefile.

Repaired area

1. Zoom in to the **vent** to the left of the statue's head until the zoom level is **100%**.

TIP Make sure the Resize Windows To Fit check box on the options bar is selected.

2. Click the **Clone Stamp tool** 🔳 on the Tools panel, change the brush type to **Hard Round**, the size to **30**, then sample the area (hold [Alt] (Win) or [option] (Mac) while positioning the pointer) just above the vent, as shown in Figure 5.

3. Click the area containing the **vent**.

4. Compare your image to Figure 6, then zoom out to **66.7%**.

TIP You can also cover a selection by clicking Edit on the Menu bar, then clicking Copy, which allows you to paste the selection elsewhere by clicking Edit on the Menu bar again, then clicking Paste.

You used the Zoom tool to get a closer look at an image, then used the Clone Stamp tool to eliminate unwanted imagery.

Create a layer from a selection and apply an Adjustment layer

1. Verify that the **Duo layer** is active.

2. Click the **Lasso tool** , change the Feather setting to 0 px if necesssary, then trace the dark triangular area of the man's poncho as shown in Figure 7.

3. Click **Layer** on the Menu bar, point to **New**, then click **Layer Via Copy**.

4. Apply an **Exposure Adjustment layer** (that is clipped to Layer 1), having an Exposure setting of **+1.21**, then collapse the Properties panel to the dock.

   Compare your screen to Figure 8.

5. Change the zoom level to **100**%, then display the **Essentials workspace**.

You made a selection which you turned into a layer, then applied an adjustment layer to it.

Figure 7 *Selected area*
Source: Morguefile.

Triangular selection

Figure 8 *Lightened area*
Source: Morguefile.

Enhanced pixels

DESIGN**TIP**

Fooling the Eye

You can fool the eye when you replace pixels in an image. Even if the replacement pixels are not completely accurate, the eye can be tricked into thinking that the image looks reasonable. For example, you can duplicate ground and sky pixels, and most viewers will accept them as looking "right." However, the reverse is not necessarily true. If you remove something from an image but leave some pixels behind, viewers are likely to think that something is wrong. For example, if you erase the figure of a woman from an image, but you neglect to eliminate all the pixels for the woman's hair, the reader's eye would probably recognize the incongruity. Remnants of dangling hair would almost certainly bring into question the accuracy of the image.

Figure 9 *Image with new layer*

Source: Morguefile.

Layer created
from selection

Correcting Color

You can make color corrections on a layer in a number of ways. One option is to make your corrections directly on the original layer. Another option is to make a copy of the original layer *before* making the corrections on the layer. You can also make your corrections using adjustment layers, and then merge the layers down when you are satisfied with the results. You can add an adjustment layer to the current layer by clicking Layer on the Menu bar, pointing to New Adjustment Layer, and then clicking the type of adjustment you want to make, or by clicking a preset button on the Adjustments panel.

Correct Colors
IN AN IMAGE

What You'll Do

Source: Morguefile.

In this lesson, you'll make color adjustments to a specific layer.

Revitalizing an Image

You may find that you are working with an image that looks fine except that it seems washed out or just leaves you in the doldrums. You may be able to spice up such an image by adjusting the color settings. By modifying the color balance, for example, you can increase the red tones while decreasing the green and blue tones to make the image look more realistic and dramatic. After you select the layer that you want to adjust, you can make color-correcting adjustments by displaying the Adjustments panel, and then clicking the type of color adjustment you want to make.

Making Color Adjustments

So, the image you're working with seems to need *something*, but you're not quite sure what. Until you become comfortable making color corrections, do everything in your power to provide yourself with a safety net.

Create duplicate layers and use adjustment layers instead of making corrections directly on the original layer. Before you begin, take a long look at the image and ask yourself, "What's lacking?" Is the problem composition or a color problem? Do the colors appear washed out rather than vibrant and true to life? Does the image's appearance support the message you're trying to convey?

Assessing the Mood

Color can be a big factor in establishing mood in an image. For example, if you are trying to create a sad mood, increasing the blue and green tones may be more effective than modifying specific imagery. If you decide that your image does need color correction, start slowly. Try balancing the color and see if that gives you the effect you want. Keep experimenting with the various color correction options until you find the method that works for you.

Figure 10 *Hue/Saturation Properties panel*

Figure 11 *Brightness/Contrast Properties panel*

Figure 12 *Color corrected image*

Source: Morguefile.

Figure 13 *Layers panel*

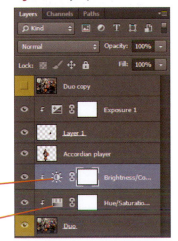

Brightness/Contrast
adjustment layer

Hue/Saturation
adjustment layer

Correct colors

1. Make the **Duo layer** active.
2. Click the **Hue/Saturation button** on the Adjustments panel.
3. Click the **This adjustment affects all layers below (click to clip to layer) button** on the Properties panel.
4. Change the settings in the Hue/Saturation Properties panel so that they match those shown in Figure 10, then collapse the Properties panel to the dock.
5. Click the **Brightness/Contrast button** on the Adjustments panel.
6. Click on the Properties panel.
7. Change the settings so that they match those shown in Figure 11, then collapse the Properties panel to the dock.
8. Save your work, then compare your image to Figure 12 and your Layers panel to Figure 13.

You adjusted the hue/saturation and brightness/contrast in the Duo layer, making the image of the accordion player stand out. You made color adjustments using adjustment layers, which you clipped to the Duo layer.

Tweak
AN IMAGE

What You'll Do

Source: Morguefile.

 In this lesson, you'll crop out unnecessary imagery. You'll also add layer styles to enhance the image and draw attention away from the background.

Evaluating What's Next

Every image has its own unique problems, and you'll probably run into a few final challenges when coordinating an image to work with other elements in a final publication or finished product. The last step in preparing an image for production is to decide what final fixes are necessary so that it serves its intended purpose.

Cropping an Image

Sometimes an image contains more content than is necessary. In the image of the accordion player, there's too much distracting imagery. Of course, *you* have to determine the central focus of the image and what it is you want the reader to see. Is the subject of the image the accordion player or both of the street musicians? If your image suffers from too much of the wrong imagery, you can help your reader by getting rid of the unnecessary and distracting imagery.

Determine the appearance of the grid

Figure 14 *Crop tool options bar*

Additional crop options

Click to set additional crop options

This type of deletion not only removes imagery, but changes the size and shape of the image. You can make this type of change using the Crop tool on the Tools panel. When you make a selection within an image, you can use cropped area settings (the Enable Crop Shield check box and the Opacity list arrow) on the options bar to see how the image will appear after it has been cropped. Figure 14 shows the Crop tool options bar with a crop area drawn.

When you click and drag the Crop tool over an area of an image, a grid appears over the selected area using the Rule of Thirds (by default). The **Rule of Thirds** divides an image vertically and horizontally into 3 parts. The intersections of the horizontal and vertical gridlines are compositional options for placing objects.

QUICK **TIP**

What's important about the Rule of Thirds is that it tells us that the best way to add interest to an image is to position objects of interest not in the center of the image, but off to the side.

Resizing versus Resampling

Sometimes the terms resizing and resampling are often confused. **Resizing** an image means that the dimensions of the image are changed, whereas **resampling** an image means that the numbers of pixels within the image are changed.

- Image Resizing: Changing the size the image will print without changing the number of pixels in the image.
- Image Resampling: Changing the number of pixels in the image.

Cropping and Resampling

Resampling and cropping both change the number of pixels in an image. Cropping always reduces the number of pixels, while resampling can increase the number of pixels. Increasing the number of pixels is called resampling up or **upsampling**; decreasing the number of pixels is called **downsampling**. While upsampling can sometimes result in an improved image, it can also result in poorer image quality because you're either increasing the size of each pixel or you're adding new pixels and your computer has to guess. **Intelligent upsampling** is an enhancement that preserves detail and sharpness while enlarging images for different print sizes.

Image Resampling and Interpolation

If you have an image that needs to be resized (either larger or smaller), you'll want to change the size without compromising the appearance of the image. You can change the image size by clicking Image on the Menu bar, and then clicking Image Size. Sure, the dimensions of the image need to change, but what really needs to happen is you need to alter the number of pixels in the image. You can do this by selecting the Resample check box.

When you select the Resample check box, the resampling process involves recalculating the individual pixel values rather than, in the case of reducing the image size by 50 percent, just throwing out every other pixel.

This resampling recalculation takes place in a number of ways that are called **interpolation methods**. Each interpolation method determines how pixels are added or deleted; each produces different results and has its own advantages and disadvantages. Table 2 below illustrates the various interpolation methods. Nearest Neighbor and Bilinear are best used for images for the web; Bicubic, Automatic, Bicubic Smoother, and Bicubic Sharper are best used for print images.

TABLE 2: INTERPOLATION METHODS		
Interpolation method	**Process**	**Advantages/Disadvantages**
Preserve Detaiils (enlargement)	Pixels are added more exactly while keeping sharp edges.	Preserves the edges of an image. Offers a Noise reduction slider for smoothing noise as you upscale.
Nearest Neighbor (hard edges)	The simplest process, used with illustrations containing edges that are not anti-aliased to preserve hard edges and produce a smaller file. A new bitmap grid is created over the original image and the closest pixel value from the original grid is given to the new coordinates.	Colors are unchanged from the original image. Coordinates rarely match directly so images can become jagged, or pixelized. Fast, but less precise, and can produce jagged results.
Bilinear	Similar to Nearest Neighbor, but averages values of four surrounding pixels, rather than just using the nearest pixel value. Produces medium-quality results.	Image is less likely to look jagged, but colors are likely to shift due to averaging.
Bicubic (smooth gradients)	The most advanced and accurate interpolation method, averaging 16 surrounding pixel values. Produces smoother tonal gradations than Nearest Neighbor or Bilinear.	Keeps more accurate tonal values, but a slower process. Used by most printer drivers.
Bicubic Smoother (enlargement)	Based on the bicubic method, but produces smoother results.	Best used for enlarging images.
Bicubic Sharper (reduction)	Based on the bicubic method, with enhanced sharpening.	Best used for reducing images. Maintains detail.
Automatic	Default interpolation method.	Sharpens more heavily than other methods.

© 2015 Cengage Learning®

Crop the image

1. Display the rulers in pixels.

2. Click the **Crop tool**  on the Tools panel.

   TIP You can also crop with perspective using the Perspective Crop tool (grouped with the Crop tool, Slice tool, and Slice Select tool). This tool makes it possible to crop while considering changing perspective.

3. Drag the **Crop pointer** from **250 X/50 Y** to **700 X/750 Y**, adjusting the crop handles if necessary so the top of the image is at **50 Y**, the right edge of the image ends at **700 X**, and the left edge of the image is at **250 X**.

   The area that will be cropped from the image appears darker, as shown in Figure 15.

4. Verify that the Delete Cropped Pixels check box is *not* selected, then click the **Commit current crop operation button** on the options bar.

   The cropped imagery is no longer visible.

   TIP You can use the Straighten feature on the Crop tool options bar to straighten an image. You can also use the Ruler tool to straighten an image by dragging a horizontal or vertical line on an object, then clicking Straighten on the options bar.

5. Hide the rulers, then resize the image with a zoom level of **100%** if necessary.

You cropped the image.

Figure 15 *Cropped area in image*
Source: Morguefile.

Shielded area will be hidden during cropping

Crop handles

New boundaries

Preview and Crop Box

When the Crop tool is selected, the crop box is automatically set to the perimeter of the active image. You can determine the crop dimensions by dragging the edges of the image. The actual image can be rotated during the cropping process by dragging *outside* the crop box: the canvas automatically expands and the crop box shrinks to fit in the image. Click outside the crop box to go into Crop mode.

While the Crop tool is active, you can change the aspect ratio by clicking the Ratio button from the options bar. (The default selection is Unconstrained.) You can also use the Ratio button to save a preset.

Figure 16 *Completed image*

Source: Morguefile.

Figure 17 *Layers panel for completed image*

Styles
applied
to layer

1. Click the **Accordion player layer** on the Layers panel, then click the **Add a layer style button** *fx* on the Layers panel.

2. Click **Bevel & Emboss**, click the **Drop Shadow check box,** accept the existing settings, then click **OK**.

3. Save your work, then compare your image to Figure 16 and your Layers panel to Figure 17.

4. Close the image file and exit Photoshop.

You applied the Bevel and Emboss and Drop Shadow styles to the layer created from a selection.

Rotate and Pan and Zoom a Canvas

Perhaps you need to rotate an image from its current axis in order to paint or draw on it. If this is the case, and you have an OpenGL enabled document window, you can click the Rotate View tool on the Tools panel (grouped with the Hand tool), and then drag any corner of the image. The Rotate View tool allows you to rotate a canvas *non-destructively*: it does not transform the image. As you drag, a compass displays in the center of the image which indicates how much rotation you have added to the original image. (The amount of rotation is also shown in the Rotation Angle text box in the options bar.) You can use the **pan and zoom feature** if you have a graphics card and your computer has OpenGL enabled (in Preferences). You can use the scrubby zoom feature to quickly zoom in and out by clicking and holding the Zoom pointer on the canvas without loss of resolution. You can pan by holding the [spacebar] while pressing the Zoom pointer. If this feature is available on your computer, you'll see the Scrubby Zoom check box on the options bar when the Zoom tool is selected.

POWER USER SHORTCUTS

To do this:	Use this method:	To do this:	Use this method:
Add layer style	*fx*, click style(s)	Duplicate a layer	Drag layer to ▢
Clear selection	[Delete] (Win) or [delete] (Mac)	Duplicate a selection and move it to a new location	▢ or ◯ or **M**, create selection, press and hold [Ctrl][Alt] (Win) or ⌘ [option] (Mac), then drag selection to new location
Clone an area	▣ or **S**, press and hold [Alt] (Win) or [option] (Mac), click sample area, release [Alt] (Win) or [option] (Mac), then click areas you want cloned	Erase pixels	▨ or **E**, drag pointer over pixels to be removed
Create an adjustment layer	Layer ➤ New Adjustment Layer ➤ type of adjustment	Magnify an area	🔍 or **Z**, then click image
Create a layer from selection	[Ctrl][J] (Win) or ⌘ [J] (Mac)	Paste selection	Edit ➤ Paste or [Ctrl][V] (Win) or ⌘ [V] (Mac)
Crop an image	▣	Select a complex object	▣ or **L**, or ▨ or **W**
Cut selection	Edit ➤ Cut or [Ctrl][X] (Win) or ⌘ [X] (Mac)	Select and delete by color	✦ or **W**, then click Edit ➤ Clear
Deselect selection	Select ➤ Deselect or [Ctrl][D] (Win) or ⌘ [D] (Mac)		

Key: Menu items are indicated by ➤ between the menu name and its command. Blue bold letters are shortcuts for selecting tools on the Tools panel.

Delete unnecessary imagery.

1. Open PS 15-2.psd from the drive and folder where you store your Data Files, then save it as **Paradise Lost**.
2. Zoom in on the metronome in the Toy Boat layer.
3. Use the tool of your choice to select as much of the metronome as possible without selecting the toy boat or telephone. (*Hint*: You can use the Add to selection button on the options bar to alter your selection or you can make multiple selections.)
4. Clear the metronome selection from the image.
5. Deselect the selection.
6. Use the Eraser tool and any size brush tip to get rid of any remaining metronome pixels.
7. Create a selection around the telephone and its cord using the tool of your choice. (*Hint*: You can use multiple selections to select this object.)
8. Clear the selection.
9. Deselect the selection.
10. Use the Eraser tool and any size brush tip to get rid of any remaining telephone pixels.
11. Sample the red color of the toy boat image near the damaged area on the hull of the boat.
12. Use the Brush tool and any size brush tip to repair the damaged toy boat (where the telephone was removed).
13. Zoom out to the original magnification.
14. Save your work.

Correct colors in an image.

1. Make the Whistle layer active and visible.
2. Create a Color Balance adjustment layer that is clipped to the Whistle layer.

3. Correct the Cyan/Red level to +73, and the Magenta/Green level to −57.
4. Create a Brightness/Contrast adjustment layer that is clipped to the previous layer.
5. Change the Brightness slider to −10 and the Contrast slider to +15.
6. Use the bounding box feature to rotate the whistle, nudge the object up using the sample in Figure 18 as a guide, then commit the changes.
7. Make the Toy Boat layer active.
8. Create a Hue/Saturation adjustment layer that is clipped to the Toy Boat layer.
9. Change the Hue slider to +45 and the Saturation slider to +60.
10. Save your work.

Tweak an image.

1. Hide the Background layer.
2. Make the Push Pins layer active.
3. Use the tool of your choice, such as the Clone Stamp tool or the Magnetic Lasso tool and the Patch tool, to remove the two shadows above and below the whistle (cast by the green push pin behind the whistle) using Figure 18 as a guide. (*Hint*: You can magnify the area, if necessary.)
4. Apply the Ocean Ripple (Distort category in the Filter Gallery) filter using the following settings: Ripple Size = 3, Ripple Magnitude = 6.
5. Display the Background layer.
6. Change the opacity of the Push Pins layer to 60%.
7. Apply the Drop Shadow style to the Toy Boat layer using the default settings.

8. Make the Push Pins layer active. (*Hint*: you can rearrange the layers to work more efficiently.)
9. Use the Horizontal Type tool to create a red type layer in the upper-right corner of the image that says **Paradise Lost**. (In the sample, a 72-point Rage Italic Regular font is used.)
10. Center the text on the type layer, adjust the baseline shift of the P and L characters to -12.24. (*Hint*: You can kern this type if you choose.)
11. Add the following styles to the type: Drop Shadow, Stroke (using RGB Red), and Bevel and Emboss.
12. Save your work, then compare your image to the sample in Figure 18.

Figure 18 *Completed Skills Review*
© Photodisc/Getty Images

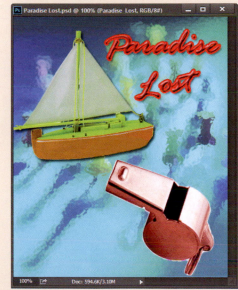

An exclusive women's clothing shop, First Class Woman, has hired you to revamp its image by creating the first in a series of print advertisements. First Class Woman has been known for some time as a stuffy clothing store that sells pricey designer originals to the over-60 set. The time has come to expand its customer base to include women between the ages of 30 and 60. Their advertising agency recommended you, having seen samples of your work. They want you to inject some humor into your creation. They have provided you with some product images they want to see in the ad.

1. Open PS 15-3.psd, then save it as **First Class Woman**.
2. Separate each of the items in the Glasses, Necklace, Bags layer into their own layers. (*Hint*: You can use the selection method(s) of your choice.)
3. Rename the layers using appropriate names.
4. Color-code each renamed layer on the Layers panel.
5. Rearrange the objects as you see fit.
6. Turn on the Show Transform Controls feature. Use a bounding box to resize the glasses, bags, or necklace, if you choose.
7. Make the Fan layer active and visible, then transform the size of the fan so it is smaller. (*Hint*: Click Edit on the Menu bar, point to Transform, then use the Scale command.)
8. Make a duplicate of the Glasses layer, accepting the default name.
9. Hide the original Glasses layer.

10. Use the Liquify feature on the duplicate Glasses layer using your choice of effects.
11. Add at least one adjustment layer, as you feel necessary. (*Hint*: In the sample, the Brightness was applied to the Bags layer and adjusted to −8, and the Contrast was adjusted to +35. In the Necklace layer, the following color balance adjustments were made: Cyan/Red level to +53, the Magenta/Green level to −65, and the Yellow/Blue level to −49. In the Roses layer, the Brightness was adjusted to −55, and the Contrast to −1.)
12. Add a type layer that says **First Class Woman**. (*Hint*: You can use any color and any font available on your computer. In the sample, a 60 pt Pristina Regular font is shown.)
13. Warp the type layer using the style and the settings of your choice.
14. Apply the styles of your choice to the text.
15. Display the Roses layer, then adjust the opacity of the Roses layer using any setting you feel is appropriate.
16. Add any filter effects you want. (In the sample, the Smudge Stick filter is applied to the Roses layer, and the Lens Flare filter is applied to the Glasses copy layer.)
17. Save your work, then compare your image to the sample in Figure 19.

Figure 19 *Sample Project Builder 1*
© Photodisc/Getty Images

Your local chamber of commerce has asked you to volunteer your services and design a new advertisement for the upcoming membership drive. The theme of this year's membership drive is "The Keys to the City." They have supplied you with an initial image, but the rest is up to you.

1. Open PS 15-4.psd, then save it as **Membership Drive**.
2. Convert the Background layer into an image layer.
3. Rename the layer using any name you want, then color-code the layer.
4. Create a new layer, then convert it into a Background layer.
5. Locate at least one piece of appropriate artwork— either a scanned image, an image on your computer, one from a digital camera, or an image from a royalty-free collection—that you can use in this image.
6. Use any appropriate methods to select imagery from the artwork.
7. After the selections have been made, copy them into the Membership Drive image.
8. Transform any imagery you feel will improve the finished product.
9. Use any method to eliminate some of the keys in the image. (In the sample, the third key from the bottom is eliminated.)
10. Add a type layer using the text and style of your choice to create a catch phrase for the ad. (*Hint*: You can use any color and any font available on your computer. In the sample, a Perpetua Regular font in various sizes is shown.)
11. Add another type layer that contains the chamber of commerce name. (*Hint*: You can use the name of the town in which you live.)
12. Add additional type layers, if desired.
13. Add an adjustment layer or layer effect to at least one of the layers.
14. Modify the layer containing the keys using any method(s) you want. (In the sample, the Opacity is lowered to 86%, and the Tiles filter is applied.)
15. Save your work, then compare your image to the sample in Figure 20.

Figure 20 *Sample Project Builder 2*
© Photodisc/Getty Images

You have seen how you can use Photoshop to take ordinary photographs and manipulate them into exciting artistic creations. You can use the web to find imagery created by many new and exciting artists who specialize in photo manipulation. To broaden your understanding of Photoshop, you decide to closely examine an artistic work, and then *deconstruct it* to speculate as to how it was accomplished.

1. Connect to the Internet and use your browser to find digital artwork. (Make a record of the site you found so you can use it for future reference.)
2. Click the links for the images until you find one that strikes you as interesting. A sample image is shown in Figure 21.
3. Examine the image, then ask yourself the following questions:
   - What images would you need to create this image? In what format would you need them (electronic file, hard-copy image, or photograph)?
   - What techniques would you use to create this effect?
   - Do you like this image? If so, why?
4. Using your favorite word processor, create a document called **Digital Art Analysis** that records your observations.
5. Be prepared to discuss your answers to these questions in a group discussion or in a presentation format.

Figure 21 *Sample Design Project*
Source: Morguefile.

Final Project¶
Digital·Art·Analysis¶

¶
This·image·was· created·by·artist· Clarita·and·was· located·on·the· morguefile.com· Web·site.·¶
        The· imagery·is· instantly· recognizable·in·terms·of·its·actual·origin,·yet·it·has·been·turned·into·line·art.·To·create· this·effect,·the·images·would·need·to·be·in·electronic·form.·If·this·is·not·possible,·any· photograph·or·paper·copy·images·could·be·scanned·and·then·manipulated·in·Photoshop.·¶

        The·following·imagery·would·be·needed·to·reconstruct·the·displayed·image:·an· open·eye,·glasses·(if·the·image·of·the·eye·did·not·have·the·glasses·already),·and·assorted· shapes·and·shadows.·Using·different·layers,·the·artist·probably·used·different·filters·to· provide·texture·and·various·adjustment·layers·to·change·the·colors·and·saturation.¶

        I·think·this·artwork·effectively·shows·how·Photoshop·can·be·used·to·manipulate· images·in·a·creative·fashion.·I·like·the·image·very·much.¶

You are about to graduate from The San Antonio Art League, a local, independent institution that trains artists in the use of all art media. Because of your talent, you have been asked to create next year's poster for the school.

1. Develop a design concept for the poster.
2. Create a new Photoshop image with your choice of dimensions.
3. Save this file as **Art School Poster**.
4. Locate several pieces of artwork—either on your hard disk, in a royalty-free collection, from a digital camera, or from scanned images. The images can show anything that is art-related and can be part of other images.
5. Create a layer for each image, then name each layer and color-code each layer.
6. Transform any imagery you feel will enhance the design.
7. Add a type layer using a style and color of your choosing that contains a phrase you like. (*Hint*: You can use any font available on your computer. A Papyrus font in various sizes is used in the sample.)
8. Add an adjustment layer to at least one of the layers.
9. Add any filter effects, if you decide they will make your image more dramatic.
10. Save your work, then compare your image to the sample in Figure 22.

Figure 22 *Sample Portfolio Project*
Source: Morguefile.

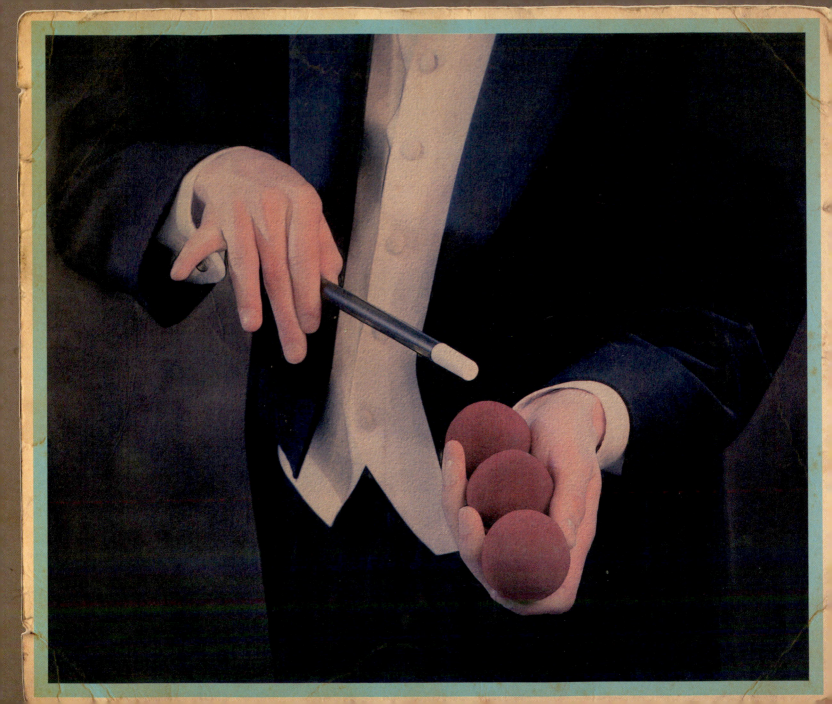

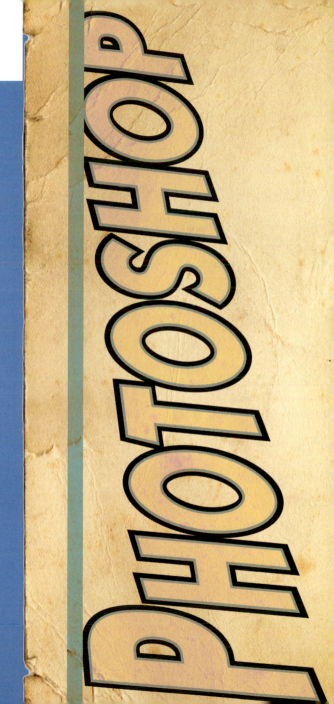

CHAPTER 16

ANNOTATING AND AUTOMATING
AN IMAGE

1. Add annotations to an image

2. Create an action

3. Modify an action

4. Use a default action and create a droplet

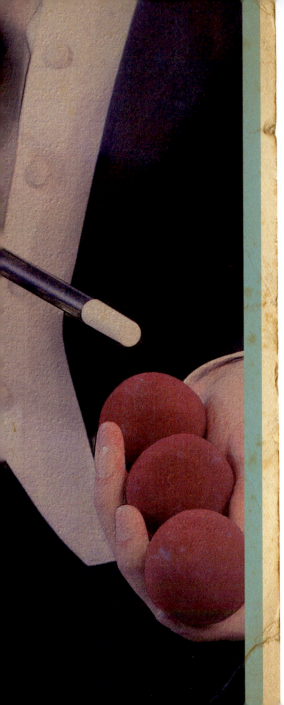

ANNOTATING AND AUTOMATING
AN IMAGE

Creating Notes

Have you ever wished you could paste a sticky note on an image, to jot down an idea or include a message to someone who will be reviewing the design? Well, in Photoshop you can, using notes.

Communicating Directly to Your Audience

By creating written notes, you can communicate directly to anyone viewing your image. You can place written comments—electronic sticky notes—right in the file. Once a note is in place, anyone opening your image in Photoshop can double-click the note icon and read your comments.

Using Automation

Have you ever performed a repetitive task in Photoshop? Suppose you create an image with several type layers containing different fonts, and then you decide that each of

those type layers should use the same font family. To make this change, you would have to perform the following steps on each type layer:

- Select the layer.
- Double-click the layer thumbnail.
- Click the Set the font family list arrow.
- Click the font you want.
- Click the Commit any current edits button.

Wouldn't it be nice if there was a way to speed up commonly performed tasks like this one? That's where automation, courtesy of the Actions feature, comes in. Using this feature you can record these five steps as one action. Then, rather than having to repeat each of the steps, you just play the action.

QUICK TIP

Many programs have a feature that records and then can play back repetitive tasks. Other programs call this feature a macro, script, or behavior.

TOOLS YOU'LL USE

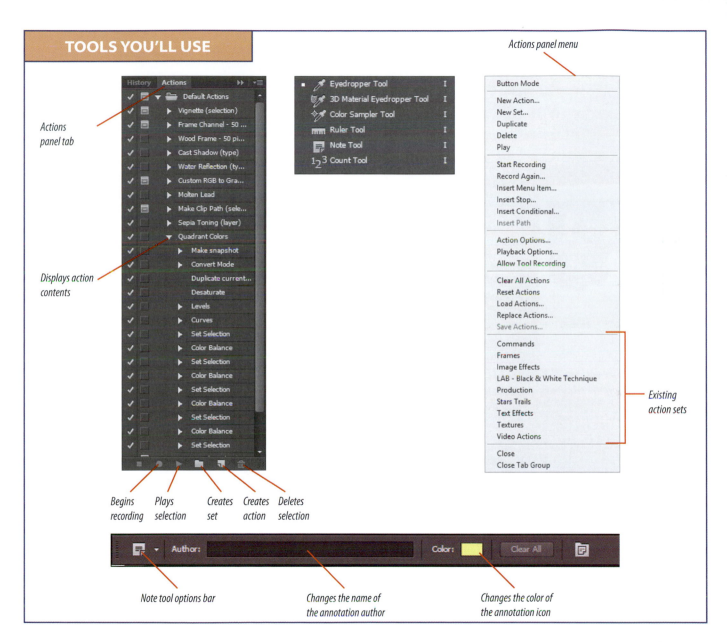

Actions panel tab

Displays action contents

Actions panel menu

Begins recording

Plays selection

Creates set

Creates action

Deletes selection

Existing action sets

Note tool options bar

Changes the name of the annotation author

Changes the color of the annotation icon

Add Annotations
TO AN IMAGE

What You'll Do

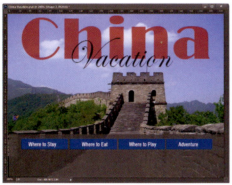

Source: Morguefile

In this lesson, you'll create two notes and delete a note.

Creating an Annotation

Annotations are similar to the yellow sticky notes you might attach to a printout. You can create an annotation by clicking the Note tool on the Tools panel (found in the Eyedropper group), clicking the image where you want the note to appear, and then typing the contents. Each note within a file has an icon that appears on the image in the document window, as shown in Figure 1, while the contents of the note displays in the Notes panel.

Reading Notes

To open a closed note, double-click the note icon. You can also right-click (Win) or [control]-click (Mac) the note icon, and then click Open Note, as shown in Figure 1. You can move the note within the image by dragging the note's icon.

> **QUICK TIP**
>
> You can differentiate between active and inactive notes by the appearance of the note icons. The icon of an inactive note has a solid color, while the icon of an active note displays a pencil.

Using the Notes Panel

The contents of a note displays in the Notes panel, which is grouped with the Layer Comps panel and can be opened by double-clicking an existing note icon, clicking the Show or hide the notes panel button on the Note tool options bar, or clicking Notes on the Window menu. Scroll bars display in the Notes panel if the contents exceed the window display, although you can resize the Notes panel by dragging any of the edges to the desired dimension. The status bar (at the bottom of the Notes panel) contains previous and next arrows that let you navigate all the notes within an image, a counter to tell you which note is currently active, and a trash can icon that lets you delete the active note.

> **QUICK TIP**
>
> You can delete a selected note by clicking the Delete note button in the Notes panel, pressing [Delete], or by right-clicking the note (Win) or [control]-clicking the note (Mac), and then clicking Delete Note.

Personalizing a Note

By default, the note icon is a pale yellow color. You can change this color by clicking the Note color box on the options bar. When the Color Picker (Note Color) dialog box opens, you can use any method to change the color, such as sampling an area within an existing image. You can also change the existing author of the note by selecting the contents in the Name of note by selecting the contents in the Name of author for notes text box on the options bar, typing the information you want, and then pressing [Enter] (Win) or [return] (Mac).

Figure 1 *Open note in an image*

Name of author appears here

Click to delete note

View previous note

View next note

Total notes

Solid color indicates closed notes

Create a note

1. Open PS 16-1.psd from the drive and folder where you store your Data Files, update the text layers (if necessary), then save the file as **China Vacation**.

2. Magnify the image so the zoom factor is **200%**, display the **Essentials workspace**, then turn off any displayed guides (if necessary).

3. Click the **Note tool** 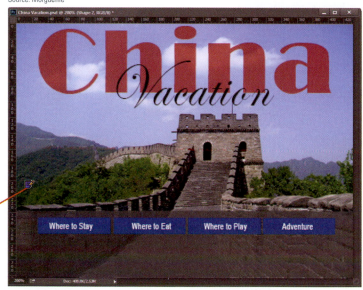 on the Tools panel.

TIP The Note tool is grouped with the Eyedropper tool.

4. Click the **Note color** ▭ on the options bar, click **RGB Blue** (the fifth swatch from the left in the first row) on the Swatches panel, then click **OK** to close the Color Picker (Note Color) dialog box.

5. If your name does not appear in the Name of author for notes text box on the options bar, select the contents of the text box, type **Your Name**, press [**Enter**] (Win) or [**return**] (Mac), then compare your options bar to Figure 2.

   The Note color is blue.

6. Display the rulers in pixels, then click the trees above the far-left button at approximately **10 X/200 Y**.

7. Type the text in the Notes panel as shown in Figure 3.

8. Click the **Show or hide the notes panel button** ▤ in the Note tool options bar, then compare your image to Figure 4.

You used the Note tool to create a note within an image. You specified an author for the note, and you changed the color of the note icon using the Swatches panel. Notes are a great way to transmit information about an image.

Figure 2 *Options for the Note tool*

Your name will display here

Click to display/hide the Notes panel

Figure 3 *Text in Notes panel*

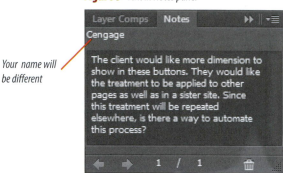

Your name will be different

Figure 4 *Note icon*
Source: Morguefile

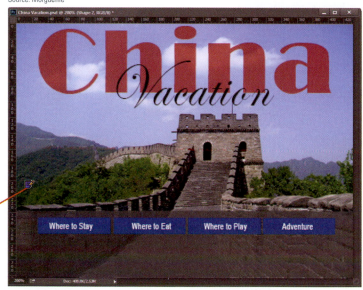

Note icon

Figure 5 *Notes panel contents*

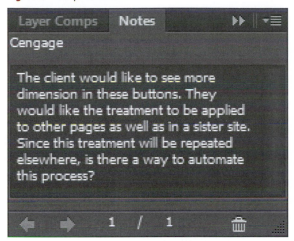

Figure 6 *Note icon in image*
Source: Morguefile

1. Click the **Show or hide the notes panel button** in the Note tool options bar.

TIP You can also expand/collapse the Notes panel using the dock.

2. Click to the **left of 'more'** in the first line of the note, type **to see**, select **to show (and its trailing space)**, then press [**Delete**].
   Compare your note to Figure 5.

3. Click the **Note tool pointer** on the image beneath the 'h' in China.

4. Type **The client may want to use another image for the next advertising cycle**.

5. Click the **Select previous note button**.
   The first note displays in the Notes panel.

6. Click the **Select next note button** in the Notes panel.

7. Click the **Delete note button** in the Notes panel, then click **Yes** to delete the note.
   One note remains in the image.

8. Click to close the Notes panel, compare your image to Figure 6, then save your work.

You modified an existing note, added a new note, viewed each of the notes using buttons in the Notes panel, then deleted the second note.

Create an
ACTION

What You'll Do

Source: Morguefile

In this lesson, you'll create an action that applies a style to a layer by first creating a snapshot that is used to restore your file to its original condition, and then recording steps using the Actions panel.

Simplifying Common Tasks

Suppose you are responsible for maintaining the ad slicks for all your company's products (and there are a lot of them). What would you do if the company decided to change their image designs so that each existing product advertisement is shown with Drop Shadow and Inner Shadow styles? (Resigning your position is *not* an option.) Instead, you can create an action to speed up this monumental task. (You can also create an action to record menu items that don't have keyboard shortcuts.)

Understanding Actions

Most tasks that you perform using a button or menu command can be recorded as an **action**. Each action can contain one or more steps and can also contain a **stop**, which lets you complete a command that can't be recorded (for example, the use of a painting tool). Actions can be stored in sets, which are saved as .atn files and are typically named by the category of actions they contain. For example, you can create multiple type-related actions, and then store them in a set named Type Actions. You access actions from the Actions panel, which is grouped with the History panel. You can view actions in list mode or in Button Mode on the Actions panel. The **List mode** (the default) makes it possible to view the details within each action. The **Button Mode** displays each action without details. You can toggle between Button and list mode using the Action panel options button.

> **QUICK TIP**
> The act of creating an action is not recorded on the History panel; however, the steps you record to define a new action are recorded on the History panel.

Knowing Your Options

You use commonly recognizable media player buttons to operate an action. These buttons are located at the bottom of the Actions panel and let you play, record and stop, as well as move forward and backward in an action.

> **QUICK TIP**
> The Actions panel displays on the icon dock in the Motion and Photography workspaces.

Recording an Action

When recording is active, the Begin recording button on the Actions panel appears red. The action set also opens as soon as you begin recording to show all the individual actions in the set.

Playing Back Actions

You can modify how actions are played back using the Playback Options dialog box, as shown in Figure 7. The playback options are described in Table 1. You can open the Playback Options dialog box by clicking the Actions Panel options button, and then clicking Playback Options. The Accelerated, Step by Step, and Pause For options control the speed at which the steps are performed.

Figure 7 *Playback Options dialog box*

TABLE 1: ACTION PLAYBACK OPTIONS	
Option	**Description**
Accelerated	Plays all steps within an action, then makes all changes.
Step by Step	Completes each step in an action and redraws the image before advancing to the next step.
Pause For	Lets you specify the number of seconds that should occur between steps in an action.

© 2013 Cengage Learning®

Create an action

1. Display the **Motion workspace**, click the **History button**  on the dock to expand the History panel, then click the **Create new snapshot button** .

   TIP By default, the History and Actions panels window is small. You can enlarge it by dragging the bottom edge.

2. Change the zoom level to **100%**, drag the **History tab** out of the Actions panel group so it displays separately to the left of the Actions panel, then rearrange the History and Actions panels so both are visible.

3. Verify that the **expand triangle** to the left of the Default Actions set on the Actions panel is facing to the right (collapsed) and that the set is closed. Compare your panel to Figure 8.

   You can click the expand triangle next to a set to show or hide the actions in it. You can also click the expand triangle next to an action to show or hide the steps in it.

   TIP When you create an action in the Default Actions set, or in any set, the action is available in all your Photoshop images.

4. Click the **Create new action button**  on the Actions panel. The New Action dialog box opens, then type **Button Drop Shadow** in the Name text box.

5. Click the **Color list arrow**, click **Yellow**, then compare your dialog box to Figure 9.

6. Click **Record**. Did you notice that the Begin recording button is displayed in red on the Actions panel and all default actions are opened? See Figure 10.

You created a snapshot to make it possible to easily test the new action. You used the Create new action button on the Actions panel to create an action called Button Drop Shadow.

Figure 8 *Actions panel with detail hidden*

Figure 9 *New Action dialog box*

Displays action detail

Creates an action

Figure 10 *New action*

The location of the action in the list might be different

Indicates recording in progress

Figure 11 *Layer Style dialog box*

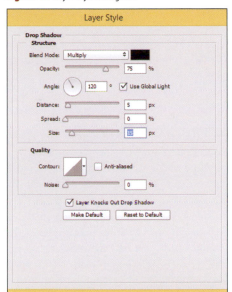

Figure 12 *Selected action*

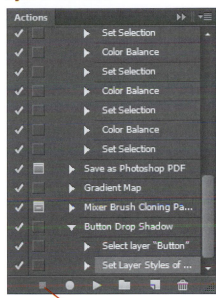

Stop playing/
recording button

Figure 13 *Modified image*

Source: Morguefile

Drop shadow
behind buttons

Record an action

1. Click the **Button layer** on the Layers panel.
2. Click the **Add a layer style button** *fx* on the Layers panel, click **Drop Shadow**, then change your Layer Style dialog box settings so they match those shown in Figure 11.
3. Click **OK**.
4. Click the **Stop playing/recording button** on the Actions panel. See Figure 12.
5. Click the **History panel**, scroll to the top (if necessary), then click **Snapshot 1**.

   The Button layer returns to its original appearance.
6. Click the **Button Drop Shadow action** in the Actions panel, then click the **Play selection button** on the Actions panel.
7. Compare your screen to Figure 13, then save your work.

You recorded steps for the Button Drop Shadow action. After the recording was complete, you used a snapshot to restore the image to its original state, then you played the action to test it. Testing is an important step in creating an action.

Modify an
ACTION

What You'll Do

Source: Morguefile

 In this lesson, you'll modify the recently created action by adding new steps to it.

Getting It Right

Few of us get everything right the first time we try to do something. After you create an action, you might think of other steps that you want to include, such as changing the order of some or all of the steps, or altering an option. The beauty of Photoshop actions is that you can make modifications and additions to them with little effort.

Revising an Action

You can modify an existing action by clicking the step that is just above where you want the new step(s) to appear. Click the Begin recording button on the Actions panel, record your steps (just as you did when you initially created the action), and then click the Stop playing/recording button when you're finished. The new steps are inserted after the selected step.

> **QUICK TIP**
>
> Because users may not know how to resume playback after encountering a stop, it's a good idea to include a helpful tip that tells them to click the Play selection button after encountering the stop.

Changing the Actions Panel View

In addition to dragging the borders to change the shape of the Actions panel, you can also change the way the steps are displayed. By default, actions are displayed in a list; the steps appear as a list below each action included in them. Figure 14 shows the actions in the Default Actions set in a list in which all the detail is accessible but hidden. (Remember that you can display the detail for each action by clicking the triangle next to the action, to expand it.)

Working in Button Mode

In Button Mode, each action is displayed as a button—without the additional detail found in the list format. Each button is displayed in the color selected when the action was created and the Play button is not displayed. In Button Mode, all you need to do to play an action is to click the button. Figure 15 shows the same actions shown in Figure 14, but in Button Mode. You can toggle between these two modes by clicking the Actions Panel options button, and then clicking Button Mode, as shown in Figure 16.

Figure 14 *Actions displayed in a list*

Toggles a
dialog
on and off

Figure 15 *Actions displayed in Button Mode*

Figure 16 *Actions panel menu*

Switches
between list and
button modes

Button Mode

New Action...
New Set...
Duplicate
Delete
Play

Start Recording
Record Again...
Insert Menu Item...
Insert Stop...
Insert Conditional...
Insert Path

Action Options...
Playback Options...
Allow Tool Recording

Clear All Actions
Reset Actions
Load Actions...
Replace Actions...
Save Actions...

Commands
Frames
Image Effects
LAB - Black & White Technique
Production
Stars Trails
Text Effects
Textures
Video Actions

Close
Close Tab Group

Understanding a Stop

In addition to containing any Photoshop task, an action can include a stop, which is a command that interrupts playback to allow you to perform other operations—particularly those that cannot be recorded in an action, or those that might change each time you play the action. You insert a stop by clicking the step *just above* where you want the pause to take place. Click the Actions Panel options button, and then click Insert Stop. The Record Stop dialog box opens, allowing you to enter a text message that appears when the action is stopped, as shown in Figure 17. You select the Allow Continue check box to include a Continue button in the message that appears when the action is stopped. You can resume the action by clicking this button. An action that contains a dialog box—such as an action that contains a stop—displays a toggle dialog on/off icon to the left of the action name on the Actions panel. This icon indicates a **modal control**, which means that dialog boxes are *used* in the action, but are not displayed. When the action is resumed, the tasks begin where they were interrupted. You can resume the action by clicking the Play selection button on the Actions panel.

Figure 17 *Record Stop dialog box*

Add steps to an action

1. Verify that the Button layer is active on the Layers panel.

2. Click the **Set Layer Styles of current layer step** (the second step) in the Button Drop Shadow action on the Actions panel.

3. Click the **Begin recording button**  on the Actions panel.

4. Click **Image** on the Menu bar, point to **Adjustments**, then click **Brightness/Contrast**. Change the settings in your dialog box to match the settings in Figure 18.

5. Click **OK**.

6. Click the **Stop playing/recording button** on the Actions panel. Compare your Actions panel to Figure 19.

   The Button Drop Shadow action has a new step added to it.

7. Turn off the ruler display, then click **Snapshot 1** on the History panel.

8. Click the **Button Drop Shadow action** on the Actions panel, then click the **Play selection button** on the Actions panel. Compare your screen to Figure 20.

You added a new step (which modified the brightness/contrast) to the Button Drop Shadow action. You then tested the modified action by using a snapshot and playing the action.

Figure 18 *Brightness/Contrast dialog box*

Figure 19 *New steps added to the Button Drop Shadow action*

Figure 20 *Result of modified action*
Source: Morguefile

Annotating and Automating an Image

Figure 21 *Modified image*

Source: Morguefile

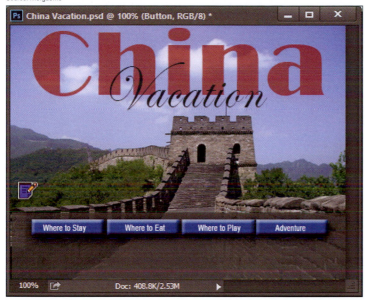

China Vacation.psd @ 100% (Button, RGB/8) *

China
Vacation

Where to Stay   Where to Eat   Where to Play   Adventure

100%   Doc: 408.8K/2.53M

TABLE 2: METHODS FOR MODIFYING AN ACTION

Modification type	Method
Rearrange steps	Move an existing step by dragging the step to a new location in the action.
Add new commands	Click the step above where you want the new step to appear, then click ⚪.
Rerecord existing commands	Click the step you want to recreate, click ▾☰, then click Record Again.
Duplicate existing commands	Click the step you want to duplicate, click ▾☰, then click Duplicate.
Delete actions	Click the action you want to delete, then click 🗑.
Delete a step in an action	Click the step you want to delete, then click 🗑.
Change options in an action	Click the step in the action you want to change, click ▾☰, then click Action Options or Playback Options.

Add steps and modify an action

1. Click the **Brightness/Contrast step** on the Actions panel (the third step in the Button Drop Shadow action).
2. Click the **Begin recording button** ⚪ on the Actions panel.
3. Click the **Add a layer style button** *fx.* on the Layers panel.
4. Click **Bevel & Emboss,** then click **OK** to accept the existing settings.
5. Click the **Stop playing/recording button** ⬛ on the Actions panel.

   The new step is added to the existing action. Table 2 describes other ways to modify actions.
6. Click **Snapshot 1** on the History panel.
7. Click the **Button Drop Shadow action** on the Actions panel, then click the **Play selection button** ▶ on the Actions panel.
8. Compare your image to Figure 21, then save your work.

You added the Bevel and Emboss style to an action, then you tested the action.

Use a Default Action
AND CREATE A DROPLET

What You'll Do

Source: Morguefile

  In this lesson, you'll use actions from other sets and create a droplet.

Taking Advantage of Actions

Photoshop actions can really help your work day by automating tedious tasks. You can add a default action to any action you've created. A **default action** is an action that is prerecorded and tested, and comes with Photoshop. You can incorporate some of these nifty actions into those you create.

Identifying Default Actions

The default actions that come with Photoshop are Vignette (selection), Frame Channel, Wood Frame, Cast Shadow, Water Reflection, Custom RGB to Grayscale, Molten Lead, Make Clip Path (selection), Sepia Toning (layer), Quadrant Colors, Save As Photoshop PDF, Gradient Map, and Mixer Brush Cloning Paint Setup. In addition, there are nine action sets that come with Photoshop: Commands, Frames, Image Effects, LAB – Black & White Technique, Production, Stars Trails, Text Effects, Textures, and Video Actions. You can load any of these action sets by clicking the Actions Panel options button, and then clicking the name of the set you want to load.

Using Default Actions

You can incorporate any of the default actions that come with Photoshop—or those you get from other sources—into a new action by playing the action in the process of recording a new one. Each time an existing action is played, a new snapshot is created on the History panel, so don't be surprised when you see additional snapshots that you never created. To incorporate an existing action into a new action, first select the step that is *above* where you want the new action to occur. Begin recording your action, and then scroll through the Actions panel and play the action you want to include. When the action has completed all steps, you can continue recording other steps or click the Stop playing/recording button if you are done. That's it: all of the steps in the default action will be performed when you play your new action.

Loading Sets

In addition to the Default Actions, the nine additional sets of actions are listed at the bottom of the Actions Panel menu. If you store actions from other sources on your computer you can load those actions by clicking the Actions Panel options button, clicking Load Actions, and then choosing the action you want from the Load dialog box. The default sets that come with Photoshop are stored in the Actions folder, which is in the Presets folder of the Adobe Photoshop CC folder.

QUICK TIP

If you want to save actions to distribute to others, you must first put them in a set. You create a set by clicking the Create new set button on the Actions panel (just like creating a Layer set). Place an action in a set by dragging it to the set folder in the Actions panel, select the set, click the Actions Panel options button, and then click Save Actions.

Understanding a Droplet

A **droplet** is a stand-alone action in the form of an icon that appears in a location outside of Photoshop. You can drag one or more closed Photoshop files onto a droplet icon to perform the action on the file or files. You can store droplets on the hard drive on your computer, place them on your desktop, or distribute them to others using other storage media. Figure 22 shows an example of a droplet on the desktop. Droplets let you further automate repetitive tasks.

Creating a Droplet

You create a droplet by using the Automate command on the File menu, an existing action, and the Create Droplet dialog box.

In the Create Droplet dialog box, you use the Set list arrow to choose the set that contains the action you want to use to create the droplet, and then use the Action list arrow to choose the action. Finally, you can choose the location on your computer where you'll store the droplet.

QUICK TIP

When placed on the desktop, a droplet has a unique down-arrow icon filled with the Photoshop logo. The droplet name appears below the icon.

Figure 22 *A droplet on the desktop*

Icons on your desktop will be different

Photoshop droplet

Recycle Bin

Adobe Creati...

Button Drop Shadow-Ca...

Automating Using Batches

There may be times when you might need to perform the same action on multiple files. Rather than dragging each image onto a droplet, one at a time, you can combine all of the images into a batch. A **batch** is a group of images designated to have the same action performed on them simultaneously. You can create a batch using all of the files in one specific folder or using all of the Photoshop images that are currently open. When you have opened or organized the files you want to include in a batch, click File on the Menu bar, point to Automate, and then click Batch. The Batch dialog box opens, offering you options similar to those used for creating droplets. You can also use Adobe Bridge as a source of creating batches by clicking Tools on the Adobe Bridge Menu bar, pointing to Photoshop, and then clicking Batch.

Include a default action within an action

1. Activate the **Set Layer Styles of current layer step** (the last step in the Button Drop Shadow action) at the bottom of the Actions panel.

TIP If your Actions panel becomes too messy, you can clear it by clicking the Actions Panel options button, then clicking Clear All Actions. To restore the Default Actions set, click the Actions Panel options button, then click Reset Actions.

2. Verify that the **Button layer** is active in the Layers panel.

3. Click the **Begin recording button** 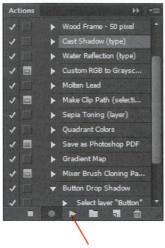 on the Actions panel.

4. Scroll to the top of the Actions panel, then click the **Cast Shadow (type) action**, as shown in Figure 23.

You prepared to insert the Cast Shadow default action into the Button Drop Shadow action. If this action had been applied to a type layer, the type would have been rasterized before the effect could be applied.

Figure 23 *Action to be added to the Button Drop Shadow action*

Plays the selected action while recording

Figure 24 *Adobe website that offers Photoshop actions*

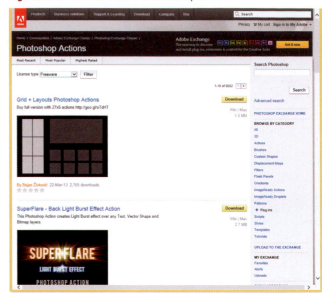

Finding Actions on the Web

Actions can be fun to design, and the more practice you get, the more you'll want to make use of them. But no matter how good you are, time is at a premium for most of us. You can find great actions on the web—and many of them are free! Figure 24 shows the Adobe Photoshop Actions website where you can explore a variety of actions that are free or available for purchase. Just connect to the web, open your browser and favorite search engine, and search on the text "Photoshop Actions."

Figure 25 *Cast Shadow action added to the Button Drop Shadow action*

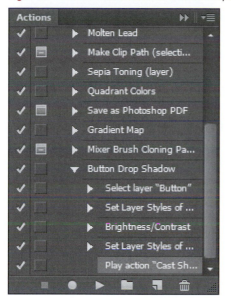

Figure 26 *Modified Layers panel*

Play an existing action in a new action

1. Click the **Play selection button** ▶ on the Actions panel.
2. Click the **Stop playing/recording button** ■ on the Actions panel. A new layer is created in the Layers panel. Compare your Actions panel to Figure 25.
3. Click **Snapshot 1** on the History panel.

TIP Some default actions create a snapshot as their initial step. For this reason, you might see multiple snapshots on the History panel.

4. Click the **Button Drop Shadow action** on the Actions panel.
5. Click the **Play selection button** ▶ on the Actions panel.
6. Save your work, then compare your Layers panel to Figure 26.

   The Cast Shadow action added a reflection beneath the buttons.

You included the Cast Shadow action in the Button Drop Shadow action. You used the snapshot to revert to the image's original appearance and replayed the action, which modified the image.

Create a droplet

1. Click **File** on the Menu bar, point to **Automate**, then click **Create Droplet**.

2. Click **Choose** in the Create Droplet dialog box.

   The Save dialog box opens.

3. Type **Button Drop Shadow-Cast Shadow** in the File name text box (Win) or Save As text box (Mac) in the Save dialog box.

   TIP If you are using a Mac, see the Sidebar on this page.

4. Click the **Save in list arrow**, then click **Desktop** (Win) or click **Desktop** in the **Favorites section** (Mac), as shown in Figure 27.

   TIP You can create a droplet and save it anywhere on your computer by clicking the Save in list arrow (Win) or clicking the location in the Favorites list in the left pane (Mac), then navigating to the location where you want to store the file.

5. Click **Save**.

6. Click the **Action list arrow** in the Create Droplet dialog box, then click **Button Drop Shadow** if necessary. Compare your dialog box settings to Figure 28.

7. Click **OK**.

You created a droplet using the Button Drop Shadow action and saved it to the desktop for easy access.

Figure 27 *Save dialog box*

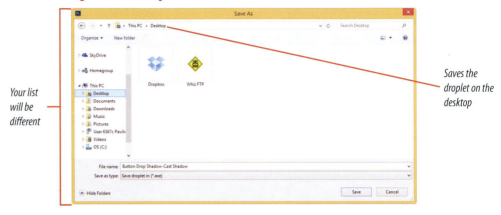

Your list will be different

Saves the droplet on the desktop

Figure 28 *Create Droplet dialog box*

Updating a Droplet for Use in Mac OS

When Photoshop creates a droplet, it's saved in the .exe format. Mac OS uses the .app format. If you're using a Mac, once the droplet is created, drag it onto the Photoshop icon on your desktop, and the app will update the droplet for use in Mac OS.

Annotating and Automating an Image

Figure 29 *Droplet on desktop*

New Droplet icon on desktop

Figure 30 *Image updated by droplet*
Source: Morguefile

Run a droplet

1. Minimize all open windows so the desktop is visible, then compare your desktop to Figure 29.
2. Maximize the Photoshop window.
3. Click **Snapshot 1** on the History panel.
4. Save your work, close the China Vacation image, then minimize Photoshop (Win) or Hide Photoshop (Mac).

TIP When Photoshop is not running, activating a droplet automatically launches the program.

5. Locate the closed China Vacation image on your computer, using the file management program of your choice, then adjust the windows so you can see the China Vacation file and the droplet icon on the desktop.
6. Drag the **China Vacation file** onto the droplet icon on the desktop.

TIP In Windows 8.x, you may have to adjust the Compatibility tab (in the Properties setting) of both the Droplet *and* Photoshop to make sure both are being Run as Administrator. You can make this adjustment by right-clicking, clicking Properties, clicking the Compatibility tab, clicking the Run as Administrator check box, then clicking OK.

The Photoshop window is restored, the China Vacation image opens, and the action is replayed.

TIP Sometimes a file automatically closes after a droplet has been applied. To see the applied droplet, you must reopen the file.

7. Display the **Essentials workspace**, compare your screen to Figure 30, then save your work.
8. Close the file and exit Photoshop, then drag the **droplet** to the location where you store your Data Files.

You returned the image to its original appearance by using Snapshot 1 on the History panel, and closed the file. Then you tested the droplet by dragging the China Vacation file onto the droplet.

POWER USER SHORTCUTS

To do this:	Use this method:	To do this:	Use this method:
Apply droplet	Drag closed Photoshop file onto droplet	Expand action detail	▶
Change name of note author	📝 or [Shift] **I**, then type name in Name of author for notes text box	Open a closed note	Double-click note icon
Change Note icon color	📝 or [Shift] **I**, click ▯, choose color, then click OK	Play an action	▶
Close an open note	Click 🗐	Record an action	⬤ , then perform tasks
Collapse action detail	▼	Record an action from another set	⬤ , click existing action in another set, click ▶ , then click ◼
Create a batch	File ➤ Automate ➤ Batch	Revert image to original appearance using a snapshot	Click History panel tab, click snapshot
Create a droplet	File ➤ Automate ➤ Create Droplet	Stop recording	◼
Create a note	📝 or [Shift] **I**, then click where you want the note to appear	Toggle Actions panel between List and Button Modes	▤ , click Button Mode
Create a snapshot	📷 on the History panel	Select next note	➡
Create an action	📄 on the Actions panel, select options, then click Record	Select previous note	⬅
Delete a note	Select note, press [Delete], or click 🗑		

Key: Menu items are indicated by ➤ between the menu name and its command. Blue bold letters are shortcuts for selecting tools on the Tools panel.

Annotating and Automating an Image

Add annotations to an image.

1. Open PS 16-2.psd from the drive and folder where you store your Data Files, then save it as **Team Players**.
2. Select the Note tool.
3. Enter your name as the Author of the note (if necessary).
4. Change the Note color to Dark Green (the fourth box from the right in the fifth row of the Swatches panel).
5. Display the rulers (if necessary).
6. Click the image at 30 X/650 Y, then type the following: **This will make a great motivational poster for our company**.
7. Close the Notes panel.
8. Hide the rulers, then save your work.

Create an action.

1. Make the A Source of Strength and Stability layer active (if it is not already active).
2. Display the Essentials workspace and the Actions and History panels, and create a new snapshot using the History panel.
3. Collapse the Default Actions set (if necessary).
4. Create a new action using the Actions panel.
5. Name the new action **Motivation**, and apply the color Blue to it.
6. Record the action using the following steps:
   a. Make the Team Players layer active.
   b. Change the font in this layer to an 85 pt Impact Regular (or another font available on your computer).
   c. Stop recording.

7. Click Snapshot 1 on the History panel to restore the original appearance of the image.
8. Replay the Motivation action.
9. Save your work.

Modify an action.

1. Select the last step in the Motivation action at the bottom of the Actions panel.
2. Begin recording the following steps:
   a. Make the A Source of Strength and Stability layer active.
   b. Change the font in this layer to a 36 pt Impact Regular (or another font available on your computer).
   c. Make the Team Players layer active.
   d. Add the default Bevel and Emboss style with Contour to the layer.
   e. Stop recording.
3. Click Snapshot 1 on the History panel to restore the original appearance of the image.
4. Replay the Motivation action.
5. Save your work.

Use a default action and create a droplet.

1. Make the A Source of Strength and Stability layer active.
2. Select the Set Layer Styles of current layer step in the Motivation action (the last step).
3. Begin recording the following steps:
   a. Make the Team Players layer active.
   b. Play the Water Reflection (type) action in Default Actions. (Substitute another action if this one is not available.)
   c. Stop recording.

4. Click Snapshot 1 on the History panel to restore the original appearance of the image.
5. Replay the Motivation action.
6. Restore Snapshot 1, then save your changes.
7. Create a droplet on the desktop called **Motivation** using the Motivation action, save your work, then exit Photoshop.
8. Drag the Team Players file onto the Motivation droplet. See Figure 31.
9. Drag the droplet to the location where you store your Data Files, then save your work and close the Team Players file.

Figure 31 *Completed Skills Review*
© Photodisc/Getty Images

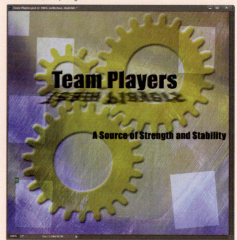

As the newest member of the Game Corporation design team, you have noticed that some of your fellow designers perform many repetitive tasks and could really benefit from using actions. One of these repetitive tasks is taking a single-layer image, converting a layer from a Background layer to an image layer, and creating a new layer. You want to make their lives easier, so you decide to create an action that completes this task. To circulate the action among your coworkers, you decide to create a droplet for this action that you can e-mail or post to the network. (*Hint*: There are a variety of steps in a varied sequence you can take to create this action.)

1. Open PS 16-3.psd, then save it as **New Layers**.
2. Create a snapshot of the current image using the default name.
3. Hide any other displayed action details you may find distracting (if necessary).
4. Write down the steps you will need to perform to create this action. (You can use a word processor or a sheet of paper, or you can use the Notes panel in Photoshop.)

5. Create a new action in the Default Actions set called **New Layers**.
6. Apply the Violet color to the action.
7. Record the necessary steps to complete the action.
8. Use the snapshot to return the image to its original condition.
9. Play the action to verify that it works as you expected.

10. If the action does not perform as expected, make any necessary modifications to it.
11. Save your work, then compare your screen and Actions panel to the sample in Figure 32. (Your steps may differ.)
12. Create a droplet for the action named **New Layers**, then save it in the drive and folder where you store your Data Files.

Figure 32 *Sample Project Builder 1*
© Photodisc/Getty Images

Annotating and Automating an Image

An anniversary is coming up for some friends of your family. You and your twin have decided to collaborate on a gift, even though you live at opposite sides of the country. You each have a great photo of the couple that you'd like to modify in the same way, using Photoshop. You decide to create a droplet (which is significantly smaller in size than a completed Photoshop image), and e-mail the droplet so that your twin can apply it to the photo. The droplet can be used to apply your proposed modifications to the picture.

1. Open PS 16-4.psd, then save it as **Anniversary Gift**.
2. Create a snapshot of the current image using the default name.
3. After examining the image, decide what changes you want to make. Write down the steps you will need to perform to create this action, including any stops. (*Hint*: You can use any of your Photoshop skills and any Photoshop features. Include any necessary color corrections in adjustment layers.)
4. Create a new action in the Default Actions set called **Image Modifications**.
5. Apply the green color to the action.

6. Record the steps you wrote down. (*Hint*: In the sample, a 48 pt Trebuchet MS Regular font is used. You do not have to include a type layer, but if you do, use any font available on your computer.)
7. Use the snapshot to return the image to its original condition.
8. Play the action to verify that it works as you expected.

9. If the action does not perform as expected, make any necessary corrections to it.
10. Save your work, then compare your image, Layers panel, and Actions panel to the sample in Figure 33.
11. Create a droplet for the new action called **Gift Image**, and save it to the drive and folder where you store your Data Files.

Figure 33 *Sample Project Builder 2*
© Photodisc/Getty Images

The Internet is a great resource for actions and droplets. You can find many actions that incorporate sophisticated design concepts. Some websites let you download actions for free, while others might charge a fee. As you perfect your skills using actions, you decide to scour the web and see what cool actions you can find.

1. Connect to the Internet and use your browser to find Photoshop actions. (Make a record of the site you found so you can use it for future reference.)

2. Download an action that you want to try.

3. Create a new Photoshop image called **Action Sample** using any dimensions.

4. Supply any imagery and/or type layers by using any electronic images you can acquire through Internet purchase, from your hard disk, or by using a scanner. Use any fonts available on your computer.

5. Duplicate the image and any type layers to preserve your original image.

6. Create a note anywhere on the image, indicating the source of the action (include the URL).

7. Create a snapshot of the image.

8. Load and play the action in the image. If necessary, click Continue or OK to accept any messages or settings in dialog boxes that open.

9. Create a droplet called **Play Downloaded Action**.

10. Save your work to the drive and folder where you store your Data Files, then compare your screen (and the partial view of the downloaded action) to the sample in Figure 34.

11. Be prepared to discuss the design features used in your downloaded action.

Figure 34 *Sample Design Project*
© Photodisc/Getty Images

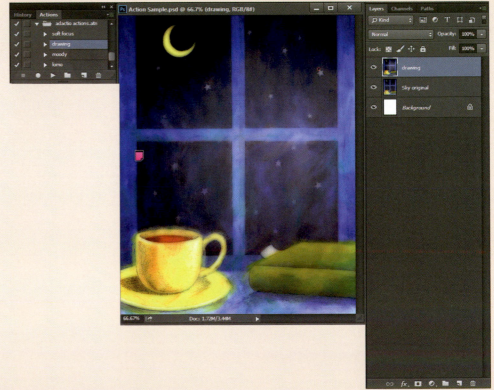

Creating an interesting design can be a challenge. As a motivational exercise, the head of your department has asked you to create an image to inspire a positive working environment using Photoshop actions, along with your raw creativity and imagination. You can choose any topic for the artwork, work with any existing or scanned imagery, and use any new or existing actions. As you determine what actions to create, think about why a series of tasks is worthy of an action. How will automating a task benefit you, your coworkers, and your organization? Think efficiency; think quality.

1. Create a new Photoshop image with any dimensions.
2. Save this file as **Game Plan**.
3. Locate artwork—either on your computer, in a royalty-free collection, or from scanned images.
4. Sketch a rough draft of your layout.
5. Add any necessary type layers using any fonts available on your computer. (*Hint*: In the sample, a Comic Sans MS Regular font is used.)
6. Create a note that lists the actions you used. (*Hint*: You can use actions created in this chapter, or you can create one or more new actions, if necessary.)

7. Write down the steps that were used in any new actions. Review the following questions: Why did you create the actions that you did? What factors determined that a task should be converted into an action?

8. Be prepared to prove that the actions work correctly.
9. Save your work, then compare your image, Layers panel, and Actions panel to the sample in Figure 35.

Figure 35 *Sample Portfolio Project*
© Photodisc/Getty Images

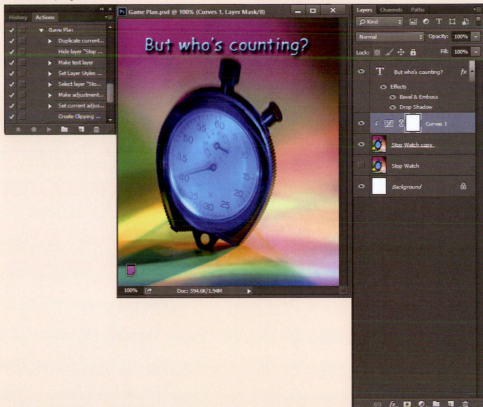

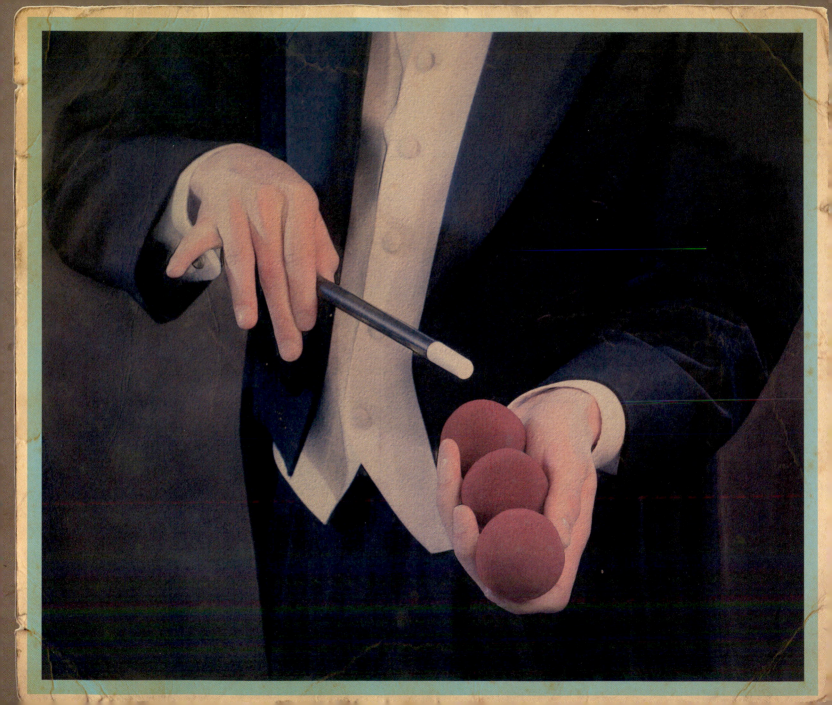

CHAPTER 17

CREATING IMAGES FOR
THE WEB

1. Learn about web features
2. Optimize images for web use
3. Create a button for a web page
4. Create slices in an image

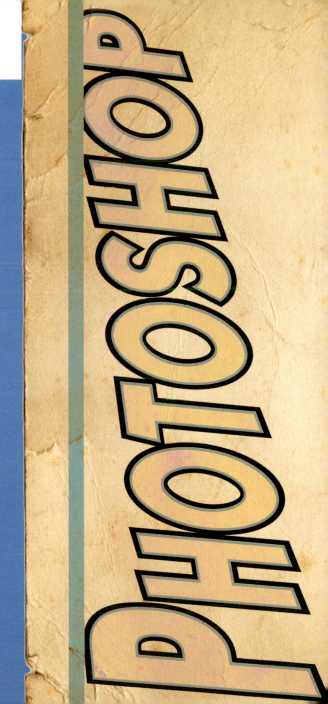

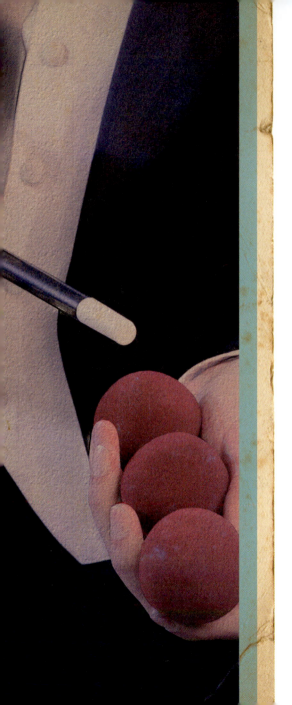

CHAPTER 17

CREATING IMAGES FOR
THE WEB

Using Photoshop for the Web

In addition to creating exciting images that can be professionally printed, you can use the tools in Photoshop to create images for use on the web. Once you have a Photoshop image, you can use additional web-specific tools and features to add the dimension and functionality required by today's web audience.

Understanding Web Graphics

Images and graphics can be tailored specifically for the web by creating buttons and other features unique to web pages. Using Photoshop, you can combine impressive graphics with interactive functionality to create an outstanding website.

QUICK TIP

Photoshop provides the capabilities for dividing one image into smaller, more manageable parts, creating more efficient web-ready files.

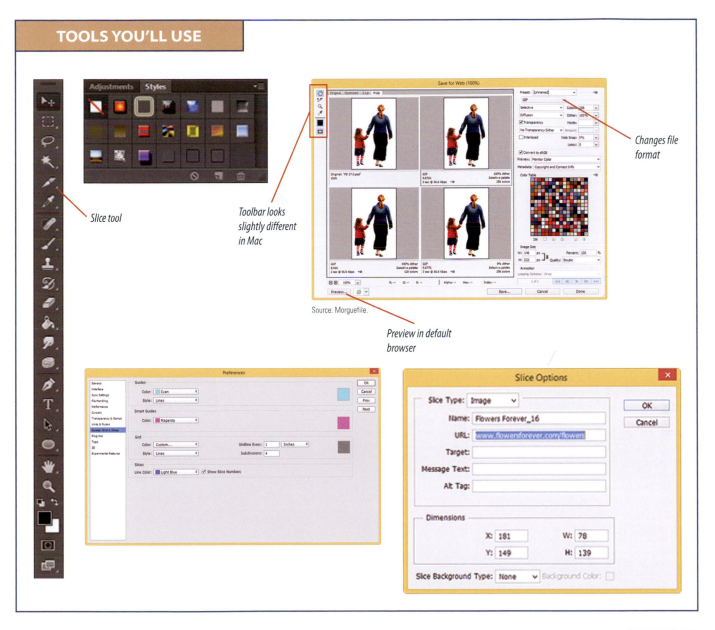

Slice tool

Toolbar looks slightly different in Mac

Source: Morguefile.

Changes file format

Preview in default browser

Learn About
WEB FEATURES

What You'll Do

Source: Morguefile.

 In this lesson, you'll open and rename a file in Photoshop, view slices, and then turn off the display of the slices.

Using Photoshop to Create Web Documents

Using Photoshop to create web documents is similar to creating any other image, except that you will optimize graphic images and include slices (subsections of an image to which you can assign additional functionality).

Previewing Files for the Web

You can add many sophisticated web effects to the files you create in Photoshop, such as slices and buttons, as shown in Figure 1. To insert and view them in a web page, you need to follow the procedures dictated by your HTML editor. **HTML** (Hypertext Markup Language) is the most commonly used language for creating web pages. You can preview most web effects directly in Photoshop. You can preview your files in your browser by clicking the Preview the optimized image in a browser button in the Save For Web dialog box.

Creating Navigational and Interactive Functionality

You can divide an image you create for a website into many smaller sections, or slices. You use a slice to assign special features, such as links and animation, to specific areas within an image. **Links** allow you to direct the reader to pages specifically related to a particular topic. A fundamental goal of website design is to encourage users to remain at your site and click the links you've provided. Thinking about the links you'll be using and how to make your pages visually appealing is key.

Figure 1 *Image with web features*
© Photodisc/Getty Images

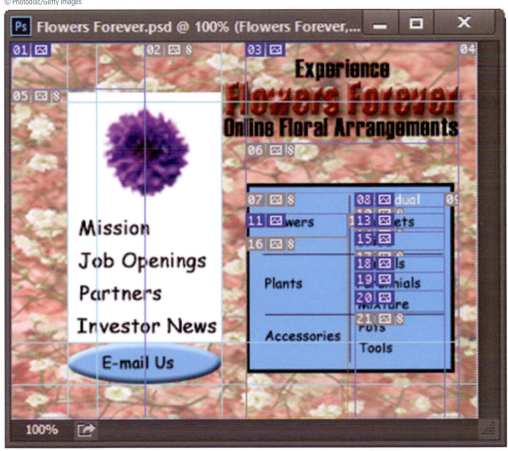

View Slices

1. Start Photoshop, open PS 17-1.psd from the drive and folder where you store your Data Files, then save it as **Shopping Heaven**.

TIP Update the text layers if you see a message box stating that some text layers need to be updated before they can be used for vector-based output.

2. Click the **Default Foreground and Background Colors button** 🔲 on the Tools panel.

3. Verify that the rulers display in pixels.

4. Click the **Slice tool** on the Tools panel.

TIP The Slice tool is grouped with the Crop tool, the Perspective Crop tool, and the Slice Select tool.

5. Display/reset the **Essentials workspace**.

6. Zoom in until the zoom factor is large enough for you to see the individual slices.

Compare your screen to Figure 2.

You opened an image in Photoshop, then displayed the document slices and the Essentials workspace.

Figure 2 *Image with slices*

Source: Morguefile.

Individual slice

Zoom level

Figure 3 *Slices turned off*
Source: Morguefile.

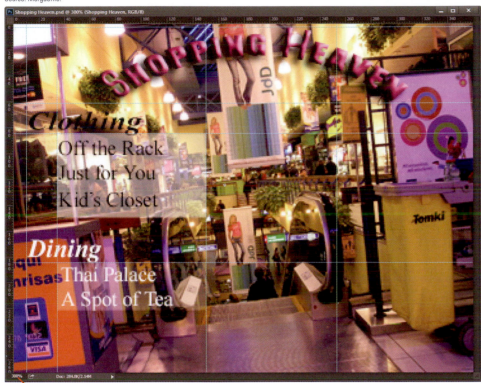

Your zoom level may differ

Turn off slices

1. Click **View** on the Menu bar, point to **Show**, then click **Slices** to deselect the command.

2. Verify that the **Zoom tool** is selected, then click the **Fit Screen button** on the options bar or change the zoom factor to **300%** (whichever looks better on your screen).

   The size of the document may change (depending on the size of your monitor and your resolution setting) after clicking the Fit Screen button. This button is just one more tool you can use to create your ideal work environment.

3. Verify that the guides are displayed, then compare your image to Figure 3.

You adjusted your view of the image, turned off the display of the slices, then verified that the guides are displayed.

Optimize Images
FOR WEB USE

What You'll Do

Source: Morguefile.

In this lesson, you'll optimize an image for the web in Photoshop. Then you'll modify the optimized image and add it to an existing file.

Understanding Optimization

You can create an awesome image in Photoshop and merge and flatten layers conscientiously, but still end up with a file so large that no one will wait for it to download from the web. An optimized file is as beautiful as a non-optimized file; it's just a fraction of its original size.

Optimizing a File

When you **optimize** an image, you save it in a format that balances the need for detail and accurate color against file size. Photoshop allows you to compare an image in the following common web formats:

- JPEG (Joint Photographic Experts Group)
- GIF (Graphics Interchange Format)
- PNG (Portable Network Graphics; supported by wireless protocol for color images)
- WBMP (a Bitmap format used for mobile devices, such as cell phones; for monochrome images only)

In Photoshop, the Save For Web dialog box has four view tabs: Original, Optimized, 2-Up, and 4-Up. The Original view displays the graphic without any optimization. The 2-Up and 4-Up views display the image in its original format, as well as other file formats. You can change the file format being displayed by selecting one of the windows

Exporting an Image

You can export an image with transparency in Photoshop by saving your file in either a PNG or GIF format, and then converting the image's background layer to an image layer. Select any elements in the layer you want as transparent, delete them from the layer, and then save your changes.

in the dialog box, and then clicking the Optimized file format list arrow. See Figure 4 for the 4-Up view; see Figure 5 to see two formats compared in the 2-Up view.

Understanding Compression

GIF, JPEG, and PNG compression create compressed files without losing substantial components. Figuring out when to use which format can be challenging. Often, the decision may rest on your desired target file size and whether color or image detail is most important. JPEG files are compressed by discarding image pixels; GIF and PNG files are compressed by limiting colors. GIF is an 8-bit format (the maximum number of colors a GIF file can contain is 256) that supports one transparent color; JPEG does not support transparent color. Having a transparent color is useful if you want to create a fade-out or superimposed effect. Because the JPEG format discards, or *loses*, data when it compresses a file, it is known as **lossy**. GIF and PNG formats are **lossless**—they compress solid color areas but maintain detail.

Figure 4 *Optimizing files in Photoshop*
© Photodisc/Getty Images

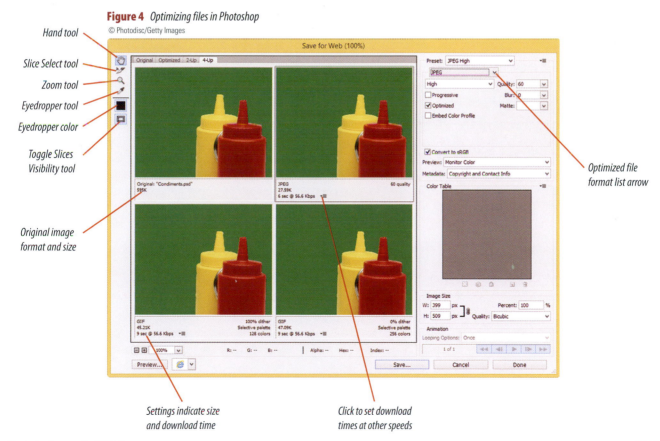

Hand tool
Slice Select tool
Zoom tool
Eyedropper tool
Eyedropper color
Toggle Slices Visibility tool
Original image format and size
Optimized file format list arrow
Settings indicate size and download time
Click to set download times at other speeds

Comparing Image Types

Figure 5 compares optimization of a photograph with a solid color background optimized in the JPEG format. If you look closely, you'll see that the GIF colors look streaky and appear to be broken-up, while the JPEG colors appear crisp and seamless. Table 1 lists optimization format considerations. Because you cannot assume that other users will have access to the latest software and hardware, it's a good idea to compare files saved under different formats and optimization settings, and preview them in different browsers and on different computers. Yes, this can be time-consuming, but you'll end up with images that look great in all web browsers.

Figure 5 *Comparing file formats*

© Photodisc/Getty Images

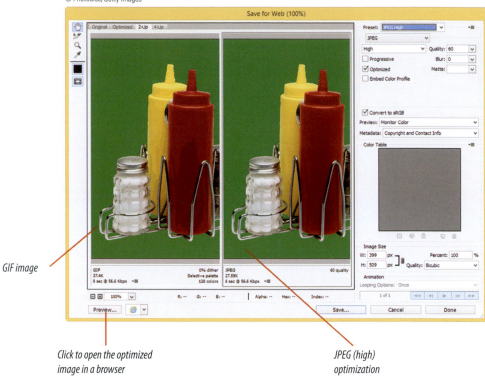

GIF image

Click to open the optimized image in a browser

JPEG (high) optimization

TABLE 1: OPTIMIZATION FORMAT CONSIDERATIONS		
Format	**File format**	**Use with**
JPEG (very common)	All 24-bit (works best with 16 M colors)	Photographs, solid colors, soft edges
GIF (very common)	8-bit (256 colors)	Detailed drawings, sharp edges (logos, vector graphics), animation, transparency
PNG (very common)	24-bit (16 M colors)	Detailed drawings, logos, bitmap graphics, transparency
WBMP (rare)	1-bit (2 colors)	Cell phones and other mobile devices without color displays

© 2015 Cengage Learning®

Figure 6 *Save For Web dialog box*

Source: Morguefile.

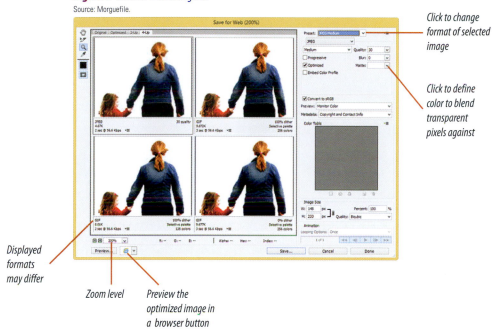

Click to change format of selected image

Click to define color to blend transparent pixels against

Displayed formats may differ

Zoom level

Preview the optimized image in a browser button

Using Transparency and Matte Options

When using the Save For Web dialog box you can determine how the Transparency and Matte options are optimized within an image. Transparency can only be applied to images using a GIF or PNG format. Using both of these tools in a variety of combinations, you can blend fully or partially transparent pixels with a color from the Color Picker or Matte menu.

Prepare to optimize an image

1. Open PS 17-2.psd from the drive and folder where you store your Data Files, then save it as **Shoppers** in the folder where you store your Data Files.

2. Click **File** on the Menu bar, then click **Save for Web**.

3. Click the **4-Up tab**.

4. Click the **Zoom tool** on the left side of the Save For Web dialog box.

TIP The zoom level is displayed in the lower-left corner of the Save For Web dialog box. You can also click the Zoom Level list arrow and select a magnification.

5. Click the **top-right image** until all four images are enlarged for optimum visibility.

TIP You can use the Hand tool to reposition the image.

6. Click the **Preset list arrow**, click **JPEG Medium**, then compare your dialog box to Figure 6.

The Save button saves the selected thumbnail in the selected format, the Cancel button resets the settings and closes the dialog box, and the Done button remembers the current settings and closes the dialog box.

TIP To complete optimization of the file, you can click the desired format in the dialog box, click Save, enter a new name (if necessary) in the Save Optimized As dialog box, then click Save.

You opened a file, then used the Save for Web command on the File menu to open the Save For Web dialog box. You observed the differences between possible formats.

Complete image optimization

1. Click the **Preset list arrow,** then click **GIF 128 Dithered**. Compare your image to Figure 7.

   TIP The Preset list arrow contains 12 predesigned settings, while the Optimized file format list arrow lets you create your own unique settings with any options you choose.

2. Click **Save**.

3. Navigate to the folder where you store your Data Files, verify that **Shoppers** is in the File name text box (Win) or the Save As text box (Mac), then click **Save**.

   TIP Click OK if a warning box displays.

   The optimized file is similar in color quality, but less than one-tenth the size of the original file (7.908K vs. 101K). Exact sizes may vary.

   TIP The optimized file is saved in the designated file format and folder. If your optimized file had spaces in its name, you would notice that the spaces in the optimized file name were replaced with hyphens.

4. Close the Shoppers.psd file without saving any changes.

   You optimized a file, then saved the optimized file using a format that greatly reduced the file size while maintaining acceptable image quality. When you optimize a file, a copy of the file is saved, and no changes are made to the original.

Figure 7 *Image optimized*
Source: Morguefile.

Click to select a predesigned format

Optimized file format list arrow also changes format

File size

Outline surrounds selected format

Using High Dynamic Range (HDR) Images

High Dynamic Range images are used in motion pictures, special effects, 3D work, and high-end photography. An HDR image is one that stores pixel values that span the whole tonal range. HDR images store linear values, meaning that the value of each pixel is proportional to the amount of light measured by the camera. Each HDR image stores 32-bits per color channel and is coded using floating point numbers. In Photoshop, an HDR image is converted to an 8-bit/channel or 16-bit/channel image mode. You can use the HDR Conversion dialog box to adjust the brightness and contrast using one of the following methods: Exposure and Gamma, Highlight Compression, Equalize Histogram, or Local Adaptation. In Photoshop, you can make this conversion by clicking File on the Menu bar, pointing to Automate, and then clicking Merge to HDR Pro. In Bridge, you can use this feature by selecting your images, clicking Tools on the Menu bar, pointing to Photoshop, and then clicking Merge to HDR Pro.

Figure 8 *Optimized file moved to image*

Source: Morguefile.

GIF image in document

Place an optimized image

1. Select the **Background layer** in Shopping Heaven.psd, then change the zoom level to **200%**.

2. Open Shoppers.gif.

3. Click **Select** on the Menu bar, click **Color Range**, then verify that the **Image option button** is selected and that the Fuzziness text box is set to **0**.

4. Click the **white background** of the image in the Color Range dialog box, select the **Invert check box**, then click **OK**.

5. Click the **Move tool** on the Tools panel, verify that the **Show Transform Controls check box** is *not* selected, then use the **Move pointer** to drag the selection to the Shopping Heaven image.

6. Drag the **Shoppers** so the top of the woman's head is below the "G" in Shopping, and below the guideline at 60Y.

7. Defringe the contents of Layer 1 using a setting of **2** pixels.

8. Double-click the name **Layer 1** in the Layers panel, type **2 Shoppers** in the Name text box, then press [**Enter**] (Win) or [**return**] (Mac).

9. Close the Shoppers.gif file, save your work, then compare your screen to Figure 8.

You opened an optimized file, selected the file and dragged it into the Shopping Heaven image, defringed the image, then renamed the layer. The optimized file will make it easier for a viewer to load in a browser.

Create a Button
FOR A WEB PAGE

What You'll Do

Source: Morguefile.

In this lesson, you'll create and name a layer, and then create a button to use in a web page. You'll add type to the button, apply a style, and then convert the type layer into a Smart Object.

Learning About Buttons

A **button** is a graphical interface element that helps visitors navigate through and interact with a website with ease. Photoshop provides several ways for you to create buttons. You can create your own shape, apply a preformatted button style, or import a button you've already created. You can also assign a variety of actions to a button so that the button completes the required task when clicked or hovered-over by someone viewing the site in a browser.

Creating a Button

You can create a button by drawing a shape with a shape tool, such as a rectangle, on a layer. After you create the shape, you can stylize it by applying a color or style, and then add text that will explain what will happen when it's clicked.

QUICK TIP

You can add a link (containing a URL) to a button so that when you click it, a new web page will load.

Saving a File for the Web

Before you can use Photoshop files on the web, you must first convert them to an HTML-compatible format. Photoshop uses default settings when you save optimized images for the web. You can specify the output settings for HTML-compatible format, your HTML editor, and the way image files, background files, and slices are named and saved. For example, to change the output settings in Photoshop to a JPEG file, click the Preset list arrow in the Save For Web dialog box, select a JPEG format and compression type, and then click the Compression quality list arrow (above the Progressive check box and only available on images in the JPEG format) and the Quality list arrow to 'dial-in' the exact settings you want. To convert a file to the HTML-compatible format, open the file in the Save For Web dialog box, click Save (located at the bottom of the dialog box), click the Format list arrow in the Save Optimized As dialog box, click HTML and Images or HTML Only, and then click Save.

Applying a Button Style

You can choose from the many predesigned Photoshop button styles on the Styles panel, or you can create your own. To apply a style to a button, you create a button shape, and then add a style. To create a button, draw a shape for the button (using the Rectangle tool, for example), and then click one of the button styles on the Styles panel or select a style name from the Style picker list arrow on the options bar. Figure 9 shows the button styles on the Styles panel. You can also modify a button with a style already applied to it by first selecting the button and then choosing a new style from the Styles panel.

Figure 9 *Styles panel*

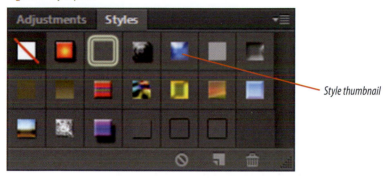

Style thumbnail

Create a button

1. Verify that the **2 Shoppers layer** on the Layers panel is selected.

2. Click the **Create a new layer button**  on the Layers panel.

   A new active layer, Layer 1, appears in between the 2 Shoppers layer, and the Shape 2 layer.

3. Double-click the name **Layer 1** on the Layers panel, type **QuickGift**, then press [**Enter**] (Win) or [**return**] (Mac).

4. Click the **Rounded Rectangle tool** in the Tools panel.

TIP The Rounded Rectangle tool is grouped with the Rectangle, Ellipse, Polygon, Line, and Custom Shape tools.

5. Verify that **Shape** displays in the Pick tool mode list arrow on the options bar.

6. Click the **Styles Panel options button** on the Styles panel, click **Buttons**, then click **Append**.

7. Using the guides as a reference to create a shape beneath the word A in A Spot of Tea, drag the **Marquee pointer** ╋ from approximately **35 X/220 Y** to **150 X/260 Y**.

   You created the shape that will be used for a button. (The Properties panel displayed when you drew the shape.)

8. Scroll to the bottom of the Styles panel list, then click **Star Glow**, as shown in Figure 10.

You created a new layer, used the Rounded Rectangle tool to create a shape, appended new styles to the Styles panel, then applied a style to the shape.

Figure 10 *Button styles*

Star Glow

Figure 11 *Button created in image*

Source: Morguefile.

Add type to a button

1. Click the **Horizontal Type tool** on the Tools panel.

2. Click the **button shape** at approximately **50 X/230 Y**.

3. Zoom in if necessary, click the **Set the text color box** on the options bar, sample the **maroon** in the existing type, then click **OK**.

4. Click the **Set the font family list arrow** on the options bar, then click **Arial Regular**.

5. Click the **Set the font size list arrow** on the options bar, then click **18 pt**.

6. Display the Character panel, click the **Small Caps button** on the Character panel, type **QuickGift**, then commit the current edits.

7. In the Layers panel, right-click the **QuickGift type layer**, then click **Convert to Smart Object**.

8. Click the **Move tool** on the Tools panel, then center the type on the button.

TIP If you have trouble using the Move tool, you can select the Move tool and use the keyboard arrow keys to center the type.

9. Save your work, then compare your image and Layers panel to Figure 11.

You added type to a button, converted the QuickGift type layer to a Smart Object, then repositioned the type on the shape.

Create Slices
IN AN IMAGE

What You'll Do

Source: Morguefile.

In this lesson, you'll view the existing slices in the Shopping Heaven image, create slices around the Clothing and Dining type, resize a slice, and assign a web address to the slice. You'll also create a new slice from the 2 Shoppers layer on the Layers panel.

Understanding Slices

You not only have the ability to work with images in layers, but you can also divide an image into unlimited smaller sections, or slices. Photoshop uses slices to determine the appearance of special effects in a web page. A **slice** is a rectangular section of an image that you can use to apply features, such as rollovers and links, and can be created automatically or by using the Slice tool.

> **QUICK TIP**
>
> A slice is always rectangular.

Using Slices

There are two kinds of slices: a **user slice**, which you create, and an **auto slice**, which is created in response to your user slice. You can use the Slice tool to create a slice by dragging the pointer around an area. Every time you create a slice, Photoshop automatically creates at least one auto slice, which fills in the area

around the newly created slice. Photoshop automatically numbers user and auto slices and updates the numbering according to the location of the new user slice. Slice numbering changes as you add or delete slices.

User slices have a solid line border, auto slices have a dotted line border, and any selected slices have a yellow border. Each user slice contains a symbol indicating if it is an image slice or a layer-based slice, or if the slice is linked. See Table 2 for a description of the symbols used to identify user slices. A selected user slice contains a bounding box and sizing handles. You can resize a slice by

TABLE 2: USER SLICE SYMBOLS	
Symbol	**Used to identify**
⊠	Image slice
⊡	Layer-based slice
⊠	No image slice

© Cengage Learning®

Creating Images for the Web

dragging a handle to a new location, just as you would resize any object.

Learning About Slice Components

By default, a slice consists of the following components:

- A colored border that helps you identify the slice type
- An overlay that dims the appearance of the unselected slices
- A number that helps you identify each individual slice
- A symbol that helps you determine the type of slice

QUICK TIP

When two slices overlap, a subslice is automatically created.

Adjusting Slice Attributes

You can adjust slice attributes by clicking Guides, Grid & Slices under the Preferences command, which opens the Preferences dialog box, shown in Figure 12. You can choose slice line color and whether to display slice numbers.

QUICK TIP

It doesn't matter which layer, if any, is active when you create slices using the Slice tool.

Using a Layer-Based Slice

In addition to drawing a slice using the Slice tool, you can use the New Layer Based Slice command on the Layer menu to create a slice from a layer on the Layers panel. This is an easy way of creating a slice *without* having to draw an outline.

Creating a Layer-Based Slice

Creating a layer-based slice automatically surrounds the image on the layer with a slice, which can be useful if you want to create a slice quickly or if you want a large slice.

Figure 12 *Preferences dialog box*

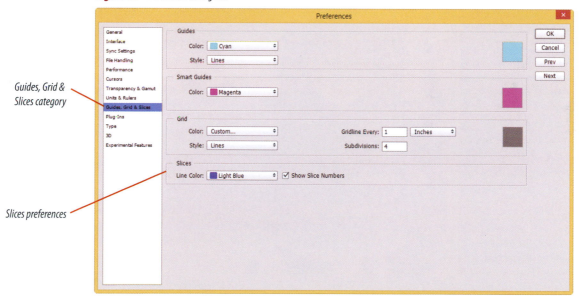

Guides, Grid & Slices category

Slices preferences

Photoshop updates the slice whenever you modify the layer or its content. For example, the slice automatically adjusts if you move its corresponding layer on the Layers panel, or you erase pixels on the layer. In Figure 13, the active slice is an image slice.

QUICK **TIP**

To delete a layer-based slice, user slice, or auto slice, select the slice, and then press [Delete] (Win) or [delete] (Mac).

Using the Slice Options Dialog Box

The Slice Options dialog box is used to set options such as content type, name, and URL for a specific slice. You open this dialog box by double-clicking a slice with the Slice Select tool. You use the text boxes in the Slice Options dialog box to assign a URL, add message text, and use the list arrow to change the slice background type. For example, you can make the slice a link in the resulting web page.

Assigning a Web Address to a Slice

You can assign a web page to a selected slice by typing its Uniform Resource Locater (URL) in the URL text box. The **URL** is the web page's address that appears in the Address box in your browser. You can designate how that web page will be displayed in your browser by entering the name of the target frame in the Target text box.

Figure 13 *Sliced image*
© Photodisc/Getty Images

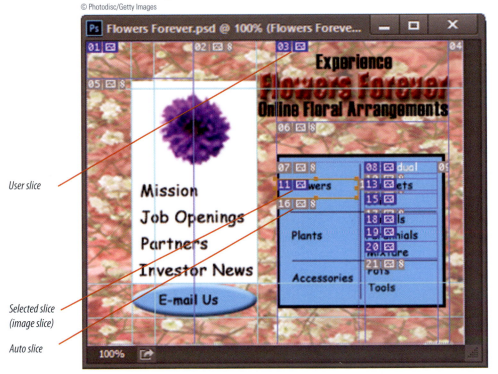

User slice

Selected slice
(image slice)

Auto slice

Figure 14 *New slices added to image*

Source: Morguefile.

Newly added slice

Selected slice

Slice numbering automatically changes with each modification (your numbers might be different)

1. Click the **Slice tool** ✐ on the Tools panel. The existing slices in the image are visible.

TIP You can also create a slice using guides. Select the Slice tool from the Tools panel, arrange guides, then click the Slices from Guides button in the options bar.

2. Drag the **Slice pointer** ✐ around the **Clothing type** (from approximately **10 X/60 Y** to **100 X/85 Y**).

3. Drag ✐ around the **Dining type** (from approximately **10 X/160 Y** to **70 X/185 Y**), then compare your slices to Figure 14.

You viewed the existing slices in the Shopping Heaven image and created two user slices, one for the Clothing text and one for the Dining text.

Create a layer-based slice

1. Click the **2 Shoppers layer** on the Layers panel.
2. Click **Layer** on the Menu bar, click **New Layer Based Slice**, then compare your screen to Figure 15.

   A new slice surrounds the 2 Shoppers layer object.

TIP Slice numbering automatically changes with each modification so your slice numbers might be different.

You made the 2 Shoppers layer active on the Layers panel, then created a slice based on this layer.

Figure 15 *New layer-based slice*

Source: Morguefile.

Auto slice generated by the layer slice

Indicates layer-based slice

Figure 16 *Resized slice*
Source: Morguefile.

*Drag handle to
new position*

Resize a slice

1. Click the **Slice Select tool**  on the Tools panel.

2. Click the **Dining slice**.

3. Drag the **right-middle sizing handle** ◄·► to **90 X**, compare your slice to Figure 16, then release the mouse button.

TIP As you drag the sizing handle, a black box displays the changing slice width in pixels.

TIP Because layer-based slices are fitted to pixels on the layer, they will not display sizing handles when selected.

You resized the Dining slice.

Assign a web address to a slice

1. Double-click the **Dining slice** with the **Slice Select pointer** .

   The Slice Options dialog box opens when you double-click a slice with the Slice Select tool.

2. Type **shoppingheavenmarket.com** in the URL text box, then compare your Slice Options dialog box to Figure 17.

   TIP Your slice number and dimensions might vary.

3. Click **OK** to close the Slice Options dialog box.

You assigned a web address to a slice using the Slice Options dialog box.

Figure 17 *URL assigned to slice*

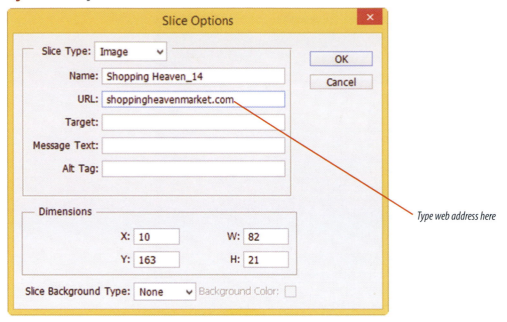

Type web address here

Figure 18 *Image with rulers, guides and slices hidden*
Source: Morguefile.

1. Click an **area outside of the slice** (but not part of another slice) to deselect the Dining slice, turn off the display of the rulers, guides, and slices, then compare your image to Figure 18.

TIP To hide slices in your image, click View on the Menu bar, point to Show, then click Slices.

2. Save your work, close Shopping Heaven.psd, then exit Photoshop.

You deselected a slice.

POWER USER SHORTCUTS	
To do this:	**Use this method:**
Create a slice	✏️ or [Shift] **C**
Cycle shape tools	[Shift] **U**
Deselect slices	Click outside slice
Fit image to screen	[Ctrl][0] (Win) or ⌘ [0] (Mac)
Hide/show rulers	[Ctrl][R] (Win) or ⌘ [R] (Mac)
Save for Web	[Alt][Shift][Ctrl][S] (Win) or [shift][option] ⌘ [S] (Mac)
Select a slice	✂️ or [Shift] **C**

Key: Menu items are indicated by ➤ between the menu name and its command. Blue bold letters are shortcuts for selecting tools on the Tools panel.

© Cengage Learning®

Learn about web features.

1. Start Photoshop, open PS 17-3.psd from the drive and folder where you store your Data Files, then save it as **Optimal Dolphin**.
2. Set the background and foreground colors to their default values.
3. Fit the image on the screen.

Optimize images for web use.

1. Open the Save For Web dialog box.
2. Display the 4-Up tab, then reposition it or zoom in or out of the image (if necessary).
3. Verify the settings of the image to the right of the original image as GIF 64 Dithered.
4. Save the file as **Optimal-Dolphin.gif** to the drive and folder where you store your Data Files.
5. Open the Save For Web dialog box, click the first GIF image after the original image, change the settings to JPEG High, then compare your image to Figure 19.
6. Use the Save button to save the file as **Optimal-Dolphin.jpg**.
7. Close Optimal Dolphin without saving changes.

Figure 19 *Completed Skills Review 1*
© Photodisc/Getty Images

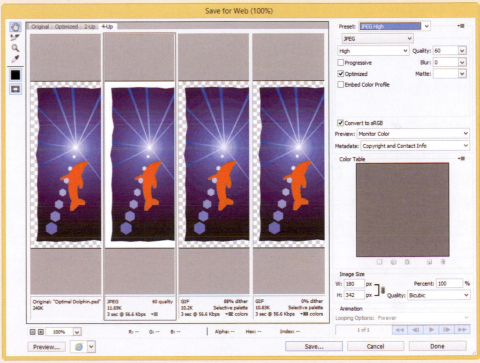

Create a button for a web page.

1. Open PS 17-4.psd, then save it as **Canine-Nation**.
2. If prompted, update the text layers.
3. Set the background and foreground colors to the default.
4. Fit the image on the screen, and display the rulers, guides, and slices (if necessary).
5. Select the Rounded Rectangle tool.
6. Activate the Board layer, then add a new layer.
7. Use the guides to help you draw a shape from 15 X/340 Y to 135 X/390 Y, then select the Woodgrain style. (The Woodgrain style is in the Buttons styles set.)
8. Select the Type tool.
9. Click the image within the button, type **Rescue** (use a White, Arial Regular Bold font of appropriate size), then center the text within the button.
10. Save your work.

Create slices in an image.

1. Draw a slice for the Train button from 15 X/150 Y to 135 X/200 Y.
2. Draw a slice for the Groom button from 15 X/210 Y to 135 X/260 Y.
3. Draw a slice for the Board button from 15 X/275 Y to 135 X/325 Y.
4. Draw a slice for the Rescue button from 15 X/340 Y to 135 X/390 Y.
5. Resize the Jack Russell slice (the image of the dog in the top-right portion of the image) so that the top is at 90 Y and the bottom is at 320 Y.
6. Type the following (fictitious) URL for the Jack Russell slice, **www.caninenation.com/jackrussell_faq .html**, then click OK.
7. Hide the slices and rulers.
8. Save your work, compare your image to Figure 20, then close Canine-Nation.

Figure 20 *Completed Skills Review 2*
Source: Morguefile.

You're intrigued by button styles, and as the designer of your firm's website, you decide to impress your boss and find a source of free button styles you can use in Photoshop. A variety of clothing buttons are shown in Figure 21: perhaps you can find similar Photoshop button styles online.

1. Connect to the Internet and use your browser to find sites containing downloadable button styles. (Make a record of the sites you find so you can use them in the future.)
2. Create a new Photoshop image and save it as **Button Samples**.
3. Create an attractive document that displays a sampler of button styles. You can use styles you've found on the web or those found within Photoshop.
4. Save your work.

Figure 21 *Sample (clothing) buttons*
Source: Morguefile.

Creating Images for the Web

Why should you care about optimizing web graphics? Everyone has broadband, right? Well actually, no…they don't. To satisfy your own curiosity, you've decided to look into the mechanics of optimization of web graphics.

1. Connect to the Internet and use your browser to find sites containing information about graphic optimization. (Make a record of the sites you find so you can use them in the future.) A sample web graphic image is shown in Figure 22.
2. Use your favorite word processor to create a document called **Optimized Graphics**.
3. Briefly summarize the information you obtained about the importance of graphic optimization, and be prepared to discuss your findings.
4. Save your work.

Figure 22 *Sample Project Builder 2*
Source: Morguefile.

Website design is not so easy as you might think. You need to find out more about design principles for websites.

1. Connect to the Internet and use your browser to find sites containing information about designing websites. (Make a record of the site you found so you can use it for future reference, if necessary.) A sample web graphic image is shown in Figure 23.
2. Use your favorite word processor to create a new document and save it as **Website design principles**.
3. Create a list of principles that you feel are most important in website design, and be prepared to discuss this topic.
4. Save your work.

Figure 23 *Sample Design Project*
Source: Morguefile.

Your employer, Green Grocer Foods (an independent organic grocery store), is impressed with your knowledge of Photoshop, and they would like you to take a 'first stab' at setting up a web page in Photoshop. The sample site does not have to contain any graphics, just type and slices that indicate where links will be placed.

1. Create a new Photoshop image, then save it as **Green Grocer Foods**.
2. Apply a color or style to the Background layer, add other colors and type as desired, and apply any necessary effects that make the sample site more attractive.
3. Add type layers that will identify departments and customer features found in the store.
4. Create slices around the type, displaying rulers and adding guides where appropriate.
5. Add at least two (fictitious) URLs to the slices.
6. Save your work, compare your screen to the sample shown in Figure 24, then hide the rulers and any guides you may have created.

Figure 24 *Sample Portfolio Project*

CHAPTER 18

WORKING WITH ANIMATION, VIDEO, & PHOTOGRAPHY

1. Create and play basic animation
2. Add tweening and frame delay
3. Modify video in Photoshop
4. Use Camera Raw features
5. Fix common photography problems

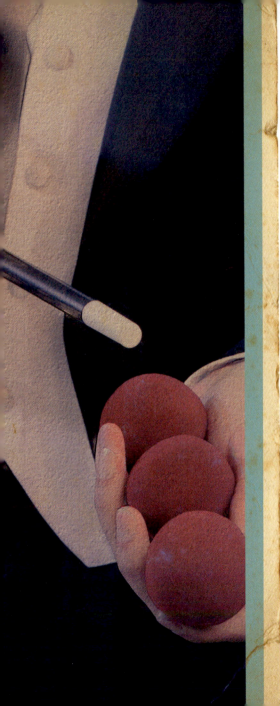

CHAPTER 18 WORKING WITH ANIMATION, VIDEO, & PHOTOGRAPHY

Understanding Animation

A quick display of an image sequence, or **animation**, creates the appearance of movement. In Photoshop, you can generate animation from your images. You can create an animation by making slight changes to several images, and then adjusting the timing between their appearances. When you convert an image to HTML for display on a web page, slices become cells in an HTML table and animations become files in object folders.

QUICK TIP

If the Timeline panel is not visible, you can display it by clicking Window on the Menu bar, and then by clicking Timeline, or by displaying the Motion workspace.

Extending Photoshop Skills to Video

Photoshop CC can be used to play and modify video. Almost any Photoshop skill you can apply to images can be applied to video clips.

And you don't have to invest in sophisticated, expensive video camera equipment to shoot video. Just about any commonly available point-and-shoot digital camera or smart phone has the capability to shoot video. (So get ready to harness your inner Scorsese!)

QUICK TIP

Video features are *not* supported on 32-bit Windows systems.

Fine-Tuning Images with Camera Raw

Images that you take with your own digital camera can be tweaked using Adobe Bridge and the Camera Raw dialog box. You can use the Camera Raw dialog box to adjust images in Raw format (as well as those in JPEG and TIFF formats) while preserving all the original image data.

TOOLS YOU'LL USE

Frame animation timeline

© Photodisc/Getty Images

Video timeline

Create and Play
BASIC ANIMATION

What You'll Do

 In this lesson, you'll create basic animation by creating timeline frames. For each newly created frame, you'll modify layers by hiding and showing them, and changing their opacity. You'll also play and preview the animation to test your work.

Understanding Animation

You can use nearly any type of graphics image to create interesting animation effects. You can move objects in your image or overlap them so that they blend into one another. Once you place the images that you want to animate in a file, you can determine how and when you want the animation to play.

Creating Animation on the Timeline Panel

Remember that an animation is nothing more than a series of still images displayed rapidly to give the illusion of motion. The Timeline panel displays a thumbnail of the animation image in each frame. A **frame** is an individual image that is used in animation. When you create a new frame on the Timeline panel, you duplicate the current frame, and can then modify the duplicate frame as desired. The layers that are visible on the Layers panel appear in the selected frame, and thus, in the animation. Here's all that's involved in creating a simple animation:

- Place images on layers in the file.
- Hide all but one layer.

- Duplicate the frame, turn off the displayed layer, and then turn on the layer you want to see.

Animating Images

If you look at the Layers panel in Figure 1, you'll see that there are images on two layers. The Timeline panel contains two frames: one for each of the layers. When frame 1 is selected, the man appears in the image; when frame 2 is selected, the woman appears. When the animation is played, the images of the man and woman alternate.

Moving and Deleting Frames

To move a frame to a different spot, click the frame on the Timeline panel, and drag it to a new location. To select contiguous frames, press and hold [Shift], and then click the frames you want to include. To select noncontiguous frames, press and hold [Ctrl] (Win) or ⌘ (Mac), and then click the frames you want to include. You can delete a frame by clicking it on the Timeline panel, and then dragging it to the Deletes selected frames button on the Timeline panel.

Looping the Animation

You can set the number of times the animation plays by clicking the Selects looping options list arrow on the Timeline panel, and then clicking Once, 3 times, Forever, or Other. When you select Other, the Set Loop Count dialog box opens, where you can enter the loop number you want.

Previewing the Animation

When you're ready to preview an animation, you have a few choices:

■ You can use the buttons on the bottom of the Timeline panel. When you click the Plays animation button, the animation plays.

■ You can preview the optimized image in your browser by clicking Preview in the Save for Web dialog box.

Figure 1 *Sample of basic animation*
© Photodisc/Getty Images

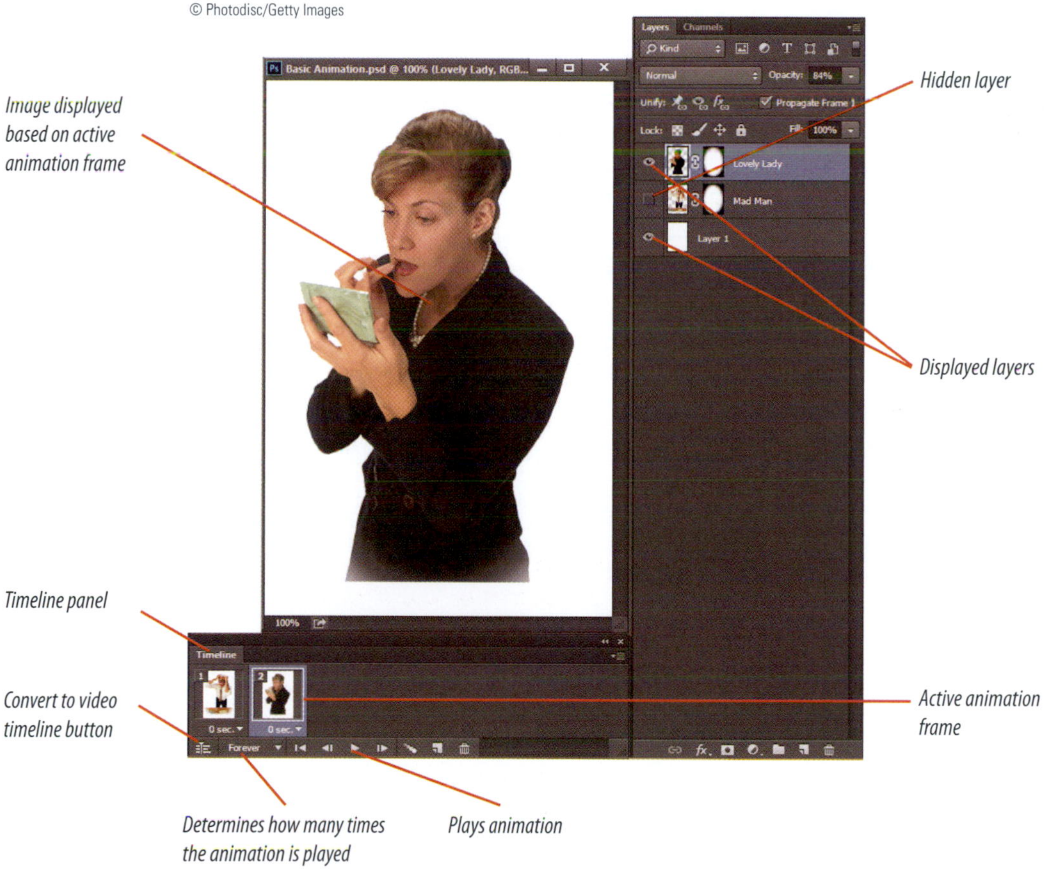

Image displayed based on active animation frame

Hidden layer

Displayed layers

Timeline panel

Convert to video timeline button

Active animation frame

Determines how many times the animation is played

Plays animation

Converting Animation Frames to a Video Timeline

By default, the Timeline panel displays frames, but you can change the panel so it shows a video timeline. You change the display by clicking the Convert to video timeline button in the lower-left corner of the Timeline panel. (Return to displaying frames by clicking the Convert to frame animation button when the video timeline is displayed.) Figure 2 shows the Video Timeline panel. As you drag the bars for each of the layers in the timeline, the image updates to show the effect of your changes.

QUICK **TIP**

If the Timeline panel displays the video timeline, the Convert to frame animation button appears. Conversely, the Convert to video timeline button displays in the (Frames) Timeline panel.

Exporting to Zoomify

Using the Export to Zoomify feature, you can post your high-resolution images on the web so viewers can pan and zoom in on them in more detail. Using this feature, your image will download in the same time as an equivalent size JPEG file. Figure 3 shows the Zoomify™ Export dialog box which you can open by clicking File on the Menu bar, pointing to Export, and then clicking Zoomify.

Figure 2 *(Video) Timeline panel*

Convert to frame
animation button

Figure 3 *Zoomify Export dialog box*

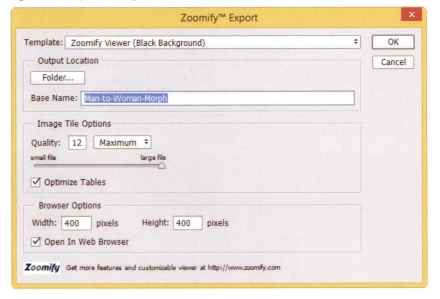

Figure 4 *Frames created on Timeline panel*
Source: Morguefile

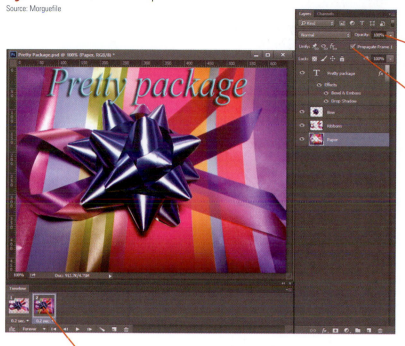

Opacity setting
of newly created
animation frame

Indicates state has
an animation

New animation frame

Figure 5 *Newly created animation frames*

New animation frame

Create and duplicate animation frames

1. Open PS 18-1.psd from the drive and folder where you store your Data Files, then save it as **Pretty Package**.
2. Display the **Motion workspace**, display the rulers in pixels, then **resize the Timeline panel** so it is no wider than the Pretty Package image.

TIP You can resize the Timeline panel by dragging it from its dock, positioning it above or below the image window, then dragging from the left or right to resize it.

3. Adjust the opacity setting of the Paper layer to **50%** on the Layers panel.
4. Click the **Duplicates selected frames button** on the Timeline panel.
   A new Animation frame is created and is now the active frame.
5. Adjust the opacity setting of the Paper layer to **100%**, then compare your screen to Figure 4.

TIP Your computer may show a different value for the time interval at the bottom of each frame, instead of the .2 sec default.

6. Click on the Timeline panel.
7. Click the **Indicates layer visibility button** on the Paper layer on the Layers panel to hide this layer.
8. Click on the Ribbons layer on the Layers panel to hide this layer.
9. Click the **Bow layer** to make it active.
   The content from the Bow layer appears in frame 3 of the Timeline panel. See Figure 5.

You created an animation frame, duplicated existing frames, and adjusted the opacity of the frames. Duplicating frames with different levels of opacity creates one of the possible animated effects when viewed in a browser.

Adjust animation frames

1. Set the opacity setting of the Bow layer to **50%**.

2. Click the **Duplicates selected frames button** on the Timeline panel, then adjust the opacity setting of the Bow layer to **100%**.

3. Click on the Timeline panel. You have now created five frames.

4. Click the **Indicates layer visibility button** on the Bow layer to hide it.

5. Click the **Ribbons layer** on the Layers panel to make it active, then click the **Indicates layer visibility button** on the Layers panel to display this layer.

6. Adjust the opacity setting to **50%**.

7. Click on the Timeline panel, then adjust the opacity setting of the Ribbons layer to **100%**. Compare your screen to Figure 6.

You adjusted the opacity of frames using the Layers panel. The adjustment of frame settings lets you simulate movement when the animation is played.

Figure 6 *Completed animation frames*
Source: Morguefile

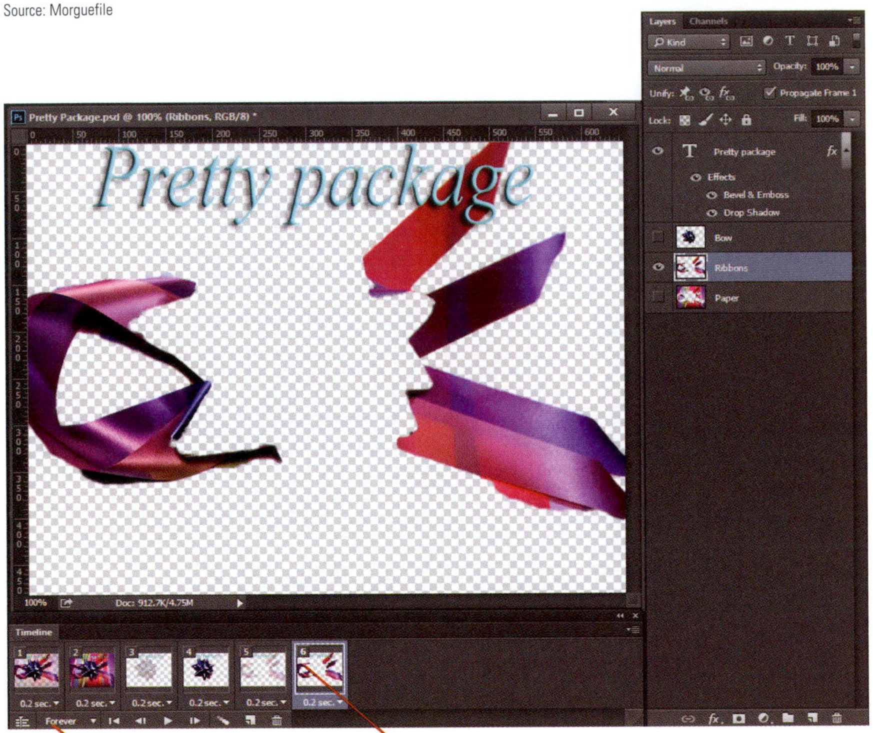

Selects looping options list arrow   New animation frame

Using Video Layers in Photoshop CC

If you have QuickTime 7.6.2 or higher installed on your computer, you can use Photoshop CC to edit individual frames of video and image sequence files. You can also edit and paint on video, and apply filters, masks, transformations, layer styles, and blending modes. When you open a video file in Photoshop CC, the frames are contained within a video layer (indicated by a filmstrip icon in the Layers panel). You can create a video layer in an active document by displaying the Timeline panel in Timeline mode, clicking Layer on the Menu bar, pointing to Video Layers, and then clicking New Video Layer from File.

Figure 7 *Animation displayed in browser*

The active frame determines which imagery displays in the browser: yours may differ

Animation automatically begins when you open the image

Your information may differ

Format: JPEG
Dimensions: 645w x 483h
Size: 78.8K
Settings: Quality is 60, Non-Progressive, Optimized on

TABLE 1: ANIMATION TOOLS		
Tool	**Tool name**	**Description**
Forever ▼	Selects looping options	Determines how many times the animation plays
◀❘	Selects first frame	Makes the first frame on the panel active
◀❘	Selects previous frame	Activates the frame to the left of the current frame on the panel
▶	Plays animation	Plays the animation
■	Stops animation	Stops the animation
❘▶	Selects next frame	Activates the frame to the right of the current frame on the panel
⬎	Tweens animation frames	Adds interim frames with incremental animation changes
❏	Duplicates selected frames	Creates a duplicate of selected frames
🗑	Deletes selected frames	Disposes of selected frames

Play animation in the image and view optimized image browser

1. Verify that **Forever** is selected in the Selects looping options list arrow, click the **first frame** in the Timeline panel, then click the **Plays animation button** ▶ on the Timeline panel.

2. Click the **Stops animation button** ■ on the Timeline panel.

   The animation stops, displaying the currently active frame.

   The Plays/Stops animation button changes its appearance depending on the current state of the animation. See Table 1 for a description of the buttons on the Timeline panel.

3. Turn off the ruler display, then save your work.

4. Click **File** on the Menu bar, click **Save for Web**, click **Preview**, then compare your preview to Figure 7. (The file will display the animation *only* if saved in the GIF format.)

TIP The first time you use this feature you may have to add a browser.

5. Close your browser, then click **Cancel** in the Save for Web dialog box.

TIP The animation might play differently in your browser, which is why it is important to preview your files on as many different systems as possible. You may need to install the Adobe Flash Player plug-in for your browser to display the animation.

You played the animation in the file, then viewed the image in a browser.

Add Tweening
AND FRAME DELAY

What You'll Do

 In this lesson, you'll add tweening to animation and adjust the frame delay for a frame on the Timeline panel.

Understanding Tweening

To create animation, you assemble a series of frames, and then play them quickly to create the illusion of continuous motion. Each frame represents a major action point. Sometimes the variance of action between the frames creates erratic or rough motion. To blend the motion *in between* the frames, you can tween your animation. **Tweening** adds frames that change the action in slight increments from one frame to the next. The origin of this term predates computer animation, when an artist known as an *inbetweener* hand-drew each frame that linked major action frames (at 24 frames per second!), and thus the term tweening was born.

Using Tweening on the Timeline Panel

You can add tweening to a frame by clicking the Tweens animation frames button on the Timeline panel, and then entering the number of in-between frames you want in the Tween dialog box. You can choose whether you want the tweening to affect all layers or just the selected layer, and if you want the image to change position, opacity, or effects. You can also specify the frame on which

you want the tweening to start, and specify the number of frames to add in between the frames (you can add up to 999 frames in a single tween). Figure 8 shows a two-frame animation after four tween frames were added. The opacity of the man is 100% in the first frame and 0% in the last frame. Adding five tween frames causes the two images to blend into each other smoothly, or **morph** (metamorphose).

> **QUICK TIP**
>
> You can select contiguous frames and apply the same tweening settings to them simultaneously.

Understanding Frame Delays

When you create frames on the Timeline panel, Photoshop automatically sets the **frame delay**, the length of time that each frame appears. You can set the delay time in whole or partial seconds by clicking the Selects frame delay time button below each frame. You can set the frame delay time you want for each frame, or you can select several frames and apply the same frame delay time to them.

Setting Frame Delays

To change the delay for a single selected frame, click the Selects frame delay time button, and then click a length of time. To change the delay for contiguous frames, press and hold [Shift], click the frames you want to include, and then click the Selects frame delay time button on *any* of the selected frames. To change the delay for noncontiguous frames, press and hold [Ctrl] (Win) or [⌘] (Mac), click the frames you want to include, and then click the Selects frame delay time button on any of the selected frames.

Correcting Pixel Aspect Ratio in Video

The **pixel aspect ratio** feature automatically corrects the ratio of pixels displayed for the monitor in use. Without this correction, pixels viewed in a 16:9 monitor (such as a widescreen TV) would look squashed in a 4:3 monitor (typical rectangular TV). You can assign a pixel aspect ratio to a document by clicking View on the Menu bar, pointing to Pixel Aspect Ratio, and then selecting a pixel aspect ratio. (Unless you are using the image for video, Square is the recommended setting.)

When you have selected a pixel aspect ratio, the Pixel Aspect Ratio Correction option will be checked on the View menu. If you've made a change to the aspect ratio, you can uncheck the Pixel Aspect Ratio Correction command to turn off the scaling correction and view the image as it looks on a computer (square pixel) monitor. Photoshop automatically converts and scales the image to the pixel aspect ratio of the non-square pixel document. Images brought in from Adobe Illustrator will also be properly scaled.

Figure 8 *Timeline panel*
© Photodisc/Getty Images

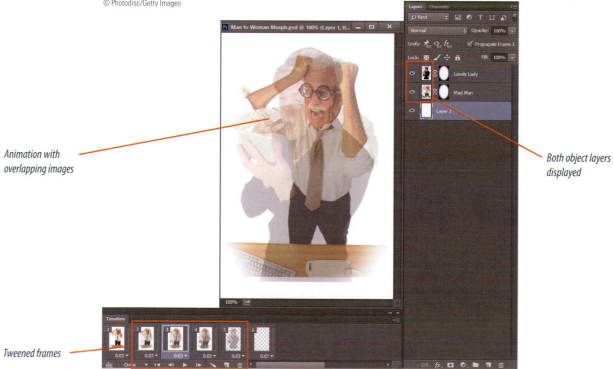

Animation with overlapping images

Both object layers displayed

Tweened frames

Tween animation frames

1. Click **frame 3** on the Timeline panel.
2. Click the **Tweens animation frames button** 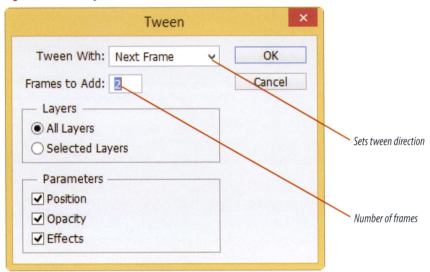 on the Timeline panel.
3. Adjust the settings in your Tween dialog box so that they match those shown in Figure 9.
4. Click **OK**.

   Two additional frames are added after frame 3.
5. Click the **Plays animation button** ▶ on the Timeline panel, then view the animation.
6. Click the **Stops animation button** ◻ on the Timeline panel, then compare your panel to Figure 10, which now has eight frames.

You used the Tweens animation frames button on the Timeline panel to insert two new frames, then played the animation to view the results. Did you notice that the effect is smoother and more fluid motion?

Figure 9 *Tween dialog box*

Sets tween direction

Number of frames

Figure 10 *Tweening frames inserted*

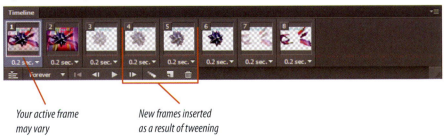

Your active frame may vary

New frames inserted as a result of tweening

Figure 11 *Frame delay menu*

Figure 12 *Frame delay in Timeline panel*
Source: Morguefile

1. Click **frame 2** on the Timeline panel.

2. Click the **Selects frame delay time button** `0.2 sec. ▼` at the bottom of the selected frame.

3. Compare your frame delay menu to Figure 11, then click **0.5**.

   The frame delay for frame 2 changes from 0.2 to 0.5 seconds.

4. Click the **Plays animation button** ▶ on the Timeline panel, then view the animation.

5. Click the **Stops animation button** ▣ on the Timeline panel.

6. Open the **Save for Web dialog box**, then click **Preview**.

7. Review the animation, close your browser, then close the Save for Web dialog box.

8. Compare your screen to Figure 12, then save your work.

9. Close the image.

You fine-tuned your animation by changing the frame delay for frame 2, then previewed the animation in your browser. It's important to preview animations in multiple web browsers on as many computers and operating systems as you can manage, so that you can see your work as others will view it.

Previewing Photoshop Documents for Video

When you're working on a Photoshop image that you plan to include in a digital video or video presentation, you can use the Video Preview plug-in (included with Photoshop) to see real-time results as you work. Because the images you create in Photoshop are made up of square pixels, and video editing programs usually convert these to nonsquare pixels for video encoding, distortion can result when you import an image into a video editing program. But with Video Preview, you can check for distortion and make changes before finalizing your image. When the Video Preview plug-in is installed, and your computer is connected to a video monitor, you can access Video Preview by clicking File on the Menu bar, pointing to Export, and then clicking Render Video. This command also lets you adjust the aspect ratio as necessary for different viewing systems, such as NTSC, PAL, or HD.

Modify Video
IN PHOTOSHOP

What You'll Do

Image courtesy of Elizabeth Eisner Reding

 In this lesson, you'll open a video file and save it in a Photoshop format. You'll apply two adjustments, apply a transition, and change the starting and ending points of the video sequence.

Playing Video

It might surprise you to know that you can play video using Photoshop CC (with QuickTime 7.6.2 or higher installed), but then again, you might have guessed that it was possible after creating animation sequences using individual frames, since video is the natural next step after working with individual images. (You can create a still Photoshop image that automatically inherits the pixel and frame aspect ratio of an Adobe Premiere Pro project. Title-safe areas will also be preserved.)

> **QUICK TIP**
>
> You can create your own video sequences using most digital cameras. You may have to modify your camera settings or flip a switch on the camera body.

Working with Video

When you open a video file in Photoshop CC, individual frames are contained in a video layer, and the layer appears in the Layers panel with a special filmstrip icon, shown in Figure 13. You can use your existing Photoshop skills (such as creating and editing adjustment layers, adjusting opacity, making selections, adding masks, painting, and cloning) on the video layer. Table 2 lists the movie file extensions that can be opened in Photoshop CC.

Frame Versus Video in the Timeline Panel

Although the Timeline panel has two modes (frame and video), you use the video mode when working with video. These mode tools, are located at the bottom of the Timeline panel, as shown in Figure 14, allow you to navigate the video sequence. In addition to the tools in the Timeline panel, you can use the spacebar to start and stop playing the video. Both modes display frame duration, but the frame mode shows

Figure 13 *Filmstrip icon in Layers panel*

Filmstrip icon in thumbnail

layer animation properties while the video mode shows keyframed layer properties.

QUICK TIP

If you convert a video sequence from video to frame animation, you will be left with a single frame in the Timeline panel.

Enhancing Video

Changes you can make to layers in a Photoshop image can also be applied to video layers. For example, you can apply adjustment layers to lighten or darken the overall look of a video sequence. Such enhancements can be used throughout a video sequence or can be controlled so that they only affect specific areas of the timeline. Figure 15 shows several adjustment layers applied to the video layer.

QUICK TIP

Video playback performance will be greatly affected by the type of video card and video RAM (VRAM) installed. For best performance, Adobe recommends an OpenGL 2.0-capable system, with a minimum of 512 MB of VRAM (1 GB recommended).

Figure 14 *Timeline panel*

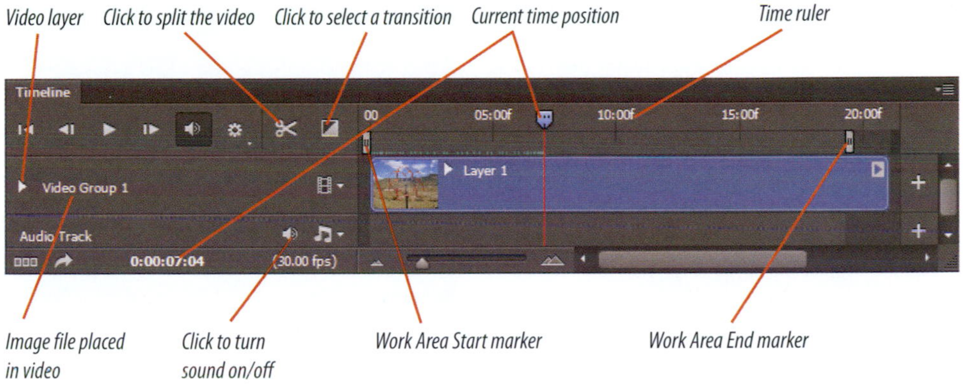

Video layer Click to split the video Click to select a transition Current time position Time ruler

Image file placed in video Click to turn sound on/off Work Area Start marker Work Area End marker

Figure 15 *Layers panel with adjustment layers applied to video*

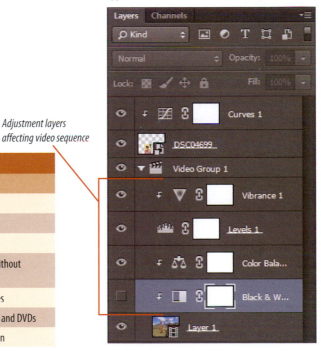

Adjustment layers affecting video sequence

TABLE 2: USABLE MOVIE FILE TYPES IN PHOTOSHOP CC		
Name	**Stands for**	**Additional information**
AVI	Audio Video Interleaved	Developed by Microsoft
F4V	MPEG-4 video file; Flash video	Streaming video
FLV	Flash video	Streaming video files
MOV	QuickTime format	Developed for Mac. Can be uploaded to YouTube without additional conversion
MPEG-1	Moving Pictures Expert Group	Used on the web for short video and animation files
MPEG-2 (with encoder)		Used for higher resolution video, digital television, and DVDs
MPEG-4		Used for compression of AV data and CD distribution

© 2013 Cengage Learning®

Apply an adjustment layer

1. Open PS 18-2.avi from the drive and folder where you store your Data files, then save it as **Coyotes.psd**.

   TIP When you save a video file in Photoshop, the file format is changed to .psd.

2. Fit the image to the screen.

3. Click the **Layers Panel options button** [icon], then click **Convert to Smart Object**.

   The filmstrip icon in the Layers panel is changed to a Smart Object icon. See Figure 16.

4. Display the **Timeline panel** if necessary, then click the **Brightness/Contrast button** [icon] on the Adjustments panel.

   TIP You can resize the Timeline panel using the Zoom slider so that the beginning and ending points are visible.

5. Change the Brightness to **40** and the Contrast to **25**, then collapse the Properties panel to the dock.

6. Click the **Color Balance button** [icon] on the Adjustments panel, change the midtones settings to **+30**, **+15**, and **+20**, then collapse the Properties panel to the dock.

7. Click the **Play button** [icon] on the Timeline panel.

   TIP You can turn the audio track on/off by clicking the Mute or unmute audio track button to the right of the Audio Track layer.

8. When you are finished watching the video, click the **Stop button** [icon], then compare your work to Figure 17.

You saved a movie file in the Photoshop format, converted it to a smart object so it can be modified later if necessary, added two adjustment layers, then played the video.

Figure 16 *Layers panel with Smart Object*

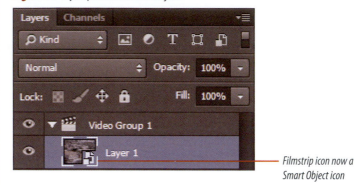

Filmstrip icon now a Smart Object icon

Figure 17 *Adjustment layers in video sequence*
Image courtesy of Elizabeth Eisner Reding

Current time position may vary

Playhead

Figure 18 *Split video tracks*

Work area
start marker

Area between
video tracks

Playhead

End of Work
area marker

Figure 19 *Modified video settings*

Image courtesy of Elizabeth Eisner Reding

Modified video settings

1. Make Layer 1 the active layer in the Layers panel, then click the **Go to first frame button** in the Timeline panel.

2. Drag the **Playhead** of the Layer 1 video on the Timeline panel to approximately **4:00f** on the time ruler, then click the **Split at Playhead button** as shown in Figure 18. (The figure has been resized for display purposes only.)

3. Click the Color Balance 1 layer in the Layers panel, then drag the **End of Work marker** of the Color Balance 1 layer to approximately **14:00f** on the time ruler.

TIP Dragging the End of Work marker affects all layers, not just the active layer.

4. Click the **Select a transition and drag to apply button** in the Timeline panel, then click **Fade with Black**.

5. Drag the transition between Layer 1 and Layer 1 copy on the Timeline panel.

6. Click , then click the **Play button** on the Timeline panel.

TIP You can also play a video by pressing [Enter] (Win).

TIP The Photoshop Open GL/GPU feature supports the smooth display of non-square pixel images.

7. Save your work, compare your screen and Timeline panel to Figure 19, then close the file.

You modified the starting and ending point of a video file, split the video layers and added a transition between the two layers, then played the video sequence.

Use Camera Raw
FEATURES

What You'll Do

Image courtesy of Elizabeth Eisner Reding

 In this lesson, you'll learn how to use the Camera Raw dialog box to make adjustments to images in the Raw, TIFF, and JPEG formats.

Using Raw Data from Digital Cameras

If you're a digital camera photographer, or have access to digital photos, you'll appreciate the ability to use images in the 16-bit **Camera Raw** format because it contains so much controllable data. Sure, the files are twice the size, but the resolution contains 65,000 data points (versus the 256 data points in an 8-bit image). Once an image with raw data is opened, the Camera Raw interface appears containing magnification and color correction options.

The Camera Raw dialog box shown in Figure 20 contains three buttons in the

Figure 20 *Camera Raw dialog box*
Image courtesy of Elizabeth Eisner Reding

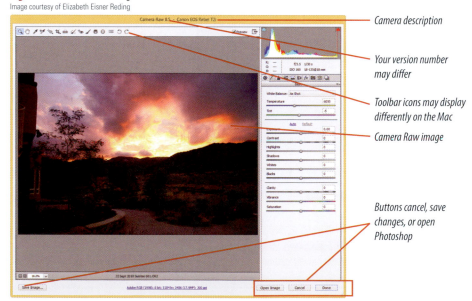

Camera description

Your version number may differ

Toolbar icons may display differently on the Mac

Camera Raw image

Buttons cancel, save changes, or open Photoshop

Working with Animation, Video, & Photography

lower-right corner: Open Image, Cancel, and Done, and one button in the lower-left corner: Save Image. The Open Image button applies the changes and opens the image in Photoshop. The Save Image button converts and saves an image in Photoshop. The Done button applies the changes and closes the dialog box without opening the image. The Cancel button closes the dialog box without accepting any changes. In addition to files in the Raw format, JPEG and TIFF digital images can also be opened using the Camera Raw dialog box, enabling you to take advantage of the same powerful setting options. To do this, right-click the image in Adobe Bridge, and then click Open in Camera Raw. You can also access this tool by clicking Filter on the Menu bar, then clicking Camera Raw Filter.

Modifying Camera Raw Images

An image in the Camera Raw file format can be opened using the Open As command on the File menu or Adobe Bridge, but the image initially opens in the Camera Raw dialog box rather than in the Photoshop window. This dialog box creates a sidecar XMP file that contains metadata and accompanies the Camera Raw file. An image that has been modified using the Camera Raw plug-in is identified with a Camera Raw icon in Bridge, as shown in Figure 21.

Using Camera Raw Settings and Preferences

The Camera Raw file format is similar to a digital negative. It contains all the information a camera has about a specific image. It is also similar to the TIFF format in that it does not discard any color information, yet it is smaller than an uncompressed TIFF. Camera Raw settings can be saved (up to 100 settings) and then applied to a specific camera or for specific lighting conditions. The Camera Raw Settings menu, found on the individual Image Adjustment tabs, allows you to save current settings and add them to the Settings menu, load saved Settings, or reset the Camera Raw defaults. You can modify settings for Temperature, Tint, Exposure, Contrast, Highlights, Shadows, Whites, Blacks, Clarity, Vibrance, and Saturation using the Basic tab.

Figure 21 *Camera Raw image in Adobe Bridge*
Image courtesy of Elizabeth Eisner Reding

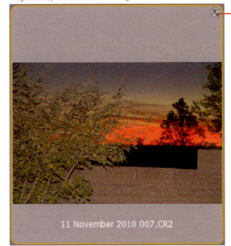

Icon indicates edits to raw file

11 November 2010 007.CR2

Using Camera Raw Adjustment Settings

Because the Camera Raw format for each digital camera is different, you can adjust the Camera Raw settings to recreate the colors in a photo more accurately. Using the Camera Calibration tab, one of the Image adjustment tabs in the Camera Raw dialog box, you can select one of six profiles. (Embedded will display as the Camera Profile if you don't have a Raw image open.) Use the Hue and Saturation sliders to adjust the red, green, and blue in the image. Camera Raw adjustments made to the original image are always preserved, so you can adjust them repeatedly if necessary. The adjustment settings are stored within the Camera Raw database file or in a sidecar XMP file that accompanies the original Camera Raw image in a location of your choosing.

Understanding the Camera Raw Dialog Box

When you open multiple Camera Raw images, the Camera Raw dialog box displays a filmstrip, as shown in Figure 22. The left panel of the dialog box, which only appears when multiple images are open, displays Camera Raw, TIFF, or JPEG files opened in the Camera Raw dialog box. The center panel displays the toolbar, the selected image, zoom levels, and navigation arrows. The right panel displays a histogram for the active image, the image adjustment tabs, and adjustment sliders.

QUICK **TIP**

You can synchronize image settings from one to many images in Camera Raw by selecting the images you want to synchronize (while in Filmstrip view) and then clicking the Synchronize button at the top of the Filmstrip pane. The Synchronize dialog box opens, displaying the settings that can be synchronized. Select the settings you want synchronized, and then click OK.

Figure 22 *Multiple open images in Camera Raw dialog box*
Image courtesy of Elizabeth Eisner Reding

View controls
Histogram
Image adjustment tabs
Click to open the Camera Raw settings menu
Filmstrip view
Image adjustment sliders
Navigation arrows
Zoom levels
Selected image

Using the Digital Negative Format (DNG)

Adobe DNG (Digital Negative format) is an archival format for camera raw files that contains the raw image data created within a digital camera, as well as the metadata that define what that data means. This format is designed to provide compatibility among the increasing number of Camera Raw file formats. The following DNG Saving options are available:

- Compatibility with a variety of previous Camera Raw versions, as well as a custom version. The Custom option allows you to choose from additional older versions of DNG that let you choose linear and uncompressed settings.
- Embed Original Raw File, which stores the entire original camera raw image data in the DNG file.

- JPEG Preview, which specifies whether to embed a JPEG preview in the DNG file.
- Embed Fast Load Data enables DNG files to load up to eight times faster.

Export Camera Raw Settings

The settings you created and stored in the Camera Raw database can be exported to a sidecar XMP file. To export Camera Raw settings, open the files in the Camera Raw dialog box, and then select the thumbnail(s) whose settings you want to export. Open the Camera Raw Settings menu in the Camera Raw dialog box (located to the right of the bar beneath the Adjustments icons), and then click Export Settings to XMP. An XMP file will be created in the folder where the Raw image is located.

Modifying Images in the Camera Raw Dialog Box

You can make many image modifications right in the Camera Raw dialog box. Some of the tools should look familiar to you, as you've already seen or used them in Photoshop. Figure 23 identifies unfamiliar tools on the toolbar. Using the Spot Removal tool, you can heal or clone defective areas of an image *before* bringing it into Photoshop. You can use the Graduated Filter and Adjustment Brush tools to change exposure, brightness, contrast, saturation, clarity, sharpness, and color.

> **QUICK TIP**
>
> The Camera Raw controls may look slightly different on the Mac.

Figure 23 *Camera Raw view controls*

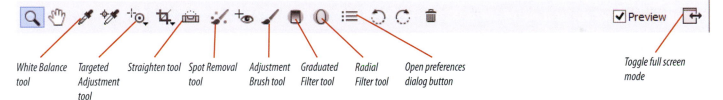

White Balance tool | Targeted Adjustment tool | Straighten tool | Spot Removal tool | Adjustment Brush tool | Graduated Filter tool | Radial Filter tool | Open preferences dialog button | Toggle full screen mode

---

Wide-Angle Correction

This feature (available in the Camera Raw 8.5 plug-in) uses adaptive projection to correct perceived distortion in photos with a large field-of-view, which matches human perception. The benefits of this feature are best illustrated in an image having many layers; there's little point in filtering an image having only a handful of layers. An Adaptive Wide Angle filter is also available on the Filter menu in Photoshop.

Layers can be filtered using the following types: kind, name (default), modification date, effect, and blend mode, as well as the logical parameters is, is not, has, has no, or color is. An image that has been filtered displays a *visual indicator*.

You can make changes to colors using tabs in the Image Adjustments area in the right panel. Adjustments you can make include the following:

- Basic: adjusts white balance, color saturation, and tonality, as shown in Figure 24.
- Tone Curve: fine-tunes tonality using a Parametric curve and a Point curve.
- Detail: sharpens images or reduces noise that degrades image quality and is visible as luminance (grayscale) noise which makes an image look grainy or color noise (resulting in stray artifacts within an image).
- HSL/Grayscale: fine-tunes colors using Hue, Saturation, and Luminance adjustments.
- Split Toning: colors monochrome images or adds special effects with color images.
- Lens Corrections: compensates for chromatic aberration and vignetting caused by a camera lens.
- Effects: simulates film grain or applies a postcrop vignette.
- Camera Calibration: corrects a color cast in shadows and adjusts non-neutral colors to compensate for the differences between camera behavior and the Camera Raw profile for your particular camera model.
- Presets: saves (or applies) sets of image adjustment settings.
- Snapshots: records the image state at any point during the editing process.

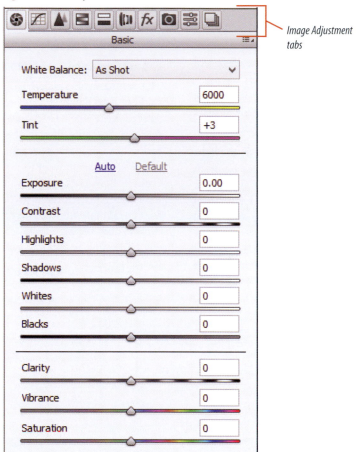

Figure 24 *Basic Adjustments tab*

Image Adjustment tabs

Changing Camera Raw Preferences

To change the preferences in the Camera Raw dialog box, click Edit in the Adobe Bridge CC menu bar, and then click Camera Raw Preferences (Win), click Camera Raw Preferences from the Adobe Bridge CC menu bar (Mac), or click the Open preferences dialog button in the toolbar of the Camera Raw dialog box. The Camera Raw Preferences dialog box lets you determine how image settings will be saved, and how default image settings are handled. See Figure 25.

Camera Raw Workflow Options

Workflow options are used to specify settings that effect Camera Raw output. These settings determine how Photoshop opens files but *does not affect* the camera raw data itself.

QUICK TIP

If you routinely use JPEGs in your workflow, you can modify the way in which Camera Raw opens your images by clicking Edit on the Bridge Menu bar, then clicking Camera Raw Preferences.

 Reducing the effect of Camera Shake

Sometimes, despite your best efforts, your image looks blurry from camera shake. Not to worry: you can fix that using the Camera Shake Reduction feature. Click Filter on the menu bar, point to Sharpen, then click Shake Reduction. The Shake Reduction dialog box launches and automatically analyzes the image, selects a region of interest, determines the shape of the blur and makes the correction.

The Detail loupe displays over the analyzed area and can be used to examine the image in the Preview window.

The Workflow options settings display as a link at the bottom of the Camera Raw dialog box. Clicking this link opens the Workflow Options dialog box in which you can change the Space, Depth, Size, Resolution, Sharpening, and whether or not you want the image opened as a Smart Object.

QUICK TIP

You can open a Camera Raw image as a Smart Object by clicking File on the Menu bar, then clicking Open As Smart Object. An existing Smart Object can be duplicated by clicking the Layer menu, pointing to Smart Objects, then clicking New Smart Object via Copy.

Figure 25 *Camera Raw Preferences dialog box*

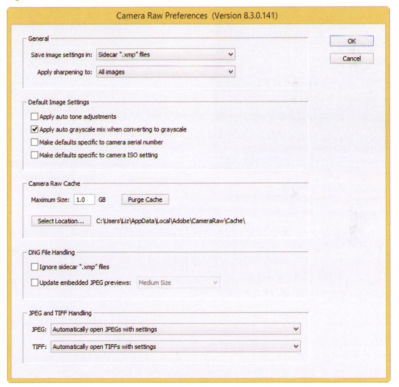

Fix Common PHOTOGRAPHY PROBLEMS

What You'll Do

Image courtesy of Elizabeth Eisner Reding

 In this lesson, you'll remove debris and blemishes from an old photograph and fix an overexposed image.

Organizing Your Images

It doesn't take much time before the photos on your hard drive number in the thousands. How will you keep track of them all? Are they all worthy of being kept? Do you really need all 10 blurry pictures of your neighbor's dog? Or can you narrow that collection down to zero?

Learn to develop a thick skin when it comes to discarding your images. Get rid of photos that make people look bad. Organize your photos into folders as soon as you upload them from your camera and apply keywords to images (in Bridge) early... before you forget.

QUICK TIP

If you plan to work in photography, *get good with Photoshop.* Use it a lot, feel comfortable with it, and know what it can do. Know your own limitations too, and learn how to evaluate the strengths and weaknesses of an image.

Images Too Light or Too Dark?

You probably have an image that is either too dark or too light in one or more areas. This can be fixed using a Brightness/Contrast adjustment layer. (If the object(s) to be lightened/darkened is complex, remember to save the selection, just in case you're not happy with the results.) The left side of Figure 26 shows an image before being adjusted; the right side shows the result.

QUICK TIP

Learn the difference between an image that's just plain lousy and one that has promise. There's a lot of information hiding in those pixels.

Curing Bad Skin (Tones)

Somewhere in your collection, you probably have a favorite photo that contains someone with skin that has an orange cast to it. This is a common problem that occurs as a result of fluorescent light. Before you trash that image, see what you can do with it in Camera Raw. (Do you remember that you can open a JPEG in Camera Raw?) Open a JPEG in the Camera Raw dialog box, and then try adjusting the Temperature slider on the Basic Adjustments tab and watch those skin tones come back to normal. When you're satisfied with the results, click Open Image and the change(s) will be applied to the image. The left side of Figure 27 shows an image before changes; the right side shows the result of the adjustment in Camera Raw.

Goodbye Rips and Folds

Personal photographs are among people's most prized possessions. And one of the unfortunate realities of print photos are the ravages of time: dirt, folds, and rips. Fortunately, with Photoshop and your bag of tricks, you can fix many of these seemingly hopeless blemishes.

Eyeglass Glare

And what about that great photo that is ruined by eyeglass glare? Don't trash it—fix it! Figure 28 shows the before and after images of a mild case of eyeglass glare that was fixed using the Spot Healing Brush tool. Enlarge the image as necessary, and then click the areas with glare. Your friends will think you're a genius!

Figure 26 *Before and after: dark areas within an image*
Image courtesy of Elizabeth Eisner Reding

Figure 27 *Before and after: skin tone correction*
Image courtesy of Elizabeth Eisner Reding

Orange skin from fluorescent lighting

Figure 28 *Before and after: eyeglass glare*
Image courtesy of Elizabeth Eisner Reding

Fix damaged areas

1. Open PS 18-3.jpg from the drive and folder where you store your Data files, then save it as **Prom Photo.jpg**, then click **OK** to accept the JPEG options.

2. Create a copy of the background layer, then zoom into the **man's face** until the zoom factor is **100%**, or more as necessary.

3. Click the **Spot Healing Brush tool**  on the Tools panel.

4. Make the **brush tip hard** with a tip size of **10**, then click the **Content-Aware option button**.

5. Begin painting the damaged area at the top of the man's face, then remove any existing dirt where necessary, including facial blemishes.

TIP Rather than trying to cover all the damage in one painting stroke, use short strokes or clicks. Remember that if you're not happy with the results as you paint/ click the areas, you can undo your step using the History panel or the (single-step) Undo keyboard shortcut (Ctrl) Z (Win) or ⌘ Z (Mac).

6. Use any skills you have learned to improve the image, including applying filters (create a SmartFilter if you do), then change the zoom display to **66.7%**.

7. Compare your image to Figure 29, save your work, then close the file.

You used the Spot Healing Brush tool to repair an image that had a variety of age-related defects.

Figure 29 *Damaged areas repaired*
Courtesy of Claire Yannotti

DESIGN**TIP**

Lighting Principles

As you spend more time taking photographs, you may start to spend more time in a studio shooting portraits. If so, you'll need to know the basics about studio lighting. As a portrait photographer, your job is to make each subject look his/her best, and one of the best ways to achieve this goal is through the use of lighting. Lighting techniques make it possible to control the harshness of the light: accentuating the positive and eliminating the negative. Table 3 on page 27 describes the four basic styles of primary lighting.

The dots of light that appear in your subject's eyes are called **catchlights**. While you might be tempted to delete these: *don't do it*. Catchlights (which should be at the 1 or 11 o'clock positions) make the subject look realistic; without them, your subject may look lifeless.

A fill light, used in addition to the main light, should generally be placed on the opposite side of the camera, and should be of lesser power and intensity. The purpose of the fill light is to control contrast and soften the shadows created by the main light. Unfortunately, the fill light may add a second pair of catchlights, which should be removed through retouching.

Background lights can be used to illuminate the background. These lights provide more depth or separation and should be placed low to the ground on a small stand halfway between the subject and the actual background.

Figure 30 *Dark areas lightened*
Image courtesy of Elizabeth Eisner Reding

16.67%   Doc: 34.3M/34.3M

Lighten dark areas

1. Open PS 18-4.jpg from the drive and folder where you store your Data files, then save it as **Relaxing at the pool.jpg**, then click **OK** to accept the JPEG options.

2. Zoom in to the image until the zoom factor is **25%**.

3. Click the **Quick Selection tool** on the Tools panel, set the brush tip size to **40**, then select the lower portion (dark) of the image.

4. Display the **Photography workspace**.

5. Click the **Brightness/Contrast button** on the Adjustments panel.

6. Change the Brightness setting to **150** and the Contrast setting to **–20**, then collapse the Properties panel.

7. Change the zoom display to **16.7%**, then flatten the image.

8. Save your work, compare your image to Figure 30, close the file, then exit Photoshop.

You used an adjustment layer to minimize contrasting light and dark areas in an image.

TABLE 3: 4 BASIC STYLES OF PRIMARY LIGHTING		
Light type	Positioning	Use(s)
Board Lighting	Light illuminates the side of the subject's face that is turned *toward* the camera	Deemphasizes facial features and makes thin, narrow faces appear wider
Short (or narrow) lighting	Light illuminates the side of the subject's face that is turned *away* from the camera	Emphasizes facial contours and is used on a subject with a round, plump face; has a narrowing effect
Butterfly lighting	Light is placed directly in front of the subject's face, adjusting the height to create a shadow directly under and in-line with the nose	Well-suited for women having a normal oval face; a glamour style
Rembrandt lighting	Light is positioned high and on the side of the face facing away from the camera (a combination of short and butterfly lighting techniques)	Produces an illuminated shadow on the cheek closest to the camera; the illuminated triangle displays just under the eye and not below the nose

© 2013 Cengage Learning®

POWER USER SHORTCUTS	
To do this:	**Use this method:**
Open an image in Camera Raw (Adobe Bridge)	Select image, ⟳
Show Timeline panel	⊞
Start animation	▶
Stop animation	◻

Key: Menu items are indicated by ➤ between the menu name and its command. Blue bold letters are shortcuts for selecting tools on the Tools panel.

© 2013 Cengage Learning®

Create and play basic animation.

1. Open PS 18-5.psd, then save it as **The Old Soft Shoe**.
2. Display the rulers.
3. Display the Timeline panel, duplicate frame 1, make the Cat Forward layer active, then drag the Cat Forward image to approximately 250 X.
4. Duplicate frame 2, then hide the Cat Forward layer and make the Cat Dancing layer visible.
5. Duplicate frame 3, then hide the Cat Dancing layer and make the Cat Forward layer visible.

6. Duplicate frame 4, hide the Cat Forward layer, make the Cat Dancing layer visible, then change the Opacity setting of the Cat Dancing layer to 0%.
7. Play the animation.
8. Save your work, then hide the rulers.

Add tweening and frame delay.

1. Tween frame 2 using the previous frame and adding two frames.
2. Tween frame 5 using the previous frame and adding one frame.

3. Tween frame 6 using the previous frame and adding five frames.
4. Set the looping option to Forever, then play the animation.
5. Set the frame delay for frames 1, 4, 6, and 7 to 0.2 seconds.
6. Play the animation.
7. Preview the animation in your browser.
8. Save your work, then compare your work to Figure 31. Your results may vary slightly.

Figure 31 *Completed Skills Review 1*
Source: Morguefile

Modify Video in Photoshop.

1. Open PS 18-6.avi, then save it as **Wind Trancer Sculpture**.
2. Convert the video layer into a Smart Object.
3. Add a Color Balance adjustment layer using the following midtone settings:
   Cyan-Red: -27
   Magenta-Green: -15
   Yellow-Blue: -48
4. Add a Brightness/Contrast adjustment layer using a Brightness of −15 and a Contrast of +30, then compare your Layers panel to Figure 32.
5. Select the video in the timeline, move the playhead of the Layer 1 to approximately 6:00f, then split at the playhead.
6. Apply a Fade transition of any duration between the Layer 1 and Layer 1 copy video tracks.
7. Play the video.
8. Decrease the work area by approximately one second at the beginning and ending of the video sequence.
9. Save your work, play the video, then compare your screen to Figure 33.

Figure 32 *Partially completed Layers panel*
Image courtesy of Elizabeth Eisner Reding

Figure 33 *Completed Skills Review 2*
Image courtesy of Elizabeth Eisner Reding

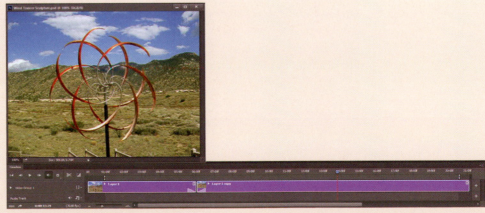

Fix common photography problems.

1. Open PS 18-7.jpg, then save it as **NM Sunset** (accepting the default JPEG options).
2. Display the Photography workspace, then zoom into the bottom portion of the image.
3. Use the Quick Selection tool (and a brush size of 40) to create a selection that includes the dark bottom portion of the image.
4. Add a Brightness/Contrast adjustment layer using a Brightness of 86 and a Contrast of -4.
5. Flatten the file, compare your image to Figure 34, then save your work.

Figure 34 *Completed Skills Review 3*

Image courtesy of Elizabeth Eisner Reding

You're about to start your own business as a photo-retoucher. In order to land an important client, you've agreed to fix a photo you happen to see on the owner's desk free-of-charge.

1. Open the PS 18-8.jpg and save it as **Graduation**.
2. Use any of your Photoshop skills to fix the image, and be prepared to discuss what you did to improve the image.
3. Save your work, then compare your screen to the sample shown in Figure 35.

Figure 35 *Sample Project Builder 1*

Image courtesy of Elizabeth Eisner Reding

You've just been elected to the board of directors of a community access TV station. Each board member is expected to serve on at least one committee. You've chosen the Community Involvement Committee, and have been asked to design a snappy, numeric countdown animation that will introduce public service announcements.

1. Obtain images appropriate for a countdown. You can draw your own numbers, use the images that are available on your computer, scan print media, capture images using a digital camera, or connect to the Internet and download images. You must include at least one other image and can include other images, as desired.

2. Create a new Photoshop image, then save it as **Countdown**.

3. Apply a color or style to the Background layer, add images as desired, and apply effects to them. (*Hint*: The Background layer in the sample has a Pattern Overlay style applied to it.)

4. Create at least three type layers with numbers for a countdown, and apply styles or filters to them as desired. (*Hint*: Each number in the sample has a duplicate with different opacities.)

5. Create an animation that makes the numbers move across the image and fade into one another.

6. Duplicate the last number so that it changes appearance at least twice.

7. Tween each animation and add frame delays as necessary, then save your work.

8. Preview the animation in Photoshop and in your browser.

9. Save Countdown as **Countdown Browser.psd**, then adjust tweening and frame delays and play it in your browser.

10. Save your work, close the Countdown Browser file to return to the Countdown image, then compare your screen to the sample shown in Figure 36.

Figure 36 *Sample Project Builder 2*
© Photodisc/Getty Images

After your first experience with creating your own animation, you and your friends are hooked. You want to peruse the full range of animation on the web. You decide to study one aspect of web animation. Your first stop will be to check out the latest in animated banner ads.

1. Connect to the Internet and use your browser to find websites containing downloadable animation. (Make a record of the website you found so you can use it for future reference.)
2. Create a new Photoshop image and save it as **Banners et al**.
3. Identify an animation that interests you by scrolling down the page or linking to one of the websites listed on the page.
4. Create a type layer named **Animation Techniques**, then type the animation techniques and Photoshop skills and features that you believe were used to create the appearance of the animation.
5. Be sure to add the following points to the Animation Techniques layer:
   - Identify how many different animations are active throughout the sequence and at any one time.
   - Identify instances of tweening and frame delay.
   - Give examples of techniques unknown to you.
6. When your analysis is complete, print the image.

7. Hide the Animation Techniques layer, then obtain images to use for your own interpretation of the animation. You can use the images that are available on your computer, scan print media, or download images from the Internet.
8. Place the images in your image, create type layers as needed, then apply the animation techniques you identified.

9. Update the Animation Techniques layer as necessary, print the image so that the Animation Techniques layer prints clearly, then compare your before and after analyses. (*Hint*: Hide distracting layers.) A sample animation is shown in Figure 37.
10. Hide the Animation Techniques layer, make the other layers active, then save your work.

Figure 37 *Sample Design Project*
Source: Morguefile

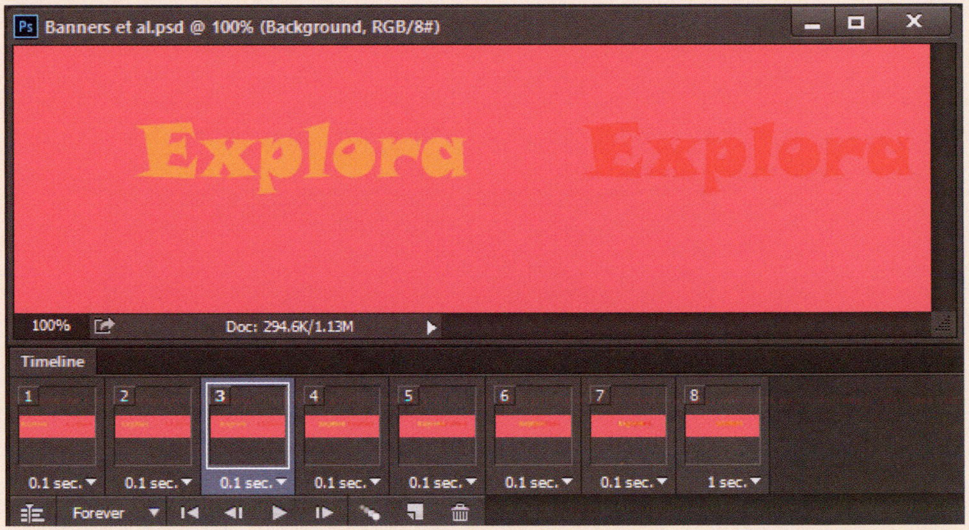

You and your team handle new product presentations for Never Too Late (NTL), an online message service that sends daily reminders to clients. NTL is teaming with an automated home electronics company to offer a new home-based service. They're going to provide an automatic wake-up call that turns on a client's computer, plays a wake-up message until the client responds, and then lists the day's important activities. You want to demonstrate a prototype that shows off the product at your next staff meeting. This prototype will transform a black-and-white line drawing into a color image as part of the wake-up call feature. You'll add appropriate sounds later.

1. Obtain images for the wake-up animation. One image should be a black-and-white image that you can easily transform to color. You can draw your own images, use the images that are available on your computer, scan print media, create images using a digital camera, or connect to the Internet and download images.

2. Create a new Photoshop image, then save it as **Wake Up**.

3. Convert the Background layer to an image layer, apply a color or style to that layer, add other images as desired, and apply effects to them. (*Hint*: The sample has three color layers that alternate as the background, two of which have gradients applied to them.)

4. Place the images that will be animated in the file. (*Hint*: The black-and-white line art is a cartoon line drawing that was filled in with color. You can color a similar image by choosing foreground and background colors on the Tools panel, selecting the Eraser tool, and then clicking the Lock transparent pixels button on the Layers panel.)

5. If you choose, create at least one type layer as desired and at least one other image or background.

6. Create an animation for the state you created.

7. Tween each animation, and add frame delays as necessary.

8. Preview the animation in your image and in your browser.

9. Save your work, then compare your screen to the sample shown in Figure 38.

Figure 38 *Sample Portfolio Project*
Source: Morguefile

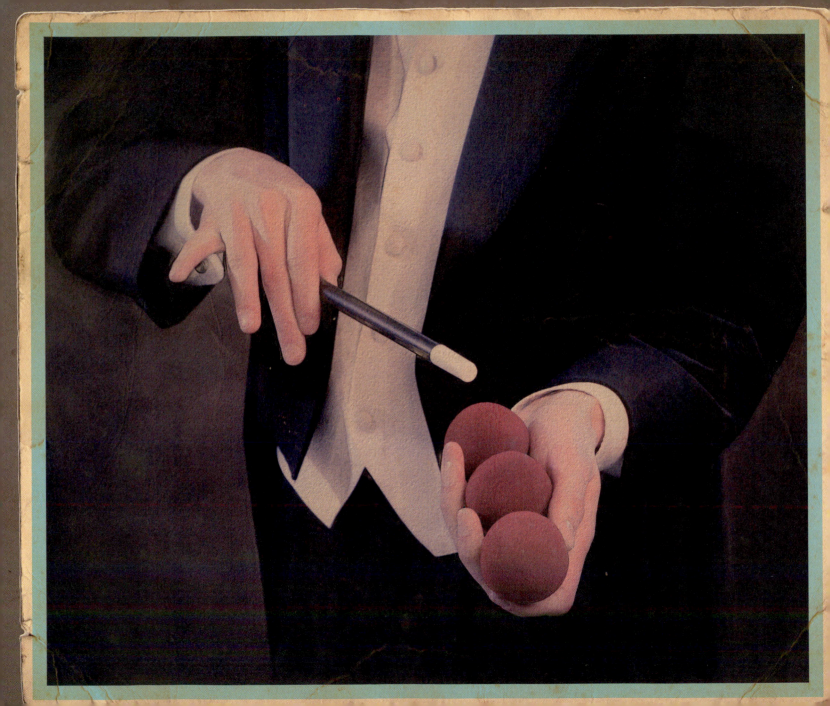

APPENDIX A

STORING AND EDITING IMAGES WITH THE ADOBE FAMILY OF REVEL APPS

1. Get to know the Adobe family of Revel apps

2. Edit images using Revel

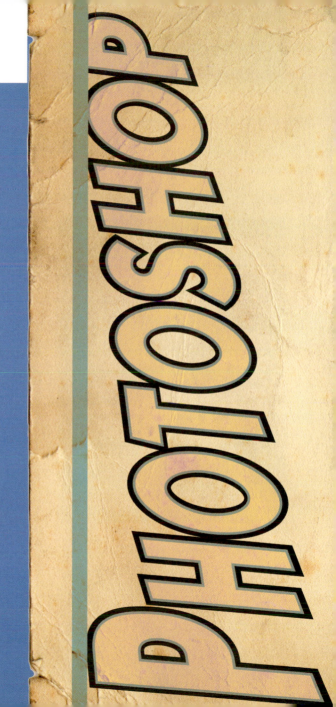

Get to know the
ADOBE FAMILY OF REVEL APPS

What You'll Do

Image courtesy of Elizabeth Eisner Reding

 In this lesson, you'll learn the basics of working in Adobe Revel, including creating a library, sorting, and sharing images.

Adobe Revel (rhymes with *bevel*) is a subscription-based photo-sharing application that lets you access and edit the same library of images on your iPhone, iPad, iPod touch, Mac, Android phones and tablets, and Windows computers. The images in Revel are stored in the cloud and automatically synced through a single subscription to all your devices and to those with whom you've chosen to share them.

> **QUICK TIP**
>
> Adobe Revel is available in free and fee versions. The free version has a 2 GB limit of photo and video storage; the fee version has unlimited photo and video storage.

Browsing your images is easy with touch-screen methods with which you are already familiar: swiping your screen, using other multitouch gestures, or navigating with a mouse. Your images can also be shared with Facebook, Twitter, and Flickr, depending on which platform you're using.

Images can be viewed in either portrait or landscape orientation.

> **QUICK TIP**
>
> Revel is a cloud-based app and its appearance and interface can and will change over time. The appearance and placement of icons may be different from those shown in these lessons.

Download Revel from the Mac App store, Google Play, or the Windows Store, launch the app, and log in using your Adobe ID and password. After you log in, thumbnails of your existing libraries display, as well as the number of photos and videos, total file size, and buttons to add and show photos. Follow the prompts to import your photos. After importing, the desktop displays the default library, as shown in Grid mode on an iPad in Figure 1. (The desktop looks similar regardless of the device you use.)

> **QUICK TIP**
>
> You can change the way library images in a selected library display by clicking Show (beneath the library name), then clicking Grid, Dates, Events, or Added By.

In Adobe Revel, you can create Group Libraries which allow you to share images with your family and friends. Within each library, you can have an unlimited number of images, which are grouped into events that are sorted in ascending order by date and time. The images in each library are limited to the JPEG format, however. (Adobe has plans to include other formats.) Each of the libraries can be shared with others (who do not have to be Revel subscribers). Non-Revel subscribers you've invited to share a library cannot create or delete a library or invite others to join a library.

The images you import into Revel are stored on your hard drive on your device and are also copied and stored on a secure Adobe Revel server in the cloud. This storage ability means that you'll use less space on your hard drive and have instant access through multiple devices.

Whomever has access to your library can view, import, modify, delete, and share your images with others. Friends and family you share images with can do whatever you can do to those images, so... share with care!

Getting to Know the Revel Family of Apps

With Revel comes a variety of apps available on different platforms outlined in Table 1. Each app has a different function, and depending on which platform you're using, you'll be able to find just the right tool for your needs. (FYI: This list of Adobe apps is ever-changing in appearance and availability.)

Figure 1 *Revel desktop on iPad*
Image courtesy of Elizabeth Eisner Reding

Tap to choose a library or carousel

Tap to change the view used to display library images

Tap to see favorite photos

Tap to see all libraries

Tap to share photos

Tap to see albums

Tap to explore older content

Tap to see comments and other activity

TABLE 1: REVEL FAMILY OF APPS						
App Name	**Description**	**iPhone**	**iPad**	**Android**	**Windows 8**	**Mac**
Adobe Revel	Photo organizer and editor	X	X	X	X	X
Adobe Grouppix	Shared photo albums	X		X		
Adobe Photoshop Elements	Easy photo editing		X		X	X
Adobe Premiere Elements	Edit video clips		X		X	X
Adobe Photoshop Touch	More advanced photo editing	X				
Adobe Photoshop Express	Edit photos on-the-go	X	X	X	X	X
Adobe VideoBite	Arranges and edits video clips	X				

© 2015 Cengage Learning®

Within each library, images are shown in groups by date. You can scroll through the list by swiping the list from right to left (touch apps) or by dragging or clicking back and forward arrow icons (Mac). An individual image can be viewed in Single image view, as shown in Figure 2, by double-clicking it or using a tap or zoom gesture. On a Mac, you can use a Magic Trackpad for multitouch gestures if desired.

QUICK TIP

Tap the screen anywhere if you don't see any buttons on the image.

When you tap the plus/minus icon, you enter Edit mode, where you can change the look of an image (just as you would with a Photoshop filter), make lighting adjustments, correct red-eye, and crop and rotate the image.

QUICK TIP

You can exit the Edit mode by tapping the Cancel icon in the upper-left corner of the Edit mode.

Figure 2 *Single image view on iPad*
Image courtesy of Elizabeth Eisner Reding

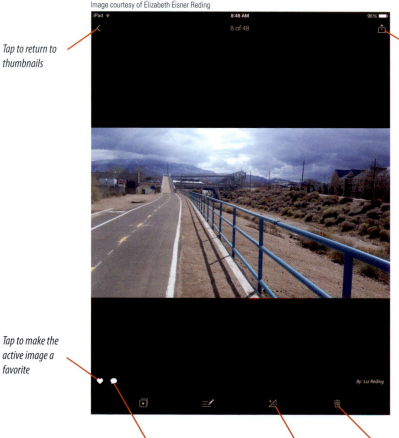

Tap to return to thumbnails

Tap to copy or share the image via e-mail or social network

Tap to make the active image a favorite

Tap to add a comment

Tap to enter Edit mode

Tap to delete

In Revel, your original image is always preserved so you can feel free in your experimentation. Even after you've saved your changes, you can revert to the original image.

QUICK TIP

You can use your device to take a photo within Revel and sync the image as soon as it's taken.

Figure 3 *Share Actions on iPad*
Image courtesy of Elizabeth Eisner Reding

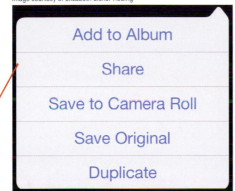

Your menu options may vary

Figure 4 *Actions panel on Mac*
Image courtesy of Elizabeth Eisner Reding

Your library name will differ

Your list may differ

Sharing Revel images

You can share any image by clicking the Share icon in the upper-right corner of Single image view. Figure 3 shows the Actions panel on the iPad; Figure 4 shows the Actions panel on the Mac.

Edit Images
USING REVEL

What You'll Do

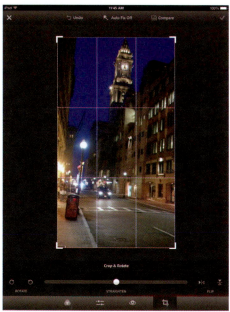

Image courtesy of Elizabeth Eisner Reding

 In this lesson, you'll learn about using Revel to make changes to an image.

Most popular file formats, outlined in Table 2, can be edited in Revel. You can make edits using the Revel app, but not on the web version (adoberevel.com). Edits made in Photoshop, Photoshop Elements, or Lightroom can also be uploaded to Revel. The intersecting circles icon (iOS) or Looks tab (Mac), shown in Figure 5, is displayed by default when you tap the plus/minus icon while viewing a single image. This mode allows you to apply one of over 2 dozen alternate appearances to your image. The first Look in the list is Normal; you can always return to the way your original image looked by selecting this option. Any choice you select can be made permanent by tapping the checkmark (iOS) or Apply button (Mac).

TABLE 2: SUPPORTED FILE FORMATS IN REVEL			
Operating system	**Photo**	**Video**	**Raw files**
Mac OS	jpg		
iOS	jpg, png	mov	arw (SONY), cr2 (CANON), crw (CANON), dng, erf (EPSON), raf (FUJI), 3fr & fff (HASSELBLAD), dcr (KODAK), mrw (KONICA), mos (LEAF), rwl (LEICA), nef & nrw (NIKON), orf (OLYMPUS), rw2 (PANASONIC), pef (PENTAX), srw (SAMSUNG)
Android	jpg, png	mp4, 3gp	
Windows 8	jpg, png	mp4, wmv	
adoberevel.com	jpg, png	avi, mov, mpeg, m1v, mpe, mpv, m2p, m2v, mpg, avc, 264, 3gp, 3g2, m4v, mp4, mts, m2ts, dv, wmv, flv, asf, tod	arw (SONY), cr2 (CANON), crw (CANON), dng, erf (EPSON), raf (FUJI), 3fr & fff (HASSELBLAD), dcr (KODAK), mrw (KONICA), mos (LEAF), rwl (LEICA), nef & nrw (NIKON), orf (OLYMPUS), rw2 (PANASONIC), pef (PENTAX), srw (SAMSUNG)

© 2015 Cengage Learning®

The slider icon (iOS) or Adjustments tab (Mac), shown in Figure 6, lets you make changes to White Balance, Exposure, and Contrast. On both the iPhone and iPad, you can use the following categories to control the edits in your photos: White Balance (for Temperature and Tint); Exposure (for Exposure, Highlights, and Shadows); and Contrast (for Contrast, Clarity, and Vibrance).

QUICK TIP

If the controls on the iPad are not visible, tap the screen and they will reappear.

Editing Photos in Revel

Edits made in Revel are nondestructive, meaning that your original image is *always* preserved. Revel applies your edits when you export a photo (Mac) or Save to Camera Roll (iOS).

In addition to all the looks you can apply and adjustments you can make, you can also fix red-eye using the Red Eye tab. Use Auto Fix to let Revel make the changes it thinks are necessary, and click the Compare button to see the before and after edits you've made.

Figure 5 *Looks tab on iPad*
Image courtesy of Elizabeth Eisner Reding

Tap to crop and straighten

Tap to remove and correct red-eye

Tap to change white balance, exposure, and contrast

Looks gallery: swipe to scroll (touch apps), point to gallery and drag scrollbar to scroll (Mac)

Figure 6 *Adjustments tab on iPad*
Image courtesy of Elizabeth Eisner Reding

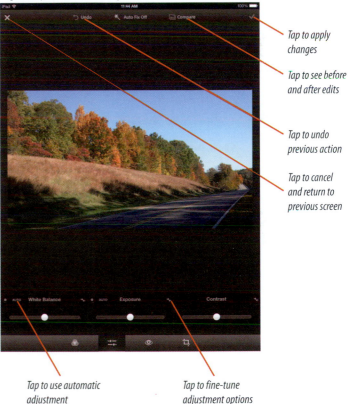

Tap to apply changes

Tap to see before and after edits

Tap to undo previous action

Tap to cancel and return to previous screen

Tap to use automatic adjustment

Tap to fine-tune adjustment options

The crop icon (iOS) or Crop & Rotate tab (Mac), shown in Figure 7, lets you rotate an image in 90° increments using the clockwise and counter-clockwise buttons in the lower-left corner of the screen.

The cropped image is shown in Figure 8. Select the Apply button to save your changes.

QUICK TIP

You can also flip an image using the buttons in the lower-right corner of the screen.

The crop icon (iOS) or Crop & Rotate tab (Mac) can also be used to straighten a crooked image. By dragging the Straighten slider to the right, the image is tilted counter-clockwise. If you drag the Straighten slider to

Figure 7 *Crop & Rotate tab on iPad*
Image courtesy of Elizabeth Eisner Reding

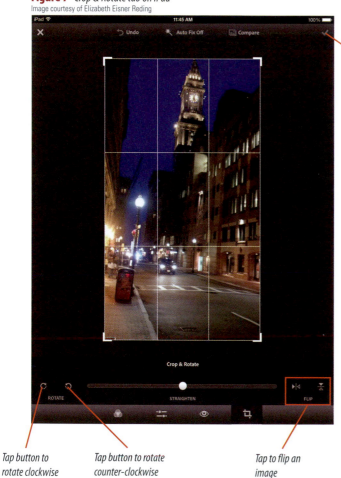

Tap to save changes

Tap button to rotate clockwise

Tap button to rotate counter-clockwise

Tap to flip an image

Figure 8 *Cropped image on iPad*
Image courtesy of Elizabeth Eisner Reding

the left, the image is tilted clockwise. You can make rotation adjustments in any increment you want using the crop icon or Crop & Rotate tab. Figure 9 shows an image being straightened by tilting it to the left (rotating it a few degrees counterclockwise).

QUICK TIP

The cropping grid can be used as a visual checkpoint to see if you've straightened the image enough. By dragging the straighten slider (*not the cropping handles*), you can pick an area (such as the flat walkway of the dock) and align it using the cropping grid (similar to grid guides in Photoshop).

As you straighten the image, you'll be able to see where and how much it's been tilted. The rectangular shape and size of the image is maintained, but the tilted areas are shown as shaded against a black background. When the cropping is applied, the shaded areas are removed, but you will still be able to revert to the original image if you choose to.

Importing Photos and Videos

You can use a variety of different apps as a source of photos and videos for use in Adobe Revel. (Keep in mind that this app changes frequently. Expect this list to change!) Presently, you can import photos and videos into Revel from the following:

- Adobe Photoshop Elements
- Adobe Premiere Elements
- Photoshop Express
- GroupPix
- VideoBite
- Photoshop Lightroom
- iPhoto

Figure 9 *Straightening an image on iPad*
Image courtesy of Elizabeth Eisner Reding

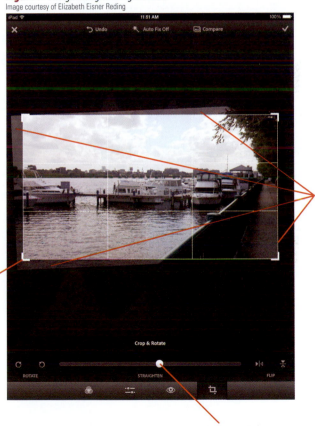

Shaded area indicates how the image is rotated

Crop image by dragging handles

Drag slider to straighten an image

APPENDIX B

PORTFOLIO PROJECTS
AND EFFECTS

1. Create a pencil sketch from a photo
2. Create a montage effect with blocks
3. Simulate a slide mount
4. Create a reflection effect
5. Fix underexposure
6. Improve a photo
7. Straighten, crop, and patch an image
8. Create a magnifier effect within a photo

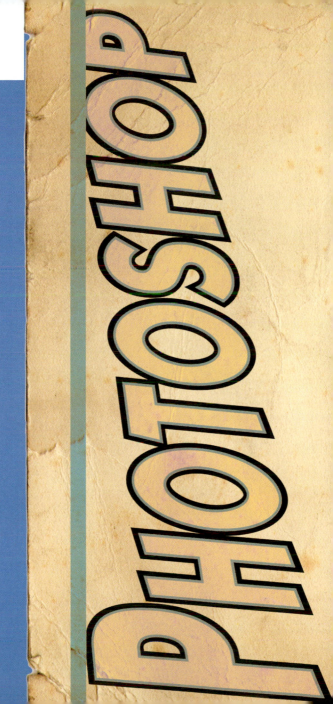

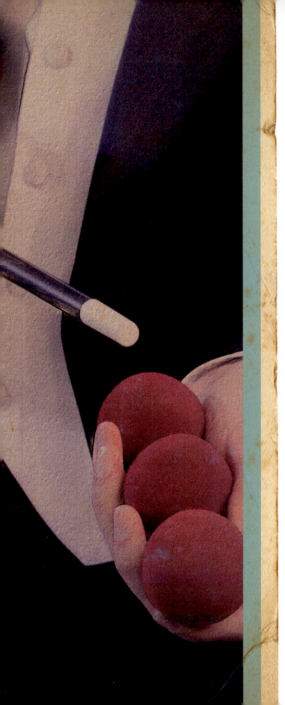

APPENDIX B PORTFOLIO PROJECTS AND EFFECTS

Introduction

Now that you've got all kinds of Photoshop skills under your belt, you're ready to discover real-world opportunities to use these skills and have some fun, too. This appendix presents eight projects that you can complete at your own pace using your own design choices. Rather than guiding you through each step, these projects suggest strategies and methods for achieving the finished product. As you complete these projects, you'll build on the knowledge you already have, and even learn a few new Photoshop tricks along the way.

Getting the Most from the Projects

Of the eight projects in this appendix, four are effects—smaller, mini-projects that you can use within other images. For example, the reflected object effect shown in Figure 1 could stand on its own or be used as a component in a larger image. The magnifier effect seen in Figure 2 could easily be used in any image. (You'll create both of these effects later in this appendix.) Any of the techniques shown in this appendix could be exaggerated or minimized. Your results will vary with the samples shown depending on how much technique is used (you may, for example,

choose to use more cropping or add more blocks to a design).

Figure 1 *Reflected object effect*
Source: Morguefile

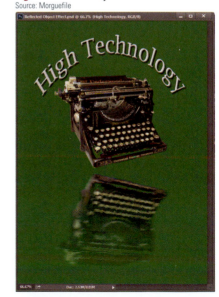

Using Multiple Skills

Like most real-life projects, the image in Figure 2 makes use of many different Photoshop skills. Look at the figure, and then see how many tasks from the following list you can identify:

- Desaturation
- Composite images
- Masking
- Making a selection
- Transforming a selection
- Reordering layers
- Cropping

QUICK TIP

Don't be afraid to use resources such as Photoshop Help and the web to find answers when you are unsure as to how to complete a task or achieve an effect.

Making Your Images Look Their Best

One of the great things about Photoshop is that you're in control. You get to decide when an image is deficient and you get to decide what to do about it. The image in Figure 3 could just have easily been left as it was—straight out of the camera. However, the statue of the children was very dark and it was difficult to make out the details. So, given that you know how to fix an image that has areas of darkness, well... who can resist!

Figure 2 *Desaturated, masked, and transformed image*
Source: Morguefile

Figure 3 *Evened areas of light and dark*
Image courtesy of Elizabeth Eisner Reding

Create a Pencil Sketch
FROM A PHOTO

Skills You'll Use

In this lesson, you'll do the following:
- Save a digital image as a Photoshop file.
- Change the color mode.
- Duplicate and invert a layer.
- Apply a filter.
- Change the blending mode.
- Use the History Brush to restore color.

Creating a Unique Look

How about this? Take an ordinary photo, and give it a look that's not realistic at all. You can do this by duplicating a layer here and there, changing the color mode, applying a filter, and then selectively restoring color. How much color you restore is entirely up to you!

> **QUICK TIP**
>
> As you work through each exercise, carefully examine the History panel of the completed project. It may help you understand the steps that were taken to achieve the final product.

Preparing for Magic

Figure 4 contains an ordinary portrait photo, but watch what happens. First, you turn this color image to grayscale mode, discarding the color information, and then duplicate the existing background layer. Next, you invert the duplicate layer. This process (which you achieve by clicking Image on the Menu bar, pointing to Adjustments, and then clicking Invert) flips the colors or tones of the active layer, so whatever is dark becomes light. Change the Blending Mode to Color Dodge. Don't panic: it looks like your image has disappeared, doesn't it? But apply a Gaussian Blur and a pencil-like sketch will be visible. Pretty cool, huh?

Using the History Brush Tool

You might be satisfied with the image the way it is, but wait—there's more! To add a little more pizzazz, you can selectively reapply some color. First, flatten the image, and then change the mode back to RGB color. Now we're going to see some magic! Select the History Brush tool from the toolbox and selectively paint areas in the image. In Figure 5, for example, the face and hair are painted, but you could paint any areas you want.

> **QUICK TIP**
>
> The History Brush tool is a source of earlier pixel data, but can only be used within a single image.

Figure 4 *Project 1 - Beginning*
Source: Morguefile

Figure 5 *Project 1 - Completed*
Source: Morguefile

Figure 6 *Project 1 – Portfolio Sample*
Source: Morguefile

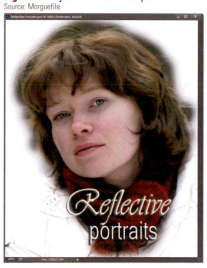

Create a pencil sketch effect

1. Open PS APP-1.jpg from the drive and folder where you store your Data Files, then save it as **Colored Pencil Sketch.psd**.

2. Use the following suggestions to guide you through completing the project:
   - Change the image mode to Grayscale.
   - Duplicate the background layer, then rename the duplicate.
   - Invert the new layer (click Image on the Menu bar, point to Adjustments, then click Invert), then use the Layer Style dialog box to change the blending mode to Color Dodge.
   - Add a Gaussian Blur filter. (A setting of 4 pixels is used in the sample.)
   - Flatten the image, then change the mode to RGB Color.
   - Create a new layer, then set the blending mode to Multiply.
   - Use the History Brush to paint the woman's face, hair, neck, and scarf. (*Hint*: The image may look like a faint pencil sketch or almost blank up to this point.)

3. Save your work, then compare your image to Figure 5.

   Figure 6 shows how this image might be used in artwork to promote a business. In this example, type was added to promote the name of a photography business.

You saved a digital image as a Photoshop file, changed the image mode, applied a filter, flattened the image, then used the History Brush to selectively restore color to the image.

Project 1   Create a Pencil Sketch from a Photo

Create a Montage Effect
WITH BLOCKS

Skills You'll Use

In this lesson, you'll do the following:
- Save a digital image as a Photoshop file.
- Add a background layer.
- Resize imagery.
- Create layers from selections.
- Add layer styles.

Keeping It Simple

Sometimes all it takes to make an image stand out is a simple technique executed with artistic flair. Take, for example, the image shown in Figure 7. This is a nice photograph as is, but with a little Photoshop sleight-of-hand, you can really make it pop.

> **QUICK TIP**
>
> Most Photoshop tasks are easy to accomplish but may take longer than you think.

Getting Boxy

The boxy effect you see in Figure 8 is not difficult to create. Once you've added a background layer and resized the initial image (in this case, the Las Vegas street scene), the real fun begins. Make the layer containing the actual image active, and then randomly pick a spot and draw a rectangle with the Rectangular Marquee tool. Create a layer from the selection using the Layer via Copy command and then add a drop shadow to the layer. Then, to add to the effect, move the layer (the one you created from the selection) so it's slightly offset from the original. Repeat this process in different parts of the image until you're satisfied with the results. As you can see from the completed image, this effect was repeated 12 times (resulting in 12 new layers). Now, that wasn't hard, was it?

> **QUICK TIP**
>
> You could automate this process by creating an action for these repetitive steps.

Figure 7 *Project 2 - Beginning*
Source: Morguefile

Figure 8 *Project 2 - Completed*
Source: Morguefile

Figure 9 *Project 2 - Portfolio Sample*
Source: Morguefile

Project 2   Create a Montage Effect with Blocks

Create a block montage effect

1. Open PS APP-2.jpg from the drive and folder where you store your Data Files, then save it as **NY NY-Vegas Strip.psd**.

2. Use the following suggestions to guide you through completing the project:

   ■ Create a new background layer using the color of your choice. (A vibrant orange is shown in the sample.)

   ■ Resize the original layer so it appears to be framed by the background layer.

   ■ Make a rectangular selection, create a layer from the selection using the Layer via Copy command, add a drop shadow or outer glow effect, then move the layer on the canvas so that it is slightly offset from the original image.

   ■ Repeat the process of creating a drop-shadowed or outer-glowed, offset layer from a selection until you've achieved the look you want.

TIP You can easily copy formatting from one layer to another by selecting the layer containing the formatting you want to duplicate, press and hold [Alt] while dragging the formatting effect(s) to the layer where you want to apply the formatting.

3. Save your work, then compare your image to Figure 8.

   Figure 9 shows how this image could be used in a promotional poster.

You saved a digital image as a Photoshop file, added a new background layer, resized an object, created layers from selections, then added layer styles.

Simulate
A SLIDE MOUNT

Skills You'll Use

In this lesson, you'll do the following:
- Use a digital image in a Photoshop file.
- Draw a shape.
- Delete a selection.
- Add a drop shadow.
- Add type.
- Merge layers.
- Resize and skew or rotate a shape.

Creating an Illusion

You've probably seen photos that look like slides in a magazine or an ad somewhere, and asked "How'd they do that?" The illusion is actually very easy to create, using a few simple Photoshop tricks. Just draw a shape, add some text, and pop in an image.

Simulating a Slide

To create the effect of a slide, you create a new layer, change the foreground color to gray and then draw a rounded rectangle shape. (You don't want to draw a shape layer or a path, and you want to fill pixels.) Draw a horizontal marquee within the rounded rectangle (this is where the slide image would appear), rasterize the shape, and then delete the selection to 'punch a hole' in the slide. Add a drop shadow to the object, and your slide is finished. You can add text to the

slide to make it look more realistic. When your slide looks just right, merge all the appropriate layers into a single slide layer.

> **QUICK TIP**
>
> You'll probably want to duplicate your blank slide so it'll be easier to use over and over. No point in reinventing the wheel!

Adding the Image to the Slide

The individual photos in Figure 10 will work fine for the individual slide images. Make sure you've got enough slide blanks, and then select each photo and drag it into the slide image. Each photo will have to be resized to fit the hole in each slide, and you may want to skew the slides to make them look scattered, rather than perfectly aligned. This gives the slides a more realistic look.

Figure 10 *Project 3 - Beginning*
Source: Morguefile

Figure 11 *Project 3 - Completed*
Source: Morguefile

Figure 12 *Project 3 – Portfolio Sample*
Source: Morguefile

Create a slide mount effect

1. Open PS APP-3.jpg and PS APP-4.jpg from the drive and folder where you store your Data Files.

2. Open a new Photoshop image with the dimensions 450 X 225 pixels, then save it as **Slide Mount.psd**.

3. Use the following suggestions to guide you through completing the project:

   - Create a path consisting of a rounded-rectangular shape, change it to a selection, then fill it with a shade of gray.
   - Knock out a rectangle in the middle of the shape.
   - Add a drop shadow to the shape.
   - Add text to the image, then merge the layers so the slide is a single layer.
   - Copy the slide layer (you may want to make multiple copies, depending on your overall design goal).
   - Insert an image in the rectangular knock-out, resizing and transforming the image as necessary.
   - Rotate or skew the slide (if that is the look you want to achieve), then make any necessary adjustments.

4. Save your work, then compare your image to Figure 11.

TIP The image on the right was converted into a Smart Object, then enhanced with the Sharpen filter.

Figure 12 shows an example of how the slides could be used in a corporate advertisement.

You created a new Photoshop image, opened two digital image files to use in the new image, created a shape that looks like a slide, knocked out a rectangle in the slide, added type to the shape, inserted an image in the shape, and rotated or skewed it to make it look more realistic. You repeated this process for all the images you wanted to present as "slides."

Create a
REFLECTION EFFECT

Skills You'll Use

In this lesson, you'll do the following:
- Save a Photoshop image using a new name.
- Duplicate a layer.
- Flip and reposition an image.
- Apply a blur filter and a distort filter.
- Apply a mask and gradient.

Understanding Illusion

So much of what we do in Photoshop involves creating an illusion. As you saw in the previous project, you can create an image that looks like a photographic slide by using what you know about how real slides look to trick the eye. In this project, you trick the eye again—by making an object look as if it were reflected in rippling water. The beauty of Photoshop layers is that you can easily duplicate objects, and then manipulate the images within selected layers. Once a layer is duplicated, it can be flipped, and then 'doctored' to display the ephemeral qualities that it might have by being reflected in a pool of water. Figure 13 shows a single object against a background, and Figure 14 shows the same object after a reflection effect was created.

QUICK **TIP**

Use your observations about real objects to create effective illusions. An object reflected in water would look blurrier than the original, maybe with some ripples, and the reflection would fade as it got farther from the original.

Creating a Reflection

You can begin creating the reflection effect by duplicating the Typewriter layer. Flip the duplicate vertically, and then drag it beneath the original. (The duplicate will serve as the reflected object.) Since a reflected object should not be a mirror-image, apply a Motion Blur filter, and then apply a Ripple filter to give it that 'watery' look.

Applying a Fade

To give the reflection a faded look, apply a mask, and then apply a gradient to the mask. If you choose, you can give depth to the surface on which the object sits, by creating a marquee on the background layer, adding a fade effect, and then (optionally) adjusting the midtone levels in the Levels dialog box. *Voila!*

Figure 13 *Project 4 - Beginning*
Source: Morguefile

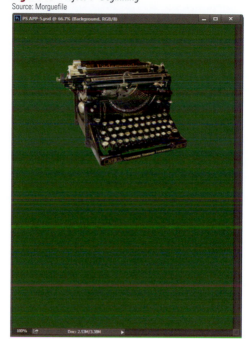

Figure 14 *Project 4 - Completed*
Source: Morguefile

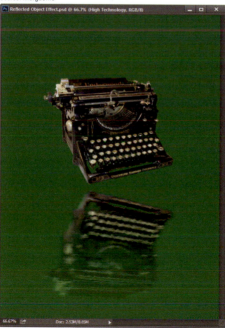

Create a reflection effect

1. Open PS APP-5.psd from the drive and folder where you store your Data Files, then save it as **Reflected Object Effect.psd**.

2. Use the following suggestions to guide you through completing the project:

   - Duplicate the Typewriter layer.
   - Flip the image vertically on the duplicate layer.
   - Reposition the duplicate layer so it appears to be beneath the original layer.
   - Apply a Motion Blur filter to the duplicate layer (having an approximate distance of 40).
   - Apply a Ripple filter to the duplicate layer.
   - Add a layer mask to the duplicate layer.
   - Draw a linear gradient from the top of the duplicate layer to the bottom of the image.

3. Save your work, then compare your image to Figure 14.

You saved a Photoshop file using a new name, duplicated and flipped an image, applied two filters, created a layer mask, then added a gradient.

Fix
UNDEREXPOSURE

Skills You'll Use

In this lesson, you'll do the following:
- Save a digital image as a Photoshop file.
- Create a complex selection, and then save the selection.
- Apply an adjustment layer.

Deciding What's Possible

The image in Figure 15 isn't bad, it's just that there's a lot you can't see because the foreground of the sculpture is too dark. Everything else is fine, it just needs a little push to get from OK to really good.

It's All About Selections

It seems that no matter what you do in Photoshop, a selection is involved. The only thing really wrong with this image is the dark foreground, so start by selecting the problem area: the children in the sculpture. Once you've got that done, save the selection, and then apply an Exposure adjustment layer (although you could also use a Brightness/ Contrast or Levels adjustment layer), and you're done.

QUICK **TIP**

Become really comfortable making selections in Photoshop; you'll be doing a lot of it! And remember to save those selections . . . you never know when you'll want to revisit an image and make more changes.

Figure 15 *Project 5 - Beginning*
Image courtesy of Elizabeth Eisner Reding.

Figure 16 *Project 5 - Completed*
Image courtesy of Elizabeth Eisner Reding.

Increase exposure

1. Open PS APP-6.jpg from the drive and folder where you store your Data Files, then save it as **Sculpture Garden.psd**.

2. Use the following suggestions to guide you through completing the project:
   - Change the Background layer to an image layer.
   - Select the sculpture of the children.
   - Add an Exposure adjustment layer.

3. Save your work, then compare your image to Figure 16.

You opened a digital image and saved it as a Photoshop file, changed the Background layer to an image layer, made a complex selection, then added an adjustment layer.

Improve A PHOTO

Skills You'll Use

In this lesson, you'll do the following:
- Save a digital image as a Photoshop file.
- Use the Content-Aware Spot Healing Brush to reduce glare.
- Paint areas to make them brighter.
- Blur areas that are not central to the image.

Looking Good in Photoshop

If only it was as easy in life as it is in Photoshop. Got a little glare? There's a tool for that. Teeth dingy? There's a fix for that too. Figure 17 is a lovely picture of two friends. The trouble is, the glare from both sets of sunglasses is a little distracting. But not to worry: if we can't eliminate it, we can at least tone it down and make it, well, a little less *glaring*. And while the background imagery isn't bad, it also doesn't add anything to the photo.

Improving on Reality

You can whiten dingy teeth by applying an adjustment layer or by simply painting them white, right? Sure, but be careful not to overdo it—you can easily make someone look ridiculous. Impossibly white teeth can look unrealistic. A better approach is either to back off the adjustment layer settings, sample a

brighter area of the existing teeth, or to find a brighter off-white that looks believable.

QUICK TIP

Remember that real-life objects are rarely made up of solid colors. That means that no one's teeth are completely one color. Look closely, and you'll see greens and blues in your teeth. This means that when coloring objects in Photoshop, you may need to mix colors rather than using only one shade.

When in Doubt, Blur

When you look at Figure 18, you can see what a difference these changes can make. Using the Blur filter on a selection, the background imagery is obscured but not eliminated.

QUICK TIP

You could also have used the Blur tool, but it seemed easier and quicker to blur a selected area with a filter.

Figure 17 *Project 6 - Beginning*
Image courtesy of Betsy Womack

Figure 18 *Project 6 - Completed*
Image courtesy of Betsy Womack

Figure 19 *Project 6 – Portfolio Sample*
Image courtesy of Betsy Womack

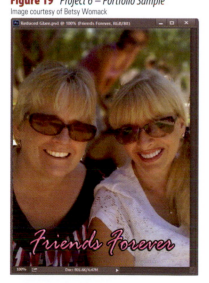

Improve a photo

1. Open PS APP-7.jpg from the drive and folder where you store your Data Files, then save it as **Reduced Glare.psd**.

2. Use the following suggestions to guide you through completing the project:

   - Duplicate the original layer, to ensure that you can always return to the original image.
   - Open a second window for the Reduced Glare image and arrange the windows (one enlarged, one at 100%) so you can watch the changes as you make them.
   - Use the Spot Healing Brush tool (with the Content-Aware setting) to reduce the glare in the sunglasses.
   - Zoom into the dingy teeth, use your favorite selection tool to select the teeth.
   - Apply a Brightness/Contrast adjustment layer to the selection.
   - Select the areas above and in between the two women, save the selection, then create a new layer via copy.
   - Apply a Lens Blur filter to the selection.

3. Save your work, then compare your image to Figure 18.

   Figure 19 shows an example of how this improved photo could be used in an advertisement.

You saved a digital image as a Photoshop file, used the Spot Healing Brush tool to reduce the glare from the sunglasses, brightened teeth using an adjustment to a selection, and blurred nonessential information.

Project 6   Improve a Photo

Straighten, Crop, and Patch
AN IMAGE

Skills You'll Use

In this lesson, you'll do the following:
- Straighten an image.
- Crop an image.
- Use the Patch tool's Content-Aware Mode.

Straighten an Image

So maybe you've taken a really great image, except for one thing... it's crooked. Using the Image Rotation command on the Image menu, you can flip an image or apply a rotation clockwise or counter-clockwise in 90 or 180 degree increments, or in increments you determine. Righting a crooked image (such as a street or building) is not always done with a single setting: you may have to use a trial-and-error method until you find just the right setting and just the right tool.

And once you find the right settings to straighten the image, you may wind up with weird-looking white bars that need removal. Not to worry: you can remove these using the Crop tool.

Content-Aware Patching

There are many ways of correcting defects in images, but one of the coolest is the Content-Aware feature on the Patch tool. Once you've selected the area to patch, select the Patch tool on the Tools panel, then make sure the Content-Aware mode is selected in the options bar. Drag from inside the selection to the area you want to sample.

Figure 20 *Project 7 - Beginning*
Source: Morguefile

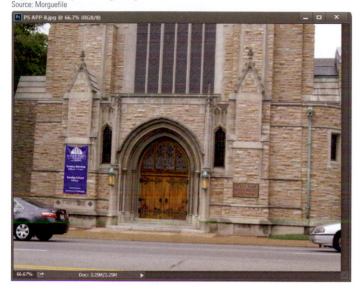

Figure 21 *Project 7 - Completed*
Source: Morguefile

Project 7   Straighten, Crop, and Patch an Image

Straighten, crop, and patch an image

1. Open PS APP-8.jpg shown in Figure 20 from the drive and folder where you store your Data Files, then save it as **West End Methodist Church.jpg**.

2. Use the following suggestions to guide you through completing the project:

   - Straighten the image using an arbitrary adjustment (—2 degrees CW is used in the sample).
   - Crop the image to eliminate the missing areas.
   - Eliminate the blue banner hanging on the stone wall using the Content-Aware feature of the Patch tool.

3. Save your work, then compare your image to Figure 21.

You saved a digital image with a different name, straightened and cropped it, then used the Content-Aware feature in the Patch tool to eliminate a banner from a stone wall.

Create a magnifier effect
WITHIN A PHOTO

Skills You'll Use

In this lesson, you'll do the following:

- Duplicate a background layer and rename the copy.
- Drag a jpg image into a psd file.
- Position an object, then crop unnecessary imagery.
- Create guides and mask a selection.
- Reorder the layers.
- Desaturate a layer and apply a clipped adjustment layer.

Creating a Unique Look

How about this? Take an ordinary photo, and give it a unique look that draws the eye to a particular person, object, or area in an image. You can do this by duplicating a layer here and there, masking a layer, resizing a selection so it fits a shape, and then using adjustment layers to emphasize certain elements.

Preparing for Magic

Figure 22 contains an ordinary portrait photo, but watch what happens. Determine the area you want to highlight in an image, and whether it will fit into the area you want to use, such as an elliptical area (like a magnifying glass). In the sample shown in Figure 22, you'd like to highlight the woman wearing glasses, and you want an enlarged version of her to display within an image of a hand holding a magnifying glass. Once you know the two images will fit together, create a layer you can use, then create a mask that reveals what you want to highlight. In order to correctly position both the area to be highlighted and the magnifier, you may need to juggle some layers and turn on/off the display of some layers while you position the layer content.

> **QUICK TIP**
>
> You might want to create some guides in order to properly shape the layer mask. (It can be hard to judge the starting coordinates when creating an elliptical marquee.)

Fine-Tuning the Imagery

Once you've gotten all the imagery in place, you'll want to transform the masked content so it fits the magnifier. You've gotten most of the mechanical work out of the way. Now, you can refine the image. You might want to desaturate the original image, and change the exposure to show off the magnified area. And let's not forget to crop any uninteresting, unnecessary, or distracting imagery. Pretty cool, huh?

Figure 22 *Project 8 – Beginning*
Source: Morguefile

Figure 23 *Project 8 – Completed*
Source: Morguefile

Project 8   Create a magnifier effect within a Photo

Create an enlarged area

1. Open PS APP-9.psd, shown in Figure 22, from the drive and folder where you store your Data Files, then save it as **Friend under glass.psd**.

2. Open PS APP-10.jpg, copy the contents of the file, paste it into the Friend under glass file, horizontally flip the image, close PS APP-10.jpg, then rename the pasted layer magnifier.

3. Use the following suggestions to guide you through completing the project:

   ■ Copy the background layer (in Friend under glass) and rename the copy friends.
   ■ Copy the friends layer and rename the copy girlfriend.
   ■ Position the magnifier over the image of the woman with the glasses, then crop any unnecessary imagery in the girlfriend layer.
   ■ If necessary, create guides that help you define the area you want to enlarge and emphasize, then create a selection and mask the selection.
   ■ Move the masked layer above the magnifier layer, then transform the shape of the masked layer so it fills the magnifier, then remove any white areas on the magnifier layer.
   ■ Turn off the display of the Background layer, then remove the saturation from the friends layer using a (clipped) Hue/Saturation adjustment layer.
   ■ Apply a (clipped) Exposure adjustment layer to the girlfriend layer.

4. Save your work, then compare your image to Figure 23.

You added an image of a hand and magnifying glass, positioned the glass over an area, created a masked layer, transformed an area so it appears to be in the magnifier, then added clipped adjustment layers to change the appearance of two layers.

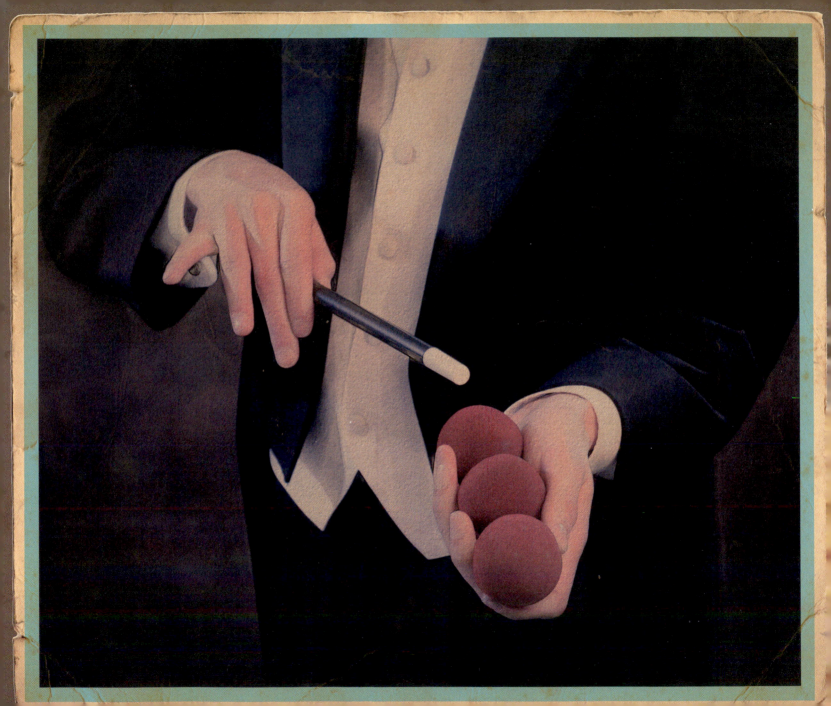

ADOBE PHOTOSHOP CC			
Chapter	**Chapter Data File Supplied**	**Student Creates File**	**Used in**
Chapter 1	PS 1-1.psd		Lessons 2–4
	PS 1-2.tif		
		Review.psd	Skills Review
	PS 1-3.jpg		Skills Review
		Print design-1.jpg	Design Project
		Web design-1.jpg	
Chapter 2	PS 2-1.psd		Lesson 1, 4
	PS 2-2.jpg		
	PS 2-3.psd		
	PS 2-4.psd		Lesson 2, 4
		your name Chapter 2 contact sheet.pdf	Lesson 4
	PS 2-5.psd		Skills Review
	PS 2-6.psd		Project Builder 2
		Critique-1.psd	Design Project
		Critique-2.psd	
		Cloud Computing.docx	Portfolio Project

ADOBE PHOTOSHOP CC			
Chapter	**Chapter Data File Supplied**	**Student Creates File**	**Used in**
Chapter 3	PS 3-1.psd		Lessons 1–4
	PS 3-2.psd		Lessons 3–4
	PS 3-3.psd		Skills Review
	PS 3-4.psd		
	PS 3-5.psd		Project Builder 1
	PS 3-6.psd		
	PS 3-7.psd		Project Builder 2
	PS 3-8.psd		
	PS 3-9.psd		Design Project
	PS 3-10.psd		
	PS 3-11.psd		Portfolio Project
Chapter 4	PS 4-1.psd		Lessons 1–4
	PS 4-2.psd		Lesson 1
	PS 4-3.psd		
	PS 4-4.psd		Lesson 2
	PS 4-5.psd		Lesson 3
	PS 4-6.psd		
	PS 4-7.psd		Skills Review
	PS 4-8.tif		
	PS 4-9.tif		
	PS 4-10.tif		
	PS 4-11.psd		Project Builder 1
	PS 4-12.psd		Project Builder 2
		Sample Compositing.psd	Design Project
	PS 4-13.psd		Portfolio Project

ADOBE PHOTOSHOP CC			
Chapter	Chapter Data File Supplied	Student Creates File	Used in
Chapter 5	PS 5-1.psd		Lessons 1–4, 6-7
	PS 5-2.psd		Lessons 5–6
	PS 5-3.tif		Lesson 7
	PS 5-4.psd		Skills Review
	PS 5-5.psd		
	PS 5-6.tif		
	PS 5-7.psd		Project Builder 1
	PS 5-8.psd		Project Builder 2
	PS 5-9.psd		Design Project
	PS 5-10.psd		Portfolio Project
Chapter 6	PS 6-1.psd		Lessons 1–7
	PS 6-2.psd		Skills Review
	PS 6-3.psd		Project Builder 1
	PS 6-4.psd		Project Builder 2
	PS 6-5.psd		Design Project
		Community Promotion.psd	Portfolio Project
Chapter 7	PS 7-1.psd		Lessons 1–4
	PS 7-2.psd		Skills Review
	PS 7-3.psd		Project Builder 1
	PS 7-4.psd		Project Builder 2
		Art Course.docx	Design Project
		Dealership Ad.psd	Portfolio Project

ADOBE PHOTOSHOP CC			
Chapter	**Chapter Data File Supplied**	**Student Creates File**	**Used in**
Chapter 8	PS 8-1.psd		Lessons 1–6
	PS 8-2.psd		Skills Review
	PS 8-3.psd		Project Builder 1
		Cleanup.psd	Project Builder 2
		Currency.psd	Design Project
		Poetry Poster.psd	Portfolio Project
Chapter 9	PS 9-1.psd		Lessons 1–6
	PS 9-2.psd		Lesson 6
	PS 9-3.psd		Skills Review
	PS 9-4.psd		
		Play.psd	Project Builder 1
		Jazz and Blues.psd	Project Builder 2
	PS 9-5.psd		Design Project
		Dance.psd	Portfolio Project

ADOBE PHOTOSHOP CC			
Chapter	**Chapter Data File Supplied**	**Student Creates File**	**Used in**
Chapter 10	PS 10-1.psd		Lessons 1–7
	PS 10-2.psd		Lessons 5–6
		Carnival ride Picture Package.pdf /Contact Sample/ContactSheet-001.pdf	Lesson 7
	PS 10-3.psd	Tools Picture Package.pdf	Skills Review
	PS 10-4.psd	/Contact Sample 2/ContactSheet-002.pdf	
		Spheroid.psd	Project Builder 1
		Perfect Oasis.psd	Project Builder 2
		My Vision.psd	Design Project
		Beach Poster.psd	Portfolio Project
Chapter 11	PS 11-1.psd		Lessons 1–4
	PS 11-2.psd		Skills Review
	PS 11-3.psd		Project Builder 1
	PS 11-4.psd		Project Builder 2
	PS 11-5.psd		Design Project
		Annual Report Cover.psd	Portfolio Project
Chapter 12	PS 12-1.psd		Lessons 1–4
	PS 12-2.psd		Skills Review
	PS 12-3.psd		Project Builder 1
	PS 12-4.psd		Project Builder 2
		Shape Experimentation.psd	Design Project
		Contest Winner.psd	Portfolio Project

DATA FILES LIST

(CONTINUED)

ADOBE PHOTOSHOP CC			
Chapter	**Chapter Data File Supplied**	**Student Creates File**	**Used in**
Chapter 13	PS 13-1.psd		Lessons 1–4
	PS 13-2.psd		Skills Review
	PS 13-3.psd		Project Builder 1
	PS 13-4.psd		Project Builder 2
		Television Station Ad.psd	Design Project
		CD Cover Artwork.psd	Portfolio Project
Chapter 14	PS 14-1.psd		Lessons 1–3
	PS 14-2.psd		Skills Review
	PS 14-3.psd		Project Builder 1
	PS 14-4.psd		Project Builder 2
		Photoshop Presentation.psd	Portfolio Project
Chapter 15	PS 15-1.jpg		Lessons 1–3
	PS 15-2.psd		Skills Review
	PS 15-3.psd		Project Builder 1
	PS 15-4.psd		Project Builder 2
		Digital Art Analysis.doc	Design Project
		Art School Poster.psd	Portfolio Project

ADOBE PHOTOSHOP CC			
Chapter	**Chapter Data File Supplied**	**Student Creates File**	**Used in**
Chapter 16	PS 16-1.psd		Lessons 1–4
	PS 16-2.psd		Skills Review
	PS 16-3.psd		Project Builder 1
	PS 16-4.psd		Project Builder 2
		Action Sample.psd(downloaded action - varies); Play Downloaded Action.exe	Design Project
		Game Plan.psd	Portfolio Project
Chapter 17	PS 17-1.psd		Lessons 1–4
	PS 17-2.psd		Lesson 2
	Shoppers. gif		
	PS 17-3.psd		Skills Review
	PS 17-4.psd		
		Button Samples.psd	Project Builder 1
		Optimized Graphics.doc	Project Builder 2
		Website design principles.doc	Design Project
		Green Grocer Foods.psd	Portfolio Project

ADOBE PHOTOSHOP CC			
Chapter	**Chapter Data File Supplied**	**Student Creates File**	**Used in**
Chapter 18	PS 18-1.psd		Lessons 1-2
	PS 18-2.avi		Lesson 3
	PS 18-3.jpg		Lesson 5
	PS 18-4.jpg		
	PS 18-5.psd		Skills Review
	PS 18-6.avi		
	PS 18-7.jpg		
	PS 18-8.jpg		Project Builder 1
		Countdown.psd	Project Builder 2
		Countdown Browser.psd	
		Banners et al.psd	Design Project
		Wake Up.psd	Portfolio Project
Appendix B	PS APP-1.jpg		Project 1
	PS APP-2.jpg		Project 2
	PS APP-3.jpg		Project 3
	PS APP-4.jpg		
	PS APP-5.psd		Project 4
	PS APP-6.jpg		Project 5
	PS APP-7.jpg		Project 6
	PS APP-8.psd		Project 7
	PS APP-9.psd		Project 8
	PS APP-10.jpg		

A

Action
A series of tasks that you record and save to play back later as a single command.

Active layer
The layer highlighted on the Layers panel. The active layer's name appears in parentheses in the image window title bar.

Additive colors
A color system, used for lighting, video and computer monitors, in which, when the values of R, G, and B (red, green, and blue) are 0, the result is black; when the values are all 255, the result is white.

Adjustment layer
An additional layer for which you can specify individual color adjustments. The adjustment layer allows you to temporarily alter a layer before making the adjustment permanent.

Adjustment panel
Visible panel that makes creation of adjustment layers easy.

Adobe Bridge
A stand-alone application that serves as the hub for the Adobe Creative Cloud. It can be used for file management tasks such as opening, viewing, sorting, and rating files.

Adobe Configurator
A stand-alone program (available as a download) that lets you create your own panels.

Adobe Creative Cloud
A fee-based membership service that includes CC tools (such as Photoshop CC, Illustrator CC, InDesign CC, and Dreamweaver CC) and services (such as Typekit and Kuler), plus new products and services as they are released.

Adobe DNG
An archival format for camera raw files that contains the raw image data created within a digital camera as well as its defining metadata. Also called *Digital Negative Format*.

Adobe Exchange
Allows you to discover and install plug-ins, extensions, and other Creative Cloud content.

Adobe Generator
Improves workflows by making it possible to extract assets (such as GIFs or JPGs) from a Photoshop image.

Adobe Mini Bridge
A less-powerful (and smaller) version of Bridge that opens within the Photoshop window.

Adobe Typekit
Part of the Creative Cloud subscription, Typekit contains hundreds of fonts which can be synced to all your Creative Cloud computers.

Alpha channel
Specific color information added to a default channel. Also called a *spot channel*.

Altitude
A Bevel and Emboss setting that affects the amount of visible dimension.

Ambience property
In the Lighting Effects filter: controls the balance between the light source and the overall light in an image.

Anchor points
Small square handles, similar to fastening points, that connect straight or curved line segments.

Angle
A drop shadow and bevel and emboss setting that determines where a shadow falls relative to the text.

Animation
The illusion of motion, created by placing a series of images in the same location and adjusting the timing between their appearances.

Annotation
A written note embedded in a Photoshop file.

Anti-aliasing
Partially fills in pixel edges, resulting in smooth-edge type. This feature lets your type maintain its crisp appearance and is especially useful for large type.

Arrangement
How objects are positioned in space, relative to one another.

Artistic filters
Used to replicate natural or traditional fine arts effects.

Asymmetrical balance
When objects are placed unequally on either side of an imaginary vertical line in the center of the page.

Attribution (*cc by*)
The simplest of all Creative Commons licenses, in which any user (commercial or non-commercial) can distribute, modify, or enhance your work, provided you are credited.

Attribution No Derivatives (*cc by-nd*)
Your work can be distributed by others, but not modified and in its entirety, with you being credited.

Attribution Non-Commercial (*cc by-nc*)
Your work can be distributed, modified, or enhanced, with credit to you, for non-commercial purposes only. Derivative works do not have to be licensed.

Attribution Non-Commercial No Derivatives (*cc by-nc-nd*)
This is the most restrictive license category. Redistribution is allowed as long as credit is given. The work cannot be modified or used commercially.

Attribution Non-Commercial Share Alike (*cc by-nc-sa*)
Your work can be distributed, modified, or enhanced, with credit to you, for non-commercial purposes only, but must be licensed under the identical terms. All derivative work must carry the same license, and be non-commercial.

Attribution Share Alike (*cc by-sa*)
The same as Attribution, except that the new owner must create their license under the same terms you used.

Auto slice
A slice created by Photoshop. An auto slice has a dotted-line border.

———————— **B** ————————

Background color
Used to make gradient fills and to fill in areas of an image that have been erased. The default background color is white.

Background Eraser tool
Used to selectively remove pixels from an image, just as you would use a pencil eraser to remove unwanted written marks. The erased areas become transparent.

Balance colors
Process of adding and subtracting colors from those already existing in a layer.

Banding (Bands)
Phenomenon which may occur during image conversion resulting in tonal edges. This effect can be reduced or removed using the Add Noise filter.

Base color
The original color of an image.

Base layer
The bottom layer in a clipping group, which serves as the group's mask.

Baseline
An invisible line on which type rests.

Baseline shift
The distance type appears from its original position.

Batch
A group of files designated to have the same action performed on them simultaneously.

Behance
A social network platform dedicated to showcasing and promotion of creative work.

Bitmap
A geometric arrangement of different color dots on a rectangular grid.

Bitmap mode
Uses black or white color values to represent image pixels; a good choice for images with subtle color gradations, such as photographs or painted images.

Bitmap type
Type that may develop jagged edges when enlarged.

Blend color
The color applied to the base color when a blending mode is applied to a layer.

Blend If color
Found in the Layer Style dialog box; determines the color range for the pixels you want to blend.

Blending mode
Affects how pixels in two separate layers interact with each other. Used to darken or lighten colors, depending on the colors in use.

Blur Gallery
An on-image, selective softening tool for generating shallow depth-of-field and tilt-shift effects.

Bokeh
A Japanese term used to describe the qualities of an unfocused area within a photo.

Bounding box
A rectangle with handles that appears around an object or type and can be used to change dimensions, also called a *transform box*.

Bridge
See Adobe Bridge.

Brightness
The measurement of relative lightness or darkness of a color (measured as a percentage from 0% [black] to 100% [white]).

Brush library
Contains a variety of brush tips that you can use, rename, delete, or customize.

Button
A graphical interface that helps visitors navigate and interact with a website easily.

Button mode
Optional action display in which each action available in Photoshop is displayed as a button—without additional detail.

C

Camera Raw
Allows you to use digital data directly from a digital camera. The file extension that you see will vary with each digital camera manufacturer. The Camera Raw feature allows you to make additional adjustments to images.

Canvas size
The full editable area of an image that can be increased or decreased in size using the Canvas Size command on the Image menu.

Catchlights
The dots of light that appear in your subject's eyes in a photo.

Channels
Used to store information about the color elements in an image.

Channels panel
Lists all channel information. The top channel is a composite channel—a combination of all the default channels. You can hide channels in the same manner that you hide layers: click the Indicates layer visibility button.

Character panel

Helps you control type properties. The Toggle the Character and Paragraph panels button is located on the options bar when you select a Type tool.

Clipboard

Temporary storage area, provided by your operating system, for cut and copied data.

Clipping mask (Clipping group)

A group of two or more contiguous layers linked for the purposes of masking. Effect used to display the image or pattern from one layer into the shape of another layer.

Clipping path

Used when you need to extract a Photoshop object from within a layer, then place it in another program (such as Adobe InDesign or Adobe Illustrator), while retaining its transparent background.

Closed path

One continuous path without endpoints, such as a circle.

Cloud computing

Allows you to share files with others in a virtual environment.

CMYK image

An image using the CMYK color system, containing at least four channels (one each for cyan, magenta, yellow, and black).

CMYK mode

Color mode is based on colors being partially absorbed as the ink hits the paper and then being partially reflected back to your eyes.

Color cast

A situation in which one color dominates an image to an unrealistic or undesirable degree.

Color channel

An area where color information is stored. Every Photoshop image has at least one channel and can have a maximum of 24 color channels.

Color decontamination

An Output option that allows you to remove color fringing around the edges of a masked image; ideal for use in extracting a subject from its background.

Color levels

The numeric values of an individual color. Also called *tonal values*.

Color management system

Keeps colors looking consistent as they move between devices.

Color mode

Used to determine how to display and print an image. Each mode is based on established models used in color reproduction. Represents the amount of color data that can be stored in a given file format, and determines the color model used to display and print an image. Determines the number and range of colors displayed.

Color model

Determines how pigments combine to produce resulting colors.

Color Picker

A feature that lets you choose a color from a color spectrum.

Color Sampler tool

Feature that samples—and stores—up to four distinct color samplers. This feature is used when you want to save specific color settings for future use.

Color separation

Result of converting an RGB image into a CMYK image; the commercial printing process of separating colors for use with different inks.

Color swatch

Changes the ambient light around the lighting spotlight in the Lighting Effects filter.

Composite channel

The top channel on the Channels panel that is a combination of all the default channels.

Compositing

Combining images from sources such as other Photoshop images, royalty-free images, pictures taken from digital cameras, and scanned artwork.

Contact sheet

Compilation of a maximum of 30 thumbnail images (per sheet) from a specific folder.

Content-Aware fill

Feature in which Photoshop intelligently fills an area in a selection. Also available in the Patch tool.

Content-Aware Scaling

Feature that lets you change the dimensions of a selection *without* changing the scale of important content.

Contiguous

Items that are next to one another.

Copyright

The right of an author or creator of a work to copy, distribute, and modify a thing, idea, or image; a type of intellectual property.

Creative Commons licenses

Licensing of intellectual property without the use of lawyers or expensive fees by Creative Commons, a non-profit organization that offers free licenses and legal tools used to mark creative work.

Crisp

Anti-aliasing setting that gives type more definition and makes it appear sharper.

Crop

To exclude part of an image. Cropping hides areas of an image without losing resolution quality.

Crop marks

Page notations that indicate where trimming will occur and can be printed at the corners, center of each edge, or both.

—————— **D** ——————

Default action

An action that is prerecorded and tested, and comes with Photoshop.

Default channels

The color channels automatically contained in an image.

Depth of field

Camera feature used to enhance the image composition; the sharp area surrounding the point of focus.

Derivative work

A new, original product that includes content from a previously existing work.

Deselect

A command that removes the marquee from an area so it is no longer selected.

Destructive editing

Changes to pixels that are irreversible and *cannot be undone* once the current Photoshop session has ended.

Device profile

A hardware description that can be created for specific devices and embedded in an image; defines how colors are interpreted by a specific device. (Also called an *ICC profile*.)

DICOM (Digital Imaging and Communications in Medicine)

A file format that contains multiple slices or frames which are read and converted to Photoshop layers, and can then be annotated or manipulated. In architecture and engineering applications, images can be overlaid, making complex analysis much easier, accurate, and effective.

Digimarc

Embeds into an image a digital watermark that stores copyright information.

Digital camera

A camera that captures images on electronic media (rather than film). Its images are in a standard digital format and can be downloaded for computer use.

Digital image
A picture in electronic form. It may be referred to as a file, document, picture, or image.

Digital Negative Format
See Adobe DNG.

Direct Selection tool
Used to select and manipulate individual anchor points and segments to reshape a path.

Distance
Determines how far a shadow falls from the text. This setting is used by the Drop Shadow and Bevel and Emboss styles.

Distort filters
Create 3-dimensional or other reshaping effects. Some of the types of distortions you can produce include Pinch, Polar Coordinates, Ripple, Shear, Spherize, Twirl, Wave, and Zigzag.

Dock
The dark gray vertical bar to the left of the collection of panels or buttons. The arrows in the dock are used to collapse and expand the panels.

Downsampling
Decreasing the number of pixels in an image.

Drop Shadow
A style that adds what looks like a colored layer behind the selected type or object. The default shadow color is black.

Drop Zone
A blue outlined area that indicates where a panel can be moved.

Droplet
A stand-alone action in the form of an icon.

Duotone mode
Color mode used to create grayscale images using monotones, duotones, tritones, and quadtones.

E

Embedded object
A copy of an object that is placed in a Photoshop image and not updated when the original is changed.

Endpoints
Anchor points at each end of an open path.

Eraser tool
Has the opposite function of a brush in that it eliminates pixels on a layer.

Erodible brush tip
A brush tip that erodes from thin to thick lines, like a crayon, to let you draw lines with a tip that can be customized using the Brush panel. The Softness slider lets you adjust the erosion rate, and the Shape list arrow lets you set the shape of the brush.

F

Fading type
An effect in which the type appears to originate in darkness and then gradually gets brighter, or vice versa.

Fair use doctrine
Allows a user to make a copy of all or part of a work within specific parameters of usage, even if permission *has not* been granted.

Fastening point
An anchor within the marquee. When the marquee pointer reaches the initial fastening point, a small circle appears on the pointer, indicating that you have reached the starting point.

Feather
A method used to control the softness of a selection's edges by blurring the area between the selection and the surrounding pixels.

Field of view
Refers to the content you want to include in an image and the angle you choose to shoot from.

File versioning
A feature that allows you to store multiple versions of your work.

Filter Gallery
A feature that lets you see the effects of each filter before applying it, and lets you apply multiple filters to a layer.

Filters
Used to alter the look of an image and give it a special, customized appearance by applying special effects, such as distortions, changes in lighting, and blurring.

Flattening
Irreversible process that merges all visible layers into one layer, named the Background layer, and deletes all hidden layers, greatly reducing file size.

Flow
Brush tip setting that determines the intensity of the tool's effect while the mouse button is held.

Font
Characters with a similar appearance.

Font family
Represents a complete set of characters, letters, and symbols for a particular typeface. Font families are generally divided into three categories: serif, sans serif, and symbol.

Foreground color
Used to paint, fill, and stroke selections. The default foreground color is black.

Frame
An individual image that is used in animation.

Framing
Centering object(s) or interest in the foreground, which gives an image a feeling of depth.

Frame delay
In an animation sequence, the length of time that each frame appears.

Freeform Pen tool
Acts like a traditional pen or pencil, and automatically places *both* the anchor points and line segments wherever necessary to achieve the shape you want.

Freeze
To protect areas within an image from being affected by Liquify tools.

Fuzziness
A setting similar to tolerance, in that the lower the value, the closer the color pixels must be to be selected.

--- **G** ---

Gamut
The range of displayed colors in a color model.

Gloss contour
A Bevel and Emboss setting that determines the pattern with which light is reflected.

Gradient fill
A type of fill in which colors appear to blend into one another. A gradient's appearance is determined by its beginning and ending points. Photoshop contains five gradient fill styles.

Gradient presets
Predesigned gradient fills that are displayed in the Gradient picker.

Graphics tablet
An optional hardware peripheral that enables use of pressure-sensitive tools, allows you to create programmable menu buttons and maneuver faster in Photoshop.

Grayscale image
Can contain up to 256 shades of gray. Pixels can have brightness values from 0 (black) to white (255).

Grayscale mode
Uses up to 256 shades of gray, assigning a brightness value from 0 (black) to 255 (white) to each pixel.

Guides
Non-printing horizontal and vertical lines that you create to help you align objects. Guides appear as light blue lines.

H

Handles
Small boxes that appear along the perimeter of a selected object and are used to change the size of and shape of the selected object.

HDR (High Dynamic Range) image
An image that is used in motion pictures, special effects, 3D work, and high-end photography, and stores pixel values that span the whole tonal range.

Hexadecimal values
Sets of three pairs of letters or numbers that are used to define the R, G, and B components of a color.

Highlight Mode
A Bevel and Emboss setting that determines how pigments are combined.

Histogram
A graph that displays the frequency distribution of colors and is used to make adjustments in the input and output levels.

History panel
Contains a record of each action performed during a Photoshop session. Up to 1000 levels of Undo are available through the History panel (20 levels by default).

HTML
Hypertext Markup Language (HTML) is the language used for creating web pages.

Hue
The color reflected from/transmitted through an object and expressed as a degree (between 0° and 360°). Each hue is identified by a color name (such as red or green).

I

ICC profile
Created for specific devices and embedded in an image, and used to define how colors are interpreted by a specific device. ICC stands for International Color Consortium.

Image-editing program
Used to manipulate graphic images that can be posted on websites or reproduced by professional printers using full-color processes.

Intellectual property
An image or idea that is owned and retained by legal control.

Intelligent upsampling
An enhancement that preserves detail and sharpness while enlarging images for different print sizes.

Interpolation methods
Ways of recalculating the numbers of pixels in an image. Methods include Preserve Details (enlargement), Nearest Neighbor (hard edges), Bilinear, Bicubic (smooth gradients), Bicubic Smoother (enlargement), Bicubic Sharper (reduction), and Automatic (best used for print images).

Interruption
A hesitation or omission in the text or design; used to guide a reader's eye to a specific area of an image or page.

J

Jitter
The randomness of dynamic brush tip elements such as size, angle, roundness, hue, saturation, brightness, opacity, and flow.

K

Kerning
Controlling the amount of space between two characters.

Keyboard shortcuts
Combinations of keys that can be used to work faster and more efficiently.

Kuler

A web-hosted application that lets you create, save, share, and download color-coordinated themes for use in images. It can be accessed from a browser, the desktop, or Adobe products such as Photoshop or Illustrator.

L

Landscape orientation

An image with the long edge of the paper at the top and bottom.

Large Document Format (PSB)

A file format for files larger than 2GB, which supports documents up to 300,000 pixels, with all Photoshop features such as layers, effects, and filters. (The PSB format can be opened by Photoshop CS or later.)

Layer

A section within an image on which objects can be stored. The advantage: Individual effects can be isolated and manipulated without affecting the rest of the image. The disadvantage: Layers can increase the size of your file.

Layer-based slice

A slice created from a layer.

Layer comp

A variation on the arrangement and visibility of existing layers within an image; an organizational tool.

Layer group

An organizing tool you use to group layers on the Layers panel. (Sometimes referred to as *nested layers* or a *layer set*.)

Layer mask

Used to hide or reveal a selection and can cover an entire layer or specific areas within a layer. When a layer contains a mask, an additional thumbnail appears on the Layers panel.

Layer set

The result of grouping layers on the Layers panel.

Layer style

An effect that can be applied to a type or image layer.

Layer thumbnail

Contains a miniature picture of the layer's content and appears to the left of the layer name on the Layers panel.

Layers panel

Displays all the individual layers within an active image. You can use the Layers panel to create, delete, merge, copy, or reposition layers.

Leading

The amount of vertical space between lines of type.

Link

Clickable text, graphic, or object that hyperlinks to a specific website and opens that website in a browser window.

Linked object

A placeholder for an object that contains a link that is automatically updated.

Liquify feature

Applies distortions to rasterized layers using distinct tools in the Liquify dialog box.

Liquify session

The period of time from when you open the Liquify dialog box to when you close it.

List mode

The default display of actions in which all action detail can be viewed.

Logo

A distinctive image used to identify a company, project, or organization. You can create a logo by combining symbols, shapes, colors, and text.

Lossless

A file-compression format in which no data is discarded.

Lossy

A file-compression format used in JPG format that discards data during the compression process.

Luminosity

The light and dark values that result when a color image is converted to grayscale.

———————— M ————————

Magic Eraser tool

Used to erase areas in an image that have similar-colored pixels.

Magic Wand tool

Used to choose pixels that are similar to the ones where you first click in an image.

Marquee

A series of dotted lines indicating a selected area that can be edited or dragged into another image.

Mask

A feature that lets you protect or modify a particular area; created using a marquee.

Matte

A colorful box (often without shine) placed behind an object that makes the object stand out.

Menu bar

Contains menus from which you can choose Photoshop commands.

Merging layers

Process of combining multiple image layers into one layer.

Mesh

A series of horizontal and vertical gridlines that are superimposed in the Liquify preview window, or an object to which 3D extrusion has been applied.

Metadata

Standardized descriptive information about a file, including the author's name, copyright, and associated keywords.

Metering

A feature that provides a photographer with a way of compensating for a variety of lighting conditions. Examples of metering are spot metering, center-weighted average metering, average metering, partial metering, and multi-zone metering.

Modal control

Dialog boxes that are used in an action, and are indicated by an icon on the Actions panel.

Monotype spacing

Spacing in which each character occupies the same amount of space.

Morph

To blend multiple images in the animation process. Short for metamorphosis.

Multiple-image layout

Layout (generated in Adobe Bridge) that features more than one image.

———————— N ————————

N-up view

A view that allows you to edit one image while comparing it with another. You can drag layers from one image to another in N-up view. Display N-up view using the Arrange command on the Window menu, then tile either horizontally or vertically until the images are in the configuration that works best.

Noise filters

Used to add or remove pixels with randomly distributed color levels; gives an image the appearance of texture.

Nondestructive editing

Alterations to an image that are *not* permanent and can be edited.

None

Anti-alias setting to which no anti-aliasing is applied.

O

Object layer
A layer containing one or more images.

Opacity
Determines the percentage of transparency. Whereas a layer with 100% opacity will obstruct objects in the layers beneath it, a layer with 1% opacity will appear nearly transparent.

Open path
A path that comprises two distinct endpoints, such as an individual line.

Optical center
The point around which objects on the page are balanced; occurs approximately 3/8^{ths} from the top of the page.

Optimized image
An image whose file size has been reduced without sacrificing image quality.

Options bar
Displays the settings for the active tool. The options bar is located directly under the Menu bar, but can be moved anywhere in the workspace for easier access.

Orientation
Direction an image appears on the page: portrait or landscape.

Outline type
Type that is mathematically defined and can be scaled to any size without its edges losing their smooth appearance. Also known as a *vector font*.

Out-of-gamut
Indicates that the current color falls beyond the accurate print or display range.

P

Pan and zoom
Ability to zoom in and out by holding the Zoom tool without loss of resolution; pan by holding the [spacebar] while pressing the Zoom tool. (Requires a graphics card and OpenGL enabled.)

Panel group
A collection of panels.

Panels
Small windows that can be moved and are used to verify settings and modify images. Panels contain named tabs, which can be separated and moved to another group. Each panel contains a menu that can be viewed by clicking the Panel options button in its upper-right corner.

Path
One or more straight or curved line segments connected by anchor points used to turn the area defined within an object into an individual object.

Path component
One or more anchor points joined by line segments.

Path Selection tool
Used to select an entire path.

Paths panel
Storage area for paths.

Pen tool
Used to draw a path by placing anchor points along the edge of another image or wherever you need them to draw a specific shape.

Perspective Warp
Feature that allows you to adjust the perspective within an image.

Picture package
Shows multiple copies of a single image in various sizes, similar to a portrait studio sheet of photos.

Pixel
Very small squares that make up an image; each dot in a bitmapped image that represents a color or shade.

Pixel aspect ratio
A scaling correction feature that automatically corrects the ratio of pixels displayed for the monitor in use. Prevents pixels viewed in a 16:9 monitor (such as a widescreen TV) from looking compressed when viewed in a 4:3 monitor (nearly-rectangular TV).

Plug-ins
Additional programs—created by Adobe and other developers—that expand the functionality of Photoshop.

Points
Unit of measurement for font sizes. Traditionally, one inch is equivalent to 72.27 points. In PostScript measurement, one inch is equivalent to 72 points. The default Photoshop type size is 12 points.

Portrait orientation
An image with the short edge of the paper at the top and bottom.

PostScript
A programming language created by Adobe that optimizes printed text and graphics.

Preferences
Options that are used to control the Photoshop environment based on your specifications.

Preset Manager
Allows you to manage libraries of preset brushes, swatches, gradients, styles, patterns, contours, and custom shapes.

Profile
Defines and interprets colors for a color management system.

Project scope
The work that needs to be accomplished to deliver a project, the complexity of which can be discussed using three variables—performance, time, and cost.

Proportional spacing
The text spacing in which each character takes up a different amount of space, based on its width.

Puppet Warp tool
Used to add natural motion to rastersized images.

———————— **R** ————————

Rasterize
The process of converting a type layer to a bitmapped image layer.

Rasterized shape
A shape that is converted into a bitmapped object. It cannot be moved or copied without compromising image quality and has a much smaller file size.

Red-Eye effect
Photographic effect in which eyes within photographs look red due to the use of a flash.

Reference point
Center of the object from which distortions and transformations are measured.

Relief
The height of ridges within an object.

Render
Transform 3-dimensional shapes and simulated light reflections in an image.

Rendering intent
The way in which a color-management system handles color conversion from one color space to another.

Resampling
Changing the number of pixels within an image.

Resizing
Changing the dimensions of an image. (The size of the image changes, while the number of pixels remains the same.)

Resulting color
The outcome of the blend color applied to the base color.

RGB image
Image that contains three color channels (one each for red, green, and blue).

RGB mode
Color mode in which components are combined to create new colors.

Rule of Thirds
A design technique used to find the best way to add interest to an image. Achieved by dividing an image vertically and horizontally into 3 parts; the intersection of the horizontal and vertical gridlines are compositional options for placing objects.

Rulers
Onscreen markers that help you precisely measure and position an object. Rulers can be displayed using the View menu.

——————— **S** ———————

Sampling
A method of changing foreground and background colors by copying existing colors from an image.

Sans serif fonts
Fonts that do not have tails or strokes at the end of characters; commonly used in headlines.

Saturation
The strength or purity of the color, representing the amount of gray in proportion to hue (measured as a percentage from 0% [gray], to 100%

[fully saturated]). Also known as *chroma*.

Scale
The size relationship of objects to one another.

Scope creep
A condition in which a project seems to have lost its way.

Screen frequency (line screen)
The number of printer dots or halftone cells per inch used to print grayscale images or color separations and is measured in lines per inch (lpi).

Screening
An illusory effect in which type appears to fade into the imagery below it.

Script
Creates external automation of Photoshop from an outside source, such as JavaScript. Also called *scripting*.

Selection
An area in an image that is surrounded by a selection marquee and can then be manipulated.

Serif fonts
Fonts that have a tail, or stroke, at the end of some characters. These tails make it easier for the eye to recognize words; therefore, serif fonts are generally used in text passages.

Shading
Collection of Bevel and Emboss settings that determine lighting effects.

Shadow Mode
Bevel and Emboss setting that determines how pigments are combined.

Shape
A vector object that keeps its crisp appearance when it is resized and, like a path, can be edited.

Shape layer
A clipping path or shape that can occupy its own layer.

Sharp
Anti-aliasing setting that displays type with the best possible resolution.

Sharpen More filter
Increases the contrast of adjacent pixels and can focus blurry images.

Sharpness
An element of composition that draws the viewer's eye to a specific area.

Sidecar file
A separate file that contains metadata and can be applied to other files as a template.

Size
Determines the clarity of a drop shadow.

Slice
A specific rectangular area within an image to which you can assign special features, such as a link or animation.

Smart Filter
A filter applied to a Smart Object that allows for nondestructive editing of the object(s).

Smart Guides
Vertical and horizontal guides that appear automatically when you draw a shape or move an object and are helpful in its positioning.

Smart Object
A combination of objects that has a visible indicator in the bottom-right corner of the layer thumbnail. Makes it possible to nondestructively scale, rotate, and warp layers without losing image quality. Can be linked *or* embedded.

Smooth
Anti-aliasing setting that gives type more rounded edges.

Snapshot
A temporary copy of an image that contains the history states made up to that point. You can create multiple snapshots of an image, and you can switch between snapshots.

Soft proof
The way an image looks on specific calibrated hardware using a color management system.

Source
The image containing the color that will be matched.

Splash screen
A window that displays information about the software you are using.

Spot channel
Designed to provide a channel for additional inks, also called a *spot color* or an *alpha channel*. A spot channel is added to an image using the Channels panel.

Spot color
A method of defining a difficult or unique color that couldn't otherwise be easily recreated by a printer.

Spread
Determines the width of drop shadow text.

Spring-loaded keyboard shortcuts
A feature that lets you temporarily change the active tool by pressing and holding the key that changes to another tool.

Status bar
The area located at the bottom of the program window (Win) or the work area (Mac) that displays information such as the file size of the active window.

Step
Measurement of fade options that can be any value from 1–9999, and equivalent to one mark of the brush tip.

Stop
In an action, a command that interrupts playback or includes an informative text message for the user, so that other operations can be performed.

Stroking the edges
The process of making a selection or layer stand out by formatting it with a border.

Strong
Anti-aliasing setting that makes type appear heavier, much like the bold attribute.

Structure
A Bevel and Emboss setting that determines the size and physical properties of the object.

Style

In type, a collection of formatting attributes that can be saved and applied to specific characters or a paragraph. When creating a customized object, there are 18 predesigned styles that can be applied to buttons.

Stylize filters

Used to produce a painted or impressionistic effect.

Subtractive colors

A color system in which the full combination of cyan, magenta, and yellow absorb all color and produce black.

Swatches panel

Contains available colors that can be selected for use as a foreground or background color. You can also add your own colors to the Swatches panel.

Symbol fonts

Used to display unique characters (such as $, ÷, or ™).

Symmetrical balance

When objects are placed equally on either side of an imaginary vertical line in the center of the page.

T

3D Extrusion

A tool for turning a 2-dimensional object (such as type) into a 3-dimensional object. Allows for rotation, rolling, panning, sliding, and scaling.

Target

When sampling a color, the image that will receive the matched color.

Thaw

To remove protection from a protected area in an image so it can be affected by Liquify tools.

This Layer slider

Found in the Layer Style dialog box; used to specify the range of pixels that will be blended on the active layer.

Tolerance

A setting that specifies the range of pixels and determines which pixels will be selected. The lower the tolerance, the closer the color is to the selection. The setting can have a value from 0–255.

Tonal values

Numeric values of an individual color that can be used to duplicate a color. Also called *color levels*.

Tone

The brightness and contrast within an image.

Tools panel

Contains tools for frequently used commands. On the face of a tool is a graphic representation of its function. Place the pointer over each button to display a tool tip, which shows the name or function of that button. An arrow in the lower-right of the button face indicates other similar tools in the group.

Tracking

The insertion of a uniform amount of space between characters.

Transform

To change the shape, size, perspective, or rotation of an object or objects on a layer.

Transform box

A rectangle that surrounds an image and contains handles that can be used to change dimensions. Also called a *bounding box*.

Tweening

The process of selecting multiple frames, then inserting transitional frames between them. This effect makes frames appear to blend into one another and gives the animation a more fluid appearance.

Type
Text, or a layer containing text. Each character is measured in points. In traditional measurement, one inch is equivalent to 72.27 points.

Typeface
See Font.

Type spacing
Adjustments you can make to the space between characters and between lines of type.

———————— **U** ————————

Underlying Layer slider
Found in the Layer Style dialog box; used to specify the range of pixels that will be blended on lower visible layers.

Upsampling
Increasing the number of pixels in an image (also called *resampling*); this can sometimes result in an improved image, or it can also result in poorer image quality.

URL
Uniform Resource Locator, a web address.

User slice
A slice created by you. A user slice has a solid-line border.

———————— **V** ————————

Vanishing Point
Feature used to maintain perspective as you drag objects around corners and into the distance.

Vector data
A shape or path that will not lose its crisp appearance if resized or reshaped.

Vector font
Fonts that are vector-based type outlines, which means that they are mathematically defined shapes. Also known as *outline type*.

Vector graphic
Image made up of lines and curves defined by mathematical objects.

Vector mask
Makes a shape's edges appear neat and defined on a layer, independent of resolution.

Vignette
A feature in which the border of a picture or portrait fades into the surrounding color at its edges.

Vignette effect
A feature that uses feathering to fade a marquee shape.

Visual hierarchy
The order in which the eye understands what it is seeing.

———————— **W** ————————

Warping
A feature that lets you create distortions that conform to a variety of shapes.

Web Gallery
In Bridge, contains a thumbnail index page of all exported images, the actual JPEG images, and any included links.

Widget
Tool that can be used to change a 3D object.

Work path
A path when it is first created, but not yet named.

Working space
Tells the color management system how RGB and CMYK values are interpreted.

Workspace

The entire window, from the Menu bar at the top of the window, to the status bar at the bottom border of the program window.

Z

Zoom factor

The amount of magnification applied to a document; displays in the document title bar and allows you to customize the view of the area you're working on.

graphics tablets, 7–18, 7–22

grayscale, converting color layers to, 11–9

grayscale color mode, 5–6

grayscale images, 5–22
    adjustments, 5–22—23
    colorizing, 5–23, 5–25
    converting color images to, 5–24
    converting to color mode, 5–22, 5–24

Group Layers command, 8–12

grouping layers, 8–12

Grow command, 4–14

guides, 3–5, 4–7—8. *See also* Smart Guides
    locking, 4–8

Hand tool, 9–31

handles, selections, 4–19

Hard Light blending mode, 5–28

hardware requirements
    Mac OS, 1–7
    Windows, 1–6

HDR Conversion dialog box, 17–12

.hdr (Radiance) file format, 1–5

HDR (High Dynamic Range) images, 11–10, 17–12

Healing Brush tool, 4–19, 4–23, 7–5

Help system, 2–2, 2–16—21
    finding information in Adobe reference titles, 2–18
    finding information using Search, 2–20
    finding new features, 2–21
    Support Center vs., 2–19
    topics, 2–16

hexadecimal values, 5–9

hiding
    layer thumbnails, 3–4
    layers, 2–13, 2–14
    panels, 1–22

hierarchy, visual, 2–14

High Dynamic Range (HDR) images, 11–10, 17–12

highlight(s), correcting, 5–29

highlight mode setting, Bevel and Emboss style, 6–20

histogram(s), 11–2
    correcting, 11–12—13

Histogram panel, 11–12—13

History Brush tool, 7–21

History Options dialog box, 10–25

History panel, 2–13, 13–14
    actions, 16–8
    deleting states, 2–15, 6–19
    limitations, 10–24

Horizontal Distortion setting, Warp Text dialog box, 13–9

Horizontal setting, Warp Text dialog box, 13–9

Horizontal Type tool, 6–28

housekeeping tasks, Bridge and Mini Bridge, 2–8

HSB color mode, 5–5

HTML (Hypertext Markup Language), 17–4

hue, 5–5

Hue blending mode, 5–28

Hue/Saturation adjustment, 8–27, 11–8—9

Hue/Saturation dialog box, 5–25

Hue/Saturation Properties panel, 15–11

Hypertext Markup Language (HTML), 17–4

Note tool, 16–6
Notes panel, 16–4, 16–6, 16–7
.nrw file format, 1–5

.obj (Wavefront) file format, 1–5
opacity, 3–2
    adjusting, 3–22
    drop shadows, 6–14
    settings, 5–30, 6–14
Open As command, 1–9
Open dialog box, 1–8, 1–12
Open EXR (.exr) file format, 1–5
Open GL, 6–22
open paths, 12–2
opening
    Blur filters, 9–7
    files. *See* opening files
    images. *See* opening images
    Liquify dialog box, 14–6
opening files, 1–8—9
    using Folders panel in Bridge, 1–12
    using Menu bar, 1–12
    using Mini Bridge, 1–13
opening images, 4–6
    Camera Raw images, 18–18, 18–19

Camera Raw images as Smart Objects,
    18–23
    multiple Camera Raw format images,
    18–19
    scanned images, 1–8
optical center, 1–28
optimizing images for web use,
    17–8—13
    compression, 17–9
    file formats, 17–8, 17–9, 17–10
    HDR images, 17–12
    image types compared, 17–10
    Matte option, 17–11
    placing optimized images, 17–13
    preparation, 17–11
    Transparency option, 17–11
options bar, 1–17
order, layers, changing, 3–5
.orf file format, 1–5
organizing photographs, 18–24
orientation, paper, 2–23
Other filters, 9–6
outline type, 6–4
Output Module, installing, 2–27
Overlay blending mode, 5–28

Paint Daubs filter, 9–11
painting
    areas, 7–9
    borders, 7–15
    finger painting, 7–16
    layer masks, 8–5, 8–9
    with patterns, 7–7
    pixels, 7–2
painting tools, 7–1—24. *See also*
        Blur tool; Burn tool; Dodge tool;
        Patch tool; Sharpen tool;
        Sponge tool
    adjusting patched areas, 7–11
    brush libraries, 7–2
    creating a patch for an area, 7–10
    Deco Pattern feature, 7–7
    fade options, 7–4, 7–8, 7–9
    patching an area, 7–11
"paintings," turning photos into, 7–19
Palette Knife filter, 9–11
pan and zoom feature, 15–15
panel(s), 1–17. *See also specific panels*
    creating your own, 1–23
    displaying, 1–17
    hiding, 1–22

selecting (*continued*)

lighting settings, 9–26

Magic Wand tool. *See* Magic Wand tool

multiple layers, 8–12, 8–15

multiple paths, 12–10

non-contiguous images, 1–10

Quick Selection tool, 4–21

by shape, 4–4—13

tools, 1–19—20

using color, 4–18

selecting colors

using Color Picker, 5–10, 5–12

using Swatches panel, 5–11, 5–12

selection(s), 3–14—17, 4–1—26

adding to, 4–15

applying Stylize filters, 9–14, 9–17

complex, moving, 4–13

converting into a path, 12–16, 12–18

converting paths into, 12–17

copying, 4–9

correcting errors, 4–6

creating, 4–4—5, 4–9, 4–12

creating alpha channels from, 10–7

creating for layer masks, 8–7

creating from Quick Mask, 8–7

creating layers from, 15–8

creating using a focus area, 8–10

cutting, 4–9

defringing, 3–15, 3–17

deleting, 4–9

deselecting, 4–5, 4–9, 4–11

fastening points, 4–5

fixing imperfections, 4–19, 4–23

flipping, 4–22

handles, 4–19

for layer masks, creating, 8–7

loading, 4–11

making, 3–14

marquess. *See* marquee(s)

mastering, 4–12

matching colors using, 5–32

moving, 3–14, 3–17, 4–9, 4–10, 4–13

pasting, 4–9

placing, 4–6—7

saving, 4–11

selecting by shape, 4–4

subtracting from, 4–15

transforming, 4–19

vignettes, 4–24—25

selection masks, refining using filters, 9–13

selection tools, 3–15, 4–2, 4–5

choosing, 4–19

by shape, 4–5

Selective Color color adjustment, 8–27

semitransparent type, 13–16

separating panels, 1–17

serif fonts, 6–4, 6–5

shading setting, Bevel and Emboss style, 6–20

shadow(s). *See also* drop shadows

correcting, 5–29, 11–12—13

creating using Transform command, 12–17

shadow mode setting, Bevel and Emboss style, 6–20

Shadow/Highlight dialog box, 5–29

Shadows/Highlights color adjustment, 8–27

Shake Reduction dialog box, 18–23

shape(s), 12–2

creating, 12–12—13, 12–14

custom, creating, 12–13, 12–14